THE COMPLETE SERMONS OF
RALPH WALDO EMERSON

Volume 4

THE COMPLETE SERMONS OF RALPH WALDO EMERSON IN FOUR VOLUMES

Chief Editor: Albert J. von Frank

Editors: Ronald A. Bosco
Andrew H. Delbanco
Wesley T. Mott
Teresa Toulouse

Contributing Editors: David M. Robinson
Wallace E. Williams
Douglas E. Wilson

THE COMPLETE SERMONS OF RALPH WALDO EMERSON

VOLUME 4

Edited by Wesley T. Mott

WITHDRAWN

UNIVERSITY OF MISSOURI PRESS
COLUMBIA AND LONDON

The publication of this volume was made possible in part by a grant from the National Endowment for the Humanities, an independent federal agency.

5 4 3 2 1   96 95 94 93 92

Library of Congress Cataloging-in-Publication Data
(Revised for volume 4)

Emerson, Ralph Waldo, 1803–1882.
The complete sermons of Ralph Waldo Emerson.

Vol. 4 edited by Wesley T. Mott.
Includes bibliographical references and index.
1. Unitarian churches—Sermons. 2. Sermons, American. I. Von Frank, Albert J. II. Mott, Wesley T. III. Title.
BX9843.E487C66 1989 252'.091 88-4834
ISBN 0-8262-0681-6 (v. 1 : alk. paper)
ISBN 0-8262-0746-4 (v. 2 : alk. paper)
ISBN 0-8262-0797-9 (v. 3 : alk. paper)
ISBN 0-8262-0859-2 (v. 4 : alk. paper)
ISBN 0-8262-0889-4 (set)

Preface

This final volume of Emerson's sermons presents those he numbered CXXXVI to CLXXI and several occasional and fragmentary sermons as well as the "Records of the Second Church, Boston" relating to Emerson's ministry. The volume includes not only the famous "Lord's Supper" sermon (CLXII—edited for the first time from the manuscript Emerson actually preached from), but also eight sermons he wrote after resigning his position at the Second Church. Emerson's continuing engagement with the pulpit is reflected both in these additional compositions and in the extensive recycling of so many earlier sermons for many years, as registered in his Preaching Record.

I thank the Ralph Waldo Emerson Memorial Association and the Houghton Library, Harvard University, for permission to publish the sermons. Over many years the Houghton staff and the Memorial Association leadership have been unfailingly helpful and gracious. I thank also the First and Second Church in Boston (Dr. Rhys Williams, minister) and the Massachusetts Historical Society for permission to publish material from the Second Church Records. The superb staffs of the American Antiquarian Society, the Boston Athenaeum, the Concord Free Public Library, the Concord Museum, and the Gordon Library of Worcester Polytechnic Institute were indispensable to my research.

Like my predecessors, I have discovered that textual editing is essentially collaborative. I am deeply indebted to the editors of *The Early Lectures* and *The Journals and Miscellaneous Notebooks of Ralph Waldo Emerson,* to the late Gene Irey, to Michael Preston, and to Kenneth Walter Cameron. It is a special pleasure to acknowledge the help of Emerson editors Ronald A. Bosco, Joel Myerson, Ralph H. Orth, and Douglas Emory Wilson. I am grateful to JoAnn Manfra, head of the Humanities Department at Worcester Polytechnic Institute, for logistical support; to Joel Brattin and Kent Ljungquist for their collegiality; and to the National Endowment for the Humanities for a travel grant and a summer stipend.

My greatest debt is to Albert J. von Frank, whose example and leadership have brought this project to fruition.

W. T. M.
January 1992

Deaths, 1830

Nov 25   Sarah   Moore, æt. 16
Dec 23   a foundling infant at house of D. R. Lilley. æt 4 weeks.

1831
                        a Portuguese Sailor
Feb. 8   Mrs Ellen Tucker Emerson.   æt. 19.   consumption.
         Mary Howard Bridge æt 23.   inflammation.
         Mrs Hannah Bell   æt 45   tumour
March   Samuel Austin – child of Seth Tucker 1 y
         Doddridge   child of Mr Owen 4 y.
                     child of Amos Allen 1 y.
April   Mrs Grace Meinzies   old age.
June 22 William Little   æt. 81.   old age
July 8   Mrs Mary Perry   Consumption.
Aug. 2   Ellis Crook   æt 71   Dropsy.
    31   Henry Augustus child of Mr H. Little æt. 13 mo.
Sept 2   Charles   Lobdell   æt 6 y.   dropsy.
    7   Francis Green   æt 81
         Lorana Howe   æt 23   Consumption
         Mrs Mary Turell æt 91
         Sarah   Lovejoy   æt 19   Consumption
    21   Robert Ambrose of Concord N.H. æt 35. killed by a fall.
Oct 20   Henry Gale   8 y 6 mo.   drowned.
Nov 5   Sarah E. child of Geo. Spinney, æt. 4 y. croup
    7   Mrs Sarah Howe, æt. 64, a Tumour.
Dec.   child of Green Smith æt 1 year
         Samuel Shaw child of S.S. Lewis æt 7 mo. consumption
                     child of Thomas White æt 5 y.
    19   William Kidder of N. York æt. 47. consumption
    28   George   child of George Whittemore æt 16 years. dropsy
                                         1

February 8, 1831: Emerson notes the death of his wife in the official records of the Second Church (Courtesy of the Massachusetts Historical Society).

CONTENTS

Preface   v

Abbreviations of Works Frequently Cited   xiii

Textual Introduction   1

An Emerson Chronology: November 1831 to January 1839   6

THE SERMONS

SERMON CXXXVI
O give thanks unto the Lord; for he is good: for his mercy endureth forever.
Who can utter the mighty acts of the Lord? Who can show forth all his
praise?   Psalms 106:1-2   23

SERMON CXXXVII
Choose ye this day whom ye will serve; as for me and my house, we will
serve the Lord.   Joshua 24:15   28

SERMON CXXXVIII
Unto us a child is born, unto us a son is given, . . . Of the increase of his
government and peace there shall be no end.   Isaiah 9:6-7   37

SERMON CXXXIX
If our heart condemn us, God is greater than our heart and knoweth all
things . . . if our heart condemn us not, then have we confidence toward
God.   I John 3:20-21   42

SERMON CXL
Let no man seek his own, but every man another's wealth.
I Corinthians 10:24   49

SERMON CXLI
Do thyself no harm.   Acts 16:28   54

SERMON CXLII
Lo I am with you alway, even unto the end of the world.
Matthew 28:20   60

SERMON CXLIII
Forgetting those things which are behind and reaching forth unto those things which are before, I press toward the mark for the prize of the high calling of God in Christ Jesus.   Philippians 3:13–14   65

SERMON CXLIV
Therefore leaving the principles of the doctrine of Christ, let us go on unto perfection.   Hebrews 6:1   71

SERMON CXLV
Why even of yourselves judge ye not what is right?   Luke 12:57   77

SERMON CXLVI
Jesus Christ, who gave himself for us that he might redeem us from all iniquity and purify unto himself a peculiar people zealous of good works.   Titus 2:13–14   83

SERMON CXLVII
And beside this, giving all diligence, add to your faith, virtue; and to virtue, knowledge; and to knowledge, temperance; and to temperance, patience; and to patience, godliness; and to godliness, brotherly kindness; and to brotherly kindness, charity.   II Peter 1:5–7   89

SERMON CXLVIII
And these words which I command thee this day shall be in thine heart, and thou shalt teach them to thy children.   Deuteronomy 6:6–7   96

SERMON CXLIX
Thy law is my meditation all the day.   Psalms 119:97   103

SERMON CL
Is it such a Fast that I have chosen?   Isaiah 58:5   110

SERMON CLI
He hath made every thing beautiful in his time: also he hath set the world in their heart, so that no man can find out the work that God maketh from the beginning to the end. I know that there is no good in them, but for a man to rejoice, and to do good in his life.   Ecclesiastes 3:11–12   116

SERMON CLII
For all live unto Him.   Luke 20:38   122

SERMON CLIII
*The Lord God is a sun and shield; the Lord will give grace and glory; no
good thing will he withhold from them that walk uprightly. O Lord of
hosts, blessed is the man that trusteth in thee.*   Psalms 84:11–12   129

SERMON CLIV
*For this commandment which I command thee this day, it is not hidden
from thee, neither is it far off—but the word is very nigh thee in thy mouth
and in thy heart that thou mayest do it.*   Deuteronomy 30:11, 14   136

SERMON CLV
What shall a man give in exchange for his soul?   Mark 8:37   142

SERMON CLVI
Charity envieth not.   I Corinthians 13:4   148

SERMON CLVII
*God that made the world and all things therein, . . . dwelleth not in
temples made with hands. . . .*   Acts 17:24–25, 29–31   153

SERMON CLVIII
And God said unto Moses, I am that I am. *And he said, thus shalt thou
say unto the children of Israel,* I am *hath sent me unto you.*
Exodus 3:13–14   160

SERMON CLIX
We can do nothing against the truth, but for the truth.
II Corinthians 13:8   166

SERMON CLX
*For this cause we also . . . do not cease to pray for you and to desire that ye
might be filled with the knowledge of his will in all wisdom and spiritual
understanding; that ye might walk worthy of the Lord unto all pleasing,
being fruitful in every good work and increasing in the knowledge of
God.*   Colossians 1:9–10   171

SERMON CLXI
*In the sweat of thy face shalt thou eat bread till thou return unto the
ground.*   Genesis 3:19   178

Sermon CLXII
*The kingdom of God is not meat and drink; but righteousness and peace
and joy in the holy ghost.*   Romans 14:17   185

Sermon CLXIII
He that believeth on me hath everlasting life.   John 3:36   195

Sermon CLXIV
*Be renewed in the spirit of your mind and . . . put on the new man which
after God is created in righteousness and true holiness.*
Ephesians 4:23–24   201

Sermon CLXV
*Howbeit when the spirit of truth is come, he will guide you into all truth:
for he shall not speak of himself; but what he shall hear, that shall he speak;
and he will show you things to come.*   John 16:13   209

Sermon CLXVI
As in water face answereth to face, so the heart of man to man.
Proverbs 27:19   218

Note on Sermon CLXVII   220

Sermon CLXVIII
*Honorable age is not that which standeth in length of time nor that is
measured by number of years, but wisdom is gray hair unto men and
an unspotted life is old age.*   Wisdom of Solomon 4:8–9   221

Sermon CLXIX
*I am fearfully and wonderfully made. Marvellous are thy works; and that
my soul knoweth right well.*   Psalms 139:14   229

Sermon CLXX
Set your affections on things above and not on things on the earth.
Colossians 3:2   236

Sermon CLXXI
*How beautiful on the mountains are the feet of him that bringeth good
tidings, that publisheth salvation.*   Isaiah 52:7   244

OCCASIONAL DISCOURSES AND SERMON FRAGMENTS

[SERMON FRAGMENT]
Brethren, if our gospel be hid, it is hid from them that are lost.
II Corinthians 4:3   253

[DRAFT SERMON ON THE EVIDENCES OF CHRISTIANITY]   256

"RIGHT HAND OF FELLOWSHIP"   262

[PRELIMINARY NOTES FOR SERMON LXXXIV]   265

"ADDRESS AT THE DEDICATION OF SECOND CHURCH VESTRY,
FEB. 28, 1831"   267

[SECOND DISCOURSE ON THE DEATH OF GEORGE SAMPSON]   272

[THANKSGIVING SERMON: FRAGMENT]
*Whoso is wise, and will observe these things, even they shall understand the
loving kindness of the Lord.*   Psalms 107:43   281

[THANKSGIVING SERMON: INTRODUCTION]
And the Lord God said, It is not good that the man should be alone.
Genesis 2:18   283

[SERMON FRAGMENT]   284

Appendix A: Records of the Second Church in Boston, Relating to the
Ministry of Ralph Waldo Emerson   285

Appendix B: Letter from the Rev. R. W. Emerson, to the Second Church
and Society   304

Textual and Manuscript Notes   307

Cumulative Index to Volumes 1–4   449

Index of Biblical References in Volumes 1–4   465

Abbreviations of Works Frequently Cited

CW   *The Collected Works of Ralph Waldo Emerson*. Edited by Joseph Slater et al. 5 vols. to date. Cambridge: Harvard University Press, 1971–.

EL   *The Early Lectures of Ralph Waldo Emerson*. Edited by Stephen E. Whicher, Robert E. Spiller, and Wallace E. Williams. 3 vols. Cambridge: Harvard University Press, 1959–1972.

J   *Journals of Ralph Waldo Emerson*. Edited by Edward Waldo Emerson and Waldo Emerson Forbes. 10 vols. Boston and New York: Houghton Mifflin Co., 1909–1914.

JMN   *The Journals and Miscellaneous Notebooks of Ralph Waldo Emerson*. Edited by William H. Gilman et al. 16 vols. Cambridge: Harvard University Press, 1960–1982.

L   *The Letters of Ralph Waldo Emerson*. Edited by Ralph L. Rusk. 6 vols. New York: Columbia University Press, 1939. Continued under the editorship of Eleanor M. Tilton. 2 vols. to date (vols. 7–8). New York: Columbia University Press, 1990–.

MHS   Massachusetts Historical Society. Papers of the Second Church, Boston.

RWEMA   Manuscript owned by the Ralph Waldo Emerson Memorial Association (Houghton Library).

W   *The Complete Works of Ralph Waldo Emerson*. Edited by Edward Waldo Emerson. Centenary Edition. 12 vols. Boston and New York: Houghton Mifflin Co., 1903–1904.

THE COMPLETE SERMONS OF
RALPH WALDO EMERSON

TEXTUAL INTRODUCTION

Sermons CXXXVI through CLXXI, together with the occasional discourses and sermon fragments, are presented here in accordance with the textual principles set forth in the introductions to the preceding volumes—that is to say, in an annotated clear-text format with full textual notes in the back matter. Items in Appendix A ("Records of the Second Church") are presented in a genetic text with some minor normalization, principally of spacing. Appendix B reprints, in the absence of any manuscript, the scarce *Letter from the Rev. R. W. Emerson, to the Second Church and Society* (Boston, 1832) from the original pamphlet printing. Ronald A. Bosco has performed an independent reading of the computer transcript against the manuscripts, and his readings were made available to the volume editor for purposes of cross-checking. Albert von Frank, as General Editor, has verified the accuracy of the entire volume and assisted with the annotations.

Copy-Text

According to the editorial principles set forth in the Textual Introduction to Volume 1 and further clarified in the Introduction to Volume 2, the editors have chosen as copy-text the earliest manuscript in an effort to present, wherever possible, the first-delivery form of the sermon. Whenever this cannot be done, as for example when the first manuscript has been heavily reworked or even mutilated in the process of a revision leading to a second manuscript, the editors are compelled to present the second version as the earliest that can confidently be reconstructed. In the present volume there are seven instances of multiple manuscripts. In two instances (Sermons CXLI and CLXII) the earlier manuscript is adopted as copy-text because revisions are relatively slight and were apparently done prior to the first delivery. In five instances (Sermons CXLIII, CLVII, CLXI, CLXIV, and CLXIX) the revisions performed on the earlier manuscripts are substantial and suggest that Emerson was reworking them with the intent of producing a distinct second version. In these cases the editors have been compelled to choose the second version as copy-text, on the grounds that it is simply impossible to reconstruct the first version from the available manuscript evidence. In one of these instances (Sermon CLVII) the earlier manuscript is incomplete. In all cases of multiple manuscripts, however, the text of the manuscript not chosen as copy-text is given in full, in genetic form, in the Textual and Manuscript Notes.

The "Right Hand of Fellowship" delivered at the ordination of Hersey Bradford Goodwin in 1830 and Emerson's *Letter . . . to the Second Church and*

1

Society (see Appendix B) are the only two documents from Emerson's ministerial career that were contemporaneously published, and in both instances the
published versions are adopted as copy-text. No manuscript of the *Letter* is
known to have survived. The revisions introduced into the published form of
the "Right Hand of Fellowship" are clearly authorial and reflect Emerson's final
determinations in regard to the text. While it is perhaps tempting to reason
analogically that the revised version of the "Lord's Supper" sermon (CLXII)
should serve as copy-text, the editors believe that nothing less than the presence
of an authorially supervised publication should overturn the general policy of
presenting the sermon as actually delivered. The historical importance of the
sermon and its delivery, and the fact that the original version was virtually
unknown to scholarship, also weighed in our decision to adopt the earlier
manuscript as copy-text.

Textual Notes

The textual notes give the manuscript reading in every case of authorial insertion, deletion, substitution, transposition, and variant reading. With the exception of the categories of silent emendation listed below, the notes also record
every instance in which a word or part of a word has been editorially supplied
or deleted (for example, to correct Emerson's accidental doubling of words), or
in which punctuation has been altered for clarity. No editorial emendations,
silent or otherwise, occur in the textual notes, the purpose of which in each
instance is to give the manuscript form using such standard symbols as are
necessary to describe the situation. (A key to these symbols appears at the head
of the Textual and Manuscript Notes.) Thus, a textual note might take this
form:

our ⟨beliefs⟩ ↑Xty↓.

The symbols indicate that Emerson canceled "beliefs" and inserted "Xty". Although abbreviations in the edited text are regularly and silently expanded (the
clear text would in this instance read "our Christianity."), the textual note is
always bound to reproduce the manuscript form. Because the expansion of
abbreviations is treated in this edition as a *silent* emendation (see the list below),
no textual note is provided when Emerson uses "Xty" or any other abbreviation
in the course of a sentence he did not revise. Put another way, the occasion for
the textual note in the example above is not the abbreviation, but Emerson's
substitution of one word for another.

Silent Emendations

1. Emerson's sermon numbers are given throughout in uppercase roman numerals, which in fact he regularly employed up to and including the earlier of
the two manuscripts of Sermon CXLIII. For some reason, he switched there-
after to lowercase roman numerals and maintained that practice until Sermon
CLXV, first delivered near the time of his resignation from the Second Church,
at which point he switched to arabic numerals.

2. Citations for biblical texts at the head of each sermon are given in regularized form, spelling out the book of the Bible, which Emerson often abbreviates, and giving chapter and verse in arabic numerals, which Emerson does not consistently use. Emerson often quotes the Bible, as indeed he quotes other sources, from memory; inexact quotations are not corrected, though punctuation may be supplied from the King James Version of the Bible for clarity when necessary.

3. The following abbreviations are expanded: altho' (although), & (and), bro't (brought), ch. (chapter), Chh. (Churches), Xt (Christ), Xdom (Christendom), Xn or Chr^n (Christian), Xty (Christianity), ch. (church), cd. (could), diff. (different), eveg. (evening), gov^t (government), hist. (history), mt. (might), m.f. (my friends), nt. (not), N.T. or N. Testament (New Testament), pd. (paid), relig. (religious), Rev. (Revelation), sd. (said), servt (servant), shd. (should), y^e (the), y^{r}s (there's), tho't (thought), tho'tless (thoughtless), v. (verse), wd. (would), wro't (wrought), yrself (yourself).

4. Numbers and numerical terms below 100 are spelled out: e.g., 1 (one), 3^d (third).

5. Missing punctuation is supplied when undoubtedly called for, as periods at the ends of sentences, commas or semicolons in series, commas or colons to introduce quotations, and question marks at the ends of rhetorical questions (silently emended from a period when necessary). Emerson's use of single and double quotation marks is preserved without imposing uniformity, but omitted marks in a pair are supplied (a textual note describes the situation if there is any doubt about where a quotation ends). Apostrophes have been supplied where necessary; if there is any doubt whether singular or plural possessive is intended, the manuscript form is given in a note.

6. Words beginning a sentence (following Emerson's period) have been capitalized; capitalized words following Emerson's semicolons (but not his colons) have been reduced to lowercase.

7. Terminal punctuation consisting of a period followed by a dash has been retained within paragraphs when it seems to have the force of a semicolon. The dash is silently omitted when it falls at the end of a paragraph.

8. Emerson's usual practice is to put commas and periods inside his quotation marks. Contrary instances in the manuscript seem to be the result of haste and carelessness, and are therefore silently regularized.

Variants, Transpositions, and Other Reported Emendations

1. Emerson occasionally inserts an alternate word or phrase above the uncanceled corresponding word or phrase in his initial inscription. This situation is always reported in the textual notes, where it takes the form /first/second/. The clear text regularly adopts the second inscription in a pair of variants unless doing so results in a reading that is objectionable on the grounds of grammar or sense.

2. Emerson's usual method of indicating transposition is to label the relevant

sentences, phrases, or words with subscript numbers 1 and 2 (or, more rarely, a and b) and to mark off the material to be transposed with square brackets. In a few instances, three elements are designated for transposition. The clear text reflects the transposed order; the original order is given (with Emerson's numbers or letters represented as superscript) in a textual note.

3. Misspelled words are corrected and the misspellings reported in the textual notes. Inconsistency in the use of British and American forms is not regularized. No attempt has been made to revise odd spellings when Emerson's version occurs in dictionaries of the period or when contemporary authority for it has been found in the *Oxford English Dictionary*.

4. Emerson's erratic punctuation has been altered in the few instances when it is likely to cause confusion. All such instances are recorded in the textual notes. All ambiguous instances in which *missing* punctuation has been supplied are recorded in the textual notes.

5. Words that Emerson accidentally omitted or that are illegible or lost through damage to the manuscript are supplied without editorial brackets in the clear text and the situation described in the textual notes. Accidentally doubled words (as well as a few deliberately used catchwords) are corrected and reported in the textual notes.

6. Notes by Emerson—either footnotes or parenthetical notes—that briefly identify the source of a quotation are given in the editor's explanatory footnotes, where they are identified as Emerson's; they do not otherwise appear in the text or textual notes. Emerson's notations concerning the date and place of delivery, irregularly given on the last manuscript page, are incorporated in the information supplied in the first explanatory footnote for each sermon as well as in the Chronology; they do not otherwise appear in the text or textual notes.

7. Emerson's use of square brackets is always reported in the textual notes (represented as curved brackets to distinguish them from editorial remarks), though they do not appear in the clear text. In addition to setting off the elements in a transposition, they are frequently used to identify the limits of an inserted passage. Emerson also used them to set off paragraphs or larger blocks of text, most likely to indicate that the portions thus bracketed could be omitted in a particular delivery. Emerson was not consistent in the form of his square brackets, and while we believe we have consistently been able to distinguish them from Emerson's parentheses, we have freely interpreted as square brackets a range of crooked and angled lines that manifestly serve the same function.

Editorial Annotations

Editorial annotations, which appear as footnotes to the text, have been kept to a minimum. For each sermon, the unnumbered first note supplies what is known about its composition and, drawing on Emerson's manuscript Preaching Record and notations on the sermon manuscript itself, information about when and where it was delivered. If substantial draft passages relating to the sermon exist in the *Journals and Miscellaneous Notebooks,* that fact is given in the first note; otherwise, the existence of briefer draft passages is indicated in the appropriate place in subsequent notes. Biblical and other allusions are identified in the numbered notes, as are Emerson's uses of sermon material in lectures and other later compositions.

Emerson's repetitions of the main Bible text in each sermon are not annotated. Phrases of common occurrence in the King James Version of the Bible, such as "the fountain of life" and "the work of his hands," for example, belong to Emerson's generally biblical rhetoric in the sermons and are not annotated. An effort has also been made to annotate passages that occur only in the textual notes, primarily to have as full a record as possible of Emerson's use of the Bible; these allusions have been included in the Index of Biblical References. The present volume contains cumulative indexes to the entire edition.

An Emerson Chronology

November 1831 to January 1839

Note: When two sermons are listed as having been preached on a particular day, the first is the morning sermon, the second the afternoon sermon. A third sermon indicates a special Sunday evening service. Emerson also delivered sermons for Thursday (or other weekday) lectures, Fast Days, Thanksgiving, Christmas, and New Year's Eve.

While Emerson (and others) often referred to Boston's Second Church as the "North Church" or the "Old North Church," it is here always identified as the Second Church. It should not be confused with another "Old North," the Anglican church associated with Paul Revere's ride; that church, which Emerson referred to as the "New North," was at this time led by Francis Parkman, father of the historian. Similarly, Nathaniel Frothingham's First Church was popularly known as "Chauncy (or Chauncey) Place"; to avoid confusion, it is regularly identified in the following Chronology as the First Church.

1831

Nov. 27	Preaches LXXI (Second Church) and CXXXIV (Purchase St.).
Dec. 1	Thanksgiving; preaches CXXXVI (Second Church).
Dec. 4	Preaches CXXXVII (Second Church) and CXXXIV (New North Church, for Francis Parkman).
Dec. 11	Preaches LXVII and XLIV (Second Church).
Dec. 18	Preaches CXXI and CXVIII (Lynn, for David Hatch Barlow).
Dec. 23	Preaches LXXXVI as a Friday Evening Lecture, presumably at the Second Church.
Dec. 24	*Christian Register:* "The Sunday evening lectures by Unitarian clergymen will commence tomorrow evening at the Rev. Mr. Emerson's church, in Hanover Street, and will be continued alternately there and at the Rev. Mr. Motte's church, at the corner of Washington and Castle Streets."
Dec. 25	Preaches CXXXVIII at the Second Church in the morning and at the First Church in the afternoon. Emerson: "The Sunday Evg lectures begin this Evg Dr Channing was to have preached yᵉ first at my church. When I told Mr Park-

man y^t he wd. not, he broke out 'With all my respect for genius that man is a plague to Christendom'" (*L* 1: 341).

Dec. 31   Preaches CXXXIX (Second Church) in the evening.

1832

Jan. 1   Preaches XCVI (Second Church) and XV (New North Church).

Jan. 8   Preaches CXL and XXXVI (Second Church).

Jan. 10   "It is the best part of the man, I sometimes think, that revolts most against his being the minister. His good revolts from official goodness" (*JMN* 3:318).

Jan. 15   Preaches CXLI and LXXIV (Second Church), and CXXI as an Evening Lecture (Castle St.).

Jan. 22   Preaches CXVIII (East Cambridge).

Jan. 29   Preaches CXLII (Second Church), CXL (New South), and XCVIII (Friend St.).

Feb. 5   Preaches CXLIII and LXV (Second Church).

Feb. 12   Preaches CXLIV (Second Church) and CXLIII (Federal St.).

Feb. 19   Preaches CXLIV (Cambridge, First Parish, for William Newell) and CXLIV (Hollis St., for John Pierpont).

Feb. 24   Preaches LXVIII as a Friday Evening Lecture, presumably at the Second Church. In a letter, Mary Moody Emerson pleads with her nephew to remain in the ministry, to leave a name to be "enrolled with the Mathers & Sewalls of that venerable City" (*L* 1:353n).

Feb. 26   Preaches CXLV and XCI (Second Church).

Mar. 1   Preaches CXLIV, a Thursday Lecture (Federal St.).

Mar. 4   Preaches CXLVI and C (Second Church), and CXVIII (Friend St.).

Mar. 11   Preaches CXLIV and CXXI (Watertown, for Convers Francis).

Mar. 18   Preaches CXLVII and LXVI (Second Church).

Mar. 25   Preaches CXLVIII (Second Church) and CXXXIV (Castle St.).

Mar. 29   "I visited Ellen's tomb & opened the coffin" (*JMN* 4:7).

Apr. 1   Preaches CXLIX and LXXVI (Second Church).

Apr. 5   Fast Day; preaches CL at the New North in the morning and at the Second Church in the afternoon.

Apr. 8   Preaches CLI (Second Church) and CXLIV (West Church, for Charles Lowell).

Apr. 15   Preaches CXLIV and CXVIII (West Cambridge).

Apr. 19	Preaches CXLIII as a Thursday Lecture, presumably at the Second Church.
Apr. 22	Preaches CLII and XCIII (Second Church).
Apr. 29	Preaches CLIII (Second Church) and LXXXI (First Church).
Apr. 27	Preaches an unidentified sermon as a Friday Evening Lecture, presumably at the Second Church.
May 6	Preaches CLIV (Second Church) and CLII (Purchase St.).
May 13	Preaches CLV (Second Church) and CLII (New South).
May 20	Preaches CLVI and XCIV (Second Church).
May 27	Preaches CLVII (Second Church), CLVI (Twelfth Church), and CXLVII (Friend St.).
May 29	The annual meeting of the American Unitarian Association (May 29–31); Emerson attends.
June 2	"Thermometer Says Temperate. Yet a week of moral excitement. . . . I have sometimes thought that in order to be a good minister it was necessary to leave the ministry. The profession is antiquated. In an altered age, we worship in the dead forms of our forefathers. Were not a Socratic paganism better than an effete superannuated Christianity?" (*JMN* 4:27). About this date Emerson sends a letter to a committee of the Second Church indicating his altered views on the Lord's Supper (*L* 1:351).
June 3	Preaches CXLIV and XCV (Waltham, for Samuel Ripley), and LXXIX, the Charity Lecture (Old South).
June 10	Preaches CLVIII and LXXXVII (Second Church).
June 11	Charles Emerson to Mary Moody Emerson: "I wish I had time & energy to give you a full account of what Waldo has been about lately—but by & by when the end has come, I may be better able to set in order the whole story—meantime be assured I respect him more than ever for his sincere & independent course" (RWEMA).
June 16	Report of Second Church Committee, responding to Emerson's letter concerning the Lord's Supper (*L* 1:351).
June 17	Preaches CLIX and LX (Second Church).
June 21	Meeting of the Second Church to consider the committee report of June 16; the report is affirmed and a letter to Emerson is drafted (*L* 1:352–53). Emerson travels to Portsmouth, N.H., with Charles (*JMN* 4:228).
June 24	Preaching Record: "Second Church vacant for repairs 6 weeks"; Emerson is visiting his aunt in Waterford, Maine (*JMN* 4:228).
July 1	Preaches CXXI and CXVIII (Fryeburg, Maine).
July 8	Probably preaches again in Fryeburg (*L* 1:353n).

July 15	With Mary Moody Emerson at Crawford's Inn at the Notch of the White Mountains; reads Sewel's *History of the Quakers* (*JMN* 4:29–33).
July 24	Charles Emerson: "Waldo . . . is for this last day or two troubled with a diarrhoea which he is nursing lest a worse thing come upon him. . . . He will preach to his *Society* (to them he has not hitherto mentioned the matter publickly,— only to the *Church*) his opinions the 2d Sabbath in August,—and will probably afterward ask a dismission—this will bring things to a legal issue. This however is not yet said to any but a few friends. . . . I had hoped Waldo was to be fixed for some years longer exactly where he is—The prospect seemed brightening & enlarging before him— But he must follow his conscience wheresoever it leads—& I acquiesce & sometimes think I am not sorry" (RWEMA; *L* 1:353n).
Aug. 19	Emerson to Mary Moody Emerson: "I have been shut up almost ever since I returned home with the meanest complaint & though I came home stronger & fatter than for years it has stripped me to bones. . . . I have not yet come to any point with my people, my explanation being postponed by my ails, and have not come to any new point with myself. . . . Ellen is beyond misfortune, & I will not invite any others to penury & disappointment if I am doomed" (*L* 1:352–54).
Aug. 26	Preaches CXLIV and XIX (Hingham, for Mr. Brooks).
Sept. 2	Preaches CLX and CLXI (Second Church).
Sept. 9	Preaches CLXII ("The Lord's Supper" sermon) and CIX (Second Church). Charles reports a crowded house at the morning service: "If the Parish were to be polled probably ¾ would be for keeping their minister on his own terms— but this will not be done—because certain of the most influential men in the Church & Society adhere to the ordinance, & would be thereby grieved & sent away—So they have chosen a committee which is to confer with Waldo & which will probably after some talk & expressions of unfeigned regret, let him go & bid him God speed. What he will do is uncertain—I think he will gather a parish of his own by & by—He behaves magnanimously to the bone— & will not print his sermon which would justify & make proselytes for him, because he does not wish to do anything in hostility to the ordinance or shocking to good but weak vessels" (RWEMA; *L* 1:355n).
Sept. 11	Emerson submits his letter of resignation (*L* 1:355–57).

Sept. 13	Charles thinks that the Church "will probably appoint a committee to confer with him—& if any plan can be hit upon by which he can stay with them & not administer the ordinance, both parties will be pleased" (RWEMA).
Sept. 16	Preaches CLXIII and XXXV (Second Church). Preaching Record: "Sent a communication to the Proprietors this day."
Sept. 23	Preaches CXVII (Second Church).
Sept. 26	Charles: "Waldo is very feeble—His people dont like to let him go away from them—At present the disposition is to make arrangements so as to keep him—He will probably stay where he is this winter—His friends are many & kind" (RWEMA; L 1:356n).
Oct. 21	Preaches CLXIV (Second Church).
Oct. 28	According to the Preaching Record, David Hatch Barlow preached this day at the Second Church, though a letter from Charles to William Emerson of November 2 clearly indicates that Emerson preached: "Did I say how well Waldo preached last Sunday? He made me laugh & feel sad—I recognized mine ancient, my real preacher & teacher. Mother & Elizabeth [Hoar] were there to hear him" (RWEMA). In the evening, the Proprietors meet and accept Emerson's resignation by a vote of 34 to 25. They further express their continuing regard for their minister, and continue his salary for the time being. Preaching Record: "This day the Proprietors voted to accept my letter of resignation of office."
Dec. 22	Emerson's Farewell Letter to the Second Church.
Dec. 25	Emerson sails from Boston aboard the *Jasper,* bound for Sicily.

1833

Oct. 7	Emerson arrives in New York on his way back from Europe (*L* 1:397).
Oct. 9	Arrives in Boston; stays briefly with his friend George Adams Sampson.
Oct. 20	Moves to Newton to stay with his mother.
Oct. 27	Preaches CLXV (Second Church).
Nov. 5	Emerson begins his lecturing career with "The Uses of Natural History," before the Natural History Society, at the Masonic Temple, Boston.
Nov. 10	Preaches CLV and CXLIV (New Bedford, for Orville Dewey).
Nov. 17	Preaches CLXIV and XCIV (New Bedford).

Nov. 24	Preaches CXXXVII and CXLIX (New Bedford).
Nov. 28	Preaches an unidentified Thanksgiving sermon (New Bedford).
Dec. 1	Preaches LXXXI and CLX (New Bedford).
Dec. 4	Ordination of Chandler Robbins as Emerson's successor at the Second Church; Emerson writes a hymn for the occasion (*JMN* 4:97n).
Dec. 8	Preaches CXLI and CXLIII (New Bedford).
Dec. 15	Preaches CXXXVII (Second Church).
Dec. 22	Preaches CLX (First Church).

1834

Jan. 5	Preaches CLIV (Friend St.).
Jan. 12	Preaches CXLI (Hollis St.).
Jan. 26	Preaches CLIV and XCV (New Bedford).
Feb. 2	Preaches CXXII and CXXVI (New Bedford).
Feb. 9	Preaches CIV and CLXIII (New Bedford). The latter sermon number is followed by a question mark in the Preaching Record, but see *JMN* 4:252.
Feb. 16	Preaches CXXIV and CXVII (New Bedford).
Feb. 23	Preaches CXXIV and CLXIV (Hollis St.).
Mar. 2	Preaches CXXVII (Federal St.).
Mar. 9	Preaches CXXVII and LXXIX (New Bedford).
Mar. 13	Preaches CLX, Thursday Evening Lecture (Plymouth).
Mar. 16	Preaches CLXV and XXXIII (New Bedford).
Mar. 21	Swedenborgian minister Artemas Stebbins tells Emerson that he (Stebbins) need not preach, since Emerson is "giving as much New Jerusalem doctrine as the people will bear" (*JMN* 4:269).
Mar. 23	Preaches CXXI and LXXVI (New Bedford).
Mar. 30	Preaches CLXVI and CXI (New Bedford).
Apr. 3	Fast Day; preaches CLX (Waltham).
Apr. 6	Preaches CLXIII (New North), CLV (Hollis St.), and CXLIX (Friend St.).
Apr. 13	Preaches CLXIV (Federal St.).
Apr. 20	Attends installation of Samuel H. Stearns as pastor at the Old South; hears his inaugural sermon in the morning, and another, from Frothingham, in the afternoon (*JMN* 4:277).
Apr. 27	Preaches CXLIX and CLXIII (Waltham, Second Church).
May 4	Preaches CXXI and CXLI (Waltham, Second Church).
May 11	Preaches CLXIV and CXXIV (Watertown).
May 13	About this date Emerson receives the first half of the Tucker inheritance, $11,600 (*L* 1:413–14).

May 14	Emerson's first letter to Carlyle.
May 18	Preaches CLXIV, CXLIX, and CXLI (Fall River).
May 25	Preaches CLXVII and CLX (Hollis St.).
June 1	Preaches CLXIV and CIV (Waltham, Second Church).
June 8	Preaches CLIII and XCIV (Hollis St.).
June 15	Preaches CXLI and CXLIX (Watertown).
June 22	Preaches CXLIX (Newton Upper Falls).
June 29	Preaches CLXI and CLXIV (Waltham, Second Church). Charles: "At Church Waldo preached soul-helpfully" (RWEMA).
July 6	Preaches CLXIV and CLX (Bangor).
July 13	Preaches CXXI, CLXIII, and CXLIX (Bangor).
July 20	Preaches CXLI and CIV (Bangor), and gives an evening lecture on Temperance at Stillwater, Maine.
July 23	Attends installation of John Maltby at the Hammond Street Congregational Church, Bangor. In the evening George Adams Sampson dies in Portland on his way to join Emerson (JMN 3:307–8; L 1:417).
July 27	Preaches CLXVI, XCIV, CLIII, and CXLIV (Bangor).
July 30	Charles: "Waldo says the Bangor folk warmed to the First Philosophy, & tease him to make them some promises. He is half inclined to hear them; I tell him if he goes as minister, I will go as lawyer" (RWEMA).
Aug. 3	Preaches CLXVIII, a eulogy for George Adams Sampson (Second Church). Elizabeth Palmer Peabody and Bronson Alcott attend.
Aug. 10	Attends the Baptist church in Newton (JMN 4:309).
Aug. 24	Preaches CXXVII and XCIV (Waltham, for Samuel Ripley).
Aug. 27	Charles reports that Orville Dewey is ill and has asked Emerson to be his successor at New Bedford (RWEMA).
Aug. 28	Emerson reads his Phi Beta Kappa poem at Harvard Commencement.
Aug. 31	Preaches CLXVI and CLXI (First Church).
Sept. 7	Preaches CLXIX and CLXI (New Bedford).
Sept. 20	Emerson: "After much conversation with the New Bedford people & Mr. Dewey I have declined going there for the coming winter & therefore I return with pleasure to our former prospect of spending the winter at Concord" (L 1:420).
Oct. 1	Edward Bliss Emerson dies in Puerto Rico.
Oct. 19	Preaches CXLI and CLXIII (Second Church, New York, where Orville Dewey will shortly be installed).
Oct. 26	Preaches CLXIV and CXLIX (Second Church, New York).
Nov. 2	Preaches CLXIX (Second Church, New York) and CLX (First Church, New York).

Nov. 9	Preaches CLXVI and CXXI (Second Church, New York), and CLX (Brooklyn).
Nov. 16	Preaches CLX (Concord).
Nov. 30	Preaches CXLIII (Waltham, Second Church) and CLVII, the revised sermon on Astronomy (Waltham, First Church, for Samuel Ripley). Solar eclipse visible this day at Waltham.
Dec. 6	Charles reports that Emerson is considering a call to Waltham (RWEMA). Bernard Whitman of the Second Church, ill since the spring, had died November 5.
Dec. 7	Preaches CLXIII (Concord).
Dec. 14	Preaches CXLIX and CLX (Sudbury).

1835

Jan. 1	Preaches CII, Thursday Lecture (Concord).
Jan. 7	Emerson: "I think when I have done with my lectures which begin shortly I shall write & print a discourse upon Spiritual & Traditional Religion, for Form seems to be bowing Substance out of the World & men doubt if there be any such thing as spiritual nature out of the carcass in which once it dwelt" (L 1:430–31).
Jan. 18	Preaches CLXIV, CLX, and CXXIV (Lowell).
Jan. 21	Preaches CLXIX, Wednesday Lecture (Plymouth).
Jan. 24	Emerson proposes marriage to Lydia Jackson, of Plymouth, by letter.
Mar. 1	Preaches CLV and CXI (Waltham, Second Church).
Mar. 8	Preaches LXXVI and LXXIX (Waltham, Second Church).
Mar. 15	Preaches CXXXVII and CXVII (Waltham, Second Church).
Mar. 22	Preaches XCIX and CLII (Waltham, Second Church).
Mar. 29	Preaches CXXIV (Waltham, Second Church) and CLXIX, revised version (Waltham, First Church).
Apr. 5	Preaches CLV, CXI, and CXLIX (Plymouth).
Apr. 9	Fast Day; preaches CL (Waltham, Second Church) and CXXII (Waltham, First Church).
Apr. 12	Preaches LXXVI and CXVII (Watertown).
Apr. 19	Preaches XCIII and CXLIX (Acton).
Apr. 26	Preaches CLXX (Seamen's Bethel, Boston).
May 3	Preaches CXLI and CXLIX (East Lexington).
May 10	Preaches CLXIV and CLX (East Lexington).
May 17	Preaches CXLI and CXLIX (Chelmsford).
May 31	Preaches CLV and CXXXVII (Groton).
June 3	Harriet Martineau "says that Mr Ware is sanctimonious, Mr Gannett popish, Unitarians in a twilight of bigotry, and that Mr Furness has a genius for religion" (JMN 5:47).

June 14	Preaches CXXIV and CLXIII (Framingham).
June 21	Preaches CXLVIII and CXLI (Framingham).
June 28	Preaches CLX and LXXVI (Framingham).
July 5	Preaches CXXXVII and CXLIII (Framingham).
July 7	About this time Emerson buys the Coolidge House in Concord for $3,500.
July 12	Preaches CXLVI and CXXXIV (Lexington). (The Preaching Record indicates Lexington, though just possibly the deliveries were at East Lexington: On September 9 Charles Follen paid Emerson $30 for supplying East Lexington twice in May and once in July.)
July 19	Preaches CLXIX (First Church, Boston) in the afternoon.
July 26	Preaches CXXXIV and CX (Waltham, First Church).
Aug. 9	Preaches CXXXIV and XCIV (Chelmsford).
Aug. 11	Attends meeting of the Cambridge Association of Congregational Ministers, held at the Old Manse. Convers Francis and Frederic Hedge among those present.
Aug. 16	Preaches CLX and XCIV (Acton).
Aug. 23	Preaches XCIV and CXI (Lowell).
Aug. 30	Preaches CLXVI and CXVIII (Lowell).
Sept. 12	Emerson delivers the "Historical Discourse" at the Concord Bicentennial.
Sept. 14	Emerson marries Lydia Jackson in Plymouth.
Nov. 1	Preaches CXVIII and XXVI (East Lexington).
Nov. 8	Preaches CXXIV and LXXIX (East Lexington).
Nov. 15	Preaches CLXIV and CXXIV (Concord).
Nov. 22	Preaches CXLIV and CXXXVII (East Lexington).
Dec. 3	Thanksgiving; preaches CXXXVI (East Lexington).
Dec. 6	Preaches CIV and XXXVII (East Lexington).
Dec. 13	Preaches XCVI and XXXVII (Waltham, Second Church).
Dec. 20	Preaches CXI and CXLVIII (East Lexington).
Dec. 27	Preaches CXXXVIII and CLXI (East Lexington).

1836

Jan. 3	Preaches CXXXIX and CII (East Lexington).
Jan. 10	Preaches CXXXVI and CXLIII (Concord). George Moore: "Today, heard some sermons of a high literary order from Rev. R. W. Emerson, in the morning, upon the duty of praise and gratitude to God for existence, and what makes existence happy—for friends—for civilization—and for providence—in the afternoon, upon the fitness of every man for some particular sphere in life, and the consequent duty of every man's studying himself in order to find out

what his particular sphere of action is. By such study, every man will sooner or later find out for what he is best fitted— and will never feel easy and happy until he does find out and enter it" (Kenneth W. Cameron, ed., *The Transcendentalists and Minerva* [Hartford, 1958], 463).

Jan. 17	Preaches CLX and CXXXIV (Weston).
Jan. 24	Preaches CLV and LXXVI (East Lexington).
Jan. 31	Preaches XCIX and XCIV (East Lexington).
Feb. 7	Preaches CXXXVI and CVIII (Waltham, First Church).
Feb. 14	Preaches LXXXI and XCVI (East Lexington).
Mar. 6	Preaches CLXVI and CLXIX (Harvard College Chapel, for John L. Sibley).
Mar. 13	Preaches CVIII and XXXIII (East Lexington).
Mar. 20	Preaches CLIII and CLXIII (East Lexington).
Mar. 27	Preaches CLX and CXLI (Lexington).
Apr. 3	Preaches CXVII and CXXI (East Lexington).
Apr. 7	Fast Day; preaches CL and reads "Martin Luther" (East Lexington).
Apr. 10	Preaches CXXVII and CLVI (East Lexington).
Apr. 17	Preaches CXII and CIX (East Lexington).
Apr. 24	Preaching Record indicates "Springfield" but gives no sermon numbers; Emerson is traveling to New York with his ailing brother Charles.
May 1	Preaches CXXXVI and CIX (Lowell).
May 8	Preaches CLX and CXXXVI (Salem, for Charles W. Upham).
May 9	Charles Chauncy Emerson dies in New York.
May 11	Emerson attends his brother's funeral in New York.
May 29	Preaches CXIV and CXLII (East Lexington).
June 5	Preaches CXIV, CLIII, and CXLIV (Concord).
June 11	"I know not why, but I hate to be asked to preach here in Concord. I never go to the Sunday School Teachers without fear & shame" (*JMN* 5:173).
June 12	Preaches CXXXIII and LXXVIII (East Lexington). Elizabeth Palmer Peabody and Bronson Alcott attend (Joel Myerson, "Bronson Alcott's Journal for 1836," *Studies in the American Renaissance* [Boston, 1978], 60).
June 19	Preaches CXXXIII and CXVII (Concord).
June 26	Preaches CXXXVII and CXXXIV (West Cambridge).
June 30	Preaches LXXVIII, Thursday Lecture (Concord).
July 3	Preaches LIV and LIX (East Lexington).
July 9	Hersey B. Goodwin, associate pastor to Ezra Ripley, dies in Plymouth.

July 10   Preaches CLII and XCIV (Concord).

July 17   Preaches CLXXI (East Lexington) and CLXXI (Concord) in eulogy of Hersey B. Goodwin.

July 21   This day or the next, Margaret Fuller comes to Concord for a three-week visit with the Emersons, their first acquaintance (*L* 2:29–30, 32n; *JMN* 5:186, 188).

July 24   Preaches CXXVII and CIV (Concord).

July 31   Preaches CLII (East Lexington). Margaret Fuller attends.

Aug. 7   Preaches CXLI and LXXXI (Concord). Reported by George Moore (see Cameron, *The Transcendentalists and Minerva*, 465).

Aug. 14   Preaches CIX and CV (East Lexington).

Aug. 21   Preaches CLXI and LXXVI (Concord).

Aug. 28   Preaches CLXVI and XXXV (East Lexington).

Sept. 4   Preaches XCIII and LXXXVII (East Lexington).

Sept. 8   First meeting of the Transcendental Club, at Harvard Commencement.

Sept. 9   *Nature* published.

Sept. 11   Preaches XXXVII and CXXXVII (Concord).

Sept. 18   Preaches XIX and LXIV (East Lexington).

Sept. 25   Preaches CXLI and CLX (Groton, for Charles Robinson). Margaret Fuller attends.

Oct. 2   Preaches LXXXIX and XV (East Lexington).

Oct. 9   Preaches LXXXIX and LXXVIII (Waltham, Second Church).

Oct. 11   Ambrose Morell writes that money has been raised to conduct public worship in East Lexington, on the condition that Emerson be in charge (*L* 2:79n).

Oct. 16   Preaches CLIV and XLVII (East Lexington).

Oct. 23   Preaches LXXIII and CXLV (East Lexington).

Oct. 30   Preaches XXVI and LXXXIX (Wayland). Waldo Emerson born at 11 P.M.

Nov. 6   Preaches C and XCVIII (East Lexington).

Nov. 13   Preaches LXX and CLI (East Lexington).

Nov. 20   Preaches CLXI and XCIV (Weston).

Nov. 27   Preaches CXXV and XCV (East Lexington).

Dec. 1   Thanksgiving; preaches XCVII, augmented with two pages from XII (East Lexington).

Dec. 4   Preaches LXXXIX and XCV (Concord). Reported by George Moore (see Cameron, *The Transcendentalists and Minerva*, 466).

Dec. 18   Preaches CXLVII and LXXXVI (East Lexington).

Dec. 25   Preaches LX, augmented with the introduction from XIII, and LXXII (East Lexington).

1837

Jan. 1	Preaches CI and LXXXV (East Lexington).
Jan. 8	Preaches LXXXII and XXI (East Lexington).
Jan. 15	Preaches CXXXVII and CXXXVI (Lexington).
Jan. 22	Preaches CXI and LXXXV (Concord).
Feb. 1	Attends ordination of Barzillai Frost in Concord.
Feb. 5	Preaches LXII and CXV (East Lexington).
Feb. 12	Preaches LXXI and LVI (East Lexington).
Feb. 19	Preaches CLIII and CLXI (Waltham, First Church).
Mar. 5	Preaches XXIII and LXXXVIII (East Lexington).
Mar. 12	Preaches XLVI and XLV (East Lexington).
Mar. 19	Preaches CXLV and CLVI (Waltham, First Church).
Mar. 26	Preaches XCV and LXXVIII (Lowell, for Henry A. Miles).
Apr. 2	Preaches XC and LII (East Lexington).
Apr. 6	Fast Day; preaches CXIII and reads "George Fox" (East Lexington).
Apr. 9	Preaches XLVIII and LV (East Lexington).
Apr. 16	Preaches XLIII (East Lexington) and CLXIV (Lexington).
Apr. 23	Preaches CLIII (Wayland, for Richard T. Austin).
Apr. 30	Preaches XLIII and CLXIII (Watertown).
June 4	Preaches CLXV (East Lexington) and CLII (Lexington).
June 13	Ministerial Association meeting at Emerson's house; Orville Dewey and Caleb Stetson among those present (*L* 2:80–81).
July 16	Preaches XXV and XXXIX (East Lexington).
July 23	Preaches XLIII and CLII (Framingham).
July 25	About this time Emerson receives the second half of the Tucker inheritance, $11,674.49 (*L* 2:87, 91–92).
July 30	Preaches CXXIII and XLI (East Lexington).
Aug. 6	Preaches XXVII and CX (East Lexington).
Aug. 8	Emerson pays John Sullivan Dwight for five weeks of supply at East Lexington (Account Books).
Aug. 20	Preaches LXXXV and CLI (Waltham, First Church).
Aug. 31	Delivers American Scholar Address during Phi Beta Kappa Day ceremonies, Harvard.
Sept. 1	Meeting of Transcendental Club at Emerson's home (*L* 2:95n).
Sept. 3	Preaches CLIX and CXIX (East Lexington).
Sept. 10	Preaches CLVII and CLXIX (East Lexington).
Sept. 24	Preaches CXXX (East Lexington).
Oct. 8	Preaches CLIX and XLIII (Waltham, First Church).
Oct. 15	Preaches CXXXVII and XXXVII (Billerica).
Oct. 22	Preaches CXVI (both parts) (East Lexington).

Oct. 29	Preaches XLIX and LIII (East Lexington).
Nov. 5	Preaches LXVIII and LXV (East Lexington).
Nov. 12	Preaches XC and CXIX (Waltham, Second Church).
Nov. 19	Preaches CLIX and CLVII (Concord).
Nov. 26	Preaches XXXVII and CXI (Weston).

1838

Feb. 4	Preaches CLV and CXLV (Concord).
Feb. 10	Attends meeting of Sunday School teachers; Henry Thoreau also present (*JMN* 5:452).
Feb. 11	Preaches XLIII (Concord).
Feb. 18	Preaches CXXXV and XCII (East Lexington). Emerson tries unsuccessfully to transfer responsibility for the East Lexington parish to John S. Dwight (*L* 2:113).
Feb. 25	Preaches CLVIII and IV (East Lexington).
Mar. 18	Hears Barzillai Frost at Concord: "At Church all day but almost tempted to say I would go no more. . . . The snowstorm was real, the preacher merely spectral" (*JMN* 5:463).
Mar. 21	Students at Harvard Divinity School invite Emerson to give an address (*L* 2:129n).
Mar. 25	Preaches CLIV and LXXXVII, "enlarged by Lect on Religion" (East Lexington).
Apr. 1	"The Divinity School youths wished to talk with me concerning theism. I went rather heavy-hearted for I always find that my views chill or shock people at the first opening. But the conversation went well & I came away cheered" (*JMN* 5:471).
Apr. 4	Emerson meets Jones Very for the first time.
Apr. 8	Preaches enlarged versions of CLIV and LXXXVII (New York).
Apr. 29	Preaches XXXVII and LXXXVII (enlarged) (Waltham, First Church).
July 15	Delivers the Divinity School Address. Among those present, besides the students, are Henry Ware, John G. Palfrey, Cyrus Bartol, Elizabeth Palmer Peabody, Theodore Parker, Andrews Norton, Jones Very, and Lidian Emerson. Among the students are H. G. O. Blake and Robert C. Waterston.
Aug. 12	Preaches CLIV and LXXXVII (enlarged) (Watertown).
Aug. 26	George Moore: "Mr. Emerson gave a general lesson to the Sab. School, upon the difference between good and bad . . . . Good is useful—bad is hurtful. Everything in nature has its use . . . . So every person should be useful in his sphere of life. He who is most useful is the best. God is the

greatest and best, because He is the servant of all—is useful to all. Every useful action brings with it its reward. Every base action degrades the actor" (Cameron, *The Transcendentalists and Minerva,* 470).

Sept. 23   Henry Ware preaches "The Personality of the Deity" in reply to Emerson.

1839

Jan. 13   Preaches CI and LXXXVII (enlarged) (Concord).
Jan. 20   Preaches CLXIX (Concord).

THE SERMONS

CXXXVI

O give thanks unto the Lord; for he is good:
for his mercy endureth forever.
Who can utter the mighty acts of the Lord?
Who can show forth all his praise?

PSALMS 106:1–2

We are called upon to give thanks. Let us respond to the call. The summons to gratitude ought never to find us unprepared. Let the sentiment of David be ours, "as long as I live I will praise him, I will give thanks whilst I have my being."[1] It should be a welcome call. It is not long that we can pay it in the world. To each one are a few thousand days; a few budding springs, and snowy winters; three or four memorable events; a few friendships formed and broken, a few gains and losses, a little store of knowledge, a bird's eye view of the agitations in the human family in what is called church and state, and our own guesses thereupon; a few irregular very unsystematic actions, some very bad ones that we wince to think on, some natural pleasures, a delighted glance or two at the sun as he rises into the morning heaven, of vague wonder at the moon and stars; a feeble interest in the future welfare of our children and friends and town and country;—and the drowsiness of age steals over our senses, the eyes fix, and the pulse stops. The friends come and mournfully lay the poor carcass in the ground; they survive and act; but the individual is gone forever. Gone. Where is he gone? The heart and the gospel say "He is not here, he is risen."[2] It is that word that puts a new face upon the whole picture; that runs back and animates the trivial passages of forgotten lives; that casts a pathos and sweetness into the whole history, and raises each incident by its relation to what is to come. Let us then adorn this fleeting being with so natural and generous a sentiment as gratitude for whatever good we enjoy. We did not make ourselves.[3] We did not make the things that give us pleasure. Let us own it. Praise is the acknowledgment that

---

Manuscript dated December 1, 1831, at Chardon Street. Preached seven times: Thanksgiving Day, December 1, 1831, at the Second Church, Boston; Thanksgiving Day, December 3, 1835, in East Lexington; January 10, 1836, in Concord; February 7 in Waltham; May 1 in Lowell; May 8 in Salem; and January 15, 1837, in Lexington.

1. Cf. Psalms 104:33 and 146:2.
2. Matthew 28:6; cf. Mark 16:6 and Luke 24:6.
3. Cf. Psalms 100:3.

whatever good belongs to the mind has its source in God. It will then differ in every mind according as its sight is opened to see good. But it is becoming to all, and for all they have.

My friends, I desire to call your attention to the first and plainest topics of gratitude. We need not go far to find them. They are close by. It was a saying of an ancient poet that Water was the best of things,4 by which he would intimate that the best things are the universal gifts. A throne, immense riches, a prodigious success, brilliant fame, belong to here and there an individual. Well, do not covet them. They have as many pangs as sweets. The best things which they who have them enjoy, are those which are common to them with men of the humblest condition. It is only in connexion with the first common riches that these rare ornaments have any value, as diamonds would not be good for any thing if there were no bread to eat. It is because they who have these things have the others, because they can think, because they have friends; home; are spectators with other men of God's world; and hope with other men, that they shall not die. It is because they can draw with their bucket from the eternal well of truth from which all the dwellers on the earth draw; it is because they have these, that these distinctions are any thing beyond the pearl of the cock in the fable.5

    1. First then I hold it to be to a rational mind a topic of thanksgiving, *that it exists*. Merely *to be*, is something; to be intelligent is much more; is so much that until sin has deformed and unblest it, it seems to comprehend all things, and to be a tautology to say, 'I am thankful that I am.' To be a spectator of what is done in heaven and earth, to witness the magnificent phenomenon of a Day— what a vast expenditure of forces; what floods of light; what amounts of attraction; what enormous journeys through space; what multitudes of orderly processes going on throughout all things at the same time puzzle and astonish us when we try to analyze the exhibition that nature offers us in a single day. Yet is all this bewildering pomp and magnitude of works done with the quiet with which a leaf falls in the forest. The morning has its wonders, and the noon, and the night. The resurrection of all men from sleep; the congratulation that smiles in all the families of the world that they yet exist under a Power which they do not make, or affect, or see. The houses are emptied and the human race are again scattered over the face of the earth.

They go out to trust again with implicit confidence the old laws, to use again the powers of nature, water, and fire, and steel, and wood, and clay, and the animals, as they did yesterday. They mix in the workyards, and the markets, and the statehouses, and the fields, and on the seas; and over all the round sun shines in the firmament enlightening, warming, cheering all, and the blaze of so many ages has not bereft him of a ray.

There is not a minute in the twenty-four hours that is not filled with miracles when once we attempt to detail and explain all.

---

4. Pindar, *Olympian Odes*, I:I; see *JMN* 6:94. Used in "Water" (*EL* 1:50).
5. The reference is to Aesop's fable "The Cock and the Jewel."

2. But to withdraw ourselves from so universal and familiar a blessing, as this great one of bare spectatorship in the world, and to come in doors to a much smaller and more precise consideration, or rather to advance from the simple blessing of *being* to the first connexion with others, I will mention another topic of gratitude which all may feel,—I mean the pleasures of Home. I am thankful that I am connected intimately with a few of my fellowmen, that we sit together at one fire, and eat bread at one table. I do not use this word in a narrow sense; it does not need that a man should own a house, or even live with his own kindred, to enjoy the general good signified by this word. All I mean is to be so related to a few as we are not to many. It is one of the intensest pleasures, to see far into the thoughts of another, and to be seen into by another,—to have a mutual interest established between a few persons in each other's thoughts, so that we feel that we are known, and that a confidence is established.

No man's life and motives are so transparent but that he is always liable to be misunderstood, and is very often misunderstood by those with whom he deals. It were an endless labor for even the most private and secluded man to set himself to clear up every doubtful word and action of his life, in the mind of every individual to whom they have gone with a false colouring. And the most sensitive is obliged to put up with a great deal of unjust personal prejudice. It is therefore coming out of shade into sunshine when he returns into the little company who know him well, who balance his virtues against his faults. A company where each is known to each; and perfect confidence reigns; and where each in his turn imparts and receives kind offices.

My brethren, this blessing of Home is greater than it seems to the heedless eye. It is the true soil where virtue flourishes. If there is any grace in the soul it will show itself there. I have known several men who were dishonoured abroad, who were revered at home as benefactors; and it has sometimes made me doubt whether all men are not at heart better than they seem; whether, since the most repulsive, disagreeable, wrongheaded persons have yet one right side, one kind aspect, we ought not to consider that perhaps many of their worst actions— hard and unjust as they appear—have a remote origin in this inward kindness, which whilst it forgets the many, spends itself on a few.

On this day of domestic recollections and joys, which is in New England the jubilee of firesides, let us appreciate the benevolence of him who formed the heart, and who has set the solitary in families.[6] Even though that little beloved company may have been thinned and the place of the dearest and most honoured is vacant yet more of comfort and instruction and hope shall issue out of the griefs of home than of the joys of the world beside.

3. Another cause of lively gratitude is a blessing a little beyond home, the acquaintance we have, near or remote, with persons of great worth. A cultivated heart and mind, a finished character, is the most excellent gift of God, the most excellent thing out of us that we can form an idea of. It is the plainest

---

6. Psalms 68:6.

revelation of God, the thing most like God, more plain and more persuasive than any book can be. How far more exciting is this spectacle of living virtues than the dead letter which describes the same virtues.[7] I look upon the persons of fine intellectual endowments and of magnanimous dispositions whom it is or has been my fortune to know, as my apostles and prophets. They perform to us the office of good angels; they show us to what height active virtue can be carried; the thought of them comes to us in the hour of despondency and of temptation, and holds us up from falling.

Now God has made no man so poor but his memory is enriched with the names of some persons to whom he looks up as signal examples of virtue. There are not only the eminent persons who are set by the course of events in the front of their age, and whose names are in all men's mouths as bywords,— the heroes and statesmen of the day, and, so that they be pure in their dangerous places, their fame cannot be too dear to us. But there are also lights not set so high that placed in obscure corners do yet cast a most useful and cheerful radiance in the limited room where they shine. Each of us knows an upright man whose interest never could convince him that a crooked course was a right one. Each of us knows some poor man of that true dignity of character that he has preserved his selfrespect and so the respect of other men under every disadvantage and the greatest misfortunes. We know some worthy woman whom evil example never could betray into the low gossip that abounds in society and to whom religion was support enough in loneliness and poverty. We know some one who never was so much afraid as ashamed to do an evil action and the sight of that friend's countenance raises our esteem of human nature. Or perhaps we have known (what more than any other invigorates our religious temper) a mind in whom faith seemed instinctive; a mind which though never too proud for engaging in the lowest occupations, yet drew in great thoughts as its natural air and lived by them; a mind which believed in its own immortality because the contrary opinion seemed absurd and inconsistent with all it knew and felt, and lived in such a lowly and perfect reverence of God that it was more jealous of his perfections than for its own destiny and resigned to be nothing at his will.

It is these good minds beyond the walls of home that seem to me to be one of the greatest mercies God bestows upon us and to demand of us therefore the most fervent acknowledgments.

4. To carry these considerations of blessings one step farther from self to kindred, from kindred to friends, from friends to mankind, it is a natural and obvious reason of gratitude our knowledge of and our connexion with all our fellowmen. Let us not stint our love and interest to ten or a hundred. Let us rejoice in the good of human society. Let us feel the warm blood that mounts in our veins in sympathy with all the blood of the Saxon race, with all of the Christian name, with all who have the gift of reason. I would feel an interest and property in the kindred civilization and arts and learning and laws and

---

7. See II Corinthians 3:6 on the "letter" versus the "spirit."

religion of England; in the liberal institutions of France, the scholar in liberty of England; in the wisdom of Germany; in the remembrances of Italy; in the patience of Spain; in the expectation of the children of freedom under every despotism; in all the virtue that fights with so much gross vice in Europe. I would feel an interest in the new dawn of commerce, and civilization and so the hope of religion in Asia, and the skirts of afflicted Africa. Let us rejoice in every acre of land won by the plough from sterile waste; in every comfort added by art to domestic life; in every discovery of science; in every victory that law gains over force; in every inch of ground won by the cause of human freedom, say rather in every battle fought for freedom, whether in the field or in senates; for, the defeats of Liberty, are only means by which she conquers more wisely and surely,—because the claim of political independence is founded on justice, and things will not rest, hearts will burn, conspiracies will be hatched, revolutions will break out, and things be confounded, until justice, which satisfies all men, be done.

Let us rejoice, brethren, in the instructive and animating spectacle which mankind present to us, in the facilities of intercourse, in the diffusion of knowledge, in the ascertaining of law, in the progress of liberty, in the triumphs of religion.

5. Finally it is a reason for praise that God is around all, embracing in his power the creation and inwardly present to every mind. Utterly unable as we are to form distinct conceptions of that Being, yet we know enough of him to fill us with a devout delight in the Divine Providence.

Let us give thanks for our religious nature, for this deep seated veneration of goodness, this invincible belief that whatever is, is wisely ordered, this love that in us is always seeking objects on which it can dwell and never finds here what it seeks, what satisfies it.

Let us give thanks for this obstinate conviction in us that in spite of all the appearances of decay in our bodily nature believes in its own accountableness, believes in duty, believes in the power of improvement without end, when it is stricken yet hopes on, when it is defeated recovers, when it has sinned repents, when life is departing triumphs. Let us rejoice in the living benevolence of Jesus Christ; in the affectionate Providence of God; in the knowledge of a future state. Let us rejoice in the nature of the soul which fits it for these, and forms it for praise. The harvest is now gathered in, and man and beast are made glad by its plenty, but it is always harvest to the soul. Summer and winter, spring and autumn make no change on its eternal nature. It gains by youth, and by age; it gains by plenty, it gains by privation, it gains by affliction, and remorse, and fear, and by the death of the body.

CXXXVII

Choose ye this day whom ye will serve; as for me and my house, we will serve the Lord.

JOSHUA 24:15

The sentiment of Love to God is the highest that can fill the soul. It is a question which every thinking being may well ask himself: what principle shall govern me? It is a question not whether any love shall govern him but what love. Shall it be idolatry or shall it be religion? It is not to choose whether he will serve or not, but whom he will serve.

I say it is not a question whether any love shall govern him, but what love. The human heart requires a God. Some god, a true or a false one, it must and will have. There exists no mind but is possessed with love either of good or of evil. It will make a god of Conscience, or of riches, or of power, or of science, or of honor, or of hatred, or of the belly. It was made through all its faculties to love, as a tree was made to bear fruit.

For every one may see, who will look at the mind as a philosopher, that whoever made us, we were made not for ourselves, but from the beginning to the end of our structure and of our progress, do plainly discover a reference to something else than ourselves.

The keenest and noblest of our pleasures is admiration. We are eager to admire. All men admire. To be without admiration of any thing is to be destitute of the mainspring of a progressive nature. We are so prone to this habit, that we make good which we do not find, and grow very dexterous in decking our idols.

Every one must have noticed the eager disposition to admire, that runs through almost all conversation. How fast does any wonderful story concerning any man's performance get abroad. It is repeated from mouth to mouth, a hundred or a thousand times, and the story never loses in one. If you have heard an eloquent oration, or seen a good book, or a beautiful face, or a fine landscape,

---

Manuscript dated December 4, 1831, at Boston, and November 23, 1833, at New Bedford. Preached eleven times: December 4, 1831, at the Second Church, Boston; November 24, 1833, in New Bedford; December 15 at the Second Church, Boston; March 15, 1835, at the Second Church, Waltham; May 31 in Groton; July 5 in Framingham; November 22 in East Lexington; June 26, 1836, in West Cambridge; September 11 in Concord; January 15, 1837, in Lexington; and October 15 in Billerica. A list of hymns headed "N.Y.C." on the first page of the manuscript suggests an unrecorded delivery in New York City.

or a worthy man, how prone are men to say not it is good, or fair, or upright, but it is the best, the fairest, the greatest they ever saw in their lives. Why do they say so? Not from an intention to deceive, but because for the time they really think so, not taking the pains to reflect, and because it is natural to the heart to give itself up to unbounded praise. Considerate persons gradually correct this habit in themselves and become more parsimonious of their praise. Why? Because they love less to admire? Oh no. But because they have corrected and extended their views of what is truly grand and beautiful. It is because they have refined on their admiration, and a more admiration has supplanted a less.

The fact is that the human heart is impatient of things finite, of a small limited merit of which it can see the beginning and the end, and loves to lose itself in the contemplation of the vast and unbounded. Did ever any body read or hear an eulogy which did not break over the strait edges of truth? Did ever any body read an essay upon a man of genius such as Shakspeare or Newton or upon a hero as Tell or Wallace or Washington that did not discover a disposition to magnify the genius or the prowess of the man?

This proneness to admiration, to an unlimited love of others, is a conspicuous peculiarity in man. It flows directly from his religious nature. It proves him to possess a religious nature. He is formed through all his faculties to love, to venerate, to adore. The improper direction of these feelings is idolatry. The right direction is true religion.

It has always seemed to me that much light upon the true intent of our faculties is got by looking into some of those remarkable sentiments which in all ages have exercised the strongest and the best influence over men, and whose only fault is that they have called out a strength of affection altogether disproportionate to their objects.

The most familiar and striking example of this tendency of the mind is in the passion of love. In young and ardent minds, as is well known, this passion increases by indulgence, and from slight preference proceeds to warm attachment, and then to extravagant devotion. The growing affection clothes its object in ideal perfections and cannot speak without hyperbole. It utters itself in expressions of selfdevotion which seem ridiculous to others, and if strictly applied to the actual characters concerned, would be so. The language of love approaches very near to the language of worship. But however extravagant the language the feeling is genuine in the mind of the lover. He really adores the excellences which he contemplates, though they are only attributes of his own mind, and do not exist, to that extent he supposes, in the character of his friend.

Every one knows, too, what heroic energy of thought and action this passion has imparted to the mind.

It ennobles and blesses the mind which feels it. "The lover," it is said, "is made happier by his affection, than the object of it can be. Like the song of the bird it cheers his own heart."[1] And it was avowed by a keen observer of human nature,

1. Augustus and Julius Hare, *Guesses at Truth* (London, 1827), 2:115-16; see *JMN* 3:297.

that "were it not for the shame that attends an unrequited affection, he should prefer to love without any hope of return for the mere pleasure of loving."[2]

Now what is it that excites this sentiment? Is it the beauty of the skin? Is it a little color or form or motion? Never. These catch the outward eye but never satisfied the human affections. These are not the objects of the true love. Its objects are certain amiable and excellent qualities supposed to reside in the person beloved; purity, truth, kindness, self-command, and wisdom. And if these qualities should increase to a great, to an infinite degree, would it not increase our attachment?

On the contrary if the opposite qualities of cruelty, falsehood, hatred, impurity, meanness should appear in one whom we love, would it not alter our feelings?

I say then that the natural object of this sentiment of love in us is infinite goodness and though the objects on which it rests in this world are imperfect, yet the passion is true and noble.

Another example of the force with which the human spirit delights to go out of itself and give itself up to another is found in the sentiment of *loyalty* or fidelity to a king, or to the chief of a clan, a passion which has given rise to some of the noblest incidents in history, and has been a very powerful spring of action. Whilst it was a graceful friendship or private attachment in the higher classes who came into the personal acquaintance with the sovereign, in the great body of people it has been frequently a far stronger principle and became a species of worship; and hundreds of times men have marched in companies or alone to certain death, without flinching, yea, and with ardor, in the cause and for the love of a man whom perhaps they had never seen but once, perhaps never, of no great merit, and possibly a person of loathsome vices.

It is related by an eye witness of Buonaparte's Russian Campaign, that, in crossing a frozen river, the ice broke, and many of the troops were lost. One soldier, after struggling a long time, being benumbed with cold, and unable to extricate himself, yet found strength to wave his cap, and cry "Long live the Emperor," and then sunk in the icy waters.[3]

The history of Europe abounds with instances of similar devotedness and perhaps oftener lavished on men of blood and crime, than upon virtuous princes. We read these incidents with a mixture of admiration and pity; admiration for the glorious dis-interestedness of the sufferer; and pity for the unworthy direction it had taken. We say the sentiment is right, but the direction of it is not right.

These facts show plainly the truth of the old observation that a man wants to feel himself backed by a superior nature, as one of the lower animals, a dog or a horse, will exert powers in the presence of man they would never exhibit for their own advantage.

2. St Evremond [Emerson's note]. See Charles de Marguetel de Saint-Denis, seigneur de Saint-Evremond, *The Works of Mr. de St. Evremond* (London, 1700–1705), 2:4; and *JMN* 6:161.

3. Philip de Segur, *History of the Expedition to Russia, Undertaken by the Emperor Napoleon, in the Year 1812* (Philadelphia, 1825), 1:91–92.

They show that the mind was made with this intent—to go out of itself and apply its affections to some other being. This hungering admiration which rather than not indulge itself will live and glow all unreturned, what is it but the rudiments of pure religion, the first efforts and directions of that affection which the Maker of the Mind demands for himself.

The Reality of which these admirations are the poor shadow, is God. Nothing else but Himself can satisfy the desire of what is vast and great, which haunts it. In both these instances, in the sentiment of love and of loyalty, the object of regard is a poor fellow creature—in the first, with a nearer view of personal satisfaction and advantage; in the second, a much more remote and contingent good. But neither of these can ever furnish the mind with a rule of action. The soul wants a pilot, a star, a stronghold amidst the vicissitudes of life to which it can repair continually for refreshment and instruction. In short it wants an object as great as its love.

But there is a third sentiment of which the mind has made a deity, which is more elevated and unexceptionable than either of those to which I have alluded and which seems to be a yet nearer approach to religion—or the worship of God,—I mean Honor. Here we get a more spiritual devotion. This is not a homage paid to any man or any woman, but to a simple sentiment. It is a respect paid by proud men to what they think is graceful and becoming; what is approved in the judgment of honest and generous men. It was a delicate sense of right which, when seated in a noble breast, quick and correct in its judgments, was no unfit representative of the law of God. For, take the high definition of Honor which a true poet has given:

> "Say what is Honor? 'Tis the finest sense
> Of justice which the human mind can frame
> Intent each lurking frailty to disclaim
> And guard the way of life from all offence
> Suffered or done."[4]

If it were so,—if, in the hearts of all who appeal to it, it were this pure tribunal, then it were sacred, and its decisions would chime, as far as they went, with the decisions of the gospel. Far be it from me,—it is not in my heart,—to breathe one word of disparagement against this pure sentiment wherever it has been refined of vulgar error and has extended its jurisdiction over all the parts of life. It was said of Andrew Fletcher, in whose heart it ruled, that "he would give his life to serve his country but would not do a mean action to save it."[5]

And in a dark age I rejoice that it had power to form single characters, an image of courtesy and truth, a man without fear and without reproach.

---

4. William Wordsworth, *Poems Dedicated to National Independence and Liberty,* part 2, XVII, lines 1–5. See *JMN* 6:205.

5. Sir James Mackintosh, *A General View of the Progress of Ethical Philosophy* (Philadelphia, 1832), 205. See *JMN* 6:157 and 205. Fletcher (1655–1716) was a Scottish patriot.

There are memorable words and sacrifices which it hath dictated which make our hearts glow within us and which I will not cavil at because of the name honor. In noble breasts it rises often to a religion, though without the name of Jesus of Nazareth. And then arises an unexpected coincidence of sentiment between these heroes of the world and the heroes of the gospel. Anthony Collins, an unbeliever in the Christian miracles, was accustomed to confess his unqualified admiration for the character of St. Paul, who he said had the sentiments of a true and perfect gentleman.[6]

And if any man of honor shall tell me that his code is such to him as to exclude every action that the sternest morality would exclude, I shall think he is a Christian without knowing it. Though the misfortunes of education may have given him false associations with the Bible, he has read the original edition of it in his heart. I shall say to him in the language of the poet,

> "Here you stand,
> Adore and worship when you know it not,—
> Pious beyond the intention of your thought,
> Devout above the meaning of your will."[7]

But whilst this sentiment of Honor like the other sentiments we have considered shows the natural tendency of the soul, and whilst it has prompted such pure and lofty sacrifices, yet considered as a Rule of life it is open to very serious objection. It is not in all men what it is in the purest bosoms. Though it may be a religion to one man it is a worship of devils to another. The service of it in Sidney's mind is the service of God, but in Buckingham it is lust and pride.[8] This arises from its uncertain foundation. For who is the umpire that determines what is and what is not consistent with honor?

It is the collective sense of the great multitude of persons of standing in the world. It is the speech of men exalted into a god. Of course it is liable to all the caprices and imperfections and vices of society. And beside its uncertainty it very rarely extends its authority to all classes of actions. It has been found that they who held this law in respect and would die rather than do a cowardly or a miserly action, have yet been intemperate and licentious. It is insufficient to the wants of the heart and of the life of man. It is good in the street but what can it do in the closet? It will serve, it may be, in laborious and perplexed action;— but how will it urge and sustain the mind in intellectual labors, in the acquisition of truth? It is good to act with the brave and the industrious,—but what can it do for those who are excluded from action, who are only called to suffer?

6. Anthony Collins (1676–1729), friend of John Locke, was an English deist and controversialist. Emerson's source may be the entry for John Shute Barrington in *Biographia Britannica*, 2d ed. (London, 1778–1793), 1:626.

7. William Wordsworth, *The Excursion*, IV, 1147–50. See *JMN* 3:192.

8. Sir Philip Sidney (1554–1586) was widely regarded as the model of chivalry; for the contrasting figure of Buckingham, see *Sermons* 1:264.

It is remarkable that all these sentiments are of the most beneficent and unexceptionable character that they exalt the soul which feels them, but the direction of them all is unworthy. The sentiment is infinite and so always outruns and belies the object, which is finite. One worships a friend of another sex. One worships a king. One worships the speech of his fellowmen.

These sentiments which we have considered are powerful and in their degree noble principles; they have produced and are producing the welfare of society; they shame our selfishness. But their objects are not equal to the capacity and destiny of the human soul. It seems to me they serve a higher use than to make the present order and advantage of Society, they acquaint us with our own powers and wants. From the delight and the superior efficiency which we find in surrendering ourselves to a sentiment, we discover that the soul was made to go beyond itself for its objects; to apply itself to more than its own benefit; to lose itself in the love and seeking of infinite good. They point at and prophesy a higher principle to be the love and object of devotion to the soul, that is, God. The sentiments are natural and they are infinite, but the objects to which they are applied are finite and very unworthy. Our earthly friends baulk and disappoint our affection. We have invested them with perfections that are not theirs. Much more do the great men whom we choose for our leaders and patrons. The extremest spirit of party would not now teach us to die for the cause of a political leader. And as to honor, its foundation is too narrow and its being too artificial and limited to fill the desires and exercise the faculties of the soul.

But carry out these sentiments to their greatest extent, enlarge these desires and exercise these faculties to the utmost, and they become the love of God.

Let me then present to your thoughts another sentiment by which the human mind can be controlled, that of faith in God, and compare it with these imperfect sentiments.

My friends, you are so familiar with the words 'faith in God' and so accustomed to hear as things of course what is said in the pulpit that I hardly can hope to get for this thought that freshness of effect which even the oldest thought will derive from the effort to bring it home to our own mind. Yet I could wish that this sentiment might be compared by you as a principle, a rule of action, with the confessedly beneficent sentiments to which I have alluded. I could wish that every soul that hears me would explore the sense of that word 'faith in God' and see whether possibly it do not contain a beauty and value as yet unknown to you.

If it seem to any ardent mind a noble devotion to be in heart and in soul the bondsman of your friend, or of some great man, or of your honor, I entreat that one to come with me and visit an infinite and immortal beauty—a most intimate and perfect Friend, a law which is the fountain of Honor—to accompany me within the doors of his own soul and by humble watching, he shall find there is a source of all truth of all generous and humane affections, a source of power to produce great and beneficent changes in the world. There, in the soul, in the eternal Temple of God—he who watches his thoughts will find that he can at once make a calm solitude in the midst of the thickest multitude and yes and the sweetest society in total solitude.[9]

I believe there are degrees of this feeling known in great hearts which have something more heroic, more truly sublime, than any thing which the sentiments of love, of loyalty, of honor ever dictated.

Consider how the pious man worships. He seeks not the approbation of one or two erring creatures but invigorates himself with the thought that the Eye which fills the universe with light and searches the darkest secret of space, rests benignantly upon him, sees in his mind with approbation every good intention, long before yet it has bloomed into action. He considers that a powerful and earnest Benevolence watches in the creation and sends its bounty as in ceaseless waves of light from the centre to the circumference of things. He steadies his steps with the thought that in all the immensity of nature there is no lawless particle, there is no decay, there is no malice, that is not watched and overruled.

But the perception of God's power is the least affecting thought to those that know him best. The heart must have the relation of personal love. "I fear God," said the pious Thomas Browne, "I fear God, but I am not afraid of him."[10] Nothing is known of him until we have become acquainted with the serious and sublime pleasure of opening to him the council chamber of our own thoughts, of treating him as the holy Friend whose praise atones for all censure and whose censure spoils all praise; to whom we make a solemn appeal whenever we are injured by men, and feel, that,—come what sufferings soever,—even unto death, his power and justice will make all things equal, and justify us in the end.

Then when this faith hath got rooted—when it has become the ruling motive,— it fast becomes an object of exclusive attachment. Then it comforts the wretched, it unchains the slave, it is father, mother, friend, house, and home to them who are destitute of all.[11]

The heart in the sight of God feels that all earthly distinctions are annihilated. What are the greatest inequalities in human lot, before him, but varieties of discipline? And moreover his sight converts the worst losses and pains into angels and helpers; for the happiest man, in God's eye, is the man of humblest and sweetest temper, and that perfection is formed in obscurity, and dependence, and disappointment. The heart that is touched with this celestial impulse amid its own afflictions rises with gratitude to its Author and without one repining thought asks for higher blessings upon those who are better endowed and better placed in life. To feel that he is low, causes him no regret; for the thought springs in his mind—Can the favoured child of his election love him so well or cling to his will with the submission of the shrunken sufferer pinched by poverty and sensitive to the touch of error and shame? No, an angel knows not

---

9. Cf. "Self-Reliance" (CW 2:31): ". . . but the great man is he who in the midst of the crowd keeps with perfect sweetness the independence of solitude."

10. Slightly misquoted from Sir Thomas Browne, *Religio Medici*, part 1, sec. 52, in *The Works of Sir Thomas Browne*, ed. Simon Wilkin (London, 1852), 2:403.

11. Cf. Mark 10:29-30.

the height and depth and breadth of resignation like him who, stript of all and satisfied that in him is no strength, yet exults in all that is good and fair; he has a property in all through his relation to God. The peace and joy that belong to deepest suffering are the miracles of faith.

I find in the book of the Acts one of the sublimest passages in human history. "At midnight in the prison Paul and Silas prayed and sang praises unto God."[12]

And is it not a practical principle as it affects our active powers? for the good man leans upon omnipotence, yes and borrows of omnipotence in the prosecution of his undertakings. I mean what I say. Surely the future will wear a new face to him who considers that he may rely on a Divine help in every virtuous design, that a good cause is always strong with more than the help of man, that unexpected succors spring up from a thousand quarters, and, mainly, out of his own faculties;—in a right cause they multiply themselves, they grow wiser than they were; there is more fire in his eye; more activity in his imagination; his understanding hath a greater reach; new truth opens, greater courage appears, until he discovers in his own experience the truth that a humble man in the single service of conscience hath literally infinite force and becomes the voice and the hand of God.

Finally the faith in God opens the understanding of the mind and explains the seeming contradictions of the gospel.[13] It shows how the poor in spirit have the kingdom of heaven or true happiness, how the pure in heart see God, how they that mourn are comforted by lasting consolations, how the hungry are filled and the persecuted triumph.[14] For the greatest sacrifice requires the highest faith and the highest faith is the most intimate union with God.

And as this faith increases, it continually makes the conscience more clear-sighted and the affections more pure. An observation of the secrets of nature does not operate to diminish our admiration of her laws nor does an affectionate watching of the moral laws lessen our wonder or our love.

My friends there are two questions which a sincere mind will ask in contemplating this principle: Are we assured of its truth? and Is it practicable as a rule of life?

In the first place, Is it founded in fact? Is there evidence enough to make it reasonable that finite men, atoms as we are in the immensity of being, ignorant as we are of the powers that surround us, should put our trust in an unseen infinite Mind? I say that our constitution answers the question, that we are in our fabric God believing, God worshipping creatures, that the common sentiments of men do grope after some great object on which they may rest and depend and for lack of such object they waste themselves on unworthy substitutes, that if the sentiment of love be analyzed it will be found that it is always necessarily drawn to wisdom and goodness and repelled by sin, that therefore it does point at and prophesy an infinite object, and therein conspires with all the instincts of nature and all the conclusions of reason.

12. Acts 16:25. These two sentences are repeated from Sermon XLIII (*Sermons* 2:22).
13. Cf. Luke 24:45.
14. Cf. Matthew 5:3–10.

And is it practicable? Is it possible that so vast a thought should be brought down to be the common food of the mind,—should be made familiar enough to be an ever present motive and rule? It is practicable, for it has made thousands good and happy under assaults and suffering. It is practicable; for, which of us does not remember in the past years of his life some elevated moments in which this principle did animate him to thoughts and acts of genuine worth? It is practicable, if we seek God in the right place; if, instead of seeking a Thunderer in the sky, we realize that a good man is the clearest manifestation of him, and that therefore Jesus Christ, a poor benevolent Jew, was declared the express image of his person,[15] if we understand the sublime doctrine that the pure in heart shall see him;[16] and so instead of painfully seeking him in external miracles, realize, that, the heart becomes pure by his influence, that the pure heart is united to him, utters his word, beams his glory, is a vehicle through which his spirit passes.

Ah, brethren, I fear we are strangers to ourselves. Amid the clamors of our passions, amid the din of this world's affairs, we do not heed the thunder call of a superior Nature which pleads with and warns us from within. When I say it is practicable, I know I have a witness in every one of your hearts which hath affirmed the same thing many times and put it beyond a doubt. Let me exhort you then to lend an ear to all the good and sacred promptings that hitherto you have withstood, to prefer the good of your whole character to any petty present gratification; to prefer an hour of humble earnest dealing with yourself—humble earnest endeavor at improvement, aiming at the friendship of the Eternal Spirit, to all the praise and advantages which men can confer. For these will pass away with the breath that is in your nostrils.[17] That is eternal.

15. Hebrews 1:3.
16. Matthew 5:8.
17. Cf. Genesis 2:7 and Isaiah 2:22.

_____

Unto us a child is born, unto us a son is given,
x x x x Of the increase of his government
and peace there shall be no end.
ISAIAH 9:6–7

On the return of this religious festival, welcome to the lovers of God and of man, we are naturally led to look at the rise and progress of Christianity as an external event, i.e., in its aspect upon society. This day and every day the Christian thanks God for the gift of his Son as a Saviour to himself. But this day more than other days invites the mind to the thought of what Christianity has done for the healing of the nations,[1] whether it has been a blessing, and how it compares with other events which have extensively affected mankind.

There are several great eras in history usually marked as moments when great impulses were impressed on the human race, occasions when mankind seemed to derive a new spring from some leading event, and which operated with wonderful force in improving the arts, the social institutions, and the morals of men. These events were usually the establishment of some new Kingdom, whether by discovery of a new region or the ruin of an old one. One of these events, beyond all comparison the most striking and permanent in its effects, is, the introduction of Christianity. And, as if in allusion to these events, and by a natural image, it is continually called by Jesus and by his disciples, a Kingdom.

An ancient historian and philosopher considers the Invasion and Conquest of the East by Alexander the Great one of the most bright and pleasing pages in the history of the world.[2] And he gives sound reason for his opinion. It had the effect of uniting into one great interest the divided commonwealths of Greece, and infusing a new and more liberal public spirit into the councils of their

---

Manuscript dated December 25, 1831, at Chardon Street. This Christmas sermon was preached three times: December 25, 1831, at the Second Church, Boston; on the afternoon of the same day at the First Church, Boston; and December 27, 1835, in East Lexington.

    1. Revelation 22:2.

    2. The civilizing effect of Alexander's conquest of the East is praised in "The First Oration of Plutarch Concerning the Fortune or Virtue of Alexander the Great," in *Plutarch's Morals,* ed. William W. Goodwin (Boston, 1870), 1:480–82, where Alexander is called "the chiefest of philosophers" (481). Though generally more critical of Alexander's flaws in "The Life," even there Plutarch notes his benevolence upon being "acknowledged king of all Asia" (*The Lives,* ed. John and William Langhorne [New York, 1822], 5:237).

statesmen. It carried the arts and language and philosophy of the Greeks into the sluggish and barbarous nations of Persia, Assyria, and India. It introduced the arts of husbandry among tribes of hunters and shepherds. It weaned the Scythians and Persians from some cruel and licentious practices to a more civil way of life. It introduced the sacredness of marriage among them. It built seventy cities and sowed the Greek customs and humane laws over Asia and united hostile nations under one law. It brought different families of the human race together with whatever present disadvantages yet with eventual advantages to both.

In this manner the Macedonian invader was made useful to the world. Much the same thing might be shown of the Roman conquerors.

It cannot be denied that there is great justice in this opinion, that these turbulent men were instruments of great benefit to the world. However unwilling we may be to call such selfish persons benefactors of mankind we cannot but acknowledge that they have been made under the control of Providence instruments of real and extensive good. The same thing may be said of Cyrus, of Caesar, of Charlemagne, even of Attila; they have been, as Attila called himself, "Scourges of God,"—destroying rotten institutions, planting new and vigorous ones, sharpening the intellects, multiplying the resources, raising manly virtues, promoters of new and unknown commerce between most distant nations, and communicators, on a large scale, of the good of one part of the human family to a greater number.

But we cannot fail to observe that whether this benefit done to mankind be more or less, mankind owe no thanks to these rude benefactors. The good was done by God, not by them; the good grew out of evil, as, in modern times the great fire of London finally extirpated the Plague from that city. The benefit was not incidentally contemplated by these men. They were moved by a self love almost insane, to make themselves famous by plunder and murder on whole communities and so have been proverbially denominated *madmen*. They had each of them their pretence—in their age, or to themselves, it seemed a sufficient plea,—but it is no longer fit that we should be cheated, and call murder and robbery by sounding names.

We commemorate this day another great impulse which acted upon the human race, attended by all and more than all the good effects of these without their mischief. These were attempts to establish universal empire. But the kingdom whose foundations we commemorate, the Prince whose nativity the nations celebrate today and which likewise seeks to attain universal empire, is an element of human good of a very different character. This religion has been not indirectly but directly the tamer of savage man, the civilizer of civilization; the purger of the intellectual eye; the friend of order; the inspirer of liberty, the softener of the heart, the sweetener of domestic life. It has elevated the character of woman. It has been the children's friend. More than this, it has raised the character of man and the level of human life by presenting nobler objects of thought, initiating the inquisitive soul into the mysteries of spiritual nature.

The nature of this impulse was spiritual. It consisted in proposing a real object to the mind, namely, the attainment of a perfect character. What is it, that, from that day to this, has moved the hearts of all men where his name was known? The image of a perfect man. This thought has haunted them in all places, and all the variety of action, to form themselves anew in his likeness. A child was born in a manger in a Jewish inn. As he grew in years he grew in favor with God and man, and exhibited a consummate moral character.[3] And this was the blessing he left, and the heaven whereinto he called men. He set this far above all the wonders of supernatural power. "Rejoice not," he said, "that the devils are subject to you but that your names are written in heaven."[4]

This is the gift of God to men, the daystar that hath shined in our hearts, the image of spiritual perfection proposed to us as a rule for ourselves.[5]

I wish to ask your attention to some circumstances of difference which separate by an unmeasurable interval the impulse given to mankind by vulgar heroes and that given eighteen centuries ago by Jesus of Nazareth.

1. First, that whilst their usefulness was accidental, very small part of it proceeding from their design, and none of it projected in the beginning of their enterprize, the whole good wrought by Christianity came within the original intention of him who was born at Bethlehem. He *came* to redeem men from the power of sin unto God. It was his direct purpose to work the great effect which we now see is being wrought. His purpose was every whit as vast as its accomplishment, and the word that seemed like the dream of enthusiasm uttered by a Jewish peasant to a little knot of Jewish peasants on the Mount of Olives, "Go preach to all nations the kingdom of heaven,"[6] is now, as it goes on to its fulfilment, the proof of its divine authority.

2. Secondly; the good wrought by him is unmixed. He stood separate from men in this, that he sought only their good, that he sought no selfish good which is found in others' harm.

He sought good ends by good means. And his instructions and his doings were free from any mixture of evil. The whole force of his action upon the history of man is beneficent. And this widely separates him from the best of men.

Is it said that strife and persecution have attended the progress of his religion from the beginning and that he himself declared that he came to set men at variance and bring a sword?[7]

He indeed foresaw and announced the sad consequence that should come from the abuse of his name and of his truth. And wars have been called Holy and thousands of thousands slain under colour of his name. Yet who does not see that he is not accountable for one angry word men have uttered in dispute

3. Luke 2:52.
4. Luke 10:20.
5. Cf. II Peter 1:19.
6. Cf. Matthew 10:7.
7. Matthew 10:34–35.

nor for one drop of blood that has flowed in what was called his cause? It was not his cause. For there is not a warrant in his precepts for the least act of intolerance but the whole spirit and expression of all his commands is that of unlimited love. If men have persecuted, they never learned it of him. If they have used his name they blasphemed it. If any member of his church from his ascension until now has thought or spoken uncharitably of any other it was not Christianity but the want of Christianity that gave rise to that thought or word.

This is the triumphant ground on which Christianity stands before the world, that, the faults of her defenders are not her faults, but it is because they are no better Christians that they stand charged with any sin.

The cause of Christ in any nation or in any individual depends for its present purity upon the state of the recipient. Whilst he assumes its name, if there is a preponderance of evil in him, that is the reason why his actions are no better; but if he have the religion of Christ in him,—one spark of genuine virtue at the bottom of his heart,—it will work itself pure, it will work off the scum of flesh and sin that mix with it, and every day he shall present a truer likeness, a better disciple.

3. In the third place I wish to direct your attention to the means by which it is spread. The condemnation of other great movements in society have been the corrupt means by which good ends even have been wrought. Even in the best cause. How is it that Christianity goes on from nation to nation? Analyze the force of this divine principle and you shall see that still as at first it is propagated and can be propagated only by means like its ends. We vulgarly compute the number of Christians on the globe at 235,000,000. But when you come to find among these swarming nations the numbers of those who in any true sense can be said to live by the law of Christ, these numbers disappear. Take away first all those who in every Christian land openly oppose the institutions and the principles of Christ. Then take away all who though they do not openly oppose the gospel pay no regard to it in speculation or in practice. Then take away all those who give to its forms an occasional mark of respect but who neutralize the good they do on one occasion by gross violations of its spirit on others, and come down to that handful of good men who steadily walk in the light and work under the law of Christ, to whom their faith is their comfort, whom it directs in the use of earthly good and when earthly blessings fail them is in the place of earthly blessings, the fervent faithful souls to whom the pleasures of contemplation and devotion are dear; who have found the inward world more glorious than the outward; to whom the command of conscience is an overmatch to all the baits of pleasure or avarice; whose daily work is that of kindness; whose solace is selfcommand; whose hearts embrace the interests of others and the society of spirits. And you find but a few, a handful. But it is this slender residue that are the hosts and heroes of its cause.

It is these men, these doers of the word.[8] It is still at this day as it was at the

8. James 1:22.

first, the Word made Flesh, the Word of truth made Flesh or realized in the actions of good men that reconciles men to God.[9] It is the manifest superiority of a good act over a bad act when men see it performed that wins the soul. It is not armed men nor political advantages nor any thing of this world that is to carry on the victories of the gospel but only the principle of Christianity itself, the life of Christ as far as it is formed in our hearts. And each one of us in proportion to that goodness that resides in us and not in proportion to that goodness not in us is a missionary preaching to the world the glad tidings of great joy.[10] And so we yet whenever we are assisted to a virtuous act do fulfil the command, Go preach to every creature.[11]

4. Of the increase of his government and peace there shall be no end. The other impulses on the world have spent themselves. The empires of Cyrus and Alexander and Caesar and Napoleon have crumbled. But of his government there shall be no end. For it is the reign of truth and virtue. Truth always wears out falsehood. Humility in the long run will be better than pride. Honesty is the best policy. And Love in time will prevail over any hatred. But all evil passions are in their nature temporary and transient. And therefore the gradual progress and triumph of meekness and righteousness, of holy affections and the good cause, is sure.

Then it is sure because his reign is a reign in the individual mind and it is progressive there as it is in the world; it is a mustard seed, a little leaven,[12] a gracious word, a humble prayer, a charitable act first that takes root and spreads and becomes a good habit and then shows us the good of more, and we form good resolutions and enter upon the threshold of holy living. And we see at once that there can be no end to this course, to the increase of the government of Christ on our hearts, to the increase of peace in our minds.

And on this day does it not seem a rational object of prayer and of hope that the kingdom of heaven, the doctrine of righteousness and temperance and judgment to come, shall yet be preached to all nations, shall rise to a far greater authority among the nations that now own it and shall be welcomed by them that now sit in darkness?[13]

Does it not seem to humble piety in the sight of God an object of hope that of the increase of his government and peace there shall be no end until all the evil that groans and suffers and sins throughout all his moral creation shall be purged and overruled for good—till all evil shall pass away and be swallowed up in Infinite good? Until all the present means and helps of the soul shall be set aside by higher, until Jesus shall deliver up his kingdom to the Father and God shall be all in all.

---

9. Cf. John 1:14.
10. Luke 2:10.
11. Cf. Colossians 1:23.
12. Matthew 13:31, 17:20, Mark 4:31, Luke 13:19, 17:6, I Corinthians 5:6, Galatians 5:9.
13. Cf. Matthew 4:16 and Luke 1:79.

CXXXIX_____

*If our heart condemn us, God is greater
than our heart and knoweth all things
x x x if our heart condemn us not,
then have we confidence toward God.*

I JOHN 3:20–21

The last sun of another year has set. It has poured over the nations of this hemisphere its melancholy light, admonishing them that another orbit of the earth is about to be fulfilled; another season of action ended; another portion of their decreasing life cut off. It has gone down to multitudes of men in darkness and thick gloom. The finest parts of the world are shaken with civil alarms and the fear of change. Others have been crushed and downtrodden by the dragoons of military tyrants.[1] Others suffer under natural evil. A frightful plague, baffling the remedies of human science, has ravaged Asia, Northern and Central Europe and now threatens the South and the East.[2]

In our own country the air we breathe is surcharged with pestilence which is swelling every hour the numbers of the dead and the living are pinched with the cold of a premature and unrelenting and fatal winter.[3] These are the public

Manuscript dated December 31, 1831, at Chardon Street. Preached twice: at the Watchnight service, December 31, 1831, at the Second Church, Boston, and January 3, 1836, in East Lexington.

1. In France, the new government of Louis Philippe faced violent labor unrest, notably among the silk weavers of Lyons. In Switzerland, massive demonstrations were held for the franchise. Reform riots in England had been reported in the Boston papers as recently as December 27. During the summer, the papers had been full of reports on the Polish rebellion and the successful Russian efforts to suppress it, culminating in the fall of Warsaw on September 8. Closer to home, Nat Turner's slave revolt in Virginia in August had shocked the entire country.

2. A cholera epidemic that began in India in 1826 would reach Scotland by 1832. The Boston *Daily Evening Transcript* for December 27, 1831, reported that the disease had reached Sunderland, England. Emerson's cancellation of "England" from the sermon manuscript may have resulted from a notice in the issue of December 29 calling into question the accuracy of the first report.

3. Smallpox had been reported in nearby Lynn, Massachusetts, in July and in Amherst in December, but the immediate cause of Emerson's concern was an outbreak of influenza. On December 23, the *Transcript* reported a total of 76 deaths in Boston for the week ending December 17: "This is the largest number since the settlement of Boston, even in Yellow Fever times. The excess is attributed to the number who died of the prevailing coughs and colds, or disorders induced thereby." Emerson's observations about the prematurely frigid weather are also confirmed in the *Transcript:* "We have heard it remarked that no winter has commenced with so much rigor as the present since 1798" (December 19). On December 31, the same newspaper carried a notice that "There will be religious

griefs. But what town or what individual on the face of the earth has not his own burden that makes the departure of the sun of the last day sad? And now whilst the stars are rapidly measuring the few remaining degrees to bring this period of time to its close, let us bring our work to a close and make up our account with ourselves and with God.

In this clouded evening they seem to read over again the story of their misfortunes. How many have seen in this year their strength weakened, their substance wasted, their hopes shattered, their families desolated? How many have lost all that was dear in life and the remnant of life seems but a poor afterpiece not worth attention? How many have lost ground in the race of duty and usefulness and feel that they are losing ground? But on the other side there are many bright lines and pleasant events and good deeds. If we have suffered, we have enjoyed, if we have erred, we have learned much. There is much to commemorate.

And I propose to use these moments in considering

1. What is Time for
2. What record remains of its use
3. What account that record bears.

1. What is a year? What is Time? Time, simple vacant duration, is nothing. What is Time to each of us? Only our actions, only our sufferings, only our virtues and vices. Time always was, but not to us. The shoreless starless eternity before the world was, when as yet we slept in the foreknowledge of God, is nothing to us; is less in our account than the meanest moment we have trifled away. The whole era of creation before our birth, the crowded events of dated time are just as little, though hereafter we may hang with interest upon their events when the history of heaven shall be read to us. Time to us is even less than our little day—to most of us much less than our warm, living, eventful, accountable span of thirty, fifty, or seventy years. For time is measured by its use. The only record that remains of time once gone is what was done in it. The value of time to every being is more or less according to its nature. Time is money to the merchant.[4] Time is wisdom to the student, and affection to the lover, and success to the just, and torment to the indolent, and folly to the fool. (The frivolous try to kill time and in so doing they kill themselves. The diligent gains time and thereby lengthens life.) Time to every being has a different value, determined always by its nature.

Time to fire is its fuel; time to grass is its growth; time to animals the play of their bodily functions.

Time to angels is the ministry of knowledge and love. Time to God is the execution in parts and detail of infinite purposes.

And Time to man, the child and image of God,[5] is the imitation and resem-

---

services at Mr Emerson's Church THIS EVENING" immediately below a report that the temperature at sunrise that day had been thirteen degrees below zero.

4. Benjamin Franklin, "Advice to a Young Tradesman" (1748), in *Benjamin Franklin: Writings,* ed. J. A. Leo Lemay (New York, 1987), 320.

5. Genesis 1:27.

blance of God, the growth and use of his spiritual nature, the exercise of our faculties. Time to us is the discharge of our duties; it is benefits done to our friends; it is forgiveness extended to our enemies; it is humility and industry and faith and prayer and love.

Now, my friends, the question comes back to each of us (in the setting sun, in the rising stars, in the moaning wind,) what has been our use of so much time? Have we spent well the year that is now closing? And it is worth an effort of attention to each of us that we should considerately and truly answer this question.

2. Does any one suppose that there is any difficulty in getting an answer to this question? Does any one suppose that any uncertainty or obscurity rests upon it? There is none. There can be none. The answer may be had by any one who will seek for it in terms far more intelligible than language can convey. And this is the fact to which I wish to call your consideration. Do you say, how shall I remember every day and the unheeded passage of so many hours? Hour steals on hour and day on day as silently as flake follows flake upon the surrounding snow drift. I have sometimes tried to do my duty and sometimes I fear I have neglected it, but I cannot tell now what I have done with my time. How can one keep a record of the innumerable trifles that make up a year? Ah, my brother, there is an Annual Report. There is a day book, an hour book. You are yourself the record wherein every line is drawn, every fact is set down, every moment of the year has its history written. Each of us has come up here bearing in his own bosom a secret verdict of praise or shame. For our present state of mind is nothing but the result of all our action; and nothing that we have done, neither any good, neither any evil is so small, but it is represented in the actual condition of the soul. Go into the chambers of the human mind and see what consummate art with which the Maker hath secured justice to it, hath put reward to virtue and penalty to guilt beyond the reach of accident. Observe that in every virtuous action you have done you are the person benefitted. Have you given to the poor? You are enriched by a kinder heart. Have you abstained from an act of spite and revenge, and forgiven the obnoxious person? Do you think it comforts him? It is you that are comforted and exalted. Have you reined in your appetites? You have got the rare power and honor of self-command. Have you forborne to make unworthy compliances by making which you might have bettered yourself in a worldly point of view and now you are poor? So great as was the temptation, just so great is the increased elevation of your mind. So much more powerful and honorable are you on the scale of moral beings. You have gained new fame with all spirits. And so are all the currents of your action turned back upon yourself.

On the other hand have you struck at any man's fair fame? you have wounded your own. Have you refused charity? you have contracted your heart. Have you reproached your brother and laughed in your sleeve that your insult had galled him? you have soured your own temper. You have let in a devil into your mind. Have you defrauded your customer? take care—it is yourself whom you have cheated. Have you got the means and allowed yourself the indulgence of a more delicate table? I am afraid you have only got a new master. Unless you think you are a gainer by turning your honest, true, generous, temperate self out of doors to make room for a false, dishonest, intemperate, contemptible self. This is the very wonder of our constitution. Men don't regard it, but still it is not the less admirable. You say you think virtue has a reward in the next life, and vice pays its penalty then, and do not perceive that in the moment of the good act, the reward attends it; in the moment of the crime the punishment is born. In the very act of getting rid of impurity, purity is received; in the very act of getting rid of hatred, you are rewarded with love. Thus you have never done a single act, great or small, good or evil, but whatever other effect it wrought, it wrought its full effect upon you. Every action reacts on yourself. And so, as you have gone on from morning to night through a year of days, acting or forbearing to act, each single determination of your will and of all the forgotten passages of the year contributed its part to make you what you are. Nothing is lost but every particle is worked up into the formation of the man himself.

Ask yourself then, my brother, where is the record of the year? Your own mind, the arrangement of your thoughts, your habits, and your principles, are the answer. Nothing can be more distinct than its language. The thunder is not so loud. Hearken to the verdict. If our hearts condemn us not, we have confidence toward God. If our hearts condemn us, God is greater than our hearts and knoweth all things.

There is no escape from it. There is no cowering down under the shelter of families or churches or in the shadow of the frailty of the human race. This unerring judgment singles you out from all other beings. The righteousness of the righteous shall be upon him and the wickedness of the wicked shall be upon him.[6] It separates husband from wife and brother from sister and father from child.[7] We sit together, we are bred together, we have listened to the same instruction and converse together every day,—still in the sight of God we part and stand alone. We are what these actions have made us and the society of the universe cannot hinder or share the independent self approbation or self condemnation of every mind.

3. Now brethren in view of these two facts which we have considered, first, that time is to be valued according to the nature of the being, and second, that each of us has brought to this house an unerring record of the past year, let us proceed each to ask himself before God 'how he has spent it?'

In order to this you must answer the question whether your capacities have been occupied on objects worthy of them. Whether any part of your nature has been suffered to lie inactive. You must look forward to what must befal you, death,—and see if you are armed to meet it. You must separate yourself from others and compare yourself no longer with the dregs of custom but with that shining image of perfect goodness which lives in your mind, that star that shines

6. Ezekiel 18:20.
7. Cf. Matthew 10:35 and Mark 13:12.

more gloriously the more steadfastly you look at it, that mirror of God in the soul.

Especially bend your thoughts upon death, for it is the best test of just views. As long as you look only at the scenes and groups of common life, you are likely to be deceived as to your own merit. You seem to yourself to play your part as well as they, and so we keep one another in countenance in our miserable deficiencies. But therefore God wrote this assurance on nature, "Thou shalt die," to be an everlasting remembrancer and counteraction to the weight of flesh. Contemplate then the fast approaching event of death. If you turn pale at it, if there seems to you any terror in the thought, especially if you find it seems an eternal night—then you have not spent the year well—then you are not yet alive—you have noble faculties which you have never used[8]—you are not yet born into the spiritual world. The best part of your being is yet wholly unknown to you, perhaps is every day farther from being known.

And for this reason, that if death seems dreadful, it is because a man has not an acquaintance with his soul. He can only perceive that he has a soul or an immortal part by using it. But if he is accustomed to find all his gratifications in meats and drinks and the other pleasures of the senses, why of course the death of the body which is the seat and instrument of all his pleasures must appear to him the end of his pleasures. Not being accustomed to use his soul except as a servant to the body, he has no assurance that he has a soul; and though he thinks perhaps that he believes in his immortality, it is all a word in his mouth, it has no root in his heart. If he thought at all on the subject, that man would doubt and deny his immortality.

On the other hand if your heart has been opened to the love of others, and you have learned to set at nought your own interest in seeking another person's, if you have learned to think patiently and accurately, aiming always to settle what is true, if you have learned to prefer truth to every opinion of your own, if you have so far conquered yourself as to feel that no advantage you can think of is any temptation at all to draw you from a known duty; if you have found out that the pleasure arising from a difficult act of self command is more than a compensation for the pleasure you refused; if the purpose not to commit any fault at any time (i.e., the aim at perfection which Jesus Christ proposed) has come to be a purpose in your mind; if you have learned to see beauty in the commandments and evidence accumulating from every object in nature, raying out from every object—of a designing Wisdom and Love which is the source of your life—then, my brother, you have spent the year well, then death will have no terror to you for you will see plainly that you have an existence and objects wholly independent of death. They do not spring from the body and will not die with the body. By use of your soul you have learned its glorious nature and Jesus revealing immortality seems to you a friend confirming your own thought.[9]

Thus hath God provided a lasting record of virtue and vice in every mind.

8. See *JMN* 3:167 and *Sermons* 2:225, n. 6.
9. With the preceding two paragraphs, cf. *JMN* 3:312–13.

Thus hath he provided that no water shall be spilled, no crumbs wasted, no blood shed that shall not call him to witness. Brethren, if our hearts condemn us not, we have confidence toward Him, if our hearts condemn us, God is greater than our hearts, and knoweth all things. We may be indifferent, if we are so mad, we may be indifferent to what has been done with the period of time whose last moments we are spending, but we ought to know that here is an unerring register of all its hours, the idle and the busy, the improved and the abused,—there is a register, and we may read it if we will.

But once more the great interest of this hour and of this doctrine is that they are only introductory to a greater period and a greater truth. Tomorrow is a new day. Tomorrow is a new year. Neither time nor truth will stop when this year ends. The year is an epitome of life. The judgment which is thus written for each is only a prophecy, or rather it is the beginning, the first announcing thunders of the Judgment which God shall pass upon every soul that he hath made. If God shall spare us to another day our temptations will be as numerous and as strong, the motives to duty as urgent, the consequences of action as certain as they have been hitherto.

There is no vacation to duty. We shall have as many enemies and as much and more to do. The more time is gone the less remains. There is no time to be lost then in reconciling yourself to your own heart, in securing the approval of your own conscience to the whole of your life. For this is the verdict of God. It is all a vain waiting which men have when they go up and down the world talking as if there were any uncertainty in the decision of the day of Judgment or as to the verdict of God. We ourselves hold the pen; we ourselves write down the doom; we write it every day. We have written it now for another year. Doth it say, "Well done good servant!" or doth it say, "Depart ye cursed"?[10] According to that which is written it operates upon us, it is infusing sweetness or turning into bitterness the waters of life.

The interest of this thought is that thus it will go on forever. If we live tomorrow we shall go on weaving our own web, determining our own doom, and every day and every hour our hearts, if we consult them, will declare in plainest terms our future fate.

I exhort you then, devote the last hour of the year to communion with our hearts, to learn what now are their changing characters, what is their love; which way their impulses point, to God or from God. Let us remember his mercy. Let us remember his chastisements. To some of us it has been a weary year, months of suffering and gloom. God grant that we may find our faith full and strong; then shall every day be blessed, then every bitter hour of fear and anguish and selfreproach and grief yet bear good fruit and out of darkness light shall shine,[11] and this span of earthly time departed shall be a symbol and prophecy of the eternity of heaven.

If therefore on faithful dealing with yourself you find that there is peace

---

10. Matthew 25:21, 23, 41.
11. Cf. II Corinthians 4:6.

within, and that all the future is bright with duty and joy and hope, God shall multiply to you his peace and joy.

But if you know that your days are unhappy, that you have no love for your fellowmen, no pleasure in yourself, Oh then make haste to make your peace with your own heart whilst grace and hope are granted, before your habits are irretrievably fixed, before the new temptations which sin creates have led you further, before growing depravity has blinded your eyes and sealed your ears and hardened your heart.

Brethren, The night is far spent, the day is at hand.[12] The only redemption that is yet in our power to make of a year not so well spent as it should have been, is to hallow its last moments with a pious vow that shall hold us when it is gone, that shall save to virtue the time which yet it may please God to grant us to save the year whose air we have not yet breathed, whose inviolate hours as now they are spread all bright before you it lies with you to pollute or to bless.

12. Romans 13:12.

CXL

Let no man seek his own,
but every man another's wealth.

I CORINTHIANS 10:24

I choose these words as the foundation of some remarks I have to offer upon that noble part of our constitution which draws us to form strict relations of attachment to one or to a few of our fellowmen. The scriptures paint in pleasing colours the friendship of David and Jonathan in the old Testament and, in the new, the sacred friendship of Jesus and John.[1] But more than by example and more than by special precept they have sanctioned these alliances inasmuch as they have raised and refined the soul, and whatever refines the soul increases its capacity and its relish for friendship.

Every view of our social condition is cheering to a good mind. All evil is resolved in one system of morality into self love. All good into the spirit of self sacrifice. And it is plain that all selfish passions are mean, and all social ones, i.e., all that seek the good of another as such, are noble. The fear of death is unworthy a man. Would you know the remedy? Go and see the death of one who spends the last breath in devoted serving of others, and you see the ruins of human nature clothed with beauty and all the meanness of death taken away. It may be recommended to us as a practical rule, the golden rule of Christ,[2] that when unawares we are surprized with any cowardice, either in the apprehension of death or of evils on this side of it, let us take refuge in immediately applying ourselves to an active interest in the welfare of those persons who have the nearest claims upon us: it will bring courage and conscience and God to our aid.[3]

As if introductory to the stricter society of minds, how kindly and wisely has

---

Manuscript dated January 8, 1832, at Chardon Street. Preached twice: January 8, 1832, at the Second Church, Boston, and January 29 at the New South Church, Boston. Emerson mined this sermon for an abortive lecture on Friendship, composed no earlier than March, 1834; see Karen Kalinevitch, "Emerson on Friendship: An Unpublished Manuscript," *Studies in the American Renaissance: 1985,* ed. Joel Myerson (Charlottesville: University Press of Virginia, 1985), 47–61.

1. The story of David and Jonathan is told in I and II Samuel. New Testament scholarship in Emerson's day scarcely distinguished among John, son of Zebedee, "the disciple whom Jesus loved," and the authors of the Gospel of John, the Johanine epistles, and the book of Revelation. This composite John was believed to have died at Ephesus at an extremely advanced age.

2. Matthew 7:12 and Luke 6:31.

3. Emerson borrows this paragraph from Sermon CIV (*Sermons* 3:84).

God arranged the natural societies of human life! "The child is born by the side of his father and there he remains."4 He is brought up in the company of his equals, thrown, without any effort of his own or of his natural guardians, into company the most agreeable and the most useful for him. As the youthful man grows mature, the company of his associates is always kept full, and when he comes to manhood and when he comes to gray hairs, even though he has walked with his friends in all the journey, he is hardly conscious of having made any effort in their selection. They have been given him as his parents were given him by the Divine Disposer, and when some were removed from his side, others have joined his circle.

So universal are these laws that the world has hardly heard of a man or a woman who was absolutely alone.

Some of these companions are worthy, some are unworthy. There are all purposes for which we form and cherish these ties, for consanguinity, for family pride, for interest, for gossip, for love of knowledge, for love of virtue, for love of pleasure, and into all a portion of personal attachment enters. We use them as we use all things, for good or for evil.

These are the offices of that little company that every man finds himself connected with in the world. But to draw a little narrower circle and to consider the office of virtuous friends.

We hardly consider how much we live with our friends, how much we are indebted to them for this insensible influence. It is present when they are absent. In the silence of night, in solitary thought, in the gloom of discontent, in the stress of temptation they talk with, they exhort, they succor us.

But the better men they are, the better friends they will be. If those with whom you live have these virtues, you will eat of the fruits. No man becomes better without becoming more affectionate, for this is one of the highest rewards God has proposed to his children, the indulgence of an affectionate temper.

As many friends as a man hath, so many times is his presence multiplied, for all these see for him, hear for him, act for him in all places where they go. It is a true enlargement of a man's being, for their experience is trusted like your own, and their virtues impose obligations upon you. A true friend is another self. The arms of friendship reach round the world.

A true friend is the ideal object which every human mind seeks and with an earnestness proportioned to its improvement. And of the difficulty of that search one who knew it well observes: "Though a man may almost everywhere meet with men sufficiently qualified for a superficial acquaintance, yet in this where a man is to deal from the very bottom of his heart, without any manner of reservation, it will be requisite that all the springs and wards be neatly and truly wrought, and perfectly sure."5

4. Montesquieu, *The Persian Letters,* trans. J. Robert Loy (New York, 1961), 179. See *JMN* 2:325. Used in Sermon CLXVI and in "Society and Solitude" (*W* 7:10).
5. Montaigne [Emerson's note]. See "Of Friendship," in *Essays of Michael Seigneur de Montaigne . . .* , trans. Charles Cotton (London, 1693), 1:300.

But whilst all men are familiar with the image of a perfect friendship, whilst all ardent minds have so keen an appetite for it, is it not strange that it is so seldom realized? realized, I mean, in the highest degree. It was the saying of a wise man, "O my friends, there is no friend."[6] And I cannot but think that every one of us must have remarked in his own experience the strange solitude in which every soul lives, in this world, let our acquaintances be as many and as intimate as they may. Few men communicate their highest thoughts to any person and this not from a desire to withhold them; by no means; but because they do not find persons proper to receive them. It is not what is in us, that alone determines what we shall say to our companion, but also what is in him and his capacity to understand us. We live with people for years to whom we never impart things we think of every day.

Moreover there are those, in whose capacity and kindred sentiments we have the highest confidence, to whom the secrets of the thought are no more imparted for they are always intrenched behind a wall of separation which we cannot describe or account for but only feel. And in true and tried attachments to those who stand next to the heart in place there is a limit to our confidence and mutual understanding. It is not voluntary, it is involuntary. We cannot get at the mind of each other.

And hence, we see men moving about in the crowded streets every day intent as others upon their several business, who never speak to any whom they meet of that of which their souls are full. Have you not yourself thoughts which you have never imparted? Has not the wonder of your own existence here as a man among men, ever startled you as the most impressive and amazing of facts? And is it not generally in proportion to the elevation and value of your thoughts that you find difficulty in selecting persons to whom you may confide them?[7]

Yes, we give the time of the day to all men; we speak of our common necessities, we express good will to all. And yet we go about the earth most truly strangers and pilgrims.[8] Among his friends a man feels unknown.

For I suppose that every man is in some sort a different person to every one of his acquaintance. You speak with every one on those topics only in which you both have an interest and involuntarily you confine the discourse in the manner as well as in the matter to what is equally interesting to you two. You meet one with whom your discourse does not go beyond the signs of the sky and the state of your health. You meet another of nearer acquaintance or of larger information and the discourse takes a greater range of domestic and public events.

You meet a third with whom you have sympathy in regard to the same literary and religious institutions and whilst you talk of them still the remarks limit

6. Aristotle, quoted in "Of Friendship," *Essays of Michael Seigneur de Montaigne . . .*, trans. Charles Cotton (London, 1693), 1:296; cf. *JMN* 6:161.

7. With the three preceding paragraphs, cf. *JMN* 3:272–73. The reticent figure of the last of these paragraphs is there identified as Emerson's parishioner and friend, George Adams Sampson.

8. Hebrews 11:13; Emerson repeats the phrase "strangers and pilgrims" in "Friendship" (*CW* 2:115).

themselves to the institutions. Or perhaps there are a few or a chosen one with whom you speak freely of your nature and expectations, yet still—always, I believe—with a limit. And if a mind of higher order, more able to answer exactly what you would ask, should converse with you, you would then deal with thoughts which have never yet parted from the silence of your own consciousness; things which you recognize but have not expressed.

Thus it happens that the best part of our nature is not known or shared. Yet were these thoughts made for communication as much as light for the eye or air for the lungs. This is attested by the hungering for sympathy that is manifested by every mind in proportion to its powers. What then? Shall these powers go to the grave and perish unknown; and shall these desires remain forever unsatisfied? No; it is a maxim of the wise so abundantly confirmed by all experience that it has become a maxim of the ignorant, that "nothing was made in vain,"[9] least of all, that which is best and noblest in our nature. These unsatisfied desires intimate a future state; they promise a gratification yet to come. We hold out the hand of affection to embrace friends in the spiritual world. This restless love, ever seeking its object, points to a future state and to exalted companions, as much as the folded wings of the poor caterpillar indicate that one day it shall cease to creep along the ground and shall rise into the air with new form and increased powers. Who can reflect upon the intense delight which we feel our social affections are capable of bestowing if ever they should be brought into perfect exercise and observe the insurmountable barriers that time and sickness and death and distance and different education put to any free and continued action of them here, without having his confidence increased in the good that awaits the faithful servant, and his mind enlightened as to the nature of that good?

So distinct is this desire, so steady is its increase with the improvement of the mind, that it is capable of becoming a sublime motive to virtue. It were a noble aim to aspire after the friendships of the spiritual world yet in the dust and smoke of this. And in the measure of the elevation of a man's character will this become a practical end. When you feel the pulse of virtue to be low, when you are tempted to a small sin, to acts of self indulgence, to vanity, to a cowardly compliance with custom; when conscience speaks with a faint warning and you ask yourself why you should always struggle against the stream? why it is not better, as others do, to give yourself up to the strength of the tide?—oh then persist; feel that you are contending in the cause of all the good, for by this steadfast service you are forming yourself for the fellowship of those who are now all over the creation serving the same law, and by force of virtue you shall be brought near to each other.

Certainly the sympathy of all the good is a noble and a certain reward to virtuous effort. And if moral laws hold in the next world as in this (and why they should not, being independent of the body, no reason appears,) that sym-

9. See *Sermons* 1:84, n. 17.

pathy is increased by the progress of the soul. Let it not then afflict you that you are for the time separated from those who should act and think with you, or that in the present imperfection of minds you are a stranger in the counsels of your nearest friend. Persevere in God's work and be assured the wants of the heart shall be supplied.

What if you are separate? Remember it is not neighborhood but affinity that is the cement of minds. Minds that have reached the same elevation, wherever they are, act with like aims and have one cause. They are all at one, by a common faith; unknown to each other are helping each other; and by doing the same things, and by their love of God, are doing more to strengthen their regard than would be done by years or ages of intercourse under the same roof.

Once more; I put the inquiry whether this anxiety to find a mind so perfect, one that shall be equal to all the offices of friendship, capable of a perfect confidence, open as the day, full of wisdom, and full of tenderness, does not lead us to a yet higher thought, that, nothing less than the all perfect mind can supply the cravings of man; that God is the Friend, whom always we seek; and that he has formed the soul capable of entering into the most intimate relations with him; and whether this be not the just light in which to regard him as the Friend of the soul? If it be true that our thoughts of God are always more or less worthy as are our own characters, is it not the effect of our partial views and many offences that he has been clothed by us with so much dread and removed to so terrifick a distance? Has he not made these affections for the contemplation and enjoyment of himself, and when we become more obedient shall we not perceive the meaning of the revelation that "God is Love"?[10]

10. I John 4:8, 4:16.

CXLI

Do thyself no harm.

ACTS 16:28

I use these words not in the sense in which they are employed in the passage of sacred history from which they are quoted but to express a general moral law which may be made to comprehend the whole of our duty.

Every commandment of religion truly considered is not so much God commanding man as it is a higher part of man contending against a lower part, or rather the whole against a part. It is the brain contending with the belly. It is the soul contending with the flesh. Plainly spoken, the voice is, Do thyself no harm. And as all our duties may be viewed under their relation to self, this is the beginning and end of religion.

Few men consider how sacred a possession is locked up within the narrow boundary of a human frame. If that which we must do and what we do every day, and that which we might do be considered, it will be seen that Heaven, Hell, Judgment, the knowledge of all truth, the possession of indefinite power, and the love of innumerable beings, the choice of blessed or of accursed society are therein contained. And by reason of the retributions which in the nature of things are affixed to every act, a man is in some sort the Providence to himself which dispenses the events of his life.

When men come to consider the great significance of this self, to consider how much power is lodged in it, how much trust committed to it, they will feel the importance of the maxim, Do thyself no harm, that this is the sum of religion. God in his government is not seeking to glorify himself, but to benefit us. Our wrongdoing does not dishonor him but hurts us. And in magnifying our little actions as if they affected the whole order of things, we act like children who think you see or lose them as they open or shut their eyes. We are the universe to ourselves but nothing to the universe. We can benefit ourselves. We can hurt or destroy ourselves, but none else can harm us.

Sermon CXLI exists in two manuscripts, one dated January 15, 1832, at Chardon Street, and another, substantially revised, dated December 8, 1833, at New Bedford. The revised text is given in the Textual and Manuscript Notes. In all, Sermon CXLI was preached fourteen times: January 15, 1832, at the Second Church, Boston; December 8, 1833, in New Bedford; January 12, 1834, at the Hollis Street Church, Boston; May 4 at the Second Church, Waltham, for Bernard Whitman; May 18 at Fall River; June 15 at Watertown; July 20 at Bangor, Maine; October 19 at the Second Church, New York; May 3, 1835, at East Lexington; May 17 in Chelmsford; June 21 in Framingham; March 27, 1836, in Lexington; August 7 in Concord; and September 25 in Groton.

Do thyself no harm. No power in existence can harm a virtuous mind. If it could be supposed that instead of the benevolent power that governs the world, we should be exposed to the tyranny of supernatural agents, if as the Indian and the Greek poets fabled, the gods were subject to like passions as we are, and should pursue with hideous calamities an innocent man—do we not see, that so long as he preserved his integrity he would have a friend, a refuge in his own breast, from the most tremendous evils; would keep a certain everlasting superiority to all that mere physical power could do against him? I put this incongruous and impossible case as the extreme one, and the more willingly because something like it is supposed in the popular theology,[1] that there are elect persons and reprobate persons who enjoy grace and suffer punishment without regard to merit. I say that here in the mind is an eternal refutation of such dogmas in the clear perception we have that nothing can work us mischief without our own connivance.

But nothing can be more gross than such an imagination of God. He cannot harm you because it is more alien to his Nature to wrong you than it is to your own Will. He is Love;[2] and He cannot be any other for this very judgment which the mind forms of his nature, it draws from its own constitution, reasoning from the work to the workman.

No; God does not, cannot harm us. Much less can any other. But we open the door by which mischief enters. No external power can much afflict us, whilst we have this approving testimony within. But when that fails—when the kingdom within is divided against itself[3]—when I am accused by myself—then I fear, then I am tormented, then is there no refuge in the Universe left to which I can repair, and whilst I am at war with myself, all the good of nature is lavished on me in vain, the peace and the glory of the whole creation, the possession of knowledge, the pleasures of Society can yield me no good. It is like the face of the heavens reflected in troubled water, which must return a broken image.

Do thyself no harm. All nature seems to me written over and over with this lesson. I find the doctrine in the writings of the wise and the proverbs of the multitude. It is the observation of the East and of the West. On the tomb of Nushirvan the ancient monarch of Persia was written, "Thou shalt be paid exactly for what thou hast done, no more, no less."[4] In the writings of St. Bernard I find the following sentence. "Nothing can work me mischief except myself. The harm that I sustain I carry about with me, and never am a real sufferer but by my own fault."[5]

It is the burden of the revelation which God has made to man by Jesus Christ,

---

1. That is, in Calvinism.
2. I John 4:8, 4:16.
3. Cf. Matthew 12:25, Mark 3:24-25, and Luke 11:17.
4. See *JMN* 6:215; used in "Ethics" (*EL* 2:152–53) and "Compensation" (*CW* 2:64).
5. *Pious Breathings, Being the Meditations of St. Augustine . . . [with] Select Contemplations from St. Anselm and St. Bernard,* trans. George Stanhope (London, 1818), 401. See *JMN* 3:339, 4:86, 210, and 6:93–94; used in Sermon CLXIX and in "Compensation" (*CW* 2:71).

that as ye judged ye shall be judged, as ye render ye shall receive.[6] It is that echoed by the apostles: Who is he that can harm you if ye be followers of that which is good?[7] That which a man soweth shall he reap.[8]

And if men will read rightly the lesson of their own experience it will show them that we are perfectly safe from all but ourselves, that we can never receive any harm except by doing it, that all things from the least to the greatest as they touch man are retributive and that every moment is a Judgment Day.

There is no such thing, a reflecting mind sees, as fortune. The most casual and contingent events, clouds, winds, disease, are bound in strict chains of cause and effect. The greater is our knowledge, with the more certainty do we predict events from seeing their causes and if we were more wise should see the certainty of more occurrences that now take us by surprise. There is nothing fortuitous in the events that daily occur bringing happiness and misery to thousands. They eat of the tree they planted. As we grow wiser we learn to avoid more dangers and reap more benefits; all that we suffer from is not avoidable but we might save ourselves much pain by greater heed to what we do.

Each quality of the mind, as each plant, bears its own fruit, bears it always, and never bears any other. Temperance never produces the effect of intemperance. Hatred never produces the effect of love. Servility is never confounded in its consequence with independence. Honor is different from dishonor in its beginning and middle and end.

And in their success men see this very plainly. A man who has been industrious, frugal and prudent enjoys his growing estate with keen satisfaction because he sees he is reaping his own fruit. He is very well pleased to say to his children or his friends that he has worked and watched and studied and waited for this and that the same force is in the same virtues for them.

And none of us ever attained any great object of our ambition, I suppose, without being very willing to see and acknowledge our own fair share of merit in the same.

But the moment that instead of good we receive evil, we cease to see the effect of our own doings. We think then it is caused by others. We complain of being unfortunate, we complain of our fellowmen who have wronged us, or we speculate upon the inscrutable decrees of Providence that so chasten those whom God loveth.[9]

We will not see that we have opened our own breast to the dart that has hit us; that we foresaw long ago the hour that has come upon us; that we neglected the means offered of securing our good, that we yielded to a temptation of which now we pay the penalty and we blame our luck or our fellowmen. There is no luck and your fellowmen are not the wrongdoers.

We loudly blame our bad luck or just as often the mismanagement of other

6. Matthew 7:2; cf. Luke 6:37-38.
7. I Peter 3:13.
8. Galatians 6:7.
9. Cf. Hebrews 12:6.

men for misfortunes which the clearsighted observer sees to be the natural effect of some subordinate part of our own character. "The industrious man who appears at first sight to have been ruined by the misconduct of others or by some unexpected disturbance in the business of society, may in reality owe his ruin to a want of prudence. He is sure he has been diligent but the observer is sure he has been wasteful. The natural consequence of his industry was prosperity, but the natural consequence of his imprudence was loss and misfortune. We must not expect that the exercise of one virtue will be followed by the beneficial consequences of all, neither must we conclude that the indulgence of any vice will be pursued by unmixed evil, and destroy the good effects of better qualities."[10]

Whilst thus we ought to feel that we are accountable for many things with which we tax Providence I am not so rash as to affirm that all outward misadventures befal us by our own fault. Those on whom the tower of Siloam fell were not more sinners than others.[11] Virtuous men are the sons of sinful men and inherit the diseases of their parents. Risks must be incurred by good as well as bad merchants and the wind and sea are no respecters of persons.[12] And death comes into the worthiest family by doors which no skill or diligence could keep shut, and takes away the sweetness of life from the survivors. We mistake in expecting fruits different from the seed we have sown. The proper fruit of virtue is not wealth but peace of mind, the love of God and of good men. The proper fruit of industry and frugality is not health but a larger income.

How is it then that none can harm us but ourselves if thus always we are liable to evils which no foresight and no virtue can elude? It is because these evils are only apparent and not real. Because there is no real evil but that which touches the mind. The loss of property is to *fail* as a merchant, but is not necessarily to fail as a man. The loss of friends is a severe privation, but may bring out new resources in the heart. The loss of health and the approach of death are necessary steps in God's order to the glorification of the soul.

These evils are obviously outward and may every one subserve the advantage of a well ordered mind, teaching, purifying, invigorating it, and then they are no more evils, but disguised goods. The loss of character, the loss of selfcommand, the loss of benevolent disposition, the loss of purity, the loss of simplicity of speech and of action—these are real evils. These defile a man. And all these are losses that can only befal us by our own consent.[13]

It is only by a steady confidence in the strict and immutable connexion between moral causes and effects, by perceiving that a man is better for every

10. V. Formation & Publication of Opinions, p.   [Emerson's note]. See "Essay V: On Inattention to the Dependence of Causes and Effects in Moral Conduct. Part II," in Samuel Bailey's anonymous *Essays on the Formation and Publication of Opinions* (Philadelphia, 1831), 166.

11. Luke 13:4.

12. Cf. Acts 10:34.

13. This and the previous paragraph are perhaps the earliest formulation of Emerson's doctrine that "Evil is merely privative"; cf. "Ethics" (*EL* 2:155) and "The Divinity School Address" (*CW* 1:78). On "These defile a man," cf. Matthew 15:18, 20, and Mark 7:15, 20, 23.

good act and impoverished by every bad one, that we can come to see the importance of this practical truth.

Every action you perform, whomsoever else it may affect, mainly affects yourself, well or ill according to its nature. You cannot do a good action so secretly but it will brighten and beautify your character with a glory as manifest as that which shone on the face of the man of God. You cannot do a mean action but it shall sensibly affect the impression you make upon men and shall seem to hiss you as you walk in the street.

A man cannot be under a greater delusion than to think that any outward good can atone for a sacrifice of principle. The outward good is temporary and can hardly be said to belong to the man. The sacrifice of principle is permanent and of the man himself. Again the advantages to be gained depend much on the opinion of men into whose society you only occasionally come, but the advantages sacrificed are by yourself with whom you are always present.

Therefore brethren, let us give heed to the warning of nature and revelation exhorting us to be wary of our actions, to look a little farther ahead than we are wont to do to the consequence and see how sorely we are losers by what we think we have gained.

Do thyself no harm by the indulgence of any evil habit. You cannot be enriched by ill gotten gain but grow poorer. You cannot be honoured by any false pretension but are degraded. You cannot be refreshed by any intemperate morsel or draught but are chewing poison.

Do thyself no harm by neglecting any duty to others. It can be done perhaps for them by others; the loss may be repaired; the pain of your neglect consoled; but who shall repair the loss or console the pain to you? Who can restore the peace of faithfulness to you or open your contracted views?

Do thyself no harm, for thou art making thyself—thou art making a being which shall have no end. Look at the opening future and walk wisely, warily, in every step. I am afraid no man considers how much of his being depends on his free will. Yet every one knows the effect of certain actions to produce fixed habits; the effect of certain postures to alter the form; the effect of the disposition in giving expression to the face; the effect of our general tastes in determining the selection of our companions, of our books, of our pursuits, and amusements; and lastly the effect of all these in determining what objects shall attract our attention in the general aspect of society. Does it not follow that wherever we go, we only converse with those objects that are like ourselves? so that we do not so much see the general world which God made, but only a world of our own eye. Every man has peculiar thoughts, peculiar dreams, peculiar set of friends, and peculiar purposes. He is creating day by day a world for himself.

Let him feel that he cannot possibly meditate too much the steps he is taking, the friends he is choosing, the habits he is forming, for it is as if he was making the world in which he shall live.

In the enlarged view of self which we have taken it is plain that the cause of a man's self is one with the cause of God. I have spoken of self as it is presented to us by that inward monitor which seems to be the voice of our maker speaking to us from within in stifled tones often and very faint when we neglect them, but always becoming more distinct as they are more obeyed. From the first dawn of reason to the day of death, it uses one voice that always is prophetic of a future state for which this being is to be thus carefully guarded and kept. If thou wouldst live forever do thyself no harm.

CXLII

Lo I am with you alway, even unto the end of the world.

MATTHEW 28:20

The manner in which religion is presented to men in the infancy and ruder state of society is by *authority*. Men very ignorant and very prone to serve their passions can only be deterred from gross vices by alarming menace and by the offer of tempting rewards, and so all over the world we find that savage and semisavage nations have had a religion of this character, which said, 'Thou shalt do this:' 'Thou shalt not do that:' and held out a bait to these who would obey, and the sternest threatenings to those who should disobey, ruling men not by reason but by authority.

Now this happens not I suppose because God speaks thus to man, but because man thus represents God as speaking. The voice of God does not go out of his prophet as it came in to him but takes a new character from the prophet's mind, just as the sun's rays in passing through a glass do not come out pure but blue or red or green according to the colour of the medium.

If you give the same instruction to many men they will communicate it to others in a very different manner and each tinged with the peculiar qualities of his own mind.

And so in the night of the early ages men had imperfect views of God's providence. The prompting in his own mind which Abraham or Noah or Moses felt each expressed as faithfully as he could, but it seems to us to convey a very inadequate notion of God. It represents him not as the God of the world but as the tutelary genius of that people; not as the unchangeable and allwise but as subject to the passions of a man. This I suppose is the defect not of the Revelation that was made him but the unavoidable effect of the rude mind that received it.

In a more advanced state of society men outgrow these gross views of God and his Providence and become prepared for truer views. The commandment ceases to be given in hostility, God ceases to be regarded with terror. The commandment comes to man recommended to his reason, seen to be good. God shows himself to his mind as his Friend. No harm or confusion arises from

---

Manuscript dated January 29, 1832. Preached twice: January 29, 1832, at the Second Church, Boston, and May 29, 1836, in East Lexington.

60

this change of aspect, as if it took off any wholesome restraint, for our ideas of God do not suit themselves only to ages but just as much to individual minds. The good man sees God to be good. The bad man sees him to be terrible. A bad man cannot form any image of kindness in God, for whilst he retains his evil thoughts he finds the whole course of things hostile to him and reaps pain and disaster and remorse and fear at every step.

The laws of the world are immutable and he that is not in harmony with them cannot but be crushed by their irresistible force. Whoso falleth upon them shall be ground to powder.[1]

And at the same time Christendom is filled with churches of different creeds each of which meets the wants of some one class of minds from the most gross and sensual to the most spiritual worship and every mind falls into that which is best for him.

Such is the progressive character of faith that it opens before us, and is always wide enough for the greatest progress of man. We are not come to the mountain that may only be touched but we are come to Mt. Sion, the city of the living God.[2]

When the reason of man has been developed he is not capable of being guided by authority, but by reason. It is not by violence that he is to be driven to worship, but by showing him the loveliness of obedience, the reasonableness and truth and advantage of religion. Any other course is like the insane persecutions of former days when men were dragged to the stake and there offered the alternative of the mass or the fagot.

1. Apply these remarks to the manner in which Jesus Christ is regarded by Christians. Much of the reluctance which is felt by men in yielding that veneration which is due to so exalted a character is owing to the mistaken manner in which their teachers have attempted to extort regard.

If you would awaken in one man favorable sentiments towards another, you would not go to him and say, 'You must love him. It is your duty and penalties will follow the neglect of it. How this man will hate you and execrate you! You are a wretch, an outcast from society if you do not reverence his actions.' I suppose it will be agreed this would be the mode of all others least likely to bring him into those dispositions you desire to produce.

No, you would rather show the amiable qualities of the man in question. You would represent the kind sentiments he entertained for him to whom you spoke; you would not hint at an obligation, but would stimulate the desires of your companion by painting the happiness that would flow from a relation of friendship to so elevated a mind.

Is it not just as unsuitable to compel men to love Christ? The human heart can never be cowed nor commanded into love of any being. The exaltation of

1. Matthew 21:44 and Luke 20:18.
2. Cf. Hebrews 12:18-22.

the being does not make any difference. Love is in its nature the same and always spontaneous. It will grow up inevitably in every mind for those beings which resemble it.

Therefore cease to require of us a different regard to Jesus from that which we should pay to the same goodness and wisdom in one of our brethren. We do not know any other elements in rational nature than these two. Let us love him as we would love one who kept the law and therefore gave it, who abased himself and so was exalted, who was tempted as we are yet without sin.[3]

Let us not suppose that God has appointed him to unnatural and arbitrary offices, but that he simply benefits us as he is more good and wise than others, not in some new and peculiar way. We ought to feel that there is and can be nothing better than moral perfection, that the moment it is perceived that Jesus Christ is the Teacher of human duty his plan and character become infinitely worthy and Godlike. Then eternity enters into his purposes. Then he is the same to us that he was to his immediate disciples. And to use the words of the text, he is with us alway.

2. Secondly; there is another and more obvious sense in which the memorable declaration of Christ at the conclusion of his ministry may be understood.

By his memory. It is a beautiful provision by which God has made men useful after their death by the record of their acts and words. Jesus was known, living, only to a few thousands of his countrymen in an obscure district of the Roman empire. But to how many millions of millions has the knowledge of him come and operated with unrivalled energy upon their minds? How many churches, how many sects, how many nations of men have been familiar with all the details of his humble life? The nations that confessed him first have been swept from the earth, and their cities are only found by the coloured dust in the desart. His name and church have been conveyed from Asia to Europe, from Europe across the ocean to America, and are now moving west till they meet his cradle in Bethlehem, and the lapse of so many ages has not effaced one trait in his character from the knowledge of men. But better than the numbers who know him a little, think on the greatness of those who love him much. What a legacy to the human race was a character whose bright recollection should prompt such a numberless amount of good actions; should fill the world with proverbs of rectitude, like this, "Do unto others as you would have others do to you";[4] should build so many hospitals; should found so many schools, and churches; should form so many characters.

And what end do we see to this? The cross is gaining its peaceful victories every year and every day. The memory of Christ has lost none of its virtue. And thus he fulfils his word; Lo I am with you alway even to the end of the world.

3. There is another sense in which the declaration of Jesus may be understood. He is present and helpful to his disciples always by his religion: not only

3. Hebrews 4:15.
4. Matthew 7:12 and Luke 6:31.

by his example but by his truth. He frequently uses, as is well known to you, his own name for the truth which he taught, Christ for Christianity.⁵ 'I am the way and the truth and the life;' 'No man cometh unto the Father but by *me*,'⁶ that is, by that holiness or Godlikeness which I inculcate. And that energy is undiminished. The same efficacy is in purity to reveal God, in humility to enter heaven, in love to cause us to be loved, in sorrow to purify, in penitence to avert judgment, in temperance and righteousness to obtain a rich reward, now as then. Heaven and earth may pass away, but one jot or one tittle from the moral law shall not pass,⁷ and thus is Jesus with you alway to the end of the world. Let it be considered too that this promise reaches also those who love the same cause though the name of Christ never came to their ears.

4. I do not know but by many it will be thought that these three heads exhaust the subject, but I cannot help adding my conviction that there is a fourth sense in which Jesus is present to his faithful disciples: I mean by personal presence.

Men are not sufficiently affected by the duty of guarding their thoughts. The goodness of how many stops short with their actions and does not regulate the sources of action? Men think they have a retreat in the silence of thought, that its privacy is perfect and defies all but the eye of God. But perhaps that door is not shut so close as we imagine. And perhaps already the windows of heaven open upon our self communion and all spirits behold us.

We know in this preliminary state, here in the entrance and porch of our being, very little of spiritual laws. Still they must always possess the highest interest to every serious mind and we should give heed to the least intimations that we find concerning them.

There is another view which has always had some currency in the world, that spirits have an unseen, an unconscious connexion in proportion to their likeness of affections. Our spirits lie in the spiritual world as our bodies in the natural,⁸ and that as every particle in the material world acts upon every other so every spirit acts and is acted upon by all. As St. Paul said, "though I be absent in the flesh I am with you in the Spirit,"⁹ as if his love of the same things, his prayers or good wishes which are the substance of prayers, wrought the same effect of aid and love at a distance as at hand. So this expression is not wholly disused among us: to be with you in spirit. There may be more than a metaphor. He did such a thing in the spirit of Washington, in the spirit of Howard,¹⁰ and in poetry, which is only more true as heated language, we familiarly say the spirits of the great and good gather round a hero. It was a saying of the Stoics that if a wise man did but lift his finger in Rome all the wise men on earth were benefitted thereby.¹¹ I mention these circumstances to show that there is in the

---

5. Emerson alludes to his own exposition of this point in Sermon XCV (*Sermons* 3:36).
6. John 14:6.
7. Matthew 5:18; cf. Mark 13:31 and Luke 21:33.
8. Emerson is adapting a remark by Fénelon; see Sermon CIV, *Sermons* 3:88, n. 11.
9. Colossians 2:5.
10. John Howard (1726–1790), English philanthropist and prison reformer.
11. Cf. Montaigne, "Of Vanity": "The *Stoicks* say, that there is so great Connexion and Rela-

human mind, an obscure perception of the doctrine entertained by some Christians that all our wishes act upon others and that in the measure of our efforts to be good we are associated with the good not only in the natural but in the spiritual world, that they act on us and we on them and thus not only doth the Eye of Him who seeth from the beginning to the end pervade our souls but the holy child Jesus, the benevolent, the perfect son of man, dwells with us alway, composing more of our strength and peace and purposes than we have powers to discern. I propose this view merely for consideration, that all our wishes and thoughts of others have some effect upon others. And if, as I hold, that principle of philosophy be as sound as it is noble, that whatever is most desirable is true, the moral universe is one great family, included in God as the waves are contained in the ocean.

My friends, it will be seen that in any view of this subject it depends on us how intimately and how long Christ shall be with us. He is not with the proud, with the covetous, with the backbiter, with the intemperate, with the sensualist.

He is with the humble, the generous, the diligent, the thoughtful, the self improver. Meantime if he is not with us, he is against us.[12] If he came to teach the eternal laws of our being it is then strictly true as the New Testament assures us that he shall judge every human soul.[13] Let us feel then that a cheerful hope allied to all the laws of our nature draws us to him. Let us see the divine benignity with which he hath loved us beforehand and repair to him that he may lead us to the Father.

---

tion amongst wise Men, that he who dines in *France*, nourishes his Companion in *Ægypt;* and that whoever does but hold out his Finger, in what part of the World soever, all the wise Men upon the habitable Earth feel themselves assisted by it" (*Essays of Michael Seigneur de Montaigne . . .* , trans. Charles Cotton [London, 1693], 3:315–16). See also *JMN* 3:324 and 328. Used in Sermon CLXX and the "Right Hand of Fellowship" (see p. 263 below).

12. Matthew 12:30.
13. See Matthew 25:31–46; cf. Acts 10:42 and 17:31.

CXLIII _____

*Forgetting those things which are behind and
reaching forth unto those things which are before,
I press toward the mark for the prize
of the high calling of God in Christ Jesus.*
PHILIPPIANS 3:13–14

The Christian doctrine of the immortality of the soul gives the greatest importance to all the events of this life as they in some degree affect the whole being of the soul.

Men in general are so entirely occupied with the particulars, as to give no attention to the general course of their life. But although they consider more the effect of single actions, and do not take heed that the course of life shall be serviceable on the whole, God does. And if men would regard it, it would comfort them to see that all this apparent disorder of innumerable unconnected actions, resolves itself into a great order, and is made by the Divine Wisdom to produce the most beneficent results. Look at the great throng in your streets. Consider the variety of callings and pursuits. Here is one man toiling with a hod on his shoulder, and another with his saw and tools; a third with his books; a fourth driving bargains at the corners of the streets; another teaches the young; another spreads his sail from the wharf toward the sea; another heals the sick; another draws a map; another interprets the law; another is hasting to his entertainment and to dangerous pleasures; another is led to the jail between officers; another takes his seat on a bench to judge him. They do not perceive who make up this sad and cheerful scene, that they are placed in these circumstances to learn the laws of the Universe, and that these various implements and callings serve the same use as the child's slate and spelling book, wherewith he also learns his lesson, murmuring all the while at the necessity, and does not yet perceive that for his own good, and not for another's, it is taught him.

Preached seven times: February 5, 1832, at the Second Church, Boston; February 12 at the Federal Street Church; April 19 as a Thursday Lecture, presumably at the Second Church; December 8, 1833, in New Bedford; November 30, 1834, at the Second Church, Waltham; July 5, 1835, in Framingham; and January 10, 1836, in Concord. The idea for the sermon is sketched in a journal entry for January 19, 1832 (*JMN* 3:319–20). A heavily revised early version, the source at least of the first two deliveries, is given in the Textual and Manuscript Notes. A listing of hymns headed "N.Y.C." on the first page of the revised manuscript suggests an otherwise unrecorded delivery in New York.

It is quite important to our peace of mind and in order to the improvement of our time that we should sometimes take this general view and settle it as well as we can in our minds for what purpose we were sent into this life, where each is performing his part. The convictions of reasonable men will be much the same. On reflexion all will probably agree in the conclusion that God has put us here from the oldest to the youngest as little children to be instructed by his Providence and by his Word in things necessary: that here he is unrolling before the eyes of each one of us the great chart of his creation, that we may rightly learn its extent and our true place in it. He is leading each one through a series of events—now placing you in one company; now in another; now appointing you to labor; then to rest; then to sickness; then to honour; drawing out your affections, gratifying them, disappointing them; he is leading each one through this sunshine and shade—as so many lessons in his school to call out successively each of the faculties, and fit every mind for the duties now unknown to us of the next world.

It well deserves attention how fit are the various employments of men not only to keep them from the misery of idleness but to engage and invigorate their faculties, to form the virtues,—in short, to educate the man. It deserves attention how much every one is indebted to his calling for his powers and for his enjoyments. And it is curious to observe how complex is the action and reaction of a man upon his profession, and of his profession upon the man.

Under this main design two particular purposes are answered by the general distribution of the work of society into various professions, and by each man's attention and ability being confined to some one; *first,* his more efficient action is gained to the common good; and, *secondly,* his own powers are revealed to him, and gradually he is shown what his own peculiar talent is, which is every man's true and eternal calling from God, his Maker.—It is to some remarks upon this last topic that I wish now to request your attention. I would persuade you to forget what is behind, to reach forth unto those things which are before, and press toward the mark of the prize of your high calling. I would second that divine voice which in each of your hearts is calling you to reflect that you were made for no mean or finite purpose—that your present employments are not the ends for which you were created; that the common pursuits and professions of life are all prospective; they are merely means by which you are led to the knowledge of your own powers and therefore of your duties.

On account of the remarkable effect which particular situations and duties have been observed to work in some men, a great deal more power has been usually ascribed to things outward than belongs to them. We hear a great deal of the empire of circumstances over the mind, but not enough of the empire of the mind over circumstances. Both expressions contain truth, for the mind is capable of commanding, and of being commanded by circumstances. In the fact that the human character is much affected by the accidents of country, parentage, and the like, we trace the Divine Wisdom operating a progressive education of the race. At the same time it were treachery to our souls to overlook the other fact,—the power of man over his condition, which bespeaks the great gift of God in the endowment of the human race with liberty. Circumstances are of the greatest importance as instructers, but they suppose a pupil. To say, they make the man, is to say, the air makes the sound, which it only conveys; or, that it is the winds and not the pilot that brought the ship into harbour.

It is not to be denied that all men are much influenced by the fortune of their birth and early associations, and many men are passive under these influences. A man is born under the shadow of ancient institutions by the side of whose strength, his own strength is insignificant. Men are observed to be of their fathers' religion. Men frequently follow, especially in old countries, their fathers' profession. And so it is said, man is formed by these institutions. But observe, on the other hand, how strong is the effect of individual character in each man to change the complexion of the same pursuits in his hands. In a degree, he always is affected by the nation, age, family, profession, friendships, he falls upon; but he exerts influence, as well as receives it. And that, in proportion to the strength of his character.

It may be questioned whether every man is not born with a peculiar character, or, having a peculiar determination to some one pursuit or one sort of usefulness. If he cultivate his powers and affections, this determination will presently appear. If he do not, he will yield to those influences under which he first happens to fall; but as his character opens, there will be a constant effort on the part of his mind, to bend his circumstances to his character.[1] Hence we continually see men of strong character changing the nature of a profession in their hands. What different men have figured under the name of a *soldier,* from the bloody savage who was brother to the tiger and the wild boar, to the pious and gentle patriot who saved his country. How different has been the profession of the ministers of religion, as it has fallen upon different men. One is a soldier, one a statesman, one an adviser of the king's conscience, one a dispenser of ceremonies, one an almsgiver, one a beggar, one a petty tyrant, one a preacher, one a pastor.

How many separate professions are contained under the name of merchant or lawyer,—each individual pursuing those parts only or chiefly for which his talents most qualify him.

At present, society is served by a limited number of professions, and each man according to his temper or the temper of his friends, is thrown into one of these. But as society advances, no doubt, these pursuits will be indefinitely multiplied, and instead of a few professions, there will be almost as many callings as individuals. Such is the diversity of characters and tastes, that if every individual should follow his own inclination, all places would be filled and society no loser. For one man loves agriculture; another, commerce; another, learning; another, art; one would live on the mountains; another on the sea;

1. Cf. *JMN* 3:324.

another in the mine; one has skill in speech; another, the brain in the hand;[2] one loves a crowd; another prefers to sit alone. Even now we sometimes see an individual forsake all the usual paths of life and show men a new one better fitted than any other to his own powers. And as any man discovers a taste of any new kind or any new combination of abilities he tends toward such places and duties as will give occasion for their exercise. And this, because great powers will not sleep in the human breast. Every thing was made for use. Great powers demand to be put in action, the greater they are with the more urgency. Every man is uneasy until every faculty of his mind is in freedom and in action; and hence arises a constant effort to take that attitude which will admit of this action.

Hitherto men have exercised their reflexion so little upon this matter, that you see only rarely a man exactly suited to his profession. Often men grow grey in a vocation for which they appear almost wholly unqualified, and its duties, of course, are discharged without love, and not only so, but men in that condition are but half themselves;—talents unused slumber in them. On the other hand, we sometimes see an individual who seems to have fallen exactly into his right place. And what perfect satisfaction appears in his air and behaviour; how harmoniously all his powers are developed, and with what increased efficiency he works!

Every one well knows what difference there is between doing things with all one's heart, and doing them against one's will. If every person were engaged in those employments he preferred, would not the wheels of society move with better speed, and surer effect? Would not more be done, and all be done better? And what an increase of happiness! for all labor would be pleasure.

These remarks are founded on the doctrine, which I believe gains faith in every man's mind with his habits of reflexion, that every individual mind has its assigned province of action,—a place which it was intended by God to fill, and to which always it is tending. It is that which the greatest cultivation of all his powers will enable him to do best. It is what that particular person was made to do. Every just act, every proper attention bestowed upon his mind, makes this aim more distinct to him. It may be hidden from him for years. Unfavorable associations, bad advice, or his own perversity may fight against it. But he will never be at ease, he will never act with efficiency until he finds it. Whatever it be, it is his *high calling*. This is his mark and prize. This is permanent, and of an infinite scope. All other callings are temporary,—are only means to bring out and present distinctly before his eyes, this one. Many mistakes may be made in the search, but every man who consults himself—the intimations of the Divine Wisdom in his own mind,—will constantly approach it. It is that state in which all the powers of the man are put in use. And he who is steadfastly enlarging his views of what is true, and heroically doing what is right, is fast advancing

2. Samuel Taylor Coleridge, *The Friend*, ed. Barbara E. Rooke (Princeton, 1969), 1:420. See *JMN* 4:115; used in "Trades and Professions" (*EL* 2:117).

toward this end. It ought to be matter of serious reflexion to every man, to ascertain what is his true vocation, whether he has yet found it, whether he fulfils all its duties; and in order to this end he ought to respect every doubt, every misgiving, every preference that touch his pursuits and not dismiss them till he has fully weighed and proved them.

This end, this his high calling,—let it be sacred in each man's mind. Let every soul rise to the perception that it was designed by the great Father of all for a peculiar good,—not to be benefitted only in common with nations, or with families, but as an individual. Be content, then, humbly and wisely to converse with yourself; to learn what you can do, and what you cannot; to be deterred from attempting nothing, out of respect to the judgment of others, if it be not confirmed by your own judgment. Never take for granted a common opinion against the promptings of your own heart, considering that another age will reverse all unfounded opinions, and settle them anew. Nor ever consider that your ties in life, your obligations to your family, or to your benefactors, or to your creditors, or to your country, shut you out of your true field of action by forbidding you to correct the errors of choice of pursuit into which you have fallen. For, you may constantly be tending towards this your use *through* all the common occupations and relations of life,—may constantly, by force of will, be bending them to that. The more distinctly we become acquainted with our powers and destiny, the more effectually do we exert ourselves to give that direction to our common employments. The less do we serve our circumstances, and the more do they serve us.

Furthermore; God will always give us freedom as fast as we are fit for it. He who has adopted a great purpose with ardor postpones every thing to it. It becomes to him father and mother and house and lands.[3] If his circumstances will admit of it, he bends them to this purpose, if not, he breaks them to it. Such a person forsakes the places and employments that under other circumstances it would be his duty to fill. The force of the feeling is his justification. He who does not feel his call with the same force, remains where he is.

Or if indeed there be any who feel a painful disproportion between their character and their condition, and yet are fixed in their present relations by chains too strong to be broken, their hope is in the eternity of their nature and in the omnipotence of God. Circumstances change, Heaven and earth pass— but the soul endures.[4] There is no knot of misfortune which death cannot untie. The Christian faith teaches us that death will bring to all who deserve it much more freedom than they now possess.

Once more, this the high calling of every soul is not in heaven, or over the sea, or existing in a heated imagination or in a remote future; it may be served in this life as well as in the next; it begins to be served whenever a man begins to act according to his conscience and he is leaving it whenever he violates his con-

3. Cf. Mark 10:29-30 and Matthew 10:35-37.
4. Cf. Matthew 5:18, 24:35, Mark 13:31, and Luke 16:17, 21:33.

science. Their true calling leads some men to the sea and some to the compting house; some to meditation and some to incessant bodily activity; leads some men to command and some to follow; one to strenuous opposition to all the usages of society, and another to diffuse joy and peace around a single hearth.

Finally the high calling of every mind is full of glory and joy and sweetness. Every man likes to do what he can do well. But this is to do what God made you to do best. It is no trifling, no easy, no short work. It is a work that demands severe exertion, your head and your heart, and it never will be done. But then it brings the strength it needs, for it is embraced with the whole affection of the soul. It makes the day bright. It clothes the world with beauty, and the face of God with smiles. It is a path without an end, that beginning in the little pursuits of this world, leads up to God's right hand,[5] to pleasures forevermore.

5. I Peter 3:22. The third chapter of I Peter was the scripture reading that accompanied the sermon in at least its first delivery.

CXLIV

Therefore leaving the principles of the doctrine of Christ, let us go on unto perfection.

HEBREWS 6:1

The great height of Christian doctrine,—I had almost said, the great paradox of Christian doctrine—is the commandment "Be ye perfect as God is perfect."[1] Is it not a great—is it not an enormous requisition? Yet it agrees with the nature and with the hopes of the mind. It falls in with the whole constitution of man, and his condition in the world, by making the cause of *religion* one with the cause of *self-improvement*.

There are many men who speak and act with a degree of foolish petulance when the admonitions of religion are addressed to them, as if to them they did not belong; as if, such had been their education or such are their avocations, that they have no time or will for any thing more than immediately concerns them, and these thoughts are for those who have leisure to attend to them; as if any man or any woman could have any business so pressing as the work of self cultivation or as if this responsibility could touch any one person more than another. Who is not bound by it? And whose business is it that you keep the commandments? Is it God's? Your obedience cannot profit Him. Is it Man's? Surely we shall all be the better for your virtue, but the good will get on to heaven without you; yes, and sometimes by the instrumentality of your vices. They shall be the occasion of good actions; and the bad will not be troubled that you are no better than they. No; it is not the primary concern of mankind— or of any class, or any individual. It is not the church's business, it is not the minister's business, it is not their calling but yours. It is the dear concern of your whole nature and can touch no other, as it touches you.

It seems to me that this exhortation to progress as it is the most powerful

Manuscript dated February 1832, at Chardon Street. Preached fourteen times: February 12, 1832, at the Second Church, Boston; twice on February 19, at the First Parish Church, Cambridge, in the morning, and at Hollis Street Church, Boston, in the afternoon; March 1, a Thursday Lecture, at Federal Street; March 11 in Watertown; April 8 at the West Church, Boston; April 15 in West Cambridge; June 3 at the First Church, Waltham; August 26 in Hingham; November 10, 1833, in New Bedford; June 29, 1834, at the Second Church, Waltham; July 27 in Bangor, Maine; November 22, 1835, at East Lexington; and June 5, 1836, in Concord. Emerson sketched out the idea of the sermon on January 12, 1832; see *JMN* 3:319.

1. Matthew 5:48.

appeal so it is of the most universal application that can be addressed to the human mind. It appeals to Christian, and Jew, and Pagan, to the believer and to the unbeliever, and, in a degree, even to those who have no hope beyond this life. It appeals to all. But to those who believe in God,—to those with whom the precepts of religion have weight,—the exhortation to self improvement will speak with greatest force. For, in that measure in which we have right views, will this duty appear plain.

The world is deceived by very false notions respecting the religious character. There is no such thing as an unimproving religious character. If it do not improve, it is not religious. No languid piety can be agreeable to God. He did not make this struggling mind—these powers of accurate thought—for nothing; it is not an occasional sentiment, it is not a good book, it is not a prayer, it is not a religious Sabbath, that will satisfy him, or exercise these powers. But he made man to become a more exalted servant of *His* will every day. He made him to serve Him with *all* his powers. He made these lungs to suck in air, and these understandings to drink in knowledge no less; this memory to receive and retain; this judgment to try words; this moral sentiment to be refined; this religious heart to carry a more filial and abiding trust; these active powers to journey from duty to duty without end. And the best prayer and praise which we can offer is to show him every day purer actions, more skilful hands, wiser judgments, fuller memories, and fairer and more perfect souls.

In asking your attention to the duty of self improvement I shall speak 1. of the call which God utters to you in your condition and in your nature. 2. I shall offer some practical considerations upon the extent of our duties.

Do you not hear the voice of Providence as it speaks to you with unexampled distinctness, in the wonderful multiplication of the means of improvement, in the profuse distribution of books, in the provision of written and oral instruction; which send knowledge begging to every man's door, and in the plainest and most accessible forms? Instead of the jealousy which, in old times, excluded all but a favoured few from every school of science, now, men of every profession and every trade are besought to read and to hear, yes, and to become instructors in their turn.

Do you not hear the voice of Providence as it speaks to you in the course of events; the remarkable agitations of the times; the singular freedom of the institutions amidst which you are born,—singularly favorable by the removal of all those barriers which obstruct the progress of men elsewhere, to whatever degree of energy is in your character; inviting you, as men never before were invited, to chuse the place you will fill, the duties you will discharge; setting up everywhere the rewards of merit, and saying, So much exertion shall receive so much honour; Sow what you will you shall reap the same.[2]

This singular freedom of our condition permits every man to take the place he wills to take. I would not speak loosely. I do not mean that a man can

2. Job 4:8; cf. Galatians 6:7.

propose to himself with any certainty to attain an exact measure of influence or to fill a given office for which he resolves to qualify himself. This is not a proper aim, and he may be defeated; but he may choose in what sort of usefulness he will serve his fellowmen and to what extent. And if he choose, he shall so serve them. If he do not find opportunities, he will make them. If he cannot serve by a public function, he will serve the same cause by a private one; if not by office, by the press; if not by the press, by his daily discourse; or if he is a silent man, yet by actions, by money, and by vote. In the innumerable modes of lawful and useful employment, let each man chuse well and pursue steadfastly and fear not but place, means, and occasion of service will be supplied him in that kind he loves. Now this freedom of choice of pursuit which exists among us is a great progress on the immoveable state of society of former times, when the ways of private influence were few and similar and often hereditary and may be to our minds an emblem of what is done in that 'eternal country,' where all of us shall choose by strong determination of character our own peculiar duties in the spiritual world.

But all these means, this accumulation of motives and facilities, and this increased liberty of action were not given without meaning. A strict account is taken of all. And if we have more gifts, a greater usury will be demanded of us, than of the savage or the slave.[3]

Hear, then, this call of the times, of society, of good men, of your own soul, and set about the work of self-improvement. Let us see what we are doing and how fast we advance. What is the fruit of each new week and month. If this inquiry were brought home to each of us we should find, I doubt not, that many of us were adding a little every year to our capital in trade, some ornament to our houses, some conveniences to our families at home. Time is making us more skilful in our business, and more ambitious too of extending our connexion, and getting up in the world. But—is it making you a wiser man, in any true and noble sense? Is it making you better? Is it making you more reconciled to inevitable misfortunes; more brave to bear disaster; more generous in your views and actions towards men; more able to entertain yourself innocently alone; more just in your judgments, and more firm in the apprehension of death?

If not, I fear you are making great haste in a wrong road; all your steps must be retraced; much of your skill is to be unlearned. You have mistaken the object of living.

I have alluded to that voice which speaks to us from our condition. Much more emphatic is that which speaks from our nature.

Consider, brethren, with what purpose God has given us Reason. He has not given us Reason with the intention that we should shut its eye, and live by custom instead. He has not given us Reason, with the intention of leading us by other super-natural lights, if we please to neglect the lamp we have. He intended

3. Cf. Luke 12:48.

that we should call ourselves to account, when he made us "a law to ourselves";[4] that we should make our lives pass in review before us; that we should correct our faults, that we should cherish our virtues, that we should cultivate our talents, not that we should acquire habits with blind inconsideration. Reason was given you for this use, to judge. It was given us, to this very intent that we should not slide insensibly into habits, which, by our constitution, exercise so despotic a control over our happiness and degree of efficiency,—but should form our habits deliberately as what shall be our good or our evil angels. It was given that you may not be a solemn trifler in an old routine of engagements, business, pleasure, company,—going where you are wont, without ever being able to give a good reason why you are doing these things, what you seek in this company, and what result time is to show for all your work; but that you may see your end in it, your great interest in it, and work like a man, and not as the ox without understanding.[5] Reason was given that you might make your own habits, and not take them from others; that reason might preside at their formation, and not chance.

There is a passage in the writings of Dr. Paley, bearing upon this subject, full of practical wisdom, that well deserves the careful attention of every one who is in earnest setting himself to the improvement of his character.

"The art," he says, "in which the secret of human happiness in a great measure consists, is, to *set* the habits in such a manner, that every change may be a change for the better. The habits themselves are much the same; for whatever is habitual, becomes smooth, and easy, and nearly indifferent. The return to an old habit is likewise easy, whatever the habit be. Therefore the advantage is with those habits which allow of indulgence in the deviation from them. The luxurious receive no greater pleasure from their dainties, than the laborer does from his bread and cheese; but the laborer, whenever he goes abroad, finds a *feast,* whereas the epicure must be well entertained to escape disgust. Those who spend every day at cards, and those who go every day to plough, pass their time much alike;—intent upon what they are about, wanting nothing, regretting nothing, they are both for the time in a state of ease; but then whatever suspends the occupation of the cardplayer distresses him; whereas to the laborer, every interruption is a refreshment. And this appears in the different effect which Sunday produces on the two, which proves a day of recreation to the one, but a lamentable burden to the other.

"The man who has learned to live alone, feels his spirits enlivened, whenever he enters into company, and takes his leave without regret. Another who has long been accustomed to a crowd experiences in company no elevation of spirits nor any greater satisfaction than what the man of retired life finds in his chimney corner. So far their conditions are equal; but let a change of place, fortune, or situation separate the companion from his circle, his visitors, his club, or coffee

---

4. Romans 2:14.
5. Cf. Psalms 32:9.

house, and the difference of advantage in the choice and constitution of the two habits will show itself. Solitude comes to the one clothed with melancholy; to the other, it brings liberty and quiet."[6]

The use of these observations is manifest. Every one can apply the moral for himself. Set your habits with moderation. Make them such as shall not in the first days exhaust the sweetness of life. They proceed on the supposition that life has a limit, and the enjoyments of man have a limit, and that it is obviously wise to set our habits on such a key as we can hold; not to live too fast, but to have a prudent reference to our threescore years and ten.[7]

But I wish to urge a farther extension of this doctrine, from the pursuit of a fugitive well-being to the attainment of everlasting good. The use I wish to make of this doctrine, is, *that we should set our habits as immortal beings;* that we should set our habits at such a key as we can hold forevermore.

We must get rid of this confused idea entertained of the future state,—that it is so different from any thing in our experience, as that it will almost confound our identity, and learn to consider it as only the progress of which this is the outset. I believe it happens to all reflecting persons, that their views of the future state of the soul, alter very much as their religious character improves, and harmonize more, and not less, with their experience in this world. The truth is, we are not to form one set of habits of worldly prudence, so as to secure the most enjoyment *here,* and another set of habits to ensure happiness hereafter,— but we must set all our habits whilst on the earth, for our whole being, that is, for all the future, and not for the seventy years of man.

Would you know then what is your true condition? You have only to enumerate honestly to yourself your customary sources of enjoyment, and see how many of them are such as will survive the body: If you are accustomed to intellectual pleasures; to think patiently; to study the works of God; to master your appetites; to exercise kind affections; to make yourself useful; to worship the Divine Providence;—then death does not threaten any of your main satisfactions; you will continue to do the same things hereafter. But if all your enjoyments are of the table, or of display, or of covetousness, or of debauchery,—then these things manifestly cannot survive the life of the body; they must presently have a final stop—and you are yet unborn into the life of God.

Now this is a plain rule which all of us can apply very easily to ourselves, to see that our pleasures are such as can last us forever. Thus the habit of speaking the strict truth may be formed which will be as beautiful in heaven as it is on earth. The habit of accurate discrimination between our own thoughts, will not have less value a thousand years hence than it has today. The habit of self-command will always inspire respect. The habit of benevolence is excellent

6. Paley's Moral Philosophy [Emerson's note]. Emerson may have found the passage in William Paley, *The Principles of Moral and Political Philosophy,* 5th ed. (London, 1788), 1:36–37, or, more likely, in Dugald Stewart, *The Philosophy of the Active and Moral Powers of Man,* in *The Works of Dugald Stewart* (Cambridge, 1829), 5:538–39, where it is quoted. See *JMN* 3:201 and 319.

7. Psalms 90:10.

among the angels. And every just conclusion and every kind action hath its principle in the spirit, not in the flesh; in the spirit which is beautified by it. And so peruse with a critical eye every part of your life, drag every practice to the light, and judge them all by this test of their durability. Observe, too, that the present life is raised and sweetened by all these courses which look at immortality.

When it shall be considered as it deserves that the mind is the seat of contentment, how indifferent are many of those circumstances commonly esteemed so essential,—will not a greater self-cultivation make great wealth of less account in men's estimation? How much more time does almost every man spend in the acquisition of property than is necessary for the supply of his first wants, in order that he may procure those superfluous conveniences or ornaments which the pride of life has caused to be thought necessary,—losing of course so much time to pursuits wholly intellectual and to improving social enjoyment, which would be very welcome indeed to many men who thus labor, and who regret what they think their absolute exclusion from them.

Let every one consider this anew for himself and see whether leisure for the employments of the soul be not a great want enough to be supplied at the price of a magnanimous resistance of some of the opinions or customs of society, whether a plainer dress, or plainer diet, or a humbler house be too great a price to pay for thought and freedom.

Let us obey then the prompting of God which urges us to redeem the time;[8] to signalize these days and months which roll over us by virtues, by knowledge acquired and communicated, by usefulness. Let us from the height of the calmest reason see if we are adding any more to the amount of human comfort, than we were in former years; whether any of the ways in which we had done mischief are stopped; whether our employments have become more worthy, more fit to show to men, and angels, and to God, as the best return we can make for the gift of Reason. Well would it be with us, if every night we would renew this inquiry, if every week we would make this comparison. Then when in our turn sickness and death shall come to each of us, we shall smile to discover, that an inward health blooms in us, which no pestilence can infect, that a spiritual man has been formed within us by the discipline of good and evil, who lives and acts by principles which shall not pass, though heaven and earth pass away,[9] and who is supported and cheered and led on by his love and trust in God.

8. Ephesians 5:16 and Colossians 4:5.
9. Cf. Matthew 5:18, 24:35, Mark 13:31, and Luke 16:17, 21:33.

CXLV

Why even of yourselves judge ye not what is right?
LUKE 12:57

It is often remarked that the acquisitions of the wisest men of one generation become the property of the whole people in the next. It was once known only to two or three persons that the earth was a sphere, a fact now taught almost all the children in Christendom. Three hundred years ago, only one man believed that by sailing west from Europe, land might be found. We live upon that land. It is only a little while ago that the circulation of the blood was discovered by Harvey: now it is known to all.[1]

In the same way, every thing truly valuable that has ever been made known by any man, comes presently to be known to many, and in course of time to all. No man has ever gone so far beyond his fellowmen in his attainments but the children of a later age were able to master what was most valuable in his knowledge. This fact shows us that though all men are capable of knowing the same things, yet may one man go by mere dint of thinking a century in advance of his fellow men.

So also is it in morals. I hope it will be admitted that there is some progress of society in virtue from the rudest ages, when it is considered that idolatry, polygamy, the endless fighting, and some other vices of savages are entirely without example in our times among civilized nations. A single savage, or two or three, more pure and wise than the tribe, discerned the folly and guilt of these practices and abstained from them. Now no man thinks it a hardship that he cannot kill his neighbor for every hard word. And all men with one voice would execrate the proposition to introduce among us the horrid licentiousness and cruelty of the New Zealanders.

That is to say the great body of the people have risen to the same degree of virtue that belonged to the most wise and pious individual of some former age. Or in other words, though all men are capable of the same virtue, yet has one man arrived at it a century sooner than the multitude. All knowledge was

Manuscript dated February 26, 1832. Preached four times: February 26, 1832, at the Second Church, Boston; October 23, 1836, in East Lexington; March 19, 1837, at the First Church, Waltham; and February 4, 1838, in Concord. The sermon grew out of journal entries for January 21 and February 6, 1832; see *JMN* 3:321 and 325–26.

1. William Harvey (1578–1657), English physician.

once a private opinion. "The Christian religion," says Milton, "was once a schism."[2]

Let us reason from the past to the present. Let us believe the same progress is now going on that has always proceeded. Certainly we see in these facts what a divine economy is in our power, that by the use of our intellectual and moral powers we may outstrip the tardy progress of the race and anticipate future centuries in the short term of our mortal life. Hence arises the sacred duty of judging for ourselves, and this is the duty I wish to urge.

Is it thought that the right of private judgment is pretty well established in the world, and needs not to be insisted on? In matters of speculation perhaps it is, and yet it has been very reluctantly admitted; but in matters of practice it is not to any thing like its just extent. Few men feel at liberty to exercise a free and original judgment upon the whole course of their actions. Most men surrender the greatest part of them to be governed by the custom of society.

But the rule of the gospel is, 'Go into thy closet and shut the door, and consider thyself in the presence of God.'[3] This is a practical rule which results from all the instruction of the New Testament. And I am led by it, brethren, to offer you some reasons why we should judge of ourselves what is right, and some remarks upon the obligation and advantage of that duty.

1. First it is important that you judge for yourselves what is right on account of the insufficiency of any other tribunal. It is of great importance that you judge for yourself because the world is full of errors which find shelter under the authority of great names. What is the defence that is always set up for every enormity which good men wish to root out? Why, that a great deal better men than we, have borne with it, and therefore, there must be some good in it. War seems to us not shocking, such great and good men have played at that game. Bigotry has been upheld a thousand years, because pious men have caused men to die for difference of opinion. Censoriousness has saints to recommend it, and is hardly yet found out to be a fault. Entire disuse of the highest powers of the intellect does not seem to us any great negligence, because eminent men have gone to their graves without using half their powers. Other great men have allowed themselves in gross habits of self indulgence. And there is hardly any vice which has not the authority of some admired name. Of course, were it not for the existence of some court of appeal in the hearts of individuals, all vice and ignorance would be entailed on society forever by the means of the virtues of heroes.

But it is said, Have we not the Sacred Scriptures? are they not a sufficient guide? Let it be remembered that when we say the Scripture is a sufficient rule of conduct we necessarily understand the aid of human spirit to interpret it. And so it means more or less according to the sharpness of our eye to read. This will appear from the fact that the Scriptures have been received and read in the

2. *Areopagitica,* in *The Works of John Milton,* ed. F. A. Patterson (New York, 1931-1938), 4:321. See *JMN* 6:183.
3. Cf. Matthew 6:6.

same ages when the enormities I have alluded to, were allowed without scruple by the best men.

There seems therefore no precept so important as that a man should get his principles nowhere but in himself. There is no other way for you to arrive at the voice of God but by patient listening to your own conscience. Even Jesus reveals God's will to you by outward message which your own reason must explain and enforce, but your own reason is the voice of God himself which speaks to you and to all mankind without an interpreter. Why do we say it comes from God, it is the child of God? Partly, to be sure, because the human race from a mysterious antiquity that has no record have so informed us, but chiefly because the mind recognizes all over the creation thought and design like its own, and so declares that however great is that being who made and animates this world, He must be of the same sort as itself, it is a ray of the same light.

Settle it then deeply in your mind that it is accountable for its opinions; that as it has been made capable of judging of all that is offered to it, so it is its solemn duty to receive nothing however ancient or venerable without examination; that it must dispose all its thoughts in one of two classes, either that which it has laid up for consideration, or that which on good reason it has approved. You are to bring to the trial, your whole order and course of life; your daily work; the details of your business; your domestic habits; the company you keep; the projects you entertain; the institutions you support; the party in the state to which you attach yourself; and all the opinions which you hold with respect to common usages and to the various public and private affairs that are transacted every day before your eyes.

Settle every thing anew for yourself, especially whatever things are esteemed finally settled.

Examine what others omit to notice. Take nothing for granted. That strikes you in hearing the discourse of a wise man, that he gives you new views of the most trite and familiar subjects, showing that it is the habit of his mind to let nothing pass without question, but to prove every thing for himself, as good chemists are said to bring to the crucible whatever others throw away. Indeed there, *in the common things,* is always the field of the most splendid discoveries. The greatest triumphs of science have been to show why a stone falls, and what the air is made of, and what water is, which a hundred generations had never thought of considering. It is what is immediately under our eye, what we see and do every day, that passes unnoticed, whilst our thoughts are inquiring about angels or inscrutable mysteries or obscure controversies or distant countries. Consider how many ages men acquiesced peaceably in the distinction of hereditary ranks.

Consider how long Slavery has passed for an innocent institution,—till within fifty years. See how long an army of drunkards has been permitted to bring all sorts of mischief upon every successive generation of mankind and men never imagined it could be prevented. It is only recently that capital punishments have been diminished; only recently the use of torture abolished. Only recently that

decency and discipline have been introduced into Prisons. It is but yesterday
that education has reached the vagabond boy that formerly was trained in the
street for the pillory. And so with Sunday schools; and Bankrupt laws; and
Farm Schools; and Asylums for the Blind, and the Dumb, and the Insane. These
are evils that have been felt from the foundation of the world, and never was it
suspected that they had remedy or alleviation until now.[4] What hinders that
more be done? Do you suppose these expedients have exhausted the evils or the
means of relief? It is only that eyes of love and understandings of discernment
have scrutinized things which other men passed by without inquiry. And the
world still is very far from perfect and is abused by great delusions which every
man will do much to remove, who is superior to acting from custom and acts by
principle. Mankind are under nearly as much delusion now as to the uses of
power and wealth as they were formerly with respect to the worship of idols, or
the necessity of orders of nobility.

The whole world runs now after power, it is sought as an ornament instead of
being received as a trust. The greatest men of this age are those who figure in
the highest places of political action. This will not always be so. Already the
esteem of men is shared by these persons with another class of competitors,
those, namely, who have added to the stock of natural truth, who find out the
secrets of the elements; the untiring inquirers who penetrate the laws of matter,
and ascertain the hidden truths of mathematical science in its application to
population or to mechanics or to astronomy, the men of genius who charm the
world with poetry or with art, the philosopher who expounds the causes of all
and the symmetry of things. These already divide with kings and legislators the
reverence of mankind, and in the progress of opinion when the majority of
mankind shall have imbibed a taste for knowledge shall more deserve and obtain
more.

And in like manner with regard to Wealth. Men, it is to be hoped, will some
time act with more reason in the pursuit of wealth. Now they labor fifty or sixty
years to make and increase their fortune and then it is time to die. They cannot
well do otherwise; for, life to the great majority of men does not appear to have
any greater charm than that deference which they see every where paid to wealth.
But when the mind has been made to taste other pleasures, when the sweetness of
acquiring knowledge and the beauty of truth have once been revealed, will not

4. In a journal entry of November 10, 1830, Emerson developed this idea, first broached in
Sermon LIX, after reading a sermon by Francis Wayland on Sunday schools (see *JMN* 3:208–9,
272). The American Temperance Society was founded in Boston in 1826. The Boston Prison Discipline Society was at this time a strong advocate for prison reform (see *Sermons* 2:68, n. 3). Agitation for improvements in the common schools of Massachusetts led to the creation of a State Board
of Education in 1837. The American Sunday School Union was established in 1824, though the
institution itself was developed earlier in England by Robert Raikes and Catherine Cappe (see
JMN 3:282). Imprisonment for debt, as a matter of federal law, was abolished in 1832. Work with
the handicapped was centered at the Perkins Institute for the Blind in Boston; Samuel Gridley
Howe joined the staff in 1832. Also in that year treatment of indigent insane persons in Massachusetts was revolutionized with the completion of the State Lunatic Asylum at Worcester, a
project devised and led by Horace Mann.

men strictly limit their exertion to the attainment of property as a means, instead of pursuing it, as now, for its own sake?

Do not then think that 6000 years have settled forever all that can be thought or said touching poverty and riches. It is still open to new and better judgments. Form your opinions for your own peculiar case, as if it were an exception to that of all mankind; and do not begin by considering it as forever settled that to be poor is to be wretched. Every reasoning man has some facts in his mind which invalidate the vulgar opinion, and incline him to think that the poor are as happy as the rich. Their greatest misfortune is that they borrow to their own harm the common opinion, that they are poor in their own conceit as well as in outward circumstances.

There are many rich who would be happy if they were poor; there are many poor who would be unhappy if they were rich. And certainly the capacity for intellectual pleasures makes a very great difference in judging of what is necessary for comfort and will make a man content with much less. Consider therefore whether a little that a righteous man hath is not better than the treasures of many wicked.[5]

Do not take it for granted that you need many thousands to make you easy in your circumstances because other people think so, but strictly examine whether the true sources of your satisfaction cannot be secured with half so much or the tenth part.

So think also of sickness and health. In putting sickness on the list of miseries, do not overlook the fact that the greatest blessings of health belong equally to sickness as to health, the power of discerning truth, and of acting right, and a firm religious belief.

So think especially of the use of your intellectual powers. Do not neglect the precious treasure the author of Wisdom has given you in the power of acquiring truth. It is some comfort to observe that men always value what wisdom they have. It is supposed that the man does not live so base as to exchange the least intellectual power for the wealth of the world. Yet how slow to augment this treasure admitting of indefinite addition. In another age, what men think now is a tolerable proficiency in knowledge will be pitied as extreme ignorance.

In short, carry this sharp discernment into the whole circle of your duties. Separate yourself from the judgments of men and by the simplicity of your desire to know and do the right, carry, as it were, the eye of God to every part of your life. If we would do this resolutely, it would give a new face to many duties. For we are very apt to hold our heads up, where we ought to blush, to consult our own interest where we should be seeking another's, and to live as if there were no other life, by a foolish following the custom of society. I might give many instances of this depraved judgment if time permitted. Every pious man has sometimes perceived the perfectness of the law of love, has believed it to be the best peacemaker of the world, that it could vanquish every enemy. Yet in

5. Cf. Proverbs 10:2.

many cases very worthy men act on the contrary opinion: Every thing must be done, every law broken sooner than one submit to the least injustice. But why, said Paul, do not ye rather suffer yourselves to be defrauded?[6] There are worse things than being defrauded; Defrauding is worse, and Malice, and Slander. We ought to feel that the true check upon our benevolence to a man who injures us, is the benevolence we owe to our families and to society and which enjoin us to resist aggression when it becomes outrageous. But the violence of a man should never put out of your mind or abridge in any degree your duty to serve him as far as you can.

But it would be utterly vain to attempt to give instances in every kind of the erroneous judgments that prevail in the world and which demand to be reversed by the better judgment of independent, conscientious, reasoning men. The fact is most men are too timid when they feel differently to say so, and they suppose they must be wrong when the probability is they are right. These considerations should teach us that we ought to give careful entertainment to every motion in our minds that condemns a practice which we allow.

Finally, does any one fear that a too great reliance on one's self and an obstinate questioning of every practice and institution might beget danger to faith and to virtue? Oh no. We might say, if they will not bear the test let them fall. But fear not. God has provided too surely for faith and virtue in the constitution of man. Generations perish, opinions change, but the testimonies of his power and love, which spoke to the eye and soul of the first generation, speak also to ours. There is the sun in the heaven and the eternal revolution of the heavenly host. Here is this divine economy of nature around us, every year better understood and the more admirable the more it is comprehended. Here is man who unites all wonders in himself by understanding them all, but in his farthest progress to true wisdom he never gets beyond the first truth that the only explanation of all things is God. It is beautiful to see after so many perverse revolutions of opinion the decided religious tone of all the science and all the philosophy of our age. All that religion demands for itself is that the whole truth may be fully and fairly viewed. It is the spirit of all the instructions of the great teacher and Friend of the human race, that we should serve the truth and it will make us free.[7] Why even of yourselves judge ye not what is right?

6. I Corinthians 6:7.
7. John 8:32.

CXLVI

Jesus Christ, who gave himself for us that he might redeem us from all iniquity and purify unto himself a peculiar people zealous of good works.

Titus 2:13–14

Jesus Christ came to redeem men from all iniquity. His prayer was 'Deliver us from evil.'[1] And he lived and died with this design. It is the work of God. The whole course of Providence viewed with the eye of reflexion and of faith has this for its object, to assist man in the work of self cultivation.

Nothing is more admirable than the adaptation of the world to the formation and education of the human soul. An attentive and pious eye may trace a providence that like a guardian genius takes up the infant when he enters into life,—feeds, exercises, instructs him; awakens, one by one, the powers that slumber in his breast, and, only employing one sort of helps as long as they are useful, quits these for a new and better series as soon as he is fit for them. This guardian never deserts him whilst he does not desert himself, but is always operating more and more to emancipate man and enable him to stand alone. The perfect man is a law to himself.[2]

Let us separately consider a few of the successive stages of this discipline.

1. In the first place the material world is curiously adjusted to the formation and residence and the improvement of man. 'Tis a house convenient for his habitation. Its texture is suited for his habitation, neither sinking under his feet from softness nor impenetrable to his plough. Its elements are suited for his food. Its air is suited for his respiration. All these might have been much otherwise. The chemist has tried the experiment of respiration with numerous gases and found none that can support life so long as the gas we breathe. Another observation is much more singular: The air we breathe is made up of two gases called oxygen and azote which is found to be a mixture of four parts of one, and one part of the other. Now these airs can be mixed in any proportion whatever. They have been mixed by experimenters in different proportions, and breathed, and it is found that no other mixture will support respiration so well

---

Manuscript dated March 4, 1832. Preached twice: March 4, 1832, at the Second Church, Boston, and July 12, 1835, at Lexington or, possibly, East Lexington.

1. Matthew 6:13 and Luke 11:4.
2. Cf. Romans 2:14.

as four parts and one part. Now what keeps this invariable proportion no one has yet discovered.[3]

2. In like manner the cultivation of the earth and the pursuit of his necessary accommodations upon it, which make up all the great variety of arts and trades, are admirably adjusted to the unfolding of all his powers. As the child among his playthings is said to be learning the laws of natural philosophy, so is the artificer among his tools and in all the exigences of his profession becoming acquainted with the laws of eternal truth and thereby acquiring greater power— that is, greater freedom. But, secondly, the natural world is also his first instructor in *moral* laws. It teaches him temperance. It forbids him excess. It holds up a premium to virtue. It extorts a severe tax from vice.

3. But a far more important aid than any appertaining to material nature is afforded to each individual in the aid which Society furnishes to the moral sentiments.

The common sense of mankind has been in some systems set up as the standard of right and wrong. And this might do if it were possible to ascertain what would be the impartial sentiment of every individual.

But the common sense of nations has sanctioned every sort of crime. One nation commends parricide, another theft, another polygamy, another self-murder.

Even in the best days of the best nation, public opinion has never been so pure but it has connived at very gross offences. It has permitted practices which the conscience of the virtuous individual condemns. It is altogether too fluctuating, unworthy of being the criterion of right and wrong.

The true standard must forever be the reason of every individual. By this all other tests must be tried, by this only can others address themselves to us.

But whilst the moral sentiments of our fellow men in every place allow particular vices, in the majority of cases they are always just and are far better than no law. Whilst therefore it will not do to make so uncertain a tribunal the rule of right, yet none can be blind to how great advantage it is to men that whilst reason in the individual is yet only in infancy and speaks with a stifled voice, the first steps of virtue are upheld by a dependence on the moral sentiments of the community.

This happens first by necessity. The young man who has his bread to earn must conform himself, willing or unwilling, to the good customs of the community. He must be honest or he will not be trusted; he must be temperate or he will come to want; he must be kind or he will find no kindness. A free indulgence of his

3. Emerson used this paragraph in "The Relation of Man to the Globe" (*EL* 1:32–33), where he identifies the experimenter as Sir Humphry Davy (1778–1829). See Davy, *Elements of Chemical Philosophy* (Philadelphia and New York, 1812), especially 130–32, 146. Emerson borrowed this edition from the Harvard College Library on September 22, 1828, though at some point he acquired the 1812 London edition. Emerson's father, William, made similar observations in the lecture "Respiration," in *A Discourse, delivered in the First Church, Boston, on the Anniversary of the Massachusetts Humane Society. June 9, 1807* (Boston, 1807). The elder Emerson commended "the great Dr. Priestley, and the celebrated Lavoisier" (8), but in a note credited "Mr. Davy" with a more exact knowledge of the subject.

passions would quickly bring down upon him the arm of the law, in which the moral sentiment of the community embodies itself.

By these gross restraints he is kept from doing himself injury whilst yet his power of self restraint is very weak.

By and by he gets above the fear or the need of the law. Most men would feel injured at the intimation that they abstained from assaulting or defrauding other men or from gratifying any criminal passion out of regard to the terrors of the penal law. And a great part of society do not need the terrors of the criminal statute. If the law was abolished against murder, murder would be as rare among them. But they do not so soon get above the restraints of public opinion, which makes the law.

The moral sentiments of our fellowmen have a mighty influence in assisting the formation of virtuous character. This influence can hardly be overestimated. It affects insensibly almost all action. It affects in a greater or less degree the moral judgments of every individual from the highest to the lowest. There is hardly any man of that degree of courage as to fly in the face of the unanimous opinion of his contemporaries. Even those who have advanced so far as to acquire fixed principles of action, who practise many virtues for their own sake, do yet obey in many things the voice of society, abstain from or perform things out of compliance with a custom which it would cost too much fortitude to withstand.

Yet this is not virtue; what is the strength worth of a thousand individuals who all are kept from falling, only because they lean upon each other? Place them in a new situation, where this restraint shall not be felt, or give them opportunity of sinning in secret, and it will be presently seen how miserable a foundation such virtue has. Yet has this its uses. It has proved a safeguard in the most dangerous period of life to thousands whom it allured into good habits, into the near acquaintance with virtue, and the opportunity and the power to give it their deliberate preference, and their steadfast devotion. Who is he that cannot remember with gratitude the occasions when he has been indebted to this influence for his safety? It will be admitted to be one of the strongest foreign aids which God has furnished virtue.

He is yet far from the kingdom of heaven who seeks no higher merit than to satisfy society,[4] who is content to live with that decency and innocence which public opinion requires, to be as bad as he dares. To act from example, to act with reference to the consequences of our action in this life is to take the shadow for the substance, a secondary for the primary principle.

There is a time in the progress of a good man when he begins to feel the unworthiness of finding his rule of right out of himself. He begins to feel the superiority of the law of the mind to all laws, and to prefer the calm judgments of his own reason to the opinion and practice of the whole world. What a vast step is this to true freedom. He is exchanging the yoke of a thousand masters to

4. Cf. Mark 12:34.

come under the rule of one. He is exchanging the yoke of laws of authority for a commandment which shows its own end. The commandment is a lamp to the feet.[5]

Does it seem to any that we make light of the opinion of mankind? that there is a degree of arrogance and therefore of falsehood in condemning entirely the reference to the judgments of other men and the vulgar doctrine that we must do so and so for the sake of example? Let me draw what I conceive to be the true distinction on this question and define what I think the true deference which we owe to the opinions of others. I will suppose that a sincere man has made up his mind that it is right for him to do something which the common opinion of good men disapproves. But in going forward to execute his purpose he is disturbed by finding the whole mind and heart of the community or of the best part of the community arrayed against him. What is its natural and just effect? Why this, that it leads him to reconsider the whole action, to go over again with more careful thought, the steps by which he came to his conclusion, and perhaps he will find that there is some flaw in his reasoning; that what so shocks mankind ought also to shock himself; that it is neither good for them, nor good for him; and so he shall desist from his design. I do not think that this unwillingness to outrage the feelings of society, which is strongest in the best men, exists there in vain, but that God would give virtue this outwork, this opportunity of consideration and of reconsideration. But if, at last, with the best light, and in perfect simplicity the man still approves his action, let him go and do it though he go alone.

But even with those who have reached ground and aim to act from principle the moral sentiments of other men are not without use. For every man has some defects in his education, some blind side in his understanding, and if he were allowed to stand too much on the sufficiency of his own judgment would be likely to adopt some errors.

But the independent judgments of other virtuous men are a wholesome check upon prejudice as well as an unspeakable encouragement when they confirm our own. "Already," it has been said, "my opinion has gained infinitely in force when another mind has adopted it."[6]

4. The next great help in aid of the soul lies in an external religion. By external religion I mean not one of forms but one which represents God as external to the soul. Mankind have regarded God as powerful genius whose thoughts and ways very much resembled their thoughts and ways. They have supposed that the reward of virtue was a distinct reward like a prize given at a school, that the punishment of vice was an external infliction.

The religious phraseology of the world is framed on these ideas. Virtue is enjoined by commandment and Vice is forbidden by threats. Men almost expected

5. Psalms 119:105.
6. The sentence is slightly misquoted from Carlyle's anonymous article "Characteristics" (*The Edinburgh Review* 54 [December 1831]: 359), where Carlyle has translated it from Novalis, *Die Schriften* (Berlin, 1826), 2:104. See *JMN* 4:15 and 5:29. Used in Sermon CLXVIII and in "Society" (*EL* 2:101).

to see God walking in the clouds. They called the thunder his voice, and the storm his manifestation. They saw his hand in the spasms of disease or the fate of the wretch on whom mankind rose in vengeance, but they did not feel the divinity stirring in the mother's heart and the child's thirst for knowledge.

All of us know the power of these religious views. They are received into the mind when no other could have authority. They are then sufficient for the soul: they hinder from vice; they lead to justice, temperance, and to the beginnings of a holy life. They furnish an anchor to the soul.[7] They supply occupation to the thoughts. They powerfully move on the young mind and satisfy the affections and infuse a wholesome dread of sin and a desire and delight in well doing.

But they must lead to higher and better views. It is only the porch of the temple. It is a poor service of God that is paid from fear of punishment or from hope of reward. We must be led from the erroneous worship of God that kneels to a supposed deity above the stars to know Him who was, and is, and shall be;[8] Him who is the life and order of the universe; Him who makes our being every moment; Him who imparts himself to us in our Reason and who is best honoured in its use. We must be led to a spiritual worship, to a love of truth and virtue for their own sake. We must understand that by them we are to approach God and see God, nay to become more largely partakers of his nature.[9]

We must be led to a religion in which we shall not regard the approbation of God as one thing and our own approbation as another and feel that we have God to serve and please as well as ourselves, but shall come to perceive that in the soul he is most present, that right reason and pure love are the most we know of him, that his right worship consists in the constant acknowledgment that our individual life flows from him continually as light from the sun.

My friends, I think we ought to regard these wonderful provisions as aids to the formation of God's great work, a human soul. And only as aids. God is operating forever to lead the soul to freedom. The first steps of the process are got from the material world, which is fitted to raise and discipline the body so as to give the soul external freedom. The next support is found in the moral sentiment of mankind, which acts as a strong barrier coming between the soul and the worst temptations. By this, man is enabled to preserve his youth and ignorance from overthrow before yet he is made acquainted with religious motives. The next aid is the beneficent discipline of religion as first it is received into the mind, a severe and hallowing principle but like the others wholly insufficient by itself.

But if the soul cooperate with God, who furnishes these helps, it is led from external religion to internal, from the religion of Moses to the religion of Christ; from the letter of the gospel to the spirit,[10] to the doing of God's will from love. The design of God is to make the soul sufficient to itself. He has most richly

7. Hebrews 6:19.

8. Emerson echoes the "Gloria Patri": "Glory be to the Father, and to the Son, and to the Holy Ghost; as it was in the beginning, is now, and ever shall be, world without end. Amen."

9. Cf. II Peter 1:4.

10. Cf. Romans 2:29 and II Corinthians 3:6.

endowed it. He has made it capable to know its own happiness and misery. He has kindly lent it in its feebleness these outward supports. If it will accept his goodness and use every effort to advance, one by one these helps become useless and fall off; the soul advances until it is filled with light and love, and becomes a heaven in itself. In the sublime words of the Apocalypse: And there shall be no night there, and they need no candle, neither light of the sun, for the Lord God giveth them light.[11]

Judge then by the greatness of these means of the greatness of the end. God is setting before every soul that he hath made a great work, an interminable progress. Think worthily of your destiny. Do not rest in the means but advance unceasingly to the freedom and power to which he calls you.

I conclude with two reflexions.

1. Virtuous action must be secured, if the man would be happy or safe. Surely it is best to act well from the highest motives, but it is and he feels virtuous conduct in itself to be of immense importance—as virtuous conduct tends to virtuous principle. Let not a man therefore presume to cast off the restraints of public opinion, because he says it is a very unworthy motive to act from, unless he receive the restraints of the higher law within his own breast. For Virtue he must have, and let his own knowledge of what will most effectually bring his actions under its law be the measure of his advancement.

2. These are given as aid, not as strength itself; that must be from within or nowhere. The help of omnipotence is vain but for your own disposition and effort to raise, redeem, deliver yourself. We must work out our own salvation.[12]

Let us then joyfully accept the unspeakable gift of God; let us perceive his presence; let us acknowledge his aids; and assured of the Divine protection so long as we desire it, let us use our diligence to obtain strength; to go on from lower motives to more excellent; from innocence to virtue; that he may deliver us from evil,[13] and purify unto himself a peculiar people zealous of good works.

11. Revelation 22:5.
12. Philippians 2:12.
13. Matthew 6:13 and Luke 11:4.

CXLVII

And beside this, giving all diligence, add to your faith, virtue; and to virtue, knowledge; and to knowledge, temperance; and to temperance, patience; and to patience, godliness; and to godliness, brotherly kindness; and to brotherly kindness, charity.

II PETER 1:5–7

St. Peter begins this rich catalogue of graces by congratulating the church upon the great and precious promises which the power of God has made to them, to the end, he says, (and the words are remarkable) "that ye might be partakers of the divine nature."[1]

The first thing that strikes one on an attentive perusal of this passage is this magnificent inducement to right action thus quietly and simply presented, that ye might be partakers of the divine nature.

Christianity has been sometimes represented as the obscure and narrow dogma of a few Jews very low in life and contracted in their thoughts. And if humble circumstances had any thing to do with contracted thinking, it would be very just to condemn them unheard. But this is for the outward eye to try to judge of what belongs to the inward.

The truth is, the disciples were poor Jews, but surely it is no new thing in the world that poverty and truth should dwell together or that genuine virtue should be found in unlearned men. So far from its being narrow, never was any thing so noble and commanding before presented. The very attraction which has drawn the best minds in the world to the reverence of the gospel has been its great and precious promises, its exalted views of the human soul there shown to be on the pattern of the divine and most beloved of all his works by the great parent.

Has any theory of life ever been presented by any poet or any philosopher

---

Manuscript dated March 17, 1832, at Chardon Street and May 27 at the Friend Street Chapel. Preached three times: March 18, 1832, at the Second Church, Boston; May 27 at the Friend Street Chapel; and December 18, 1836, at East Lexington. The sermon draws on a lengthy journal entry for March 10, 1832; see *JMN* 4:4–5.

1. II Peter 1:4.

more enlarged than this which Peter presents as the practical motive to every member of the Christian Church, "that having escaped the corruption that is in the world, ye might be partakers of the divine nature"? And to what ends is his zeal directed? to what ends is this motive to animate them? See particularly whether he has a jewish zeal; speaks the language of a craft or sect. Does he stir them up to sectional spirit? to a peasants' war? to a conspiracy against the powerful or the rich or against the public order? No; but to accomplish themselves in a circle of virtues; to make themselves perfect men and perfect women. Not add to yourself wine and oil, friends and fame. No, nor yet Samaria, and Idumea, and Tyre, and Sidon.[2] But add to faith, virtue; and to virtue knowledge, and to these temperance, patience, godliness, brotherly kindness, and charity.

Certainly this is the attraction, this is the evidence of Christianity, that it does not appeal to anything that is low or local or temporary but to our inmost and best feelings. This is the ground of our unshaken confidence in its progress and triumph over all opposition and sin, its perfect coincidence with the moral nature of man.

Let us proceed to a further examination of the Apostolic advice.

I do not think that this is, or that St. Peter meant it should be, a systematic list of the Christian virtues. It is neither a complete list nor is the arrangement quite perfect. It is not the way of the Apostles to write like scientific moralists. They wrote what they thought would be useful. They had particular churches or persons in their eye. He speaks of those virtues that were in the situation of himself and his brethren most needed and most loved.

Yet the enumeration will appear more just by a nearer examination of it and a correction of some trifling errors that have crept into the translation.

1. *And beside this, giving all diligence.* This is incorrectly rendered. It should run, *And to this very end bend all your strength*[3]—to the end, that is, of becoming 'partakers of the divine nature.'

2. *Add to your faith, virtue.* What is the meaning of faith? Every careful reader of the New Testament will perceive that this term is used in different passages with some difference of signification and that it is a matter of some nicety to settle its import in the general use. The simplest meaning is *belief.* "Felix heard Paul concerning the faith in Christ."[4]

But belief depends on evidence. It is not voluntary. No man is praised in common life for his simply believing a story of which the facts have been vouched to him nor blamed for disbelieving a story of which not a particle of evidence has been shown him. Why then is faith represented as a virtue in the gospels and epistles? "Thy faith hath saved thee."[5]

2. Samaria, the northern kingdom of ancient Israel, or its capital city; Idumea (or Idumaea), the southernmost region of Judea, Israel's southern kingdom; and Tyre and Sidon, Phoenician seaports north of Israel.

3. "And with this very view, employing your utmost earnestness" Wakefield [Emerson's note]. See Gilbert Wakefield, *A Translation of the New Testament,* 2d ed. (London, 1795), 2:301.

4. Acts 24.24 [Emerson's note].

5. Luke 7:50, 18:42.

A comparison of the uses of this word will show that faith means more than historical belief, that it is used in the sense of *a perception of spiritual things*. Now this is a discernment that can only belong to a virtuous mind. He that sees the beauty of humility, of benevolence, of self denial, must have some portion of those virtues which he who does not see their beauty wants. When Jesus therefore praises the faith of particular persons, he would say, "So virtuous is your state of mind that you are able to acknowledge that divinity in my character which these depraved Pharisees cannot see. You are fit objects for outward healing."[6]

In this sense faith implies a degree of virtuous character. It did then and does now. Certainly the Christian revelation will show more marks of truth and authority to a good than to a vicious man. Observe, however, this exclusively regards the internal evidence of Christianity. The external must stand or fall by their own character as mere historical proofs of any other fact. But in the sense of a cheerful acceptance of the truth taught by Christ, Peter puts it at the beginning of his list. *Add to your faith, virtue*.

But so comprehensive a term as virtue would seem to render unnecessary those which follow, for temperance is virtue and patience and charity.

And the word here translated virtue, though a general term, yet in the ancient languages expresses particularly the virtue of fortitude or courage, the most shining merit in the savage character. And in the Greek language it retains much of that meaning and is used to denote that quality so that the passage is more justly read, Add to your faith in Christ *fortitude*.

And to fortitude, knowledge. Faith and Fortitude. Faith and courage to defend it are not enough; that the soul be without knowledge is not good. These virtues themselves of course presuppose some knowledge, and they can have no great force except with the progress of the intellectual nature. For knowledge, understand, then, the exercise of the intellect whereby it is obtained. And most right and welcome it is, that the first teachers of this divine truth should come with this early and earnest exhortation to intellectual cultivation upon their lips. Add to your faith and fortitude the power of thought, that you may give a reason for your faith and your hope. Let not this word fall to the ground. It does not rest upon the authority of Peter alone. It is the voice of all your experience.

What say these powers of your mind, of which you cannot think meanly when you observe, which tally so perfectly with the same powers in the very greatest minds, that you understand all they say, and sympathize with all they feel? What says your observation of men? Is it not true that he who knows more, is always the master of him that knows less? Is not he that knows more, a free man, and he that knows less in bonds to his ignorance? Is not he that knows more, the benefactor, and he that knows nothing apt to be useless, or hurtful to the state? Does he that knows more or he that knows less make the best son, father, magistrate, agent, friend? Is it knowledge or ignorance that finds its way

6. The "quotation" is, of course, Emerson's own construction, but cf. Matthew 9:28–35.

so surely to the poorhouse and the penitentiary? Is it knowledge or ignorance that is laying open the secrets of nature, the laws of matter, and accumulating every day the irresistible evidence of the wisdom and love of the Creator, that is making revelation more probable to the last days than to the first and justifying the first spontaneous thoughts of the human heart by the exact deductions of the head?

Finally what say these wonderful powers of your own mind, which, every one of them, grow by use, and perish by disuse; which hunger and thirst after knowledge; the memory which remembers better, the judgment that discerns better, the active powers that work more readily for every exertion they make?

They all say, Add to your fortitude knowledge. Buy wisdom and sell it not: search for understanding as for hid treasures.[7] Fear and scorn this unreflecting unreasoning way of life; the life of example; the servitude of custom; the living in a herd. Awake to the power of thought, the use of reason. Go alone; commune with your own heart, and open there the fountains of truth. Add to fortitude knowledge.

Have you any knowledge which you think you could spare, and if you had a thousand times as much do you think you should not value it all? Well, then, do not grudge any exertion, any sacrifice of time or ease, that will help you to add to it.

And to knowledge temperance. This is a cardinal virtue. This is a virtue that has to do with what is so coarse and earthy in our nature; the opposite vice is so disgusting that it is very apt to be passed over in the pulpit without particular consideration for fear of being offensive. And in conversation it is not permitted except in the most general terms to condemn it. And yet, standing as it does in human nature at the very doors of the temple of the body, so that without this virtue there is no room for any other to enter and no exclusion for any vice, and the temptations to violate it are so many and so ever-present, that too much attention can not be called to it. A trumpet of alarm should sound in every ear of man or woman: Be temperate. In its largest sense and indeed in the sense in which the apostle here uses it, it means self command and applies to all the natural appetites.

To speak only of what is commonly reckoned temperance. Suffer me to descend for a moment to so gross a subject as the evil of intemperate eating. The efforts of society in suppressing the abuse of ardent spirits appear to have been attended with unexpected yet blessed effects. Honor to the faithful men who have achieved thus much positive good and pardon all slight deviations from delicacy in the means of accomplishing so great a good. But, here is an evil to which all are at all times exposed and which society does not frown down. There are no societies to suppress this intemperance and none can be. I said that nothing more needed to be enforced and thundered in our ear than this counsel. And this seems to have guided the Divine Providence in the multiplying without

7. Cf. Proverbs 2:3–4 and 23:23.

end the motives and warnings that lead us to abstinence. God has set up round intemperance fences and beacons to scare. With how many sharp pains, with what lasting diseases, lasting how frequently to a sad posterity who thank your excess for gout and atrophy, a dull brain, weak eyes, and shattered nerves. It is the way to Want. How faithful is the picture when the Prodigal Son looked wishfully at the husks which the swine did eat.[8] It seems to me in that animal which faithfully follows man into every climate, the Supreme Friend of man had designed to provide a perpetual lesson upon gluttony to turn the stomach of men from so grovelling a vice. In the contempt men feel for the vice, is a sharper antidote. In the humiliating degradation of the offender, the most effectual check.

But the solicitations of appetite return every day; the gratifications are always at hand; the most wakeful virtue sometimes slumbers; the sanction of innumerable examples, the easy excuses with which society furnishes you and which your conscience is ready to admit, all these make vain the warnings of Scripture and reason except in a few brave followers of the right.

Let me then speak in seconding the exhortation of Peter to the young, whose habits are not yet chains of steel which they cannot put off but with their body, and hastily enumerate the motives from the lower to the higher which enforce selfcommand.

In the first place let it be considered that ancient observation has shown a mysterious yet habitual connexion between sensuality and all that is most hideous in human nature. It has been noticed that there is in history a close connexion between sensuality and cruelty, which though not always distinctly traceable in individuals is yet very easily seen in large masses of men, by an unknown process hidden in the depths of our nature, and which makes devils of malice out of men who have gratified their pleasant tastes.

Next consider the entrance which Intemperance administers to all evil. How it bereaves you of purity of thought; of contentment; of kindness; of power to think; of energy to act; yea and of strength to resist the worst sins.

> Swinish Gluttony
> Ne'er looks to Heaven amid his gorgeous feast
> But with besotted base ingratitude
> Crams, and blasphemes his Feeder.[9]

Consider then the whole advantage of Temperance, not only negative but positive. Temperance is an estate. The abstinent man is richer by his selfcommand than he is by his income. The wealth which other men eat and drink and are the worse for it enables him to be magnificent in good expenses of charity and of taste. It is an estate not liable to decay and of no cost.

8. Luke 15:16.
9. John Milton, *Comus,* lines 776–79; see *JMN* 4:5.

Consider in the next place among the lower praises of temperance whether there be in the world any more illustrious ornament which a man can wear. It is continually in use and note and all men are judges of it. It does not need, like your words, to be translated into another language to be intelligible.

It does not need any explanation to make it admired by savages, by kings and nobles, by the multitude or by wise men. If you wear a diamond I will not deny it may be a pretty ornament, and attract much attention; but a thief may pilfer it and it is gone forever, though it cost you much. But the kingly decoration of a temperate habit no man can take from you, and no law compel you to conceal it. No change in fashion can make it of less current value than it has now. It will be a perpetual letter of recommendation, and really possesses the virtues falsely ascribed to amulets, that of making the bearer healthful and beloved.

But to come to higher ground. Temperance hath a clear head and a cheerful heart; it adds to the means and to the disposition of beneficence; highest of all, it comes to be loved for its own sake, filling the mind with extreme delight in the victory it gains over the body; when you are temperate you are always conscious that it is well pleasing in the eye of God, and you are prepared for contemplating all holy and happy things.

Therefore add to knowledge Temperance.

And to temperance patience. But what are these virtues if they cannot endure, if they melt away with the first heats of temptation or you are laughed out of them by the first scorner you meet, or they are wearied down by the dull routine of common days. You must have patience. Essential to a good mind is the power to persist in its purposes, the adherence to its duty in spite of pain and time and change. You live among the dying and must lose them today and tomorrow go away yourself. Add therefore to temperance patience. But whence can this come? By piety toward God, which is the meaning of *godliness* in our text.

And to patience godliness. This signifies the reference of all our duties and all our being to the one great thought of God. He is immensity and Eternity. He is Wisdom and Power and Love and in him all particular beings are lost as drops in the sea. The introduction of God into the mind gives foundation and subsistency and perfection to all the virtues. It includes also the duty of worshipping him in social and in private service.

And with piety to God, brotherly love, or the love of our family, our friends, (and usually in the epistles) of all Christians. Finally, *And with brotherly love charity.* Charity is used here to extend the benevolence to the greatest degree, to make it comprehend nations—all mankind and, further, the brute creation. And thus far having carried his notion of duty the apostle stops. Let me read over the list.

God has given us exceeding great and precious promises, that we, escaping the corruption that is in the world, might become partakers of the divine nature. Now to this very end bend your whole strength. Add to your faith fortitude and to fortitude knowledge and to knowledge temperance and to temperance pa-

tience and to patience piety toward God and to piety toward God love of your
brethren and to love of your brethren love of the whole world.

My friends, I may leave this exhortation to speak for itself. Does it need any
miracles or any examination of the original tongue to satisfy your mind that these
are words of truth and soberness and uttered in conformity with the will of God?
No; it is no matter who spoke them, or when, or where. Wherever they go, they
carry on their face the mark of divine authority. Wherever they are obeyed, they
will fulfil their work, and make men partakers of the divine nature. What is most
material, is, that we should perceive their application to us, as full and close as to
the first ear that heard them. And it would be well if every day we would repeat
them meditatively in our chambers, until we could compare the whole passage
with our whole character without any shame.

CXLVIII

And these words which I command thee
this day shall be in thine heart, and
thou shalt teach them to thy children.

<small>Deuteronomy 6:6-7</small>

It is proposed on the next Sabbath to remove the Hancock Sunday School to the Vestry of this church and so to bring it more immediately under the eye and we hope the interest of this Society.[1] No Christian, no philanthropist, no lover of his country, no parent, can see without pleasing emotions the prosperity of the general undertaking, of which this is a single branch, which has struggled up from slender beginnings in half a century to its present commanding importance, as a means of influence in our social system. I embrace therefore with pleasure the occasion of calling your attention to some of the good qualities of this youngest benefactor of our species.

I shall ask your attention to a brief review of the most conspicuous advantages of this institution.

1. It is an institution for *children*. It may seem unnecessary to speak to this point and yet it is not without importance.

The world is full of projects for the benefit of men and women. Books, churches, lectures, lyceums, societies, commerce, agriculture, manufactures,— all are addressed to these classes and aim at their good. But all with partial effect. Men and women make up their opinions and habits pretty early, and not easily alter them. A habit is stronger than a hundred reasons. All reformers act on this belief. They who are seeking to rid the world of intemperance are not so sanguine as to hope to reform sots. But they hope to persuade the rising generation to wholly abstain and so make the next age temperate. And so with those who would introduce any general improvement in the manners or morals of any people have reckoned it prudent to begin with the young.

But more especially this institution which aims at a moral reformation of Society by means of more familiar and systematic religious instruction, comes to the young. It has its apology in the character of that age. The religion of

Manuscript dated March 25, 1832, at Chardon Street. Preached three times: March 25, 1832, at the Second Church, Boston; June 21, 1835, in Framingham; and December 20 in East Lexington.

1. Supported by the Second Church, the Sunday School had been meeting at the Hancock School for girls on Hanover Street.

children is proverbial. The young child's mind naturally and cheerfully receives the knowledge of God as the tender sprouts of plants lean toward the light.

Out of the mouths of babes and sucklings God's praise is perfected.[2] Where is the mind that has never been touched by the eager affection with which the little child imperfectly utters the great name of God; the readiness with which the forming conscience assumes its office in the youngest breast; the premature sense sometimes of their opinions; and above all that light of true divinity that won the heart of Jesus to them shining in their simplicity, affection, trust, and obedience? Who ever saw the young human flower untimely cut down and all its earthly beauty blasted without the most pleasing assurance that the unstained life passed back into the fountain,

"that its Creator drew
Its spirit as the sun the morning dew."[3]

We say commonly, It is never too late to learn. With more emphasis we may say, It is never too soon.

No children are too young who have seen one summer and one winter to receive a moral or an immoral impression. The only way to be safe and begin early enough, is, never to permit any other than a right impression to be given. It is recorded of that wonderful people, the ancient Spartans, that when Antipater would make a treaty with them, and demanded fifty children for hostages, they made answer, that, "they would rather give him twice so many grown men," so much did they value the loss of their country's education.[4] And let it be the praise of this institution that it secures to society whatever good it attempts, by being beforehand with the enemy, by preventing with good the approach of evil. It is one of the excellent anecdotes in the life of Pestalozzi, that, after he was compelled by misfortunes to give up his Asylum which he had established for destitute children in his house at Neuhof, he yet comforted himself that all was not lost, that the seeds of knowledge and virtue had been planted in the breasts of a hundred poor children, and, go where they might, through the mountains of Switzerland, he calmly trusted their timely growth with God.[5]

I see with hope the ear of childhood won to highest duty and holiest truth. With joy I see it saved the bitter tears of remorse, the sad toils of reformation, by

2. Matthew 21:16; cf. Psalms 8:2.

3. John Dryden, "On the Death of a Very Young Gentleman," lines 25–26; see *JMN* 2:275 and 6:165.

4. Montaigne, "Of Pedantry," *Essays of Michael Seigneur de Montaigne* . . . , trans. Charles Cotton (London, 1693), 1:210. The anecdote is marked in pencil in Emerson's copy.

5. The anecdote, together with a version of the entire paragraph, occurs in Sermon CXXVIII (*Sermons* 3:230). Emerson's source is Edward Biber, *Henry Pestalozzi, and His Plan of Education; being an account of his life and writings* (London, 1831), 17. Emerson borrowed the volume from the Boston Athenaeum on March 23, 1832, though his use of Biber's work in Sermon CXXVIII shows that he had access to it earlier.

making its first steps right. It is a work on which the Son of God will look down with pleasure: the deliverance of the little ones he blessed out of the offence that must needs be in the world.[6]

And his confidence was as just as it was sublime. Never was a sincere word utterly lost.[7] The good principle that has been instilled, is present when the teacher is absent. It survives when he dies. It hinders from transgression, and even when it can not hinder it mitigates the crime and brings penitence after it.

2. The next advantage of these institutions is that they admit of a personal instruction of every individual child. This I conceive to be their peculiar excellence. They do not instruct schools or classes, but every child. It is, I believe, the uniform practice of Sunday Schools that the classes shall be no larger than to allow the teacher to give the most intimate attention to each one. A class consists of four, five, or six children. This circumstance, it is obvious, makes a most important difference between these and every other school, and makes the instruction truly parental. For it is most true of this teaching which is moral, that it is indispensable to its success that the disposition and habits of thought of the child should be known and humoured in order to any real intercourse with his mind. Faithful instruction is like those sorts of work which cannot be done by machinery but must be done *by hand*. Arithmetic and grammar may be taught well enough in classes but the moral discipline to be effectual must be given to each particular child.

And this is seen in another view.

No one can be much acquainted with children without discovering that a boy or girl shows a very different character alone, from that which the same child exhibits in the company of other children. One who is inexperienced in the care of children and who goes a stranger into a large school, is very apt to be disheartened by the appearance of idle, stupid, impracticable habits; the readiness with which children conspire together in frivolous teazing of their teacher; he thinks he sees malignity and obstinacy and he leaps to the disagreeable conclusion that no impression can be made upon this prematurely corrupt mass. It only needs that he should be intimately acquainted with each one to have this impression wholly effaced from his mind. It is a rule of education as of policy, Divide and Conquer. As they are seen separately and the character of each individual disclosed, it shows itself plastic and amiable and inquisitive; and the most disagreeable and obstinate child is found to be capable of good humor and application.

The very expressions children use in their games attest, to an attentive mind, the same fact, if I may be pardoned for alluding to what some may think trifling. A child at play with his mates says, *you know me,* which is no obscure intimating the confidence each child feels that he who knows him best will like him best, or, that, under his faults, there is goodness and truth.[8]

6. Matthew 18:7.

7. Mme. de Staël, *Germany* (London, 1813), 3:401. The entire paragraph is adapted from Sermon CXXVIII (*Sermons* 3:230).

8. See *JMN* 3:309.

This individual character, this goodness at the bottom of the heart, the Sunday School teacher may seek and find. It will always come when it is called for by simplicity and kindness. Yet many and many a child is suffered to grow up a bad boy full of vulgarity, ignorance, and selfishness, for want of strong and frequent appeals made to this inmost soul. And I count it one of the greatest benefits of this system that it tends to establish so close a confidence between teacher and pupil.

On this fact indeed must always depend the efficacy of a Sunday School, which will vary too in every class—I mean the degree of personal acquaintance which the teacher forms with his pupils. It enables the teacher to discern and call out whatever is peculiar and original in the powers of the child far beyond what the ordinary school routine can admit of. Thus he becomes the discoverer and encourager of merit, by the freedom and flexibility of its teaching, teaching genius and virtue to know itself, and giving it the most safe and serviceable direction. An acorn, it has been said, needs but a handful of earth to become an oak but that handful it must have, or it will perish.

3. The next peculiarity of Sunday Schools is one that marks an era in the progress of mankind. It is that they are founded on the principle of *love*. The almost universal principle on which the discipline of schools has rested is Fear. It has been thought and still is thought that the order of a school cannot be maintained without a degree of severity. In former days the almost uniform system was stern discipline. A very sensible improvement in this respect has already taken place. Certainly by the great majority of teachers, or until an entire revolution in the mode of teaching, a coercive system must be used.

In the last generation, however, lived a man who cherished, and, in his own practice, unfolded and exemplified another mode of teaching, and who seems to me the true model and guide of the religious teacher; I mean of course Henry Pestalozzi, the celebrated Swiss schoolmaster. And it is only in the accounts that are preserved of his life and his teaching that any adequate conception can be formed of the power of this principle. This man was inspired with a passionate attachment to children and with this an ever-present conviction that they were capable of being made to act from reason and from benevolence. This faith was to him schoolhouse, and food, and books, and apparatus. He lived by it and taught by it. It could not be wearied out or laughed out or persecuted out of him.

At first it was necessity as well as choice that made this principle so great in his eyes. "The whole of his school apparatus consisted of himself and his pupils."[9] He began at Stantz with the care of the worst children of the worst parents. They were vicious beggars and he was poor. He had abundance of prejudice to encounter. The only means therefore by which it was possible for him to gain any ascendancy over his pupils was an all forbearing kindness.[10] The few instances of discipline which he used with good effect, we are told, "far from convincing

9. Biber, *Henry Pestalozzi*, 33.
10. Biber, *Henry Pestalozzi*, 29–30.

him of the necessity or propriety of punishment, on the contrary proved to his mind the extraordinary power of love, which if it be once established as the basis of the relation between teacher and child penetrates the heart of the latter even when the former assumes for a moment the character of wrath (the measure of his forbearance being exhausted by an excessive offence)."[11]

"At Stantz in the midst of his children he forgot that there was any world besides his asylum. And as their circle was an universe to him so was he to them all in all. From morning to night he was the center of their existence. To him they owed every comfort and every enjoyment, and whatever hardship they had to endure he was their fellow sufferer. He partook of their meals and slept among them. In the evening he prayed with them before they went to bed, and from his conversation they dropped into the arms of slumber. At the first dawn of light, it was his voice that called them to the light of the rising sun, and to the praise of their heavenly Father. All day he stood among them teaching the ignorant and assisting the helpless, encouraging the weak and admonishing the transgressor. His hand was daily with them, joined in theirs. His eye, beaming with benevolence, rested on theirs. He was to them a father and they were to him as children.

"Such love could not fail to win their hearts; the most savage and the most obstinate could not resist its soothing influence. Discontent and peevishness ceased; and a number of between seventy and eighty children, whose dispositions had been far from kind, and their habits anything but domestic, were thus converted, in a short time, into a peaceable family circle, in which it was a delight to exist."[12]

He thought that in the world a great deal was learned about things and he wished to teach the things themselves. "He taught deeds of faith and love instead of abstruse creeds. Instead of building up a dead mind and a dead heart on the ground of a dead letter he drew forth life to the mind and life to the heart from the fountain of life within and thus established a new art of education in which to follow him requires on the part of the teacher not a change of system but a change of state."[13]

It was objected by some visiters of his house that the children were not taught by rule and could not compare in their knowledge of textbooks with children of ordinary schools. One of his pupils remarks: "Though there was in it little or no method there was much life; the children felt excited, attracted, interested, stimulated. They had no tasks to get, but always something to investigate, or to think about: they gained little positive knowledge, but they increased daily in the love of knowledge and in the power of acquiring; they might have been at a loss if called upon to quote texts in support of any particular doctrine of Christianity but in the practice of its virtues they were perpetually exercised."[14]

11. Biber, *Henry Pestalozzi*, 32.
12. Biber, *Henry Pestalozzi*, 34–35.
13. Biber, *Henry Pestalozzi*, 33.
14. Biber, *Henry Pestalozzi*, 39–40.

But all who would see the energy of this principle, must examine the history of this remarkable man and the extraordinary change in the public sentiment of Europe effected by him.

It was something new in the world that a man of genius should be able to throw so much beauty and delight over an occupation oftener esteemed either irksome or mean. It was the power of love. But that which makes these narratives chiefly interesting to us is the peculiar applicability of his principles and his modes of teaching to the *Sunday School*. There are no punishments; the whole basis of its order is love. The child knows well that nothing but kindness has brought the teacher to the place, and he is inspired by the same feeling. The most pleasing relation of confidence is established between them which a person of common discretion can hardly fail to turn to the best account for the child's present and lasting welfare.

4. I might point you to the advantage that will flow out of this instruction, if well dispensed, into other schools; and yet that is not the least of its advantages. It was said of Pestalozzi that "he became the pupil of pupils in order that he might become the teacher of teachers."[15] But this need hardly be specified as it is one of many good effects; for it will be a fountain of good sending out streams of blessing in every direction. Too much can hardly be expected from this institution, if it were made to yield all it can. What would be too much if the intelligent young men and young women should with any unanimity lend themselves to this work, establishing between themselves and the whole population of children relations of personal friendship and confidence, and a recognition of mutual obligation to the greatest truths and holiest duties. The celebrated Leibnitz was wont to say that he did not despond of reforming mankind when he saw how much education might be reformed.[16] What would be too much to expect from this training up for the next age an entire nation of well informed, affectionate, and virtuous minds? They would purify the world. They would introduce a healthy action into the whole social frame of mankind. They would reform the Reformation. They would deliver liberty. They would remove those ancient corruptions and malpractices that now fill all the ways of life with temptation so that men complain they must transgress to get their bread. They would fan the ardor of knowledge and piety, and sanctify unto God a peculiar people zealous of good works.[17]

5. Allow me in the last place to speak of an advantage to the teachers of the Sunday School. I will not now speak of that real benefit that the habit of instruction brings to the instructor from the fact that knowledge is a property which is always increased the more it is imparted. Nor to the fact which yet deserves notice, that you are making in your class four or five faithful friends whom it

15. Biber, *Henry Pestalozzi*, 39.

16. See *JMN* 4:327, 5:234, and *The Topical Notebooks of Ralph Waldo Emerson*, vol. 1, ed. Susan Sutton Smith (Columbia, Mo., 1990), 136; used in "Address on Education" (*EL* 2:199) and "Education" (*W* 10:133).

17. Titus 2:14.

will always give you pleasure to meet, but I would call the attention of all who have time and attention to bestow on this charity to the highest reward, which you shall deserve and obtain: namely the consciousness that you have for the sake of usefulness given up a portion, which perhaps you could ill spare, of the day of rest to this holy work of humanity, that you have sacrificed your inclinations to this at first unpleasing duty.

That teacher has the consciousness of having served in the most effectual way his country, the consciousness of the approbation of God, and that pure delight which always accompanies a conquest over one's self. This testimony in his own breast will better enable him to explain to those children the true nature of heaven than all the commentaries on earth.

This is the charity, Christian friends, which this day we present before you. We ask parents to bring their children and to come and witness their progress. We ask the interest of all and we ask the assistance of those who have the time and the will, in this great work of philanthropy. I have spoken of the institution in reference to what it may be, not what it is. It may be as cold and useless as the most selfish heart would be content to see it, and surely will be, if neglected; but it admits beyond all question of being an organ of immeasurable good. And we earnestly entreat of any one whose heart beats with the desire of usefulness to come and give his help to the direct end of giving instruction, forming good virtues, and so contributing even the most insignificant part, if such efforts can be called so, to the promotion of everlasting good.

CXLIX

Thy law is my meditation all the day.
PSALMS 119:97

Nothing seems more important to our success in the formation of religious character than that we should be possessed with a thorough conviction that we can be what we would be, and then that we should direct our exertions to the attainment of particular virtues. We must know the exact amount of the demand upon our way of living before we can heartily engage in any cause. We must know that the improvement is practicable, and we must know where to begin.

For this reason it is always the part of prudence in seeking to improve ourselves to concentrate our endeavours on one point, and that within the range of common observation. It were better therefore that the mind be not fatigued and bewildered by vague desires of angelic perfection, but whilst we keep steadily in view that there is an infinite career before us, that every harvest is to be only new seed, and every goal a new starting post, let us be content with contriving the improvement of single days, let us brighten the domestic virtues, and not take it too easily for granted that we must leave our religion at church when we go home, or at least leave it at home, when we go to the counting house, or the workyard.

Especially never let it be imagined that any way of life is too humble and vulgar for virtue. No error is more common and none is more gross. This is the very blindness of the Jews who expected Christ to come in purple and gold, with armies and plenty, and rejected him for the very reason that he offered them only eternal power and eternal prosperity. Herein indeed is the divine mark of spiritual good, its universal fitness to all conditions and all minds. And a clear perception of this fact is a sort of test of our spiritual growth. Until a man sees this fact clearly, he is yet far from the kingdom of God.[1] We hear and say every day that Jesus Christ preached his gospel to the poor; what else does this mean than that he enjoined a way of life which the poor and the rich could

---

Manuscript dated April 1, 1832, at Chardon Street. Preached fourteen times: April 1, 1832, at the Second Church, Boston; November 24, 1833, in New Bedford; April 6, 1834, at the Friend Street Chapel, Boston; April 27 at the Second Church, Waltham; May 18 in Fall River; June 15 in Watertown; June 22 in Newton Upper Falls; July 13 in Bangor, Maine; October 26 at the Second Church, New York; December 14 in Sudbury; April 5, 1835, in Plymouth; April 19 in Acton; May 3 in East Lexington; and May 17 in Chelmsford.

1. Cf. Mark 12:34.

alike attain? Every one has read the child's story called "Eyes and no Eyes,"[2] the story of two children who walked in the same road and one found it full of pleasing objects and the other very dull, disagreeable. It is a good illustration of the truth we are considering. In the very same objects at the very same time two persons with different minds see, one a world of beauty, and the other a series of vexations. And so I fear few men turn their thoughts to the consideration of the divine beauty that may be made to shine in the homeliest details of common life. "Good workmen," it is said, "never quarrel with their tools."[3] And God's workmen, who are *virtuous men,* will contrive to do his will with any materials, how sad or obscure soever they may be. They will make poverty or plenty, pain and ease, business and solitude, alike subservient. They will rear the fabric of moral good on its pillars of fortitude, of temperance, of benevolence, and justice,—the house not made with hands,[4] on the foundation of any circumstances, and under every sky.

My friends, it seems to me it would be a worthy ambition for each of us to set himself down with that diligence with which we enter on any new project or business enterprize, or main affair of life, to see what new degrees of virtue we could introduce without hindrance into the circle of our ordinary habits; to begin with the lowest; to make our course of life cleaner and sweeter, more decorous, then more pure, then more beneficent; then more holy.

And this is my design in the present discourse, to consider how a man may make God's law his meditation all the day;[5] to speak in turn of some of those duties which every man can cultivate in his own house in the humblest or the highest sphere, to notice those means, which the Divine Bounty has given to every child he has made, to elevate and beautify the humblest condition with a glory from heaven: to excite, if it were possible, in every one of us attention to himself; to arouse in each down to the youngest the sublime ambition of that good man who, not emulous of others, is emulous of himself, and determines that every day shall be better.

And the first of these virtues for whose cultivation every condition affords room is self-command.

Self Command in that limited sense in which it concerns itself in the absolute subjection of the animal nature to reason, which enjoins Temperance in sleep and food, and chastity.

Philosophers have prescribed the same rule with regard to sleep as with regard to food—that we should always sleep a little less than our inclination would permit. All mankind have agreed in declaring the morning favorable to calm reflection. It is naturally due to gratitude and to forethought. It hallows

2. "Eyes and No Eyes; or, The Art of Seeing," in John Aikin and Mrs. Anna Letitia Barbauld, *Evenings at Home* (London, 1792–1796), Twentieth Evening. Emerson refers to the story again in "The Uses of Natural History" (*EL* 1:18).

3. Byron, *Don Juan*, I, cci, 6; see *JMN* 3:285 and 325. Used in "Ben Jonson, Herrick, Herbert, Wotton" (*EL* 1:350).

4. II Corinthians 5:1.

5. Psalms 119:97.

the day of him who uses it for devotion. The Lacedemonians were accustomed to offer sacrifice betimes in the morning that they might gain, they said, the ear of the gods before their enemies.[6] The story has a good moral. Let us gain the ear of God by good thoughts before our enemies, the passions, have hidden his favor from us.

Why need I praise Temperance (of which I had recent occasion to speak somewhat in detail)?[7] And yet in this connexion I must say one word. Let no man who desires true greatness, let no mind fired with ambition neglect this virtue. Here are laurels to be won. Here is a martyrdom to be endured in resisting the daily returning allurements to indulgence which not one in a thousand has the dignity and the vigor to finish. If any young person desires to raise himself in his own esteem, to feel himself arrived at the dignity of a rational being, to be master of his hours and his faculties, health in his veins, peace in his sleep, and benevolence in all his thoughts, let him conquer the disposition to excess and delicacy in his food and drink. A few ounces, twelve or fourteen, of solid food experience has found sufficient for health and vigor,[8] and no cautions and no means are ridiculous that have for their end so excellent a moral purpose. Its reward is with it.[9] "To Temperance," says the moralist, "every day is bright."[10] And it has been observed to increase the means and the disposition of beneficence.

Now here is a virtue that may be practised at any time by any person. The consciousness of its possession will console one in the weariest day and most disagreeable circumstances and give dignity to the thoughts of the poor, the forsaken, and the injured.

Another virtue which comes within the circle of domestic life and which all men might attain in greater degrees, is *personal independence*. This virtue is far more easy and natural to us, a free and educated nation, than to any other nation on earth. And I suppose no people ever were more jealous of their civil rights than we are. But of our moral rights, of those which the law does not and cannot defend, we are culpably heedless. We lean one upon another for our opinions and practices in moral conduct. We feel no shame in preferring the opinion of society to our own. We see men in society whose eyes and whose actions seem to ask leave of other men to live. And the great mass of our common views and acts are really such as we have never settled for ourselves, but have adopted as what is done by those next us. Now there is but one way to personal independence, namely, a deliberate use of a man's own reason; for we cannot act by chance, and must lean upon that of others or our own. This way is strait and narrow and few there be that walk therein.[11] But if a man will

6. Emerson read Xenophon's account as repeated by David Hume in *Philosophical Essays* (London, 1817), 2:382; see *JMN* 2:335.

7. In Sermon CXLVII.

8. Emerson verified these figures for himself; see *JMN* 4:6.

9. Cf. Isaiah 40:10.

10. Samuel Johnson, *The Idler*, no. 11 (New Haven, 1963), 2:39. See *JMN* 6:124 and 163; cf. *JMN* 3:255.

11. Matthew 7:13-14.

consider how much mortification and sense of inferiority and painful suspense he suffers, who acquires the bad habit of now lending an ear to one and now to another adviser, and changing his opinions with the moon, instead of the firm and respectable self satisfaction of the man who knows what he shall do and why he shall do it, he will think it worth his while to consider with care beforehand what the truth is, what his duty is in regard to those things which occur every day.

Perhaps the most familiar example of the defect of this virtue is in the false shame with which people are affected at the notice of any inferiority in their dress or condition in comparison with the same things of another. A man considers the better fashion of his neighbor's garments and then condemns his own. Let him change them for better, he will find his uneasiness still excited by some new observation. Does he wish a final deliverance from these belittling anxieties? Let him consider that the only way to improve the fashion of his own dress is to forget his neighbor and work out faithfully his own duties: command his tongue, eat a lighter meal, rise earlier, work harder, do more benefits, and more strictly adhere in his acts to the decisions of his own judgment. He will be agreeably surprized to find that this is really a way of improving the fashion of his garments in the eyes of all men. Nothing is more pliant than our associations with external appearance of men. And any high degree of merit in a man seems to shine in every feature of his face and give expression to his very clothes.

It is a consoling truth that God has given every thing necessary to every mind. He has done better than to give us all things—in giving us the power to obtain all things. And it is the part of wisdom no less than of piety to be content and thankful in our lot, convinced that our true interest is to be sought not in peering enviously round to see what others have or do, but in manfully staying at home and opening the unfathomable mines of our own thoughts. Know thyself.[12] Let each consider that whilst he is occupied in meek yet persevering reflexion upon his duty, privately comparing his own thoughts in the sincere wish to know what is true and what is right for him, he is really advancing in the scale of being. That humble soul is attaining to true dignity and honor such as will be acknowledged not only in the little company of his kinsfolk and acquaintance but in every society of God's rational children among whom he shall be called to act.

There is another accomplishment that belongs to ordinary life, which is a grace rather than a virtue, and if it have not much merit, has great value—I mean, Tranquillity of mind. It is too much neglected. Jesus looked at the lilies, and said, Behold how they grow! they toil not, they spin not, yet God careth for them.[13]—God feeds *us* by giving us the powers of thought and action whereby we may feed ourselves. Now when a man has used his abilities in whatever

---

12. For this injunction, inscribed on the temple at Delphi, see Sermons XXVII (*Sermons* 1:226) and XLVII (*Sermons* 2:41–42). Used also in Sermons CLV and CLXV.

13. Luke 12:27; cf. Matthew 6:28.

channel they lie, whether in study, in trade, in agriculture, in manual labor, has done what he could, well, in the hours appointed to work, let him compose himself with the thought that in the sight of God, he is better than the lilies. With a cloudless brow and a serene mind, let him return to his family, and lie down at night, and arise in the morning, calm in the belief, that he rests upon the lap of the Divine beneficence, and that he is never for one moment forgotten or forsaken.

But to rise higher in the scale, the next duty of which the occasions occur in every dwelling and every day, is *benevolence*. It is so comprehensive a virtue that no man fulfils its whole law, and yet every man may very much improve his practice in this respect. I will not point you to those extremely unhappy persons whose life is a hindrance to human enjoyment,—who pour out the gall of their endless discontent and ill will upon all whom they are permitted to afflict—they sow the wind to reap the whirlwind,[14] and hatreds and retaliations are the harsh instructors by which they must be reclaimed; but which of us does not sin at home against the law of love? Good men and good women break it. They that make progress in self command, in diligence, in independence of character, are apt to be made vain by virtue. They are apt to forget the claims of inferiors, and be overbearing and unfeeling.

Alas, who is he that can accuse his brother? We are amazed at the persecuting spirit that blazed up in other days when public opinion allowed it to use the ax and the fagot. But it is very impertinent for us to wonder at the bigotry and violence manifested in those times. Every man may read the history of it in himself when he is contradicted and silenced in argument by a person whom he had always reckoned his inferior. This malevolence we may trace in our deport-ment to our associates. And how many people imagine that in transactions where they pay money, that circumstance entitles them to make any outrage upon the feelings, much more any neglect of the convenience of the other party?

And many a person grows grey at the fire side in a good repute of Christian virtues in a total oversight of the truth that the basis of the relation between master and servant, or master and apprentice is benevolence and not opposi-tion. We see glaring instances of this peculiar defect in those whose hearts seem to overflow with pity for many objects of distress and who would be shocked to be taxed with uncharitableness. It admonishes us pointedly of that necessity that every one who would live wisely, should sternly bring up the entire course of his conduct to the bar of his reason.

Benevolence—charity—love—these words are often in our mouths, but the principle must pervade the whole man who would really raise and bless his life. See if you are useful. For that is what you were made for. See whether they love you most to whom you are best known. "If our friends appear to look upon us with little interest, if our arrival is seen without pleasure, and our departure

14. Hosea 8:7.

without regret, instead of charging them with want of feeling we should turn our scrutiny upon ourselves."[15]

If God has given you the power to do favors, to be the benefactor of your friends, look carefully to see whether you have exercised that trust tenderly, and have done all you could to soften the pain of dependence. But be your means ever so little, the fireside can tell you your character, and if love is your principle it will make evermore its silent eulogy. "To see," said an acute observer of men, "to see the same countenance, however defective in form, constantly preserving an expression of tenderness amidst all the cares and disappointments of life, to hear language of uniform kindness and be the object of nameless acts of regard, can hardly fail, whatever other circumstances may operate, to beget feelings of reciprocal affection."[16] And, I add, can hardly fail to create kindness in more than one heart, to throw sunshine on the faces of all who approach us, to reprove bitterness, to call out charity, and add to the amount of human happiness.

I must leave to your own reflexion—and it well deserves the self examination of each of us—the numerous applications of this principle to our household, our friends, our dependants, our townsmen, to strangers, to persons of different religious or political opinions from ourselves, and to the whole world.

But it may be the fountain of unceasing kindness and usefulness in every house and every company.

"My son," said the dying husbandman, "be always planting a tree; it will be growing when you are sleeping."[17] *Always be setting a good action to grow,* is the advice of a divine thrift. It is bearing you fruit all the time,—knitting you to men's hearts, and to men's good, and to God,—and, beyond this, it is benefitting others by remembrance, by emulation, by love.

But, finally, the narrowest sphere of action, the meanest condition, or the most crowded life admit equally of the sublime feeling of love to God, the highest feeling of the human heart. And this great emotion makes all conditions equal and glorifies the lowest occupation. And when I speak of this principle as one for daily life I am not, I hope, thought by any to speak of that which is uncertain and visionary. I have neither understanding nor love of unreasonable rapturous religion. I mean by love to God what must issue from the severest reason when it considers the whole of man. It must then feel that we are wholly derived from something wiser and better than ourselves, and that every moment. No man feels self existent. And as by more comprehensive and more minute observation it deduces a better knowledge of the good God by which all things live, it warms with love and adoration and perceives the duty of submit-

15. Essays on yᵉ Formation & Pub. of Opinions [Emerson's note]. The reference is to Samuel Bailey's anonymous *Essays on the Formation and Publication of Opinions,* "Essay V: On Inattention to the Dependence of Causes and Effects in Moral Conduct. Part I." (Philadelphia, 1831), 159.

16. Bailey, *Essays on the Formation and Publication of Opinions,* 161.

17. "Jock, when ye hae naething else to do, ye may be aye sticking in a tree; it will be growing, Jock, when ye're sleeping" (Sir Walter Scott, *The Heart of Midlothian,* chapter 8 [New York, 1906], 92). See *JMN* 3:314; used in "Prudence" (*EL* 2:317).

ting to his will. And that acknowledgment of the Deity should make a part of every thought, should be the habitual state of the mind.

In a good mind, my brethren, in a mind which is cultivated by the exercise of all these virtues, this love of pure Wisdom and Goodness will be delighted in as a privilege, will be welcomed as a heart cheering revelation and not reluctantly rendered as a debt.

These are some of the virtues which we may cultivate every day. It would be easy to add to their number or show more applications of these, but the task would have no end. But will not these suffice to show us that the shortest day or the most eventful affords room for many good works and that true greatness and goodness are entirely independent of worldly condition? I need not remind you of the blessed effect of these virtues,—how they bind you to your friends,— make you unspeakably dear to them;—how they excite in the breasts of all wise and good men among whom you are known, the liveliest interest in your welfare; yea, how they help and encourage all good spirits known or unknown to you in or out of the body. Jesus in heaven sympathizes with you and God draws near to you in every pious endeavor. To practise these virtues would be to meditate on God's law all the day. Let us be wise in season. Let us redeem the time.[18] Let us feel that there are spectators enough of our virtue, if it were only God and ourselves; objects enough, if it were only our own family circle; occasions enough, if it were only the day we are now spending.

18. Cf. Ephesians 5:15–16.

Is it such a Fast that I have chosen?

ISAIAH 58:5

Great difference of opinion exists among those who are at the pains to consider the question at all, as to the general expediency of the religious anniversary we are assembled to keep. It is rightly regarded as a question wholly of expediency, and not by any esteemed one of ritual obligation, founded upon any precept of the Mosaic or of Christian law. Its friends esteem it as an invaluable institution of the fathers of New England, which it would argue degenerate posterity who should suffer it to fall into disuse; as a highly becoming accommodation of the apostolic usages to these late times of the Christian church; as a carrying on of the sacred history of the world; as another verse of the penitential psalm of centuries making music in the ear of God, finally as a consecration of our privileges by a devout solemnity and as a means of public and personal piety.

On the other hand many considerate and pious persons think that the actual state of the public feeling with regard to the Fast Day—the great indifference with which it is viewed by a majority of the community and the injury done to the public morals by any unnecessary holiday increased in this instance by the gross inconsistency between nominal use and the real abuse by multitudes of this day— warrant them in desiring that an end should be put to it, or, what would much better meet the views of many, that a Sabbath day at this season of the year should be set apart to the particular duties of penitence and public remembrances.

However time and the change of religious opinion may settle these questions, that which I am anxious should be felt by all of us in relation to the whole matter, is, that although the Day and its uses are forms, they are not mere forms. Fasting is a form; Humiliation is a form; Prayer is a form; yet they all represent and cover *things.* And though it may be of almost no importance whether you keep this form, or change it, or drop it,—it is of extreme importance, that you do not lose the substance. For, rightly considered, these venerable usages are of no local or accidental origin, but are as old as the world and have their roots in the nature of man.

"Men are not made truly righteous by performing certain actions which are

---

This Fast Day sermon was preached four times: twice on April 5, 1832, at the New North Church in the morning, and at the Second Church, Boston, in the afternoon; April 9, 1835, at the Second Church, Waltham; and April 7, 1836, in East Lexington. Observance of official Fast Days had become increasingly unpopular, as evidenced by the rejection, in July 1832, of Henry Clay's proposal for a national Fast Day. Democrats, led by Jackson, opposed it on the grounds that it violated the separation of church and state.

externally good, but men must have righteous principles in the first place and then they will not fail to perform virtuous actions."[1]

And I propose to consider each of these three particulars in detail that our attention may be fixed on the fact that they all are not occasional but duties of perfect and perpetual obligation.

1. Fasting. This ancient and universal custom is found to have prevailed as a religious rite in all the ancient nations. It was peculiar to no one form of religion. It grew up naturally in every place where man endeavoured to recommend himself to the Supreme Being by superior virtue. For what is it? what is its essence? The principle on which this and the kindred practices depend, is *the subjection of the body to the soul.* It was the aim of lawgivers who would form a heroic people; of philosophers who would train the mind to the pursuit of the true and the beautiful; and of the devout who would lead the soul to God. And the records of the human race are adorned with the triumphs of this principle in every age. It has been the ornament of the world. It is almost incredible the power of the human will to bear privation and pain. However misapplied, however ostentatious, however disfigured with some vices, were the various orders of self denying men, the Nazarite among the ancient Jews, of the later Essenian, the Pythagorean, the Spartan, the Stoic, the Christian monk, all from the naked sage in ancient India down to the self tormenting order of Latrappe,[2] they all conspire to teach in their various ages, modes, and lights, one noble lesson, the superiority of the soul to the body, its power not only of abstaining from bodily delight, but of sustaining every form of bodily torture with unalterable serenity.

The Gymnosophist no doubt was not wise in forsaking men to spend his dreary days in hunger and penance in the desarts of India.

The Spartan boy was wrong who in obedience to the false honour in which he was educated concealed the gnawing fox in his bosom till he fell down dead.[3]

1. The statement is Martin Luther's, slightly misquoted from Joseph and Isaac Milner, *The History of the Church of Christ* (Boston, 1809), 4:281–82. Used in "Martin Luther" (*EL* 1:120).

2. All members of ascetic sects. The Nazirites (Nazarites), a biblical Hebrew sect, avoided drinking wine or cutting their hair, and typically expressed their possession of "the Spirit of the Lord" ecstatically. The Essenes lived in Palestine from the second century B.C. to the second century A.D. They adopted simple eating habits, wore white, shared property, and professed the immortality of the soul; some were celibate. Pythagoreans followed the teachings of the historically elusive Pythagoras in stressing the immortality of the soul, and the mystical significance of numbers. Spartans were renowned throughout ancient Greece for the self-denial and discipline on which their military prowess rested. Trappist monks belonged to a reformed branch of the Roman Catholic Cistercian Order established c. 1663 by the Abbot Armand de Rancé at the monastery of La Trappe in Normandy. The order was characterized by extraordinary dietary austerity and by complete silence. The term "naked sage" corresponds to the literal meaning of "Gymnosophist," mentioned below, and refers to a sect of philosophers in India who dispensed with clothing and aimed to do specific good each day. They are mentioned by Plutarch in his "Life of Alexander," *The Lives,* ed. John and William Langhorne (New York, 1822), 5:274.

3. This anecdote from Plutarch, "The Life of Lycurgus" (*The Lives,* ed. John and William Langhorne [New York, 1822], 1:128), is recounted by Sir Thomas Browne in *Pseudodoxia Epidemica,* book 7, chapter 18, though Emerson's more likely source is Montaigne, "Defence of Seneca and Plutarch," in *Essays of Michael Seigneur de Montaigne . . . ,* trans. Charles Cotton

The Pythagoreans' abstinence from animal food, and rigorous diet on beans and pulse grew out of an idle superstition concerning the brute creation.[4]

And the poor Christian fanatic called the Stylite who lived thirty years on the top of a pillar on which he could not lie down—was guilty of a piece of ridiculous extravagance.[5]

And yet is there any page of human history which the good mind contemplates with more delight than the unimpeachable testimony borne by these facts to the glorious nature God has lodged in the human frame, which in its devotion to what it thinks agreeable to Him can achieve these miracles of endurance, and bring every appetite, and passion, and tear, and every shrinking nerve, under the sovereignty of an absolute Will? In view of these things, in view of the armies of pilgrims and friars clothed in hair, fed on husks, and undergoing every cruel form of self appointed penance, let us check our boastful spirit. Let us not be too forward to deride them until we have endured half so much in a good cause as they bore in that of superstition.

Let not a worldly and delicate generation clad in soft clothing, sit in judgment upon the sinewy martyrs who would have walked through fire or have been screwed to the rack to get the knowledge and the liberty which we enjoy but never earned. Let us not condemn them for these victories of savage fanaticism until we have shown some faint resemblance to their power in working out the ends of truth and humanity.

Rather let us be armed with the same mind. Let us feel the debasement of a subjection to our animal appetites. Let us in the might of a good motive overcome them. Let us keep a perpetual Fast from every excess. Let us, out of reverence to our great Author, bring our passions under the control of that Conscience which is his Representative in our minds.

To this end let us cultivate the cardinal virtue of Temperance. He fasts rightly who always is abstemious. And if there were no higher motives a person of generous ambition would be strict in his diet out of very love of the purity and self possession which temperance enjoys. The sense of independence it gives is a luxury worth ten times all its sacrifices. How many things do I not want, said Socrates.[6]

Epicurus for an experiment confined himself to a narrower allowance than that of the severest prisons of his time to capital offenders, and found himself at ease in a stricter diet than a man in the worst condition needs to fear.[7]

(London, 1700), 2:627.

4. Pythagoreans were for the most part vegetarians because they believed that the soul was reincarnated in animals; an exception was made, however, for animals traditionally offered in sacrifice, which could be eaten. Emerson is mistaken about the beans; the Pythagoreans maintained a taboo against eating them.

5. Saint Simeon Stylites (390?–459) was a Syrian Christian monk, the first to practice asceticism by standing continually on top of a column (Greek *stylos*).

6. Diogenes Laertius, *Lives of Eminent Philosophers*, 2:25; quoted in Samuel Johnson, *The Idler*, no. 37 (New Haven, 1963), 2:116, and *The Adventurer*, nos. 67 and 119 (New Haven, 1965), 2:384–85, 466. With this paragraph, cf. *JMN* 4:5–6.

7. Emerson seems to have duplicated the experiment in the week before the first delivery of the

But then higher motives urge us to this virtue than a vain pride. And these are the time it saves, the mastery it gives us over still grosser propensities, the increase of our means and dispositions of benevolence, and the desire to present ourselves pure and improved beings in the sight of him who when he gave us this animal nature gave us reason to rule it.

2. Humiliation. The second duty of the day is Humiliation. And what is this? It has been a form. Men were required to cover themselves with ashes, to wear sackcloth, to bow themselves in the dust, to cry like a leper, Unclean! Unclean![8] All these were signs and may be dispensed with, but the thing they symbolized is as needful for us as for them, namely the acknowledgment of unworthiness; of sin; of being less than we ought.

And this certainly is a sentiment that eminently belongs to our dependent and erring nature. Self-conceit is the mark of a feeble mind, and of contracted affections. Wisdom, on the contrary, is always humble, according to the ancient sentence that he who was called the wisest of men was so only because he knew that he knew nothing.[9] And true holiness is always humble. For true wisdom and holiness have this in common that they have their eye fixed on the Divine Perfection, and the more it opens itself to their insight the more low and unworthy do human excellences seem, and the more black are human vices.

It is a tribute paid to the Christian virtue Humility that all the forms of good society in every civilized country continually require acts and words of self abasement in all who move therein. 'Humble' is the very byword of politeness. It has been well said, these forms are but the shadow of the Christian virtue, but they ought to satisfy men, that that quality cannot be despicable which all whom they respect, affect to possess.

The true office of every good mind is a jealousy of itself, a constant comparison of its performance with its duty and an anxious penitence for every wrong step. This is real humiliation, and it should be not a rare, not an annual act, but a permanent principle.

3. Prayer. The third office for which the day is marked, is prayer. And prayer too is a form, how often a hollow and worse than fruitless form! but not the less it contains a reality. Indeed nothing is more real, more effectual than our prayers. They move heaven and earth. Does any one remember that the effectual fervent prayer of the righteous man availeth much?[10] Alas! the prayers of the wicked man are not less frequent nor less effectual. For, if any one considers what is real, not what is apparent, and reflects upon the purely spiritual nature of God,

---

sermon; see *JMN* 4:6. Epicurus's dietary self-control is mentioned in Plutarch, "Life of Demetrius," in *The Lives*, ed. John and William Langhorne (New York, 1822), 7:35, and in Montaigne, "Of Cruelty" and "Of Experience," *Essays of Michael Seigneur de Montaigne . . .*, trans. Charles Cotton (London, 1700, 1693), 2:154 and 3:535. Emerson owned volumes 1 and 3 of the 1693 second edition; his second volume was from the third edition.

8. Leviticus 13:45.

9. The reference is to Socrates; see Plato, *Phaedo* 96A–99D. Cf. Milton, *Paradise Regained*, IV, 293–94, and *JMN* 1:210.

10. James 5:16.

he must perceive that the prayers of men are not the forms of words they address to the name of God in the church or at their bedside; these are only vehicles of prayer. And if these are only strings of words, if they do not express one single real desire of their hearts, they are only so much wasted hypocritical breath; these are not prayers, but the true prayers are the daily, hourly, momentary *desires,* that come familiarly into the soul, flow from its permanent will and are welcomed, the sincere habitual wishes that occupy our minds at morning and noon and night. These are the true prayers which every soul utters, and these prayers God is every day granting to the righteous man and to the sinner, yes, some of them to the destruction of our health of body and all peace of mind.

These are the effectual prayers, but these are not often right prayers. The right prayer is when the soul accompanies those petitions which we think it just and becoming to offer in the family or at the church to the Almighty. The right prayer is the habitual reference of the soul to God, a constant acknowledgment, which makes a part of every thought, that we are wholly his work, and wholly bound to do his will. An acknowledgment and a desire which extends beyond ourselves to our friends, to all with whom we have intercourse, to our country, and to mankind.

And here again it will be seen that this is a lasting duty, a constituent part of every thought.

On these considerations, brethren, it appears, that Fasting, humiliation, and prayer are real duties of perpetual obligation. We should keep a perpetual fast by temperance; we should make perpetual Humiliation by the grace of humil-ity; we should make perpetual Prayer, by never being absent from the thought of God. And if we do these things, it will be of little consequence in what manner the Annual Fast is appointed and kept or whether it is dropped. And if this day shall awaken the recollection of these duties in our minds, it will have answered a good purpose.

Let it not be forgotten, however, that the occasion was to our ancestors one of *social* and *political* commemoration; that they bore their country on their prayers to God, and fasted for the sins of the land as for their own sins. And this too is a perpetual duty. We ought to be always sad and ashamed of national sins. We ought never to lose sight of the truth that national offences are private offences carried out and represented at full length, so that men shudder at the vice when seen at full length which they tolerate and indulge in miniature, as the traveller in mountain countries is sometimes terrified at the apparition of his own shadow magnified on the mist.

This surely is no reason for silence and apathy respecting the public affairs. It becomes every reflecting American to consider that the silence and modesty concerning public measures and men, which is often a great duty in old king-doms where an idle word may be a spark thrown into a mine, are entirely misplaced in this country where every man, having by his vote and his influence a measured share in the government, is really responsible, in that proportion, to God and to men for the acts of government. And since this is so, if a great outrage is done to equity; if in the administration of the government, the strong oppress the weak; if a sanction is given in high places to licentious manners; and we hold our peace or approve such government by our vote, we have our part in that wrong as truly as if our tongues gave the counsel, our hands signed the instrument, or our feet ran to execute it. Let every man say then to himself—the cause of the Indian, it is mine; the cause of the slave, it is mine; the cause of the union, it is mine;[11] the cause of public honesty, of education, of religion, they are mine; and speak and act thereupon as a freeman and a Christian.

But at the same time, let him be also careful, step by step with his censure of the public vices, to censure and reform his own, in the conviction, as we have said, that the public wrongs are only private wrongs magnified. This will temper his condemnation of the public evils, and at the same time prove their most effectual remedy.

This then, brethren, is the Fast that God has chosen, not one of rare occurrence but of daily observance; not one of forms but of things; not one of public remembrance merely, but of public contrition founded on private contrition.

I would that we might keep this fast, as in the eye of Him with whom one day is as a thousand years, and a thousand years as one day.[12] Let us use this day as a token or memento to remind us of this eternal duty. Let us be temperate, let us be humble, let us offer just prayers unto God, and when presently he shall call us out of time into the eternal state, we shall be found meet for the inheritance of the saints in light.[13]

11. Effects of the Indian Removal Bill were being felt in the West, where the Black Hawk War was about to start, and in the South, where tensions between white settlers and the Seminole Indians were mounting. William Lloyd Garrison's recently established *Liberator* was effectively calling attention to "the cause of the slave." States' rights agitation would result in the Ordinance of Nullification, passed by South Carolina in November 1832.

12. II Peter 3:8.

13. Colossians 1:12.

CLI

He hath made every thing beautiful in his time:
also he hath set the world in their heart,
so that no man can find out the work that
God maketh from the beginning to the end.
I know that there is no good in them, but for
a man to rejoice, and to do good in his life.

Ecclesiastes 3:11–12

On the last Sabbath our attention was directed to the commanding obligation of the common duties.[1] I wish now to point your attention to some common pleasures with which God rewards such observances, to the abundance of that good to which every one has access.[2] It is often said there is no rose without its thorn.[3] Would it not be more becoming and more just to say, there is no thorn without its rose, no evil without its use? Our ambitious desires in looking out for satisfaction to the various parts of our nature slight that which is familiar and at hand, until it has become a sort of distinction of wise men—the simplicity of their pleasures. 'Few men,' it is said, 'know how to take a walk.'[4] And those whose range of pleasures has been much contracted by chronic disease or other disqualifications have observed that they learned to find the same amount of gratification from trifles as once they drew from larger matters.

Solomon says in a passage in which the meaning is more full than plain that

---

Manuscript dated April 8, 1832, at Chardon Street. Preached three times: April 8, 1832, at the Second Church, Boston; November 13, 1836, in East Lexington; and August 20, 1837, at the First Church, Waltham. Emerson's famous indictment of traveling in "Self-Reliance" (*CW* 2:46) is anticipated here.

1. In Sermon CXLIX (Sermon CL was given on Fast Day, Thursday, April 5).
2. Cf. II Corinthians 9:8.
3. Among the numerous sources for this literary commonplace Emerson may have recalled Robert Herrick's "The Rose": "But, for Man's fault, then was the thorn, / Without the fragrant rose-bud, born; / But ne'er the rose without the thorn." See Thomas Fuller, *Gnomologia: Adagies and Proverbs . . .* (London, 1732), no. 3625.
4. Samuel Johnson attributes the remark to a "French author" in *The Rambler*, no. 5. See *The Rambler*, ed. W. J. Bate and Albrecht B. Strauss (New Haven, 1969), 1:28. Used in "Prudence" (*EL* 2:324) and "Country Life" (*W* 12:142, 158).

God hath made every thing beautiful in its time, and hath set the world in man's heart.

It is most true in the sense that he hath given every mind access to the whole world of pleasure and of knowledge and virtue.

I shall offer some remarks, 1. upon the abundant enjoyment open to us by the senses, 2. upon the solid good which is accessible to every man even of the most limited opportunities, 3. upon the alleviation he has provided for every sorrow.

1. First; the senses are inlets to an immense amount of good. These five systems—the sources of knowledge—possessed by the meanest of mankind often in the greatest perfection, yet not the less the dependence of all—how do they seem to extend our existence from the dark, silent, solitary nook of being to a possession and society in all the Universe which they reveal to us! The eye makes the sun in the firmament, and all it enlightens in some sort, mine; the ear makes the melody of the world, the cheerfulness, and sense, and piety which men express, mine; the taste, the touch, and the smell, each have a scarce less wonderful office in this benevolent economy. Is it not true that in this way God has made the good otherwise given to each one, the property of all; that it is the same as if a new world had been created for every man and so that he has given to each of his children all things richly to enjoy.5 Brethren, if it were possible we could witness in another the possession and use of these senses without having them ourselves, we should reckon him a god; and here is all good freely given to you, if only you have at the bottom a thankful heart. Let us accustom ourselves then to reflect upon the right use of the senses, and their common organs.

Look at that famous engine, the human *hand,* 'the instrument of instruments,' the tamer of nature, without whose division into fingers, philosophers say, man would still be a beast roaming the desert. Why need I refer to the rare marvels it has executed under the genius of the painter, the sculptor, the engraver, the architect? See rather what it has accomplished for yourself—the daily cunning, the untiring industry of this excellent servant. 'It was the comparing the mechanism of the hand and the foot, that led Galen, who was a skeptic in his youth, to the public declaration of his opinion, that intelligence must have operated in ordaining the laws by which living beings are constructed.' And the passage is so remarkable that I quote it at length from a modern medical writer. "In explaining these things, I esteem myself as composing a solemn hymn to the great architect of our bodily frame, in which I think there is more true piety than in sacrificing hecatombs of oxen, or burning the most costly perfumes; for I first endeavour from his works to know him myself, and afterwards by the same means to show him to others, to inform them how great is his wisdom, his goodness, his power."6

5. Cf. I Timothy 6:17.
6. Galen apud Abernethy p   [Emerson's note]. Quotations in this paragraph are from John Abernethy, *Physiological Lectures . . . delivered before the Royal College of Surgeons in the year 1817* (London, 1817), 152–53. See *JMN* 4:10–11.

So of the eye. It is a trite sentiment which all of us repeat that blessings are not valued till they are lost,[7] and of none more familiarly spoken than of the eye. It is feelingly presented to us when they lose the organ who have known how to put it to a good use. There is a striking instance of this in the case of Galileo, the celebrated astronomer who invented the telescope and discovered by means of it the moons of Jupiter, the ring of Saturn, the fact of the revolution of the sun on its own axis, ascertained by noting the motion of his spots. He lost his sight in the year 1636, six years before his death. He lost his sight—he who had boasted that he would never cease using the senses God had given him in declaring the glory of his works. "Alas!" he says in a letter to one of his friends, "I am totally and irreparably blind, so that this heaven, this earth, and this universe, which with wonderful observations I had enlarged a hundred and thousand times beyond the belief of bygone ages, henceforward for me is shrunk into the narrow space which I myself fill in it. So it pleases God, it shall therefore please me also."[8] The loss of Galileo's sight was felt by the intelligent men of Europe as a public calamity. "The noblest eye is darkened," said Castelli, "which nature ever made, an eye so privileged, with such rare qualities, that it may with truth be said to have seen more than all those who are gone, and to have opened the eyes of all who are to come."[9]

The same calamity befel Milton,[10] who had used his sight for other but not less noble purposes. I quote these eminent instances because the sympathy which we feel with these sufferers, shows us plainly to what great purpose these organs may be put, which we are in general content to set so little by, to show by conspicuous examples how vast is the value of an organ which all possess when directed by diligence and knowledge and virtue; and that by means of this universal gift whatever God hath made of beautiful or grand, and hung in heaven, or planted on earth, he hath made for all.

2. But, in the next place, it deserves our special consideration that not only what is pleasing and beautiful but all that is really useful is to be found by every man at home. It was said in censure of a travelled man, 'Here is he who gave away his own lands to see those of other men.'[11] It is true in more than the letter. It is very apt to be true that a man gives away his own wisdom and virtue to be amused with seeing how other men live. Not to see their virtue, but their vice. It needs more than to *go into a land* to see its wisdom and virtue. These do not lie,

7. "Blessings are not valued, till they are gone." Thomas Fuller, *Gnomologia*, no. 989.

8. John E. D. Bethune, "Life of Galileo," in *Lives of Eminent Persons* (London, 1833), 75. See *JMN* 3:328, where the editors note that Emerson had access to an earlier form of this publication and read it in February 1832. It was first published separately in London in 1830, and reprinted in Boston in 1832.

9. Bethune, "Life of Galileo," 75. Used again in "The Uses of Natural History" (*EL* 1:18). Benedetto Castelli (1578-1643) was a student, colleague, and loyal friend of Galileo. A professor of mathematics at the Universities of Pisa and Rome, he was an authority on hydraulics and optics as well as astronomy.

10. See *JMN* 3:328.

11. Slightly misquoted from Shakespeare, *As You Like It*, IV, i, 21-22. See *JMN* 3:322 and 6:127.

like its mountains and cities, open to the vulgar gaze. These are secluded behind sacred walls. It must be likeness of character that can find access to them.
It must be an illuminated eye that can explore a nation's wisdom. It must be a
worthy man that will be permitted to converse with its worth.

I should be glad if it were rightly seen by us, what is certainly true, that it is
those only who were wise at home that grow wise by going abroad. For you very
often may hear people lamenting that they had no advantages when young, or
they had always been confined to a secluded life, and the like, and the young
are apt to repine because they cannot see the world, and to admire and envy
the information displayed by intelligent persons who have been abroad and
enjoyed great trusts. True Wisdom says to you, Use the advantages you have—
opportunities come to every man.

You admire the knowledge and manners of those who have seen the world
and know so much more of men. They got it, however, not by peering about all
over the world, but by minding their business. In the steadfast attention to all
the details of their profession, they met this information. And if a man will stay
in his own place, and if he will resolutely and strenuously discharge all the
duties of his relations, he will get as much instructive experience, as much
commanding knowledge, not the same facts but facts that teach the same truths;
equal knowledge of men, equal skill in counsel, equal power of virtue. 'Seest
thou a man diligent in his business? he shall stand before kings, he shall not
stand before mean men.'[12]

You expect by being much abroad to learn human nature,—as if to become
acquainted with man, it were necessary to know all the individuals upon earth.
There is a book of human nature laid open in your own house of which you
have hardly read the first characters, and always you will find that you get much
more of this knowledge from a thorough acquaintance with a few persons, than
from thousands observed superficially. 'We are a sufficient spectacle,' said one
of the philosophers, 'each to the other.'[13] Indeed it is enough to know yourself,
and by that interpretation to read all the rest of the Volume of man. 'As face
answereth to face in water, so the heart of man to man.'[14]

I would not press this point of self knowledge beyond what is natural and
true, (for I know we need the help of others to know ourselves). Far be it from
me to discourage any one from the desire of obtaining and using every the
widest variety of opportunities of enriching and varying his experience of men
and affairs. I congratulate rather every one upon such advantages. I only would
have it distinctly considered that true wisdom of every man consists in cultivat-
ing the observing power, and not in multiplying the opportunities of observation, and to remark that every man's means of knowledge are more than he has

12. Proverbs 22:29. A draft of the first half of this paragraph appears in *JMN* 3:322.
13. Attributed by Seneca to Epicurus. Emerson's source is almost certainly Bacon's "Of Love";
see *The Works of Francis Bacon,* ed. James Spedding et al. (London, 1857–1874), 6:397, and *JMN*
3:12, 19.
14. Proverbs 27:19.

used. I will ask any one who is greedy of opportunities of extensive observation, whether it were not wiser to let God judge for us in this matter, to trust the order of Providence which supplies every eye which keeps its place, with its fair share of opportunity as well as every mouth with its food. God has provided every man with twenty or thirty companions and two or three hundred acquaintances as by way of specimen of the varieties of human character and as a large book wherein he may read his own nature as it were magnified, where he may and ought to see painted in bright colours the beauty of every virtue and the deformity of every vice.

Consider also that every body's occasions in the ordinary circumstances of life provide him with much variety of intercourse so that it is rare to meet with a grown person who has not been present in all the principal scenes of human life. To almost every one, in the pursuit of his own calling and the care of his own family, have come the various *times* enumerated by Solomon of feasting, funerals, marriage, worship, war, and disease.[15] He is obliged to see the statehouse, the college, the almshouse, the court, the jail, the camp, ship, stable, mine, and mountain, sometime in his life; to travel many hundred miles by land and water. Keep your eyes open and God will provide you with opportunity. Moreover, have you never observed that all these things give far more entertainment and true advantage when taken as they rise in your way, 'no duty left, no calling broke,' than when you make it a distinct object to seek them? If you go out of doors to look at the moon or a star, they will not yield the eye half that pleasure which they give you when you avail yourself of their cheerful light on your own affairs.

And why is all this? Because God hath set the world in man's heart. For this reason, that the outward world and all that it contains, was designed in God's plan only as a shadow or type of the world within. The heart, the soul, the immortal nature is the object for which other objects exist, and he who makes himself acquainted with the properties of this nature by self cultivation advances by large steps to a comprehension of every thing else. He has the key by which all else can be explained.

3. But, once more; as we have all beautiful and noble pleasures at command and also whatever is truly valuable, so I add that the final contentment of the soul consists in this, that no sorrow is without its alleviation. There is no affliction, we commonly say, but might be sorer. No loss is total. Commonly there is some, generally there is much external alleviation. But if there is none, the mind always can find one in itself. This has been the unspeakable gift of the Christian revelation, to acquaint the mind with its own nature, and its relation to God, and chiefly its aim hath been to perfect the mind in holiness, so that it should itself feel the force of these consolations, should feel its immortality, and should be able to mount to the height of a perfect trust.

---

15. Ecclesiastes 3:1–8. A draft of this paragraph and part of the previous one occurs in *JMN* 3:322.

And why and how is this, that in a full perception of our frailty and insignificance, wherever there is religious principle we are yet able to stand the assaults of the worst sorrow, and feel that nothing is remediless, that we cannot be forsaken? It is because our fountains drink of the Sea. It is because we feel and know that somehow we are connected with God; that his life flows into us; that the expression current in every age of the world, 'God in us,' has real meaning;[16] because we feel that whilst we are worthy, we cannot perish; and whilst *he* exists, we cannot be wronged, because, though for moments the mind may despond, yet it recovers itself the next moment; for it is its nature to *hope,* and think well of things. And what do we mean by *its nature,* but the incessant prompting of the Eternal Spirit whose Will makes the nature of all beings through all time? Why art thou cast down, o my soul, and why art thou disquieted within me? Hope thou in God; he shall yet save me, who is the health of my countenance.[17]

Therefore, brethren, let us rejoice as wise men. Let us feel the fulness of truth in that declaration of the Scripture, 'No good thing will be withheld from them who walk uprightly.'[18] Let us open our eyes to the bounty of God in nature, in society, in the intellect, and in the heart. Especially let us delight in the riches of his gifts to virtue. Let us feel that to every soul is an infinite treasure in itself. Let us make no delay and spare no pains to explore the depths of our own nature, to expel the sensual passions that hide happiness and God from us, and so bring in a divine contentment with every condition, an armed mind, a heart prepared to welcome every change it shall please God to send us in all the future.

16. Emerson perhaps alludes to Luke 17:21, in which Christ is reported to have said that "the kingdom of God is within you." This suggestion of divine immanence was of much importance to Emerson, though scholars as early as Gilbert Wakefield, whose work Emerson consulted, had objected to the King James translation, asserting that a more accurate rendering might be "the kingdom of God is in the midst of you" (see Wakefield, *A Translation of the New Testament,* 2d ed. [London, 1795], 1:196). The allusion may also be to the definition of "Emmanuel" in Matthew 1:23: "God with us." Although Wakefield concurred with this King James rendition, Emerson had recently redefined the verse in more radically experiential terms as "this literal Emmanuel *God within us.*" See *Sermons* 2:24 and Wesley T. Mott, *"The Strains of Eloquence": Emerson and His Sermons* (University Park, Pa., 1989), 68.

17. Cf. Psalms 42:5, 11, and 43:5.

18. Psalms 84:11.

CLII

For all live unto Him.

LUKE 20:38

There is a sentiment of trust in the wisdom and goodness which upholds the frame of nature, that arises so naturally from every *general* view of our condition and the order that surrounds us, that it is worth every person's attention to put himself often in that train of thought which gives birth to it. We need general views, to support us in the consideration of particular calamities. If the storm beats against our windows, and covers with gloom the whole face of nature around us, we are apt to forget that the skirts of that cloud reach over only a small tract of country, and that half the world is basking in sunshine. And if we suffer under present affliction our mind naturally fixes upon our disaster to the exclusion of all the cheerful and glorious views, which the world offers us. The natural remedy for this overestimate of private griefs is in the contemplation of the Universal Providence of God, who is ever bringing good out of evil and who furnishes in the magnificent works he has spread before the eye of every human being a sufficient pledge that its own well being shall not be forgotten.

No situation in life is wholly forlorn. Winter has its joys; the savage has his advantages; sickness its resources; and the sharpest affliction, some solace. Where there is nothing else, there is hope. How significant is the proverb, 'As long as there is life there is hope.'[1] And it is not grateful nor becoming in us to cherish a desponding temper amid the rejoicing of the morning stars and the shouting for joy of the sons of God.[2]

In this view, let us attend to the weighty declaration made by Jesus in his conver-

---

Manuscript dated April 22, 1832, at Chardon Street. Preached eight times: April 22, 1832, at the Second Church, Boston; May 6 at the Purchase Street Church; May 13 at the New South Church; March 22, 1835, at the Second Church, Waltham; July 10, 1836, in Concord; July 31 in East Lexington; June 4, 1837, in Lexington; and July 23 in Framingham. The theme of order in nature is anticipated in a journal entry (*JMN* 3:311–12). For the delivery of July 10, 1836, in Concord, Emerson added a brief eulogy (see the Textual and Manuscript Notes) for Hersey B. Goodwin, associate pastor to Ezra Ripley. Goodwin had died in Plymouth the day before. On July 31, 1836, Margaret Fuller accompanied Emerson to East Lexington and attended the service (see *L* 6:309–10, n. 2).

1. The proverb can be traced back to Cicero, but Emerson's immediate source may again be Thomas Fuller, *Gnomologia,* no. 5689.

2. Cf. Job 38:7.

sation with the Sadducees;—"He is not the God of the dead, but of the living; for all live unto him." Let us open the truths contained in this declaration.

I. All live unto God, by being the objects of his present care; by deriving their being and beauty from him. There is so much beneficent design apparent in the creation, so much that blazes all over it in light, and speaks in all sound, that when our attention is once engaged to it, we feel as if all distrust was culpable, as if it were pusillanimous in us to fear, when the sparrow and the rose are not forgotten.[3]

He is the life of all things and the significant marks of design everywhere are his image and superscription. Whatever is good is given to all. The sun shines for all.

"The sleepless ocean murmurs for all ears."[4] But each spectator is commonly more affected by *particular* manifestations of divine providence; by considering one at a time. We go naturally to those whose evidence cannot be brought into controversy by the most skeptical. Every understanding, not depraved, is sensibly affected by those marks of design which our hands can handle, and our eyes can see;—by contrivances such as we should have used ourselves, if we had supernatural power.

An evidence of this kind, the human mind can take in at once, and compare it with its own work, and is conscious of a sensation of agreeable surprise. Who can see the countless processes tending in nature at the same moment to good, to preservation, to pleasure, to beauty, without joy? There is something more than beautiful—even affectionate, in the manner in which the vegetable race is perpetuated by this wilderness of flowers, not one of which but shows, when brought to a minute examination, peculiar elegance or utility of form or color; and not the commonest weed but has its continued existence ensured by provisions that set at nought all cavilling explanations, and all imitation. There is no token of a tyrant's hand in the cheerfulness of the human constitution. The readiness with which man, when not disturbed by passion, yields to smiles and laughter. The plays of children, the display of unmixed delight, the capacity of being pleased with every trifle—do they not prove kind intention?

To this point I quote with pleasure the remarks of Paley: "The contemplation of universal nature rather bewilders the mind than affects it. There is always a bright spot in the prospect upon which the eye rests: a single example, perhaps, by which each man finds himself more *convinced* than by all others put together. *I* seem, for my own part, to see the benevolence of the Deity more clearly in the pleasures of very young children, than in any thing in the world. The pleasures of grown persons may be reckoned partly of their own procuring, especially if there has been any industry or contrivance or pursuit to come at them, or if they are founded, like music and painting, upon any qualification of their own acquiring. But the pleasures of a healthy infant are so manifestly

---

3. Cf. Matthew 10:29.
4. William Wordsworth, *The Excursion*, IX, 212.

provided for by *another,* and the benevolence of the provision is so unquestionable, that every child I see at its sport, affords to my mind a kind of sensible evidence of the finger of God, and of the disposition which directs it."[5]

And all the beautiful instances of exact calculation and divine art with which animated nature abounds and of which it is but one continuous manifestation prove the same thing. I shall allude to a few particulars of this kind.

There are few instances so striking or beautiful as modern inquiry has discovered in the cell of the bee.[6] That small builder which has been the little moralist of all ages has not yet perhaps yielded all its instruction. The bee in the formation of its cell has to solve a problem that would puzzle many architects to form it, cells of a determinate capacity, but of the largest size in proportion to the quantity of matter employed. And its success is admirable. What has chiefly attracted attention is the care with which the base of the cell is constructed, which is not plain but made of three pieces which are parts of three cells on the other side. It was found that these angles, which might have every variety, were 109 degrees the larger and 70 degrees the smaller. Reaumur, the naturalist, proposed to a skilful mathematician, who was ignorant of these experiments, to determine by calculation, what ought to be the angle of a cell with so much room and so much strength so that the least possible wax should enter into its construction. The geometrician found the greater angles should be 109, and the lesser 70 degrees.

Not less wonderful is the delicate mechanism which the microscope discloses in the smallest fly, in which a distinct organization is added to guard its limbs from injury by the shock of alighting from a rapid flight; the equally singular structure by which it is enabled to bring the pressure of the atmosphere on its tiny feet and so walk upon the wall without falling. Throughout nature, there is no slighting the lesser works. The oyster is as fit for his uses, as the brain of man. The same attention is vouchsafed to the wants of the insect as to the formation of the globe. So that naturalists inform us that there are 25000 hexagonal lenses in the head of a fly, or possibly the same number of distinct visual organs.

All nature is full of these tokens through all its kingdoms. But why pick a few grains from the mountain? Why enumerate a few out of innumerable particulars?

The invariable composition of the atmosphere, formed by the mixture of the same elements in the same proportions;—the uses of snow to protect the earth in winter from the deadly effect of cold;—the remarkable exception in the case of water to the general law by which bodies expand in heating and contract in cooling. (Water is a singular exception to this law, expanding when it freezes. If

5. Natural Theology [Emerson's note]. The quotation, however, is from William Paley, *The Principles of Moral and Political Philosophy,* 10th American ed. (Boston, 1821), 64.

6. Emerson's discussion of bees and flies draws on a journal entry of April 2, 1832 (*JMN* 4:9), which in turn draws on readings in John Abernethy, *Physiological Lectures* (London, 1817), especially 265. The celebrated discovery of René Antoine Ferchault de Réaumur (1683–1757) regarding the shape of bee cells was widely discussed (see *JMN* 4:253, n. 14, 6:207, and "The Uses of Natural History" [*EL* 1:20]).

it did not, when a lake or sea were once frozen it would never melt.) The relation of the vegetable to the animal world; the perfect design of the human form; the exact ratio of equality which is observed in the number of the sexes in the human race; and every new discovery, and every old observation, confirm the ancient maxim that "in wonder all philosophy begins and in astonishment ends."[7]

When I extend my view from particular good to the general progress of *man*, to the intellectual life of so many, when I see all the treasures of history, when I consider the great virtues that have been exhibited, the various talents, the unconscious cooperation of nations and ages to effect great purposes, when I call to mind all that was sublime in thought and sweet in speech and brave in action, that has passed upon this planet, when especially I bring to mind the true hearts, the clear minds, the irreproachable characters we have known, and when, further, the mind after becoming aware of the exhaustless resources and tenderness that are exhibited in the whole economy of so many races of beings as inhabit this world, comes to find that this globe bearing so costly a deposit, is an unnoticed atom in the sublime profusion which has scattered systems like sand over unbounded space;[8] and yet one law of mutual attraction reigns through all, as the sign of one power, it is persuaded that a power exists in which all have their common origin and guard, that a common source embraces the whole in its omnipresence. All live unto him. To him the fields grow and the animals move. To him the ocean rolls. To him heaven and its hosts of spheres revolve in everlasting order.

The mind in this contemplation of a scene so vast is overwhelmed with a sense of its own littleness. It has but yesterday come out of silence into this sounding creation, and it saith, 'Who am I, that amid all this stupendous scene of power and love should be thinking of myself, and anxious about my little lot, and unwilling to trust my fate to the arrangements of an Universe so incomprehensibly glorious? All live unto God, and in Him whose being is the law and foundation of all, whose presence unites the whole, the orb of fire to the creeping worm, I find myself secure.'

It is vain to say these observations are too far off; they are mere statements of fact within the reach now of every man. And I see not how any person of sound mind can steadily contemplate them without some degree of increased trust being produced in his mind. If the thought of God seemed too vast for him before, he will see it is rational here; if the doctrine of a divine Providence seems not supported by the facts of his daily experience, it will seem well grounded and not to be avoided in this glance at the Whole.

7. This paragraph is developed from a list of "Instances of Design" recorded in Emerson's notebook Encyclopedia (*JMN* 6:206–7). Emerson may have encountered the "ancient maxim" in Samuel Taylor Coleridge, *The Friend* (1818), vol. 3, "Essay XI," where he quotes Aristotle and Plato. See Barbara E. Rooke, ed., *The Collected Works of Samuel Taylor Coleridge*, vol. 4.1 (Princeton, 1969), 519.

8. An allusion to Edward Young, *Night Thoughts*, "Night IX," line 2312; see *Sermons* 3:192.

In this sense 'All live unto God' in his creative and providing love, which makes the life and order of all nature.

II. In the second place, the words of the text affirm the immortality of the soul. This was in the mind of Jesus. God is not God of the dead, but of the living; for all live unto him. It is the consolation of mortal men. Why should it be thought a thing incredible that God should raise the dead? Why should I doubt the recovery of my life, who see this annual resurrection of nature from the dust; who see the south wind blow and green herbage run over the late regions of winter? Why should I doubt the recovery of life in another state, who have seen the little worm weave its own tomb, and after a few months of darkness and sleep, reappear in a new and more excellent form, and traverse the atmosphere on painted wings? Why should I expect the stroke of death on my soul, which is wholly unlike my body, and is just prepared to live, when my body begins to sink? He spoke wisely who on being asked if he did not fear to die? replied, 'No, I see no reason for dying.'[9] There is no intimation of death in the soul, as there is in the body. It collects grace and strength and knowledge as it draws near to its departure. It goes down to the door of the tomb collected and cheerful. It is now just ready to live.

But above all, why should I fear death, environed as I am by a wisdom and power that I see everywhere triumphing over death? Shall I in the face of heaven and earth circumscribe God's power, and say, it is unequal to produce anything more than my eyes behold. Shall I put limits to my confidence in Him by whom I live, and say, 'I can trust his love in the earth, but I cannot trust it beyond the mouth of the grave'?

Why should I fear for another's life? for the weal of a soul that is passing from the earth, and leaving its clay to fall and mix with the dust? Shall I doubt that the favored child of God who but a few weeks since drew from him the breath of spiritual life, animated that now silent clay, and led it about among men; devoted it to useful labors; to friendly actions; built up by its aid the outward works of temperance, of education, of the state, and of the church, which spoke to me of truth, of duty, of immortality,—shall I doubt that this soul which loved these things so well loves these things no longer because the flesh which imprisoned it imprisons it no more?

Shall I believe that He who hath made nothing in vain, hath wasted this profusion of excellent influences on the education of a creature that comes to nothing at last? He is all life and in Him shall all be made alive.[10] He will not suffer the soul to see corruption.[11] He who brought again from the dead his own son will bring us also with him.[12]

But this truth has far more conviction in it when we look for natural life in connexion with spiritual life.

9. Not located.
10. I Corinthians 15:22.
11. Psalms 16:10.
12. Cf. Hebrews 13:20.

III. All live unto God—All souls by moral life. As the powers of man are opened he becomes conscious of possessing very different powers. He presently perceives that he has a moral nature having laws wholly its own yet as fixed and as harmonious as the laws of matter. He conceives a respect for moral laws which material nature never commands. The last seems to fade away into a mere type and allegory by which his mind is instructed in things spiritual.

When a man begins strongly to feel the obligation of duty; when he begins to see the beauty of right actions, and to hate vices; when he begins to feel his debt to his Maker; there is such a growth and enlargement in his mind that he calls it a new life by emphasis; as if first he began to live. All the parts of his character acquire balance and energy, he becomes useful to his fellow men to the whole extent of his powers; so that he is born again.[13]

When the soul becomes filled with the love of God; with the desire of infinite good; hungers after truth and righteousness,[14]—it has become possessed of a new hold on existence; it feels that it is nearer to God; it participates in his nature; it so rejoices in him, in doing his will, that it begins to regard his will as the supreme good, and not its own private interest, and is willing to suffer and to be nothing so that may be all.[15]

The private feelings begin to be absorbed in a great public regard, and the desire to dictate our own wishes is supplied by an entire confidence that no evil can befal us under the government of God.

Where this state of mind fully takes place it is not immortality expected but commenced. This soul has passed from time into eternity whilst yet the body is among living men. This is true life, for it is not the desire of continuing to exist but the desire of doing those works and enjoying that knowledge which give life all its worth.

No man can thus live unto God, when it becomes the habitual act of his will, without knowing it and rejoicing in it. This is to be what we were made for. This is to pass from death unto life.[16] This is to have character for imbecility, wisdom for ignorance, self-command for animal indulgence; love, for a cold, selfish, injurious existence.

This then is the highest sense in which man lives unto God. Thus heaven lives unto him and all its host of holy beings and thus every soul lives unto him in proportion to the progress it hath made.

Thus, brethren, we have confidence before God that all live unto him, the whole creation in his omnipresent care; the human soul after the death of the body; and lastly in its virtue after the death and before death because this event has nothing to do with its true *life,* which is virtue, holiness.

My friends, let these thoughts comfort us. Let us retreat upon them in every

13. Emerson interprets the doctrine of the second birth, announced in John 3:3. Cf. John 3:7 and I Peter 1:23.

14. Cf. Matthew 5:6.

15. An echo, apparently, of a position held by Samuel Hopkins; see *Sermons* 2:33, n. 5.

16. John 5:24.

hour of sadness, in every momentary doubt. He is great enough surely that we should trust him, nor is our venture so large in the Universe but we may safely lose sight of it in seeking the good of the whole. Above all let us accustom ourselves to remember that it is *unto God* that all live; and that the soul without God in the world, without obedience to him, without love of him, is but the dead-alive. Let us praise him for the past; let us trust him for the future; and let us draw nigh to him in heart as to the Fountain of all life and blessedness.[17]

17. Cf. Psalms 36:9, Proverbs 13:14, 14:27, and Revelation 21:6.

CLIII

*The Lord God is a sun and shield; the Lord will
give grace and glory; no good thing will he
withhold from them that walk uprightly. O Lord
of hosts, blessed is the man that trusteth in thee.*

PSALMS 84:11–12

A sentiment which finds expression continually in the Sacred Scriptures and which finds expression in the mouth of every pious person, is, that God is all sufficient for the human soul, that those who attain any good measure of the love of God cannot be impoverished or weakened or wounded, for that sentiment is more than life to them and all external things are accounted vile in comparison. This sentiment is the inspiration of the Psalms. This is the sense of that noble strain of prophecy which has been the vehicle of devotion in every age. 'Although the figtree shall not blossom neither shall fruit be in the vines; the labour of the olive shall fail, and the fields shall yield no meat; the flock shall be cut off from the fold and there shall be no herd in the stalls; yet I will rejoice in the Lord,—I will joy in the God of my salvation.'[1] This was the angel that ministered alway unto Jesus.[2] And Paul and Peter and James and John act and speak under the strong influence of the same feeling.

If the power of that sentiment be truly so great, it is most needful and shall be welcome to us. Every day at least shows us our want of such a resource. It is true the beneficence of God has provided in the cares of every day among industrious persons a refuge from sorrow. We are happy or at least insensible to misery whilst we are occupied. But the mind sometimes labors to understand itself. We demand a better happiness than comes from ignorance, or diversion. We would understand our happiness and see if it is made of such stuff as will last, or be cloud. We are so constituted that deception is resented by us as an insult, and we do not wish to be gratified at the expense of our reason.

But not only is it fit that rational beings should explore the sources of their

---

Manuscript dated April 29, 1832. Preached seven times: April 29, 1832, at the Second Church, Boston; June 8, 1834, at the Hollis Street Church; July 27 in Bangor, Maine; March 20, 1836, in East Lexington; June 5 in Concord; February 19, 1837, at the First Church, Waltham; and April 23 in Wayland, Massachusetts.

1. Hab[akkuk] 3, 17–18 [Emerson's note].
2. Matthew 4:11 and Mark 1:13.

satisfaction and see if they are genuine, it is also necessary. The labor of your hands will not at all times afford you pleasing occupation, the toil of the eyes in study will not carry with it peace of mind, nor will the multitude of amusements, no, nor social pleasures always gratify.

There are times when the spirit in man will obstinately question itself, and will not be pacified by any thing but truth. Every one sometimes calls himself to account and compares the present day with the past hope and sees very clearly a great difference between the promises of his youth and the performance of his manhood, sees distinctly that through all the pretension and apparent activity of his life his soul is not becoming more mature or more happy; he sees it with pain,—and blessed is he, if he is not able to drown that whisper of conscience in the tumult of politics or commerce. It makes itself heard in every worthy soul above the din of the world, and God is always giving it aid by drawing the curtain of darkness over us every night, and sending us continually into solitude.

But besides this obstinate self scrutiny which occasionally comes to all, and which makes all things bitter, all men are exposed and in turn suffer from misfortunes. Their peace of mind, their self satisfaction, is put to severe trial. That which they most prize is taken away. Unforeseen and bitter mortifications await them in the prosecution of that which they have most at heart. They have enemies who hinder them from sleep. They lose their employment and livelihood; their health is wasted; or, dear friends are removed from them by death, or the altered character of their friends has ceased to make their life a source of happiness to them.

These infirmities of our nature and crosses of our condition give inestimable value to this promise of religion. It is the claim of religion that it is a consolation, a medicine, the oil of joy, the anchor of hope.[3] And I invite you, my friends, to consider the import of that promise, and the manner in which it may be fulfilled to us.

1. The way in which God satisfies those who seek him is through and by means of their performance of his commandments. This is a resource which is sure, and to which every moral being may have recourse. I see around me in the world a great many persons who are called unfortunate, who have lost those friends on whom their earthly hopes rested, or who have grown up to that age which is expected to provide for itself and whom yet circumstances prevent from so doing.

I see those who far removed from want are yet from leisure and the opportunity of comparing their situation with others far more keenly sensible of a solitary or dependent condition; I see people who without any fault of their own are yet excluded from the sympathy of others; I see disappointed men in whose hands every project fails; I see lonely and unhappy women; I see age left childless; and the invalid of many years; I see the oppressed debtor; the suspected, the friendless, and the mourner.

---

3. Isaiah 61:3 and Hebrews 6:19. For "the oil of joy," see also *JMN* 3:309.

Now whilst these various classes of sufferers deeply excite your pity, and really cast a gloom by their sorrow over every man's view of life, yet I think no person of reflecting mind fails to see that these sad conditions cause more affliction than they ought because the sufferers do not draw from the fountains of comfort within their reach. That circumstance in their case which most forcibly awakens your pity, is that they are often wholly unconscious that there are pleasures accessible to them, that will set them far above pity.

They sit complaining or they occupy themselves in drawing a miserable relief from trivial and momentary circumstances whilst the true and infinite relief is quite within their reach and quite overlooked.

See how shallow are the ordinary wells of human consolation. A perpetual comparison of circumstances. The mourner enervated by his grief yet considers that the departed object of his love has escaped from this or that mortification to which he and others are exposed; or that in his loss he is not quite destitute— his friend is more a sufferer; or that his pride has still certain recollections and certain accomplishments to lean upon; or that his friends will become more to him, and occupies himself in gathering up his wrecked affections within a narrower circle. But presently he contrasts his solitude with the gratified affections of others and his sorrow returns. The victim of a cruel or fatal disease strives to compensate himself for the enjoyments that are taken by a critical inventory of what is left. His outdoor labors and amusements are gone, but he multiplies the indoor works; he finds as much amusement in small things as once he found in great; he makes an occupation for his thoughts even of his disease and the watching of symptoms and hopes of favorable turns employ his attention, but his pale cheek grows paler at the approach of the robust form and glowing cheek of youth.

But more an object of pity than the mourner or the invalid is that of the servile dependant on society, those unhappy men and women, whose eye is ever upon place in society, who neglecting the intellectual and moral resources within their reach, have set their ambition upon success in the world, upon connexions, high society, unexceptionable appearance, and influence. They compare their condition with that of others, whence come hard thoughts, painful feeling of inferiority, servile manners, and continual dwarfing of themselves, and thus ever live in a little circle of trifles out of which possibly no refreshment, no generous aims, no improving influences can ever issue. Especially if any signal misfortune has come upon such persons as the loss of property or disease, you shall sometimes hear from them sentiments most impertinent and betraying miserable ignorance as if the individual thought himself hardly dealt by.

To all these sufferers Religion utters one and the same word. You are seeking relief, peace of mind, in alteration of circumstances: You seek in broken cisterns that can hold no water.[4] In your character find consolation. Fear God and keep his commandments, and you shall find rest to your soul.[5] Be a ministering angel

4. Jeremiah 2:13.
5. Ecclesiastes 12:13; cf. Jeremiah 6:16 and Matthew 11:29.

to the wants of others. Withdraw your eye from too close a criticism on your own *lot*, compared with that of others, and fix in upon your *duties*.

If you have been defeated in your exertions hitherto, thus shall you repair your loss, by the very highest success. If your children, your friends, the objects of your dearest regard have been taken from you,—thus shall you be a friend of the human race. If you have been wounded by the unworthiness of those whom you loved,—in this opening acquaintance with new worth, with virtue, with usefulness, you shall become aware of the presence of a multitude of friends and helpers. If your condition is a dependent one, thus shall you soar from dependence to independence, from independence to active usefulness. Instead of watching and repeating the smile and frown of those whose favor is fashion, you shall be yourself a giver of honor, the resource of the friendless, the counsellor of the young and ardent; one whose opinion everywhere commands respect, because it is not your nor any man's opinion, but drawn from the Source of Truth.

And thus in the first place does God satisfy the soul through the keeping of his Commandments.

Occupy yourself in forming and executing plans of progress. Can there be a nobler employment for man or angel than to make a soul more perfect? There are persons who have transmitted their names to all ages by spending months and years in watching the revolutions of a star, in observing the habits of a bird, or in detecting the secret organization of an insect or a plant. Shall these persons have our respect who have only found out some law of an inferior nature; how much more glorious is the study of the virtuous man who occupies himself not upon an animal or a plant but upon an intelligent mind,—not in finding what it is, but in making it what it should be, in recommending himself to the Supreme Being by finishing his work after his design.

Who is forlorn? Who is unhappy? Come to the noble and blessed employments which religion offers you and you shall find rest. Come and contrive how you can increase the happiness of your household. Earn the respect of those whose respect is worth much, because they see you every day. "Real virtue," said an ancient moralist, "is most loved where it is most nearly seen, and no respect which it commands from strangers can equal the never ceasing admiration it excites in the daily intercourse of domestic life."[6]

That man does not need to go out and seek God but brings God home to himself who does not ask any praise or any reward for his virtues but adores the loveliness of the virtues themselves; who sees in his own experience that patience, humility, courage, and love are company and entertainment enough in his own breast. Him I call rich; that soul I call endowed in man or woman who by poverty or affliction or love or happy influence of God has been so far forced into acquaintance with itself that it has become aware of the spiritual dominion

---

6. Plutarch [Emerson's note]. The quotation is from an unidentified translation of "The Life of Pericles"; see *JMN* 3:323. Cf. *The Lives,* ed. John and William Langhorne (New York, 1822), 2:115.

of every human mind. He can never again despond. Henceforward he is introduced into sublime society. Henceforward he can wave the hand of adieu to all
things he coveted most. Henceforth he is above compassion. He may not yet
take possession of his treasure. He may be often and long interrupted. But he
will return to it. He never can forget it is his. Him I leave in his heaven and all
others I call miserably poor.

A cheerful diligent love, an efficient philanthropy, is the water of life,[7] without money and without price, which Heaven offers us. But whilst it is open to
all I do not affect to represent it as a common attainment. Let no one think that
this rule of benevolence, so simple and so oft repeated, is often fulfilled or
easily. It is wonderful how difficult its observance is. It is wonderful how deeply
hid are the simplest truths. It needs great selfreliance, power of persisting, and
extreme watchfulness to obey the command to love our neighbor a single day.[8]
We set out in the morning with a thorough conviction that it is the true interest
of mankind, that that law should be invariably observed. But presently when we
come to act, we hear something thrown out concerning a proper pride, or the
necessary degree of spirit; or we are checked by some of those proverbs of a
pitiful prudence which abound in conversation and which, however excellent to
guard the young against Vice, to hinder idleness, passion, dissipation, become
mischievous when they are turned against Virtue. These alarm our selfishness
and shake our purpose and straightway we forget our morning principles, and
conform ourselves to the expectation of an evil world. But we come back again
ere long through some painful mortification to a new conviction that love is the
Universal law; that with the lowly is perpetual peace; that God striketh down
the proud; and we learn that implicit reverence is due to our first thoughts.
"First thoughts," said an old maxim, "come from the Divinity;"[9] and it is an
observation of modern moral philosophy that "first and third thoughts coincide."[10]

Does any one then find many misfortunes in his or her condition? Try this
remedy of obedience to the commandments according to the advice of the Old
and New Testaments. Who is he that desireth life and would see *good* days? Let
him refrain his tongue from evil and his lips that they speak no guile. Depart
from evil and do good. Especially shall peace be found in works of kindness.[11]
Love is the fulfilling of the Law.[12] He that dies in hot blood never feels the
wound,[13] and he that is directing all his attention to the happiness of others does

7. Revelation 21:6, 22:1, 17.

8. Leviticus 19:18; Matthew 5:43, 19:19, 22:39; Mark 12:31, 12:33; Luke 10:27; Romans 13:9;
Galatians 5:14; James 2:8.

9. Francis Bacon, *The Advancement of Learning,* in *The Works of Francis Bacon,* ed. James
Spedding et al. (London, 1857–1874), 4:473. See *JMN* 4:308 and 6:220; used in "The Heart" (*EL*
2:284).

10. Dugald Stewart, as quoted in Augustus and Julius Hare, *Guesses at Truth* (London, 1827),
1:143. See *JMN* 3:265, 310, 4:292, and 6:220.

11. Cf. Psalms 34:12–14 and I Peter 3:10–11.

12. Romans 13:10.

13. Used in Sermon CLXIII and "The Uses of Natural History" (*EL* 1:22).

not feel the petty evils that make others wretched. It is the remark of an eminent foreign writer that "the sorrows of the soul the Understanding can do nothing, the Reason little, time much, resolute activity everything to heal."[14]

2. In the second place this obedience to the commandments of God is the true and only way by which the soul is introduced into a personal relation to its Maker. It does seem necessary to our peace of mind that we should feel that we as individuals have our part in the divine love, that the Spirit of the Universe is not unmindful of us.[15] But we know nothing of God by description, only by our own likeness to him.[16] We form just conceptions of him by doing his will. Obedience is the eye that sees God. By obedience, enlarged thoughts of his Providence take possession of the mind and we not only consent to but exult in submission to his ordination. There is a love and trust in God to which virtue alone can introduce us, which is capable of being, and has a thousand times been, a principle of daily life.

God was not less an infinite and omnipresent spirit to Jesus Christ than he was in the mind of the philosophers, yet by the habit of holy contemplation and of renouncing his own will to walk in the line marked out by duty or regard to God, he so far realized the idea of God as to reveal him as a person and a Friend. Is it not a truer account of God that is given us by the discourses of Jesus in St. John's Gospel than can be found among all the speculations of the sages or poets? Yet there the heart finds a being whom it can adore as well as the intellect, an object which fills and exalts its faculties. Look back to the happiest hours and best actions of your life and you shall find it was when the Unknown God was made known, when you heartily referred yourself to him, when every morning and every evening you conferred with Him upon every plan of life, and when you studied alone or in company to approve yourself to his Eye.

It is the precious distinction of our nature that we are able to make all that is seen and sensible obedient to the unseen and spiritual, to make this mortal serve the Immortal, to make this obscure insignificant child of clay, in a sphere of action so little as each of us occupies, yet govern every step and every word by the Will of Him who liveth forever and ever and so to unite an atom as it were to the Universe.

This feeling may seem extravagant to the unhallowed understanding; but a deeper reason, a closer observation of God's works, leads to the discovery that the Author of all has been guided by benevolence in every work of his hands and that in all things he is training up his intelligent offspring; that with him is no great, no small; that every act of obedience, every emotion of resignation and love in the human heart is witnessed and accepted by the Father of Spirits with more favor than whole burnt offerings and sacrifices.

Cannot we therefore, my friends, console our griefs and elevate our way of

14. Source not located; used again in Sermon CLXI.
15. Cf. Psalms 8:4 and Hebrews 2:6.
16. Cf. Genesis 1:26.

living by this sublime worship? Cannot we live unto God?[17] Cannot we introduce some portion of this heavenly rule, this law of angels, into the abodes of
the sons of men? This was the grace and truth which Jesus brought from God.
As far as we receive it we are his disciples. When it enters freely and fully into
our souls we cannot sin and we cannot suffer. And so we shall have entered into
heaven.

17. Cf. Luke 20:38.

CLIV

For this commandment which I command thee this day, it is not hidden from thee, neither is it far off—but the word is very nigh thee in thy mouth and in thy heart that thou mayest do it.

DEUTERONOMY 30:11, 14

He that keepeth the commandment keepeth his soul.

PROVERBS 19:16

Great peace have they that love thy law and nothing shall offend them.

PSALMS 119:165

In these simple yet venerable sentiments which abound in the old and in the new Testament lies the value of the Scriptures. We hear with approbation from the depths of antiquity, from the fathers of the ancient world, these attestations of a law which is sacred to us and true to the latest generation. Heaven and earth pass away but one jot or one tittle of the divine law in the human heart shall not be made vain.[1] This law is the feeling of duty.

The most remarkable property of our human nature is the feeling of duty. It pervades us all as one man. It is in every one of us, however you have been bred, whatever is your lot. It pervades all men. There never was a man of sane mind

---

Manuscript dated May 6, 1832. Preached seven times: May 6, 1832, at the Second Church, Boston; January 5, 1834, at the Friend Street Chapel; January 26 in New Bedford; October 16, 1836, in East Lexington; March 25, 1838, again at East Lexington; April 8 in New York; and August 12 in Watertown. For the last three deliveries it was coupled with Sermon LXXXVII, and each time one or the other sermon (the Preaching Record is unclear) was enlarged with additions from the lecture "Religion."

1. Matthew 5:18.

who did not know the distinction of right and wrong. There never was a man who found pleasure in whispering to himself that he was cruel, or base, or lewd, or dishonest. There never was a man who did not feel that he owed obedience to this law of duty. There never was a time when this law did not exist. Before the mountains were brought forth, it was; when the mountains are worn down, it shall remain. Wheresoever there is intelligence there it must live.

It is universal and it is immutable. It is subject to no birth or death or change. And herein is it to man the proper foundation of all repose of mind.

1. And this is the first point to which I would ask attention, that it is the rest and centre of the soul. We see around us a continual change of outward things. The eye is giddy almost with the unceasing sight of revolution in nature and in man. Not less rapid and unceasing is the change in the thoughts and characters of men. One age pursues one folly and the next age pursues another and the third age laughs at both and has follies of its own. And so every individual man may remember things which he chased with the devotion of a child, which have long lost all interest to him and he wonders how he ever thought them important. We so often alter our purposes, and things look so different to us at different times, that we should soon come to doubt if there were any such thing as truth, whether all opinions, if the whole of life and the whole of history, were not some great Vision which would depart as it came, without cause;—if all were not, as some philosophers have taught, a picture and not a reality. We should be tempted to give up acting upon any settled purpose of life and meditate upon the shifting prospect before us and be puzzled and disheartened by the din and contradictions which the world presented.

But God has provided a remedy against these treacherous doubts, a regulator in the human constitution, a provision for repose of mind and selfsubsistency in the feeling of Duty. Amidst all changes, this is the same. This was to the first age what it is to ours. Amid the changes of the individual this is fixed,—commands his youth, and his grey head. There never was an hour nor a crisis when this law did not distinctly command one course to be adopted, and assure man with an authority impossible to dispute, that, eternal advantages waited on the course of conduct it enjoined.

Observe the relation of moral truth or this law of duty to those questions of religious opinion which have turned the world upside down. Men live and die for another man's opinion; they work with the sword and the pen; they will postpone every personal gratification, they will turn to wormwood all the kindness of life, for the establishment of some strange dogma—that the souls of infants are unregenerate, that Faith comes by Justification or Justification by Faith, some arbitrary particular assertion concerning the nature of man or the character of God, or the office of Christ; and they cannot persuade their antagonist and the dispute and the doctrine are wholly forgot in the next generation. But the simple principles of right action are received by all without controversy; are understood by the most ignorant; and whatever doctrine the disputants teach must always include them. These are the first foundations of all religion, and run under all the forms in which man ever worshipped. It is strange that men do not see that there is more of God and religion in them than in doubtful and obscure questions of faith though they should be discussed and cleared up by the tongues of angels.[2] "I am wiser than the ancients," saith David, "because I keep thy law;"[3] and the most ignorant and humble disciple who implicitly follows the line of duty is wiser than all the doctors of Westminster or Rome or Geneva.

Yes, here is the true centre of the soul in this immoveable principle. This allays all perturbations of mind, all doubts. This is a rock foundation which gives steadiness and everlasting peace to him who rests upon it.

2. The feeling of Duty is not only the principle of equipoise and stability in the soul, it is also its solace. Look around you, brethren, at all those whom the misfortunes that fly so thick in life have wounded. If the houses of our friends were unroofed, we should find many tragedies as full of bitterness in the domestic history of those we meet every day, as any that history records or fiction paints. We should find the fair hopes of parents destroyed. We should find the brilliant expectations of young persons suddenly and strangely changed; the flush of youth is gone, the joyfulness of its behaviour exchanged for the negligent manners of hard life, limited opportunities and without conversation. There is the fair bride who departed from her father's house a vision of beauty now changed and reserved, with little to remind you of an hour so hopeful, much altered now to endless cares, sad with misfortunes, afflicted by unkindness, bereaved, widowed, childless.

We should find friends separated, and those who thought labor sweet when it was shared with a friend, toiling alone. There are many whom unforeseen misfortunes or the imprudence of others or some apparent unsuitableness to the wishes and characters of other people seem to threaten with poverty, and their dependent family instead of being a source of happiness becomes a source of unhappiness.

We should find the ravages which sickness had made; a soul of fire imprisoned in a bilious or nervous frame, a countenance that seems to say—When will it end?

Not by death. O do not mourn for the cheek that is pale, for the earthly hopes that are disappointed by Death. Think on the thousand sufferings that are saved: Say rather, Blessed are they who have passed the trial and are gone into God, who are removed forever from worldly pollution, from bad advice, from vicious example, from fatal mistakes, from momentary crimes, and long contrition; do not mourn for the saved, for the redeemed, for the angels. But I will tell you for whom you shall mourn. There are deeper miseries than these. There are those from whom these precious friends are taken. They who are too solitary or too old to find new friends in their place. There are those whom the crimes of

2. Cf. I Corinthians 13:1.
3. Cf. Psalms 119:100.

others have darkened and dishonored. There are those who wear out the years of middle life in whom you recognize no vestige of their former self. They hardly can themselves.

One adequate consolation remains to these infirmities and disasters: the sincere veneration and faithful practice of duty. He that sets up this principle in his soul hath a burning and shining light.[4] He that serves this law, not only bears his troubles better, but removes his troubles. He not only removes his troubles, but he casts the responsibility of his condition off from himself upon the Divine Providence, and makes God accountable, so to speak, for the events of his life. He casts himself with a generous trust upon the Omnipotence of God and it never shall be wanting to him.

Out of this fidelity, out of this homage to Duty, spring to him a thousand advantages. A sweetness flows from it back into his heart that flavors all the waters of life. No man is good alone. As the communion with God gave a light to the face of Moses which caused his face to shine upon the beholder,[5] so will a faithful doer of duty amidst the most unpleasing works have a serenity of countenance and of temper that will make way for him wherever he goes into the heart of those he converses with. He will impress them with reverence. They will hide their vices from him. They will bring out from the soul their inmost thoughts to meet a spirit so pure and happy. And the exhibition of pure thoughts and actions is soothing and invigorating again to him and makes his labor light. It scatters flowers in his path. And the world in which he lives is far different from the world in which the cold, the sensual, the proud man lives, even though they inhabit the same house or sit at the same board.

Every being is contented whilst it moves in its appointed place and exerts the faculties which God entrusted to it. And Duty is the *place* of the soul and a sufficient resource in the worst calamities.

3. And this leads me to say, in the third place, that this royal law, this devout reverence of Duty, is not only a rest and a solace, but is also a principle of improvement. He who walks in the way of duty walks in a path that ever widens and never ends. It begins for each man in few and small things. It concerns itself at first only with his relations to those who are next to him. As he advances in life, it widens this circle around him, and extends its law as far as his relations extend, to all spirits with whom he has to do. But its growth is not only by multiplication of its objects, and the enlargement of its sphere. Far otherwise. A king is not better than a master of a family because his acts affect more persons. No, the improvement is in the fidelity of its observance, not the extent of its application. Man, finite, partial, ambitious man, cannot too often consider that his duties begin at home,[6] that he is a poor patriot who is a negligent father, that an unfaithful friend is not to be praised for his philanthropy, nor the un-

4. John 5:35.
5. Exodus 34:35.
6. Cf. "Charity begins at home, but should not end there." Thomas Fuller, *Gnomologia*, no. 1085; also in John Ray, *A Compleat Collection of English Proverbs* (London, 1737), 86.

grateful son to say in his defence that he has visited the prison and relieved the poor. For when was public virtue found where private was not? Can he love the whole who loves no part? He be a nation's friend who is in truth the friend of no man there? Certainly the place where each of us can accomplish the most good or evil is our own house and among our kindred. And in proportion to their nearness to you and dependence upon you does your duty bind you to be the benefactor of your fellowmen. No measure of a man's merit is so unerring as the estimation in which his family hold him.

It begins there but there it does not stop. In its nature it is diffusive. It visits with good will and then with benefits its neighbors, its country, and the whole world.

But as these demands of duty are complied with the soul is rewarded by a better knowledge. It serves God with its eyes open, and sees the good of serving him. The difficulties of virtue disappear. He that goeth forth and weepeth bearing precious seed shall doubtless come again with rejoicing bringing his sheaves with him.[7] There is no pleasure in the Universe comparable, we may boldly say, to the consciousness of improvement in virtue. Well may there be joy in heaven over the repenting sinner;[8] he feels the fulness of that joy in his own mind. Ask him who has risen superior to a gross temptation,—who has mastered himself and persisted, and won the victory, for what he will compound with his enemy and restore his conquest and come again into captivity to his evil passion? Not any pleasures, not any possessions can be any bribe. He will tell you, the simple feeling of superiority to that temptation is the sweetest pleasure he has ever known, and has more instructed him in the nature of heaven than all the Scriptures.

He that steadily aims to do his duty constantly gains on himself. There is no truer word than that of Solomon: 'The commandment is a lamp, the law is a light.'[9] It ever shows a more and more perfect way. And thus by its permanence and at the same time by its progress, it declares to us its divine nature and the immortality of that soul of which it is the law.

Does not the existence of this principle in the breasts of all who were ever born, this representative of sovereign power enlightening and directing every man who cometh into the world,[10] speak plainer than any words, and than all other works, the truth that God is and that he is a rewarder of them that seek him?[11] See what this law of Duty is. It amounts in every instance to forbidding the doing of harm and enjoining the doing of good. To serve it, is really to serve all beings that exist. Can such a law exist without meaning, or does it not force you to believe,—though you know not why—in a beneficent, wise, adorable Author, giver of the law and former of your nature?

7. Psalms 126:6.
8. Luke 15:7.
9. Proverbs 6:23.
10. John 1:9.
11. Hebrews 11:6.

And if the law is in our breasts, is it not to be obeyed? My friends, if it is the source of all repose of mind, of consolation, and of improvement, let us keep it. Here is something apart from all controversy and above it.

And how is it to be kept? Ask yourself and wait. It is not in heaven that thou shouldst say, who shall go up to heaven and fetch it to us that we may hear it and do it, nor over the sea, but in thy mouth and in thy heart that thou mayest do it. To do your duty is a plain commandment and every day will make it known to those who really would know it.[12]

My friends, much of life is dark and painful. Much of doubt and uncertainty is in every general course of action, in every public enterprize. Over all the future God has drawn an impenetrable veil. But one thing we see plain and clear, that humility, and love, and truth, and temperance, are always beautiful; that the sunshine of God's favor and of human respect never sets on them, that we can and ought to discharge those obligations which God has imposed on each of us. These things let us perform. However painful it may be at the time, to do the bidding of conscience, we know well that when it is done it will applaud us, it will comfort, it will strengthen us, it will have helped us forward in our everlasting progress.

12. Deuteronomy 30:11–14.

CLV

What shall a man give in exchange for his soul?

MARK 8:37

No one can be much conversant with the moral writings of the present day without observing the very different light in which man is regarded from that in which the teachers of the gospel have been accustomed to hold him. Human nature is now spoken of with tenderness, and respect, and admiration. It was for ages treated in sermons and ethical books as only worthy of pity or execration. It was ashamed of itself. And even at this day a great deal of the theology of the time holds the same language, accounting it a sin to speak kindly of so sinful a being, as if it bred self sufficiency and sloth.

My friends, God did not give us this wonderfully endowed nature for us to be ashamed of it. I thankfully accept the wondrous gift of being at my maker's hand. I am not going to confound my sins with my nature as God made it, and because I repent of them, lampoon my constitution. I think well of mankind. I think reverently of their nature. I hope highly concerning their destiny. I think he who despises a man knows not what he despises. I must think he is a stranger to himself. He has not meditated on that unfathomable mystery which every man's own self is; he has never estimated its vast resources, its capacity of good, its boundless meaning, or he would not have applied to it such false and impertinent sentiments.

I know that they who have used or who use this language employ self in a different sense and mean only to condemn man as he is, not as he ought to be. But that is the error which should be corrected, the habitual view of man in this partial and injurious aspect, ungrateful to God and repressing every good hope of the soul. No man should permit himself to be ignorant of that precious treasure which is committed to him in an earthen vessel.[1] No man should think of his being with levity,—but rather with awe. By much reflexion he will come to understand the sentiment which filled the mind of Jesus, 'What would it

---

Manuscript dated May 13, 1832. Preached eight times: May 13, 1832, at the Second Church, Boston; November 10, 1833, in New Bedford; April 6, 1834, at the Hollis Street Church; March 1, 1835, at the Second Church, Waltham; April 5 in Plymouth; May 31 in Groton; January 24, 1836, in East Lexington; and February 4, 1838, in Concord. A list of hymns headed "N.Y" on page 1 of the manuscript may imply an otherwise unrecorded ninth delivery in New York.

1. II Corinthians 4:7.

profit a man to gain the whole world and lose his own soul? or what shall a man give in exchange for his soul.'

And I design in the present discourse to present the dignity of the human soul among the works of God, under three views which probably some time present themselves to every mind.

1. To him who seeks the truth, the more he thinks, the more strange does nature appear, until soon he is lost in astonishment. A single thought is a country wide enough for an active mind.[2] I throw myself in mere amazement upon the thought of God, which I seem to see realized in the Universe, and I find no end to the contemplation. That is *one thought,* only one state of the human mind. But what is, (truly considered,) the measure of self, the possessor of all these thoughts? Add up all that is contained in the depths of one man's consciousness. Let me ask of each of you, my friends, of each of you the effort of thought to consider one moment the whole that is contained in the being you call yourself. Is it not all being? Is it not,—not only all that you have,—but all that you know; all that you love, and all that you imagine? What were God's blessed creation to you if it existed and grew far from you, separate? It might exist and shine to all eternity, unknown. You should be one being, that another; but now has he brought and set it within your consciousness; somehow by his almighty power, he has extended the limits of your mind around the earth and the heavens, around the sun and the moon and the stars and the formless space. There they are in your mind, or how could you know them?

You are conscious of all these things, are you not? Well then, in your conscious self are contained the Heaven, in you are the objects of love and of desire, the images of your friends, the society of the living, the remembrance of the dead, the sublime motives of action to the future, and more than all, God dwells in you—the Father with the child.[3] The single fact that the mind is capable of forming and cannot help forming an idea of one who made it, yet is distinct from it; and, that it is wholly bound to love and serve the wisest and best of all beings,—the Creator of this glorious nature, the Supreme Good, God—seems to ennoble the whole work. And ever and forevermore as a man's knowledge is increasing, and his motives of action are purified, this consciousness enlarges and embraces more facts, more truths, more regions of nature within its ample horizon.

This is a man—the image of God.[4] And is this stupendous work of the divine wisdom to be trodden in the dust, and spit upon, and called reprobate and accursed? Say rather with David, I am fearfully and wonderfully made and that my soul knoweth right well.[5]

But will any say, 'Such an immense view of human consciousness though it

2. *JMN* 4:14.
3. Cf. John 14:10-13.
4. Cf. Genesis 1:26.
5. Psalms 139:14.

may be metaphysically true yet is not capable of being familiarized and acted upon. It bewilders me when I apply it to particulars.' Be it so. I only offer it by way of suggesting to our meditation that central mystery of our being which so many men live and die without considering. It seems ungrateful—unworthy— to be a part of God—to be possessed of an infinite nature—to be a perceiving mind—and never to convert these divine faculties to any other purpose than of feeding and entertaining the body. Never to reflect—never to become aware of the astounding wonder of simple being as a man among men.

But it is not necessary to insist upon this view.

2. In the next place, in a less comprehensive and more common view of human nature, man is too noble a being to be slightly esteemed. To drop this view of his all-embracing consciousness, and consider him as commonly he accounts himself, as one among many creatures—God hath put all things under his feet.[6] He is the image of God in the lower world. What were the world without man? He is the head and termination of the visible scale of nature. All below seem to point at him, to tend towards him, each from a less perfect to a more perfect nature, and his existence binds all together. He is the eye and intelligence to which their forms and order are suited. He is the interpreter of nature and the priest of the world. The incense and praise which other beings offer up in dumb show, man makes vocal and plain by seeing their excellence and understanding their use. They are an alphabet out of which he forms language. The shell which the sea casts up on the beach, cannot admire its form or the splendor of its colors. Man can.[7] And why was the cup of the lily so exquisitely carved, and the petals of the tulip so richly dyed? Why all this divine *taste* (let me so speak) displayed in the architecture and the decoration of the world? Was it for the eye of horses, and eagles and bats, or for the discerning, measuring, educated eye of man?

Moreover it is that which alone resides in man, it is *moral nature*, which affords the key by which the works of nature are to be read. They seem all to be hieroglyphicks containing a meaning which only that can decipher. There is no form in nature but seems to be the expression of something in mind.

Thus all the beasts appear to be expressions of particular qualities, good or bad, which are attributes of man, and so have always been used from the beginning until now as a fable to instruct man in a pointed manner. The ant, the bee, the dog, the fox, the swine, as they meet the eye of man wherever he goes forth to his labor, are mute instructors in his own duties—pictures in which he sees the good and evil of his own life.[8]

Judge how capable man is of mastering all this knowledge, of commanding

6. Psalms 8:6.

7. On May 3 and May 11, 1832, Emerson commented on the shells collected by his brother Charles (*JMN* 4:13–14).

8. The paragraph derives from a journal entry for April 2, 1832 (*JMN* 4:9), and is in turn developed in "English Literature: Introductory" (*EL* 1:220–21) and in the "Language" chapter of *Nature* (*CW* 1:18).

nature through observing its laws, by seeing what he hath already done. Men go to and fro and knowledge is increased.[9] The animal, the vegetable, the mineral kingdoms are searched and put under contribution for the convenience and luxury of man. And they are explored not only for profit but for the delight which the knowledge gives. The electric fire is tortured to discover its birth-place and cause, the magnet is incessantly importuned to reveal its laws, every salt, every earth is weighed and analyzed. The bird on its bough no longer sits unnoticed, nor the insect under a leaf. The small violet in the grass is not now neglected. What is too far for the eye to see the telescope seeth, and the micro-scope what is too small.

> "'Let us make man.'—With beauty clad,
> And health in every vein,
> And Reason throned upon his brow,
> Stept forth immortal Man."[10]

But why speak of the triumphs of science? Do they not sometimes seem nothing and less than nothing when we see with how much misery and vice they coexist? Undoubtedly there have been great men both heroes and sages; but the world is full of men who are neither very good nor very wise. Is there not more to shame us in the view of profligacy, of selfishness, of stupidity, than to encour-age and delight us in the view of his merits?

I asked just now whether a creature so highly endowed was to be spit upon and called reprobate and accursed. But it is a question of much more interest and cogency whether such a being will make himself reprobate and accursed, whether he who concentrates in himself, by God's mercy, all the riches of heaven and earth shall squander on low passions this divine inheritance and do what he can to unman, to uncreate himself.

3. But the third reason which excites unspeakable gratitude in view of the nature of man is, because whilst I see and lament all the vices of individuals, I see running through all the individuals and under the vices of each individual a common nature which is pure and divine. Vices, follies, are superficial, pecu-liar, personal—the permanent general nature of man is upright.

When our Saviour speaks of the repenting prodigal, he says, *And when he came to himself.*[11] To come to himself, then, is not to come to vices but to come to truth and goodness. Himself, the inmost self, is a pure nature in every man. So when we say, 'Know thyself,' 'Reverence thyself,' 'Be true to thyself,'[12] we do not surely mean—study trifles, be conceited, follow your whims, but we mean know, love, and obey virtue.

9. Daniel 12:4.
10. These lines have not been identified and may be Emerson's own.
11. Luke 15:17.
12. See Sermon CXLIX, n. 12, as well as *Sermons* 1:226, n. 2, and 2:42, n. 4. Used also in Sermon CLXV.

In every individual a large portion of the thoughts which engage his attention seem to reside in the surface of his mind and never enter the interior of the man. These superficial thoughts are those which form the subject of common conversation. Compliments, the news, the common places respecting the market, the weather, and the neighbors are of this sort; he is conscious of no effort in this conversation—he could talk about them half asleep. To be always engaged in them is as bad a discipline for the mind as those trades are for the frame which occupy the fingers, instead of work that exercises the whole body.

Present to him a higher topic, a measure affecting the commercial relations of large bodies of men—political liberty,—the welfare of thousands and millions, the diffusion of knowledge, the interests of a science—these topics strike deeper and in discussing them he is conscious of calling more of himself into action.

But a man's thoughts upon a right, a duty, an affection, a moral principle, when he rouses himself (as most men do seldom and reluctantly) to reflexion,— go deepest of all. They search his whole nature and come from his inmost self. He is conscious of having really thought and acted. These thoughts stir the great deep within him, and it is only when he has occupied his mind upon such subjects that he becomes aware of the grandeur of his nature, and conscious of the immortality of the soul.

Moreover those thoughts which are superficial are local and personal; would be unsuitable to any other time or place. Those which move the man from the bottom of his soul are equally interesting to all men. Carry the gossip of your street to Rome or Japan and it would be unintelligible. But your conclusions respecting right and wrong, the laws of the mind, the end of man, which command your own interest at all times have an equal interest for all men that ever were on earth. Moses and Socrates and Confucius and Fenelon think the same thing. Justice, love, purity, truth are intelligible to all men, and have a friend in the bottom of the heart of every man. Thus is the inmost self the universal nature of man. Thus is there within all a man's errors and all his peculiarities, a divine principle.

(The superficialities—the littlenesses and the vices of each individual—are like minerals or plants found only in one or a few places. Principles are like the granite foundation of the soil which rises highest in Alpine peaks and is found under all other strata at the bottom of mines, or like the atmosphere which envelopes all or the electricity which is ever present throughout nature.)

It is this inmost self, this common human nature where these principles have their seat, which commands my reverence. I cannot chuse but honour it. It seems to me God in man. I think that it is not possible that too much study and respect should be bestowed on this nature which is in every son and daughter of Adam, that no unclean thing may be suffered to enter and defile this holy of holies—this place of God in every human mind.

Therefore, brethren, we preach the worth of the soul, its infinitude, its capacity of knowledge and virtue—not surely to excite and gratify a wretched vanity by an ostentatious exhibition of our treasure, but for the practical effect which such contemplations can hardly fail to produce. The survey of what we have received ought to inspire the most solemn feeling of gratitude and of responsibleness. Open your eyes, my friend, to the wonders of your constitution that you may never despond of a being so gloriously endowed nor believe that such a work can be forgotten or forsaken. Know yourself, moreover, that you may see what you are capable of doing and therefore what you owe to God. Finally you cannot think too highly of your nature in order that you may know what unspeakable mischief you do when you admit sin into the soul. Compared with this there is no real evil. Poverty, sickness, mutilation, the loss of friends are not evils inasmuch as they do not hurt this inmost self. The loss of an eye or a hand, deafness, palsy, or the rottenness of the lungs, may be well endured if there is inward health. But crime is calamity which strikes at that heart and soul. A crime kills the life of your life; it lays waste the inner world—it tends to separate you from God and make your return difficult, separates you from the sources of thought and freedom and enslaves you to the outward and perishing and contemptible. What good will it do you? It will give you some single, short, shameful gratification but it will hurt yourself. It will please the body or the superficial thoughts; it will shame and hurt the glorious inhabitant. Above all remember that the outward perishes, the inner is renewed day by day.[13] Is it the good man or the evil man that has the strong conviction of his own immortality? Is it in our good or in our evil hours? It is by thought and virtue only that we are capable of life when these members return to dust. Is it wise then as we look into the infinite future that opens before us to make our reason and our virtue less? Will our prosperity make us richer, will the power we possessed or the good opinion of the whole world make us better beyond the gates of death? What will it profit a man if he shall gain the whole world and lose his own soul? Or what shall a man give in exchange for his soul?

13. II Corinthians 4:16.

CLVI

Charity envieth not.

I CORINTHIANS 13:4

Charity in the enlarged sense given it by St. Paul comprehends the Christian character. The Christian heart envieth not. St. Paul and the sacred writers in general frequently admonish men of the guilt of envy, and denounce against it the judgments of God. It is set down among the foremost sins and threatened with the sorest condemnation.

Yet it sounds to some as if it were only written in books. Envy—men say—Who envies? and will almost deny the existence of such an old world vice.

But it is not that it is set down in the Bible that it commands our attention, any more than the tithe or the phylactery of the Pharisee,[1] but this evil is still alive; this snake has bitten us; the disease creeps in our vitals.

In the sense in which envy is often used, that of covetousness—wishing we could appropriate to ourselves the advantages of other people—stealing in thought—I do not think it very common. The advanced state of civilization and the consequent sureness of the laws of property make it fruitless and therefore rare to entertain such wishes with respect to outward wealth; and the impossibility of acquiring another's virtues by wishing keeps men commonly from such folly.

But if envy be the wishing to annihilate advantages in which we had no share; wishing that the success which has befallen a neighbor had not befallen him; wishing that he may come to harm;—a guilty joy in the disaster that befals him;—if that be envy which looks askance at the elegant manners, the rising reputation, the prosperous family, the advantageous connexions of an equal, and strikes us with coldness at hearing too much praise of him—in short if envy be the hatred of superiority—then, I had almost said, there is none without it. It is too conspicuous every where.

There is a constant array of classes of society, of parties in the state and of individuals against each other founded on this unhappy principle. Who can see without pain how constant and active a jealousy exists against the rich, the well

---

Manuscript dated May 20, 1832. Preached four times: May 20, 1832, at the Second Church, Boston; May 27 at the Twelfth Church, Boston; April 10, 1836, in East Lexington; and March 19, 1837, at the First Church, Waltham. The source of the sermon is a journal entry for May 18, 1832 (*JMN* 4:19).

1. Matthew 23:5.

born, the eminent, against them who have wrought out their success by the sweat of their face and the courage of their heart;[2] against men in office by men out of office; against those who know much by those who know little; against the happily connected by those who are alone?

Indeed if one set out to notice all the instances of this bad affection that take place around him it will make his heart sick at the swelling catalogue.

If you talk with any man upon the existing institutions in society, it is likely you will not run over many topics before you come to something which revolts him; he does not like that man or that set of men or that law, or that college, or that corporation. Why? for no reason that can at all justify his rooted hostility, but a general impression that they know more or have power or intercourse and enjoyments above his own. And that seems to him reason enough.

(One man is vexed at a High School and another would write down the dead languages and a third is afraid of the manufacturers.)

At this moment, a new order of fanatics in the kingdom of France propose under the name of religion and philanthropy to destroy the machinery used in the arts, to take away the property from the hands that hold it and distribute it anew according to their own better judgment.[3]

In our own country who can fail to see and regret the spread of this malevolent feeling. It puts on the cloak of patriotism and stalks through the land. If any interest prospers, it is called a favoured interest, and denounced. If any institution, even of learning or of charity, is well conducted and successful, somewhere a voice of accusation and menace is raised against it. If any district of the country thrives more than its neighbor, that is reason enough why its neighbors should combine against it. If any man hath a bright and spotless name, that is reason enough why the idle and selfish should hoot at it as dogs bark at the moon. And the amount of it is that we should regard with a settled aversion every person who owns any advantage which we have not. They have no objection to any advantage which they possess, oh no; none more prompt to defend it. Dr. Johnson said, "Sir, your levellers wish to level *down* as far as themselves, but they cannot bear levelling *up* to themselves."[4] What right has this man, it says, to be more courted or better served than I? I don't like it that he should be drawn in his carriage whilst I walk afoot. I don't like to have his opinion quoted when mine is not. I don't like to have him elected to offices. I am tired, like the Athenian, of hearing Aristides called the Just.[5]

2. Genesis 3:19; cf. *JMN* 4:10.

3. Emerson alludes to unrest in Lyons, where in November and December of 1831, some 550 people died in the course of violent protests by skilled silk weavers. Long threatened by preindustrial pressures, such as regulation by an increasingly powerful merchant class, artisans found themselves reduced from elite to wage laborer status. Urban artisans throughout France were frustrated by the lack of change following the Revolution of 1830, in which Charles X was supplanted by Louis Philippe.

4. James Boswell, *Life of Johnson,* ed. George Birkbeck Hill and L. F. Powell (Oxford, 1934), 1:448.

5. Plutarch, "The Life of Aristides," in *The Lives,* ed. John and William Langhorne (New York, 1822), 3:158; see *L* 1:120.

This is envy; this is the evil eye; this is that which Solomon calls 'rottenness of the bones.'[6] This is that whose fruit, St. James saith, is 'confusion and every evil work.'[7] This is that curse from which Jesus came to redeem you. He taught that the old commandments were to be kept in the *spirit* not in the *letter* merely.[8] He taught that to indulge licentious *desire,* was to commit adultery. He taught that to *covet* thy neighbor's good was to *steal;* that to *hate* thy neighbor was to kill.[9]

He came to teach love, to abase self, to make each seek with hearty good will the advancement of the other. In the morality of the gospel therefore envy is spiritual robbery. It is murder. It is the mother of quarrels and long spite and bloody revenge. Carry it out to its full length—it would destroy society, for where would it stop? When would it come to the end of every superior gift which art or nature had given until it had made an end of art and nature? In that disastrous period when this principle usurped the sceptre of power in the French Revolution, the ferocious mob conceived such a hatred of the superiority of the order of nobility that they abolished the distinction of rank and confiscated their estates; but they presently found that the dignified manners of the peers remained though the titles were gone, and to prevent being put out of countenance by their superior elegance of deportment they determined to cut off all their heads.

And such must be the operation of this principle wherever it rules. It is a war upon all merit. It would unmake this fair fabric of civilization. It would demolish all the architecture and besmear all elegance; it would burn, it would strip, it would defile, it would brutify, it would pluck up man's superiority to some purpose and send him back again to the woods and the beasts.

This feeling of malevolence in great, avowed, extravagant indulgence is very rare or the world would be uninhabitable; but the least degrees of it, good men think they may indulge—a mere reserve and coldness at a rival's praise—or, what seems blameless, a regret at the prosperity of the undeserving,—are common. Upon the whole subject I have two general remarks to make.

  1. That this feeling is founded in error; that it argues utter ignorance of the true sources of human happiness in the desire of an impossible thing, to draw another's happiness to itself.

It was said by a great moral poet that "he who hath contempt for any living thing hath faculties which he hath never used";[10] it may with equal justice be said, "he that hath envy." He has not yet found out the everlasting truth that the only good that any man can obtain he must get by the cultivation of himself. There is a time when every reflecting man becomes aware of this truth, that he must take himself for better for worse as his portion, that though the wide

  6. Proverbs 14:30.
  7. James 3:16.
  8. Cf. Romans 2:29 and II Corinthians 3:6.
  9. In the Sermon on the Mount, Matthew 5, especially verses 21-22 and 27-28. Emerson makes a similar observation in Sermon CXXXIII (*Sermons* 3:255).
  10. The quotation occurs, without attribution, in *JMN* 3:167. See also Sermon LXXXII, n. 6 (*Sermons* 2:225).

creation is overflowing with good, no particle can he add to himself but through his toil bestowed on that spot,[11] and that the law given at the gates of Eden is true forever: 'In the sweat of *thy* face shall thou eat bread all the days of thy life.'[12] It is not what is given to you, much less what is taken from others, that can make you wise or happy,—but it is the state of your own mind, the knowledge, the self command, the power and disposition to help others that reside there that make your well being.

(It is the temper you have cultivated in yourself that enables you to draw satisfaction or pain from the events of life and the characters of others.)

Nor can the prosperity of a wicked man ever make him the proper subject of a good man's envy but only the more of his pity.

2. The hatred of any appearance of superiority is not only founded in a misapprehension of the true seat of happiness but it is itself a perpetual torment. It lives on its own sufferings. It eats mortifications. It is a lively image of hell. It shuts you out of the Paradise of God, makes you incapable of receiving pleasure from all the glorious and beautiful objects with which God surrounded you. It shuts you out of the Paradise of human perfections. How could God have made more ample provision for your gratification? All the noble characters, the informed minds, the eloquent orators, the beautiful persons, the ingenious artists, the delightful companions with whom the Creator hath adorned and blessed the world are occasions of chagrin to your depraved heart.

God set you in the midst of your fellows to receive and impart in equal measure, as the heart perpetually receives and perpetually returns the blood to the system. This disposition would see nothing and believe nothing better than itself. It would love nothing. It only loves its little self. Like that incarnation of Selfishness with which it pleased God to visit mankind in the person of Napoleon, it would have every object it sees a mere mirror to bring back its own wretched image. It would read nothing on every house top, on every arch, and on the sky if it could but the syllables of its own name. And so all prosperity turns sour at its touch. It pines and gnaws itself. It is a sad uncomfortable inmate.

But if any evidence were wanting to show the guilt and folly of malevolence, let it be found in the delight with which the mind contemplates the manifestation of the opposite temper. Far from the low, stingy, venomous spirit that looks upon all that others enjoy as so much taken from itself, Christianity taught the divine secret of converting all the happiness we witness into our happiness. It teaches me to enjoy the virtue, genius, beauty, riches, health, favor, triumph of my fellows as so much kindness done to me—so much pain spared to me—so much occasion to me for gratitude.

I exhort you therefore: Cultivate, my friends, this generous good will. It is essential to your happiness and to your usefulness. Can any possession, any

11. See *JMN* 3:208. Used in "The Protest" (*EL* 3:101) and "Self-Reliance" (*CW* 2:27–28).
12. Genesis 3:19; cf. *JMN* 4:10.

talent, bestow upon a good man half the pleasure he derives from rejoicing with those who rejoice?[13] Let us be willing that other people have virtues, and bless-ings. Let us delight in them. Far be it from us to cast censure or doubt upon their deserts. A man without virtue is ever ready to suspect the purity of others, but he who is conscious of his own worth believes and reveres the worth of other men. Blessed as the life of an angel on earth is the course of that man who never forgives any sin to himself yet apologizes for every offence of another, surveys with unmixed satisfaction all men's advantages, and even out of the midst of his own defeats offers up ardent thanksgiving for other men's joy. Truly he that loveth is born of God, and dwelleth in God, and God in him.[14]

13. Romans 12:15.
14. I John 4:7, 12–13.

*God that made the world and all things therein,
seeing that he is Lord of heaven and earth,
dwelleth not in temples made with hands; neither
is worshipped with men's hands as though he
needed any thing, seeing he giveth to all life and
breath and all things. . . . Forasmuch, then, as we
are the offspring of God we ought not to think
that the Godhead is like to gold or silver or
stone graven by art and man's device. And the
times of this ignorance God overlooked but now
commandeth all men every where to repent.
Because he hath appointed a day in which he
will judge the world in righteousness by that
man whom he hath ordained, whereof he hath
given assurance unto all men in that he hath
raised him from the dead.*

ACTS 17:24–25, 29–31

The remarkable spectacle we have witnessed loses nothing of its interest from the fact that it was yesterday predicted to us in every particular. What was prediction yesterday is now fact. But Nature never disappoints us. What impresses one man as grand or beautiful makes a kindred impression upon all men. And though we see the sun every day and always walk by his direct or

---

Manuscript dated May 27, 1832; revised introduction dated November 30, 1834, at Waltham. Preached four times: May 27, 1832, at the Second Church, Boston; November 30, 1834, at the First Church, Waltham, on the occasion of the solar eclipse; September 10, 1837, in East Lexington; and November 19 in Concord. Emerson substituted a new introduction for the second delivery; since some original matter was lost in the revision, the text given here corresponds to the sermon as delivered in Waltham. Journal sources include entries for May 23 and 26, 1832 (*JMN* 4:24–27).

reflected light, though every grain of wheat we eat and every drop of blood in our arteries and every bodily function is as strictly related to that distant orb as is the act of respiration to the air, this we forget in the munificent flood of his daily light, but let a shadow creep once in an age upon his southern limb and blot by degrees the light and men are seized with an instinctive dread which all foresight does not wholly remove.

It seems as if they anticipated the fatal consequence should that shadow continue to cover his face. This life, this organization, which throughout the animal and vegetable nature of our globe beats as one heart, would freeze and stop; the rejoicing nations would be still enough and the shade that covered the earth would be the pall of death to her children. Those who have seen an eclipse are likely never quite to forget how indispensable is that luminary not to beauty but to being.

This rare and striking appearance suggests many useful reflexions. Perhaps the most obvious is a feeling of joy at the fact that it was predicted. It reminds us impressively of the powers of the human intellect. What a contrast between the littleness of the observer and the magnitude and duration of the laws he observes. Compared with the great bodies in the heavens the astronomer on the earth seems a mere eye sailing in space round the circle of its small orbit. What is he to weigh the formidable masses, to measure the secular periods, to fix the faithful laws by which they all have been governed and shall be in all past and all future time!

But a better reflexion shows us no occasion for pride. This human mind is but a derived light from the source of wisdom as yonder sun is but a spark of his enkindling. It is only the knowledge of God that unites this bright outward Creation of brute matter to the brighter inward Creation of intelligent mind. The passage which I have read from the New Testament is valuable because it serves as one out of many to show that the Scriptures claim to come from the same Being that made the heavens and the earth;[1] that the God of nature and the God of the Bible are affirmed to be the same; that the Father of Jesus Christ is the Divine Providence in whose wisdom and love all beings are embosomed.

Since this is so, since the records of the divine dealings with men claim no other origin than the author of nature, we may expect that they are to be read by the light of nature; that more knowledge of his works will enable us.

There are many considerations that associate astronomy with the history of religion. It is always at hand as the visible image of every exalted sentiment. Religion in the later ages suffering from the caprices and errors of men wanders often far from her object into strange paths and the attempt is resisted as a sort of violence which strives to reunite Religion with the love of nature. Yet the song of the morning stars was really the first hymn of praise and will be the last;[2] the face of nature, the breath of the hills, the lights of the skies, are to a simple heart the real occasions of devout feeling more than vestries and sermon hearings,

1. Revelation 14:7.
2. Cf. Job 38:7.

and are those natural checks that are ever exerting an insensible influence to hold us back from fanaticism and keep us within sight of the true God.

Then the aspects of the heaven cannot fail to affect all opinion, especially these speculations. These aspects are so prominent. In the beginning of society in mild climates of South Asia when as yet man had not built magnificent towns, Nature made the riches and the shows of men. What perfection and elegancy in them! Nothing else in nature has the grandeur and influence upon the mind. How delicately at sunset come out these sparks in the vault. The changes which touch us touch not them. From Time, which they measure, they suffer not. There is the light sphered in the same vessels which contained it (not in Archimedes' or Ptolemy's time) but when the first Syrian shepherd noted down with a savage's imagination the figures he saw nightly sketched in the sky, yes and for what inconceivable periods before the human race was. We are new comers into space. Our planet is gray and scarred with wrinkles of immense age, but its inhabitant is a novelty in the cheerful eternity, long ago as bright as now, into which we are born.

And hence it naturally happened that the heavenly bodies were the first objects of idolatry. Symbols of power and beauty, they were readily understood by the perverted to be power and intelligence themselves, and let the proverbial phrases still current in common speech attest how obstinate was the opinion that the stars exercised moral influence upon the lives of men.

If a large class of men are less sensible to impressions of beauty, still to them the heavens were at hand as illustration for all argument. What questions do they not suggest? Let me ask the younger members of this assembly, have you ever settled it in your mind and do you believe that space is really boundless? You cannot deny the fact without absurdity and in words you do admit it without hesitation, but I persist in asking, Do you believe it? Dwell a moment on that gigantic thought until you feel the difficulty of the question; until you discern that the first conception which this Science presents to man is a space upon whose area all the worlds of God are a mere dot, and the boldest imagination of man or angel can only enter upon its margin. All that exists is lost in the bosom of its great night.

Thus impressive and animating are the first aspects of the science.

But an important result of the study of astronomy has been to correct and exalt our views of God, and humble our view of ourselves.

In all ancient speculation men were accustomed of course to take man for the type of the highest beings, and suppose whatever is intelligent and good among God's creatures must resemble human nature. Even God himself, the infant religion of all nations has clothed in human form, and idolatry imputed to him the passions as well as the person of man. Astronomy corrects all these boastful dreams and demonstrates that whatever beings inhabit Saturn, Jupiter, Herschel, and Mercury, even in this little family of social worlds that journey like us around the sun, they must have an organization wholly different from man.[3]

3. Herschel, named for its discoverer, Sir William Herschel (1738–1822), astronomer to George

The human race could not breathe in the rare atmosphere of the moon; nor the human blood circulate in the climate of Uranus; nor the strength of man suffice to raise his own foot from the ground in the dense gravity of Jupiter.

Each of the eleven globes therefore that revolve round the sun must be inhabited by a race of different structure. And to suppose that the constitution of the race of yesterday that now plants the fields of this particular planet, should be the pattern for all the orders that people the huge globes in the heaven is too improbable to be entertained.

Rather believe that the benignant Power which has assigned each creature to its own element, the fish to the sea, the bird to the air, the beast to the field, has not less nicely adjusted elsewhere his creatures to their habitation and has enriched other seats of his love with other and perhaps far more excellent endowments than he has granted to mankind.

In the next place the science of astronomy has had an irresistible effect in modifying and enlarging the doctrines of theology. It is known to all to whom I speak that until a few hundred years ago it was the settled opinion of all men that the earth was stationary in space, and that the sun and stars actually moved round it every day as they appear to do to the eye. The host of heaven were esteemed so many lanthorns to illuminate and set off the residence of man. It is only since the time of Galileo and Newton it was learned that the little ball on which we live spins upon its own axis to produce this appearance, and that it is at such a dizzy distance from the stars which were supposed thus revolving for its ornament, that it is not visible from them; and not only the earth but the whole system also to which it belongs, with the great sun in the centre, are perhaps too minute for observation from those remote luminaries.

Why need I repeat to you the swelling amount of distances and magnitudes of the stars with which calculation amazes us? They go in the pages of the Almanack into every house and shop. Every mind in the civilized world has caught the general results. Every heart responds to the pious hymn:

> Yet not to earth's contracted span
> Thy goodness let me bound;
> Nor think thee Lord alone of man,
> When thousand worlds are round.[4]

When the solar system had been correctly explained to us we found ourselves journeying in a comparatively small opaque planet around a single star and quite too inconsiderable to be noticed amid the millions of burning suns which the telescope revealed. It was the effect of this new knowledge, to make an

III, was an early name for the planet Uranus, which Emerson refers to a few lines later by its present name. Emerson's speculations on the inhabitability of other planets may owe something to Bernard le Bovier de Fontenelle's *Conversations on the Plurality of Worlds* (1686), which he could have seen in the London edition of 1809 (see *JMN* 6:9, n. 13).

4. Alexander Pope, "The Universal Prayer," lines 21-24.

equal revolution in religious opinion, as in science, for it was impossible to regard the earth any longer, as the only object in the care of Providence.

It had been the belief of many generations that God from all eternity had foreseen the fall of man and had devised in his councils a method by which man might be saved.

The second being in the Universe, it was represented, undertook to save them, and in the vain imagination of man the scheme of his redemption, as it was called, occupied the attention of God and of angels as if there were nothing in being but men.[5] 'The earth,' in the strange language of an old divine, 'was the scaffold of the divine vengeance.'[6]

Now this system of theology was every way suited to the ancient system of the heavens. It could not but happen that the telescope should be fatal to both. I regard it as the irresistible effect of the Copernican astronomy to have made the theological *scheme of Redemption* absolutely incredible. The great geniuses who studied the mechanism of the heavens became unbelievers in the popular doctrine. Newton became a Unitarian.

In spite of the awful exhibition of wisdom and might disclosed to their eyes— the present God—in spite of the natural expectation which dictated the sentiment, The undevout astronomer is mad[7]—the incongruity between what they beheld and the gross creeds which were called religion and Christianity by their fellow countrymen so revolted them that the profound astronomers of France rejected the hope and consolation of man and in the face of that divine mechanism which they explored denied a cause and adopted the belief of an eternal Necessity as if that very eternal necessity were any thing else than God.

In the next place, whilst the removing this veil from the creation and enabling man from the little globule in which we are embarked to send his eye so far into the surrounding infinity has at first had the very natural effect to shake down the systems of opinion which churches and doctors had built and to cast a portion of doubt upon all, this evil was balanced by an opposite beneficial tendency. The investigations of the last two hundred years have brought to light the most wonderful proofs of design—beneficent design—operating far and near, in atoms and in systems, reaching to such prodigious extent both of time and space, and so perfectly answering their end, that the mind cannot weigh them without ever-increasing surprise and delight. One inquirer ascertains that in a course of years the earth's moon has deviated from her orbit by slow increments that begin to become sensible, and alarms men by showing the future fatal consequence to the earth of these eccentric movements. A more searching observer ascertains by observation and analysis that these irregularities must from the form and relation of the two bodies be periodical, and that when, after a long course of years, they have attained their maximum, a con-

5. If Adam and his posterity are reckoned one being, as the doctrine of original sin requires, Christ is then the "second being."

6. Attributed to Jacques Saurin (1677–1730), French Protestant preacher (see *Sermons* 1:110, n. 5).

7. Edward Young, *Night Thoughts,* "Night IX," line 769.

trary motion takes place and restores the equilibrium. It is the glory of La Grange to have demonstrated that all the irregularities which take place in our system are periodical, an error on one side being compensated by an exactly equal error on the other, and fluctuate between fixed and impassable limits, that there is no ungoverned orb, no loose pin, no lawless particle through all the heights and depths of the City of God.[8]

Cheered by these results we come to feel that planet gravitates to planet and star attracts star, each fulfilling the last mile of its orbit as surely in the round of space as the bee which launches forth for the first time from its dark cell into light, and wandering amidst flowers all day, comes back at eve with unerring wing to the hive. It is the same invisible guide that pilots the bee and pilots the planet, that established the whole and perfected the parts, that giveth to all beauty, and order, and life, and usefulness.

And I thus say, my friends, that to the human race the discoveries of astronomy have added vast meaning to the name of God. Once God was understood to be the governor of this world. Now they perceive him to be an Infinite Mind. An awful, an adorable Being, yet as affectionate in his care as he is surpassing in Wisdom.

I proceed to say that as this enlargement of our religious views—this correction of error—and this more generous consideration of God's government comes to our minds inevitably by the progress of this science, so it cannot be doubted that it was designed. Though slow, it was the sure result of the divine faculties with which man is endowed. He who made the eye and the light and clothed the globe with its transparent atmosphere did thereby teach his creature to observe the stars and write their laws. Thereby he opened the heavens to them to reform their religion and to educate the mind. By the mild, affectionate yet thrilling voice of nature he evermore leads them to a higher truth, and rewards every exertion of their faculties by more just knowledge of Himself.

And finally what is the effect upon the doctrine of the New Testament which these contemplations produce? It is not contradiction but correction. It is not denial but purification. It proves the sublime doctrine of One God whose offspring we all are and whose care we all are. On the other hand, it throws into the shade all temporary, all indifferent, all local provisions. Here is neither tithe nor priest nor Jerusalem nor Mount Gerizim.[9] Here is neither Jew nor Greek.[10] Here is no mystic sacrifice, no atoning blood.

But does it take one charm from the lowly grace of Christ? does it take away any authority from his lips? It abridges what belongs to persons, to places, and to times but it does not touch *moral* truth. We are assured in any speculation we may indulge concerning the tenants of other regions in the wide commonwealth of God, that if we could carry the New Testament to the inhabitants of other

8. Emerson comments on the work of Count Joseph Louis Lagrange (1736–1813) and Pierre Simon Marquis de Laplace (1749–1827) in "The Naturalist" (*EL* 1:72).

9. A sacred mountain first mentioned in Deuteronomy 11:29.

10. Galatians 3:28 and Colossians 3:11.

worlds we might need to leave Jewish Christianity and Roman Christianity, Paul and Apollos and Cephas and Luther and Socinus,[11] but the moral law, justice and mercy would be at home in every climate and world where life is, that we can go nowhere but wisdom will be valuable and justice venerable and humility suitable and diligence useful and truth sacred and charity divine.

The largest consideration the human mind can give to the subject, makes moral distinctions still more important, and positive distinctions less. It will not teach any expiation by Jesus; it will not teach any mysterious relations to him. It will teach great, plain, eternal truths. It will teach that he only is a mediator, as he brings us truth, and we accept it, and live by it; that he only saves us, by inducing us to save ourselves; that God now commands all men, all spirits, every where to repent, and that such principles as Jesus Christ inculcated must forevermore be the standard by which actions shall be judged.[12]

It is, brethren, a glorious confirmation that is brought to our faith, the observation that it agrees well with all the new and astonishing facts in the book of nature. It is good to perceive that the beatitudes of the sermon on the mount will be such to all intelligent creatures.[13]

The Scriptures were written by human hands. God intends by giving us access to this original writing of his hand to correct the human errors that have crept into them. Let us yield ourselves with a grateful heart to the instruction that comes from this source and not repine to find that God is a greater, wiser and more tender Parent than we were wont to worship.

We shall not less distinctly see Jesus to be the gracious instrument of his bounty to instruct men in the character of God and the true nature of spiritual good; the teacher, and, by his teaching, the redeemer of men. But we shall fulfil the intent of Jesus by rendering the praise to God. The hour will already have arrived in our hearts when means and instruments shall have done their office and when God shall be over all and through all and in all.[14]

11. Apollos, an eloquent Jewish Christian from Alexandria (Acts 18:24–19:1), and Cephas, Aramaic for "rock" and thus Jesus' name for Peter (John 1:42), were both known to Paul and are mentioned in I Corinthians. Laelius and Faustus Socinus, sixteenth-century Italian theologians, denied the divinity of Jesus. Unitarians were frequently called Socinians.

12. This is Emerson's earliest statement explicitly denying a supernatural role to Jesus. With dramatic repercussions, he went on in the Divinity School Address to define Jesus as a great moral guide and therefore one of "the true race of prophets" (CW 1:81).

13. "The Sermon on the Mount must be true throughout all the space which the eye sees & the brain imagines but St Paul's epistles, the Jewish Christianity, would be unintelligible" (JMN 4:26). For the Sermon on the Mount, see Matthew 5–7.

14. Cf. Ephesians 4:6.

And Moses said unto God, Behold when I come unto the children of Israel and shall say unto them, The God of your fathers hath sent me unto you; and they shall say to me, what is his name? What shall I say unto them?

And God said unto Moses, I am that I am. *And he said, thus shalt thou say unto the children of Israel,* I am *hath sent me unto you.*

Exodus 3:13–14

The scriptures abound with sublime descriptions of the Eternity of God. That belief lies at the foundation of all religion. The human mind by its nature is a believer in the eternity of its author. For it is so made that it cannot get rid of the notion of infinite time. It sees its own life to be a point in that wide stretching duration before and after which must be, though our faculties are quickly lost in trying to conceive it. And it gives a sensible relief to the mind in the whirling rapidity with which change succeeds change in all the objects around us to repair to this fixed thought, this rock of ages,[1] this point of central repose.

Man sees himself one individual in a countless crowd and sees his generation to be one individual of a countless succession of generations that are gone and that are pressing after. And it would fill him with dismay if he could suppose that the destinies of all are ruled by a succession of governors, if there was succession in heaven as well as in earth, if the laws of nature were new moulded, if the counsels of divine power were subject to change. No; he gets the belief of the divine Unity by seeing the record of one law, one Nature, one truth, one goodness, subsisting from age to age at the centre of all the moving world. The *heart* remains though the members alter.

Manuscript dated June 10, 1832, at Chardon Street. Preached twice: June 10, 1832, at the Second Church, Boston, and February 25, 1838, in East Lexington. Emerson's critique of a merely "historical religion" in the present sermon anticipates his argument in the Divinity School Address of 1838.

1. This phrase, which is not biblical, appears to have originated as the title of a hymn by Augustus Montague Toplady (1740–1778).

But this faith in the doctrine of the eternity of God is not a mere intellection. I do not think it is a doctrine of the head alone. It is a moral doctrine. It is a practical doctrine, and until it becomes such it is inert; it may amuse or amaze the understanding but it will do no good. It was revealed to us to exercise a salutary influence upon us. It was revealed to correct certain great errors into which man is prone to fall. And it is in this light, brethren, that I desire to present it to you.

It is a vulgar error and a great one that men group themselves together in their religious views. They think of God as speaking to the human race or to the Jewish people or to the Christian church and not as speaking to each individual man. And so the popular religious views represent Adam in terms as the 'federal head' of his race and that when he fell all his posterity sinned, and all rose in the second Adam. They literally interpret the words of St Paul: As in Adam all die, so in Christ all are made alive.[2]

Brethren, is it not so with us? Is there not an unconsidered impression remaining on our minds that our religion consists in great part in what was said and done to and by Abraham and Moses and David, consists a good deal in our belief of ancient facts on which the moss of centuries has gathered?

Is it not true that we are looking upon ourselves as late comers into a world once honored by divine dispensations whose freshness is now past away?

Men make their religion a historical religion; they do not transfer it from their bibles to their own life; they see God in Judea and Egypt, in Moses and in Jesus, but not around them and within them; they see his footsteps in the ancient world but they do not see him now holding them up in life.

We want a living religion. As the faith was alive in the breast of Abraham and of Paul so I would have it in mine. I want a religion not recorded in a book but flowing from all things, not laid up in my memory but controlling my life. We want a religion that is vital through all its institutions and forms. We want a religion that will go as far as our knowledge, enjoyment, action and temptation go and present the image of God to us every where.—It is to this want of the heart that the eternity of God is preached. It is to this error of searching traces of the divine mind in other ages and other worlds that God saith, I am thy God.[3] That is eternal which is not liable to injury from time or external causes. And every man in his nature carries a conviction more or less dim of such a nature from which his own proceeds.

What brings us together in this house from Sunday to Sunday? Not a conspiracy against law and order: not a concert of hostile measures against other men: not a convention of political agents to raise or to supplant a party, not a meeting to arrange speculations in trade, not the patrons of a voyage of discovery nor the learned met for a lecture of science nor even the benevolent for the care of a hospital: No; we have assembled for nothing that ever the eye saw or the ear

2. I Corinthians 15:22.
3. Cf. Psalms 50:7; the formula "I am the Lord your God" occurs throughout the Old Testament.

heard.[4] We come to think of our origin; to trace the stream of life and thought to its unseen source; to ask whence we came and *who* is that whence; to contemplate a sublime thought, the Idea of God; to worship it, and to open our minds to receive the practical influences of this grand thought so that it shall command our feet, our hands, and our lips. This thought more or less distinctly appears in every human breast. The human mind is so framed that when it is in healthful action the thought of God appears in it as inevitably as a music box plays the tune for which it was constructed. The human soul is set to that anthem.

Christianity has made the name and character of God *in words* so familiar to us that we do not know how much is in education and how much in our constitution. For that reason I derive a satisfaction that is very dear to me in every just conception of God I find in the pagan. I love the story of the poor Indian squaw who is said to have prayed in her own language, "O thou great Everywhere heal my sick child!"[5] I delight in the story we have received from the Greeks of Bias king of Priene, of whom it is said that when his city was invaded by an enemy and the inhabitants were flying in every direction with what was most valuable of their property—they saw that Bias walked emptyhanded. He was asked why he did not also carry his goods with him? He answered, I do carry my *goods* with me. But he had nothing in his hand; he had nothing in his robe. He bore them in his breast not to be seen by the eye, inclosed in the narrow dwelling of his mind which could not be overtaken by the runners of the enemy nor stolen by their strength nor stabbed by their swords nor burned by their fagots—the goods of the Idea of God, of an incorruptible conscience before him and a clear sense of his love and protection.[6]

Whilst this idea dwells in the mind of each, do you not see that it tends ever to detach him from all others and deal with him alone? Souls are not saved in bundles. No, the world, the universe preaches to me and to every man by myself, by himself alone. Whilst I contemplate this Divine soul in me must not I look upon God?[7]

My reason and experience teach me to look upon God as not more the Father of Abraham or Isaac or Jacob than of the babe an hour old. The infinite love of our Creator contains us all. Every thing teaches us that he is no respecter of persons but has provided unlimited good for every one of his children.[8] He has so formed us that whilst we are parts of a social system we are each of us independent of all, detached in his sight from all and communicating directly with him. His life flows into each of us.

As each mind makes improvement it becomes in a degree separate from his

4. Cf. I Corinthians 2:9.

5. See *JMN* 6:178.

6. See Cicero, *Paradoxa Stoicorum*, "Paradox I," in *De Oratore*, trans. H. Rackham, 2 vols. (Cambridge, 1960), 2:261. This paragraph and the one preceding are borrowed from the "Address at the Dedication of Second Church Vestry, Feb. 28, 1830"; see p. 268 below.

7. Apparently an allusion to Exodus 3:6, as the next sentence more certainly is.

8. Acts 10:34.

brethren. An entire system of instruction has been provided by God for each one. "He who has been born," said one, "has been a first man," i.e., has passed through all the experience which Adam knew in Eden.[9]

And see how he reveals his eternity to you. Have the channels of the divine love been blocked up? Has he forgotten to be gracious?[10] Is he less present than ever before? And when the cloud shall break does the sun send forth a less cheerful beam than on the first morning when he rose in the heavens upon the eyes of Man in the garden? Is not the whole miracle of nature as glorious to our eyes as it was to the first age? is it not more impressive inasmuch as we understand it a little better? Does the strength of nature seem at all exhausted or the world exhibit any sign of decay? Is not the smallest leaf in the woods as delicately finished and the finest structure of animal life as skilfully adjusted to its objects as when God saw all things were good?[11]

Is there any remissness, any obstruction? On the contrary, God stamped his work with an impress of eternity. Has not the diligence of man discovered a thousand remedial processes on every side by which injurious tendencies are constantly counteracted? Do the faculties of man fail? Is he not armed every year with more power through accumulating knowledge? Or has reason faltered in her seat or have the social affections forsaken him or have generous sentiments disappeared from his heart? Does not virtue move the same approbation now as it did in the old times and is not cruelty or meanness as sternly condemned? Do not good actions as surely obtain their reward of inward peace and are not good ends sought by good means as sure of success? Why then do we say God created the world 6000 years ago?[12] The foundations of things stand strong.

What hinders then that you should see the beneficence of God as active in behalf of you as of the most favored of his children? Does it not cheer you to see the arms of God's benevolence now outstretched to embrace you; that the motives of grace now animate you, that the love of purity flows as purely from him into your heart, when in good seasons you have opened it, as into the newly inspired human clay?[13] There is nothing antiquated in his government. The offer of pardon and heaven is continually renewed.

Every moment the mighty creation of God reappears. It flows a new wave every moment from the abyss of his power and love. Every moment is a new world. We do not see the sun by the light which left his orb in the time of Abraham but the new light that sprang from his globe this very hour. And so we perceive truth not by what it was but what it is. Thoughts never lose their immortal youth. Moral truth does not grow old. The gospel of Jesus Christ has

---

9. Thomas Carlyle, "Signs of the Times," *The Edinburgh Review* 49 (June 1829): 458. See *JMN* 6:93; used in "Modern Aspects of Letters" (*EL* 1:384).

10. Psalms 77:9.

11. Genesis 1:31.

12. According to the calculations of James Ussher (1581–1656), Irish scholar and archbishop of Armagh, the world was created in the year 4004 B.C.

13. Cf. Genesis 2:7.

gathered no decrepitude from the weight of ages. Humility, temperance, love, faith, purity lose none of their force to please and to purify by the lapse of years. The kingdom of heaven is always new.

As his creation is renewed so should his worship be renewed continually.

It is this perpetual renewal of his work that to our reason marks the Eternity of God. Time with him is not barren duration but never-ceasing life. He breathes his life through all things as much at this hour as in all the past. We believe he is eternal; that with him is no past, and no future but a perpetual Now. He has not spent his kindness upon other generations, it is new and infinite still for us. And how do we know this?

How but by his works? By the same works that made him visible to the first men. By the world and by ourselves. In his best work, the human mind, he has left such a constitution that it obstinately demands a cause of every thing and will worship a Maker of some sort or other. We did not make ourselves[14] and therefore whatever faculties each has, whatever enjoyments, whatever relations to others, the whole amount of our being is to him the pledge of God's power. So much as I am—be it more or less—so much is God to me. I suck in that life from the source of life. Well then, just so much let my acknowledgment be. And that acknowledgment is religion. I understand religion to be an acknowledgment from the heart that our whole being is derived from God, and so is to be used according to his laws.

For this reason, that man has not made much progress which does not perceive that instead of God becoming farther off with time he is present every moment; that the arguments of his wisdom and benevolence are every moment accumulating, that all things that exist are using persuasion with the soul to obey him. Nor have we just views of God until they animate every act of our life.

Our religion ought not always to look backward but to be the worship of a God now revealed to us. The condition of men is always changing. Every man that is born is a new being in some respects different from any other. He needs a different worship; he cannot utter his feelings in the same words or forms that served the man of another education and a former age. So is each age a new one, has enlarged views of God's Providence; is born under a ripened dispensation by receiving a collected influence from all that went before. The forms and faith of other ages cannot serve it. It continually endeavors to worship more plainly, more directly, with fewer errors, with fewer mediums to offer its homage.

Finally the liveliest image of God's eternity to our apprehension is our own spiritual nature. The changes that we witness in nature, the concealed sun, the changing season, the event of death, suggest to our minds the possibility of far greater changes. Perhaps the beautiful creation we behold is to last forever. Perhaps it is not. The supposition of its being blotted out from the space where now it shines involves no contradiction. But not so with spiritual things. The

---

'14. Psalms 100:3.

goodness of Him who made them cannot change. Truth is eternal, every virtue is eternally beautiful. Moral truth does not grow old. It was the opinion of the ancient nations that it was given to some favored men to drink the waters of immortality. We are taught the meaning of that fable. He that acquires the Christian virtues is drinking in an eternal nature.[15] He that seeks truth and follows it wherever it may lead him, he that is humble, he that loves and serves his brother, he that subdues his own appetites out of a love and delight in doing God's will, he is approaching the true God, he is being born again.[16] He is eating that flesh which is meat indeed and drinking that water which giveth life.[17] Therefore, brethren, let us occupy ourselves in drawing nearer to the Source of life. Let us in the moment of time we have here to spend deal justly, love mercy, walk humbly.[18] Let us feel that one act of pure genuine kindness is better in the eternal world than all the[19]

The Scriptures teach it.

This is eternal life, that they should know thee and Jesus Christ whom thou hast sent.[20] To know God is to offer this perpetual acknowledgment. To know Jesus Christ I understand to be the same thing. It is Jesus who has made us acquainted with God, who has taught us his spiritual and parental character and given us distinct and affecting instruction respecting his commandments. Thus and thus only as the Teacher and Friend who leads us to the Father has he become to us Christ, the wisdom and the power of God.[21] To know him, to accept and follow him, is then indeed eternal life.

---

15. Cf. John 4:10–14.
16. John 3:3 and 3:7.
17. John 6:54–55.
18. Micah 6:8.
19. Emerson left the sentence incomplete.
20. John 17:3.
21. I Corinthians 1:24.

CLIX

We can do nothing against the truth, but for the truth.

II Corinthians 13:8

'What is truth?' was the question of Pilate.[1] What is truth? is the question put by many persons of narrow understanding and bad heart, with no more sincerity than he. What is truth? again asks many an anxious disciple, and though he would be glad at heart to know, yet desponds of an answer.

Infinite wisdom alone can tell what it is. Man can only tell what it is his mind seeks.

The word is used in many senses but in the large sense of this question, it refers to the knowledge of the constitution of the world, it refers to what is already discovered and what is yet discoverable.

Truth is that which time is always bringing to light. Truth is that which began to be shown to the first man in the first moment of his existence and was gradually disclosed to him from that hour—an ever increasing amount—till he returned to the dust.[2] It was more largely disclosed to his posterity, and still more liberally to theirs. Truth is that which every man who lives, does something to increase. All events contribute to it. All men. The failures, the miseries, the deaths of men as much as their achievements. This is the treasure that never is diminished. This is the cause that never goes backward. Battles are fought for it—but whoever loses, this always conquers. Men hate it and fight against it and the more they crush it down, the more they become its proofs and witnesses. Or they love it, and aid it, and die for it, but it never dies, and lives and prevails forevermore.

Truth is what is already known. But in order to knowledge there must be the perceiving mind as well as the fact observed. And strange it is to see how from the beginning, God has never left himself without witness,[3] but has provided and preserved a sufficient number of men in every age as his watchmen, his secretaries, his priests in the earth, so that in all the barbarism and blood into which men have sunk, in every hour there were some to serve as connecting

---

Manuscript dated June 18, 1832, evidently an error for June 17. Preached four times: June 17, 1832, at the Second Church, Boston; September 3, 1837, in East Lexington; October 8 at the First Church, Waltham; and November 19 at Concord.

   1. John 18:38.
   2. Cf. Genesis 3:19 and Ecclesiastes 12:7.
   3. Acts 14:17.

links, keepers and transmitters of the accumulation of past experience, to the inquisitive generations that were rushing into life.

Every man's life tends to make something probable. The like results in a thousand men make the same thing more probable. The like result in all men of every age and climate make the supposition certain, that is, show a truth. As truth is thus the constitution of the world—the laws of the world—it is obvious, it is just as much manifested by the ruin of those who live in opposition to it, as by the happiness of those who love it and promote it.

One meaning of the word Truth is that which I have mentioned,—the whole mass of ascertained facts concerning nature, whether outward or inward, whether human or divine. But this is only half of Truth;—no—not half,—this is an infinitely small part of Truth. This is only the whole amount of that which is certainly known by all the men in the world,—but the other part—the larger sense of Truth—is—that which remains to be known. It is that which is behind the veil which every human hand is at all times striving to lift.[4] It is that which every moment doth something to uncover. It is that which is only shown to be a vaster amount by every approach that is made to it. It is the plan of which all beings are the parts. It is the hidden Will of God. It is the cause and the Effect. It is the nature of God. It is that which we seek for in infinite duration.

This then is truth,—the knowledge of God's mind, the real ends and order of his works—a knowledge which leads ever inward from appearances to facts, from facts to causes, from causes to the first Cause.

The next fact which calls our attention in this connexion, is, that this knowledge is wholly agreeable to the nature of man.

Truth is agreeable to the nature of man, that is to say, the nature of the world is wholly suited to the nature of man. He seeks it, he is only happy when he knows it and lives by it.

The child as he sits in your lap demands impatiently if your story be true. The youth is pained by the thought that the brilliant adventures that have delighted him in a romance never happened. Moreover what is the secret of his delight in a romance or a poem? Is it not that there is a real truth running along under all the fictions—namely that merit is successful, that vice is punished, that there is an attempt throughout to administer justice to every character, whilst in the real world around him the same result is not so apparent? The mind is convinced that such an order must be, is true, and therefore delights in the fiction where it is.

If this order were contradicted throughout a narrative—if it were not faithful to the laws of the mind, it would weary and disgust.

Truth is agreeable to the nature of man. Ask your own hearts, brethren, if it be not that which you were made to seek, to love, to glorify, to live by it, and yet to seek it without end. What is this power of thought? What are all these spiritual faculties? What is this obstinate conviction that something is true more than we see; and that it can be known by us; and this unceasing endeavor to find it?

4. Cf. II Corinthians 3:14-16.

Truth is so agreeable to the nature of man that every man feels deception to be a gross insult put upon him. The most stupid are sensible of this affront and a man of generous soul can easier forgive his fellow creature who plunders his property or injures his person than him who deceives him.

We had rather know the true than the pleasant. The sentiment is sometimes uttered by orators in speaking of what they approve.—'If this be delusion, let me die deluded.' But do we not always feel it to be a false sentiment, unmanly, unsound? A secret whisper within the soul condemns it. Even on the worst supposition the mind can form of the truth,—suppose there were no God— suppose there were no hope for man—suppose there were a hideous and endless chaos—yet would every brave and elevated mind prefer the gloom of knowledge to the joy of delusion. Even on this worst supposition—

But we know better—the human mind knows better than to admit such fears. The reason why it prefers the truth to delusion, is, because it has an immoveable conviction that the truth is better than any falsehood. We have an instinctive belief that the truth is glorious, lovely, desirable. Every step we make in knowledge convinces us that error is disagreeable and mean, and that every correction of it is pleasing. We have an unalterable persuasion that what is true is best. The true and the best mean the same thing.

That is a great part of the argument in every mind for the being of God and the immortality of the soul, that it is very desirable those facts should be true; that nothing can be conceived which is so urgently demanded by the desires of the mind as these facts. And this is an argument which continually persuades us.

Thus when we have seen a few instances of the ill success and shame that usually follow fraud, we say with great assurance that Honesty is the best policy. What do we mean? We say and we believe that not only in our little neighborhood but every where and for all beings it is true. Why? not surely that we are entitled to make any such sweeping conclusion from the few cases we have witnessed, but because we see it would be far the best that it should be so, and as soon as the mind perceives this, it affirms the general law, with perfect confidence.

In short, we are made for truth. He that has much is wise, he that loves it is holy, he that practises it is just; he that opposes it ruins himself.

If these things be admitted, 1. that truth is the knowledge of the law of the world; 2. that truth is agreeable to the nature of man; we shall be prepared to receive the declaration of the apostle, 3. that we can do nothing against the truth, but for the truth.

It almost always happens when an individual embraces an opinion different from our own on any question reckoned by us important, that our first feeling is an emotion of alarm—perhaps of hostility to the individual—certainly a desire to crush as quickly as may be, the pernicious doctrine. This is especially applicable to those who deny any doctrine which we receive. The best men are filled with apprehension lest the cause of truth should suffer, lest the founda- tions of man's faith in the invisible world should be sapped and shaken and an indefinite series of evil consequences follow. And it is against this fear, this unfounded panic, that I would urge the just sentiment of Paul. Good men should not allow themselves in it. The opinions we advance, be they right or wrong, can do no harm. We can do nothing against the truth, but for the truth.

For, consider, brethren, I pray you, what truth is—that it is man's observation from age to age of the operation of God and his slow and always improving reasonings from this observation to what is the Divine character, that this observation is drawn as well from men's errors as their knowledge. The men themselves make a part of the spectacle—the men themselves and what became of them—we see whether religion made better men than irreligion, and are led gradually to irresistible conclusions—to truth which we do not make but only see.

And I ask whether it is not pusillanimous to suppose that such atoms as we are can reverse or alter God's truth? Must not that stand on its everlasting foundations and be made known more and more, alike by our exertions for, and our exertions against it? It argues an unworthy diffidence of God's strength, it shows a secret unbelief in that truth which we clamorously defend, when we imagine that what we please to say or to think, can be of any consequence to hinder its progress in the world.

It marches on at its own pace uncontrollable by us. We can help it. We can diffuse it. The feeblest voice that ever gave impulse to the air may borrow the force of thunders in its behalf, but stop it we cannot; here we are powerless.— We fall upon it and it grinds us to powder.[5]

They who fear its overthrow have not yet their eyes opened to its reality. They who fear the overthrow of the truth by any false opinion do not really believe in any truth. They must think the doctrines they reverence to be a house of cards which stands only by the general agreement of men not to blow upon it. For this is the eternal distinction between truth and error, that one bears and defies examination and always brightens under it and the other loves the dark.

It is this doctrine then that I would earnestly press upon you, that truth is a reality, that religion is a reality, something as positive and manifest as the sun, and no more to be weakened or destroyed by discussion of any thing or everything relating to it, than the light of that orb can be diminished by the disputes of philosophers on the earth concerning its nature.

Once more, the appointed way in which truth is found out, is by comparison. We put the truth and the falsehood side by side, before the mind can recognize the right. Inquiry, doubt, comparison, these are the very doors through which truth is sought. Moreover the only condition on which truth is offered to every human mind in its constitution, is, that it shall leave all and follow it.[6] The embrace of what truth we see, gives always the title to more. Follow the glimmer and you shall come to the sunshine.

Well now, do you suppose that the means of getting truth can be hurtful to the

5. Matthew 21:44 and Luke 20:18.
6. Matthew 19:27, Mark 10:28, Luke 5:11.

truth, that going forward is going back, that health is suicide? Suppose what
you will—but do not, I beseech you, imagine that the honest opinions of any
mind can ever fatally mislead it, much less injure others; that our doubts or
denials can ever dim the blazing characters in which our good God has written
his wisdom and love upon his works or shake the convictions of reflecting
human beings in the divine truth of Christianity. It is not that I wish to shield
any opinion from examination. There is no harm done in the warmest opposition to any opinion—let argument be met by argument, but do not apprehend
evil from any opinion to the cause of truth, whilst we remember that He whom
all of us serve, who worketh in Eternity not in time, is serving his cause by us
and turning our evil to good, that he formed us to seek through doubt and
examination the truth, and that his arm of protection is never withdrawn. Do
not have the presumption to believe that in our span of time we can touch that
wisdom which ages have opened. Do not doubt his care of his dearest cause.

Rather, brethren, let us render thanks to God for the great inheritance to
which our minds are born. Let us thankfully accept so much knowledge of Him
as time has yet revealed. Let us rejoice in the discoveries of his moral character
which Jesus makes and which our hearts confirm. Let us rejoice in that ever
enlarging view of his nature which our increasing knowledge of his stupendous
creation suggests. And let us receive this truth in a becoming spirit, to the end
for which it is given, that is, to lead us to ever active contemplation and search
after the whole will of God. Believing that though we can do nothing against
the truth, we may do something for it, let us adopt that other divine sentiment
of Paul; Brethren, I count not myself to have apprehended or to be already
perfect, but this one thing I do, forgetting those things which are behind, and
reaching forth to those things which are before, I press toward the prize of my
high calling.[7]

7. Philippians 3:13–14.

CLX

For this cause we also . . . do not cease to pray for you and to desire that ye might be filled with the knowledge of his will in all wisdom and spiritual understanding; that ye might walk worthy of the Lord unto all pleasing, being fruitful in every good work and increasing in the knowledge of God.

Colossians 1:9–10

These affectionate and noble sentiments of the Apostle deserve much attention. His best prayer for his friends is that they may increase in the knowledge of God. It is the best prayer we can make—for ourselves or others. For it comprehends in itself all real good.

My Christian friends, I gladly seize the first occasion of meeting you since the repairs of our church were completed, to read this lesson from the writings of St. Paul.[1] It is pertinent surely to our recent return to this ancient house, to consider the purpose for which churches are erected and worship is instituted.

But it is so great and good a desire that it hath a commanding, a perpetual pertinence, and I would gladly adopt the sentiment if it were the last lesson I should be permitted to read you out of the holy scriptures—"that ye might be filled with the knowledge of his will in all wisdom and spiritual understanding; that being fruitful in every good work, ye might increase in the knowledge of God."

Does not the thought sometimes occur to us that God is unknown in the

Manuscript dated September 2, 1832. Preached nineteen times: September 2, 1832, at the Second Church, Boston; December 1, 1833, in New Bedford; December 22 at the First Church, Boston; March 13, 1834, as a Thursday evening lecture in Plymouth; April 3 (Thursday) as a Fast Day sermon in Waltham; May 25 at the Hollis Street Church; July 6 in Bangor, Maine; November 2 at the First Church, New York; November 9 in Brooklyn; November 16 in Concord; December 14 in Sudbury; January 18, 1835, in Lowell; May 10 in East Lexington; June 28 in Framingham; August 16 in Acton; January 17, 1836, in Weston; March 27 in Lexington; May 8 in Salem; and September 25 in Groton. Margaret Fuller attended the last delivery.

1. The church had been closed for six weeks for repairs. Emerson used the time to visit his aunt, Mary Moody Emerson, in Waterford, Maine, to tour the White Mountains, and to consider his position on the Lord's Supper.

world; that He is forgot by whom are all things?[2] Men do not even desire this species of knowledge and esteem the subject dull.

But what avails it to compass sea and land as men do in pursuit of the means of living, if all the while there is no mark which we aim at, no reason for living, no hope of continuance? What avails it to collect all knowledge of the origin and progress of states, if we see not and ask not why men exist at all? What avails it to penetrate the motives, admire the characters, imitate the manners of our fellow men—to understand human nature, as it is called,—if the master spring which moves them all, lies unobserved? What avails it, to govern men, to be mightily ambitious to direct events and persuade men to an exact order of life, if our own bosom is in disorder, is without a pilot, without a hope, without a law? What avails life, what avails action, what avails sense, and all these blessed faculties we have inherited of conversing by eye and ear, and hand and thought, with all this goodly universe, if the whole seems to us an unreal and unaccountable riddle?

And such it is to him who has not yet learned to see God manifested in his works. But to every man who looks beyond the present moment to a continued being; to every one who is capable of seeking in facts for a reason, it should be a continual study—to increase in the knowledge of God—to arrive at some settled convictions respecting his nature and laws which will stand fast amidst the changes to which his condition is exposed.

And this has God provided for in the constitution of the human mind. He has made its religion to keep pace with its powers. It is precisely as natural for the good mind to have worthy notions of God, as it is for the savage to worship devils. Describe to me the god he worships, and I will describe to you the man.

It is therefore an important truth, that every step taken in the knowledge of God, is also a step gained in real humanity, that the more just are your views of God, the better is your ability to discharge well all the duties of a man. This will more plainly appear by considering the successive steps (which I think admit of being clearly marked,) whereby men ascend to the knowledge of God. I propose to consider the successive ideas by which our religious progress is ascertained that we may see, each for ourselves, what errors yet cleave to our own views. For the knowledge of God is not a knowledge, as is often supposed, to which we are born, and that the children of Christians will be Christians, but there is a process which each individual mind must go through. Only by his own reflexion, only by his own virtue, can a man grow in the knowledge of God. And in the bosom of Christianity you may find as false views of God as those which are taught on the banks of the Ganges.

With such purposes then suffer me briefly to enumerate a few of the successive steps by which men arrive at the knowledge of God.

1. The first great hint which God gave men from heaven to lead them to the

---

2. Hebrews 2:10.

truth was to forbid the worship of images.[3] This is a very important moment by which man is admonished to cease to look in every thing that shines or to listen in all that thunders for the Invisible and Omnipresent. He is the Soul within all nature. Indeed this is the only mode by which the Omnipresence can be taught, to deny his preference of any finite thing, be it sun or moon or marble image. What spectacle of gorgeous pomp can compare in sublimity with that which is familiar to our experience, an assembly of men gathered to an empty house—without a statue, without a symbol, without a picture, to see nothing, to transact nothing, to receive nothing that belongs to the senses, but to worship a Being Invisible, by exercising their thoughts in contemplating their blessings and their duties! What could make it more sublime unless that in each single mind this purpose was carried into effect! I need not, I suppose, add a word to show that this step is as important in civilization as it is in religion; for idolatry and ignorance go hand in hand, and though there have been nations of polite and learned idolaters, it was only when the form of image worship had long survived all belief in their real power.

2. The next step that is taken in the right knowledge of God, is, the disuse of sacrifices. The use of oblations was permitted and enjoined on men in the early ages so long as the childish mind of the world required the perpetual admonition of the Senses to hold it steady to the remembrance of God and his commandments; and for the same purpose they were required to offer something which had value in their own eyes. This practice ran rapidly to excess and to cruelty. A hundred sheep or a hundred oxen were frequently slaughtered before an idol, and this presently was exchanged in more ignorant communities for human victims. Reflect one moment on what must be the true character of that Divine Intelligence in whom we all live[4] and you will see how certainly it was the effect of a better knowledge of him to show the utter unsuitableness and unreasonableness of killing a man or of killing a beast in his honor;—that it was not done in his honor; that they knew not what they did;[5] that they did not pour out blood to God, but to their imagination of God. Yet was this practice a most valuable exemplification and introduction to the great moral truth that all high attainments, all true heroism, can only exist by self-denial and self-sacrifice. To lead men from this earthly to a heavenly worship, to the giving up of themselves from the butchery of beasts, seems to have been the wise and merciful end of the Jewish economy. And the conviction that God is not to be propitiated by the steaming altar, the hour when the voice is first heard in the mind, 'Bring no more vain oblations'[6] shows the dawning of a good day of reason and humanity.

3. Perhaps the next step in the mind's progress is, its arrival at the truth, that, not power, but benevolence is the basis of the Divine character; that God is not a

3. See Exodus 20:4.
4. Cf. Acts 17:28.
5. Cf. Luke 23:34.
6. Isaiah 1:13.

tyrant; that he is as much displayed in the sunshine as in the lightning; that the
sport of a child is as much a manifestation of God's power as the mechanism of
the heavens or the heaving Sea; that the great object every where sought, always
sought, and always successful, is, universal good; that Evil is made to minister
to this end as directly as what is called good; that Evil is only good unfinished;
that the vices of Nero and Domitian are made as efficacious benefactors of
mankind as the virtues of the Antonines. Savages try to appease by worship the
spite of evil spirits. The Greeks and Romans built temples to the Furies, and
averted their faces when they passed by them in the belief that these divinities
did not wish to be looked upon. They try to reconcile this evil with the good
intention of the Divinity, by supposing a Fate, a Destiny, which even the gods
cannot move. Still later, the idea is presented that God punishes men by means
of natural evils and that fire, poverty, pestilence are his judgments.

But when a more extended observation has been taken of events, and it is seen
how inseparably good and ill are mixed, it begins to be seen, that out of all evil
issues good; that our misfortunes are our best friends; and the obvious inference is that there is one Governor, and that Want, Difficulty, Affliction, are the
rough but needful masters which he has provided for the teaching of man.

Then man learns to say in its fulness of meaning, 'My Father!'

And surely it needs not be shown that this advancement in the knowledge of
God is an advancement in humanity. For how does it infuse a divine courage
and cheer into the heart in face of every danger. It removes the terror of death
and the dread of the future. We see that we belong to a system in which every
error is repaired, every loss is compensated, and the happiness of the meanest
member is not too low for the care of the Infinite Mind.

4. Another important era in this opening of the human mind to the sight of its
Maker, is, the discovery that God is not to be worshipped by specific acts but by
the conformity of the whole character to his laws. This is a very high point and
very slowly reached. Whilst God is thought to be only a little more powerful
and a little more wise than a man, men imagine that he is pleased with honors
and deceived by forms; that he loves ascriptions of praise, and punctuality in the
performance of set rites or duties which he has enjoined. They therefore are
punctual at prayers but dissolute in their thoughts; they give alms but they
break their word; they have great respect for God's name and his churches and
his ministers but they are idle and selfish and fraudulent.

But the moment the thoughts are enlarged to perceive that God does not look
at us from afar, but literally animates us, that we breathe and act and think from
his bounty, we become sensible that we might better hope to hide our thought
from ourselves than from him, and of course, that my whole being lying open in
the sunshine of his presence, it is the whole being and not a single act, and that
perhaps a false act, which must serve him. Socrates said that the gods prefer
integrity to charity,[7] a saying which shows a great insight into the nature of

7. See *JMN* 4:39, 6:93, and 6:179. Used in "Natural Religion" (1869); see Clarence Gohdes, ed.,

God. And where this truth is understood and felt, that soul is on its way to all good.

And it cannot be doubted that the reception of this doctrine will promote the improvement and happiness of man upon earth. For it strikes the blow at all hypocrisy, at all inconsistency, at all mixture of character.

5. After all these doctrines respecting the divine character have been received, there still remains the greatest truth—greatest in mystery and greatest in practical effect,—this namely, that God is within us.[8] It is the tendency of all the instruction we receive, whether by the Scriptures or by the cultivation of our minds, to withdraw our search after God continually from without and to make us more and more sensible that the brightest revelation of the Godhead is made in the depths of our own soul. It is not our soul that is God, but God is *in* our soul.[9] I pretend not to understand the way of it; I know not how to set this great and blessed truth before you in precise statements—but we all feel, or may feel, that there is a sense in which the language of the Apostle is true, that, "we are temples of the Holy Ghost, and that the Spirit of God dwelleth in us."[10] There is something in us which is higher and better than we. There is something in us which never consents to any wrong; a voice of authority which our disobedience never hurts, whilst it always hurts ourselves; a voice which is in unison with the law of nature, and with the same voice in the breast of every man. This pure and holy inmate of every human breast, this Conscience, this Reason,—by whatever name it is honored,—is the Presence of God to man. It is our door of access to the Father. It is our tie to everlasting life. Here if we seek God, we shall find him.[11] By renouncing all other laws and by a devout listening to this oracle, a man shall be guided to truth and duty and to heaven.[12]

My friends, it is possible you have made much advancement in the knowledge of God and have not yet come to realize this truth. Alas! Who is he that doth, who that can domesticate this sublime sentiment in his mind? We live too much to the senses, we cultivate the great principles too little, to be able to identify any life of any man with the direct impulses of God. And most men are revolted by the expression that 'God dwells in the soul.'[13] And yet who has not at some time felt its truth? Every man knows that the most absolute obedience to the inward law is the greatest height of virtue, and something very distinct from selfishness. Every man knows that there is a constant call from within to the improvement of every faculty compared with which any other command is faint as an infant's voice. Every man knows that there is a praise *here* that rewards a good action, to which the eloquence of angels would be cold. Every man knows that there is a majesty in his bosom with whose support he could stand out

Uncollected Lectures by Ralph Waldo Emerson (New York, 1932), 50.

8. Cf. Matthew 1:23 and Luke 17:21; see also Sermon CLI, n. 16.
9. Cf. I Corinthians 6:19.
10. I Corinthians 3:16.
11. Matthew 7:7 and Luke 11:9.
12. Cf. John 16:13.
13. Cf. John 14:17, Romans 8:9–11, and II Timothy 1:14.

against the whole universe, and that he is weak because he is at discord with himself. He believes in spite of all the seductions of present pleasure to which he yields, that no man was ever benefitted by a bad action, and that no man was ever harmed by a good action. Every act of obedience to this authority within, is a step into the light of truth and into a union with other men. Every act of disobedience is a loss of wisdom and an offence against other men.

But chiefly consider, that, every day and every hour this inward Teacher and Sovereign is more and more manifested to the heart that obeys and loves and worships Him; that ever and forevermore peace and joy and strength and knowledge are multiplied to the good man out of this Temple in his soul. He is attended always by the resplendent image of perfect goodness. He is comforted always by the friendship of the eternal Spirit. He fears himself more than the whole world. His least actions, his closest retirements, shine with light from heaven. And finally so strict is his union with God that he is incapable of any fear, for he clearly sees that disease or death cannot reach the life he lives.

If this mode of acknowledging God's presence be strongly conceived, it will help us to understand the remarkable language in which Jesus Christ always spoke to men of God. He worshipped the Father as he appeared to him in his own heart. He felt that his own being was derived from one Source with the sun and moon, with man and beast. He felt that one law prevailed throughout the whole, one love animated all, and that only by a faithful, an affectionate obedience to that law, could God be approached, be known. And so the whole of his instruction down to the last sublime act of sacrifice, was to make men submit the outward to the inward, the flesh to the spirit.

And is not this earnest endeavour to seek the eye of God within ourselves, a benefit to man in the daily business of life? Will not the Utilitarian like this? Is it not to redeem him from a thousand errors, and to set up before him a clear light? Is it not to provide him with an inseparable Friend and Governor? Is it not to withdraw his roving eye from fantastic expectations of happiness and to show him the only real happiness he is to seek and the only real misery he is to shun?

And if all men could increase in the knowledge of God to this point, would not the evils that vex the world melt away as mists in the sun? And the movements of men in society would be as true and harmonious as the revolution of the stars.

My friends, let it be our prayer and endeavour to increase in the knowledge of God—to gain some nearer approach to him who is this moment as much as at any past moment the Giver of our life. (The good man is the best picture or shadow of God. And this is that revelation of Him which we are everywhere in the Scriptures taught to expect, that 'the pure in heart shall see him';[14] that 'those who do his will shall know him.'[15] Jesus Christ is therefore called the

14. Matthew 5:8; cf. *JMN* 4:39.
15. Cf. John 7:17.

'Express image of his person.'[16]) I beseech you then, let us lay it to heart, that the best possession we have is this privilege of immediate access to God; let us reflect that by every right act and right thought he makes himself more known to us; that by a patient unremitting attention to the faintest whispers of duty, we shall expel every adversary from our breast and unfold new graces and enjoy new delight and become more faithful vehicles of his Will until our whole soul becomes one refulgent mirror of the presence and power and love of God.

16. Hebrews 1:3.

CLXI

In the sweat of thy face shalt thou
eat bread till thou return unto the ground.

GENESIS 3:19

Never was any prophecy more strictly fulfilled than this ancient word. If this be the curse which fell upon Adam, it cleaves to all his posterity. The alleviation that is in it we are slow to own. It is an old observation that 'Poverty is a good which all hate.'[1] We lament the necessity which drives us all as with the cart whip to our labor. A little respite, we say, a time to take breath. What is life for if it is all to be spent in toil? But our complaints are not heard or are not regarded; the stern law is still enforced and the earth is incessantly shaken with the din of human industry.

We see the fulfilment of the divine sentence with our eyes. We fulfil it with our own hands. In the villages, in the cities, see this army of strong men which pours out of the doors of every street when the sun rises. Hear the incessant noise of their thousand trades all day long. Go into the countinghouse and see the unwearied pen of the clerk, the anxious brow of the merchant and the diligent feet that run to and fro on his errands all day. On every wharf, in every

---

The earlier of two manuscripts is dated September 2, 1832; the second manuscript, prepared for the second delivery, is dated September 2, 1832, and June 28, 1834. Preached eight times: September 2, 1832, at the Second Church, Boston; June 29, 1834, at the Second Church, Waltham; August 31 at the First Church, Boston; September 7 in New Bedford; December 27, 1835, in East Lexington; August 21, 1836, in Concord; November 20 in Weston; and February 19, 1837, at the First Church, Waltham. George Moore reported the Concord delivery in his diary: "Mr. Emerson preached. Text, in the morning, 'By the sweat of thy face shalt thou eat bread all the days of thy life.' He 1st spoke of the necessity of labour to develope our physical faculties. It is labour—constant, untiring labour—which educates the hand of the watch-maker, the artist, &c.—and it is this labour, which gives health and beauty to the body. As soon as any parts of our frame cease their motions, their activity, disease begins. It is labour that renders life pleasant. What were we placed in this world for unless to labour? Men often look upon labor as a great evil—whereas it is their greatest good, when rightly considered. The greatest benefactors of the world have been men of the greatest labour, and oftentimes men who have been obliged to labor from want. 2. Labour is as necessary to develope our moral faculties, as physical. 3. Labour is necessary to make men *useful* and *wise*. The common salutation 'how *do* you?' shows that life, by universal consent, should consist in action" (Kenneth W. Cameron, ed., *The Transcendentalists and Minerva* [Hartford, 1958], 465–66). Emerson planned the sermon as early as the first week in April, 1832; see *JMN* 4:10. The revised earlier version of the sermon is given in the Textual and Manuscript Notes.

1. Emerson's source is Vicesimus Knox, *Elegant Extracts . . . in Prose*, 7th ed. (London, 1797), 2:1031. See *JMN* 4:10 and 16.

shop, office, manufactory, ship, there is still the same labor under new forms, the toiling of the brains and the sweat of the face. Or go under the domestic roof—and observe the cares of every family,—the endless duties of the laboring woman, of the mother, the wife, and the maiden. Leave the town, and walk into the fields—you have exchanged the machinery but the farmer works as hard as the mechanic. Or cross the seas, travel to the north pole or go southward to the line and wherever the human race hold any possessions, enjoy any comforts, the same painful means are every where the price of bread.

In the sweat of thy face shalt thou eat bread all the days of thy life.

On this day which suspends these labors it will not, I hope, be lost time to consider this necessity of our condition, to observe narrowly what advantages accrue from it, nay whether it be not altogether an advantage. I believe the effect of meditation upon the laws of our condition is to reconcile every reflecting person to his own part in the common doom, and to make the hum of labor sound more cheerfully in his ears.

Moreover the circumstances of some men release them, if only their nature would also release them, from this necessity. And the temptation continually presents itself to every man to forego some of the good he might obtain for the sake of being set free the sooner and the oftener from his task.

But we cannot do without it. The circumstances of some men may seem to release them from the immediate necessity. But it is pressing upon us all. It was said by William Penn, "If thou dost not want labor for food, thou mayest for physic."[2] It may be safely asserted that no man exists who has not some labor appointed him. That is his labor to which his peculiar gifts, means and opportunities call him, whether it be the use of the sword, the plough, the loom, the pen, the map, the helm or whatever implement. He may work without using his hands. Some of the most diligent workmen that ever lived and some of the most productive workmen too have been men of study. But in some manner he must work. If he does nothing, why is he here in this active universe of God? Our very salutation of one another is How *do* you? as if to live it needed to act.

It therefore belongs to us all to examine a law which touches all, and a better understanding of the influences which this law exerts upon our condition is always modifying and may come at last to reverse our opinion and our practice in important respects.

1. Labor produces the health and perfection of the faculties. It is a natural law that man should labor, and like other natural laws is made known to us by our instincts and its obedience secured by rewards and penalties. Man is throughout his structure designed for labor as manifestly as a fish is formed to swim or a bird to fly. The health of the body and mind can only by labor be gained and secured. This instruction is given even in the involuntary functions. It is written all over this wonderful frame; it is writ on every limb and artery and nerve: *This*

2. *The Select Works of William Penn*, 3d ed. (London, 1782), 5:127. Emerson borrowed this volume from the Boston Athenaeum from June 11 to September 20, 1832.

is for use. There is not an organ, a bone, a drop of blood in our anatomy that has not its prescribed office. The heart beats at the centre day and night, year after year, and never stops till the soul is called from the flesh. The lungs heave as long. And disease begins the moment one member ceases to perform its function. Not less is it true of the voluntary actions of the frame. The still hand becomes numb. The life of every sense and limb depends on its use and the finer powers that seem to mediate betwixt the body and the soul, health and cheerfulness, exist only in the active frame. Inaction for a short time would produce inconvenience, continued disease and in a longer time death.

It is not only needful to the health but to the perfection of the powers that they should be employed. 'A full grown man,' says the political economist, 'is an accumulated capital.'[3] The practice of years has qualified him to produce effects more surprizing every day and that would seem, if the intermediate steps were not seen, and only his first and last works compared, quite miraculous. The education of the hand alone to its miraculous dexterity—the production of such a machine as the watchmaker's hand or the surgeon's, the engraver's hand or the painter's or the sculptor's—is sufficient illustration of the fact that labor is necessary to the perfection of our physical powers. Not less striking is the power which the eye acquires by use. Educated hands and eyes have changed the face of the earth.

Yet are these attainments, which the bodily organs owe to labor, scarcely to be compared with the advantages which the intellectual and moral faculties derive from the same source.—To consider at present the subject of intellectual labor would lead us too far. I proceed at once to a new consideration.

2. I esteem it an all important moral influence of industry that it makes men safe. The safety of a person engaged in lawful labor is so conspicuous when contrasted with the dangers of the idle, that the price at which it is bought seems cheap. Though this is true it needs an interpreter that more pricks the attention. Working in your calling is like dwelling in a sanctuary which no enemies dare approach. Walls of stone or an army of guards are a less sure defence from danger, than is the discharge of our duties. Would you be safe from an enemy? Work in your calling. Your diligence shames his malignity, puts him in the wrong, makes his enmity an impertinence. Would you be revenged of your enemy? Work in your calling and you are nobly avenged;[4] you are rising above him all the time, for the man that is diligent in his business, shall stand before kings; he shall not stand before mean men.[5]

Would you be safe from enemies from whom no walls, no garrison can protect you,—from your own passions? Work in your calling. To this conclusion concur all the opinions of all men. All experience testifies the greatest peril

3. Emerson lists this among quotations from Edmund Burke in Blotting Book I (*JMN* 6:25), though its source has not been located.
4. "Would you be revenged on your enemy, live as you ought & you have done it to purpose" (Knox, *Elegant Extracts,* 2:1033); cf. *JMN* 4:17, 20, 212.
5. Proverbs 22:29.

to be the peril of idle hands. (It is a coarse but a significant saying that the devil tempts others, but the idle tempt the devil.)[6]

For repose so sweet to labor is very quickly irksome and the faculties must be employed in good or evil. It is not a choice between inaction and work but between doing good or doing harm. By our nature work we must. We are miserable without excitement. The head will be busy and the body in motion and if you do not provide them honest employment they will carve out mischief for themselves. If you will not furnish the brain with innocent subjects, it will be a shop of mischievous purposes, of unfriendly thoughts, of foul imaginations.[7] There is no virtue can be preserved in sloth.

The idle man: you know him in the street by his roving eye, by his discontented, malevolent expression. He meddles with his neighbors' affairs to their hurt. But benevolence is just as naturally generated in the breast of the industrious man. He comes from his desk or work-room, and looks abroad with senses and soul ready to draw keen enjoyment from every object. There is refreshment to him in the face of the sky, in the fragrant air, and in the countenance of man. They remind him of the thousand thousand cheerful works that have proceeded around him, whilst he has been engrossed with his own. He has a right to take pleasure in every improvement that is the fruit of their industry, for he has not been wanting in his place. He has not been soured or belittled by the gossip of the bar-room. He is spotless from the crimes into which the idlers have been drawn. He has not wrought himself into a fever in the little politics of the parish. He has not bound himself by rash promises with rash men to any criminal engagements; he has not made himself obnoxious to men, nor to the disapprobation of God.

And a higher safety than mere impunity is herein provided. We are wonderfully protected. We have scarce a weakness but we are made at sometime to see that it is a source of strength. Not a misfortune, a hindrance, an enemy, but somewhere is productive of singular advantage to us. After struggling unwillingly enough through years of poverty and hard labor, the mind perceives that really it has come the shortest road to a knowledge of its own powers and duties, to a scene and occasion of lofty exertion, that though the frosts of want were not good for leaves and flowers they were good for timber. The mind has ripened to what strength of character. It has been saved from what polluting and narrowing associations. It has been lifted into what higher region of sentiments. And thus God brings us by ways which we know not and like not to true success.

3. And this leads me to say that this our necessity of laboring makes us more than innocent, it makes us useful and wise. It makes men useful to others and then to themselves, and out of this self-good, accrues again a larger benefit to the world. It is a good thing amid the manifold temptations of the world, to do

6. Knox, *Elegant Extracts,* 2:1025; see *JMN* 4:10.
7. Cf. Shakespeare, *Hamlet,* III, ii, 88–89.

no harm; it is far better to do it a great service. And what benefactor has been so efficient, so clear-sighted, as this painful Necessity that constrains us to toil? Who is it, I pray you, who have done all the good that is or has been on earth? It is the Poor.[8] Poor men and poor women laboring for their bread with wits sharpened by their wants, pinched by cold, driven by hunger, straitened by debt, striving to make their wants fewer and their labors more lucrative. These have been the benefactors of the world. It is these stern necessities that we are ashamed of and which we lament,—that have invented all the arts and multiplied the comforts and finished the great improvements of social life. Every thing great and good cost labor and watching and contention and sacrifice. And every individual in the whole working community in whatever manner his hands may have been employed, who has done his duty through the day, may feel the lively satisfaction of having contributed his part to the prosperity of the state.

It makes you useful by making you wise. It is giving you that higher usefulness which nothing but experience can give. It is said Nothing can be truly known until it has been lived.[9] Who is it that is skilful but he that has made many trials before? Who is it that is sure to succeed but he who has already learned to his cost what are the errors on this side and on that?

Again, industrious habits make a man useful, by the additional energy they give to his will. It is observed that industrious men have more leisure than that class of men who are called 'men of leisure.' The superior vigor of their habit enables them to throw off better fruits from their recreation than the most serious exertions of the indolent could produce.

And what can be said more than to say it makes men useful? Is not that the high point which every truehearted man always sets before his eyes—to arrive at the consciousness of usefulness—to come to the perception that he is doing that he was fitted to do; that which (to speak faithfully) he can do better than any one else; to perceive that he is not without God in the world—a cumberer of the ground[10]—but in his own place the visible image of God, a vehicle between God and his fellowmen of many and multiplying benefits. Have you to whom I speak ever formed any higher wish in your best moments, than to be the centre of pure and extending influence? Without it, what is life, what is wealth, genius, knowledge, culture? To serve nobody, to live without effect, is poverty indeed. He that does nothing is poorer than he that has nothing.[11] It is the object for which the noble minded live. And it is never long pursued in vain. A man is valued as he makes himself valuable.[12]

And this usefulness and perception of usefulness continually increases. God

---

8. In a journal entry for May 12, 1832, Emerson proposed to "write a sermon upon Blessed Poverty. Who have done all the good in the world? Poor men" (*JMN* 4:16).

9. Not located.

10. Cf. Luke 13:7.

11. Emerson lists this sentence among "My Proverbs" in *JMN* 6:197; see also *JMN* 3:254, 4:10, and 4:12.

12. Knox, *Elegant Extracts*, 2:1028. See *JMN* 4:15, 17, and 5:46. Used in Sermon CLXXI, "Modern Aspects of Letters" (*EL* 1:382), "Trades and Professions" (*EL* 2:125), "Literature [First Lecture]" (*EL* 3:206), and "Spiritual Laws" (*CW* 2:89).

rewards fidelity day by day. His power is increased; his acquaintance with himself is increased; his knowledge of human nature and human duty is increased. The great truths of religion are opened to him who works in his own vocation with a single mind as in a book. One does not need to study many volumes, nor to run over many lands, nor to be acquainted with hundreds of men, and variety of manners, in order to learn what is necessary. There is a religion of common sense that lies in the mind of simple men who have had no other instruction than their bible and their daily observation in a very confined business, which is yet sufficient for the guidance of the man in the questions of common duty. For God has provided that the conscience, the domestic god,[13] the eye of the soul, should grow up in man in every condition and therefore has prepared the experience which it must use to grow like grass in every place. Every one has his own way of getting it. Books supply it to the scholar; courts supply it to the statesman; the ways of children to the schoolmaster; the course of the season and the growing corn to the farmer; and the petty details of the smallest employment in which one is habitually engaged speak a moral language to every man and are preachers to him of his duties.

Need I add that labor is the consoler of our griefs, that the hard master assumes sometimes the face of an angel and by faithful, serviceable employments weans us from griefs that threatened to overwhelm us? A keen observer of men has remarked: The sorrows of the soul the understanding can do nothing, reason little, Time much, but beneficent activity every thing, to heal.[14]

Thus we have seen that labor makes men healthful, innocent, useful, wise. It is our teacher in the laws of nature and of our own constitution. Very important influences upon man are confided to it. If we accept its instruction we owe it a great debt. As I have said, it gives us even an acquaintance with the highest speculative truths.

Yet, saith Truth, one thing thou lackest.[15] It needs that we not only work but think; think upon our work. Let a man distinguish his usefulness from the usefulness of a windmill or a waterwheel. Let his efficiency be voluntary. Let him have foresight and satisfaction of his work. Let him work in his calling with the design to produce good and with joy let him see it produced. This elevates his labor instantly, though it were the meanest, to a spiritual dignity. This introduces into the most obscure employments the sublimity of a religious act. If man will add to his labor the habit of reflexion; if he will observe and acknowledge these good influences in a condition he once thought so unhappy; if he will admit the great sentiment of duty into the petty details of his employment; if he will thus make that toil which was begun from want an offering to God, then is the laborer blessed from on high: then is his work crowned; and in his soul he shall hear the voice, 'Well done! good and faithful servant.'[16] Then are his endeavors steps in a path which has no end. His fitness for this life is

13. "Conscience is the domestic god"; see *JMN* 6:49, 51.
14. Source not located; used again in Sermon CLIII.
15. Mark 10:21; cf. Luke 18:22.
16. Matthew 25:21–23.

fitness for all life. His true preparation for this world is a preparation for all the worlds in the government of God. And the bitterness of the primal curse, 'In the sweat of thy face shall thou eat bread,' is converted into the fulness of blessing.

The continual effort of the divine Providence is to make man a law to himself.[17] He who has so far mastered himself as to need not the stimulus of necessity or of ambition to provoke him to action but prescribes his own task from the love of action has answered the purposes of his discipline on earth and is fit for the society of the blessed.

Therefore, brethren, seeing that the constitution of this world makes all our work benefit the workman, makes us more strong, more safe, more useful, more wise, for all our labor,—let us be diligent in our business;[18] let us comply with God's law; let us not be weary in well doing.[19] Above all, let us by our faithful and thankful disposition call down on our endeavors the divine benediction. Then go forth to your duties, how high, how humble soever,—to your shop, to your work-yard, to your office, to your household,—and everywhere feel that you are by these present temporary works training up yourself for higher duties, for a heavenly society, for endless usefulness.

17. Romans 2:14.
18. Proverbs 22:29.
19. Galatians 6:9 and II Thessalonians 3:13.

CLXII

The kingdom of God is not meat and drink; but
righteousness and peace and joy in the holy ghost.

Romans 14:17

In the history of the Church no subject has been more fruitful of controversy than the Lord's Supper. There never has been any unanimity in the understanding of its nature nor any uniformity in the mode of celebrating it. Without considering the frivolous questions which have been hotly debated as to the posture in which men should partake or whether mixed or unmixed wine should be served, whether leavened or unleavened bread should be broken, the questions have been settled differently in every church, who should be admitted to partake, and how often it should be prepared. In the Catholic Church once infants were permitted and then forbidden to partake. Since the ninth Century, bread only is given to the laity and the cup is reserved to the priesthood. So as to the time. In the fourth Lateran Council it was decreed that every believer should communicate once in a year at Easter. Afterwards three times—But more important have been the controversies respecting its nature. The great question of the Real Presence was the main controversy between the Church of England and the Church of Rome. The doctrine of the Consubstantiation maintained by Luther was denied by Calvin. In the Church of England Archbishops Laud and Wake maintained that it was a Eucharist or sacrifice of thanksgiving to God,

---

The original manuscript of Sermon CLXII, the so-called "Lord's Supper" sermon, is dated September 9, 1832, the date of its only delivery, at the Second Church, Boston. Shortly after the event, Emerson prepared a second manuscript, a revised fair copy, perhaps with a momentary intent to publish, but certainly for circulation among interested friends. It was this copy that Emerson conveyed to Cyrus A. Bartol in 1857 (*L* 5:81–82) and which subsequently became the source for the sermon's publication in Octavius B. Frothingham's *Transcendentalism in New England* (New York, 1876), 363–80. This was the only regular sermon of Emerson's to be published during his lifetime. Subsequent printings, in the posthumous Riverside and Centenary editions of the complete works, derive from Frothingham's text. The text presented here is edited from the manuscript that Emerson actually read to his congregation.

The Quaker background of the sermon has been studied by Frederick B. Tolles ("Emerson and Quakerism," *American Literature* 10 [May 1938]: 142–65) and Mary C. Turpie ("A Quaker Source for Emerson's Sermon on the Lord's Supper," *New England Quarterly* 17 [March 1944]: 95–101). Turpie described the extensive use that Emerson made of Thomas Clarkson's *A Portraiture of Quakerism*, 3 vols. (New York, 1806), the first two volumes of which Emerson borrowed from the Boston Athenaeum on June 11 and took with him on his retreat to the White Mountains.

Cudworth and Warburton that it was not a sacrifice but a feast after a sacrifice, and Bishop Hoadly that it was a simple commemoration.[1]

If there seem to you an agreement in this last opinion among our churches it is only but of yesterday and within narrow limits.

And finally it is now near 200 years since the society of Quakers denied the authority of the supper altogether and gave good reasons for disusing it.

I allude to these facts only to show that so far from the Supper being a tradition in which all are fully agreed, there has always been the widest room for difference of opinion upon this particular.

Having recently paid particular attention to this subject, I was led to the conclusion that Jesus did not intend to establish an institution for perpetual observance when he ate the passover with his disciples;[2] and further to the opinion that it is not expedient to celebrate it as we do. I shall now endeavour to state distinctly my reasons for these two opinions.

An account of the last Supper of Christ with his disciples is given by the four Evangelists, Matthew, Mark, Luke and John.

In St. Matthew's Gospel (26:26) are recorded the words of Jesus in giving bread and wine on that occasion to his disciples but no expression occurs intimating that this feast was hereafter to be commemorated.

In St. Mark the same words are recorded and still with no intimation that the occasion was to be remembered (14:22).[3]

St. Luke, after relating the breaking of the bread, has these words: 'This do in remembrance of me' (22:15).[4]

In St. John, although other occurrences of the same evening are related, this whole transaction is passed over without notice.[5]

Now observe the facts. Two of the evangelists (namely, Matthew and John) were of the twelve disciples and were present on that occasion. Neither of them drops the slightest intimation of any intention on the part of Jesus to set up any thing permanent. John especially, the beloved disciple, who has recorded with minuteness the conversation and the transactions of that memorable evening, has quite omitted such a notice.

Neither did it come to the knowledge of St. Mark, who relates the other facts.

1. The paragraph draws on Thomas Clarkson, *A Portraiture of Quakerism* (New York, 1806), 2:291–93. William Laud (1573–1645) was archbishop of Canterbury from 1633 until his impeachment in 1640. William Wake (1657–1737), made bishop of Lincoln in 1705, was elevated to archbishop of Canterbury in 1716. Ralph Cudworth (1617–1688) was perhaps the most prominent of the Cambridge Platonists; his writings include *A Discourse Concerning the True Notion of the Lord's Supper* (1642). William Warburton (1698–1779) was an editor of Shakespeare, friend of Alexander Pope, and bishop of Gloucester; his writings include *A Rational Account of the Nature and End of the Sacrament of the Lord's Supper* (1761). Among the writings of Benjamin Hoadly (1676–1761), bishop of Winchester, is *A Plain Account of the Nature and End of the Sacrament of the Lord's Supper* (published anonymously in 1735 but widely known to have been his), which explains the rite as exclusively commemorative.

2. See *JMN* 4:30.

3. This and the preceding paragraph draw on Clarkson, *Portraiture*, 2:357.

4. Actually Luke 22:19.

5. Clarkson, *Portraiture*, 2:358. See John, chapters 13–17.

It is found in Luke alone, who was not present. There is no reason, however, that we know for rejecting the account of Luke.[6] I doubt not that the expression was used by Jesus. I shall presently consider its meaning. I have only brought these accounts together that you may judge whether it is likely that a solemn institution to be continued to the end of time, by all mankind, as they should come, nation after nation, within the influence of the Christian religion, was to be established in this slight manner, in a manner so slight that the intention of remembering it should not have caught the ear or dwelt in the mind of the only two among the twelve, who wrote down what happened!

Still we must suppose that this expression—This do in remembrance of me—had come to the ear of Luke from some disciple present. What did it really signify? It is a prophetic and an affectionate expression.[7] Jesus is a Jew sitting with his countrymen celebrating their national feast. He thinks of his own impending death and wishes the minds of his disciples to be prepared for it and says to them, "When hereafter you shall keep the passover it will have an altered aspect in your eyes. It is now a historical covenant of God with the Jewish nation. Hereafter it will remind you of a new covenant sealed with my blood. In years to come, as long as your people shall come up to Jerusalem to keep this feast (forty years) the connexion which has subsisted between us will give a new meaning in your eyes to the national festival as the anniversary of my death."—I see natural feeling and beauty in the use of such language from Jesus, a friend to his friends. I can readily imagine that he was willing and desirous that when his disciples met, his memory should hallow their intercourse, but I cannot bring myself to believe that he looked beyond the living generation, beyond the abolition of the festival he was celebrating and the scattering of the nation, and meant to impose a memorial feast upon the whole world.

But though the words *Do this in remembrance,* to which so much meaning has been given, do not occur in Matthew, Mark, or John, yet many persons are apt to imagine that the very striking and formal manner in which this eating and drinking is described intimates a striking and formal purpose to found a festival. This opinion would easily occur to any one reading only the New Testament, but the impression is removed by reading any narrative of the mode in which the ancient or the modern Jews kept the passover. It is then perceived at once that the leading circumstances in the gospel are only a faithful account of that ceremony. Jesus did not celebrate the passover and afterwards the supper, but the supper *was* the passover. He did with his disciples exactly what every master of a family in Jerusalem was doing at the same hour with his household. It appears that the Jews ate the lamb and the unleavened bread and drank wine after a prescribed manner. It was the custom for the Lord or master of the feast to break the bread and to bless it, using this formula, which the Talmudists have preserved to us, 'Blessed be thou O Lord who givest us the

6. Clarkson, *Portraiture,* 2:360.

7. Clarkson, *Portraiture,* 2:360. The discussion of the Passover that follows draws from Clarkson, 2:339–47.

fruits of the earth,'[8] and to give it to every one at the table. It was the custom for the master of the family to take the cup which contained the wine and to bless it saying, 'Blessed be thou O Lord who givest us the fruit of the vine,' and then to give the cup to all. Among the modern Jews, a hymn is sung after this ceremony, specifying the twelve great works done by God for the deliverance of their fathers out of Egypt. And Jesus did the same thing.

But why did he use expressions so extraordinary and emphatic as these: This is my body which is broken for you. Take, Eat. This is my blood which is shed for you. Drink it.[9] They are not extraordinary expressions from him. They were familiar in his mouth. He always taught by parables and symbols. It was the national way of teaching and was largely used by him. Remember the readiness which he always showed to spiritualize every occurrence. He stooped and wrote on the sand.[10] He admonished his disciples respecting the leaven of the Pharisees.[11] He instructed the woman of Samaria respecting living water.[12] He permitted himself to be anointed, declaring it was for interment.[13] He washed the feet of his disciples.[14] These are admitted to be symbolical actions and expressions. Here in like manner he calls the bread his body and bids the disciples eat. He had used the same expression repeatedly before. The reason why St. John does not repeat the words here, seems to be that he had narrated a similar discourse of Jesus to the people of Capernaum more at length already (John 6:27). He there tells the Jews—'Except ye eat the flesh of the Son of Man and drink his blood ye have no life in you.'[15]

And when the Jews on that occasion complained that they did not comprehend what he meant, he added for their better understanding, and as if for our understanding, that we might not think that his body was to be actually eaten, that he only meant we should live by his commandment. He closed his discourse with these explanatory expressions: "The flesh profiteth nothing;—the *words* that I speak to you, they are spirit and they are life."[16]

Whilst I am upon this topic I cannot help remarking that it is very singular we should have preserved this rite and insisted upon perpetuating one symbolical act of Christ whilst we have totally neglected others, particularly one other which had at least an equal claim to our observance. Jesus washed the feet of his disciples and told them that 'As he had washed their feet, they ought to wash one another's feet, for he had given them an example that they should do as he had done to them.'[17] I ask any person who believes the Supper to have been

---

8. Clarkson, *Portraiture*, 2:340. The remainder of the paragraph draws on Clarkson, 2:346.
9. Cf. Matthew 26:26-28, Mark 14:22-24, and Luke 22:19-20.
10. John 8:6-8.
11. Matthew 16:6-12, Mark 8:15-21, Luke 12:1.
12. John 4:7-15. See also Clarkson, *Portraiture*, 2:266.
13. Mark 14:8; cf. Mark 16:1.
14. John 13:5. See also Clarkson, *Portraiture*, 2:294.
15. John 6:53. See also Clarkson, *Portraiture*, 2:348-50.
16. John 6:63.
17. John 13:14-15. Emerson's discussion of the washing of the feet also draws on Clarkson, *Portraiture*, 2:294.

designed by Jesus to be commemorated forever, to go and read the account of it
in the other gospels, and then compare with it the account of this transaction in
St. John and tell me if it is not much more explicitly authorized than the supper.
It only differs in this, that we have found the Supper used in New England and
the washing of the feet not. If we had found this rite established, it would be
much more difficult to show its defective authority. That rite is used by the
Church of Rome and the Sandemanians. It has been very properly dropped by
other Christians. Why? 1. Because it was a local custom and unsuitable in
western countries, and 2. because it was typical and all understand that humility
is the thing signified. But the passover was local too and does not concern us;
and its bread and wine were typical and do not help us to understand the love
which they signified.

These views of the original account of the Lord's Supper lead me to esteem it
an occasion full of solemn and prophetic interest but never intended by Jesus to
be the foundation of a perpetual institution.

It appears however from Paul's Epistle to the Corinthians that the disciples
had very early taken advantage of these impressive words of Christ to hold
religious meetings where they broke bread and drank wine as symbols.[18]

I look upon this fact as very natural in the circumstances of the Church. The
disciples lived together; they threw all their property into a common stock; they
were bound together by the memory of Christ and nothing could be more
natural than that this eventful evening should be affectionately remembered by
them; that they, Jews like Jesus, should adopt his expression and his type, and
furthermore that what was done with peculiar propriety by them, by his personal friends, should come to be extended to their companions also. In this way
religious feasts grew up among the early Christians. They were readily adopted
by the Jewish converts who were familiar with religious feasts, and also by the
Pagan converts whose idolatrous worship had been made up of sacred festivals
and who very readily abused these to gross riot as appears from the censures of
St. Paul. Many persons consider this fact, the observance of such a memorial
feast by the early disciples, decisive of the question whether it ought to be
observed by us. For my part I see nothing to wonder at in its originating there;
all that is surprizing is that it should exist amongst us. It had great propriety for
his personal friends to remember their friend and repeat his words. It was but
too probable that among the half-converted Pagans and Jews any rite, any form
would be cherished whilst yet unable to comprehend the spiritual character of
Christianity.

The circumstance however that St. Paul favors these views has seemed to
many persons conclusive in favor of the institution. I am of opinion that it is
wholly on this passage and not upon the gospels that the ordinance stands. A
careful examination of that passage will not I think make that evidence so

---

18. I Corinthians 10:1–31 and 11:20–34. Emerson's discussion of Paul's view also draws on
Clarkson, *Portraiture*, 2:368–82.

weighty as it seems. That passage, the eleventh chapter I Corinthians, appears to be a reproof to the Corinthian converts of certain gross abuses that had grown up among them, offending against decency not less than against Christianity: accusing their contentiousness; the fanaticism of certain of their women; and the intemperance into which they had fallen at the Lord's supper. The end he has in view, in that Chapter, and this is observable, is not to enjoin upon them to observe the supper, but to censure their abuse of it. We quote the passage nowadays as if it enjoined attendance on the supper, but he wrote it merely to chide them for drunkenness. To make their enormity plainer he goes back to the origin of this religious feast to show what that feast was out of which this their riot came and so relates the transactions of the Lord's supper. *I have received of the Lord,* he says.[19] By this expression it is often thought that a miraculous communication is implied, but certainly without good reason if it is remembered that St. Paul was living in the lifetime of all the apostles who could give him an account of the transaction, and it is contrary to all experience to suppose that God should work a miracle to convey information that might be so easily got by natural means. So that the import of the expression is that he had got the account of the Evangelists, which we also possess.

But the material circumstance which diminishes our confidence in the correctness of the apostle's view is the observation that his mind had not escaped the prevalent error of the primitive Church, the belief namely that the second coming of Christ would shortly occur, until which time, he tells them, this feast was to be kept. At that time the world would be burnt with fire, and a new government established in which the Saints would sit on thrones; so slow were the disciples during the life and after the ascension of Christ to receive the idea which we receive that his Second Coming was a spiritual kingdom, the dominion of his religion in the hearts of men to be extended gradually over the whole world.

In this manner I think we may see clearly enough how this ancient ordinance got its footing among the early Christians and this single expectation of a speedy reappearance of a temporal messiah upon earth, which kept its influence even over so spiritual a man as St. Paul, would naturally tend to preserve the use of the rite when once established.

We arrive then at this conclusion: 1. That it does not appear from a careful examination of the account of the Last Supper in the Evangelists that it was designed by Jesus to be perpetual. 2. It does not appear that the opinion of St. Paul, all things considered, ought to alter our opinion derived from the Evangelists.

I have not attempted to ascertain precisely the purpose in the mind of Jesus. But you will see that many opinions may be entertained of his intention all consistent with the opinion that he did not design the ordinance to be perpetual. He may have foreseen that his disciples would meet together to remember him and seen good in it. It may have crossed his mind that this would be

---

19. I Corinthians 11:23.

easily continued a hundred or a thousand years, as men more easily transmit a form than a virtue, and yet have been altogether out of his purpose to fasten it upon men in all times and all countries.

Admitting that the disciples kept it and admitting Paul's feeling of its perpetuity, that does not settle the question for us. I think it was good for them. I think it is not suited to this day. We do not take them for guides in other things. They were, as we know, obstinately attached to their Jewish prejudices. All the intercourse with the most persuasive of teachers seems to have done very little to enlarge their views. On every subject we have learned to think differently, and why shall not we form a judgment upon this, more in accordance with the spirit of Christianity than was the practice of the early ages?

But it is said, Admit that the rite was not designed to be perpetual. What harm doth it? Here it stands generally accepted under some form by the Christian world, the undoubted occasion of much good; is it not better it should remain?[20] This is the question of Expediency.

I proceed to notice a few objections that in my judgment lie against its use in its present form.

1. If the view which I have taken of the history of the institution be correct, then the claim of authority should be dropped in administering it. You say, every time you celebrate the rite, that Jesus enjoined it, and the whole language you use conveys that impression. But if you read the New Testament as I do, you do not believe he did.

2. It has seemed to me (yet I make the objection with diffidence) that the use of this ordinance tends to produce confusion in our views of the relation of the soul to God. It is the old objection to the doctrine of the Trinity that the true worship was transferred from God to Christ or that such confusion was introduced into the soul that an undivided worship was given nowhere. Is not that the effect of the Lord's Supper? I appeal now to the convictions of communicants and ask such persons whether they have not been occasionally conscious of a painful confusion of thought between the worship due to God and the commemoration due to Christ. For the service does not stand upon the basis of a voluntary act, but is imposed by authority. It is an expression of gratitude to him enjoined by him. There is an endeavour to keep Jesus in mind whilst yet the prayers are addressed to God. I fear it is the effect of this ordinance to clothe Jesus with an authority which he never claimed and which distracts the mind of the worshipper. I know our opinions differ much respecting the nature and offices of Christ and the degree of veneration to which he is entitled. I am so much a Unitarian as this, that I believe the human mind cannot admit but one God, and that every effort to pay religious homage to more than one being goes to take away all right ideas. I appeal, brethren, to your individual experience. In the moment when you make the least petition to God, though it be but a silent wish that he may approve you, or add one moment to your life—do you not—in

20. See Emerson's concession to the positive influence of the rite in *JMN* 4:30.

the very act—necessarily exclude all other beings from your thought? In that act the soul stands alone with God, and Jesus is no more present to the mind than your brother or your child.

But is not Jesus called in Scripture the Mediator?[21] He is the Mediator in that only sense in which possibly any being can mediate between God and man, that is an Instructer of man. He teaches us how to become like God. And a true disciple of Jesus will receive the light he gives most thankfully, but the thanks he offers and which an exalted being will accept are not compliments, commemorations—but the use of that instruction.

3. To pass by other objections, I come to this: that the *use of the elements,* however suitable to the people and the modes of thought in the East where it originated, is foreign and unsuited to affect us. Whatever long usage and strong association may have done in some individuals to deaden this repulsion I apprehend that their use is rather tolerated than loved by any of us. We are not accustomed to express our thoughts or emotions by symbolical actions. Most men find the bread and wine no aid to devotion and to some persons it is an impediment. To eat bread is one thing; to love the precepts of Christ and resolve to obey them is quite another. It is of the greatest importance that whatever forms we use should be animated by our feelings; that our religion through all its acts should be living and operative.

The statement of this objection leads me to say that I think this difficulty, wherever it is felt, to be entitled to the greatest weight. It is alone a sufficient objection to the ordinance. It is my own objection. This mode of commemorating Christ is not suitable to me. That is reason enough why I should abandon it. If I believed that it was enjoined by Jesus on his disciples, and that he even contemplated to make permanent this mode of commemoration every way agreeable to an Eastern mind, and yet on trial it was disagreeable to my own feelings, I should not adopt it. I should choose other ways which he would approve more. For what could he wish to be commemorated for? Only that men might be filled with his spirit. I find that other modes comport with my education and habits of thought. For I chuse that my remembrances of him should be pleasing, affecting, religious. I will love him as a glorified friend after the free way of friendship and not pay him a stiff sign of respect as men do to those whom they fear. A passage read from his discourses, the provoking each other to works like his, any act or meeting which tends to awaken a pure thought, a glow of love, an original design of virtue I call a worthy, a true commemoration.

4. In the last place the importance ascribed to this particular ordinance is not consistent with the spirit of Christianity. The general object and effect of this ordinance is unexceptionable. It has been and is, I doubt not, the occasion of indefinite good, but an importance is given by the friends of the rite to it which never can belong to any form. My friends, the kingdom of God is not meat and drink. Forms are as essential as bodies. It would be foolish to declaim against

21. I Timothy 2:5; cf. Hebrews 8:6, 9:15, and 12:24.

them, but to adhere to one form a moment after it is outgrown is foolish. That form only is good and Christian which answers its end. Jesus came to take the load of ceremonies from the shoulders of men and substitute principles. If I understand the distinction of Christianity, the reason why it is to be preferred over all other systems and is divine is this, that it is a moral system; that it presents men with truths which are their own reason,[22] and enjoins practices that are their own justification; that if miracles may be said to have been its evidence to the first Christians they are not its evidence to us, but the doctrines themselves; that every practice is Christian which praises itself and every practice unchristian which condemns itself. I am not engaged to Christianity by decent forms; it is not saving ordinances, it is not usage, it is not what I do not understand that engages me to it—let these be the sandy foundation of falsehoods. What I revere and obey in it is its reality, its boundless charity, its deep interior life, the rest it gives to my mind, the echo it returns to my thoughts, the perfect accord it makes with my reason, the persuasion and courage that come out of it to lead me upward and onward.

Freedom is the essence of Christianity. It has for its object simply to make men good and wise. Its institutions should be as flexible as the wants of men. That form out of which the life and suitableness have departed should be as worthless in its eyes as the dead leaves that are falling around us.

And therefore, though for the satisfaction of others I have labored to show by the history that it was not intended to be perpetual, though I have gone back to weigh the expressions of Paul, I feel that here is the true way of viewing it. In the midst of considerations as to what Paul thought and why he so thought, I cannot help feeling that it is labor misspent to argue to or from his convictions or those of Luke or John respecting any form. I seem to lose the substance in seeking the shadow. That for which Paul lived and died so gloriously; that for which Jesus was crucified; the end that animated the thousand martyrs and heroes that have followed him, was to redeem us from a formal religion, and teach us to seek our wellbeing in the reformation of the soul. The whole world was full of idols and ordinances. The Jewish was a religion of forms; the Pagan was a religion of forms; it was all body, it had no life,—and the Almighty God was pleased to qualify and send forth a man to teach men that they must serve him with the heart;[23] that only that life was religious which was thoroughly good, that sacrifice was smoke and forms were shadows, and this man lived and died true to this purpose, and now, with his blessed words and life before us, Christians must contend that it is a matter of vital importance, really a duty, to commemorate him by a certain form, whether that form be agreeable to their understandings or not.

Is not this to make vain the gift of God? Is not this to turn back the hand on the dial? Is not this to make men, to make ourselves, forget that not forms but

22. See *JMN* 3:25. Used in *Nature* (*CW* 1:8) and "Experience" (*CW* 3:31).
23. Cf. Matthew 22:37, Mark 12:30–33, Luke 10:27, and Ephesians 6:6.

duties, not names but righteousness and love are enjoined and that in the eye of God there is no other measure of the value of any one form than the measure of its use?

There remain some practical objections to the ordinance which I need not state. There is one on which I had intended to say a few words, the unfavorable relation in which it puts those persons who abstain from it merely from disinclination to that rite.

Influenced by these considerations, I have proposed to the brethren of the church to drop the use of the elements and the claim of authority in the administration of this ordinance, and have suggested a mode in which a meeting for the same purpose might be held, free of objection.

They have considered my views with patience and candor, and have recommended unanimously an adherence to the present form. I have therefore been compelled to consider whether it becomes me to administer it. I am clearly of opinion that I ought not. This discourse has already been so far extended that I can only say that the reason of my determination is shortly this—It is my desire, in the office of a Christian minister, to do nothing which I cannot do with my whole heart. Having said this, I have said all. I have no hostility to this institution. I am only stating my want of sympathy with it. Neither should I ever have obtruded this opinion upon other people, had I not been called by my office to administer it. That is the end of my opposition, that I am not interested in it. I am content that it stand to the end of the world if it please men and please heaven, and shall rejoice in all the good it produces.

As it is the prevailing opinion and feeling in our religious community that it is an indispensable part of the pastoral office to administer this ordinance, I am about to resign into your hands that office which you have confided to me. It has many duties for which I am feebly qualified. It has some which it will always be my delight to discharge according to my ability wherever I exist. And whilst the thought of its claims oppresses me with a sense of my unworthiness, I am consoled by the hope that no time and no change can deprive me of the satisfaction of pursuing and exercising its highest functions.

CLXIII

He that believeth on me hath everlasting life.

JOHN 3:36

It is a presumption against a doctrine that it produces gloomy impressions. Wisdom is goodnatured. Truth is cheerful. God is Love.[1] It is remarkable how dark and sanguinary are the pictures of heaven that have been drawn by heathen nations. Nothing exceeds the atrocity which the Eastern idolaters ascribe to their divinities. The more civilized nations had a less frightful representation of the state of the dead, and the assembly of the Gods. It is a great improvement to come to the Old Testament. With all the imperfections of the Jewish mind, the God of Moses and David is one who loves and benefits men. He delights in the shining sun, the fruitful field, the strong man, the young child; his wrath is never arbitrary; his thunders always ready to turn aside. Still, that favored people give very imperfect views of the Divine Providence. And he is strangely painted as laughing at the calamity of evil men and as the vindictive destroyer of many nations.[2]

Christianity makes men acquainted with him as the Father, and introduces the sublime doctrine of his dwelling with man,[3] and that under the name of the Comforter.[4] If this doctrine were faithfully preached, if it were steadily carried out, if the access of every man to the Father were brought home to the mind, it would infuse a courage and joy into the human heart which all the evils of life would not abate.

Although the manuscript carries the date of the sermon's first delivery, September 16, 1832, it is also marked "Palimpsest" on the first page, indicating that it is a revised version. No earlier manuscript survives. Preached ten times: September 16, 1832, at the Second Church, Boston; February 9, 1834, in New Bedford; April 6 at the New North Church, Boston; April 27 at the Second Church, Waltham; July 13 in Bangor, Maine; October 19 at the Second Church, New York; December 7 in Concord; June 14, 1835, in Framingham; March 20, 1836, in East Lexington; and April 30, 1837, in Watertown. A draft of the sermon appears in *JMN* 4:40–42.

1. I John 4:8 and 4:16.

2. All of these images occur frequently in the Old Testament; with the last, however, cf. Proverbs 1:26–27.

3. See, for example, Matthew 1:23, John 14:17, Romans 8:9, I Corinthians 3:16, and II Timothy 1:14. The Old Testament also describes God as dwelling with man; see, for example, Exodus 25:8, 29:45–46, and Numbers 35:34.

4. In a general sense this conception of the deity is common to the Old and New Testaments; see, for example, Psalms 23:4 and 86:17, as well as Isaiah 49:13, 51:3, and 51:12. Cf. Matthew 5:4 and II Corinthians 1:3–7, 7:6. St. John, however, gives an entirely new meaning to the concept in John 14:16, 14:26, 15:26, and 16:7.

But it has not been preached.

Christianity has not been represented, at least not uniformly nor usually, as the Comforter, but has notoriously been connected with stern and sad images. It has oftener been a trumpet of wrath or a funereal dirge than an affectionate pleader with the human heart. How strictly associated has it been with sickness and death; death is the time for people to become Christians. It holds the pall at funerals, and when it is called in at other times, it is expected to be very grave and to keep its finger pointed and its eye lifted upward as if not at all interested in any thing here and only belonging to another world.

Is not this so much presumption against the truth of such views of Christianity? Jesus did not go through the world with his finger on his lip, telling men they must prepare to die. He never did as his ministers have often done. He never speaks of death except in speaking of his own. He was a teacher of living. He would lead men to do that which was before them, and instead of looking to the future look to the present, and death, instead of being the foreground, absolutely disappears from his view. To present Christianity as a preparation for death, is a departure from his spirit and is unnatural and pernicious. The faults of religion and religious men grow out of this error. It is not in man to keep down the overflowing joy which God caused to issue from the heart: it is not in reason and sense to despise the glorious picture which is new created every moment around us, and he who thinks his religion demands of him to despise the present and look forward for felicity must suppress his natural feeling and injure his powers or else play the hypocrite and feign to hate what he loves.

Here is an error that embarrasses the mind of very good persons. They cannot bring themselves to consider the very event of death with any satisfactory feeling nor obtain such a lively faith of what shall follow it as to beget any feeling of desire of that event. And they blame themselves that they have no such desire. I do not think God meant we should. To seek it, is to strive against nature. It is not a desire of death that is the high point we are to reach, but indifference to it. And these are the two points I wish to consider. 1. That our business is not dying but living. 2. That the only information which God has given us of the other world is not of that sort as to withdraw us in the least from the duties or enjoyments of this.

1. The language that is heard in the world is 'Remember thou must die. In the hot pursuits of life, never forget they must shortly terminate.' I do not like this language. I say, What have I to do with death? What is death? In the midst of sickness or danger, in the immediate apprehension of death, it affords me nothing definite on which my thoughts can rest. I will dismiss it forever. God has given me other vocation. He has set duties before me which, with his help, I will discharge as long as I exist. A great man wrote upon a tomb, "Think on living."[5] That sentiment is in accordance with my nature and with Christianity.

5. The quotation is from Goethe, *Wilhelm Meister's Apprenticeship,* trans. Thomas Carlyle

The moment I recall my thought from the emptiness of death, and fix it on something to be done, I feel a sensible relief.

Set yourself to do with your might what is before you.[6] There lies your duty, your excellence, your whole concern. What advantage accrues from contemplations of death? You remind me of my mortality; you present vividly before me the unpleasing images of disease; my stomach is affected with creeping sympathies of mortality; my fears are excited; but what is done for my soul? a low fear possesses it and paralyzes it. What is the remedy? What, but to present it with images of noble action, to set before it pressing motives and present duties. It then sets out with dignity and joy in the midst of pestilence and feels a lofty indifferency and contempt for death; feels that death is nothing to it. A soul engaged in serving another in the last moments of life, or doing any thing really worth doing dies like a soldier in hot blood who never feels the wound.[7]

The true difficulty lies not in getting ready to die but in getting ready to live here. That life which men say and think would do very well if there were no other world, the life of sensual indulgence, of hatred, fraud, and meanness, is not well for this world, is not fit for any world.

Good men say, 'Get ready to die.' How shall I get ready? I know not what shall be. God has hidden from me the secrets of the other world. It seems to me therefore grossly defective to urge people to a good life *because their future wellbeing depends upon it.* That is not the right reason. They may with great propriety ask for the evidence.

No, the true reason why they should lead a good life is perfect now; it is its own evidence; you weaken your cause if you attempt to show the advantages of it. And the ground of our conviction in its being best for the future is because it is best now.

This doctrine is taught us by reason and by scripture. God has shut down upon the future world an impenetrable veil, which no man has been permitted to raise one moment, and no one in heaven has raised it for man. To what end? Certainly not, as some men say, that there is no future. Our entire ignorance of what the mode shall be is no more argument against the future state than the apparent deadness of the egg is a proof that it shall not be a bird, or the want of intelligence in the human embryo a proof that it shall not be a reasoning, speaking man. No, the stern forbiddal from Divine Providence of all intercourse between that world and this is no reason at all for doubting its existence but is a most significant admonition to men. What but this, that, we should confine our attention to the present; that we should do those things which we have faculties for doing; and not waste our energies in fruitless conjectures,

---

(Boston, 1828), 3:142. Emerson borrowed volumes 1 and 2 from the Boston Athenaeum on August 13 and 16, respectively. He may also have seen it in Carlyle's "Goethe's Portrait," *Fraser's Magazine* 5 (March 1832): 206. See *JMN* 4:40–41 and 4:88, the latter a journal entry of 1833 in which Emerson returns to the subject of this sermon. Used in "Immortality" (*W* 8:328).

6. Goethe, *Wilhelm Meister's Apprenticeship,* trans. Thomas Carlyle (Boston, 1828), 3:4.

7. Used in Sermon CLIII and "The Uses of Natural History" (*EL* 1:22).

regrets or aspirations for the unknown and the inaccessible. He teaches us by this necessity this great truth, that, the best preparation for the future is ability for the present life, that in appointing our first faltering steps to be taken here, he has not neglected to consider our whole being, but has accommodated man to his world, his world to man, and both to the vast perspective of the future to which he has opened the eye of the soul.

The true fitness for this is preparation for that, because a true fitness for this is a training and maturing of the man himself—the extrication of his powers from the inactivity in which they were folded, and acquainting him with their use, and so he is fitted for any theatre of action. And you have no right to slight any duty because it is temporary. The world is temporary, but the duty belongs to the soul, which is eternal. Too much dignity cannot be given to the part we play here. It can never be too deeply felt that the best preparation for death and heaven is the just, kind, unremitted discharge of our trusts on earth.

This way of considering the matter may show us how unreasonable are those wishes that are so often expressed by the survivors concerning the departed. A sudden death is always regretted as without preparation. We quote particular expressions with great satisfaction intimating their willingness to approve some religious form, or the love they exhibited for the church, or the intention to perform a specific act.

The expressions of pious sentiment uttered in the last hours are grateful to us. Far better in my judgment if the memory could go back to inadvertent words and acts of kindness, to a word which never was broken, to a patience that never was worn out, to a temperance that never forgot itself, to an industry that increased from year to year. Beyond all comparison better, would be the clear light that went out from an improving character and compelled us also to improve than without it, would be the fame of sainted piety and continual prayer.

2. It is the same general truth that lies at the bottom of all spiritual views of heaven and makes the distinction between them and the popular views. It has been the vice of Calvinism to *describe* heaven. Every uncultivated people have had their high coloured pictures of heaven. It has been represented as wholly different from this world, different I mean in its mode of being, its employments, its appearance. So different that skill to live here, was no skill to live there. It has been described in such terms as lead men to say, 'Yes, I should like it very well, if I could be sure it was so.'

But as soon as men reflect, they begin to perceive that they have another and very different means of learning something of that other world, that instead of a painting from the imagination, they are already in possession of the very materials out of which it is to be created; that instead of guessing at it as at some fabulous and uncertain good it is forming itself in the very circle of their ordinary powers and actions, that it is revealed to them solely by the powers which are to make it. Go into your own bosom, into that undiscovered world and into the experience of every day. These powers and these powers alone contain the revelation of what you can do and can become. It is writ in no book. It can never be foretold or imagined. They are your heaven or they are your hell. What do you know of heaven? any thing by *description*? any thing by the parabolic painting of the New Testament? If you examine it, you will find that Christ only describes what is true of God's Providence now in this world; and that is true of all you know of heaven; that is precisely your way of learning any thing about it; that, whenever you have supplanted an error in your own mind by a just sentiment, whenever you have arrived at the knowledge of some reformation in religion, in manners, in politics, that ought to take place and you are assured must sooner or later take place in society,—you have then acquired so much knowledge of heaven or of the true state of happy souls.

I am afraid these things are apt to be spoken and to be heard as general propositions without a direct application. Heaven is not in the sky, nor is the opening of its gates to be announced by trumpets of archangels and thunders of melody. It is where you live and in what you say and do—in homely duties, trivial particulars. It is in being good to wife and children and servants that the kingdom of heaven begins. It is in dealing punctually with your creditor, and not holding out false hopes to young men.[8] It is in keeping your word with those who will not reproach you if it is broken. It is in forming your own judgment upon questions of duty. It is in preferring a just act to a kind one, and a kind act to a graceful one. It is in perceiving your responsibleness for the growth of all your powers and the most efficient direction of them to the good of men.

It seems to have been the design of Christ to teach us that duration was not life, that our immortality did not consist in continuing to breathe, but in disclosing that part of man which has nothing to do with decay. As fast as this character is formed within you, have you not a new perception of something durable? A character, in the Christian ethics an upright benevolent character, is life. A habit of action strictly conformed to the laws of God, a habit of action breathing philanthropy, is the very opposite of mortality. This is the sense of the whole teaching of Christ, that *he was life*.[9] The whole stress of this revealer of immortality is laid on this, not that you shall endure so many ages or suns, but—Do the will of my Father,[10] keep the commandment; be pure; be meek; live well. Sin is death; obedience is life. He that believeth on me, that is, he that obeyeth me, shall never die.[11]

And this falls in, how perfectly, with the view we have taken, that the employments of the other world have the same relation to us as the employments of this, so that death is nothing, and we ought rather to speak of our *whole being*, than of the *future* state.

Let us take this truth then home to our own breasts. Let us feel that our

8. Emerson alludes to this compunction in dealing with apprentices in his eulogy of George Adams Sampson (see Sermon CLXVIII below).

9. Cf. John 11:25.

10. Matthew 7:21; cf. Mark 3:35.

11. John 11:26.

business is not death but life, the most earnest, faithful and useful life, if it can be, a perfect life. Let us not believe it possible to die. Let us not fear the pestilence though it walk in darkness or smite at noon.[12] Above all, let it not hinder us in any work of active love. The Cholera may kill the body; let not the fear of the Cholera kill the Soul. We are to act, doubtless, in our care of our health as if there were no other world. We should be punctilious in our care. We do not else observe the design of Providence. But the animal life itself is never to be valued at the price of the least duty. It is to be fearlessly risked at any moment at the call of a duty, for that is the life of life. Oh let not existence be valued when that which makes the value of existence is lost. It is only the consciousness of good intentions, the knowledge that we are beloved by our friends and deserve to be beloved, that can persuade an honorable mind to pray that its being may be prolonged an hour. But to outlive your own respect,—to live when your acquaintance shall shrug their shoulders and count it a disgrace to you the breath that is yet in your nostrils—I shall be glad to be told what is the pleasure, what is the profit, that is worth buying at such a price.

No; let none to whom thought and virtue are sacred fear to die. Let us believe that the character is not so wonderfully disciplined—this inward life by this outward world—to a vain purpose. Let us fear no disease, no accidents, by which not the life itself, but only its vehicle can be impaired. Believe in God that happy is the lot of those to whom the unspeakable secrets of the other state are disclosed. When our own hour comes, when every medicine and means has been exhausted, we are then to say to the angel, Hail! All hail! and pass to whatever God has yet to reveal to the conscious spirit. Why should we dread to die when all the good and the beautiful and the wise have died, and earth holds nothing so precious as that which it has lost?[13]

Why should we dread to die if in our lives we are faithful to our duties? and if not, we should dread to live. Let us apply ourselves to God; let us lay ourselves in the lap of his love who is the Source of life and feel assured that we can never perish.

12. Psalms 91:6.
13. With this and the preceding paragraph, cf. *JMN* 4:37.

CLXIV

Be renewed in the spirit of your mind and . . . put on the new man which after God is created in righteousness and true holiness.

Ephesians 4:23–24

There are some contemplative men who flatter themselves that juster views of human nature are gaining ground than have yet prevailed. It is thought that men are beginning to see with more distinctness what they ought to be, that is, what true greatness is. What was called greatness, they have discovered to be an imposture.

If it be true that we have better views of the right cultivation of the human Character, then, indeed, it is left to us, to commence the best of all works. Nations long before us have made desolating wars and gained bloody victories. Others have invented useful and elegant arts. Others have reared grand temples and beautiful palaces. Others have bred great kings terrible to their enemies and to their subjects;—have produced ingenious artists, inspired poets, eloquent orators, wise judges, brave soldiers, rich merchants, great benefactors, learned scholars. Let them all have their due praise. To us has been committed by Providence the higher work of forming *men,*—true and entire men. A finished man—who has been?[1] Men are everywhere, on the land and on the sea, in mountains and mines; cities and fields swarm with them. They are reckoned by thousands and myriads and millions. Yet where to find one who is that which he should be,—that which his Maker designed; one who is only as good as the idea we carry of a good man within our breast. Survey the whole circle of your acquaintance, of your neighborhood, of your town, and, if you can, fix upon

Two manuscripts of Sermon CLXIV exist: a heavily revised earlier version, dated October 21, 1832, which carries the title "The Genuine Man" (added in pencil), and an untitled and undated later version, probably prepared for the second delivery, but certainly read from for the ninth delivery in New York, as evidenced by the hymn citations. Preached thirteen times: October 21, 1832, at the Second Church, Boston; November 17, 1833, in New Bedford; February 23, 1834, at the Hollis Street Church; April 13 at the Federal Street Church; May 11 in Watertown; May 18 in Fall River; June 1 at the Second Church, Waltham (see *JMN* 4:294); July 6 in Bangor, Maine; October 26 at the Second Church, New York; January 18, 1835, in Lowell; May 10 in East Lexington; November 15 in Concord; and April 16, 1837, in Lexington. The earlier version is given in the Textual and Manuscript Notes.

1. Cf. *JMN* 4:54. The theme of the "genuine man" is introduced in the journal on August 18 and 19, 1832 (*JMN* 4:37–38).

one complete man; a man independent of his circumstances; one who hath a mind which fills and satisfies your idea of the perfection of human nature; one whom you venerate *as a man;* whose value to your eye consists entirely in the richness of his own nature, in the ability and dispositions you believe him to possess and not in the noise of his reputation, or the name of his family, or the office he fills, or the large estate he enjoys.

There is nothing for the most part less considered than the essential man. The circumstances weigh much more with us. A striking example of this is found in men in public life. Ordinarily when we speak of great men, we mean great circumstances. The man is the least part of himself.[2] We hear the wheels of his carriage, we see the company that walk with him. We read his name in the public prints. But *him,* the praised, the blamed, the enriched, and accompanied,—that is to say, the soul of him, we know not. There are persons who almost live in the statehouse, who scarcely walk but in a procession, and whose names are always in the newspaper,—and yet, of whose real character we are in nearly total ignorance. Hence it happens that the eminence which is acquired in society is often merely artificial, and comes to be attained by persons of mediocrity if not of inferior character.

But not only an inferior man is thus often magnified, but men of real ability owe to this noise and pomp the largest part of their eclat. It aids and doubles their greatness. Whichever way the great man turns, whatever he saith or doth, he is never considered on his naked merits; his fame wins for him, argues for him, commands for him. Who can resist this influence, and feel that the reason of a popular idol is really no more weighty than our own?

Consider what happens when we meet a person who has had what is called great success in life. The imagination is first excited and the judgment a little shaken by the renown of his name. Then he is announced by all sort of cheerful and respectful attentions. Then every word comes loaded with the weight of his professional character. Then there is still another fence of fine, plausible manners, and polished speech; and the men are very few who have the firmness of nerve to go behind all these inclosures, and, with an undazzled eye, penetrate unto, and measure, and weigh the man himself; and the men are fewer still, who can bear the scrutiny. Behind all this splendid barricade of circumstances, is often found a poor, shrunken, distorted, almost imperceptible object, who, when exposed, is found helpless and unhappy.[3]

Is it not true, brethren, in your experience, that thus the man is the least part of himself? Arts and professions, wealth and office, manners and religious connexion are screens which conceal lameness and imperfection of character. The eye is so entertained with the outward parade that rarely does any body concern himself with the state of the real person that moves under it all. The whole world runs after externals, and the soul, that is, the substance, is overlooked. But

2. "Ovid says, 'The girl is the least part of herself:' of himself as certainly the man is" (Walter Savage Landor, *Imaginary Conversations,* 1st ser., 2d ed. [London, 1828], 3:220). See *JMN* 4:44.
    3. Cf. *JMN* 4:51.

this is more than a mere speculation upon character: the reason why I beg your attention to it, is because it touches us all so nearly. I am afraid there is none of us who is not in some degree dazzled by these trappings of man,—none who is not continually in danger of mistaking them for the substance.

In the most private condition, the same mistake is made. A failure in trade is called ruin, though it may only call out the faculties and resources of the spirit. The death of a parent or relative on whom the subsistence of a family has depended is thought to cut off their prospects in life. How many families are brought up in the belief that an advantageous connexion in life is essential to the comfort and respectability of women, and so they hasten into unhappy connexions, ignorant of the sublime powers that dwell in the soul, the only source of real happiness and respectability in any situation. And, in general, the wisdom or folly of young persons is thought to be determined by the exclusiveness of their regard to their interest,—casting aside all consideration of good or evil influences upon their character.

It seems to me, brethren, as if we wanted nothing so much as the habit of distinguishing betwixt our circumstances and ourselves;—the habit of rigorous scrutiny into our own daily life, to learn how much there is of our own action, and how much is not genuine, but imitated and mercenary; the advantage of arriving at a precise notion of a genuine man such as all good and great persons have aimed to be; such as Jesus designed to be, and to make many become; such, in short, as, in the language of the Scriptures, is, "the New Man, created after God in righteousness and true holiness."

And so I beg your attention to this topic, and if, by chance, I speak to any person earnestly engaged in the formation of his own character, let him compare and correct my account by his own experience, whilst I aim at pointing out the characteristics of *the genuine man*.

1. And, in the first place, he is a man who feels an interest in himself. In general, as I have already said, nothing is less thought of. To some persons it may sound strange, that we say people do not think enough of themselves. Does not the apostle Paul, they say, teach that a man ought not to think highly of himself?[4] Do we not say of a selfish or a vain man that he thinks too much of himself? There are two ways of speaking of self—one when we speak of low and partial self, as when Paul said, Let none think too highly of himself; and the other, when we speak of the whole self—that which comprehends a man's whole being; that of which Jesus said of the prodigal son, "And when he came to himself—";[5] and, in that sense, when you say of a man that he thinks too much of himself, I say, No, the fault is that he does not think of himself at all. He has not got so far as to know himself. He thinks of his dress, he thinks of his money, he thinks of his comely person, and graceful manners, he thinks of the pleasing things he is to say and do—but the eternal reason which shines within

4. Romans 12:3. With this paragraph, cf. *JMN* 4:49.
5. Luke 15:17; see Emerson's discussion of this text in Sermon CLV.

him, the immortal life that dwells at the bottom of his heart,[6] he knows not; he is not great enough,—not good enough,—not man enough to go in and converse with his own thoughts. Possibly he is so utterly unacquainted with himself,—has lived so on the outside of his world, that he does not yet believe in its existence.

But if a man has any desire of improvement it is indispensable that he should believe in the powers and worth of his own nature, because, the very means and condition of all improvement is the raising a great counterbalance to the desire of riches, of popularity, and the love of life—in the desire of his own perfection. Far from being daunted when he comes in contact with the display of great estates, rich furniture, and the imposing luxuries of the world, it is necessary he should feel that there is something in him which is as great,—nay,—much greater than any of these. He should feel, that, whereas the consequence of most men now depends on their wealth, or their popularity,—he is capable of being, and ought to become, a man so rich and so commanding by the simple force of his character, that his wealth or poverty would be of trifling importance,—that his solitary opinion and his support given to any cause whatever would be like the acclamation of nations in its behalf. He cannot esteem it too highly—since all true greatness consists, as we shall see, in the development of this inward nature, the raising it to absolute sovereignty over him.[7] We wish that a man should hold it in such veneration that he can easier sustain the contempt of all his friends than his own contempt.

But men are apt to hear these representations with distrust and say, 'Yes, but have I the right to trust myself so far?—A strong self-reliance will do very well for men of original mind,—but for me, for most men, it seems safest not to leave the beaten track.'—My friend, and I speak from the deepest conviction to every person who hears me,—You are an original mind. You have a higher right to speak your own thought and to act it,—however obscure, or indigent, or unlearned,—than any eminence of station or any *forms* of education can confer; for, you derive that right from the Creator of the world who made you a new being. There are thoughts in your breast, that never existed in any other soul. The plan and determination of your character is novel and peculiar in the Universe. If you are a stranger to that originality and strength it is because you never give it play. It is because you depart from your own convictions, and copy other people, and say what they say, and so you have not found out what you are. And you cannot hope to make any progress to real power, until you realize this secret strength,—this right of leaning upon your own mind and the duty of obeying it.

2. This self-regard identifies itself with a regard for truth; for truth in every sense,—truth of speech, truth of thought, and truth of action. And so it is a second mark of the genuine man that he speaks the truth.

6. *JMN* 4:52.
7. *JMN* 4:52.

He speaks the truth. In our intercourse with the world we are obliged to make much allowance for what is said out of complaisance, and what is said from self-interest. Indeed, what is meant by "knowledge of the world?" does it not signify—'being suspicious'—not confiding too much in kind words and first impressions? And it is painful to see how much dissimulation exists. There are some people who never appear to speak from their thought—very well behaved people too, to whom it never seems to have occurred that a thought rises in the soul for any other purpose than to be suppressed. They never act themselves. They are always plotting. They always have one meaning on their lips and another at heart, often not so much from a design to deceive as to make themselves agreeable to their company. There are persons who really never hear with the ear their real intents. They never put off the mask, and whilst everyone wonders why one should take so much unnecessary pains, they are content to carry that cartload of dishonesty from morning till night, winter and summer, for forty years and more.

From such painful folly, it is refreshing to come into the presence of the genuine man. It seems to him needless and irksome. This duplicity shows that the person practising it has not yet learned to ascribe any importance to the good or evil opinion of the soul within but is absorbed instead in a regard to external considerations. And then is ashamed and seeks to conceal them. But where the mind has no low ends, and is acting with its own consent—it assumes no veil,—it needs none,—but goes to its object openly, and by the shortest way. It was nobly said by an old Roman, when some masons offered for ten talents to build a house such that nobody in the city could look into it, "I will give you twice so much money," he replied, "if you will build me a house so that all Rome can see every part of it."[8] It was well said by George Fox the Quaker, "That which I am in words I am the same in life." It was to the same purpose that an eminent religious teacher of the last generation, Emanuel Swedenborg, said of his writings, "that they would be found another self."[9]

But by the genuine man I understand something more than a man who speaks the literal truth. There is a rarer virtue than this, a higher service of truth which is the source of this, namely, the trusting his own thoughts and following their guidance. He is not accustomed to adopt his motives or modes of action from any other, but to follow the leading of his own mind like a little child.

Most men act from a great variety of motives, sometimes from principle, sometimes from prejudice, sometimes from the expectations other people have of them, sometimes from calculation, sometimes from superstition. The genuine man is always consistent, for he has but one leader. He acts always in

---

8. Plutarch, "Political Precepts," in *Plutarch's Morals,* ed. William W. Goodwin (Boston, 1870), 5:103.

9. The quotations occur together in a journal entry of August 18, 1832 (*JMN* 4:37). The Fox quotation is from William Sewel, *The History of the Rise, Increase, and Progress of the Christian People Called Quakers,* 3d ed. (Philadelphia, 1823), 1:460. Swedenborg's statement is paraphrased from Nathaniel Hobart, "Life of Swedenborg," *New Jerusalem Magazine* 2 (1828–1829): 36.

character, because he acts always from his character. He is accustomed to pay implicit respect to the dictates of his own reason. As he therefore speaks what he thinks, he acts his thought. He acts simply and up to the highest motives he is acquainted with.

And such an elevated love of truth flows directly into action.

3. I therefore account it a third characteristic of the true man that his action corresponds to his speech. Having one ruler and not many, all parts of him are consistent. He makes a single impression on every side. He gives himself with heartiness to the affairs which engage his attention, following the advice of the apostle,—himself a high example of this sincerity,—"Whatsoever ye do, do it heartily, as unto the Lord, and not unto men."[10] And here perhaps arises the greatest difficulty which such a character must contend with. The world is already made when he was born: the professions are fixed; the customs of business are long ago settled; and if he would get a comfortable subsistence among them and live at peace with his neighbors, he must not quarrel even with abuses, but must conform, and take the world as he finds it. No: every man who exerts himself can do something to correct abuses, and to bring his way of life, whatever it may be, into harmony with his conscience. Witness a thousand thousand sacrifices that only this cause of Temperance has occasioned. Nothing is impracticable to men in earnest. The genuine man finds his way to that mode of action for which he is fitted (and every one is peculiarly fitted for some one) and conforms that mode to him instead of conforming himself to corrupt modes, and moves therein with freedom and joy. No man can do well what he does with half his heart. He has chosen his pursuit, and engages in it with the energy of love.

It is quite important to observe that more is required of you than to say and do what is agreed on all hands to be right. I have said, Every man is an original mind. It follows, that there is some peculiar merit which it is yours to seek and find. You must work after your own fashion, and not after that of any body else. You must be virtuous and wise in your own way, as much as you must speak in your own tone, and not mimic other people's. The first resolute efforts at a virtuous life, are often embarrassed by vain attempts to cooperate in those good works which are most in vogue. There are, perhaps, many benevolent projects,—certain plans of instruction, or of charity, or of public reform, which interest the community, but which fail to affect you. Let them alone. If you have given them a fair examination, and doubt their efficacy, or are satisfied that you have not power to forward them, do not praise them because they are popular and because other people think they ought to have your support. Do not use a stronger expression in commending the best cause than your own feeling will justify. Do not put at risk the integrity of your own character, and neutralize the force of your own talents by giving a half support to any thing which, however good it may be, is not good for you,—is not the place appointed for you. There

10. Colossians 3:23.

is something—be assured, there is something—which does seem to you good and wise. Praise that; aid that; give yourself to that; and not the less because you find yourself in the minority, no, nor even if you should find yourself alone.

It is wonderful the amount of moral force which strict consistency of character—the habit of regarding not only what is true in words, but what is true for himself, a fit object for his advocacy—bestows upon the words of a single-minded person. You feel that it is not he who speaks, so much as truth and reason which speak through him.[11]

4. One more mark of the man we describe is his fearlessness and habitual tranquillity. God rewards those who obey him with peace. The person who implicitly follows the leading of his own mind casts off from himself the responsibility of his words and actions and throws that responsibility upon God.[12] Whilst a man rests upon the simple perception of the rectitude of his action, he has nothing to do with consequences. He is above them. He has nothing to do with the effect of his example. God will take care of his example. He is following God's finger and cannot go astray. Whilst I walk according to my conscience I know I shall never be ashamed. When I have adhered to it, I know my conduct is capable of explanation though I may have wholly forgotten the circumstances.

I have enumerated some of the traits of this desirable character. I wish it was in my power to show the striking contrast to the tameness and slavishness of our ordinary habits that is presented by a life thus springing ever fresh from an active mind; to show the grace and the power of a man not hampered by little fears nor mean ambition but walking in the world with the free step of Adam in the Garden, which was all his own by the highest right; a man who when known is found to unite every endearing sportive grace to a sublime self-subsistency.

I see fragments of this character every where; they make the sweetness and virtue of society, but the individual in high or in humble life who holds this purpose steadily before him—how rarely is he found.

Finally, in answer to any, if such there be, who shall say, 'This quality of genuineness or truth of character is good, but is there not something better?' I will add the remark that the conviction must be produced in our minds that this *truth of character is identical with a religious life;* that they are one and the same thing; that this voice of your own mind is the voice of God, that the reason why you are bound to reverence it is because it is the direct revelation of your Maker's will, not written in books many ages since nor attested by distant miracles but writ in the flesh and blood, in the faculties and emotions of your constitution; that the reason why the Bible is sacred is because its commandments are affirmed and sanctioned by this inward Guide and light. This is the New Man who is to be formed—the end of the life and teaching of Jesus; Jesus did not conform to the corruptions of the times, to the way of the world. He did not

11. In a journal entry of late September 1832, Emerson relates this point to his recently deceased friend, George Adams Sampson; see *JMN* 4:44, where the editors incorrectly identify "Sampson."
12. *JMN* 4:43.

teach as the Scribes but departed at once from them to obey that inward teaching, the God in him which is also in us,[13] and until this conviction is wrought
and acted upon, a man can never be said to have fairly set out on his journey of
improvement, for this alone can teach him how to blend his religion with his
daily labor, so that every act shall be done with the full consent of his head and
his heart.

How many men now regard their business as so much interruption, as so
much injury to their religious life? Their religious character is something separate from their daily actions. If instead of this each man worked in his favorite
calling in the way and according to the principles of his own inward Teacher—
and therefore with *love*—if he saw in every day's labor that he was thereby
growing more skilful and more wise; that he was co-operating with God in his
own education, so that every dollar he earned was a medal of so much real
power,—the fruit and the means of so much real goodness; if neither his working hours nor his rest were lost time, but all was helping him onward,—would
not his heart sing for joy? Would not the day be brighter and even the night light
about him? Would not company be more pleasant and even solitude be sociable
and his life reveal a new heaven and a new earth to his purer eyes?[14]

What is the practical use of the views we have taken? This and this only—Be
genuine. Be girt with truth.[15] Aim in all things, at all times, to be that within,
which you would appear without. Commune with your own heart that you
may know what it means, to be true to yourself, and follow that guidance. God
would have you introduce another standard of success than that which prevails
in the world. When you go home at night and cast your thoughts upon your
condition, fix them upon your character: instead of asking whether this day has
made you richer, better known, or what compliments you have received,—you
shall ask—am I more just—am I more patient—more wise—more useful?—
what have I learned? Then you will have an interest in yourself. You will be
watching the wonderful opening and growth of a human character, the birth
and breeding of an angel that has been born but who never will die,—who was
designed by his maker to be a benefactor to the world, and to find his own
happiness in forever enlarging the knowledge, multiplying the powers, and
exalting the pleasures of others.

13. Cf. Matthew 7:29 and Mark 1:22.
14. Cf. Revelation 21:1.
15. Cf. Ephesians 6:14.

CLXV

Howbeit when the spirit of truth is come, he will guide you into all truth: for he shall not speak of himself; but what he shall hear, that shall he speak; and he will show you things to come.

JOHN 16:13

One of the keenest enjoyments of human life is to return home. It has lately been mine. After a short absence spent in continual journeyings among the most interesting monuments of the ancient and the great cities of the modern world God has blessed my eyes with the sight of my own land and my own friends.[1] I cannot tell you, my friends of this religious society, with how much pleasure I see you again and learn of your welfare and of your virtues. I am touched by emotions that are more than pleasant in seeing again this well-known company of men and women standing together in the same connexions.

I meet you conversing with the same persons with whom I was wont to find you. I am moved with gratitude when I have again found together the husband and wife, the father and children, brothers and sisters, the betrothed, the beloved,—and mark how cunningly these affections of ours root themselves around the heart-strings, and tie the lives, the characters, and the destinies of men together. And I pray God, long to preserve to you the joy and protection of these dear and wholesome associations.

As I have seen you in the streets, and in your dwellings, so now I am permitted by your favor to address you once more in our ancient sanctuary. And as it has been my grateful duty heretofore to provoke you to a good life by suggesting religious sentiments,—let me once more—for one short hour—find my accustomed place in your thoughts;—once more let me invite you to the primal truths, again let us communicate the joy and peace of believing, let the power and love of the Highest overshadow us and amid the evils we suffer or fear, let us

---

The manuscript carries a title added by Emerson in pencil: "A Discourse preached at the Second Church in Boston Oct 27. 1833.—" The same date occurs at the end of the manuscript, which has, as well, a substitute conclusion dated March 15, 1834. Preached three times: October 27, 1833, at the Second Church, Boston; March 16, 1834, in New Bedford; and June 4, 1837, in East Lexington. Much of the second half of the sermon draws on a lengthy journal entry composed on October 21, 1833 (*JMN* 4:92–93).

1. This was Emerson's first sermon after his return from Europe eighteen days earlier.

find a respite and sanctuary in those sublime truths which are to be studied rather than comprehended. Brethren, I am one of those who esteem the good will of the meanest to be of some importance. I value the friendship of good men as the best gift they can bestow and so I would cultivate yours by being associated in your minds with those thoughts which are most dear to the best men, and have had the highest worth to each of us in our most virtuous hours.

No topic has seemed to me more suitable than the consideration of the prospects of society in reference to religious instruction. Before I parted from you I anxiously desired an opportunity of speaking to you upon the subject of that change which seems to be taking place under our eyes in the opinions of men on religious questions; of that Teaching which all men are waiting for, and of that Teacher who has been predicted and hath not yet come.[2] The lapse of a few months has in no wise lessened the interest of these questions, and the present condition and prospect of this church may even lend them greater pertinency.

I think I cannot overrate the dignity and interest of this inquiry for it refers to the highest want of the soul. The greatest gift of God is a Teacher and teaching is the perpetual end and office of all things. Teaching, instruction, is the main design that shines through the sky and the earth. It is the end of youth, of growth, of play, of studies, of punishment, of pleasures, of misfortunes, of sickness, of contests, of connexions, of professions—the purpose of all—all teach us something,—yes, even sin and death,—and that lesson is the reason of their coming. The end of living is to know; and, if you say, the end of knowledge is action,—why, yes, but the end of that action, again, is knowledge. He that has no ambition to be taught, let him creep into his grave. What is he doing among good people? The play is not worth the candle. The laborer is not worthy of his meat. The sun grudges his light, and the air his breath to him who stands with his hands folded in this great school of God, and does not perceive that all are students, all are learning the art of life, the discipline of virtue, how to act, how to suffer, how to be useful, and what their maker designed them for. It is this persuasion only, that can invest existence with any dignity or hope or raise man above the brutes.

And this will do it. If you discern that every step you take not only enables you to make another, but also brings you within reach of influences before inert, that your life is like the Day, which not only shows more objects every moment, but also brings out new properties in every particular object, you will then accept Instruction as the greatest gift of God, and anxiously put yourself in the attitude of preparation.

I must not stop to notice the careful provision that has been made from the earliest times for keeping alive in the world the knowledge of God, nor to consider the remarkable intimations among the ancient heathen nations, and still more among the Jews, of mankind's general expectation of a Teacher to

2. In a journal entry for October 24, 1833, Emerson discusses the "teacher of the coming age" (*JMN* 4:93–94).

come. I hasten to consider the memorable expressions of Jesus Christ on this subject as they are recorded by John, and one of which I have taken as a text. They show that he looked upon a Teacher in the light in which all wise and good men have regarded that good, as the greatest gift of God, and as ministering to the highest want of the soul.

He assured his disciples that he had much more truth to make known to them but that they could not bear it now; but that after he had departed from them, and by his departure, he would send them another Teacher, who would guide them to farther revelations, and that under this guidance, they who believed on him should be able to do greater things than he did.[3]

What is the meaning of all this? He would tell them that God was not yet known in his world, that the divine truth was not opened and could not be opened to the Jewish mind, but that by his death, they would cease from their shallow and fanatical expectation of an Israelitish conqueror, the bandages would be torn from their eyes, and on their despair the light of the true heaven might dawn.

Here are promises whose sense deserves to be more unfolded. That a Teacher shall come. Who is that Teacher? Let Jesus answer—Even the Spirit of Truth.[4] He would say, that there is a constant effort of the Divine Providence for the instruction of man. Time, the great teacher, is always uttering his lessons— heard or unheard—in the ear of man. Every day is exposing some of the falsehoods that have deceived us. Truth endures and is manifested every moment, from day to day, from age to age, ever since the crimson light of the first morning awoke the first man, the Almighty Father accumulates knowledge in the mind of the race from endless sources—from continual communication— from tradition, from scripture, from comparison of events, from personal experience, from every one of countless occurrences the growing treasure is poured into the world, as the globe itself receives the rays of millions of stars which beam upon it from all the concave firmament around.

The Teacher is one, namely, the Spirit of truth, but He speaks by a thousand thousand lips, in all countries, in public and in private places, to mankind. He is never silent. There is no one so remote but he is addressed by him. To drop all personification—the progress of society, the simple occurrences of every day, are always instructing men, undeceiving them, and every event big with what crimes and misfortunes soever, carries with it this beneficent effect, that an experiment has been tried which need not be repeated in the sight and for the sake of the human race. Thus the first Revolution in France was esteemed a great calamity. It is now a page of cheerful wisdom to Europe and to America. And as with one sort of truth so with the highest,—the relations, namely, of man to God and the character of God; that is continually being revealed. The rival churches that have risen and disputed, the pious and humble pastors who have labored, the fanatics who have exaggerated doctrines fundamentally true,

3. John 14:16–21.
4. John 14:17, 15:26, 16:13.

the infidels and scoffers who have assailed with success the corruptions of Christianity, have all done service to the great cause of truth, which is the Teacher of the human race.

1. Let us inquire in the first place what is the true light in which the life and labors of Jesus should be regarded. The perspective of time, as it sets every thing in the right view, does the same by Christianity. We learn to look at it now, as a part of the history of the world; to see how it rests on the broad basis of man's moral nature, but is not itself that basis. I cannot but think that Jesus Christ will be better loved by not being adored. He has had, as we all know, an unnatural, an artificial place for ages in human opinions—a place too high for love. There is a recoil of the affections from all authority and force. To the barbarous state of society it was thought to add to the dignity of Christ to make him King, to make him demigod, to make him God. Now that the scriptures are read with purged eyes, it is seen that he is only to be loved for so much goodness and wisdom as dwelt in him, which are the only properties for which a sound human mind can love any person. As the world grows wiser, he will be more truly venerated for the splendor of the contrast of his character to the opinions and practices of his age; he will attract the unfeigned love of all to whom moral nature is dear, because he planted himself, in the face of the world, upon that sole ground; showing a noble confidence in the reality and superiority of spiritual truths, that simplicity and at the same time enthusiasm in declaring them, which is itself one of the highest merits and gives confidence to all the lovers of the same truth.

But I ask whether it will not come to be thought the chief value of his teaching—whether it will not come to be thought the greatest value of Christianity—more than any single truth which it inculcated—the general fact that it was a brave stand made for man's spiritual nature against the sensualism, the forms, and the crimes of the age in which he appeared, and those which preceded it?[5] The value of his particular lessons is something less to us than it was to his contemporaries, because like every wise and efficient man he spoke to his times in all their singular peculiarities. His instruction is almost as local, as personal, as would be the teaching in one of our Sunday Schools. He speaks as he thinks, but he is thinking for them. And it is the great mark of the extraordinary force of his mind that notwithstanding this occasional character his sayings have a fulness of meaning, a fitness to human nature and an universality of application which has commended them to the whole world.

But in this respect their value is equal to us and to them and to all men, as a great affirmation of the beauty and excellence of moral truth,—a disclosure of that inner world of man whose existence, once admitted and beheld, opens an entrance for all the particular doctrines of divine truth.

I say it is the distinction of Christianity that it is the most emphatic affirmation in history, of the existence of the spiritual world.

5. Cf. *JMN* 6:183.

And in this way as Jesus was the apostle of moral nature by word and by act—living and dying—in this way was he the Teacher, the benefactor of mankind, as one who saw, and proved by his actions that he saw clearly and steadfastly an inner world, compared with whose glories the brightness of external nature is mean, and the luxuries of the senses worthless. And this I think is the light in which we are to look at the recorded teaching and example of Jesus.

2. In the second place, What has been its subsequent history? A history of growth. A great deal more truth was yet to be made known. Christianity is the most emphatic affirmation of spiritual nature. But it is not the only nor the last affirmation. There shall be a thousand more. Very inconsistent would it be with a soul so possessed with the love of the real and the unseen as Christ's to set bounds to the discoveries in that illimitable region. None knew better than he that every soul occupies a new position, and that if the stars cannot be counted, nor the sea sands numbered,[6] much less can those moral truths be numbered and ended, of which the material creation is only the shadow. He never said, All truth have I revealed—but all that which was committed to me. He plainly affirms the direct contrary. I will send you another Teacher, another Comforter, even the Spirit of Truth, he will guide you into all truth.[7] He promised that continual effort of the divine Providence which is always instructing those who are in the attitude of scholars.

Christ tells them that they are not now fit to hear what he is ready to announce, but that they shall hereafter be ready, and the future Teacher shall tell them more and greater things than he. He affirms the fact that the essential condition of teaching is a ripe pupil. The wisest Teacher can impart no more than his disciple can receive. The rapid flashes of celestial thought must wait the tardy expansion of the worldly mind. No teacher can teach without the hearty cooperation of the scholar. This, as I have already intimated, crippled his communications of moral truth. There is much, as every one knows, of what is called *accommodation* in his discourses; that is, they are clothed in the manner of speaking and in the manner of thinking of the times; otherwise, they would have been altogether rejected by that perverse generation to whom he spoke,[8] and of whom he was obliged to say, that, the very reason why they would not believe him, was that he told them the truth. "Because I tell you the truth, ye believe me not."[9]

He has always in his mouth expressions of his sense of the littleness of the present and strong assurance of the greatness of the future. His word is a

6. Jeremiah 33:22.

7. See note 4 above. For the "Comforter," see John 14:16 and 16:7.

8. In the manuscript Emerson wrote "perverse stiffnecked generation" and then canceled "stiffnecked"—perhaps because the term would too emphatically import the accusatory tone of Acts 7:51. Emerson had been admonished several times by Henry Ware, Jr., for accommodating his discourse too much to contemporary modes of speaking and thinking; Emerson may further have felt that his own communications of moral truth had been crippled by a certain inaptitude on the part of his parishioners.

9. John 8:45.

mustard seed—it is a little leaven,—it is a single pearl[10]—but with a prophet's eye he sees that the omnipotence of truth is in it, and beholds already its prolific effects—he sees it quicken in the minds of good men and run like something endued with life from soul to soul, from house to house, from land to land,— searching, agitating, educating society,—touching with sympathy all heroic minds, and preparing hearts to conceive and tongues to utter yet more lofty and significant revelations. "Greater things than these shall he do."[11] We see with our eyes the verification of his promise. We see the enlargement of religious truth in its effects. In the place of the unsupported virtues of solitary individuals that sparkle in the darkness of antiquity, of the little, stingy, rapacious inter- course of that day—a few Corinthians, a few Romans creeping round the shores of the Mediterranean for piracy and conquest, the nations of the globe are brought together by pacific and equitable commerce; liberal, humane, Chris- tian associations are correcting the manners and relieving the sufferings of vast masses of men. Bible societies, Temperance societies, Sunday Schools, Peace societies, Seamen's societies, Associations for the correction of Prison Disci- pline, for the diffusion of useful knowledge, for the abolition of slavery, and every other benevolent enterprize,—are they not all the fruit of the life and teaching of that lowly Nazarene?

I look upon them all as illustrations of the power of this conviction of which I speak in the human soul. Great and manifold as these institutions are, do they not have their origin in the fact that some men (according to the saying of Jesus) have strongly felt that 'it is better to give than to receive'[12] and that they them- selves were commanded to seek the welfare of other men? (A human mind once persuaded of a simple abstract proposition becomes the servant of that thought and puts the whole material creation as far as its power reaches into subjection to it. And a few men persuaded of the same thing will cooperate and by cooper- ation make more intense each other's conviction and soon exert a power that multiplies itself in a compound ratio and produces such effects as we behold. I rejoice as others in these effects, yet, brethren, I rejoice with no spirit of noisy exultation. I believe that the truth itself which is thus operative is worth more, far more, than all its effects. For there is in all moral truth that fruitfulness, that inborn creative force, that ever unfolding power that promises to act upon human society with an energy which nothing can adequately represent.)

3. I have said, in the first place, that Christianity was, whilst its Author lived, a defence of spiritualism against sensualism; in the second place, that it has been bearing fruit like its seed ever since by producing benevolent institutions and good men. In the third place, I wish to call your attention to the change it is now working.

There is a solemn interest settling upon the future which may well withdraw our interest from what is already around us, were it far more excellent. The

10. For "mustard seed," see Matthew 13:31, 17:20, Mark 4:31, and Luke 13:19 and 17:6; for "a little leaven," see I Corinthians 5:6 and Galatians 5:9; for the "pearl," see Matthew 13:46.
11. John 14:12; cf. John 1:50.
12. Acts 20:35.

dawn is reddening around us, but the day has not come. The Teacher is teaching but has not finished his word. That word never will be finished. It was before the heavens and shall be after them. But a part of this message is spoken this day and every day. There are truths now being revealed. There is a revolution of religious opinion taking effect around us, as it seems to me the greatest of all revolutions which have ever occurred, that, namely, which has separated the individual from the whole world and made him demand a faith satisfactory to his own proper nature, whose full extent he now for the first time contemplates. A little while ago Men were supposed to be saved or lost as one race; Adam was the federal head and, in books of theology, his sin was a federal sin which cut off the hopes of all his posterity. The atoning blood of Christ, again, was a sacrifice for all, by which the divine vengeance was averted from you and me. But now, men have begun to feel and to inquire for their *several stake* in the joy and the suffering of the whole. What is *my* relation to Almighty God? What is *my* relation to my fellow-man? What am I designed for? What are my duties? What is my destiny?—The soul peremptorily asks these questions—the Whence and the Why—and refuses to be put off with insufficient answers.

It is because so many false answers have been offered that in many earnest, well-intentioned men, reason has been so far shaken from her seat, that they have assorted with the infidel and the Atheist so called. The questions are now again presented, because the wonder of the surrounding creation begins to press upon the soul with the force of a personal address.

And what is the answer?

Man begins to hear a voice in reply that fills the heavens and the earth, saying, that God is within him, that *there* is the celestial host.[13] I find that this amazing revelation of my immediate relation to God, is a solution to all the doubts that oppressed me. I recognize the distinction of the outer and the inner self,—of the double consciousness,[14]—as in the familiar example, that I may do things which I do not approve; that is, there are two selves, one which does or approves that which the other does not and approves not; or within this erring, passionate, mortal self, sits a supreme, calm, immortal mind, whose powers I do not know, but it is stronger than I am, it is wiser than I am, it never approved me in any wrong. I seek counsel of it in my doubts; I repair to it in my dangers; I pray to it in my undertakings. It is the door of my access to the Father. It seems to me the face which the Creator uncovers to his child.

It is the perception of this depth in human nature—this infinitude belonging to every man that has been born[15]—which has given new value to the habits of

13. Luke 17:21.
14. The concept of the "double consciousness" figures prominently in Emerson's early lectures and essays. See "The Transcendentalist": "The worst feature of this double consciousness is, that the two lives, of the understanding and of the soul, which we lead, really show very little relation to each other, never meet and measure each other" (*CW* 1:213). See also "John Milton," *EL* 1:161 (used in "Milton" [*W* 12:276]); "Lord Bacon," *EL* 1:325; and *JMN* 5:475 (used in "Demonology" [*EL* 3:155] and in "Demonology" [*W* 10:8]).
15. Emerson elsewhere attributes this concept to the Quakers; see Sermon LXXXIV (*Sermons* 2:235, n. 8).

reflexion and solitude. This has caused the virtue of independent judgment to be so much praised. This has given its odour to spiritual interpretations. Many old and almost forgotten maxims have been remembered up from where they lay in the dust of centuries and are seen to beam new light. Such are the old pregnant maxim, 'Know Thyself,'[16] 'Est Deus in nobis agitante calescimus illo.'[17] The stoical precept, 'The Good Man differs from God in nothing but duration,' Bonus vir nil nisi tempore a deo differt.[18] The inscription on the gate of Athens, "But know thyself a man and be a god."[19]—"Revere thyself."[20]

And let me add that in this doctrine, as deeply felt by him, is the key by which the words that fell from Christ upon the character of God can alone be well and truly explained.

Read by the torch of this faith, it seems to me, those discourses shine with heavenly meaning. The Father is in me—I am in the Father. Yet the Father is greater than I.[21]

I anticipate auspicious effects from the farther opening of this faith upon the public mind, from the studies and the actings of good men in the course wherein its light will lead them. It will be inspiration to prophets and heroes.[22] It will be day without night. It will be power to the hands and wisdom to the understanding and society to the solitary. In a particular manner will not the increased clearness of the spiritual sight produce a great reform in the tone and character of our public religious teaching? Will it not put an end to all that is technical, allegorical, parabolical in it?

My friends, I shall not now attempt to portray the glory of that latter church which a truly spiritual faith shall have formed and shall enlighten, but I must press earnestly, affectionately, upon each of you, my own conviction of its worth. I would urge upon you the cultivation of this religious frame of mind—much meditation upon spiritual truths, especially upon these convictions of the unfathomable depth of the soul and its union with its source. In them only all real strength is found, and all those great traits which we admire in eminently wise and good men, all the supports of magnanimity and trust, all the incentives to a noble daring; in fine, the foundations and the framework on which a solid, regular, well-balanced character can be reared, which shall be able, if called, to

16. The maxim is traditionally attributed to Solon; see *Sermons* 1:226, n. 2, and 2:42, n. 4. Used also in sermons CXLIX and CLV.

17. "There is a god within us. It is when he stirs us that our bosom warms" (Ovid, *Fasti*, book 6, lines 5–6); see *JMN* 3:12, 139, and *JMN* 4:29. The lines are also quoted by Victor Cousin in his *Introduction to the History of Philosophy* (Boston, 1832), 165.

18. Seneca, "De Providentia," *Moral Essays*, trans. John W. Besore (London and New York, 1928), 1:6; used in Sermon LVI (*Sermons* 2:90), Sermon CIV (*Sermons* 3:88), "Ethical Writers" (*EL* 1:359), and "Plutarch" (*W* 10:312).

19. Plutarch, "The Life of Pompey," in *The Lives*, ed. John and William Langhorne (New York, 1822), 5:113. See *JMN* 4:212.

20. Edward Young, *Night Thoughts,* "Night VI," line 128.

21. John 14:10–11 and 14:28. Emerson actually wrote, "I am the Father" rather than "I am in the Father": certainly a careless error.

22. Cf. *JMN* 4:94.

act a part with vigor and success; if otherwise, to look with calm superiority at the disturbances of the political world,[23] at domestic disappointments, or at want and sickness,—which shall be able to go lonely through life, unhonoured, with unappreciated virtues, yet bate no jot of heart or hope, finding sufficient sympathy and applause in God only. I said that Christianity was a brave stand for spiritual truth against the sensualism of ages. A life which it has formed is a miniature of itself. A good life is a brave stand for spiritual truth against sensualism and skepticism, for the simple reason that every good act is a preference of the whole to a part; of the future to the present; of God to men.

It is the same part of our nature, the spiritual faculty, that suggests the belief that death cannot harm you. This soul converses with the past and the distant, and the future, and is conscious that its thoughts have no relation to time or to corruption. A stronger and stronger word of assurance comes from the undeceiving inward Monitor, who speaks as with the voice of the whole creation. I perceive no terrors, no shrinking in that inmost shrine at the approach of death; the fear is external to it,—in the lower faculties,—in the senses;—but all is calm within.

May this faith, this expectation of the Teacher, this effort to receive him, this divine spirit of truth, which is at once the prophecy and the fulfilment, animate them who teach and them who hear. Brethren, may it touch with fire the lips that are to speak to you—please God—for many long and happy years.[24] I rejoice in the pleasing prospects of our church. Its peace and prosperity will always be near my heart. And so farewell, my friends, and may the pastor whom God shall send you, find as much indulgence—as much tenderness at your hands, as I have found, even when we have differed upon matters of subordinate importance. May he be a true teacher of the living word. May he do that which I have desired. May he aid in communicating to your minds that peace which the world cannot give nor take away, by leading you to a nearer knowledge and love of God and habitation in him.

23. Emerson, who opposed Andrew Jackson's reelection in 1832, perhaps alludes to the crisis over the Bank of the United States, from which public deposits had been withdrawn earlier in the month.

24. The image is of the Pentecost, Acts 2:3. The Second Church Proprietors were slow to appoint a permanent successor to Emerson, and it is not clear that they had yet, in late October, settled on Chandler Robbins, who would be installed on December 4, 1833.

CLXVI

As in water face answereth to face,
so the heart of man to man.

PROVERBS 27:19

Nothing is more admirable than the kindness and wisdom which have arranged the natural societies of human life. "The child is born by the side of his father, and there he remains."[1] He is bred in the company of his equals, thrown without any effort of his own or of his natural guardians into company the most agreeable and the most useful to him. As the youthful man grows mature, the troop of his associates is always kept full, and when he comes to manhood and when he comes to gray hairs, even though he has walked with his friends in all the journey, he is hardly conscious of having made any effort in the selection. They have been given him as his parents were given him by the Divine Disposer, and when some were removed from his side others have joined his circle.

Thus every man, even from the manner in which he enters the world, finds his being intertwined with others. He sees around him faces which resemble his own; he is called by the same name as others; he has similar qualities of character. He soon comes to feel a deep interest in the prosperity of certain persons; he returns daily and hourly to their society. He needs it as he needs bread. Their aversion would make him unhappy.

But he cannot be long in discovering another fact no less certain, that, notwithstanding all this dependence, each man is, by his consciousness, separated wholly from all other men; that, dearly bound to others as he is, he is yet wholly alone. When from the jarring opinions of men he withdraws into self-communion, he finds that the whole world is as nothing before that interior Self, and his dearest friend as remote from it as his enemy. Mixed as we are in close contact, conversing with each other, conspiring with, influencing, helping, hurting each other, yet is every man's consciousness an incommunicable privacy in the abyss of being.

Only the first four pages of the manuscript of Sermon CLXVI have survived. Preached seven times: March 30, 1834, in New Bedford; July 27 in Bangor, Maine; August 31 at the First Church, Boston; November 9 at the Second Church, New York; August 30, 1835, in Lowell; March 6, 1836, at the Harvard College Chapel; and August 28 in East Lexington. On March 22, 1834, Emerson spelled out the polarities of "Self reliance" and "the ministry of our friends to us," themes he continued to explore in his journal for the next week and beyond. See *JMN* 4:269.

1. See Sermon CXL, n. 4.

Here then is a twofold nature in every individual. From this strange dualism arises, as his habits of reflexion ripen, an apparent conflict of duties which embarrasses the minds of conscientious persons; to settle, namely, the conflicting claims of solitude and society.

Our language may differ, but the great questions of human life come home to every man to be pondered and decided. I am now speaking to persons of different condition, character, early education,—yet I believe I speak to none, arrived at years of reflexion, who has not at some time debated with himself the question whether his real advantage lay in seeking or avoiding society;—whether it were wise to seek or even to accept the opportunities which offered of making new acquaintance. The wise have said—he himself has observed—that society is dangerous; that no one can be popular without conceding his independence and his originality; that recollection and sobriety belong to the closet; that friends are the thieves of time;[2] that Wisdom is the fruit of solitude and silence.

On the other hand, it is no less true, that our duties are ever calling us to active intercourse. What right have you to give yourself up to barren contemplation? Nothing is so manifest as the duty of serving others. And all the great philanthropic objects are accomplished by action and by joint action. Nay, by a degree of accommodation and some compromise of private judgment and conscience.

I am persuaded that many young persons who appear at ease in society, have yet their own secret struggles to undergo. The soul is not yet awakened to which this question has not presented itself. I believe it is to be fully answered only by a full understanding of what we seek in society: what was the design of our Creator in making us social. And it is with a view to the light that this inquiry sheds upon our social duties, that I invite your attention to the question, What are the offices we perform to each other—the lowest and the highest uses which man subserves to man?

2. Bacon, *The Advancement of Learning,* in *The Works of Francis Bacon,* ed. James Spedding et al. (London, 1857-1874), 5:34; see *JMN* 6:189.

NOTE ON SERMON CLXVII

No manuscript of Sermon CLXVII is known to survive. The Preaching Record indicates that it was delivered only once, on May 25, 1834, at the Hollis Street Church in Boston.

CLXVIII

Honorable age is not that which standeth in length of time nor that is measured by number of years, but wisdom is gray hair unto men and an unspotted life is old age.

WISDOM OF SOLOMON 4:8–9

The language of friends over the closing grave of a beloved person is wont to be partial. There is an uneasiness frequently that nothing can be said; that, whilst the great endowments proper to every man, have passed away from the flesh, we only know that our brother has been merely passive to the common influences that act on all men and our desire to apologize for and defend him, utters itself in affectionate expressions.[1] But, although the language of bereavement is not fully to be trusted, the intensity of the emotion is a test of the greatness of our loss. We are not shocked but by what ought to shock us. When we are grieved and deprived of hope, it is too much assurance of the reality of the merit that is withdrawn.

Whilst, however, we readily use strong expressions for common griefs, yet men are slow to appreciate sterling worth that falls under their own observation. Every thing human is in the act of unfolding. That which we see is only the promise of more which shall be, and so comes to be disesteemed by comparison with its own future. Then a strictly private life has no seal of public praise set upon it, such as office and fame bestow, which seem to give leave to commendations. And a good life falls in so naturally with the order of the world that we see it as we see the sun shine and the rain fall, without attention.

And so it happens that good men stand around us unregarded, and men of

Manuscript dated August 3, 1834. Emerson's eulogy for his close friend and parishioner, George Adams Sampson, who had died suddenly on July 23 while traveling to meet Emerson in Bangor, Maine, was delivered once, August 3, 1834, at the Second Church, Boston. Elizabeth Palmer Peabody and Amos Bronson Alcott were in attendance. Peabody commented: "But *words* would vainly essay to do justice to his apotheosis of Sampson. His expression—his tones—his prayers—his readings of Scripture—his sermon which was an elaborate exposition of the character—in a subdued & chastened manner of setting it forth—which cannot be described—will live in my soul forever & ever—And *I know that man* as well as I could have known him had I been his acquaintance on earth" (*L* 1:417n). See also Emerson's untitled Second Discourse on the Death of George Sampson (p. 272 below).

1. Cf. *JMN* 4:57.

wise life depart from us without being held for what they are. But let it not be so
with us. The true hero is the good man. I should be ashamed to express a
respect for Cato and Aristides and Washington and see virtues which all ages
had unanimously pointed out to me, and have no eye to discover the very same
virtues when they appeared among my own acquaintance and in the performance of ordinary duties. I should then feel no security that if Cato and Aristides should reappear in the world I should have penetration enough to discover
them. The prophet is still without honor in his own country,[2] and it is likely that
Jesus would be popular and admired in no age that the world has seen.

Nevertheless there is some progress. A good man is tolerated, is honored
among us. The emotion which the sudden death of a faithful man in the vigor
of his early manhood has awakened in the community is a proof of this. But I
say these things because now that I look back upon him and see how excellent
he was, it seems to me strange that he was not more remarked and admired. We
possess friends as if we had a right to their virtues and talents, unconscious of
the greatness of the gift until it is withdrawn. Their death alone reveals to us the
dependence we had placed on them, the increasing value of their influence to
society. Then first we are shamed by our own neglect. Then we look forth at the
remainder of our own road with a gloomy feeling that in losing our companions, the journey has lost its charm.

The application of these observations is but too obvious. O my friends, we
have lost a friend. A man has died in the midst of us who has been for years a
beloved son of this church, an active, useful, honored member of this religious
society—a man without a fault—I might almost say—so utterly unable am I,
after five years intercourse with him, to remember in him anything to censure.
He had no exemption, however, in his constitution or in his circumstances from
trial and from falling. Others may know therefore of his failings. I speak on
deliberate reflexion, when I say, they are not known to me.

What attraction is in this character! How it pleads with us in behalf of its own
virtues! There is strong propriety in speaking of him here. A good man conse-
crates the places in which he acts, and this church has been the scene of his pious
affections, of his lowly yet ardent devotion, of his manly and deep meditation.
Moreover I speak of him gladly here, because by many in this place he was well
understood, and by all in some degree; and I anticipate the strictest confirmation of my own thoughts of him, from those to whom he was best known. Most
of all, I desire to speak of him here because he was that character which we
come to the house of God to consider and to seek after; because here was a man
who had neither literature nor wealth nor power, but who spent his whole life in
common duties, in plain sight—in the streets, in his family, in well known
societies, in committees on schools, on politics, or on charities, and who had
not therefore any peculiar protection from temptation, but who did succeed in

2. Matthew 13:57, Mark 6:4, Luke 4:24, and John 4:44.

exhibiting a beautiful, unspotted life in the very thick of the crowd,[3] a man sent among us, as if to give the lie by his clear life to the vulgar pretence that the life of a man of business is not compatible with adherence to principle. His was.

Suffer me then, my friends, to speak of some of the leading traits in a character which was the common treasure of us all. The events of Mr. Sampson's life were few and nowise remarkable. It is the character that gives them all their interest. I shall not attempt to recount them. I shall speak of the features of his soul as they occur to me, in that prominence which presented themselves to the observer.

Mr. Sampson was a lover of truth. He was, if ever any was, thoroughly sincere. He was, of course, as all such persons must be, a man of guarded lips. So anxious was he to leave a correct impression that if your professions outran his own feeling, he shut his lips and did not respond to your expressions. I have heard him say that if his commercial correspondence were searched through, he did not think there would be found in the closing of any letter, a compliment of words that overstepped his feeling. This was not a mere precision, an extreme regard to literal correctness which puckers up the mouth only, and tyrannizes over words and syllables, whilst it overlooks deception in manners and actions; his care was that the truth should be told in all respects.

He saw clearly the consequences of deception and so impatient was he of them that he strongly disliked any usage which seemed to hold out hopes that were not to be made good. The holding out false hopes to young men, seemed to him so much the effect of the common relation of master and apprentice, that he thought much was to praise in the practice of hiring assistance in counting houses.

He saw the consequences of deception. And yet I may say, he loved the truth for its own sake, without a calculation of consequences. He never deceived himself or others by using words for reasons. And with the habit of such minds, sought in every conversation the simple truth with such steadiness that his words became things, and possessed the cogency of facts.[4] They who have had the happiness, as many have, to hear him speak in religious associations or in private conversation upon practical questions, will readily remember the persuasion that accompanied his discourse; how far remote was his tone of remark from any thing like speechmaking, but following the fact so evenly, step by step, that he seemed only to give it voice.

I have often had occasion to remark, and as I have said it during his lifetime, I may well say it after his death, that, so simple was his love of truth, so entirely unmixed with any wilfulness, that when he spoke upon any question of duty, his sentences had much more than the weight of an individual opinion: it was

3. Cf. James 1:27.
4. Emerson notes with approval Sampson Reed's contention, in his "Oration on Genius" (1821), that in heaven language will be "one with things" (see *JMN* 5:51). In an 1831 journal entry he noted that "in good writing words become one with things" (*JMN* 3:271).

not his opinion; it was no man's opinion; it was as if truth and justice spoke through his lips.[5]

This respect for truth which pervaded all he did, and bred in him perhaps an occasional discontent at the forms of society—had a deeper source than any computation of consequences. It sprang from that noble instinct of the best minds which nothing but truth can satisfy. There are minds which lose the desire to be thought great, in the desire to be what they were made to be; men who feel the mystery of existence; who see that a living man is encompassed round with an eternity which no thought of ours can penetrate; his own being lies like a point in the great abyss of the Past and the Future; and at the same time seeing from the order and the tenderness in the surrounding creation, that the Omnipotence which has placed them here, and made them such, may be trusted—they preserve a temper conformed to this faith. It would belie their conviction of the wonder that envelopes us, if they should be dogmatic or proud. They are so great as to be meek; too great to be capable of an arrogant word or look. At the same time, they keep alive a habitual curiosity touching the first questions,—why they exist? whither they tend? and the like; and the single fact that they have once awaked to so large thoughts confers a constant dignity upon all their ways of thinking and acting, for, the knowledge of things absolutely great, makes trifles seem to be trifles. Our friend's demeanor was marked with a sweetness and playfulness which to those who knew the depth of his character, indicated the patience with which he watched for the morning that is to break upon the night of our life;—the morning which has indeed broken upon him.[6]

Aware of these infinite relations of human nature, he conformed his life to them. He had, if I may so speak, no surface action. Whatever he did was the act of the whole man. He had no courtesy that did not spring from love; no firmness, that was not sense of duty; no modesty, that was not humility; no cheerfulness, but it was trust; no attention to your words, but it was love of truth. Thus was he all principles. And but for the even balance of his own qualities, one would have been tempted to say that a man so earnest was out of place in such a selfish and superficial world.

It was to be expected of such a man that he should cultivate his own powers; and this he did. He believed in every man's merit. He rejoiced in all the good he saw. He sought with simplicity all such places, books, or men, as promised to afford him valuable information, and listened with a candor and self-abandonment, that offered the very fairest scope to any who advocated a good cause, to make him their own.

But this love of truth would not let him be satisfied with any thing else. He never clung to any society or habit or friend, because they had been fit for him,

5. Emerson attributes to Sampson a number of the qualities of the "genuine man." See *JMN* 4:44 and Sermon CLXIV, n. 11.

6. Perhaps a recollection of the peroration of Sampson Reed's "Oration on Genius," with its allusion to Isaiah 21:11-12.

after they had ceased to be so. He sought steadfastly growth; to arrive at truth; to do the best; and whatever promised to aid him in these respects, was sure of his attention, whencesoever it came. He did not ask what reputation it had, he would have scorned to ask; for he believed that something existed independently of all opinion—of all men's support or opposition; and therefore the *worth* of any sentiment was wholly independent of its good or bad reception in the world.

He was severe to himself and suspicious of remaining stationary. He had a strong relish for all speculations that had truth for their object, and his masculine understanding was not to be imposed upon. It courted frankness by its own entire sincerity. Never any man gave his companion more of that satisfaction to which an eminent foreigner alludes in saying, "Already my opinion has gained infinitely in force, in sureness, the moment another mind has adopted it."[7] His conviction doubled your own. The only limit to the value of his assent was the warmth of his friendship, which led him to overestimate the opinions and the actions of those whom he loved.

The manner in which I should speak of him from my own recollections of his conversation would lead one not acquainted with him, probably, to augur unfavorably of his talents for action. It would be most unjust to him; and it is, I am inclined to think, precisely this equal fitness for contemplation and for action, that most distinguished him, for this man who has left us was not a recluse, but known probably to most persons only in the capacity of an active and skilful merchant. He was diligent in his business,[8] and master of its details, and whilst it cannot be concealed that he was so haunted by aspirations after the invisible and eternal, as to give him some distaste for his daily pursuits, that distaste, I believe, was not to be suspected by any the smallest negligence in the duties of his calling.

There was nothing in his manners or appearance to distinguish him from other men devoted to business. He neither had nor affected any singularity.[9] He gave himself to it and sought to understand its principles as well as its details and both thought and read upon the main questions of Political Economy.

In like manner he felt and discharged his duties as a citizen in no formal way but heartily: suspicious of his own prejudices he listened heedfully to men of the other party, to see if their measures could not be defended. He was a man to be depended on to the last, and though very far from a rash and angry partisan, was yet one who should not quit his post when thankless or dangerous duties were to be done. He valued his own time too highly to permit himself to seek or to accept offices; but the very important duties of the Primary School Committee he shared for years with faithful attention, and not only gave his time but the support of his warm solicitude to the teachers and the schools.

7. Novalis, as translated by Carlyle in "Characteristics," *Edinburgh Review* 54 (December 1831): 359; see Sermon CXLVI, n. 6.

8. Proverbs 22:29.

9. Emerson quotes a similar comment about Sir Isaac Newton in Sermon XLIV (*Sermons* 2:28).

The same benevolence led him to an active part in the Sunday School Society, Boston Port Society, in several religious and charitable associations, and in many committees where prudence and energy were demanded.

In all, his influence was of the best kind. His stability of character inspired confidence. He neither obtruded nor withheld his opinion but contributed his full share to every judicious movement. He seemed to value these societies not only for their objects, but as they afforded him incidentally an insight into the minds of the good and wise men who are usually found in such associations; a knowledge for which he had an insatiable thirst.

In this view he is indeed to be lamented. The influence of a virtuous man accumulates day by day, and who of us but has glanced with delight at the wholesome effects which this man should work for long and happy years—as the assured property of the community? It is such men that are the cement of the state, for wherever he went, there went a self-educated, earnest, devout man, whom to know was to love, who increased the confidence of good men in their principles, commanded respect from the evil minded, and kept even the fainthearted and cynical in humor with the world. Who could despond of the success of any good cause, who knew that such a man was living in the midst of society?

How shall I speak of him as a friend,—since the truest statement of his generous carriage would sound like exaggeration to strangers, and they who have enjoyed his confidence, do not need to be reminded of his true and noble heart. All of us who knew him are the debtors of his love. His idea of friendship is a part of his character. It haunted him like a passion.[10] He has carried it with him, all unsatisfied, into that spiritual world whither he is gone. His whole life might be called, a search after a friend. There was no sacrifice he would not count it a joy to make for the sake of those he loved. I may say his friendship was a species of religion; for he was accustomed to say, that the habit of recalling the image of a reverenced friend, was a powerful restraint upon any unworthy purpose.

Much less shall I venture to describe him in the dear relations of son, of husband, and of parent. God alone can comfort them from whom in his Providence he hath taken such a lover and friend. But he will comfort them by the riches of his memory; by the alway returning blessing which descends upon the house and the children of the righteous; by the desire and endeavor to replace his excellent influence in their own.[11]

The religious opinions and acts of such a man are wont to be inquired after with interest, yet it would be a sort of injustice to speak of them separately from his character. His religion was indeed dear to him; but it was not a form, but a life. The sentiments of gratitude and of accountableness, were never absent from him. The desire to attain clear and lively thoughts of perfect Wisdom and

10. Cf. Wordsworth, "Lines Composed a Few Miles Above Tintern Abbey," line 77.
11. Emerson assisted Sampson's widow and children, particularly Hillman B. Sampson, who boarded for a while with Emerson after he moved to Concord and whose tuition at Bronson Alcott's Temple School Emerson paid.

Love, still followed him from year to year. He considered himself not as having attained but always strove to attain. From year to year his mind was formed in a religious frame. He meditated on the New Testament with hunger and thirst to attain clearer conceptions of the Infinite Father. Especially was the life and character of Jesus Christ grateful to him when, in the advancement of his thoughts, he had come to contemplate him in the relation of a friend. But prayer and church-going and every outward act were animated continually by new thoughts from his active mind, else, so impatient was he of any hollowness in actions, that he could not have endured a religion that did not admit of progress with his mind. I should do wrong if I did not say that religious forms did engage his earnest attention. He was slow to change them. He suspected himself if he found them ineffectual. He speculated much about them. He was curious of the experience of others. But he loved the substance so well as to discern between a true and a false form and to embrace every form in the arms of his charity.[12] At one time, it was an object of his ardent wishes to devote himself to the profession of religious teaching, and it was only what he deemed an imperious necessity in his circumstances, which at that time deterred him. He listened to every preacher of every sect with open heart. He forgave everything in his preacher but insincerity. He loved those best who presented the Providence of God in the most simple and affectionate relations to man, and the words 'praise' and 'glory' he thought contributed little to the life of a prayer.

And thus he went on with a visible growth from month to month. He scarce made the same mistake a second time. He so lived in the present duty that we hardly separated him from his deeds, to see what excellence was dwelling with us.

Of a strong constitution of body and of mind, of temperate and punctual habits, it would scarcely occur to any observer that he would die before the common age of man. As a friend has remarked to me, there was nothing in him to suggest an early death except the perfection of his character. "Whom the gods love, die young,"[13]—was a most ancient observation, too sharply confirmed in the passing hour. He has gone in his youth, in his excellence, desired by all, attended by the veneration of the young and the blessing of hoary heads. He has gone into that world where age is counted not by years but by virtues. He is gone into that invisible assembly whither always his religious eye was directed with an insatiable curiosity. He is gone in to the fellowship of joy, himself an unstained soul, to dwell with all that is pure and noble, with truth and love which he adored. He is gone to be another bond between the natural and the spiritual world; to speak from those without, to those within the veil. He has gone into the God whom he adored. The eternal love of God go with him, as we know it will.

But we go back to weary days and nights, to sorrows, defeats and world-

12. Sampson was on the Second Church Committee that in 1832 had considered—and rejected—Emerson's views regarding the Lord's Supper. The position of particular committee members is of course not known.

13. Plautus, *Bacchides*, IV, vii, line 18. Cf. Byron, *Childe Harold's Pilgrimage*, canto 4, stanza 102.

liness. No, not if the memory of this brave Christian is cherished by us. Such a man is to be praised by virtuous actions. His monument is in good thoughts and kind deeds that are excited in those who love him, and God will not have sent our brother amongst us wholly in vain, if the fragrance of his virtues, shall have persuaded us of the eternal beauty of truth and goodness.

CLXIX

I am fearfully and wonderfully made.
Marvellous are thy works; and that
my soul knoweth right well.

PSALMS 139:14

When an Asiatic prince came to Paris, and was asked what seemed to him most surprizing in that capital, he replied, "to find himself there."[1] With better reason, a man might say that, to himself, his own existence in the world was more amazing than any other fact. I believe few persons perceive the marvel of their own constitution; and yet it is more wondrous than any fiction that was ever conceived. "Truth is strange—stranger than fiction."[2]

The fine contrivance in every part of our frame, the perfect fitting of the members and the admirable working of the whole machine, transcend all praise: then the fitness of man to the Earth; and his peaceful dwelling among the cattle, the birds, and the fish, turning the Earth into his garden and pleasure ground; the round of the seasons, and the universal order—is all set down in the books. This external fitness is wonderful;—but I doubt if to those who saw this only, it would ever have occurred (in the first instance) to remark upon the marvel. It has been said with some ingenuity of conjecture, that without the phenomenon of sleep, we should be atheists; because if we had no experience of the interruption of the activity of the Will, "we could never be brought to a sense and acknowledgment of its dependence on the Divine Will."[3] With more assurance it may be said of the things apprehended by the senses, that they are so nicely grooved into one another that the sight of one suggests the next preceding, and

---

Preached eight times: September 7, 1834, in New Bedford; November 2 at the Second Church, New York; as a Wednesday Lecture, January 21, 1835, in Plymouth; March 29 (revised version) at the First Church, Waltham; July 19 at the First Church, Boston; March 6, 1836, at the Harvard College Chapel; September 10, 1837, in East Lexington; and January 20, 1839, in Concord. Two manuscripts exist, both undated: a heavily revised earlier version, the source of the first three deliveries, and a later version, which here serves as copy-text. See the Manuscript and Textual Notes for evidence concerning the date of the second manuscript and for a complete transcription of the earlier version.

1. Not located.
2. Byron, *Don Juan*, XIV, ci. See *JMN* 3:193, 216, 248; 4:24; and 6:191.
3. "Sleep," *New Jerusalem Magazine* 6 (November 1832): 88. The author of this anonymous article was Sampson Reed. See *JMN* 4:56 and 6:171.

this the next before, so that the understanding in the study of the things themselves would run forever in the round of second causes, did not the soul at its
own instance sometimes demand tidings of the First Cause. Were there not
graver considerations to be remembered there is something almost comic in
seeing such a creature as is a man growing up with perfect senses and faculties,
and going in and out for seventy years, amid the shows of nature and humanity,
making up his mouth every day to express all degrees of surprize at every
impertinent trifle, and never suspecting all the time that it is even singular that
he should exist.

But superficial views will not always satisfy us. It will not always suffice us to
ask why this bone is thus terminated, and be answered that it may fit that
socket; or why this animal is thus configured, and be answered that the residence and the food of the animal requires such frame,—but the question starts
up and almost with terror within us, why the animal or any animal exists? to
what farther end its being has regard beyond this nice tissue of neighboring
facts? Why organization—why order exist? Nay, why the interrogator exists,
and what he is?

The bare fact of your existence as a man is one of such bewildering astonishment that it seems as if it were the part of reason to spend one's lifetime in a
trance of wonder,—altogether more rational to lift one's hands in blank amazement, than to assume the least shadow of dogmatism or pride.

"Let others wrangle," said the pious St. Augustin, "I will wonder."[4] It is
related of the wisest man in the ancient world, the Athenian Socrates, that, on
one occasion, he stopped short in his walk, and stood stockstill in a rapture of
amazement from sunset to sunrise.[5]

But we may be conscious of the mystery, without always saying so. Certainly;
and a man might be well forgiven his omission to express his admiration of that
which *is,* if his way of living indicated any sense of his powers and relations.

But see the oddity of his demeanor. This little creature set down—he knows
not how—amid all the sublimities of the moving Universe, sharpsighted enough
to find out the movement of the sphere he inhabits, and of the spheres in the
depths around him; and not only so, but capable by intellect and affection, of
acting upon remote men as upon himself: Yes, and from his little hour, extending the arms of his influence through thousands of years and to millions of
millions of rational men: Nay, by means of Virtue, of entering instantly upon a
life that makes the whole grandeur of the Creation pale and visionary.—Yet this
little creature—quite unmindful of these vast prerogatives—struts about with
immense activity to procure various meats to eat and stuffs to wear, and, most
of all, salutations and marks of respect from his fellows. He seems to think it
quite natural he should be here, and things should be as they are;—so natural as
not to deserve a second thought: and the moment he has got a neat house to sit

---

4. "Alii disputent, ego mirabor"; quoted in Robert Leighton, *Select Works* (London, 1823),
2:xvi. See *JMN* 3:193 and 6:220.
5. This incident is recounted by Alcibiades in Plato's "Symposium."

down, and to eat, and to sleep in, he is so possessed with a sense of his importance that he not only thinks it more excellent than if he knew the whole order of the Creation, but he expects impatiently great deference from his fellow men.

We go so gravely about our ordinary trifling employments, that we are apt to lose the sense of the absurdity of much that we do. We allow, by our acquiescence, a man that has more houses and ships and farms than his neighbors to assume consequence in his manners on that ground: Although we know very well when we ponder the matter that if instead of a few thousand acres of land or a score of ships or houses he owned the entire property of the world, he would be as much in the dark, as mortal, and as insufficient to himself as he is now. He could not then solve so much as one word of the vast mystery that envelopes us; he would not have a particle more of real power. In the great All, he would be the insect he is now. Yet the extent and consistency of the world's farce keeps each particular puppet in countenance, and we go on in the universal hunt for station and land and horses and ships and stocks and attentions and compliments,—hiding the inanity of the whole thing in the multitude of the particulars. Is it not as if one should have a nest of a hundred boxes, and nothing in the last box?

And hence the wise laughter of the ancient philosopher Democritus, who made a jest of all human society and pursuits. No wise man, he said, could keep his countenance in view of such folly.[6]

But why call it ludicrous? Is it not necessary that we should acquire property? Yes. We have animal wants, which must be supplied. Commerce—a net woven round every man—grows out of them. Every man should do his part, one should sow the field, and one weave the cloth, and one draw the contracts, and one build the ship, and one plough the sea, and one throw the harpoon. There's much that is wonderful, but nothing that is ludicrous in this, simply considered. The ludicrous part of it, is, in the acting as if it were just that for which we lived, and the entire oversight of the end, for which this is the means. The proud man, the sensualist, the denier of divine power, the avaricious, the selfish,—by such earth-worms the wonder of our being is not perceived: they are merely the highest class of animals, and like ants and horses and elephants they do not perceive anything extraordinary in their life.

And what remedy? What can save us from this capital error, or repair it?—The exercise of Reason, the act of reflexion, redeems a man at once out of this brutishness. The man who reflects is a man, and not an animal. The ox knoweth his owner and the ass his master's crib, but my people doth not know nor consider.[7] I take it to be a main object of that education which this world administers to each soul to touch the springs of wonder in us, and make us alive to the marvel of our condition. That done, all is done. Before, he was so wrongheaded, so at discord with things around him, that he was ridiculous: now, he is

6. See Montaigne, "Of Democritus and Heraclitus," *Essays of Michael Seigneur de Montaigne . . .* , trans. Charles Cotton (London, 1693), 1:514.
7. Isaiah 1:3.

at one with all. He accepts his lot: he perceives the great astonishment.[8] He adores. Awaked to truth and virtue—which is the twofold office of Reason—he passes out of the local and finite, he inspires and expires immortal breath.

By the act of reflexion man perceives 'that he is wonderfully made.' Moreover, as we shall presently have occasion to notice, the chief distinctions of his condition begin with that act.

Let me for more accurate consideration separate a few of the particulars that amaze the contemplative spirit.

1. See how cunningly constructed are all things in such a manner as to make each being the centre of the Creation. You seem to be a point or focus upon which all objects, all ages concentrate their influence. Nothing past but affects *you*. Nothing remote but through some means reaches *you*. Every superficial grain of sand may be considered as the fixed point round which all things revolve, so intimately is it allied to all and so truly do all turn as if for it alone. This is true in the lowest natures to the least leaf or moss. Look at the summer blackberry lifting its polished surface a few inches from the ground. How did that little chemist extract from the sand bank the spices and sweetness it has concocted in its cells? By any cheap or accidental means? Not so; but the whole creation has been at the cost of its birth and nurture. A globe of fire near a hundred millions of miles distant in the great space, has been flooding it with light and heat as if it shone for no other. It is six or seven months that the sun has made the tour of the heavens every day over this tiny sprout, before it could bear its fruit. The sea has evaporated its countless tuns of water that the rain of heaven might wet the roots of this little vine. The elastic air, exhaled from all live creatures and all minerals, yielded this small pensioner the gaseous aliment it required. The Earth by the attraction of its mass determined its form and size; and when we consider how the earth's attraction is fixed at this moment in equilibrium by innumerable attractions, on every side, of distant bodies,—we shall see that the berry's form and history is determined by causes and agents the most prodigious and remote.

What then shall we say of the manner in which one man is made the centre round which all things roll, and upon which all things scatter gifts? Let us take one from the crowd—not one of the children of prosperity, but a poor, solitary, virtuous man—the humblest who is capable of reflexion.

He stands upon the top of the world: he is the centre of the horizon. Morning and Evening lavish their sweetness and their solemnity upon his senses; summer and winter bring to him the instruction of their harvests and their storms. All that he sees and hears gives him a lesson. Do not the ages that are past, report their experience for his tuition, and millions of millions of rational spirits epitomize their fate for his behoof? Is he not continually moved to joy or grief by things said a thousand years ago? He understands them. His soul embraces the act or the sentiment as if it were done or said for him only. Is not his condition

8. Cf. Mark 5:42.

different for every one of the men that has acted upon the world? See how much Luther—See how much Columbus, Newton, Grotius, Jefferson, Franklin—has affected his condition: And all the inventors of arts. Do they not give him the unshared total benefit of their wisdom? Does not Socrates, and Solomon, and Bacon, and Shakespear counsel him alone? Jesus lives as for him only. God exists for him only, and Right and Wrong, and Wisdom and Folly, the whole of Pleasure; and of Pain; and all the heaven of Thought. Are they not all poured into his bosom as if the world had no other child?

The perfect world exists to every man,—to the poorest drover in the mountains—the poorest laborer in his ditch. Quite independent of his work are his endowments. There is enough in him (grant him capable of thought and virtue) to puzzle and outwit all our philosophy. The history of one man,—inasmuch as it is searching and profound,—is as valuable as the history of a nation. Thoroughly acquaint me with the heart of one living man,—though the humblest,—and what can Italy or England teach me more with all their wars and all their laws? Sharpen these obtuse perceptions of ours and show us the motives, the fancy, the affection, the distorting and colouring lenses that pauper makes use of,[9] and the redeeming power that still sets him right after countless errors, and that promises him a kingdom of heaven whilst he shuffles about in his barnyard, and we shall be able to do without Tacitus and Clarendon.[10]

2. Thus is each man placed at the heart of the world. But that is only half of his advantage. That is to receive influence. There is more in him. He is not designed to be an idle eye before which Nature passes in review, but is by his action enabled to learn the irresistible properties of moral nature, perceived dimly by the mind as laws difficult to be grasped or defined, yet everywhere working out their inevitable results in human affairs, whereupon if a man fall they will grind him to powder.[11] There is nothing in material nature (certainly nothing in fiction) so splendid and perfect as the law of Compensations—the law according to which an act done by any moral being draws after it its inevitable fruit which no chance and no art can elude. The nature of these laws, their extent, their omnipotence he can learn only by *acting,* and observing how they determine and reward every action. The Creation is so magically woven that nothing can do him any mischief but himself;[12] an invisible immortal fence surrounds his being, which defends him from all harm he wills to resist; the whole Creation cannot bend him whilst he stands upright; but, on the other hand, every act of his, is instantaneously judged and rewarded: the lightning

9. In "Experience," Emerson asserts not that we *use* but that we *are* "colored and distorting lenses" (*CW* 3:43).

10. Edward Hyde, first Earl of Clarendon (1609–1674), author of *The History of the Rebellion and Civil Wars in England,* which Emerson read in the six-volume Boston edition of 1827. Emerson admired Clarendon's skill in drawing "characters" (*JMN* 5:246) and seems to have regarded him as a moral historian in the tradition of Cornelius Tacitus.

11. Matthew 21:44 and Luke 20:18. With the next sentence, cf. *JMN* 4:313.

12. See Sermon CXLI, n. 5; a version of this sentence occurs in "The Sovereignty of Ethics," *W* 10:197.

loiters by the speed of retribution;[13] every generous effort of his, is compensated by the instant enlargement of his soul; his patience disarms calamity; his love brightens the sun; his purity destroys temptation; whilst falsehood is a foolish suicide and destroys belief;[14] selfishness separates itself from the happy human family; idleness whips itself with discontent; malice multiplies its foes. So that ever it seems that each individual is solicited by good and by evil spirits, and he gives himself up to them whose bidding he does, and they labor to make him more entirely their own, and induce him to confirm his last action by repetition and by fresh energy of the same kind.

To open to ourselves—to open to others these laws—is it not worth living for?—to make the soul aforetime the servant of the senses acquainted with the secret of its own power; to teach man that by self-renouncement a heaven of which he had no conception, begins at once in his heart;—by the high act of yielding his will that little individual heart becomes dilated as with the presence and inhabitation of the spirit of God.

3. Shall I select as a third trait wherein the miracle of our being is specially manifested, and one which only begins with reflexion, this, that the exercise of Reason turns all our Evil to good. Thus the moment Reason assumes its empire over a man, he finds that he has nothing low and injurious in him, but it is, under this dominion, the root of power and beauty. His animal nature is ennobled by serving the soul: that which was debasing him will now prove the sinews of his character; his petulance is the love of order; out of his necessities grows the glorious structure of civilization. Nay, what trait he blushes for and reckons his weakness because it is different from other men whom he admires, is probably what he should throw himself on his knees and thank God for, as his crowning gift. For there is somewhat peculiar in every man which is on that account apt to be neglected but which must be let grow and suffered to give direction to the other faculties if he would attain his acme and be dear and honorable to his brethren. He finds that whatever disadvantages he has labored under; whatever uncommon exertion he has been called to make; whatever poverty; what sickness; what unpopularity; what mistake; yes, even what deep sin he has been given up to commit; when once he is awakened to truth and Virtue, penetrated with penitence, touched with the veneration of the Almighty Father and stung with the insatiable desire of making every day his soul more perfect, then, all these, the worst calamities, the sorest sorrows, are changed, are glorified—he owns his deep debt to them, and acknowledges in them the omnipresent energy of the God who transforms all things into the divine.

And what is this Admiration to which we would excite the soul? What is it but a perception of a man's true position in the universe and his consequent obligations? This is the whole moral and end of such views as I present. I desire a man to consider faithfully in solitude and silence the unknown nature within

---

13. *JMN* 6:48; used in Sermon LVII (*Sermons* 2:96).
14. The phrasing is borrowed from Edward Gibbon. See *JMN* 2:102; cf. *JMN* 5:282.

him that he may not sink into his own contempt, and be a spectacle of folly to the wise. I would have him open his eyes to true wonder, that he may never more be agitated by trifles. I would have him convinced that by the act of his own will alone, can that which is most worth his study be disclosed to him. I would have him perceive that the unreflecting laborer is but a superior brute; that the reflecting laborer only is a man. Let him consider that all riches, though convenient to the senses, cannot profit *himself,* but that a true thought, a worthy deed, puts him at once into harmony with the real and eternal. Let him consider, that, if he loves respect, he must seek it in what really belongs to a man, and not in any thing accidental such as fortune or appearance. Instead of making it his pride to be announced as a person of consideration in the state, or in his profession, or in the fashionable world, or as a rich, or a travelled, or a powerful man, let him delight rather to make himself known in all companies by his action, and by his discourse, as one who has attained unto self-command; one who has thought in earnest upon the questions of human duty; one who carries with his presence the terrors and the beauty of justice; and who, even in the moment when his friends ignorantly censure him, is privy to the virtuous action he has performed, and those he has in hand.

What is this admiration? Is it not the fountain of religion in the soul? What is it but an acknowledgment of the Incomprehensible—a response to the Wisdom and Love which breathe through the Creation into the heart? What does the world suggest but a lofty Faith that all will be, that all is well, that the Father who thus vouchsafes to reveal himself in all that is great, and all that is lovely, will not forsake the Child for whom he provideth such costly instruction— whom every hour and every event and Memory and Hope educate? What does it intimate but presages of an infinite and perfect life? What but an assured Trust through all evil and danger and Death?

CLXX

Set your affections on things above and not on things on the earth.

Colossians 3:2

This is one of those noble exhortations which flow directly out of the Christian gospel and which it addresses to all classes of men. It is not addressed to any one class of men, but the Spirit of God saith to Man everywhere of whatever creed or name or race or colour or condition, Set your affections on things above.

I regard this expression of the apostle as a very good definition of Religion. Religion is an affection set on things above. The very command will send a thrill of joy into the humble heart. You can't hear the command without a feeling of congratulation for it implies the fact that this inhabitant of the earth is capable of divine sentiments, is related to higher worlds. Here is an address to the poor, to the tormented, to the bereaved, to the tempted, and not less to the successful, the honored, the great, and the good. Set your affections on things above.

This is one of those sentiments which make us feel our common nature, the equality, the brotherhood of men, how different soever may be our employments and relations. The moment we are addressed as religious beings, all minor distinctions, however large they look, all disappear.

It is a very pleasing fact that those subjects on which men have the greatest variety of opinion and the least sympathy are those which are of least importance, and those subjects which are of most importance are those which bring them all to one mind. Upon the various affairs of common life, upon trades, politics, news, business, men entertain such different views, one thinks of first importance what the other does not care a button for, that each often finds the other's conversation wholly uninteresting, but on the question of duty, of right, of the danger and mischief of sin, upon the joy and power of Faith—when these topics are brought home to them, they shall all think one thing.

I choose gladly this broad sentiment now that I am permitted to say a few words to my fellow christians in the Seamen's Church. There is no class of men,

Preached once, at the Seamen's Chapel (or Bethel), Boston, April 26, 1835. The regular minister at the Bethel was "Father" Edward Thompson Taylor, whom Emerson called "that living Methodist, the Poet of the Church" (*JMN* 4:381).

my brethren, whom their peculiar employment has so strong a tendency to detach from their fellow men as you. The seaman may naturally be expected to be very different from the landsman. All his circumstances are strange and some of them very disadvantageous.

Whilst other men stay at home and protect themselves at leisure against the occasional arrival of danger, the sailor goes out to encounter the most certain and terrific perils to which the race of man is exposed. One voyage may bring him tempest, frost, famine, pestilence, pirates, shipwreck, foreign captivity, and is almost certain to bring him some of them. Whilst to other men the heat and cold are tempered by the gradual changes of the year, the sailor rushes from climate to climate on the wings of the wind. In a few weeks he passes from the West Indies to St. Petersburg, from the dikes of Holland to the mountains of Peru, from the pepper and spice islands to the green pastures of the Northern Whales. Going round the earth like a planet the sea shuts him up in his little wooden ark in a stricter confinement than the state's prisoner suffers who has the liberty of a yard. Whilst other men sleep warm in their beds he is acquainted with the night as well as the day. And the storm that drives other men within their doors calls him out of his poor forecastle to hard and dangerous work. Upon the slippery deck or aloft between the clouds and the water, in a wind and darkness, he can't breathe, can't see, feeling his way along the yards to tie another reef. He is a traveller without the advantages of travelling, for what chance has he who works in port as well as at sea to become acquainted with foreign countries, their customs and language and religion? Go where he will he sees only sailors, in Turkey, in China or in Spain. In like manner he is confined month after month to the same round of labor and the same little room without the advantages of residence and home.

Yes and that I regard as the most serious disadvantage of the sailor's life: that from having no fixed residence he is apt to feel himself a stranger everywhere. His pursuits are so peculiar that when he sets his foot on his native land he yet feels as if nobody in the crowd, upon the wharf, or in the streets, felt any interest in him. But let him come into the Church. Let him sit down with his fellowmen and hear what the Spirit of God says to them all and he will no longer feel like a wanderer, a man without home, without friends, without brothers, for what the Spirit saith to one it saith to all: Set your affections on things above and not on things on the earth.

And truly, brethren, if you will meditate upon all the meaning that is contained in this exhortation you shall find it more than a compensation to you for every present disadvantage and a source of increasing satisfaction, for it is nothing less than the whole blessing of a religion or Divine life.

Set your affection on things above. That is, on things spiritual, not on things mortal. But don't imagine he means things out of reach, things future, things imaginary. O no, he means things real, things very near, things now present. He means things not seen by the eye of the body, but by the eye of the soul—but not the less real, but the more real for that.

How far off is Heaven? is it above the stars? Is it some remote region of angelic climate? Ah, it is here in this house, I hope: here, I trust, in many a heart its kingdom is already begun. Where love is, there it is: where justice and purity are, there it is. Where patience and Hope with eye looking to God are, there it is.

And so in the Scriptures generally what is said to be *above* is to be understood as that which is *within*. As the Word of God is said to be in our mouth and in our heart,[1] and as God is said to speak unto the hearts of men. The Arabians have a proverb, "Darken the five windows that the house may shine."[2] Withdraw yourself from all the objects of the five senses, from all that can be seen, smelled, heard, touched, or tasted, to those things which appertain to spirit, namely Conscience, Duty, and Love, or as Jesus says, the Kingdom of God is within you.[3]

A religious life begins with enjoining duty. In duty all religion begins. That is the first and last test of a true faith. Nothing is so deep in man as his convictions of right and wrong. There are some tribes so barbarous they have no name for God, but none where they do not know that truth is better than falsehood and love better than hatred.

The sense therefore is the same as if it said, set your affection on things within you. Now you are made happy or miserable by meats and drinks, by idle amusements, by foolish company, by sinful pleasures. But separate yourselves from these and lean upon your own mind for peace. Go in and learn the joy of a good conscience. Go in and listen to the voice of God in your own heart. When he says, My son, answer, Here am I, Lord, what wilt thou?[4]

I propose to consider some of the truths that give value to this exhortation of the Apostle:

  1. That the Religious sentiment makes the force of Duty
  2. That it is the source of Contentment
  3. A ground of Union with men
  4. An immortal good.

I. The service which true Religion renders us is to engrave the laws of Duty upon our mind.

Here we are in this wonderful world and a great deal of work is to be done in it. A great house always makes a great deal of work. God is a wise householder and requires all that is practicable to be done in his family. To every pair of hands in the world, therefore, is its own part assigned. And to every one that which he has power to do. You are not expected to bustle about like a vulgar housekeeper and prate of the thousand things that you have to do and wish you

---

1. Cf. Romans 10:8–10.

2. Quoted in William de Britaine, *Human Prudence; Or the Art by which a Man and a Woman May Be Advanced to Fortune, to Permanent Honor, and to Real Grandeur*, ed. Herman Mann (Dedham, Massachusetts, 1806), 73. See *JMN* 6:90 and *Sermons* 1:376.

3. Luke 17:21.

4. Cf. Acts 9:6 and 9:10.

had a thousand hands to do them and enlarge upon great plans of generosity and distant charity you propose to accomplish and convert the heathen and reform the world, but if you have once truly received this divine light in your mind it will make you calm, thoughtful and diligent, it will make you true to those to whom you are most nearly bound, it will make you a pious child, a faithful husband, a true speaker, a faithful payer of debts, a man of honest and friendly sentiments, a good citizen. Whatsoever your calling is on the sea or on the shore, the divine affection comes in and says, My son, Do that Duty.

Its first effect is by making us value our inward peace above all price, to set us at work to remove those bad actions from our life which we condemn in ourselves. Its end,—the end for which the affection on things above was planted in us—to make a happy world, and therefore it is always removing stumbling blocks and creating helps. Forevermore is it found on the side of Duty.

II. An affection set on things above is a source of Contentment.

If a man has just heard a piece of good news, he does not mind much how the wind sits. If he is very happy he does not feel the cold or care for a little rain. Well now, is it not a great art to drive away little sufferings with great joys, small anxieties with high thoughts: on the sea to remember God: hurrying in a tent over the waters to feel that we belong to the human race, to an immortal race, and that we are wholly engaged to serve them?

Man of many sorrows, in duty is your medicine.[5] Poor Man, it is your wealth.

I should be glad if I could do any justice to this great subject, the real consolation which religion can offer you. There are in the poorest man's life moments when he laments that he has been defeated; it is no great matter if the work of the world is done by other hands, if they are honored by use and I am shoved aside. Blood like mine flows in the veins of kings and statesmen, orators, great merchants and manufactures who carry on the whole business of the earth. I have such hands, such a tongue and such faculties as they. I am sure I should enjoy their great reputation among men and all their splendor of living with as keen a relish as they. Yet whilst they are announced wherever they go by the bowing and smiles of all whom they meet, I am unknown and treated as a common person and I don't think I should be missed from the crowd if the sexton should make my bed in six feet of earth tomorrow or if I should drop overboard into the mouths of the fishes in the sea. Well, the poor man may sometimes sing this sad song and the streets look cold and very lonely to him, and his own apartment cheerless and even the heat of his fire has a sort of sadness in it.[6] But now let his heart be raised and opened, let his thoughts have been called to the good God who is always speaking in very faint tones in his heart.

Ah! it will wonderfully change his view. He will say, What in his sight are the distinctions I think so much of? What before him are rich men and poor men?

5. Cf. Isaiah 53:3.
6. See *Nature* (CW 1:10): "To a man laboring under calamity, the heat of his own fire hath sadness in it."

All are poor enough. What before him is all the mighty work which these men do and brag so much? Perhaps he regards one poor prayer more than an empire made up of fraud and avarice and lies. Indeed, indeed, I am afraid that the men who have as they think done the most in the world, made the most noise with their great enterprizes, might shrink to think how little and nothing their work is to any real and good end. Ah, we think a great deal of what we do with our pompous societies and corporations and public and private influence, but we are mere tools in God's hand, and perhaps after all a very different thing is done from what we think to do, and perhaps they play the most important part who seem to do the least. There are calm moments when the sky of the soul is no longer overcast, when God shines in and trifles disappear and we have a vision of his sufficiency and of our insignificance and of the truth that entire trust and gratitude are our fittest thought. Then enters the great God into the heart of mortal man.

Yes, see how religion satisfies us with our place. It teaches us that with God is no high, no low, no great, no small; that if we do our duty in that place where we are we are counted worthy. He has given us a call to one or another work by giving us a talent for it. If we obey that call then he approves us. The place is no concern of ours. By doing what we could, we shift the responsibility off our shoulders and God assumes it all.

And so it begets in him all tranquillity of mind. Jesus looked at the lilies and said, Behold how they grow. They toil not; neither do they spin.[7]

Now when a man has used his talents in whatever vocation they lie, as master or servant, as merchant or laborer or seaman, has done what he could well in the hours appointed to work, let him compose himself with the thought that in the eye of God he is better than the lilies. With a cloudless brow and a serene mind, let him lie down though he make his bed in the hollows of the Atlantic, and again let him arise calm in the belief that he rests on the lap of the Divine Beneficence, and that he is never for one moment forgotten or forsaken.

III. It is a ground of union with men.

It is the constant tendency of sinful life to separate us from our fellow men; though it seems to bring us into contact with them, yet it really separates us by making us seek all the time to confine our enjoyments. Ambition, Avarice, Intemperance, Fraud, Anger, Slander, do these seek the good of other people? But all the Virtues tend to the good of all, and so to join all together.

If therefore you would have the happiness that comes from strict union with men, set your affections above.

I am afraid the seaman, as I have already intimated, feels sometimes alone in the crowd—the poor man—feels alone; they do not seem related to men as others do.

But judge not by appearance.[8]

---

7. Matthew 6:28. Emerson actually wrote: "They toil not &c" and may have had in mind the slightly different wording of Luke 12:27 ("they spin not"); in either event, he might have gone on: "and yet I say unto you, that Solomon in all his glory was not arrayed like one of these."

8. John 7:24.

The worldly man, he often who seems the most strictly tied to his fellow-men for he deals with hundreds and thousands and causes gangs of negroes to plant sugar for him in the islands and hundreds of Irish laborers to dig for him in his road or his canal and scores of truckmen and stevedores to run to and fro upon the wharf and the best seamen in the country to sail his ships, and many spy-glasses on the coast of England or up the Baltic are watching for his expected sail—This man who seems to be the centre of activity to thousands of men, he is not united to his race; this man is often really solitary and secluded from all, for he merely employs these persons at the price of so much bread to work for him; he cares not for them nor they for him; he pays great attention to a few people round him whom he calls his friends, but really that is interest also; he is quite selfish. In his own family even for whose good all his exertions seemed made he is only bent on securing his own comfort; he grudges to his poor relative the benefit he yields him; he is awaiting the death of others with frigid calculation as bringing him their substance or else relieving him of an expense. He, then, who has never yet known the sweetness of joyful benevolence, him I call solitary, for like an island cut off by the barren sea from all men's feet is he. And he is social and he only who has seen God, who in secret rejoices in God's presence and who thanks him for the happiness which he does not share.

Is it not true, the moment God enters my soul the mountains that severed me from my brethren vanish. I share with them a common reason as I breathe with them a common air. As one sun warms us so I participate with them the compassion of God. There is no man to whom I do not bow down as God's image,[9] and good men who really shine with something of God's own lustre I love and serve, and so no longer am I separate from my brethren but threads of relation run from me to every man and from every man to me. Then first society exists and the Spirit of God around and within speaks out of the cloud,[10] Behold how good and pleasant it is for brethren to dwell together in unity![11]

In saying that the religious sentiment is a ground of union, my thought is that whilst you indulge religious thoughts—whilst you pray—your heart is united by that very act to what is deepest in the heart of every man. Some good influence goes out from you to them. Nay, it seems to me that a man wholly unknown who sits among us with his heart filled with love to God, though that man were dumb, yet is he not alone. Him the earth rises to honor, the heavens bow to meet him. Yea, the angels bless him and associate themselves with him. The ancients said that if the wise man lifted his finger all the wise men were benefitted thereby.[12]

9. Genesis 1:26–27.

10. Matthew 17:5, Mark 9:7, Luke 9:35.

11. Psalms 133:1.

12. Montaigne, "Of Vanity," *Essays of Michael Seigneur de Montaigne . . .* , trans. Charles Cotton (London, 1693), 3:315–16. See Sermon CXLII, n. 11. On two previous occasions in the winter of 1832, Emerson in his journals suggested an analogy between this "Stoical precept" and the Swedenborgian doctrine that spirits associate (*JMN* 3:324 and 328). See Sermon CXXVII (*Sermons* 3:225, n. 8) and Kenneth W. Cameron, "Emerson and the Motif that 'Spirits Associate,'" *ESQ* 12 (3d Quarter 1958): 45–46.

IV. Finally, it is an immortal good. That is the distinction of all spiritual benefits. But I entreat you to consider what this immortality means. It is not because God has promised as a reward to any action or affection that its duration shall be prolonged. It is not because it is written on the pages of the Bible that the just shall live forever that I say an affection set on things above is everlasting, but because a religious frame of mind declares itself immortal. We perceive that Truth, Justice, Love have nothing to do with Time. They were before the world was, with God,[13] and the bosom wherein they dwell partakes of their eternity. The Gospel of Jesus Christ has gathered no decrepitude under the weight of ages.[14] The very knowledge of eternity which we have is derived from our religious states of mind. In them is life; they are Life itself.[15]

Who will care when fifty years hence we are all dead and gone what voyages or journeys we made, what good fortune or accidents we met, what feasts and frolics we had, what quarrels or lawsuits or connexions, how we lived or how we died? Nobody in the world. We shall be mere names on a town clerk's record in the village where we were born or died or on a gravestone. And even so will most of these incidents appear to us. But the clear perception, the earnest acknowledgment which sometime you made of God's tender providence, could that be made known to your fellow-men, would not grow old and fade. It would seem fresh and worthy at all times and partake an immortal savor. All the rest of our life will shrink up and these few moments in which we earnestly dwelt with God and gave our days to him will be the immortal part. The thoughts of David are as fresh now as ever.

Yes, because the same thoughts and affections will be at that hour the bread we eat, the work we do, among the angels in heaven.

And now, my brethren, may I not congratulate you that we are made partakers of this heavenly gift, of a religious life, of the life of God in the soul of man?[16] Is it nothing that amid the most unpleasing duties, under the harshest masters, in the obscurest place, a truly divine joy may come and dwell with you, that this poor man driven shivering, laboring, sweating over the earth is yet capable of a sublime peace and power compared with which the majesty of all material things is poor?

Set your affections on things above. Deny your appetites. Deny your passions and you shall find that a greater pleasure comes from resisting the allurements of sensual pleasure. Temperance, Chastity, Integrity have greater joys than Intemperance, Lust and Fraud. O then, my brother, invite the Spirit of God to come and take up his abode in your lowly breast by seeking him with diligence.

Life is very short; if today one devout thought has passed through your mind—

13. Cf. John 17:5 and 1:1.
14. *JMN* 2:313; cf. "The Poet," line 293 (*W* 9:320).
15. Cf. John 1:4.
16. The allusion is to Henry Scougal's *The Life of God in the Soul of Man* (London, 1677), which Emerson read in the Boston edition of 1823.

O, fix it there. O, comply with its intimation. If it is repulsed, it may never return. Make your heart on this Sabbath a little chapel where the hymns of angels are sung, the prayers of saints arise, where good actions are resolved and love to God and man joins this one poor heart to the whole earth and the whole heaven.

CLXXI

How beautiful on the mountains are the feet of him that bringeth good tidings, that publisheth salvation.

Isaiah 52:7

The wisdom of God has provided in the various talents of men for the greatest good of society. Men please themselves in the choice of their pursuit, and by means of the great diversity of tastes, the whole work of the world is done. Some men are fond of manual labor; others to contrive work for many hands; others to ride; others to sail; one to cast accounts; one to till land; one to speak; and one to write. All men may see how by this division of labor society is better served than if each man attempted to do all things by himself. Among these various offices is that of observing, recording and communicating truth. This office has never been quite neglected but always administered with more or less fidelity.

All men have an interest in the faithful administration of this office. At the same time it is not a coveted office. It has no external guards, but very few persons have that constitution of mind and body which qualifies them to take pleasure and to serve society in this vocation. Solitude and self-communion are to many persons as disagreeable as a jail. It needs a peculiar genius. It has its own immunities and also its own painful taxes like the rest of human works. But the delivery of the talent is the call,[1] and where it is possessed it is the manifest good of society that it should have free passage into all minds.—For it is as plain that spiritual truth is opened to one not for his private behoof, but in

---

Preached twice: on the morning of July 17, 1836, in East Lexington, and in the afternoon of the same day in Concord. The sermon is a memorial for the Reverend Hersey Bradford Goodwin, junior pastor to the aged Ezra Ripley at Concord: in effect Emerson's minister. Goodwin died at Plymouth on July 9 at the age of thirty. On July 10, Emerson commented on Goodwin's death in passages added to Sermons CLII and XCIV, delivered at Concord at Ripley's request. Emerson had delivered the "Right Hand of Fellowship" at Goodwin's ordination in 1830 (see below). Further details may be found in Kenneth W. Cameron, "Emerson's Ideal Clergyman—Hersey Bradford Goodwin," *ESQ* 12 (3d Quarter 1958): 39–44. This is the last sermon in Emerson's numbered sequence.

1. See *JMN* 3:223, where this proposition is attributed to Abraham Tucker (pseud. "Edward Search"), author of *The Light of Nature Pursued*, 7 vols. (London, 1768–1777). Used in "Ethics" (*EL* 2:147) and in "Spiritual Laws" (*CW* 2:82). See also Sermons XXXVIII (*Sermons* 1:294) and CXV (*Sermons* 3:153).

trust to be communicated to all, as it is that corn and apples do not grow for their own use. One man may see and teach truth better than another, but the truth belongs to every other as much as to him. It is the manifest interest which comes home to my bosom and to every man's bosom that there should be on every tower watchers set to observe and report every new ray of light in what quarter soever of heaven it should appear and their report should be eagerly and reverently received.[2] Merely in a low economical view, inasmuch as just views of duty are the very best police for preserving civil and social order, it is as much our interest that the truth seeker and speaker, the prophet and the priest, should be freed from all hindrance in their office, as it is that the producer of bread or the weaver of cloth should be free in their work. And inasmuch as thought and affection are those things for which we live, we may better eat hard food and wear skins and mats, than suffer the soul to famish for want of truth or be unclothed with divine affections.

Every light which God imparts to the mind of a wise man, every discovery he makes, every conclusion he announces is tidings to each of us from our own home. His office is to cheer our labor as with a song by highest hopes.

In speaking thus of the service which is rendered by those who give us what is called in the Scriptures, the Bread of Life,[3] that is, religious truth, I am very far from confining my remarks to any profession in society. I am speaking most certainly of a class, but of a natural not an artificial class. Not of men wearing certain titles and garb, and visibly exercising the offices of the church, but of the real priesthood, not made by man but by God, composed of individuals in every age of the world, in every country, in every condition and calling, who, out of love to the human soul, speak to men of its concerns: of the pious line of Jewish teachers whom their religion seems truly to have made wisest of men; of the teachers of wisdom among the Greeks and Romans, especially of the Stoic sect; of Jesus, the instructer not of a nation but of human nature, and whose offices and works differently presented and extolled in different ages do more and more in the light of time melt into the one office of the Teacher;[4] of all who, since, in any place, have borne witness of truth and justified the ways of God to man.[5] These who show us how noble a being is a man when he gives heed to the promptings of the law within him: these, who reach out a helping hand to us, to lift us out of the Slough of Despondence,[6] out of the mire of the senses, who give us aid against ourselves, beautiful on the mountains are their feet, honorable in human memory are their names.

Even more touching because they come more within reach of the affections,

2. Cf. Isaiah 52:8 and 21:6–12.
3. Cf. John 6:35 and 6:48.
4. In the Gospels, Jesus is often referred to as "Rabbi," or teacher; see, for example, John 3:2. Moreover, the term "Master," commonly applied to Jesus in the King James Version, generally becomes "Teacher" in the Revised Standard Version. In I Timothy 2:7 and II Timothy 1:11, Paul refers to himself as a teacher.
5. Milton, *Paradise Lost,* I, 26.
6. The "Slough of Despond" in John Bunyan's *Pilgrim's Progress.*

are those among our own contemporaries and acquaintance who belong to this class. I appeal to the experience of every reflecting person in this congregation and ask whether your past life has anything more charming than the sweet service of the scattered company of four or five or six persons who in the course of years have most powerfully ministered to your highest wants. I may be mistaken but I incline to the opinion that in the course of Providence, care is taken to bring the opportunity of spiritual discourse, either private or public, to every individual, and that those persons to whom this gift is committed and who are of different calling and perhaps as often found out of the pulpit as in it are friends whose value steadily rises in our regard with time and comes at last to be preferred to all other society. They characterise the world. I speak of the class of natural preachers, men of inward light, whose eye is opened upon the laws of duty, and the beauty of holiness and who love to declare what they study. They are plain men and wise; they elevate, they cheer us. We feel in their presence how frivolous are the distinctions of fortune, and their voice is far from the voice of vanity, of display, of interest, of tradition, men who believe and therefore speak, who speak that they do know.[7] They feel and they make us feel that the Revelation is not closed and sealed, but times of refreshment and words of power are evermore coming from the presence of the Lord;[8] that neither is the age of miracles over and forever gone; that the Creation is an endless miracle as new at this hour as when Adam awoke in the garden.

We are continually forced to make comparisons between the world as it is, and the world as it ought to be. In a perfectly natural state of society, undoubtedly these persons and these alone would be the priesthood, or as we say, the professional clergy. But the gratitude of men to these teachers was naturally expressed in supplying their outward wants. The superior gifts of this class of men made them, in ages when the multitude of the people were little enlightened, the depositories of civil power, the trustees of property collected for institutions of learning or charity or worship. Hence the office came to be sought for its property and its power, the old forms were easier preserved than the spirit of wisdom and love which had created them. Then as the church became outwardly rich it became inwardly and really poor. And men feel the spirit of that ancient mourner of a degenerate church who said, "Once we had wooden chalices and golden priests, now we have golden chalices but wooden priests."[9]

Moreover, the clergy of each age and state of society is undoubtedly a fair representative of the mind of the people. According to the mind and heart of the people are the priests they elect and love. What a change has been effected in the religious institutions of Christendom during the last three centuries! The nominal Christian Church had been adulterated with the worst spirit of the pagan

7. John 3:11.
8. Acts 3:19.
9. The source of this anecdote has not been located; it is used in the late lecture "The Preacher" (W 10:229).

idolatry. A proud, lording, imperious clergy, used the conscience of men, which always inclines them to reverence what pretends to come from God, as the tool of their own selfish purposes. The Reformation in all countries and societies where it had free course broke in pieces that hateful tyranny.

Yet whilst the laws and ranks in which this iniquity was embodied perished, deep traces of the old error long remained. It is well known to all men how great a revolution has been going on, down even to this day, in the character and position of the clergy in this country.

The clergy of the last generation were accustomed to speak and feel as if they were the shepherds of a flock; as if they assumed the responsibility of the souls of their congregation; as if they were to communicate to the people what doctrines the people should believe, the blood of souls was on their skirts,[10] and the parish was a small territory, and over the souls therein, the pastor was and would in heaven continue to be a sort of president and spiritual captain. Men were supposed to be saved or lost as one race.

This language is so recent that it hardly surprizes the ear. But what a revolution has been completed in the hearts of men! Men have begun to feel the unworthiness of being saved or lost in their federal head, of hearing souls disposed of in bundles, and have begun to inquire each for his several stake in the joy and suffering of the whole. What is *my* relation to the Supreme Being? What is *my* relation to my fellow man? What am *I* designed for? What are my duties? What is my destiny?

A view more adequate to the divine nature of the soul is taken. Of course the position of the preacher is equally changed. He comes as a friend to provoke his brother to good works. He no longer dictates doctrines. He now solicits your attention to truths which engage him and therefore should engage you. He drops all shadow of a claim of authority over you. Neither God, nor Christ, nor apostles, nor fathers, nor bishop, nor presbytery have given him the least particle. His whole right to address you is the friendly one that you have invited him to do so, founded in a conviction of the strictly common nature of all men; as face answereth to face in water so the heart of man to man.[11]

This change may sometimes give rise to regret on both parts. It may sometimes seem both to minister and people that he has lost something of useful influence in the loss of the accidental and traditional respect which attached to him and that one restraint more is taken away from a community whose love of freedom is prone to degenerate into licentiousness. But I am inclined to think that nothing is worth defending which rests upon a false basis; that we always gain by putting our respect to others purely on the footing of character, and that what remains of the minister's influence upon his people is more genuine and powerful than all that is taken. When sanctity attached to the office and the officer, it is true that a man of selfish and sinful life might still exercise some

10. Jeremiah 2:34.
11. Proverbs 27:19.

salutary influence on a congregation through forms and words. Now the benefit is neither more nor less than the amount of thought and the degree of piety
which he has and imparts.

The influence of this is real, is appreciable, is inevitable. It is as sure as the
attraction of matter. An ounce of iron will balance an ounce, let it be high or
low, cold or hot, ever so much divided, or in whatsoever shape. And in like
manner a principle of justice, a principle of benevolence, a principle of temperance, seated in the heart of a man, will extort the love and reverence of men
everywhere and at all times. The minister finds himself not possessed in advance of the confidence of people. That impatience and jealousy which appears
in this country against any sort of prescription is sometimes directed at him. He
may even find the virulence of that ignorant love of liberty which assails every
existing institution pointed at him. He may have railing and opposition from
those whose pecuniary interest or whose evil habits are directly attacked by his
virtuous exertions. But a good man is willing to wait and make his own reputation. As to the virulence of the ignorant he is willing to have the check and
admonition of jealous eyes laid upon him for a season, and a good man is
always cheered by a perfect confidence that the principles in which he lives are
the salt and soul of society, will be found to work better than any others in the
end and will put all others to shame. And as for railing and opposition there is
an end to these. All the devils respect virtue.[12] Such is the majesty of a truly
devout and faithful spirit that its enemies will speedily be silent and ashamed
and a prevailing virtue will go forth from it to subdue and reform the offender.
The humble disciple of Christ who in these days assumes the pastoral office,
shall find that no weakness has crept upon any of the principles of Christ. They
have all their omnipotence yet. He shall find that lowly perfect love, which temptation cannot seduce nor opposition wear out, is a more powerful preacher to the
soul of men than all tongues and all ecclesiastical powers and all superstition.

I rejoice in this because it puts the minister on a perfectly natural basis. By
taking him out of an unnatural attitude it allows him to assume the erect position, it permits the minister to be a man. It teaches him that stern but invigorating truth which calls out whatsoever is divine in us, that a man is valued as he
makes himself valuable.[13] If it takes away artificial respect it removes all the
fences that separated the minister from the people and teaches him to use all the
forces of mutual understanding and benefit which the Creator gave man to act
upon his fellow.

My friends, I have thus at length described the position and relations of the
pastor in our community, because in so doing I think I describe the character
and influence of our brother and pastor whom God has recently taken unto
himself. You have already heard this day the traits of his character from his

---

12. See *JMN* 5:150, 203, 282, and *JMN* 6:385; used in "Religion" (*EL* 2:94) and "Spiritual Laws"
(*CW* 2:92). The aphorism appears to be Emerson's own, though it may derive from James 2:19.
13. Vicesimus Knox, *Elegant Extracts,* 2:1028. See Sermon CLXI, n. 12.

venerated friend, who knew him much better than I, and to whom he was naturally so dear.[14] I have only endeavoured to add to his portrait a view of those circumstances into which he fell, or rather, among which he had to chuse his lot. This office of the Christian pastor, as I have described it, bereft of all external authority or privilege, yielding no emolument which could make it attractive to a man of talents, this office which was only an opportunity of plain usefulness, and which in usage adds to its duties of religious instruction an active and laborious interest in the schools and the religious and social libraries, this humble office he was content to qualify himself for, to seek, and to accept. That fact, that he assumed it, already makes known to us the complexion of his character. It shows him to be a man not ambitious of wealth or consideration, but who felt that he could find his satisfaction in a mild and limited beneficence. The imperious spirits, fond of power, that in a former age would have entered the church find nothing there now to tempt them. They are now the demagogues of the bar-room and of the caucus, and the church is relieved of their turbulence.

Mr. Goodwin had from infancy been remarked for an amiable and devout spirit, a youth and a man of conscience, not afraid to own and to defend and to act upon his opinion, nor yet so much a lover of his opinion but that he loved truth more. He had pleasing manners and great ease of communicating his thoughts, and these qualities determined, no doubt, the choice of his profession. You are all witnesses for him whether he acquitted himself therein as a just and wise man. He was a social, friendly spirit, not wrapt up in himself but entering with ready sympathy into the situation of others, whether happy or unhappy, and his hands were prompt to extend relief to want according to his ability. He aimed at fidelity in the discharge of his duties and did not spare himself. I have the testimony of others as well as some observation of my own to vouch for the independence of his character; that he was not to be intimidated by opposition and was rather likely to concede more than was due to his regard for his friends than to be deterred from his path out of fear of offending. His piety was a natural love of the Divine Goodness and attended him as a good angel from his earliest youth. He was a good scholar and used the leisure which his profession gave him in making himself acquainted with the best popular books.

To these qualities of the inner man he added no mean gifts as a writer and public speaker. Something of felicity there was in his address, in his voice, in his power of expression that seems everywhere to have caught the attention and affection of religious assemblies. He was a singular favorite in all the neighbor-

---

14. Ezra Ripley had eulogized Goodwin at a Concord parish meeting moderated by Samuel Hoar on July 10, and those remarks became the basis for an obituary published in the Concord *Yeoman's Gazette* on July 16. Unless Ripley spoke again at Concord on July 17, the reference must be to remarks at East Lexington. See Kenneth W. Cameron, "Emerson's Ideal Clergyman—Hersey Bradford Goodwin," *ESQ* 12 (3d Quarter 1958): 42–43.

ing churches, and I remember to have heard in the city of New York, where he preached but a single half-day, that there was a very strong disposition in the Society to invite him to settle with them.[15]

There was in Mr. Goodwin a sensibility which heightened his interest in the virtues of his friends, and at the same time made him suffer a good deal from any exhibition of hardness of heart, or of the licentious and ribald spirit which loves profanity and disorder and which ought to move in a good man only compassion for the offender. But even for men of this stamp the influence of the mild virtues, of patience, of kindness, joined with perfect honesty and courage is sure in the end to have weight and effect. It is not in man to resist the power of integrity, and the steadfast intention of kindness. They who scoffed in the presence of the good man are men also and will honor him when he is gone. His words, his deeds will sink into their memory and may yet be restraints upon their passions and warning voices to recal and save them. And all on the contrary who sympathized with his just and gentle spirit, who loved with him everything that was generous and good, will derive new force to every good and holy affection in them from the remembrance of his discourse and counsel and unspotted life. And thus in a twofold manner the memory of the just is blessed.[16]

My friends. It is not without design that we are made the subjects of a various discipline and that to us as to every generation a peculiar instruction is sent. If we are sent within the influences of a more liberal church, if our lot is cast in an hour when old traditions and usages have lost some of their power and the mind has not yet attained a clear sight of a perfectly spiritual church, it is because there is a necessity for our education and redemption that such things should be. Let us give these things no careless glance. Our weal and hope are in them. And if a good man of lowly and loving heart, of gentle manners, and of pure life, has pleaded with us in behalf of God and the interests of our eternal nature, let us give earnest heed, for he was sent to us, and the use of the talent will be asked at our hands.[17]

15. Emerson refers to the Second Unitarian Church in New York, where Orville Dewey of New Bedford accepted a call in late 1834. Emerson's brother William, who belonged to that church, was involved in the protracted negotiations.

16. Proverbs 10:7.

17. Matthew 25:14–30.

OCCASIONAL DISCOURSES AND SERMON FRAGMENTS

[SERMON FRAGMENT]

Brethren, if our gospel be hid, it is hid from them that are lost.

II CORINTHIANS 4:3

It is a remark borne out by every day's experience that nothing really worth having is cheap. Nor need the remark appear a paradox. Life itself is cheap. The sea, the air and the earth teem with it; and human life is cheap and our cities are oppressed by the redundant population. Whether Nature were always as profuse of this gift, or what slow progress of prodigious periods ripened these elements to the production of man, and so whether life can in the Universe be called a lavish gift, we do not know. Or how valuable is mere animation, how much worth to the insects of a summer day, to all the tribes of beasts, the drudges or the game of man, whether this existence is truly desirable we do not know. But for the existence of man a higher price is paid, even where that price is lowest, namely in barbarous nations. The daily toil of the parent from year to year for the subsistence of himself and his offspring, the strongest exercise of his mind to procure and keep a good footing in society, the surrender of his independence to a government, the kind deeds done with a view to conciliate the goodwill of the fellowship of savages to his child, the anxious watching, the continual counsel, the fond affections, all these constitute purchase money paid for a life, by one individual in barbarous society without going back as we might to enumerate all the costs of the gradual formation of that imperfect league which is still competent to most of the purposes of society, competent to the defence of the nursling from the fury of the elements, from the fangs of the wolf and the knife of man. Yet this is a state of life which to civilized men seems almost worthless. And the great and noble advantages of civilized and elegant institutions are fully considered in the burdens which Providence in view of these lays upon its children.

But it is not my intention at this time to follow out the details of this expanding discussion. It will be found in all its particulars to correspond faithfully to

---

This undated fragment on compensations was surely never part of a completed and delivered sermon. On the basis of a single common passage (see n. 2, below), the editors conjecture that the next item, here called "Draft Sermon on the Evidences of Christianity," was an attempt to rewrite the present sermon. Granting this conjecture, the present sermon would seem to have been written in the fall of 1826.

the general statement that all things are administered on a system of Compensations.

The scheme of Compensations is that Constitution of nature in reference to man upon which we build our convictions of a superintending Providence. It is a great law and greatly administered, overlooking in the great prosperity of its ends a small adversity in its means; and (it must be distinctly observed) bringing the good which was purchased by the toils, counsels, sacrifices and lives of a host of good men into the bosom of their country, not perhaps till a second, a third or a tenth generation has trodden down the sods upon the graves of all who suffered that the Cause might prosper. We shall presently advert to the manner in which the equity of the law is brought about in reference to that man who lives on the usury of another's virtue and toil. But in all instances the provision holds that at whose cost soever good may come great objects must be purchased by great sacrifices.

The best thing in the world, the New Testament and the Christian Religion, rests the genuineness of its history, by a sort of appeal to this principle, on the streams of the purest human blood that was shed to seal its authenticity. And what is that commentary that has come down to us with continual accession of light from all the passages of ecclesiastical history to interpret its doctrine and disencumber it from the profane dogmatism of bigots or of false pastors who wrested it to apologies for their worldly ambition—what is that commentary of defence and reformation as it subsists in the enlightened mind of the Christian who reads that book, and how was it procured but by the blood, by the murder, of holy men?

Perhaps the next best possession of man is the Constitution of our own Country, of which we should remember that only a small part of its cost can be truly said to have been proffered in this country. We do daily justice to the merits of our fathers, to the pilgrims, the champions of religious, to the patriots, the martyrs of civil, freedom. But the hundreds and thousands of valiant patriots who perished among us, were sons of those who in the parent country had been, for centuries, directing their eyes and their whole energy to these lofty ends, so that great as the price paid in this country was, it was a portion only of the ransom of human Right which we have received. And in view of this rule of God's Providence, it has always forcibly struck my mind, that it was out of a sort of obedience and acknowledgement of this high and melancholy necessity that America has yielded up her vast indigenous family, tribe after tribe, to the haughty Genius of Civilization, who cannot found his noble structure on her shores, but at this stern forfeiture of a national existence.

The same remark may be extended to all the objects of human desire. Is aspiring youth desirous of setting itself side by side with genius and experience by obtaining a distinguished Education? He must spend much and travel far, he must acquire painful habits, he must live an anchorite in the pleasures of the world, he must read, and think, and write; he must jealously separate a number of years to his object,—a considerable portion of his life, to this preparation for the duties of the remainder. Or is the idol, Honor? or is it Wealth? Is it honourable Love? is it dishonourable Pleasure? Is it the fame of Science, or the skill of Art? All men are aware of the amount of time and pains by which the good must be bought. And no man can doubt that these difficulties thus inwrought into the texture of worth were *intended* to stand in that connexion. I reverence in this the high ordination of Providence which does not consent to levity or sloth, but which by setting a high rate on all the leading objects of human desire, exercises, hardens, and ripens the great faculties of man into a health and power equal to their destiny, mighty enow to survive the sun and outshine the stars.

If such an economy, such a parsimony in the dispensing of its riches, be the habit of Divine Providence it certainly was not to be expected that the benefits accruing to men from the religion of Jesus Christ should be bestowed on a more lavish rate of bounty. The history of human opinions, the history of the Churches, does indeed shew us that such an expectation has been for ages accounted an orthodox doctrine. It has been thought unworthy of the Deity to *measure* his bounty, to give for equivalents, and hence has been compounded that dogma which more than any other offends against sense and justice and pure religion, that God did from Eternity elect his uncreated children into the Church of his Son and into the Society of Heaven before all consideration of their contingent character, of temptation and resistance, of virtue and vice, and that this high foreordination is not reversed by any excesses of deep and daring iniquity that may deface the history of the chosen servant.[1] But we all know too well how tragic a story is the story of human opinions—a tissue of folly and extravagance; of genuine principles carried to an insane excess; of depraved sentiment. We know this by a too faithful experience (it is chronicled in the blood of martyrs) to permit us to attach any weight to these traditionary opinions when they contravene our own knowledge of God's ordinary action upon men. The gospel brought by Jesus Christ offers to men the most precious advantages. The human mind had gone in many sensual ages into habits and pursuits foreign to its destiny and its happiness. The character of nations stood at a very humble level of moral elevation. Few individuals in each, preserved a sacred regard to the dictates of natural religion, and the mass of society in a state of dreary ignorance and tremendous moral delinquency[2]

1. Emerson here attacks the Universalist position.
2. The manuscript breaks off in the middle of a sentence at the bottom of page 8; this passage is given in full, however, in the next item: see "Draft Sermon on the Evidences of Christianity," n. 1.

[DRAFT SERMON ON THE EVIDENCES OF CHRISTIANITY]

The freedom of inquiry is the most precious right we possess as intellectual beings. Each new adventurer in the ways of the world, is unfaithful to himself, if he consent to take upon trust the opinions of his fellowmen in regard to topics of daily discussion, of common interest to society. Most of all is he unfaithful to himself if he servilely put the reins of his understanding in the hands of society upon the question of his life and death, the nature and intent of his existence and the venerable secrets of the invisible world. There is a praiseworthy flexibility of character of great value in life, a spirit of accommodation that meets unruffled the crowd of good and evil accidents of which so much of life is made up—an even temper slow to admire and slow to repine, the gift of nature often, but an element that ripens into the dignity of a virtue. But this is not one of the offices of that virtue, to surrender the freedom of opinion. For in the relations in which every man stands to God, he stands alone. The opinion of all mankind upon his merits is accounted nothing; the vices of all men cannot excuse his Vice, the virtues of all men alter not his Virtue. Before God he stands alone. There is to him a solitary law, a several universe. It is not therefore so much a matter of high moment as it is the one grand object for which he was made and placed in the world that we chalk out for ourselves by the aid of the lights which God and man have shed over the scene, the path in which we will walk, the duties we solemnly judge to be required of us towards God and Man and ourselves.

But in the Providence of God there are those who are called to a greater obligation still, to a responsibility not for themselves alone, who are called to furnish these very lights to other men, which God has appointed in aid of these judgments which it behoves us to make. It must readily be felt with what anxious circumspection, such men ought to walk, how diligently they should choose between truth and falsehood when their unfortunate choice involves the ignorance and peril and misery of so many more than themselves.

It is with reason, therefore, that those who in these times find themselves disposed to take up the sacred office of interpreting to men the oracles of God, set themselves to examine those Scriptures in which it is pretended they are contained to see how far they are entitled to this authority.

And what are the pretensions of that Religion which numbers among its votaries all the civilized nations of the globe? These we must briefly state. The

---

The manuscript is undated, though the text draws heavily on journal passages of late September or early October 1826 (*JMN* 3:47–50).

human mind had gone in many sensual ages into habits and pursuits foreign to its destiny and its happiness. The character of nations the most refined stood at a very humble level of moral elevation. Few individuals in each preserved a sacred regard to uncertain dictates of natural religion, and the mass of society in a state of dreary ignorance and tremendous moral delinquency passed to their great account.[1] But in the midst of this perplexing darkness a Teacher appeared in the world who pretended to a very great supernatural authority. He came to preach Repentance and offered to the penitent everlasting life. He anticipated the work of the other world by informing men of the nature of the other world. They saw what it was, and felt what it demanded. He came, he said, to reconcile a guilty world to his Father in heaven. He taught a system of doctrines in perfect unison with the moral code as it had been developed by the great masters of pagan philosophy. He revealed a character of God more august and affecting than had yet entered the human conception. It was not only infinite and perfect, it had an aspect also towards man: it was paternal.

These mighty truths were not left to the hazards of neglect, they were obtruded by miracles on the notice of men. He appealed to these as the express testimony of Heaven in behalf of his authority and the death of this Messiah was followed by a miracle the most astonishing on human record. It is altogether needless to recapitulate this renowned history. The mass of evidence from the care with which it has been collated is more entire and satisfactory than any other portion of history as distant could boast, and more convincing but for the great deduction that is always made and rightly made upon accounts of miracles. This evidence is internal and external. The labour of divines in so many generations has done ample justice to these demands of their faith both in the exhibition of its evidence and the answer to objections. There are still, however, a few remarks which I may be indulged in making that bear upon this point.

There is an objection to Christianity that is continually repeated, that all the dismal history of opinions, that have misled the human mind under the sanction of its name, conspire to throw doubt on the pretensions of the dispensation. It cannot be denied—the avowal is on every page of ecclesiastical history—that the most gross superstitions have been defended as the most precious doctrines which Jesus Christ came into the world to teach. These insane tenets have been sanctioned by councils and sealed by blood. An age went by; a revolution in men's minds took place, and these famous dogmas are pleasantly quoted in literary anecdote and are speedily forgotten. And now another set of opinions is taught in councils and illustrated in pulpits; but what security that these are more genuine than those that went before, or that another age may not treat them with the same irreverence? And in this shifting spectacle is not a doubt thrown upon the gospel itself, which is represented to different ages in such contradictory lights?

---

1. The preceding three sentences are from the "Sermon Fragment" immediately above.

We think the objection which charges the errors of Christians on the dispensation of Christianity rests on false views of the nature of Christianity. There came into the world a communication from God, informing men of the immortality of the soul and that future happiness and misery depended entirely on the choice they should make in this life, between good and evil. These simple and majestic doctrines which were rather confirmations of the secret suggestions of the moral sense than novel oracles were eagerly caught up by the numbers who in the beginning beheld the stupendous powers to which the Messenger appealed as the token of his authority. They were from their very simplicity and elevation so puzzling to the depraved and superstitious mind of the times that to the mass of the new believers it is evident they were recommended by the merits of their Teacher rather than their own. It is not the habit of the human mind to pass hastily from ignorance to wisdom, but slowly—reluctantly to receive truth for falsehood—and by the nature of association with a continual effort to incorporate the new truth to the old error. 'No doctrine,' it is observed, 'comes forth out of any mind in precisely the same hue and state in which it entered.'[2] The early believers, therefore, as is well known, adhered with the purest intentions to most of their early opinions, to which they reconciled as well as they were able the doctrines of Christ. When in the sequel Christianity became the religion of nations the corruption of its doctrine became more inevitable from the circumstance that there were other reasons besides the love of truth which attracted professors to its ranks.

But it is not only true that the errors of Christians cast no shadow on Christianity. It is also a beautiful and famed part of its evidence that its influence on men's minds continually operates to purify them and exalt their views of this divine revelation. It never was apparent to the mind at first what is the extent of this spiritual blessing. It is the *Way* before it is the *Life*.[3] It is the *Guide* to Truth, not the truth itself. It has always been divesting itself of the false opinion of men like casting off the outer bark of human prejudice. The more men study and practise it, the more they perceive of its immeasurable value.

There are also some observations that may be made in evidence.

If Christianity had never appeared, and the best progress that may be supposed, had been made in the advancement of human reason, we think the most accomplished moralist of the present time would have been strangely bewildered in his contemplation of the human soul. Amidst the riches of all experience, he would complain of a certain moral indigence. There would be a continual war between the inference drawn from the order of the world and the order of the human mind on the one side and the want of sensible Divine interference, some solitary manifestation of Deity on the other. Here are works, here are wonders, but all in vain; they exist to no purpose. Without a proprietor they cannot beget conviction or enforce any law of obedience—in this *dumb* magnificence, this speechless universe. There arises this call from forsaken

---

2. *JMN* 6:185.
3. John 14:6.

humanity, affrighted at the solitude in which it is left, Let the Lord speak, for Here am I.[4] In such a condition natural religion would not have evidence enough to make it credible that a divine Providence existed, and human virtue would want support and human suffering would want consolation. This want makes the creation and whole condition of man an aenigma, and this want Christianity has supplied. There is certainly a great measure of evidence in this perfect suitableness of the revelation to our condition. In its purified state it makes one with the moral code. The doctrine of Immortality, the grand revelation of Christianity, illuminates and ennobles the existence of man. This solves the great question also concerning the existence of evil, for if man is immortal this world is his place of discipline and the value of pain, the uses of affliction, is then disclosed.

Such was the doctrine as it appeared to those in that time of thick darkness in which it came. There is another period we ought to regard. There was a care manifested for its widest promulgation. There is a page of history we ought to read. We may read that when the doctrine was now scattered abroad in the Roman empire, the Roman Empire was broken up. There was a movement in the world such as was not before or after, an expansion of the human family in the vast regions of Central Asia, which in its progress brought the farthest peoples of the North and East, nation after nation, into the heart of Europe, to see the uplifting of the Cross of Christ, to hear the silver trumpet of God's Revelation which had been so long sounding in those parts of the world.

There is a great evidence from history which cannot, I think, but have great force on minds accustomed to trace the dealings of Providence in human affairs, an evidence of the same sort to be found in the bloody chronicles of the Reformation, in the history of the Puritans and in the settlement of America.

But we cannot attempt to enumerate even the more striking points of the evidences. It has been made clear that miracles are the only testimony Heaven can bear to its message, that the internal evidence is faultless, that the external is as perfect as the nature of the case admits.

The authority of the Christian religion, which has in every age been assailed with every variety of argument and which has triumphed over all, has in our times been attacked upon novel grounds and with a more formidable combination of reason and learning than at any former period. In an age so conspicuous as ours for the downfall of old and venerated opinions in letters, in science, in philosophy, such opposition has reasonably excited apprehension. It is always unpleasant to be compelled to give up an opinion; to find we have been dupes of prejudice. But to give up a system of religious opinions which has been embodied with all our thoughts, which has been to us the Voice of God—by which we have lived, which taught us how to die—to make shipwreck of our faith would be an evil beyond the common depth of human suffering.[5]

The objections which the German scholars have proposed attack the founda-

---

4. Cf. Acts 9:6 and 9:10.
5. I Timothy 1:19.

tions of external evidence and so give up the internal to historical speculators and pleasant doubters. The eager appetite for novelty that rages especially in our own country, undieted, uncloyed by religious establishments and venerable abuses, will not stand on ceremony with any name or form or fact by whatsoever men or prejudices hallowed, when its genuineness is denied. There will be to good men henceforward a horrid anticipation when the majestic vision that has for ages kept a commanding check upon the dangerous passions of men—has rivetted the social bonds and brought forward so many noble spirits to the help of struggling humanity—shall roll away and let in the ghastly reality of things. Regard it as a possible event and it is the prospect of a dark and disastrous tragedy. These great and blessed mysteries which have hoarded comfort from age to age for human suffering—the august founder, the twelve self denying heroes of a pious renown, distancing in moral sublimity all those primeval benefactors whom ancient gratitude deified; the apostles whose desiring eyes saw little lustre on earth and no consolation but in extending the victories, the moral victories, of the cross, the martyrs who had found after so many sensual ages in a faith for things unseen,[6] in a moral intellection, more than a compensation for the lust of the world and the pride of life;[7] and after all these and better even than all these, the boundless aggregate of hearts and deeds which the genius of Christianity touched and inspired; the violence of fiery dispositions to which it has whispered peace; the antidote it has administered to remorse and despair; the Samaritan oil it has poured into wounded hearts,[8] the costly sacrifices and unpurchaseable devotion to the cause of God and man it has now for eighteen centuries inspired—all these must now pass away and become ridiculous. They have been the sum of what was most precious on earth; they must now pass into the rhetoric of scoffer and atheist as the significant testimonies of human folly, and every drunkard in his cups, and every voluptuary in his brothel will loll out his tongue at the resurrection from the dead, at the acts, the martyrdoms, the unassailable virtues and the traditionary greatness of Christianity. God forbid. It were base treason in his servants tamely to surrender his cause. The gates of hell will not prevail against it. But it were vile and supine to sit and be astonished without exploring the strength of the enemy. Patriots turn pale when some paper privilege, some national punctilio, is withheld or disputed to their Country, and Christians should not sit still and ignorant when the honour of their *Order,* no transient institution of one age or one realm but the Chivalry of the Universe, is trampled in the dust.

This is not the place or time (if I were able) to enter on the defence of the external evidences of Christianity. It is the continual tendency of theological science to augment and rest upon its moral evidence. That the most formidable opposition that has been encountered has only tended to perplex the historical evidence whilst it leaves untouched what is moral is certainly matter of joy. For

6. Cf. II Corinthians 4:18.
7. I John 2:16.
8. Luke 10:34.

it is the weakness and misfortune of man, that the best historical evidence is liable to great cavil and uncertainty, and the reasoning which is applied to it is of so subtile and delusive a character that it can never have the weight of solid argument from other sources. The testimony of crowds and of ages has been found on scrutiny almost worthless, and the ingenuity of scholars has thrown into irrecoverable doubt parts of history which had been reckoned best authenticated. But moral evidence, the evidence of final causes, when it can be procured, is unerring and eternal.

It is a defensible faith. Every hour of time, every mind that has applied its force to this religion, has been adding something of evidence to the mighty mass. The last hope of humanity will not perish, and with its ministers rests the high and solemn and inspiring duty to defend, to maintain and transmit it; it is not a sublime speculation. "Jesus Christ died to maintain no frigid sophisms, no abstract refinement."[9] It is eminently, above all the theologies that ever advanced a claim to human belief, a practical religion, giving to its disciples a character the nearest to perfection that a system of sentiments ever bestowed on man.

---

9. Emerson attributed the remark to Edward Everett in *JMN* 6:183.

RIGHT HAND OF FELLOWSHIP. _____

By Rev. Ralph Waldo Emerson,
Pastor of the Second Church in Boston.

The ancient custom of offering a new pastor the expression of the sympathy of the churches, is no unsuitable rite in the ceremonies of ordination, and hath a deep foundation in reason. There is no sympathy so strong as that which exists between the good, and this fellow-feeling Christianity has done all to foster.

Whilst men are in the moral darkness which vice produces, each individual is a sect by himself; each is a self-seeker, with his hands against every man, and every man's hands against him.[1] Each, forgetful of all other rights and feelings, is straining every nerve to build up his own sordid advantage, and tearing down his neighbor's happiness, if need be, to build up his own. His eye is blind, his ear is deaf to the great harmonies, by which God has yoked together the social and the selfish good of his children.

Just in proportion as men grow wiser and better, their efforts converge to a point. For, as truth is one, in seeking it, they all aim to conform their actions to one standard. When intelligent men talk together, it is remarkable how much they think alike, how many propositions are taken for granted, that are disputed, word by word, in the conversation of ignorant persons. The more enlightened men are, the greater is this unanimity, as is attested by the common wonder, when two minds of unquestionable elevation, come to opposite conclusions. As it is with the mind, so is it with the heart. As two minds agreeing with truth, do mutually agree, so, if their affections are right with God, they will be true to one another.

Christianity aims to teach the perfection of human nature, and eminently, therefore, does it teach the unity of the spirit. It is not only in its special precepts, but by all its operations, a law of love. It does by its revelation of God, and of the true purposes and the true rules of life, operate to bind up, to join

---

Delivered at the ordination of Hersey Bradford Goodwin as junior pastor to Ezra Ripley at the First Parish, Concord, February 17, 1830. Giving the "Right Hand of Fellowship" was a standard component of ministerial ordinations and signified the welcoming good will of the churches; its scriptural basis is to be found in Galatians 2:9. Emerson submitted a slightly but carefully revised version for publication in James Kendall's *Sermon, Delivered at the Ordination of Hersey Bradford Goodwin . . . in Concord, Mass., Feb. 17, 1830* (Concord: Gazette Office, 1830), 29-31. The present text reproduces the published version; a full transcription of the manuscript text, as read by Emerson, is given in the Textual Notes.

1. Genesis 16:12.

together, and not to distinguish and separate. It proclaimed peace. But it speaks first to its own disciples, 'be of one mind;'[2] else, with what countenance should the church say to the world of men, love one another.[3]

And thousands and thousands of hearts have heard the commandment and anon with joy received it. All men on whose souls the light of God's revelation truly shineth, with whatever apparent differences, are substantially of one mind, work together, whether consciously or not, for one and the same good. Faces that never beheld each other, are lighted by it with the same expression. Hands that were never clasped, toil unceasingly at the same work. This it is, which makes the omnipotence of truth in the keeping of feeble men,—this fellowship in all its servants, this swift consenting acknowledgment with which they hail it when it appears. God's truth; it is that electric spark which flies instantaneously through the countless hands that compose the chain. Truth,—not like each form of error, depending for its repute on the powers and influence of here and there a solitary mind that espouses it,—combines hosts for its support, and makes them cooperate across mountains and oceans, yea and ages of time.

This is what was meant in that beautiful sentiment of ancient philosophy, that God had so intimately linked all wise men to each other, that if one should only lift his finger in Rome, all the rest were benefited by it, though in Egypt, or Asia.[4] This is what was meant by that *one body in Christ,* of which all his disciples are the members.[5]

Sir, it is this sentiment which is recognised in the ancient and simple rite of the churches. God has bound heart to heart by invisible and eternal bands, by oneness of nature, of duty, and of hope. To us is 'one Lord, one faith, one baptism.'[6] And, in acknowledgment of these divine connexions existing between us, the Christian churches, whose organ I am, do offer you, my brother, this right hand of their fellowship. They greet you by me, to the exalted relations on which now you are entering; they give you a solemn welcome to great duties, to honorable sacrifices, to unremitting studies, and to the eternal hope of all souls. They exhort you to all pious resolutions, and they pledge to you, by this sign, their sympathy, their aid, and their intercession. They say to you, that so long as in purity of heart, you do the work of God in this vineyard of his,[7]—you are not alone, but you shall be secure of the love and the furtherance not of these churches only, but of all righteous men. In every hour of perplexity or affliction, they shall encourage and aid and bless you, by desire, and by word, and by action. And when the day of success comes to you, and you see around you in this garden of the Lord, the fruit of your virtues and the light of your example, and the truth you teach shine forth together, in that day a kindred joy shall

2. Cf. I Corinthians 1:10, Philippians 1:27, and 2:2.
3. See, for example, I John 3:23 and 4:7.
4. Montaigne, "Of Vanity," in *Essays of Michael Seigneur de Montaigne . . . ,* trans. Charles Cotton (London, 1693), 3:315–16. See Sermon CXLII, n. 11, and Sermon CLXX, n. 12.
5. Cf. Romans 12:5 and I Corinthians 12:12–14.
6. Ephesians 4:5.
7. Isaiah 5:7.

touch our hearts—we shall be glad with you, and give thanks with you, and hope for you.

Sir, it is with sincere pleasure that I speak for the churches, on this occasion, and on this spot, hallowed to all by so many patriotic, and to me, by so many affectionate recollections. I feel a peculiar, a personal right to welcome you hither to the home and the temple of my fathers. I believe the church whose pastor you are will forgive me the allusion, if I express the extreme interest which every man feels in the scene of the trials and labors of his ancestors. Five out of seven of your predecessors are my kindred.[8] They are in the dust, who bind my attachment to this place—but not all. I cannot help congratulating you that one survives, to be to you the true friend and venerable counsellor he has ever been to me. I heartily rejoice to see their labors and a portion of his resting on one who comes with such ability, and, as I trust, with such devout feeling, to the work. Suffer me, then, *as for them,* to offer you my hand, and receive with it, my brother, my best wishes and prayers for your success in your great undertaking, and for your everlasting welfare.

8. Emerson was descended from Peter Bulkeley, the town's first minister, and Bulkeley's son Edward; Emerson's grandfather, William, and William's father-in-law, Daniel Bliss, were also Concord ministers. The fifth was Ezra Ripley, who married William's widow, Phebe Bliss Emerson, and was thus not actually a blood relation. The next several sentences allude to Ripley.

[PRELIMINARY NOTES
FOR SERMON LXXXIV] _____

I wish to consider this old objection to the intellectual cultivation of the laborious classes.

It would be natural to an irreligious race of beings to leave the intellect uncultivated, but the moment the being of God and immortality of the soul was declared it should follow of course—this cultivation.

Facts. That an hour of systematic research is worth years of heedless opportunity of observation. Better go up against the wall in blank inefficiency when you pursue a thought than give up the search for a more attractive object.

A thinking community such as Milton describes in Areopagitica. Every tradesman should inform himself of the natural history of the goods, merchandise, he vended, every mechanic of the materials he wrought. It is wonderful they do not. Take the first step. 'Tis easy getting on. Then we live in a moral world. Nothing takes place here at random. Every trade has its moral. Every trade will be to a good man only a new version of his bible. There are infinite ranges for the mind in the very narrowest spheres of observation. But the preliminary condition to success here is to love the right. Heart is the seat of Wisdom.

Some great advantages to wisdom possessed by laborer. He must make his speculations tally with facts as other will not for there his habits are

Animals compelled by their instincts but man's compliment from God was the reason—the voluntary pursuit of his well-being and so we will not be angels because we are not forced to be.

It is the uniform testimony of successful thinkers that what they have accomplished best was the result of a little patient thought.

Do not fear evils of knowledge. There are none that belong to it when sought from the love of truth. It will not then be useless from finespun theories nor ridiculous from pedantry.

"We must know much in order to judge well."[1] The good man is forever the master of the bad man, and the wise of the ignorant.

What is our faith worth if we have never inquired? Much if we are good; nothing if we are bad. While you are unwise your actions cannot possibly be

The manuscript is undated but bears obvious relation to Sermon LXXXIV, delivered August 1, 1830 (*Sermons* 2:232–36). The notes must have been written within the year preceding, since Emerson draws on Washington Irving's *Life of Columbus* (see n. 2 below), which he read in September 1829 (see *JMN* 6:101).

1. This is Emerson's translation from Madame de Staël's *De l'Allemagne* (Paris, 1814), 1:61. See *JMN* 6:5 and 6:26.

systematic but must be chance-sown. Every particle of truth will be felt. It will not come to a man what the gospel intends by accident.

No man was ever encumbered by his knowledge. By numbers the general may be; by wealth the rich; by states the empire, but no man by his knowledge who seeks knowledge for its own sake.

We are only separated by a thin barrier, each of us, from worlds of science. For think how few steps there were in the process of thought which led to any of the greatest inventions that adorn the history of man. The discovery of America by Columbus, how simple and decisive are a few of the data—the ancient opinion, the sight of a human body drifted from the westward of an unknown cast of features, and the roundness of the globe, and the improbability of so much water—These facts, presented to an active mind fond of great adventure, discovered America.[2]

Discovery of the law of gravitation. Whence? An apple fell from a tree and Newton seeing it said, Why should it not fall up as well as down or sideways? How far does this power of the earth to attract bodies extend? Why not infinitely far? Perhaps the moon falls to the earth and the earth to the sun.

These two or three thoughts in each instance ended in this great and beneficent result. Now that these should come together and with sufficient probability to ensure attention required certain habits of mind which are very rare and which are not easily acquired, but which every man may in some degree and in great degrees acquire. But probably we are every one of us at all times only a few steps removed from discoveries every whit as astonishing and as valuable to us as these but we remain blind to them for want of such self cultivated habits.

Discoveries to us, for it profits me not much that so much is known, I must verify it for myself. All moral philosophy is only useful to him who has made the wisdom of others his own by diligent study, i.e., comparison of the statements with his own observation of facts.

2. Emerson's source is Washington Irving, *A History of the Life and Voyages of Christopher Columbus* (New York, 1828), chapter 5. See also *JMN* 3:176.

ADDRESS AT THE DEDICATION OF SECOND CHURCH VESTRY, FEB. 28, 1831.

Peace be within these walls! For my brethren and companions' sake, I will now say, peace be within thee! The peace of God, which passeth all understanding;[1] the love of God, made known by the mission of his son, to the reception and study whereof we have opened these doors; and the wisdom of God, the only source of all spiritual illumination,—here may they dwell, as long as these humble walls shall endure; and may He, who alone can prosper a good purpose, grant, that what shall be here thought and uttered in accordance with truth, may so intimately enter our minds, as to become substance of their substance, eternal of their eternity, and so add to our power, and our joy, for ages after these walls shall be level with the earth on which they stand!

The hall in which we are assembled has been raised by the Church of this religious Society. A small fund had been permitted to accumulate for a few years until it exceeded six hundred dollars. It was then, on a proposition of the Pastor to deliver a course of Expository lectures,[2] voted by the Members of the Church to appropriate this sum to the erection of a Vestry on land belonging to the Proprietors of the Second Church, provided the Proprietors would give them the use of the land for this purpose, and it was further voted that after finishing and furnishing the Vestry, the members of the Church would give the same to the Proprietors. At a meeting of the Proprietors this offer was accepted, and the use of the land was granted. The expenses of the building and furniture having exceeded the money at the disposal of the church, a subscription has been opened to supply the deficiency. This subscription has not yet sufficed to liquidate the debt, and the Committee will continue to receive any sums for this purpose, in a full understanding that they do not wish any sum to be subscribed that cannot be given not only without reluctance, but without the least inconvenience.

The entering into a new house, whether public or private, is one of those epochs in the life of men that always impress them. The mind's eye is filled with the future. A thousand expectations of what shall here be contrived and executed, crowd upon the thought.

Delivered on the evening of February 28, 1831.

1. Philippians 4:7.
2. See Karen Kalinevitch, "Turning from the Orthodox: Emerson's Gospel Lectures," in Joel Myerson, ed., *Studies in the American Renaissance: 1986* (Charlottesville, Va., 1986), 69-112; and Kenneth W. Cameron, ed., *The Vestry Lectures and a Rare Sermon* (Hartford, 1984). Emerson delivered the first of nine Vestry Lectures on March 8, 1831.

I invite you, friends, to consider with me the purposes to which this simple edifice has been raised, and to which we assemble to dedicate it. What has brought us together this night? What is the purpose of this and of all the former meetings we have holden in the old Vestry? What brings these persons together? Not a conspiracy against law and order—not a concert of hostile measures against other men; not a convention of political agents to raise or to supplant a party; not a meeting to arrange speculations in trade: 'tis not the patrons of a voyage of discovery, not the learned met for a lecture of science, nor even the benevolent for the care of a hospital; no; we have assembled for nothing that ever the eye saw or the ear heard[3]—we come to think of our origin; to trace back the stream of life and thought to its unseen source; to ask whence we came, and WHO is that *whence;* to contemplate a sublime Thought—the Idea of God—to worship it and to open our minds to receive the practical influences of this grand thought so that it shall command our feet, our hands, and our lips.

1. And this is the first purpose of this humble chapel. We dedicate this room to the Thought of God. A thought, which, more or less distinctly, exists, I believe, in every human breast. The human mind is so framed that, when it is in healthful action, the thought of God appears in it as inevitably as a music box plays the tune for which it was constructed. The human soul is set to that anthem.

Christianity has made the name and character of God, at least *in words,* so familiar to us, that we do not know how much is in education, and how much is in our constitution. For that reason I derive a satisfaction which is very dear to me in every just conception of God I find in the pagan. I love the story of the poor Indian squaw who is said to have prayed in her own language, "O thou great *Everywhere*! heal my sick child."[4] I delight in the story we have received from the Greeks of Bias, king of Priene, of whom it is said that when his city was invaded by an enemy and the inhabitants were flying in every direction with what was most valuable of their property—they saw that Bias walked emptyhanded. He was asked, why he did not also carry his goods with him? He answered, "I do carry my *goods* with me." But he had nothing in his hand; he had nothing in his robe. He bore them in his breast, not to be seen by the eye—inclosed in the narrow dwelling of his mind, which could not be overtaken by the runners of the enemy, nor stolen by their strength, nor stabbed by their swords, nor burned by their fagots,—the *goods* of the Idea of God—of an incorruptible conscience before him, and a clear sense of his love and protection.[5]

I know this thought is extremely imperfect and indefinable in the human bosom before revelation—but it does amount to the belief of the fact—that there is supernatural and independent power far different from and the source of all that derived power, order and beauty which we every where behold. It

3. I Corinthians 2:9.
4. *JMN* 6:178.
5. This paragraph and the two preceding are used in Sermon CLVIII.

does amount to the first great Revelation of God to Moses and to Pharaoh—"*I am.*" "*I am* hath sent you."[6] For nothing else can say *I am* in this full meaning. When a creature says *I am* he acknowledges in his thought his dependence on something else before him, out of him. He that can say *I am* of myself is the Creator.

To this great Idea then, the thought of God, the source of all we have, or are, or are to be, we have raised and do dedicate this apartment.

2. We have raised this house for the worship of God as he is *revealed* to us, for the study of his Revelation, for the study of the New Testament. In the belief that abundant light shall break forth from that book to guide us,[7] we come here to find it, to hear the voice of truth, to receive the impulses of good.

In the explanation of the New Testament very different sense is put upon its text by different Christians. As long as it belongs to me to aid you in the examination of that book, I shall, with God's help, speak what I think. I know this is easily said, but hardly to be done. The more it is considered, the more the difficulty will appear. But the blessed position into which the course of things has thrown me and those of my brethren who are called Liberal Christians in this vicinity is that we have no ties of opinion to each other. The theory we hold is the true one, that every man is a sect himself, and only unites for social worship with such as are nearest him in faith and feeling, without entering into any compact of opinion with his brethren or imposing any upon them. And it is hence more in our power than it ever was, in the history of the Church, of any class of teachers, to say exactly what we think. Please God this liberty may be a substance not a name. Please God that this room may never be dishonoured by dissimulation, or the truth hindered by the love or the fear of man!

3. In the third place, my friends, let us in our hearts dedicate this house we have raised, to the *spirit* of the New Testament and not to its *letter.*[8] Since we propose it for the school in which we, and our friends, or children, shall be instructed in the true meaning of obscure passages, in the true understanding of controverted doctrines, let us here, in our first assembling, distinctly set before us our duty, that we come hither for piety and not for speculation. We are to study the discourses of Christ and the instructions of his apostles, not to form correct opinions as an end, but as a means to correct action. We come hither not to be armed with weapons to combat others, but to establish ourselves in the knowledge of God and the Spirit of Christ. That which draws us to the gospel, that which gives authority to its words beyond all other words of instruction, is the love which glows in its pages; the immeasurably high standard which it sets

6. Exodus 3:14.
7. The phrase is found in Isaiah 58:8, but Emerson surely alludes to the famous words of the Rev. John Robinson in his farewell address to the Pilgrims departing from Delftshaven in July 1620: "For I am very confident the Lord hath more truth and light yet to break forth out of His holy Word." The quotation, found in Edward Winslow, *Hypocrisie Unmasked* (London, 1646), 97, and in Cotton Mather's *Magnalia Christi Americana* (London, 1702), book 1, chapter 3, became proverbial in New England Congregational churches.
8. II Corinthians 3:6; cf. Romans 7:6.

up for the human soul; the infinite distance at which it leaves the petty squabbles and self-righteousness and acrimony of sects, when it teaches the humble believer that God is love—; that he that loveth, is born of God;[9] that God dwelleth with the humble;[10] that he that hath clean hands, and pure heart is accepted of him;[11] and that we should be holy as he is holy.[12] In the effort to keep these commandments, I understand to consist *the imitation of Christ.*[13]

To these three things, then, let us consecrate our chapel, to the idea of God in the soul; to the study of his revealed will; and to the spirit of love and duty which is the end of that revelation.

In the confidence and with the prayer that God will permit these objects to be answered by our undertaking, I give myself up to the pleasing expectations of this hour. I will anticipate the blessing of God on a pious purpose. I sympathize beforehand in the enlarged conceptions, in the grateful acknowledgments of many young minds, on whose diligence the truth shall here dawn. I foresee the footsteps of good men, wearied with the din and the cares of trade, turning in hither for short seasons to think and to pray. I rejoice in that vital activity which here, we trust, God shall impart to our souls. I see beforehand how much good we shall begin; how much hope we shall enjoy; how many and how fervent prayers we shall offer. I know well the delight that comes from the reception of new truth, and the strength—that nought else can supply—that comes from old, familiar, fully apprehended truth. He who has large possession of truth, realizes his immortality and is not afraid of losing his truth, when he perceives death advancing on his lungs and his heart. These my hopes I see in God are well founded, whether the future use of this edifice shall fulfil them or not; for they are true, I trust, for the souls that now think with me, whether this education shall take place in these walls, or in far more noble and durable abodes not built by hands.[14]

Perhaps, brethren, there are some who think we carry our interest and hopes much too far for truth in opening this hall. There are men who acknowledge nothing more than the eye sees. As the poet said of his sensualist, he saw no beauty in the flowers,

> "A primrose by the river's brim,
> A yellow primrose was to him,
> And it was nothing more."[15]

There are men in whose eyes this edifice will receive no amiableness from

---

9. I John 4:8 and 4:7.
10. Cf. Matthew 18:4, James 4:6, and I Peter 5:5.
11. Psalms 24:4
12. I Peter 1:16.
13. Emerson owned Thomas à Kempis, *On the Imitation of Christ* (London, 1797).
14. Cf. II Corinthians 5:1 and Hebrews 9:11.
15. Wordsworth, "Peter Bell, a Tale," lines 248–50.

virtue, no sanctity from truth. It will be a tenement of wood and lime, and nothing more. I trust not so with us. The material world shall be to me what God made it, a symbol of the spiritual world. I will distinguish between things and places. A token of the dead shall be more precious in my eyes than many conveniences of the living. The house of my friend shall be dearer to me than the house of a stranger. The Lord's house shall be something more sacred, than a shop or a barn. It is the want of a spiritual eye that makes men gross and vicious. In the sensual age of Athens they gradually got rid of respect for any thing that did not touch the senses and learned to say, Perjury breaks no bones. In the sensual age of France they voted that there was no God because he was not seen. As we become wise, what is unseen begins to show more real than what is seen. As we become wise, things grow more significant, till we discern that the stars have their order, and plants their law, and stones speak,[16] and all nature is only a vehicle of truth. So in a good mind—a house dedicated to God—builded for the exposition of the books of Revelation, borrows light and character thence. It becomes a sort of country of principles, an abode of truth, a house of refreshment on the road upward where peradventure angels may be entertained.[17] Far then from us and our edifice be every profane or bigoted or selfish thought. Far from this house be a word or a wish that can war with the principles to which it is dedicated. Let us keep it holy. Remember, friends, it is to be sanctified, if at all, by our prayers. It is to be useful, if at all, by our diligence. It is to be pleasant in our memory, if at all, by the love of God that shall fill our hearts and the love of men that shall thence proceed.

16. Cf. Luke 19:40.
17. Hebrews 13:2.

[SECOND DISCOURSE ON THE DEATH OF GEORGE SAMPSON]

BRETHREN AND FRIENDS:—

The occasion on which we have met is one of very strong demand upon our Christian sensibilities. It addresses itself with great power to some of our happiest remembrances; to all which is exciting in the immediate moral interests and claims of society around us; and to our plans and hopes of future good and usefulness. Does it seem to anyone that too much is implied in these expressions? We have met to appropriate an evening to the recollection of our late lamented brother, Mr. Sampson. And *who,* it may be asked, and *what* was he, to a consideration of whose death we have separated and consecrated this hour? These are very proper inquiries; and I should be ready to meet them anywhere, and before any circle in which they might be proposed; because I believe, that, poor and low as are the principles by which character is often estimated, and poor and low as are the objects to which many are devoting their times and talents, their bodies and their souls, there are yet unequivocal manifestations among us of an increased and an increasing preparation for the admission of larger views; of higher sentiments of human duty, interest and happiness; and of principles of action more worthy of that religion, whose rule of judgment is, if any man have not the spirit of Christ, he is none of his.[1] We could give this hour to recollections of our friend and brother, because, now that he is gone, and nothing of him remains to us but his character, his example, and the influence which these have exerted, and may still exert upon us, we may not only think, but we may speak of him, as we would not have spoken of him had he still been with us; and because, in his character, his example, his spirit and influence, he has left us a treasure which we ought to hold more precious than rubies.[2] Let us then bring distinctly before our minds the inquiry, *who,* and *what* was he, to a consideration of whose character and death we have appropri-

---

George Adams Sampson, Emerson's friend and parishioner, died July 23, 1834, while on his way to join Emerson at Bangor, Maine. Emerson preached Sermon CLXVIII at the Second Church as a eulogy on August 3. Shortly afterwards, at the family's request, he delivered an entirely different discourse at a private evening memorial service. Emerson evidently gave the manuscript to the Sampsons, whose descendants had thirty copies privately printed during the Emerson Centennial in 1903. Kenneth Walter Cameron has published the *Printed Copy of Sermon Preached by Ralph Waldo Emerson on the Death of George Adams Sampson 1834,* with an introduction, in *Transcendental Epilogue* (Hartford, 1982), 2:694–702, and in *The Vestry Lectures and a Rare Sermon* (Hartford, 1984), 31–39. As the manuscript has not been located, the present text reproduces the printed copy.

1. Romans 8:9.
2. Proverbs 3:15.

ated this hour? Who, and what was that brother, so lately with us, and now gone from us? Why was he so beloved by us? And why do we delight in our remembrance of him?

I do not intend to pronounce a eulogy. It is not my object to go over the events of the life of our friend. They are as familiar to you, as they are to me. But I have said, that, in his character and influence we have a precious legacy. Let us then rightly estimate, and wisely use it. And, that we may, let us ask, and answer the inquiries, what was that character? What was that influence? What were the principles which made our friend what he was to us? What are the lessons with which his removal should impress our hearts?

May I be allowed?—Yes, I know that I may be,—to speak of character as the gospel contemplates, and would form it. There are other standards and other principles of character, than those of our religion. The world,—every country, every community, every class, every trade, and every little coterie, has its standard; and these standards are everywhere, and constantly held up, for a decision of the questions which arise, of right and wrong, of good and evil. And Christianity, too, has its standard, from which it admits of no appeal. There is now, as truly as there was in the days of the Apostles, a sense in which the *friendship* of the world is *enmity* with God;[3] a sense in which *conformity* to the world is *opposition* to God;[4] a sense in which Christians are to *crucify the world,* with its affections and lusts;[5] a sense in which the disciple is *not to be of the world,* even as his Master was not of the world.[6] What, then, is the Christian standard of character? What is the character to which Christianity would form its believers? These are great questions. There are other objects than those of the gospel, for which many who call themselves, and are called, Christians, are yet living; objects to which they give all their thought and care; and every effort for which is sending a deeper corruption into the soul. And there are other objects, which, within due limitations, are proper objects of desire and of pursuit; but our interest in which, instead of being limited and guided by Christianity, is made a principle by which we qualify, and limit, the principles and objects of the gospel. This, it seems to me, is the great and terrible error of Christians, in their expositions and treatment of the instructions and ends of Christ and his Apostles; and this practical infidelity, this unfaithfulness to the principles of our Master, has done, and is doing more to keep back, and to keep down society, and to restrain the progress of Christian truth, and righteousness, and happiness, than all which the most open, determined, and uncompromising infidelity, could have accomplished.

I recur then to the questions, the Christian standard,—what is it? The Christian character,—what are its elements? What is the principle of its vitality? Shall I attempt to bring before you such a disciple as Jesus would form, and love; a

3. James 4:4.
4. Cf. Romans 12:2.
5. Galatians 5:24.
6. John 8:23, 15:19, 17:14, 17:16; Romans 12:2.

disciple who is, according to his capacity, what Christ was; whose heart beats responsive to the heart of his Master; the breath of whose soul is the spirit of his Lord?

I have said, that the world has its various standards. And they are as changing, as they are various. The standard of the gospel, on the other hand, is the same yesterday, to-day, and forever.[7] It is no other than the rule of duty in the precepts of Christ. It is no other than the measure of the stature of the fullness of Christ.[8] Let us not deceive ourselves upon this subject. There is a truth, a justice, an honesty, a purity, a respect, a kindness, a sense of right and wrong, and of good and evil, which are of the world; which the world in one or another of its departments, sanctions, and establishes. And these may either, or all of them, be any, and everything, but the truth, and justice, and honesty, and purity, and respect, and kindness, and sense of right and wrong, and of good and evil, to which the gospel would bring its believers. Now it seems to me that we are, and can be Christians, only by adopting, and acting out, the principles by which the gospel proposes to form the Christian character. Says Jesus of his disciples, "they are not of the world, even as I am not of the world."[9] Is it asked, must we then go out of the world to find a Christian? O, no! Thank God that there ever have been and still are those, who, looking unto Jesus, and formed by his spirit,[10] and his life, amidst all the temptations of the world have given living evidence of the truth, and practicability, and power, and worth, and glory of his religion. There have been and there are those, both holy men and women, who have shown in what it is to be in the world, and not *of* the world; *in* the world, and *above* the world.[11] Have you not known such an one, and followed him from the beginning to the end of his earthly course? I bring before my mind's eye a child. His condition in life is a humble one. He has no extraordinary talents, or extraordinary advantages for the culture of the powers which he possesses. But he avails himself of his means and opportunities of improving the intellect which God has given him. His heart, his desires and affections, are early brought under Christian influences. He is a good son. He is a good brother. And he passes through the term of his apprenticeship, faithful to the master he served, separate from evil associates, and unspotted by the corruptions which have surrounded him. Here I might ask you to pause, and to dwell upon this loveliest spectacle of earth and time, a pious youth; a young man who feels what it is to be a child of God, and is striving to live as a child of God; a young man striving for a comprehension of the spirit of Christ, and daily advancing in that spirit; a young man, establishing in his heart a Christian estimate of property, of honour, and of pleasure; enlightening his conscience on the obligation and extent of Christian principles, in all their bearings upon the

7. Hebrews 13:8.
8. Ephesians 4:13.
9. John 17:14.
10. Hebrews 12:2 and Galatians 4:19.
11. John 15:19 and 17:11–16.

objects and interests of life before him; and preparing to meet the temptations and trials of life, under a conviction that he is to stand at the judgment seat of Christ,[12] and is there to be judged by the word which Christ has spoken to him. The kingdom of heaven, says our master, cometh not with observation; neither will men say, lo, here! or, lo, there![13] and of this young man, no one might say, lo, here! or, lo, there! There is nothing more simple, more unostentatious, more unobtrusive than the truly Christian character in any of its stages. It is a character which asks not for notice, and which would shrink from applause. It lives upon its thought, its sensibility of God; upon its privilege, and its freedom of access to God; upon the feeling of the harmony of its own will with the will of God. It is the kingdom of heaven in the soul. It is the spiritual, the eternal life realized with its immeasurable interests already made the paramount interests of the soul. Have you, I again ask, never known a young man so formed? Have you never seen a young man thus entering life? Yes, such an one we have seen. We have seen a young Christian enter for himself upon the active business of the world; take upon himself its varied responsibilities; take his stand among men of the world; to engage in the traffic of the world; and seek and obtain for himself a share of the objects of the world; and yet stand out from the world, a simple minded, devout, and devoted disciple of Jesus. We have seen a young Christian whom even a worldling would have honoured for his fidelity to his worldly concerns, and for the uprightness with which he transacted them, yet not less honoured and loved, with an ever growing love, by his Christian friends, for an equal fidelity to the objects and interests of the gospel and kingdom of Christ. We have seen a man of business whom a worldling would have honoured upon the exchange, yet maintaining there his Christian character. We have followed this man of business into his family, and have seen him there a Christian husband, and a Christian father. And we have been with him in the hours which could be spared from the demands of business and of his home. How were those hours appropriated? The answer to this inquiry is in the records of our Sunday schools, and in those of the associations of their teachers. It is in the hearts of hundreds of the pupils who have been instructed by him in our Sunday schools. It is in the records of almost every enterprise with which any of us have been connected, either for the extension of our religion abroad, or for its wider, and purer, and more perfect influence at home. It is in the most grateful and happy remembrances which any of us have of the intercourse, which, for many successive years, we have had in this association for mutual Christian improvement. Yes, we have known one,—we have had one among ourselves,—we have called one our brother, to whom we think we may refer as an example of a Christian character; a character formed by a sincere, though without doubt an imperfect, regard to the Christian standard, and by a sincere endeavor for a faithful application of Christian principles. We have known him, we have loved

12. Romans 14:10; II Corinthians 5:10.
13. Luke 17:20–21.

and enjoyed him. We have felt the power and the charm of his simple, true and earnest piety, and of his modest, pure, and untiring benevolence. A brief time has passed since we saw him in the fulness of strength, and the richness of promise; and we thought that he had yet much to do for the cause for which he had lived; and that we had yet much to receive and to enjoy in his cooperation with us in our labours. But the wind has passed over him, and he is gone.[14] Ought we not to pause, then, to deliberate, to take counsel with each other and to pray? Are not the life and death of our brother alike full of instruction, of excitement, and of admonition to us? O that we were all wise in the knowledge of our Father's providence;—that we understood aright the principles and objects of his dealings with us;—that, as professed followers of Christ we considered aright our latter end!

We have each of us, it may be, attempted to give some method to our thoughts, in our reflections upon our departed friend, that we might bring home to ourselves the practical influence which his life and his death should exert upon us. And I have been disposed to arrange my own thoughts under two heads, to which I will but briefly refer you; being much more solicitous to be taught by you, than to take the part of a teacher on this occasion; and anxious, too, that the beautiful character of our friend should be brought into all the lights which the knowledge, and the affections of either, and all of us, can throw over it.

I remark, then, *first,* that few, I think, have done more than was done by our friend, to furnish a practical answer,—which is the only satisfactory one,—to the inquiry, may anyone be a man of business, in any of the departments of trade and commerce; engage in the competitions of business; carry Christian principles into these competitions; and, with these principles, obtain a reasonable share of worldly property? This is a question which has agitated and troubled many minds,—on which multitudes have found it very difficult to come to any satisfactory decision; and which has led some, of highly susceptible consciences, even to relinquish trade, because it was felt by them that the only alternative was a relinquishment either of trade or of conscience.

I am aware of the complexity, and the difficulties of the query to which I have referred you. It is one of the greatest of the problems which are yet to be solved by the disciples of Christ. But I hold him to have contributed one of the highest services to our religion, and to have been one of the greatest benefactors of the circle in which he moves, who has done anything to prove that the trade and commerce, by which society is advanced in its conveniences, its comforts, and I will even add in its arts and its elegances, may be prosperously conducted in perfect consistency with a maintenance of Christian principles. I have referred you to the world's standard of right and duty and to the Christian standard of right and duty. And it is well known that they are often in direct opposition to each other. And, I need not here add,—for it will be conceded, and I trust felt by each of us,—that he has no fair claim to the name and hopes of a Christian, who

14. Psalms 103:16.

pauses upon the question, whether he should cut off a right hand, or pluck out a right eye,[15] or sacrifice any conceivable prospect of worldly profit, rather than violate a principle, by which, as a Christian, he is to be judged at the bar of God. Now I do not say, that, as a man of business, our friend was a perfect Christian. I will say nothing of him which I think would offend his humble, unassuming spirit, if he were visibly with us. But I think, and I believe it is the conviction of us all, that it was his earnest desire, and aim, and care, to be *a Christian merchant;* to seek nothing, and to do nothing in this capacity, which he might not seek and do as a Christian. There can, indeed, be no doubt, whether or not there are opportunities of accumulating wealth, of which a Christian cannot avail himself; or, whether there are means of its acquisition, which a Christian cannot employ. But are there not, still, means and opportunities left open to the Christian, by which he may hope for success, and obtain it, at a less cost than of his soul?[16] If pressed by this inquiry we must fall back upon facts, and examples; and in bringing the inquiry to my own mind, I think of very few who have given me an equally satisfactory reply to it as has been given by our friend. Nor can I conceive of many circumstances by which he, or any one, could have paid a higher tribute to our religion, or have rendered a better service to the community in which he has lived. Our brother was not, indeed, in the common sense of the term, affluent. But he was *a merchant.* As a merchant, his object was property. In seeking property he mingled with all the classes of those who are seeking it among us. He obtained the property which made him not only personally independent, but with which he was enabled to do much good, and to extend much happiness, and, yet, he kept his conscience, his soul. God grant the great lesson so inculcated may be indelibly impressed upon our memories, that in this view of our friend we may be excited to follow him as far as he exhibited himself to us as a follower of Christ.

The second remark which has forced itself upon my thoughts and sensibilities, in dwelling upon our friend, has been the benignant, delightful influence, which may be, and can hardly fail to be, excited even by the simplest and most unobtrusive Christian character, when its energies are put forth for fidelity to its sense of duty.

I have said that I do not mean to pronounce a eulogy. And certainly I do not. And yet I find it very difficult to speak of our friend, even in the most artless language of truth, without some exposure to the imputation of pronouncing an encomium upon him. I shall not be true to his memory if I do not say of him, that his was a character of very unusual moral beauty and harmony. He, indeed, knew much of the world,—as the expression is in reference to the artifices and vices of the world. Many of us will not have forgotten the expositions he has given in this society, of prevailing principles and usages, which he has here also brought to the test of the law and testimony of Christ. Yet we saw him, in

15. Matthew 5:29–30; Mark 9:43 and 47.
16. Cf. Matthew 16:26, Mark 8:36, and Luke 9:25.

himself, one of the most attractive of the examples which can be cited, of simplicity, truth, purity, kindness and devotion. I think him to have been one of the most guileless, one of the most childlike of men whom I have ever known. It is hardly possible that one should directly have demanded less than he demanded of others. And, yet, had we one among us more ready than he always was, for any and every service? Had we one among us who was heard with more respect whenever he addressed either ourselves or others; or whose opinions were better matured, or excited a better influence? And where was the secret of his power? I answer, in his very simplicity, and truth, and purity and disinterestedness, and devotion. It was in the energy of an uncompromising sense of duty, which, however, was as meek as it was enlightened, which held his own and the Christian interests of others to be the paramount interests of man, and which identified his own good and happiness with the good and happiness of others. His were the energies of Christian principles, acting in a heart prepared to receive and to apply them. I think, that, in a far higher sense than is common among us, Christ dwelt in him by faith,[17] and that his influence was the influence of an operative Christian faith. In this view of him he is precious to my thought, and a benefactor to my soul; and should he not, in this view of him, be greatly precious to each of us? He had no extraordinary natural endowments. Yet few among us have closed a more useful life, or a life suited to be more widely beneficial in its influences, than his. Yet what he was, he was made by the gospel. And what he was in character, and usefulness, will the gospel also make each of us, if we shall be equally faithful to it. Let us receive the lesson, and let us honour the memory of our friend by living in accordance with it.

Among the latest public acts of our friend is one in which I feel the strongest interest. I refer to the fact that he acted as secretary of the meeting held in this city in the last April, which resulted in the organization of a union of our churches, for the purpose of giving permanency, and increased efficiency, to a ministry at large for the service of the poor.[18] I look to this organization as an era in the history of our churches; and I trust that, with God's blessing, it is to lead to great improvements in the administration of our religion. In this connection, the loss of our brother is to myself, and my associates, a great, a very great personal loss; for no one would have served this cause more efficiently than he would have served it. My personal friendship with him began at my very entrance upon the ministry in which I am living;[19] and you will remember, as well

17. Ephesians 3:17.

18. On the Benevolent Fraternity of Christian Churches for the Support of the Ministry-at-Large, see Joseph Tuckerman, *The Principles and Results of the Ministry at Large, in Boston* (Boston, 1838); William C. Gannett, *Ezra Stiles Gannett, Unitarian Minister in Boston, 1824–1871, A Memoir* (Boston, 1875), 135–38; Octavius Brooks Frothingham, *Boston Unitarianism, 1820–1850* (New York and London, 1890), 65–66; Samuel A. Eliot, *Heralds of a Liberal Faith* (Boston, 1910), 2:103–17; and Anne C. Rose, *Transcendentalism as a Social Movement, 1830–1850* (New Haven and London, 1981), 29–32.

19. Despite his resignation from the Second Church in 1832, and despite his having embarked on a career as a lecturer, Emerson was still, of course, in 1834 a professionally active minister.

as myself, his activity in obtaining, and preparing, the upper chamber of the circular building in which the poor were first gathered for social worship under my ministry;[20] his activity, and efficiency, in obtaining for us our present chapel;—aye, and his own services there, always readily rendered when they were called for; and always rendered in a spirit, to me, and, I doubt not, to you, deeply impressive, from the obviously deep solemnity of emotion with which he never failed to address himself to God. Who that ever heard them can have forgotten his prayers in the chapel, or in this association? But I cannot go into these details. Yet they will be treasured reminiscences for which I thank our Father; and a recurrence to them will be to me for light, and encouragement and consolation and joy.

Under all circumstances, the admonitions of death are very solemn. And yet, should the most sudden death be able to surprise us? Does the gospel furnish one apology for the want of preparation for death, even in the most vigorous and the busiest hour of life? The death of no one could have come upon us more unexpectedly, than did that of our friend. And yet, have we not had line upon line,[21] both in the providence and word of God to instruct and excite us to be *always* ready? May our ears and our hearts be open to the renewed injunction which has been so impressively given us! May the voice from our brother's early grave reach our hearts, as they would not have been reached, if his life had been protracted, and if his end had been that of long and lingering disease! He would not tell us, and I dare not call you, to be what he was, except as far as we are persuaded that he followed Christ. But I may say, let his character, and life, and death, awaken us to new efforts, to be indeed, and thoroughly, Christians. Brethren and friends, our object in this association is, Christian improvement. And we need,—there is not one of us who does not need,—great improvement to be the Christians which we might, and should be. I have said, and I think, that our brother was an advanced disciple. I think that he was, as few are, "alive to God through Jesus Christ our Lord."[22] But we are to be alive to God through Jesus Christ, not merely as another may be, or is, but to the extent to which every precept, and every doctrine of his religion, exciting all its power in our hearts, can advance us. Let us not then be satisfied with the partial, and poor attainments, which will obtain for us the acknowledgment of others, that we are Christians. We may be called Christians, and yet in the view of the gospel be infidels. We may be called Christians, and yet at last may hear from our judge the sentence, "depart from me, I know you not, ye workers of iniquity."[23] May God awaken each, and all of us, to a sense of our dangers, and our duties! Brethren, the time is short, and the only test of Christian faith, is Christian holiness. We do not believe God and Christ, any further than we obey God and

20. No other evidence appears to have survived regarding Emerson's ministry to the poor, nor has the "circular building" been identified.

21. Isaiah 28:10 and 13.

22. Romans 6:11.

23. Matthew 7:23 and Luke 13:27.

Christ. This is a great truth, which is yet but feebly felt by us. Have we slumbered? Let us then awake. Are we living in the neglect of any known duty, or the violation of any acknowledged principle? Let us be aware, that, to the same extent we are unbelievers, and have no part or lot in the gospel.[24] This is the instruction which should be brought home to us by the death of our brother. This is the lesson which I believe he would give us, if he could now address us. Our hearty sympathies are with those who are nearer to him than we were, and who feel in his death a loss even greater than we feel in it. But, he, we trust, is now in glory, with the spirits of the just made perfect.[25] May we all so live, always, and in everything, that our portion may be with theirs,[26] who, through faith and patience have been made heirs of the promises.[27]

24. Cf. John 13:8.
25. Hebrews 12:23.
26. Cf. Matthew 24:51 and Luke 12:46.
27. Hebrews 6:12, 6:17, 11:9.

[THANKSGIVING SERMON: FRAGMENT] _____

*Whoso is wise, and will observe these things,
even they shall understand the loving
kindness of the Lord.*

PSALMS 107:43

We are assembled, my friends, to celebrate a festival peculiar to our own country, once peculiar to a small section of the country, but than which no institution on earth is more natural or more wise. Agreeably to an usage of near two
hundred years, the civil authority of the commonwealth calls upon us to quit
our business, and set apart this day with a deliberate purpose of considering our
enjoyments and referring them to their author. It is the duty of this day to cover
up our griefs and count our pleasures, to survey the sunny side of life; to look at
the beauty of things we are accustomed to value only for their use, to sympathize (I say it in all humility) with God when he rested from the Creation and
saw that it was good.[1]

And the manner in which the fathers of New England chose to keep this feast
seems to me as wise and humane as the purpose. Friends are assembled. Families are called together. The father sees his children once more resume their
place at his board: the brothers, whom years and engrossing affairs have long
divorced from that inseparable union in which childhood bound them, side by
side, in school and at play, and in their morning and evening prayer—return for

---

This undated manuscript combines passages from the opening portions of Sermons LVII and
XCVII. In the passage borrowed from Sermon XCVII, Emerson repeats an error (linking Hezekiah to an Assyrian rather than to a Babylonian) which he made in the 1830 first delivery of
XCVII, but which he caught in time for the second delivery in 1836, strongly indicating that the
present manuscript was composed between those years. In 1831 and 1835, he preached Thanksgiving Sermon CXXXVI (at the Second Church and at East Lexington respectively); in 1832 he had
already resigned from the Second Church, and was in any event too ill to preach. The Preaching
Record gives no indication of a Thanksgiving sermon in 1834, and indeed he seems to have spent
the holiday quietly at home in Concord. This leaves only 1833: on November 28, according to the
Preaching Record, Emerson delivered a "Thanksgiving Sermon" (uncharacteristically giving no
number) at New Bedford. Why on this occasion he would have written a new sermon, or even
supplied an old sermon with a new introduction, is difficult to understand, since no one in New
Bedford had heard any of the four Thanksgiving sermons he had in his desk. The mystery passes
into insolubility in view of the fact that the single column of hymn citations on MS p. 1 (suggesting
that there *was* one delivery) is headed "N.Y.C."
  1. Cf. Genesis 1:31 and 2:2.

a season into that old familiar bond. Sisters meet again and rejoice that the formation of new connexions has not weakened the dear tie of blood. The mystic chain of kindred which joins each individual to so many more in society, is explored again; each link is counted and brightened, and new confidence felt in the strength of the whole, by inspecting the strength of the parts.

This day the forsaken are visited, and the forgotten remembered. On such an occasion, no face comes without interest into the domestic circle, but brings with it the memory of all its years, the recollection of all its blessings.

In this pure holiday the coarse conflicts of interest for a moment are forgot; the all-pervading voice of political animosity is felt to be unseasonable; a worthier feeling in man subdues for the time his malice, his avarice and his ambition, and an hour of good humor and charity and gratitude is the last hour of the dying autumn.

Such is the feeling awakened by this anniversary through the hundreds of thousands of the people of New England. In this frame of mind, they go up to the house of God. The rational happiness of his children is pleasing to the Father of all men. The just enjoyment of his bounty is itself an act of praise.

In sympathy with the occasion I invite you then to consider our reasons for thanksgiving. Let us sing the earth's harvest hymn to the God of the harvest. Let us provoke one another to love and to praise by a careful review of the divine favors. We will unlock our treasure house and show our corn and wine, our advantages, our means, not to pride, as Hezekiah did to the Assyrian,[2] but to God, that we may make an offering of all we are and have to Him.

And first, brethren, consider whether each of us has not had some reason to acknowledge the special favor of God to himself. Twelve months are past. All nature with her countless contrivances for the pleasure of the eye, the gratification of all the senses, has fulfilled her year:—and has she brought no fruit to your basket from her harvest; no strength to your limbs from air, and sun, and food; no medicine from her herbs and drugs for your sickness? Has the cloud that fertilized every other field, dropped no rain on yours? and the wind that blew onward every other ship driven yours off her course? Have you not shared God's blessing? Have you not drank his water, and eaten his bread, and been warmed at his fire? Has not the fleece

---

2. II Kings 20:12–17. See Sermon XCVII (*Sermons* 3:46, n. 2).

[THANKSGIVING SERMON: INTRODUCTION]

And the Lord God said, It is not good that the man should be alone.

GENESIS 2:18

I congratulate you, my friends, on the arrival of this most pleasing of our national festivals, which appropriately closes the autumn of each year with a solemn union of our religious and our domestic feelings. The public acknowledgment of the bounty of God is endeared by the practice of gathering from afar the members of families into their paternal home. To none of us will the day be insignificant. Each one has his own happiness to remember and thank God for, as well as his share of the common weal. You do not need to be provoked to gratitude by a set enumeration of God's gifts to each and to all. Among the many topics which suggest themselves at this pleasant hour, I have thought that it would not be inappropriate to offer to your consideration some general views of the advantages resulting to us from our social nature, by enumerating in order some of the most conspicuous forms which the social spirit in our nature takes. On this day of religious and social joy ponder the providence that set us in families,[1] in friendships, in associations, in parties, in states.

This undated manuscript is clearly a substitute introduction for a Thanksgiving sermon, though the editors have not been able to determine when or where it might have been used.

1. Psalms 68:6.

[SERMON FRAGMENT] _____

I speak not, of course, with reference to any one sect of Christians—I have here no allusion to the effect of speculative opinions on theology. I speak of what is far above all speculation in its importance to us, and of what is common to all sects—the mistake that the punctual performance of religious exercises is religion. Now I say that I think is a very injurious misapprehension—going to produce much harm in society—because, persons of these religious habits being esteemed the votaries of religion, the world naturally looks to them to find the effects of a principle that makes such lofty pretensions as religion certainly does.

The manuscript, a single page, is undated. A version of the final sentence occurs in Sermon XLIX (*Sermons* 2:53).

Appendix A

Records of the Second Church in Boston
Relating to the Ministry of Ralph Waldo Emerson

[The "Proprietors Records" indicate that in the ballot for "Colleague Pastor," held on January 11, 1829, "Mr. Ralph Waldo Emerson had seventy four votes,— Professor [Charles] Follen four,—Mr. J. Lathrop [i.e., J. K. Lothrop] one,— and four were given in blank—" (vol. 19, p. 105). Emerson explained in a letter to his brother William that of the four votes for Follen, three were cast by a single individual who held three pews, and that this man "declares himself no wise unfriendly to Mr E but wants to wait a little" (L 1:260).]

[Letter to Emerson from the Proprietors inviting him to serve as Colleague Pastor (vol. 61):]

Dear Sir

As a committee of the Proprietors of the Second church in Boston we have the pleasure to inform you that, at a meeting of the proprietors held on the afternoon of the 10th instant [i.e., Sunday, the 11th] it was voted with great unaminity [sic] that you be invited to the pastoral care of the Society as colleague Pastor with the Rev Henry Ware—

In connexion with this vote we communicate the following which were also passed at the same meeting—
Voted, that the Salary of the Colleague Pastor be 1200 dollars be paid quarterly
Voted That when in the course of Divine Providence the connexion of the senior Pastor with this Society be dissolved the salary of the Colleague than [sic] sole Pastor be 1800 dollars payable quarterly[1]

Deposited at the Massachusetts Historical Society. Published with permission of the First and Second Church in Boston. Documents relating to Emerson in the Church's extensive archives are drawn from volume 9 ("Second Church Records"), volume 19 ("Proprietors Records"), and volume 61 ("Library of the Second Church Boston: Emerson Papers," a file of letters, clippings, and miscellanies).
   1. On Sunday, July 5, 1829, following senior pastor Henry Ware's "relinquishment of salary," a meeting was held:
   On motion of Mr Gedney King it was unanimously Voted That the salary of the Rev R W. Emerson be increased to eighteen hundred dollars per annum from the first instant, & the Treasurer is authorized to pay the same—

Meeting dissolved
Geo. A. Sampson
Clerk [vol. 19, p. 118]

The committee earnest[l]y express their hope that you may find it consistent with your views to comply with this invitation, since they believe that its acceptance will essentially contribute to the future harmony and prosperity of the Society—

We are with great Respect
Your Obedient Servants

[Emerson's letter of January 22, 1829, requesting more time to respond, is published in *L* 7:178.]

To the Gentlemen of the Committee of the Proprietors of the Second Church in Boston.

Cambridge, 30 Jan. 1829.

Gentlemen,

I enclose to you an answer to ⟨the⟩your communication to me of the 11th instant with the request that it may be read to the Society.[2]

Accept my thanks for the kind wishes expressed in your letter.

Very respectfully, your friend & servant,
R. Waldo Emerson.

Mr Mackintosh,
Mr Patterson,
Mr Adams,
Dr Ware,
Mr Emerson.

[vol. 61]

[The following letter, from volume 61, also appears in *L* 1:260–61:]

To the Second Church & Society in Boston.
Cambridge, 30 January, 1829.

Christian brethren & friends,

I have received the communication transmitted to me by your committee inviting me to the office of junior pastor in your church & society. I accept the invitation.

------

2. According to the "Proprietors Records" for February 1, 1829, Emerson's letter of acceptance was "read to the Society this afternoon, from the Pulpit, by Mr. Hedge" (vol. 19, p. 107).

If my own feelings could have been consulted, I should have desired to postpone, at least, for several months, my entrance into this solemn office. I do not now approach it with any sanguine confidence in my abilities, or in my prospects. I come to you in weakness, and not in strength. In a short life, I have yet had abundant experience of the uncertainty of human hopes. I have learned the lesson of my utter dependency; and it is in a devout reliance upon other strength than my own, in a humble trust on God to sustain me, that I put forth my hand to his great work.

But, brethren, whilst I distrust my powers, I must speak firmly of my purposes. I well know what are the claims, on your part, to my best exertions, and I shall meet them, as far as in me lies, by a faithful performance of duty. I shun no labour. I shall do all that I can.

In approaching these duties, I am encouraged by the strong expression of confidence & goodwill, I have received from you. I am encouraged by the hope of enjoying the counsel and aid of the distinguished servant of God who has so long laboured among you. I look to the example of our Lord, in all my hopes of advancing the influence of his holy religion, and I implore the blessing of God upon this connexion to be formed between you and myself.

I am your affectionate friend & servant,

Ralph Waldo Emerson.

[Account of Emerson's Ordination (vol. 61):]

At an Ecclesiastical Council convened for the purpose of ordaining Mr Ralph Waldo Emerson as ⟨colleague⟩ ↑junior↓ pastor of the Second Church & Society in Boston, March 11th. 1829.

Rev Dr Ripl⟨y⟩ey was chosen Moderator, who opened the meeting with prayer. Mr Walker was chosen scribe. The following churches were represented in the Council; viz.

First Church in Roxbury by Rev Dr Porter & Br William Fisk
Second Church in d[itt]o—Mr Flagg & Br A Draper
Third Church in do—Dr Gray & Joseph Curtis.
First Church in Dorchester—Dr Harris & Br Eben. Clapp
Third Church in do   Dr Richmond & Abel Cushing
Harvard University church—Dr Ware & Dr Webster
Concord church—Dr Ripley & Edward Jarvis & Ed. B. Emerson.
Cambridge port church   Mr Gannett & N. P Hunt.
Northborough church   Mr Allen & Deacon Jonas Bartlett
1st Church in Waltham   Mr Ripley & Jonas Clark.
1st Church in Salem   Mr Upham & Hon Mr Sprague
3ᵈ Church in Cambridge   Mr Burton & Saul White
Charlestown New Church   Mr Walker & Deacon Blanchard

Churches in Boston viz.
South Congregational Church Mr Motte & Mr Marsh
Hollis St————————Mr Pierpont & Deacon H. Bass
New South Church by Mr Young & Deacon Sam K Hewes
Federal Street (Pastors not present) by Charles Barnard delegate
12th Congregation by Mr Barrett & Lewis G. Pray.
Brattle St by Mr Palfrey & Harrison G. Otis & Henry R May.
King's Chapel by Mr Greenwood & Francis J. Oliver.
New North by Mr Parkman & Deacon John Fenno.
Purchase St by Mr Ripley & Stephen Fairbank
West Boston by Dr Lowell & Deacon Elias Haskins & Wm C. Hunnewell
First Church by Mr Frothingham & Deacon Saml Morrell.

The proceedings of the Society & the candidate respecting his call were now submitted, & were perfectly satisfactory. Testimonials of Mr Emerson's connection with the church, & of his regular approbation as a preacher of the gospel were also read before the council.

Whereupon it was unanimously voted that this council are satisfied with every thing that has been done preparatory to the ordination, & are ready to proceed to that service.

The Council then confirmed the arrangement that had previously been made for the services. Viz

>   Introductory Prayer & Scriptures by Dr Pierce
>   Sermon by Rev Saml Ripley
>   Ordaining Prayer by ⟨Dr Ripley⟩ Mr Parkman
>   Charge by Dr Ripley.
>   Right Hand of Fellowship by Mr Frothingham
>   Address to the Society by E S Gannett
>   Concluding Prayer by Mr Upham.

Council then voted to adjourn to the the [sic] ringing of the bell for the services.

>   Attest
>   James Walker, Scribe

————————————

[Entries in the Church Records for February 8 and March 11, 1829, appear to be in the hand of Henry Ware, Jr.; subsequent entries are in Emerson's hand (vol. 9, pp. 25–33).]

Feb. 8. 1829. . . . At the same meeting, a certificate of the regular standing of Mr Ralph Waldo Emerson with the first Church in this city, having been read, & his desire made known to transfer his relation to this church, it was voted, that it be accordingly transferred.

Also voted—That we, the members of the Second Church, do hereby repeat & confirm the vote given by us at a meeting of the Proprietors of pews in the meeting house, giving Mr R. W. Emerson an invitation to become Junior Pastor; & we would also express our unmingled satisfaction at the prospect of his speedy settlement amongst us as a minister of the gospel of Christ, to break unto ↑us↓ [addition in pencil] Church the bread of life.

March 11. 1829. The ordination of Mr R. W. Emerson as Junior Pastor of the Second Church took place this day. The preliminary arrangements are recorded in the Society's books. The ordaining council was composed of the following Churches: the several churches connected with the Boston Association, the church in Cambridge Port, in Harvard College, ↑in Waltham,↓ in New Bedford, in Concord, ↑in Northborough,↓ in Dover N. H., in Concord N. H., Second in Northampton, first in New York, first in Philadelphia, ↑first in Salem.↓ Dr Pierce of Brookline, prayed & read lessons from scripture; Mr Ripley of Waltham preached from the text—*Preaching peace by Jesus Christ*—⟨Dr Ripl⟩Mr Parkman of the New North made the Ordaining Prayer; Dr Ripley of Concord gave the Charge; Mr Frothingham of the First Church the right hand of Fellowship; Mr Gannett of Federal Street made the Address to the people; Mr Upham of Salem prayed. The day was fine, the assembly great, & all things done happily, decently, & in order.

[Emerson's entries follow:]

May ⟨24⟩14. The Church attended the ordination of Rev J. L. Sibley as ⟨colleague⟩ pastor of the Church in Stow. Dea. Enoch Patterson, delegate

May 20 The Church attended the ordination of Rev F. H. Hedge as pastor of the Congregational Church in West Cambridge. Br. Benj. H. Greene, delegate.—

May 10. The Second Church having received a Communication from the Mayor of Boston enclosing a ⟨r⟩letter from the inhabitants of Augusta (Georgia) representing the sufferings of that town from a fire, the Standing committee determined that a contribution shd. be taken in the Society & ⟨on t⟩accordingly, on this day $98.00 were collected.

⟨June 14.⟩ ↑June 14↓ The report of the Evangelical Treasury was read in a sermon by the Pastor as is usual at this season (though omitted the last June on account of the sickness of Mr Ware,) & by leave of standing Committee a contribution was taken in the Society. The amount was $85.00.

June 15 The Unitarian Church in Washington (D.C.) having sent ⟨on⟩ a Committee to Boston to represent their pecuniary difficulties, that they owed $6000. and if it was not paid in 18 months the Church must be sold at public auction & that they had among themselves subscribed $2400.00 on the condition that the remainder shd. be raised elsewhere—it was agreed at a general meeting of their friends in Boston to apply to each of the churches for assistance. The sum of three hundred dollars was raised by subscription in the Second Church.

Oct 24 At a meeting of the Church after Lecture a communication which had been mislaid for some time was laid before them from the Faculty of the School at Cambridge. It was accepted by them & directed to be recorded.

Copy.— "Cambridge Apr. 13. 1828.

"The Faculty of the Theological School at Cambridge regret that there has been an accidental delay in acknowledging the valuable present of books from the Second Church in Boston. The Faculty have been much gratified by this mark of attention to the interests of the School; ⟨th⟩& they request the Church to accept their grateful acknowledgments & thanks.

By order of the Faculty

Andrews Norton."

Nov 1 On application made to individuals of Second Church desiring that some contribution might be made in what manner should seem best in aid of the funds for the Free religious instruction of the poor the sum of fifty dollars was immediately raised by subscription in the Society.—

Nov 26 A meeting of the brethren of the Church having been called by the Pastor at the Table Nov. 25, it was holden this evening & the question submitted to their consideration, whether the fund of this church should go on accumulating or whether its interest shd. be expended for the poor. It was determined that at present it was inexpedient to act thereon.

It was proposed that in future the old quarterly meetings of the Church for mutual religious improvement by conversation & other means should be renewed and that the Pastor shd. give notice of such meeting from the Communion table on the last Sunday in January.

At this meeting Deacon Mackintosh requested that some one be appointed to audit his Church accounts on the first of January next. Brother Geo. A Sampson was accordingly chosen.

1830

Feb 8 In accordance with the vote of Nov 26 notice was given at the Communion on 31 Jan. of a quarterly Church meeting to be held on 1 Feb but in consequence of bad weather, it was postponed one week.

This Evg. the Quarterly meeting was held in the Vestry. About 25 persons attended. The question was discussed of the general expediency of the plan & how the⟨y wi⟩meetings wd. be rendered most useful. It was tho't best to hold them oftener than quarterly; & not to exclude religious persons who were not Church members; that the Pastor should propose for each meeting a question for discussion, & open it himself; that each meeting shd. begin with prayer, & end with singing a hymn. It was tho't best not to give notice of the meetings ⟨in⟩to the congregation, but at the Communion table. The meeting was adjourned to the first Tuesday in March, at 7 o'clock P.M.

Feb. 17 Attended the ordination of Rev. Hersey Bradford Goodwin as Colleague Pastor with the Rev Dr Ripley in Concord, Mass. Br. Charles C. Emerson, delegate.

May Attended the ordination of Rev William Newell as Pastor of the First Congregational Church in Cambridge; Dea. Mackintosh & Br. Geo. A. Sampson delegates

June Attended the ordination of Rev. Artemas B. Muzzy as Pastor of the First Church in Framingham Brs. David Patterson & Albert C. Patterson delegates.

[Proprietors Records:] June 13. 1830. . . . The Rev Mr Emerson informed the Propri[e]tors that the Meeting House in Federal Street was undergoing repairs which would prevent the Society that worship there from occupying it for several Sunday's. [Parishioners of Federal Street were accordingly invited to worship in the meantime at the Second Church (vol. 19, p. 120).]

July 7 Attended the ordination of Rev George Putnam as Pastor Colleague Pastor of the First Church in Roxbury. Brother Samuel P. Heywood, delegate.

Nov 8 A meeting of the brethren was held at the Pastor's house in Chardon St. to consider the expediency of ⟨devoting⟩ appropriating the funds of the church to the building a Vestry. It was there stated that the Pastor was desirous of delivering a course of expository lectures this winter; that there was no suitable place for the purpose, the vestry room being inconveniently situated ⟨at⟩ in the third story of the meeting house↑,↓ [comma in pencil] & altogether too small⟨.⟩; [semicolon in pencil] that the fund of the Church has accumulated to nearly six hundred dollars⟨.⟩; [semicolon in pencil] and that the additional sum necessary↑,↓ [comma in pencil] could undoubtedly be raised by subscription. The assent of the brethren present was then given to this appropriation of the money and Brothers Adams, Thompson, & Heywood, were appointed a Committee to procure estimates of the expense of such a building & to report on Friday ev^g.

12 Nov The adjourned meeting of the brethren was held this ev^g. at the Pastors house. The Committee reported that a Vestry [half a line of space left] could be built & finished of the best materials for a sum not exceeding seven hundred dollars

It was voted that the proposition shd be made to the proprietors next Sunday that the Church will build & finish a Vestry [half a line of space left] provided they will grant them the use of the land in the rear of the Church, the vestry when completed to be the property of the Society.

[Proprietors Records:] Nov 14. 1830. . . . The Rev^d Mr Emerson mentioned ↑to↓ the Proprietors that a new Hymn Book had been published recently by the Rev^d Mr. Greenwood, which he thought a much better collection of Hymns, than the one now used by the Society; & expressed his wish that the Proprietors would examine it, that it might take ↑the↓ place of the one now used by the

Society, if they should think it better, & such a change expedient.— [vol. 19, p. 124] [A committee of seven, including the minister, was appointed to study Emerson's suggestion, and on October 16, 1831, recommended the Greenwood hymnal, the Proprietors noting that it should be adopted the first Sunday in November (vol 19, p. 129).]

[Nov.] 17 The Church met at the Vestry & were informed that the Proprietors had acceeded to their request & had appointed a Committee to cooperate with the building committee of the Church. A Committee was then appointed for the joint purpose of building & completing the Vestry & of soliciting subscriptions to that end. Messrs E. Patterson, G. A. Sampson, A. Adams, G. King, & E. Thompson were unanimously chosen, with power to fill vacancies occurring in their committee.

1831 ↑Annual↓ Contribution for the Evangelical Treasury made in the Society on Sunday

Dec. 11 Annual contribution for the poor at Thanksgiving postponed to this day on account of the weather . . . $78.

1832. Oct 14. Contribution made for the relief of the inhabitants of the Cape de Verd islands, suffering from famine. $137.16

Nov 29 Annual Contribution for the Poor at Thanksgiving $95.

Amount of subscriptions & donations raised in the Second Church for the support of the General Agency of the A. Unitarian Association

On the   June 1832, in compliance with an invitation from the Pastor, the Brethren met at his house to receive a communication from him. The Pastor stated to the meeting, the views at which he had arrived respecting the Ordinance of the Lords Supper; 1. *Firstly;* that he had been led by a critical examination of the history of the rite, to the belief that Jesus did not intend in celebrating with his disciples the Jewish Passover, to institute a new & perpetual rite. He particularly presented the considerations, That not a word from the lips of Jesus intimating a design of perpetuating the rite is recorded by either of the disciples who were present at the Supper. And the expression "Do this in remembrance of me," reported by Luke alone who was not present, naturally admits quite a different & limited sense, namely, that hereafter, so long as they should come up as Jews to Jerusalem, to celebrate the Passover, they would be reminded of another sacrifice, of the sacrifice of their ⟨f⟩Friend & Teacher.

That the practice of the early Christians coupled as it is with acknowledged misconceptions & false expectations, & quite explicable from the circumstances of the converts, should not bind us.

In fine, that the turn which Jesus gave to the national feast is to be esteemed a symbolical instruction, like the acceptance of the ointment, the writing in the sand, the use of the water at the Samaritan well, the washing of the feet of the disciples, & is no more binding on us than these forms. In fact the washing of feet is much more distinctly enjoined, & so is preserved by the Church of Rome; but has been very properly dropped by the Protestant church.

2. *Secondly;* That in the view of Expediency, there existed grave objections to the present institution; 1. That it is wrong to affirm, as is commonly done in terms, a command or a request from Jesus to observe it.

2. That the rite tends to uphold in the Church erroneous views of our relation to Jesus, by leading men to confound him with the Deity as an object of worship, instead [finger erasure of unrecovered character] of presenting him to the mind as a teacher & friend.

3. That although perfectly agreeable to the oriental customs it is a form unsuitable to the feelings & modes of thought of this time & country. It was the pastor's belief, that the eating of the bread & the drinking of the wine are rather tolerated than approved by us; that to some, they were an impediment to devotion; perhaps to none, an aid. This incongruity between the act & the sentiment was his own main objection to the rite. He thought it alone a sufficient objection. He preferred to testify his regard to such a benefactor as Jesus in the freest & most affectionate forms.

4. That the importance ascribed to this particular ordinance in the church as a means of religious improvement, is not consistent with the spirit of the gospel, which is at war with a formal worship, & is eminently a⟨n⟩ declaration of mans spiritual nature.

For these reasons, the Pastor proposed so far to change the manner of administering this rite as to disuse the elements & relinquish the claim of authority, and suggested a mode of commemoration which might secure the undoubted advantages of the Lords Supper without the objectionable features.

After hearing this communication, the brethren appointed a committee to consider & report upon the subject. This Committee consisted of the following gentlemen. Dea. Mackintosh, Dea. Patterson, Mr G. A Sampson, Dr J. Ware, Mr S. Beal, Mr G. B. Emerson, Mr G. King.

On the [illegible number erased] June,[3] the brethren met according to adjournment, at the Pastors house, to hear the report of the Committee. The Pastor was not present. The Committee reported the following resolutions, which were unanimously accepted. *Resolved,*[4] That in the opinion of this Church, after a careful consideration of the subject, it is expedient to maintain the celebration of the Lord's Supper, in the present form. *Resolved,* That the brethren of this Church retain an undiminished regard to the Pastor, & entertain the hope that he will find it consistent with his sense of duty to continue the customary administration of the Supper.

On Sunday, 9 September, the Pastor in a public discourse explained to the Society his views of the Lords Supper, & informed them of the deliberation & decision of the Church. In conclusion, he stated to them his conviction that as it

3. The date was June 20; see Peter Mackintosh's letter, below.
4. This is the substance of the resolutions; the minute has been mislaid [Emerson's note].

was no longer in his power, with a single mind, to administer a rite which the usage of our churches makes an indispensable part of the Pastoral office, it became his duty to resign his charge. On the following day, he requested a dismission of the Proprietors. This request was granted by the Proprietors on the 28 October.

[Report of Committee charged with reviewing Emerson's views on the Lord's Supper (vol. 61):]

The Committee to whom was referred the communication of the Pastor of this Church, stating a change in his opinions concerning the ordinance of the Lords Supper, and recommending some change in the mode of administering it, have given to the whole subject a long and careful consideration. They wish in the first place, to express their entire confidence in the purity of the motives, in the perfect candour, sincerity and love of truth which have influenced him in making this communication, and the undiminished respect in which they hold his character as a man and a Christian. Recognizing, as they do, the grand protestant principle of the right of private judgment on matters of religious belief, they do not regard it as proper that they should, as a committee express any opinion with regard to the Scriptural authority for the celebration of the Lords Supper; believing it right that it should be left to the conscience of every individual to approach the table on such grounds as seem to him to be sufficient. But they cannot regard it as the duty of the Church to consent to any change in the mode of administering the ordinance, and they accordingly recommend that the Church respectfully signify their determination to this effect to their pastor.

> Peter Mackintosh j.
> Enoch Patterson
> John Ware
> Geo A. Sampson
> Geo. B. Emerson
> Saml Beals
> Gedney King

Boston, June 16 1832—

[Letter conveying copy of the above report to Emerson (vol. 61):]

Boston, June 21st 1832.

Rev. R. W. Emerson,
Dear Sir,

At a meeting of the Brethren of the Second Church held by adjour↑n↓ment at your house last evening, the enclosed Report of their Committee was unanimously accepted; and the same committee were directed to communicate the report to you. In their behalf I now do it, hoping it may meet with your acquiescence, if not with your entire approbation.

Be pleased, Sir, to accept the sincere regards of the Committee; and believe me to be

Your sincere friend & servt.
P. Mackintosh j.

[Letter following Emerson's delivery of Sermon CLXII on September 9, 1832 (vol. 61; also given in *L* 1:355–57)]

To the Proprietors of the Second Church.

Boston, 11 September, 1832.

Christian Friends,

In the discourse delivered from the pulpit last Sabbath, I explained the circumstances which have seemed to me to make it my duty to resign my office as your minister. I now request a dismission from the pastoral charge. On this occasion, I cannot help adding a few words.

I am very far from regarding my relation to you with indifference. I am bound to you, as a society, by the experience of uninterrupted kindness; by the feelings of respect & love I entertain for you all, as my tried friends; by ties of personal attachment to many individuals among you, which I account the happiness of my life; by the hope I had entertained of living always with you, and of contributing, if possible, in some small degree, to your welfare.

Nor do I think less of the office of a Christian minister. I am pained at the situation in which I find myself, that compels me to make a difference of opinion of no greater importance, the occasion of surrendering so many & so valuable functions as belong to that office. I have the same respect for the great objects of the Christian ministry, & the same faith in their gradual accomplishment through the use of human means, which, at first, led me to enter it. I should be unfaithful to myself, if any change of circumstances could diminish my devotion to the cause of divine truth.

And so, friends, let me hope, that whilst I resign my official relation to you I shall not lose your kindness, & that a difference of opinion as to the value of an ordinance, will be overlooked by us in our common devotion to what is real & eternal.

Ralph Waldo Emerson.

[Report of the Committee appointed to review Emerson's letter requesting a dismission of pastoral duties (vol. 61):]

The Committee to which was referred the letter of the Rev. Mr. Emerson, requesting a dismission from the pastoral care of the Second Church & Society, Report—that they have given this subject a careful consideration, and have conferr'd with their Rev Pastor concerning it—they do not perceive that any arrangement can be made by which the difference of opinion between the church & pastor can be accomodated, or by which the ordinance of the Supper can be administered in a satisfactory manner to those who have been in the habit of partaking of it.

As a committee of the proprietors however, they do not feel ready to express any direct opinion with regard to the expediency of granting an immediate dismissal, since it is obvious, that the actual relation of Mr. Emerson is to the proprietors and not to the Church, and that the proprietors have an undoubted right to retain him as their pastor under the existing circumstances, without reference to the opinions of the Church.

They recommend therefor in order to obtain an expression of the opinions of the proprietors on this subject, that the following question be submitted for their consideration. viz.

"Is it expedient that the pastoral connexion between this congregation and the Rev. Mr. Emerson be dissolved on account of the difference of opinion between him and the members of the Church, with regard to the mode of celebrating the Lord's Supper"

all which is respectfully submitted

Isaac Harris   Chairman Comm.

[On October 28, 1832, the Proprietors of the Second Church voted on the question of the "expediency" of dissolving the "pastoral connexion" (vol. 19, p. 139):]

> Whole number of Ballots   61—
> Yeas 34
> Nays 25
> Blank —   2

[On the question of dismission:]

> Whole number of ballots   54
> Yeas 30
> Nays —   20
> Blank —   4

[However, it was "Voted unanimously that the Salary of the Rev Mr Emerson be continued for the present" (p. 140).]

[The following list of admissions is in an unidentified hand (vol. 9, p. 113):]

Members of Second Church

1829	
Feb 8	Ralph Waldo Emerson from the First Ch. in Boston.
March 22	Abel Kendall Jr
	Mrs Ann M. Kendall.
	Richard W. Bayley.
	Hale J. How
	Mrs Mary L. Sampson
	David Patterson
	Albert C. Patterson.
	Hepsibah Patterson
	Sarah Ann Burditt.
May 31	Mary Mansfield5
	Nancy Howe
July 26	Ebenezer Sampson
	Mrs Harriet Sampson.
	Mary E. Cook
	Charles C. Emerson
Aug 30	Mrs Lucy Lewis
	Mrs Hannah B. Lewis
Sept 27	Maria Augusta Little.
	Sophronia Aspasia Little
	Margaretta Artemisia Little.
1830	
Feb 28	Mrs Ellen Wheelock.
	Mary Howard Bridge.
1831	
Jany 30	Eliza Hulme Fisher
	Sarah H. Green.

5. A line runs from this entry to the bottom of the column, so as to include all the entries for the remainder of the year; "These by Rev R. W. Emerson" is inscribed to the right of the line.

June 26.	Levi Bartlett.
	Harriet Bartlett.
	Mrs Eliza Tucker from Derry ⎫ N.H.
	Mrs Susan Harper ⎭
Aug 28	Mrs Polly Lewis.
	Mrs Betsey Cotting
	Catherine Robbins.

[The following list is entirely in Emerson's hand (vol. 9, pp. 127–28):]

Marriages. 1829

March 15	Minot Pratt	Maria J. Bridge.
26	Joseph Manning	Sarah Moody Kimball.—
30	Richard Thayer	Sophronia Voax.
April 16	Eben Tarbell	Caroline Parker Richards
June 2	Ellis Bennett Greene	Catherine Farrie
10	Abraham Howard	Mary Howard
Oct. 7	Nathan Storrs	Sarah James.
Nov 8	Thomas Boyd	Agnes Allen 8

1830		
April 6	Henry Orne	Sempronia Aspasia Little.
May 4	John Frost	Sarah Ann Burditt.
	Charles Barrett	Abby B. Hartt
June 8	Lewis Josselyn	Emmeline Ellis
Aug.	Samuel Clement	Maria Augusta Little.
Sept. 30	Henry Penniman	Mary Woodbridge Edwards
Nov.	Samuel Chessman	Nancy Wild 7—

1831		
Jan. 27	Rev. Artemas Bowers Muzzey	Hepsibeth Patterson.
March	Jonas Eaton	Sarah Henderson Green
March 24	Luke Chamberlin	Hannah F Sargent.
April 7	Joseph Weber	Mary Ann Webster.
April 7	Harrison Cass	Mary Perham
June 19	Ebed Whiton	Mary Ann Howe
July 7	George Allen	Mary Hancock Withington
10	Thomas Glover Phipps	Lucy Steele
12	Charles Smith	Harriet Stillman Bryant.
Sept. 8	John A. Appleton	Martha A. Wells
Oct 23	Timothy J. Roberts	Mary A. Knowlton

30	Rowland Ellis	Eliza Ann Coburn.
Nov 10	Alvin Adams	Ann Rebecca Bridge.
13	Nathaniel C. Poor	Caroline Pook
Nov 22	George L. Emerson	Sally Bordman

15

1832
April 12	William Jackson Hammatt	Ann Phillips Rogers
19	Otis Turner	Sarah Loring House
May 1	Theodore Gardner	Lucy Ann Withington
10	Henry William Squires	Caroline Humphreys.
15	Harry Hunton	Adeline Augusta Aspinwall
20	Samuel Mason	Mary Moore
29	Henry Winsor	Mary Ann Davis
30	Joseph Richardson	Caroline King
June 3	Thomas Nash	Elizabeth Wentworth
	William T. H. Duncan	Rebecca L. Butler.
Oct 16	William H. Wheeler	Elizabeth Hathorne.
17	John Trull Heard	Almira Patterson.
21	Henry Leeds	Mary Smith.
	John Tucker Thompson	Sarah Spring Bemis

1⟨1⟩4

[The following list consists of entries in Emerson's hand; in the title, however, only "1829." is in Emerson's hand (vol. 9, pp. 154–56):]

Baptisms 1828. 1829.

1829
[March] 15	James Henry	Sherlock Spooner
22	Henry Emerson	Richard W. Bayley
29	Mary Elizabeth	John A. Eaton.
April 8	Mary Greenleaf	Joseph Kidder ʃ private
19	Augustus Wilder	William Stearns ⎰ private
May 24	Henry Lyman	Brigham
	John Gorham	John G. Rogers {private
31	Mary Mansfield (adult)	
June 11	Joshua James	Joshua Ellis {private
14	Abigail Frances	George Seaver.
July 12	Sarah Jane	Jason D. Battles.
Aug. 30	Mrs Lucy Lewis adult.	
	Helen Maria	Isaac Adams

	Lewis Joshua		John Henshaw
	Lucy Elizabeth		
	&		Saml S. Lewis
	Catherine Augusta		
	Robert Lambard		J. P. Robinson
Nov 29	Elizabeth Smith	adult	
Dec. 13	William Augustus		G. P. Bangs.

Baptisms, 1830

Feb 14	Ariana	John Saville. private
28	Mary Ellen	Gill Wheelock
	William Henry	
	Caroline Brooks	
	Harriet	William Blaney. private
	Sarah Coffin	
	George Leach	
	Charles	
April 11	Abby Larkin	Abel Adams. private
May 2	Susan Mansfield	George Whittemore
16	Emmeline Josephine	Thomas Coburn. private
29	Francis Buckminster	George B. Emerson
	Edward	
	Emily	
	Ann Elizabeth	Thomas Appleton {private
	Sarah Thomas	
June 27	Emma Cordelia	Peter Mackintosh
	Maria Louisa	S. P. Heywood.
July 4	Ellis Bennett	Ellis Green
	Harriet Louisa	Jonas B. Brown. {private
9	Caroline Clapp	
	William Farrie	Henry Davis, {private
	John Ware	
25	James Edward	Eben. Goodrich.
Aug 1	Mary Elizabeth	John Center {private
	Evelina Corlew	
	Ann Frances	Abel Kendall
Sept 5	Ann Bent	Henry Ware, Jr.
	Catherine Augusta	J. P. Robinson
12	Samuel Austin	Seth Tucker
Dec. 5	Charles Hildreth	Thomas Boyd {private
26	Walter Thornton	N. C. Betton. private

1831

	Charles Levi	Levi Bartlett ⎫
May 27	Levi Bartlett	⎬ private
	Hannah Clarissa ⎫	Levi Bartlett ⎭
	Susan Walker ⎬	
July 24	Convers Reed ⎱	adopted twin children of
	Martha Eleanor ⎰	J. R. Lilley
Aug 28	Maria Ellen	G. P. Bangs
	Anne Catherine	J. L. P. Orrok. private
Sept 4	Joseph Augustus	George Seaver
8	Theodore Grenville ⎫	Samuel Ellis private
	Cora Clifford ⎬	
11	Lewis Ellis	Lewis Josselyn
Oct 23	Abby Adams	John Larkin
	Sarah Livermore	Mrs Coburn private
30	Mary Ann	J. D. Battles.
Nov 27	Normand Whitney ⎫	William Stearns. private
	Charles Alfred ⎬	

1832

June 17	Georgiana	George Whittemore
	Amelia Louisa ⎫	John G. Rogers {private
	Charles Waldo ⎬	
Sept 2	George Henderson ⎬	Spinney
	Noah Lincoln ⎭	
16	Mary Catherine	Ellis Greene

[The following list is entirely in Emerson's hand (vol. 9, pp. 176–78):]

Deaths. 1829

April	Mrs Sarah Holmes, aged 26. Consumption.
	George William Appleton. aet. 2 y. 7 mo. child of Thos. A. brain fever
	Albert, child of James Foster. aet. 1 y. nettle rash
May 17	Mary Ann, child of Francis Holmes aet 10 y. ⟨brain⟩ ↑dropsy↓
21	Mrs Fanny Butler, aged 45. Typhus fever.
July 15	Charles A. Lincoln aet. cir. 23 Consumption
July 30	child of Ebenezer Scott aet. 5 weeks
31	Joshua Ellis, aet. 60— Consumption
Sept.	Child of Capt. Henry.
Oct 7	Elizabeth infant child of Seth Simmons. aet 2 y. 4 mo
Nov.	child of W. T. Spear ⟨cons⟩

Dec. 5   Lewis Joshua infant child of John Henshaw.   apoplexy. 8 months.
     20   Mercy Brackett, aet. 73   Consumption

1830

Jan 22   Archelaus Fuller, child of S. N. Fuller (aet. 20 months) lung fever
              Catherine Augusta, child of S. S. Lewis (aet. 10 months) measles.
     25   Dorothy Percy - (aet cir. 25) apoplexy.
Feb 13   John Henry Eaton   child of Samˡ Eaton (aet 7 mo.) dropsy
⟨April⟩ March
April 13   James Alonzo, child of   Owen (aet. 21 mo.) croup
       22   James Augustus Howe   son of Capt J. H.   aet 20. Diabetes.
       30   infant still born of— Sam. N. Fuller.
March   Peregrine Padduck
June   Child of Mr Eben. N. Hunting.
Oct   Gen. John Boyd, aet.   palsy
              Jonathan Wild, aet.   consumption
              Thomas Coburn, aet.   Typhus fever
Nov 25   Sarah Moore, aet. 16
Dec 23   A foundling infant at house of J. R. Lilley. aet 4 weeks.

1831
↑a Portug↑u↓eze Sailor↓

Feb. 8   Mrs Ellen Tucker Emerson.   aet. 19.   consumption.
              Mary Howard Bridge   aet 23.   inflammation.
              Mrs Hannah Bell   aet 45   tumour
March   Samuel Austin—child of Seth Tucker   1 y
              Doddridge   child of Mr Owen 4 y.
                           child of Amos Allen 1 y.
April   Mrs Grace Meinzies old age.
June 22   William Little.   aet. 81.   old age
July 8   Mrs Mary Perry   Consumption.
Aug 2   Ellis Cook   aet 71   Dropsy.
       31   Henry Augustus   child of Mr H. Little   aet. 13 mo.
Sept 2   Charles Lobdell   aet. 6 y.   dropsy.
       7   Francis Green   aet. 81
              Lorana Howe   aet 23   consumption
              Mrs Mary Turell   aet 91
              Sarah Lovejoy   aet 19   consumption
21   Robert Ambrose of Concord N.H   aet. 35.   killed by a fall.
Oct 20   Henry Gale   8 y 6 mo   drowned.
Nov 5   Sarah E.   child of Geo. Spinney, aet. 4 y. Croup⟨e⟩
       7   Mrs Sarah Howe, aet. 64, a Tumour.

Dec.   child of Green Smith   aet 1 year
               Samuel Shaw child of S. S. Lewis   aet. 7 mo. Consumption
                                    child of Thomas White aet 5 y.
19   William Kidder of N. York aet. 47—consumption
28   George   child of George Whittemore   aet. 4 years. dropsy

                                    Deaths. 1832
Jan 28   William Roberts   20 y.   Consumption.
Feb 9   Mrs Jerusha Wardwell.   72 y.   Influenza
               Ebenezer Burditt   41 y.   Consumption
    17   Louisa Gardiner   child of J. G. L. Libbey   aet 2 y. 6 mo. Throat
               distemper
March 1   George Edward   child of I. R. Butts   aet 4 y. 6 mo   Dropsy
               Lucy Elizabeth   child of S. S. Lewis   aet. 4 y. 6 mo.   Fits.
April 27   Abby Ingle   child of S. N. Fuller aet   measles
               Mrs   Bradford aet 36   consumption.
May   John Sullivan   child of Henry N. Hooper, aet. 4, Measles
    6   Sarah Louisa   child of S. N. Fuller   aet. 7 y.   Consumption
    7   George W. Bryant 26 y.   consumption.
    8   child of   Wiggin aet. 1 y. measles.
    28   Mrs Deborah Townsend, aet.
June 2   Samuel Tuttle   aet. 62   consumption.
               Mrs   Moore   aet 72   consumption
                                    child of Mr Cline, aet. 17 months.
               Eleanor Bailey
Aug 31   Mrs Bethiah Fisher, aet. 61
⟨Aug 31⟩

APPENDIX B

Letter from the Rev. R. W. Emerson,
To the Second Church and Society.

LETTER.

Boston, 22D DECEMBER, 1832.

TO THE SECOND CHURCH AND SOCIETY.

CHRISTIAN FRIENDS,—Since the formal resignation of my official relation to you in my communication to the proprietors in September, I had waited anxiously for an opportunity of addressing you once more from the pulpit, though it were only to say, Let us part in peace and in the love of God. The state of my health has prevented and continues to prevent me from so doing. I am now advised to seek the benefit of a sea-voyage. I cannot go away without a brief parting word to friends who have shown me so much kindness, and to whom I have felt myself so dearly bound.

Our connexion has been very short. I had only begun my work. It is now brought to a sudden close, and I look back, I own, with a painful sense of weakness, to the little service I have been able to render, after so much expectation on my part,—to the chequered space of time, which domestic affliction and personal infirmities have made yet shorter and more unprofitable.

As long as he remains in the same place, every man flatters himself, however keen may be his sense of his failures and unworthiness, that he shall yet accomplish much; that the future shall make amends for the past; that his very errors shall prove his instructors,—and what limit is there to hope? But a separation from our place, the close of a particular career of duty, shuts the book, bereaves us of this hope, and leaves us only to lament how little has been done.

Yet, my friends, our faith in the great truths of the New Testament makes the change of places and circumstances, of less account to us, by fixing our attention upon that which is unalterable. I find great consolation in the thought, that the resignation of my present relations makes so little change to myself. I am no longer your minister, but am not the less engaged, I hope, to the love and service

---

Written three days before Emerson departed on the brig *Jasper* for Malta, the present letter was read from the pulpit of the Second Church by the Rev. F. W. P. Greenwood during the morning service on December 23. The Church proprietors ordered the printing of three hundred copies for distribution to the congregation, and an eight-page pamphlet, printed by I. R. Butts of Boston, duly appeared. In the absence of a manuscript, the present text is taken from the pamphlet printing. Butts also printed the letter as an ornately bordered broadside on silk; for the variants in the broadside printing, see the Textual Notes.

of the same eternal cause, the advancement, namely, of the kingdom of God in the hearts of men. The tie that binds each of us to that cause is not created by our connexion, and can not be hurt by our separation. To me, as one disciple, is the ministry of truth, as far as I can discern and declare it, committed, and I desire to live no where and no longer than that grace of God is imparted to me— the liberty to seek and the liberty to utter it.

And, more than this, I rejoice to believe, that my ceasing to exercise the pastoral office among you, does not make any real change in our spiritual relation to each other. Whatever is most desirable and excellent therein, remains to us. For, truly speaking, whoever provokes me to a good act or thought, has given me a pledge of his fidelity to virtue,—he has come under bonds to adhere to that cause to which we are jointly attached. And so I say to all you, who have been my counsellors and co-operators in our Christian walk, that I am wont to see in your faces, the seals and certificates of our mutual obligations. If we have conspired from week to week, in the sympathy and expression of devout sentiments; if we have received together the unspeakable gift of God's truth; if we have studied together the sense of any divine word; or striven together in any charity; or conferred together for the relief or instruction of any brother; if together we have laid down the dead in a pious hope; or held up the babe into the baptism of Christianity; above all, if we have shared in any habitual acknowledgment of that benignant God, whose omnipresence raises and glorifies the meanest offices and the lowest ability, and opens heaven in every heart that worships him,—then indeed are we united, we are mutually debtors to each other of faith and hope, engaged to persist and confirm each other's hearts in obedience to the Gospel. We shall not feel that the nominal changes and little separations of this world, can release us from the strong cordage of this spiritual bond. And I entreat you to consider how truly blessed will have been our connexion, if in this manner, the memory of it shall serve to bind each one of us more strictly to the practice of our several duties.

It remains to thank you for the goodness you have uniformly extended towards me, for your forgiveness of many defects, and your patient and even partial acceptance of every endeavor to serve you; for the liberal provision you have ever made for my maintenance; and for a thousand acts of kindness, which have comforted and assisted me.

To the proprietors, I owe a particular acknowledgment, for their recent generous vote for the continuance of my salary, and hereby ask their leave to relinquish this emolument at the end of the present month.

And now, brethren and friends, having returned into your hands the trust you have honored me with—the charge of public and private instruction in this religious society, I pray God, that whatever seed of truth and virtue we have sown and watered together, may bear fruit unto eternal life. I commend you to the Divine Providence. May He grant you, in your ancient sanctuary, the service of able and faithful teachers. May He multiply to your families and to your persons, every genuine blessing; and whatever discipline may be appointed to you in this world, may the blessed hope of the resurrection, which He has planted in the constitution of the human soul, and confirmed and manifested by Jesus Christ, be made good to you beyond the grave. In this faith and hope, I bid you farewell.

    Your affectionate servant,
    RALPH WALDO EMERSON.

Textual and Manuscript Notes

In these notes, a physical description of the sermon manuscript is followed by a record, keyed to the text by page and line number, of all of Emerson's insertions, cancellations, variant passages, and transpositions, as well as all editorial changes not covered in the categories of silent emendation outlined in the Textual Introduction. The text given here is a literal genetic transcription of the manuscript and therefore differs in some respects from the edited version above. Editorial matter is enclosed in square brackets, while Emerson's brackets are represented as curved. All inscription is in ink unless otherwise noted.

The symbols used in these notes are explained in the list below. Matter that immediately follows a cancellation without space or symbol of insertion, as in "⟨i⟩It" or "⟨we⟩you," should be understood as having been written directly over the canceled matter.

Symbols

⟨ ⟩	Cancellation
↑ ↓	Insertion
/ / /	Variant
[ ]	Editorial insertion
{ }	Emerson's square brackets
¶	Paragraph

Sermon CXXXVI

Manuscript: Six sheets folded to make four pages each; sewn along the left margin with white thread; pages measure 25 x 20.2 cm. Two leaves (containing a revised opening) are attached to the fascicle along the left margin with white thread; these leaves measure 24.9 x 19.8 cm and 24 x 19.5–19.7 cm. Part of the top of the first folio leaf (the original opening) has been cut off, destroying most of an inscription that seems to have read "Thanksgiving 1831." The fourth folio leaf is torn at the bottom; the lower right corner of the sixth folio leaf has been torn off, as has a small portion of the bottom of the eighth folio leaf. No words appear to have been lost.

[The following revised introduction was written for a later delivery of the sermon:]
136 [in pencil]

Whoso is wise & will observe these things even they shall understand the loving kindness of the Lord. Ps 107. 43

The book of the Psalms abounds in expressions of praise. The book is shared almost equally betwixt praise & penitence. Both sentiments are just and each implies the other. And yet ↑when our true relations as human beings are considered↓ perhaps the fittest of all our sentiments to be the habitual attitude of the mind is gratitude, still gratitude. I have heard of an eminent preacher who ⟨have⟩ had received & preached all his life the stricter doctrines of the Genevan Church & whose prayers were remarked for the ⟨special⟩ earnestness of his entreaty for specific blessings; ↑who↓ in the last years of his life ⟨he⟩ ceased to ask for any gift & his prayers became merely ejaculations of love & praise. It is related of an ancient heathen philosopher that ⟨meeting⟩ ↑seeing↓ a young man dressing himself very gaily for an entertainment he asked him whether every day were not a festival to a good man. To the religious mind every dealing of providence is full of sweetness & instruction; the universal gifts of life & the air the sun the senses & every occupation of body & mind instead of being disregarded as general are received as particular bounty, ⟨to the⟩ & have as much force to persuade it to praise as if its own name was inscribed on the gift. It does not need special days, it does not need extraordinary mercies. To those who love God it is an argument for gratitude that they are not distinguished in yᵉ diffusion of common mercy; yᵗ He sends rain on yᵉ just & on yᵉ unjust [Matthew 5:45] They worship more because these worship less. They worship the more /that/because/ the love is infinite, & makes the benefit general. Whilst others receive with open arms yᵉ gift they think more of yᵉ love.

It is however the mature heart as I have already intimated that understands the loving kindness of yᵉ Lord. It is not the first lesson that we learn. ⟨B⟩ Through much discipline through many pains regrets & mortifications we struggle at last into peace & into praise. The first aspects of life are mean & unworthy. What is our life?

Lines	Page 23
1–2	call. ⟨It⟩ ↑The summons to gratitude↓ . . . unprepared. never, ⟨while⟩ ↑Let . . . ours,↓
4–12	↑a↓ welcome call. ⟨We do not live here long.⟩ ↑It . . . are↓ A few . . . & ⟨cold⟩ ↑snowy↓ winter↑s↓; ⟨nights⟩ three . . . ↑formed & broken↓, a few ⟨reverses⟩ gains & losses, ↑a . . . knowledge,↓ . . . that ⟨cause us poignant⟩ ⟨make us⟩ ↑we↓ wince to think o⟨f⟩n, ⟨an interest⟩ ↑some natural pleasures,↓ . . . our ²friends & ¹children
14–15	↑come . . . ground they↓ survive & ⟨pursue their work⟩ ↑act;↓
16	↑The heart & the gospel say↓
19–(24)5	↑Let . . . for [end of page] for . . . enjoy. ⟨P⟩ We . . . ourselves. ⟨Let⟩ We . . . have.↓ ¶ ⟨We are surrounded on ⟨a⟩ every side by astonishment. In wonder knowledge begins & ends in wonder. ↑It is little that we can certainly know.↓ But ⟨the⟩ ↑a↓ strong instinct⟨s of men⟩ ha⟨ve⟩s led ⟨them⟩ ↑men↓ under all varieties of condition to listen to the Revelation more or less accurate preserved in the tradition or the Records of every nation ⟨declaring⟩ ↑teaching↓ the Providence of God. This connexion of man with God, this showing of the source, this marriage of the finite to the infinite, of two worlds dignifies the minutest action of man & makes praise suitable to him. Praise to God What is praise It is the acknowledgment that whatever good belongs to the mind has its source in God. It will differ then in every mind according as its sight is opened to see good ¶ But it is becoming

to all⟩ ¶ My friends ↑of his flock clothed you & the apple the melon
the vine & the olive cheered you?↓ [addition in pencil rejected as
incomplete] I . . . gratitude ⟨It⟩ We

Page 24

5–7	by. ⟨Optima res aqua.⟩ It . . . things. ↑by which he would intimate that↓ The
10	with ⟨those⟩ ↑men↓
12	value. as
13–19	It is ⟨that⟩ ↑because↓ . . . others, ⟨that⟩ ↑because↓ they can think, ⟨that⟩ ↑because↓ . . . die; ⟨that these distinctions are anything but the pearl of the cock in the fable.⟩ It . . . well ⟨from⟩ of . . . draw↑; it . . . fable.↓ ¶ ⟨Let us ⟨rejoice⟩ call to mind the first & simplest possessions, the riches of the poor, the book of those who cannot read, the health of the sick, the life of the dying, what is ⟨a⟩left when all is taken.⟩ [canceled in pencil] ¶ 1. ⟨Let us⟩ First
20–21	↑is much more;↓ . . . has ⟨made it⟩ deformed
27	analyze the ⟨Univ⟩ exhibition
27–29	↑Yet . . . forest.↓
32–35	see; The . . . earth ⟨under the light of the rising sun whom the blaze of ages has not bereft of one ray⟩. ¶ They go out ⟨again⟩ to . . . the ⟨permanent⟩ ↑old↓ . . . nature, ⟨to use⟩ water,
40–(25)7	miracles ⟨if⟩ ↑when↓ once we ⟨should⟩ attempt to ↑detail &↓ [emendations in pencil] explain all. ¶ ⟨The ⟨ball on which we live⟩ ↑earth↓ spins ⟨round⟩ upon its axis until the ⟨city⟩ ↑spot↓ we inhabit gets out of the light of the sun Th⟨en⟩at ⟨it⟩ ↑shadow↓ is called Night & the diminished light enables us to see the hosts of globes with which space is full & shows us that beautiful as are the shows of this world it is but an atom in the whole.⟩ [The bracketing and cancellation of the following sentence—done in pencil—are rejected as a late emendation. Because the canceled matter is necessary for sense and because the subsequent sentence is labeled "3." in pencil, the editors conjecture that Emerson may have revised section 2 in pencil on a leaf now lost. The original scheme of numbering the sections is retained throughout in the clear text.] ¶ ⟨↑{↓2. But . . . ↑or . . . others↓ . . . gratitude ⟨for⟩ which all ⟨or all who will⟩ may feel, I mean ↑The pleasures of↓ Home.↑}↓⟩ ↑3.↓ I am . . . connected ⟨more nearly⟩ ↑intimately↓ . . . we ⟨dwell⟩ ↑sit↓ . . . table. ⟨I ⟨will⟩ do not in my tho'ts limit this topic narrowly⟩ ↑I . . . sense↓;

Page 25

9–10	↑All . . . many.↓ ⟨But⟩ it is
16	↑even↓
18–19	And /every one/the most sensitive/
19–20	is ⟨the sunshine⟩ ↑therefore↓ coming ⟨into sunshine⟩ out of shade ↑into sunshine↓
24	the ⟨common careless⟩ heedless
26–40	known ⟨many⟩ ↑several↓ . . . they ⟨seem⟩ ↑appear↓— [emendation in pencil] . . . few. ¶ ⟨On this ↑day↓ . . . heart↑,↓ [comma in pencil]

. . . families⟩ [end of page; cancellation rejected as a late emendation]
Even . . . ↑more of↓ . . . beside. ¶ ⟨3.⟩ ↑4.↓ [rejected emendation in
pencil] Another cause ⟨for which I feel a⟩of . . . acquaintance ⟨I⟩we

40–41   ↑A cultivated heart & mind,↓ A finished character is [end of line] is
the

Page 26

1–2   like God, ⟨to all to whom it is known⟩ ↑more . . . be.↓

5   as ⟨Gods choicest gifts.⟩ ↑my apostles & prophets.↓

7   in ⟨h⟩the

12–13   bywords,—⟨political benefactors or philosophers⟩ ↑the heroes . . .
day↓,

21   gossip ⟨so often found⟩ ↑that abounds↓

24   our ⟨thoughts⟩ esteem

25–29   known ⟨a mind⟩ (/which/what/ . . . yet ⟨sucked⟩ ↑drew in↓
[emendation in pencil] in great . . . natural ⟨breath⟩ air . . . opinion
⟨was⟩ ↑seemed↓

34–35   acknowledgments. ¶ ⟨4.⟩ ↑5↓ [rejected emendation in pencil] To

40   veins ⟨st⟩ in

41–(27)6   reason. ↑{Insert X}↓ [on the facing page, a passage marked "X":] ↑{I
would . . . the ⟨pupil⟩ ↑scholar↓ . . . Germany; ⟨in the patience of
Spain in the expectation of⟩ {in . . . despotism;} . . . ↑wd.↓ feel . . .
of ⟨sad⟩ afflicted Africa}↓

Page 27

7–15   ↑of land↓ . . . ↑wisely &↓ surely,—⟨for⟩ ↑because↓ . . . be ⟨formed⟩
↑hatched↓, . . . men, ⟨is⟩be

18–21   the ⟨triumphs⟩ ↑progress↓ . . . religion. ¶ [The following paragraphs
appear to be a late addition, probably dating to 1836, and are rejected
from the clear text:] ⟨↑Furthermore,⟩ ↑I deny not that there may be
some ⟨drawbacks⟩ considerations in the political aspect of ↑the
world &↓ our own country to qualify our joy & create apprehension,
but↓ a deep consideration of the blessing will increase our sense of our
debt. ⟨We shall be more⟩It will make us careful to give the whole
amount of our exertion & influence to the ⟨right⟩ cause ↑of union &
good government↓. Is it not true that good men despond when they
see the unprincipled course of our politics, the culpable levity with
which in this country we sacrifice the future to the present, the
interests of generations to the interests of a party? Whilst yet the
union is unbroken, whilst yet the laws are respected, whilst public
virtue is yet possible, it becomes the living to lay it to heart, that ⟨a
society⟩ ↑the community↓ of which each of us is one member, are the
trustees of the welfare of the human race, and ↑be awakened to the
wholesome ⟨fear⟩ alarm↓ that we ourselves by negligence, ⟨&⟩ or
fear, or favor, are ⟨bring⟩ contributing to bring down ↑upon it↓ the
greatest calamities. ↑⟨let⟩& every one of us ⟨be⟩ learn to feel that it
is his solemn duty to give the whole of his influence the whole weight
of his ⟨words his votes⟩ ↑speech &↓ his actions to the upholding

righteousness in the state. ¶ ↑In enumerating these topics of gratitude↓
I know brethren there are those to whom ye boasted advances of art
are of little account There are those who ⟨lie⟩ racked with pain & to
whom external conveniences give little pleasure. There are some who
in ye downfall of cherishd hopes in ye bereavement of dear friends,
have no relish for their good It seems to y^m all vanity There are some
who are pinched & hindered by poverty some frightened by impending dangers mortified by regrets torn with remorse threatened with
death ↑have no power or disposition to draw pleasure from these
extended considera↓ To all these, ⟨the precious faith in an overruling
Providence ye vision⟩ there yet remains one source of joy common to
all men↓↓ [addition "⟨let⟩& every . . . men" in pencil] ¶ ⟨5.⟩ ↑6↓
[rejected emendation in pencil] Finally ⟨Let us give thanks it is a
distinct & absorbing occasion of gratitude⟩ ↑It is a reason for praise↓
. . . power, the

24–26   {give thanks} . . . ne⟨w⟩ver

31   sinned, repents,

33–34   the ⟨parental⟩ affectionate . . . state. ↑And as I began ⟨with⟩ ↑my
               enumeration of↓ these topics of gratitude with the simple blessing of
               rational existence, so I will end with the same. Let us rejoice in the
               nature of the soul which fits it to ⟨take⟩ ↑draw↓ delight ⟨in⟩from all
               these sources↓ [addition in pencil; rejected as a late emendation] Let

35–36   {The . . . beast ⟨return thanks for⟩ ↑are made glad by↓ . . . soul.}

37–38   age it gains by plenty, ⟨&⟩ ↑it gains↓

Sermon CXXXVII

Manuscript: Eight single leaves (25 x 20 cm) followed by a sheet folded to make four
pages of 24.5 x 20.1 cm; a single leaf (24.6 x 20 cm) with the lower right corner torn off; a
sheet folded to make four pages of 24.6 x 20.1 cm, with a single leaf inserted (24.6 x 20.2
cm); a sheet folded to make four pages of 24.6 x 20.1 cm; a sheet folded to make four
pages of 25 x 20 cm, but with the last leaf cut out, leaving remnants of words in ink and
pencil, and a blank leaf (24.6 x 20.1 cm) inserted; and, finally, a sheet folded to make
four pages of 25 x 20 cm, but with the first leaf cut out, leaving remnants of words in ink,
and an unstitched folio of four pages (24.6 x 20.1 cm), containing a revised conclusion,
inserted. This loose folio was once pinned between the two cut-out folio leaves and the
last folio leaf. The rest of the fascicle is sewn along the left margin with white thread. An
inscribed slip, now lost, was once attached with red sealing wax to the verso of the
second leaf. Tipped to the upper right recto of the last leaf is a scrap measuring
approximately 11.6 x 12.5 cm containing a rough outline of the sermon, perhaps used to
guide revision.

[Below Bible text:] Joshua [in pencil]

Lines   *Page 28*

2   himself what

4   ↑or not,↓

6   ¶ ↑I . . . love.↓

7–8　　　god ⟨the⟩ ↑a↓ true or a false ↑one,↓ it ²will & ¹must have. . . . is ⟨filled⟩ ↑possessed↓

9　　　↑Conscience, or of↓

10–11　　　↑It . . . fruit.↓

15–17　　　ourselves. ¶ ⟨We are eager to admire.⟩ The . . . admiration. ↑We . . . admire.↓

21　　　disposition ⟨we have⟩ to admire, ⟨running⟩ ↑that runs↓

23–24　　　mouth, ⟨ & loses in never a one.⟩ ↑a hundred . . . one.↓

25–(29)4　　　book, or a ⟨handsome⟩ ↑beautiful↓ . . . are ⟨they not⟩ ↑men↓ to say ↑not↓ . . . ↑the↓ best, ↑the↓ fairest, ↑the↓ . . . to ⟨think⟩ ↑reflect↓,

Page 29

7　　　↑corrected &↓

9　　　a ⟨better⟩ ↑more↓ admiration has ⟨uprooted⟩ ↑supplanted↓ a ⟨worse⟩ ↑less↓.

12–13　　　body ⟨see⟩ ↑read or hear↓

14–18　　　or ⟨Bacon⟩ ↑Newton↓ . . . ↑or Washington↓ . . . man? ¶ ⟨⟨It seems to me it⟩ ⟨↑This↓⟩ ⟨shows plainly the disposition⟩ ⟨↑indicates the religious nature↓ of the mind that it was formed to love & apply itself to the infinite. this is an idolatry but it is the forerunner of religion. "Admiration ennobles & blesses those who feel it. ⟨Like⟩ The lover is made happier by his [af]fection than his mistress can be. Like the song of the [bi]rd it cheers his own heart."⟩ [portions of two words obscured by sealing wax] ¶ ⟨⟨Let me⟩ To illustrate this position by considering briefly those sentiments wh. seem to be an idolatry or imperfect religion & to call out a strength of affection unsuitable to their taking yᵉ place of *love of God.*⟩⟩ ¶ This proneness to ⟨an unlimited love⟩ admiration, . . . in ⟨the nature of⟩ man.

19–27　　　nature. ⟨We are⟩ ↑He is↓ formed through all ⟨our⟩his . . . adore. ⟨But *What* is it that we are to love, to venerate, & to adore? Let us consider the objects upon which our devotion is bestowed that we ⟨what⟩ ↑may see it↓⟩ ↑⟨In it⟩ The . . . feelings↓ is idolatry↑.↓ ⟨or an improper direction of these feelings, & what⟩ ↑⟨In t⟩ The right direction ⟨it⟩↓ is true religion ⟨or their right direction.⟩ ¶ ⟨I particularly request your attention to an enumeration & examination of⟩ ↑It . . . into↓ . . . ↑remarkable↓ . . . ↑only↓ . . . objects⟨, & compare them with the true sentiment⟩↑.↓ ⟨I account them the to be a discipline a preparation for the true sentiment. They are all its forerunners & prophets.⟩ [last cancellation in pencil and ink] ¶ The

30　　　to ⟨engrossing all things in itself⟩ ↑extravagant devotion↓.

31　　　without ⟨extravagance⟩ ↑hyperbole↓.

34–35　　　↑however extravagant the language↓

37–38　　　exist, ⟨as⟩ ↑to that extent↓ [emendation in pencil] . . . friend [Between this paragraph and the next, "{Insert X}" is interlined and canceled in pencil; on the facing page, otherwise blank, is the following passage, inscribed and canceled in pencil:] ⟨↑X {Now ⟨it is true of⟩ what ↑is yᵉ true object↓ excites this sentiment is it skin deep beauty a little form or color or motion, is it not the belief that certain amiable & excellent qualities reside in its object, purity, truth, kindness, self command, & wisdom? ⟨And if these {If the qualities of cruelty falsehood hatred impurity meanness should appear in one whom we loved would it not alter all our feelings.}⟩ And if these qualities should increase to a great to an infinite degree would it not increase our attachment. On the contrary, if the opposite qualities of cruelty falsehood hatred impurity meanness shd. appear in one whom we loved would it not alter our feelings? ¶ I say then that the natural object of this sentiment of love in us is infinite goodness & though the objects on which it dwells in this world are imperfect yet the passion is true & noble}↓⟩ ¶ Every

40–(30)18   ¶ ↑It . . . be.⟨"⟩ Like . . . was ⟨said⟩ ↑⟨owned⟩ avowed↓ . . . of ⟨character⟩ ↑human nature↓, . . . loving." (St Evremond.↓ ¶ ↑Now . . . noble.↓ [last addition in ink over erased pencil; the pencil layer differs as follows: ". . . satisfied a deep affection . . . reside in its object; purity, . . . would ⟨not⟩ it not . . . in this world are imperfect—yet . . ."] [end of page] ¶ ⟨Let me ⟨give two or three specimens⟩ illustrate this position by considering two or three sentiments which seem to be a sort of ⟨imperfect religion⟩ an idolatry or imperfect religion & to be a prostitution of the affections taking the place of the love of God.⟩

⟨1.⟩ ↑Another . . . to ⟨give itself⟩ go . . . found in↓ ⟨T⟩the sentiment of *loyalty* ⟨⟨of⟩ to⟩ or . . . ↑a passion↓

Page 30

20–36   or ⟨personal⟩ ↑private↓ . . . into the ↑personal↓ acquaintance ⟨of & personal relations to⟩ ↑with↓ the sovereign, in the ⟨lower classes⟩ ↑great body of people↓ [emendation in pencil] it ⟨became⟩ ↑⟨is⟩has been↓ . . . worship; & ⟨men would⟩ ↑hundreds of times men have↓ [over "hundreds of times" in pencil] march↑ed↓ ⟨alone⟩ in . . . ardor, ⟨all for the sake⟩ ↑in . . . love↓ . . . but ⟨but⟩ once, ↑perhaps never↓ of no great merit, & ⟨perhaps⟩ ↑possibly↓ a ⟨very worthless⟩ person. ↑of loathsome vices.↓ [end of page] ¶ ⟨↑Theres no end to anecdotes of this description. Well what does it show↓⟩ [addition in pencil; canceled by being written over by the following, crowded at the top of the page:] ⟨It⟨↑It is related by Segur in his account of Bonapartes Russian Campaign that in crossing a frozen river ⟨ma⟩ the ice broke & many ⟨soldiers⟩ ↑of the troops↓ were lost One ↑soldier↓ who ↑after↓ struggled long ⟨waved his cap⟩ ↑being↓ benumbed with cold ⟨being⟩ ↑and↓ unable to extricate himself, yet found strength to wave his cap & cry Long live the Emperor, & then sunk in the icy waters.

Story in Segur's Russian Campaign↓⟩ [Below this addition, and occupying most of the page, is an earlier version of the ninth paragraph of the sermon:] ¶ ⟨Akin to this though far more familiar is the passion of love, which often uses the language of extravagance & approaches to worship. It is familiar to you all how ⟨mu⟩ universal is the tendency in the ardent imagination of youthful affection to clothe

the beloved object in ideal perfection↑s↓ & to utter the feelings in expressions of self devotion which seem ridiculous to others & if exactly applied to the persons would be so. But the feeling is genuine in the mind of the lover. He really adores the excellences which he contemplates although they do not exist as he supposes in the character of his friend.⟩ [This is followed by a passage, crowded at the bottom of the page, that concludes the anecdote from Segur begun in the addition at the top of the page:] ⟨↑We read these incidents with a mixture of admiration & pity admiration for the glorious disinterestedness of the soldier & pity for yᵉ unworthy direction it had taken. We say the sentiment is right but the direction of it is not right↓ [end of page] ↑It . . . oftener ⟨wasted⟩ ↑lavished↓ . . . right.↓

37–(31)1   ¶ ⟨It⟩ ↑These facts↓ show⟨s⟩ plainly . . . will ⟨accomplish far more⟩ ↑exert powers↓ in . . . man ⟨than⟩ they would ↑n↓ever . . . advantage. ¶ ⟨It⟩ ↑They↓ show⟨s⟩ that

Page 31

3–4   unreturned, ⟨⟨{what is it but is that which in all savage nations has elevated the heroes into gods & gave them altars & priests.}⟩⟩ What . . . of ⟨that affection⟩ pure
7–8   which ⟨hants⟩ ↑haunts↓
8–9   these ⟨ca⟩ instances . . . with ⟨far⟩ ↑a↓
11   ever ⟨serve⟩ ↑furnish↓ the mind ⟨as⟩ ↑with↓ a ⟨sufficient⟩ rule
12–14   ↑a star↓ . . . instruction, ⟨& neither of these can give it; neither of these then can be the object for which the mind was made.⟩ ↑In short . . . as ⟨the sentiment.⟩ ↑its love.↓↓ [last emendation in pencil]
16–17   either ⟨love or loyalty⟩ [canceled in pencil and ink] ↑of . . . alluded↓ . . . ↑or↓ [addition in pencil]
18–19   homage ⟨made⟩ paid . . . but ⟨a respect paid by proud men⟩ to
24   given.
31   were ⟨a⟩ sacred ⟨principle⟩, & its [cancellations in pencil]
34   & ↑has↓ extended
35–38   ↑in . . . ruled↓ [ink over pencil] . . . ¶ ↑⟨It may have rendered a man the⟩ ↑And . . . form ⟨one⟩ ↑single↓ character↑s↓ an↓ image . . . reproach↓ [paragraph added and emended in pencil]

Page 32

1–2   make ⟨the blood⟩ ↑our hearts↓
3   a ⟨sublime⟩ religion,
5–10   gospel. ⟨⟨{It was his admiration of the generous sentiments of the apostle, which made⟩ Anthony . . . miracles, ⟨say⟩ ↑was . . . character↓ of St Paul, ⟨that, "that man was so⟩ ↑whom ⟨he called a⟩ he . . . of a↓ true & perfect a gentleman↑.↓, ⟨that he should believe in miracles, if any where Paul had explicitly said, that he ⟨w⟩ had wrought one."}⟩ [brackets in pencil] ¶ And . . . ↑morality↓
13   {in . . . poet,} [brackets in pencil]
19   natural ⟨direction⟩ tendency

23   it ⟨permits the grossest sensual indulgences⟩ ↑is lust & pride↓.
      [emendation in pencil]

24   foundation. ⟨It⟩ For

31   action↑,↓ [comma in pencil; in the next sentence, the first and third
      "i" in "insufficient" dotted in pencil]

35   ↑& the↓ industrious

Page 33

1–5   ¶ ↑It . . . a ⟨woman.⟩ ↑friend of another sex.↓ . . . fellowmen.↓
      [paragraph in pencil]

6–8   degree [The word is lightly overwritten with an X in pencil, not a
      characteristic mode of cancellation with Emerson; if he meant to
      express displeasure with the word choice, he has not supplied an
      alternative.] noble principles; ⟨but⟩ [semicolon possibly altered from
      a comma when "but" was canceled] they . . . selfishness. but ⟨they⟩
      ↑their objects↓ [last emendation in pencil]

12   sentiment↑,↓ [comma in pencil]

16   The⟨se⟩ sentiments

20–21   of ⟨our⟩ ↑a↓ political

24   exercise⟨s⟩ these

24–25   God. ⟨For this the soul was made. If these loves were natural, this is as
      natural. If these were good & beneficent—this is far more good &
      useful. These were insufficient but this fills up all measure. It is a
      perfect motive⟩ ¶ Let . . . thoughts ⟨the highest⟩ ↑another↓

27–⟨34⟩3 sentiments. ¶ ⟨What is faith in God? Do I speak to any young men
      who have hungered & thirsted for a good they have not found; who
      complain that life is tame & listless who cannot sleep upon their
      pillow for the ambition that is in them to do greater actions & lead a
      higher life than they see around them? Do I speak to any in mature
      years who have not been taught in vain by experience, who have been
      touched by a feeling sense of the hollowness of those objects we are
      striving after?⟩ [canceled in pencil and ink] ¶ ↑My friends You . . .
      solitude.↓ [addition in pencil] ¶ ⟨To such I say⟩ [canceled in pencil] I

28   this ⟨name of⟩ ↑the words 'faith in↓ God↑'↓

32–33   that ⟨it⟩ ↑this sentiment↓ . . . beneficent ⟨principles⟩ sentiments

34   wish ⟨fathom⟩ that . . . would ⟨fathom⟩ ↑explore↓

37–42   be ⟨wholly⟩ in heart & in soul the ⟨servant friend⟩ bondsman . . . of
      / a leader/some great man/, or . . . that ⟨soul⟩ ↑one↓ . . . beauty—
      a⟨n⟩ [canceled in pencil] ↑most↓ . . . watching, ⟨there⟩ he . . . &
      ⟨noble⟩ humane

Page 34

1   ↑the↓ thickest multitude⟨s⟩ &

5–6   dictated. ⟨{There are depths in the human soul which only this
      emotion can fathom. I believe this principle is little known to us (We
      are not yet smit with its ravishing beauty.) I believe it is one of those
      sentiments which is kindled here in the world tho but to a spark but
      which must fill with its light & heat the soul that would be happy.}⟩

⟨{Compare this emotion excited by contemplating the wisdom & goodness that created all things, with the admiration of a mortal, a king, or the received opinion of a few men.}⟩ [brackets, parentheses, and cancellation in pencil] Consider

7–9   the ⟨e⟩Eye . . . ↑up↓on

14–15   overruled. ⟨There is no desire of the mind that is not satisfied in God there is no thought of what is glorious & excellent in moral truth no pious affection no self denial no humility but the truth thereof is first & greatest in him the source of intelligence [end of page; canceled to this point in pencil] For Whence he saith do these hopes come to me Whence this wise judgment of right & wrong Whence these illimitable desires of a good not yet known but from Him?⟩ [these three sentences canceled in pencil and ink] ¶ ↑But↓ [ink over pencil] ⟨The⟩the

24   rooted ⟨& spread abroad its branches⟩—when

25   the ⟨mourner⟩ wretched,

32–38   dependance, & ⟨m⟩disappointment . . . will⟨,⟩ with

Page 35

1–8   him who ⟨is able to view from the naked summit of age the dreary years of the past—the friendless ungenial youth passing into grey hairs & not a companion left on the face of the earth⟩ ↑⟨stript of all & satisfied that in him is no strength yet exults ↑in↓ all that is good & fair he has a property in it thro his relation to God. The peace & joy that belong to deepest suffering are the miracles of faith⟩stript . . . faith.↓ [ink over pencil] ¶ ⟨The smooth cheek of youth & the wrinkled face of age make less difference to hi⟨m⟩s eye who is pressing on to lose himself in Him with whom one day is as a thousand years & a thousand years as one day. [II Peter 3:8]⟩ ¶ ↑↑I find↓ ⟨I⟩in . . . God."↓ ¶ ⟨The good man casts himself upon God with helpless trust. He feels that the satisfactions of his past life are but the joys of infancy compared to the riches that are in store for him. for he⟩ [cancellation in pencil] ↑And . . . powers for the good man↓ [addition in pencil]

16–18   of ⟨truth⟩ ↑conscience↓ hath ⟨the⟩ literally . . . God. [end of page] ⟨distinctions are annihilated. What are the deepest inequalities in human lot before him but varieties of discipline? And moreover ⟨they⟩ his sight converts the worst losses & pains into angels & helpers, for the happiest man in God's eye is the man of humblest & sweetest temper & that ⟨comes g⟩ ↑perfection↓ is formed in obscurity & dependance, & disappointment. ⟨There are those whose⟩ ↑His↓ heart out of deepest sorrow rises with rapture to its Author ⟨& again sinks in lowest submission to⟩ ask↑s↓ for higher blessings ↑yes &↓ without one tear of repining for those who are better endowed & better placed. To know to feel how low ⟨one⟩ ↑the↓ is, ⟨is not⟩ ↑causes no↓ [emendation in pencil] regret. No; ⟨this⟩ ↑for the↓ [emendation in pencil] tho't ⟨comes soon⟩ ↑springs↓ [emendation in pencil] ⟨& that tho't is⟩ ↑in⟨to⟩ [cancellation in pencil] his mind↓—

Can the lofty child of his election love him so well, at least can it cling
to his will with the submission of the shrunken ⟨aspen⟩ sufferer,
crushed by poverty & sensitive to the touch of error & shame of short
comings? No, an angel knows not the height & depth & breadth of
resignation. ↑like him who is able to view from the naked summit of
⟨years⟩ ↑age↓ the ⟨thorny boggy⟩ [canceled in pencil] ↑dreary years
of the↓ past, the friendless ungenial youth passing into ⟨hoary⟩
[canceled in pencil] ⟨age⟩ ↑grey hairs↓ & not ⟨one to drop a leaf of
remembrance⟩ ↑a companion left on the face of earth.↓↓⟩ ¶ ↑Finally↓
[in pencil] The

27–(36)25   love [end of page; the preceding paragraph is manifestly complete; at
this point two leaves have been cut out, with the following inscriptions
legible on the stubs (leaf 1, recto)]: h / w / & / [these three lines in
pencil, followed by two lines apparently blank] / a to / & turn /
conso / a vi / outwa / soul / [leaf 1, verso:] if / ble / [two lines
blank?] / ly / ave / id / us / [three lines blank?] / man / but his / you
/ these few / object / [leaf 2, recto:] / [illegible] / F / ↑We↓ fee / the /
the / f / the / he / wh / de / so / no / [leaf 2, verso:] ing / man? / en
/ s / [two illegible line ends] / ible / edy / fflic / ants / tried /
thwarted / & be not / But cleave / ↑the head↓ / . It / courage / evil /
for / for the / hile we / as long / with / [end of page; the remainder of
the sermon, on loose sheets, is evidently a revision, possibly composed
for the third delivery:] ¶ ↑My friends . . . eternal.— ¶ 2^d C. Dec
1833↓

29   principle Are
31   place Is
31–32   Is ⟨it a reasonable⟩ there . . . men ⟨as ignorant as we are⟩ atoms
40   an ⟨unlimited⟩ infinite object. & therein

Page 36

2   mind↑,—↓should [addition in pencil]
6   worth ⟨⟨{which gave & give him real pleasure.}⟩⟩ [brackets in pencil]
              It
7   instead of ⟨hunting⟩ ↑painfully seeking↓
16–17   not ↑heed↓ ⟨the Celestial Visitor who⟩ the . . . ↑with↓ [last addition
              in ink over pencil]
18–19   practicable↑,↓ [comma in pencil] I know I have a⟨n advocate⟩
              ↑witness↓ . . . thing / {a thousand} / many / times
21–22   gratification⟨,⟩; [semicolon dotted in pencil]
23–24   Spirit↑,↓ [comma in pencil] . . . & ⟨consideration⟩ ↑advantages↓
24   For th⟨is⟩ese will

[Following the end of the sermon, on a scrap of paper attached with sealing wax to the
last leaf:]
    There is no such thing as atheism
    But only choice of theisms
    The whole structure of man is theistical
    Witness the universality of Admiration

Consider particularly the sentiments of
1. Love; 2. Loyalty; 3; Honour
These are deifications
But are these sufficient principles? No
They prefigure & point at the true principle which is the love of God. ↑Carry either of
them out ad infinitum & it becomes that.↓
⟨The⟩ Describe the greatness & applications of this sentiment.

[On the page to which the scrap above is affixed:] plurima nix

Sermon CXXXVIII

Manuscript: Six sheets folded to make four pages each; folios stacked and sewn along the
left margin with white thread. Pages measure 25 x 20.2–20.3 cm.

[Above Bible text:] CHRISTMAS 1831

[The following passage, inscribed in pencil above the first paragraph, was composed for
the third delivery, December 27, 1835, at East Lexington, and is therefore excluded from
the clear text:] ↑Day before y was celebrated by a large portion of Xdom as yᵉ festival of
yᵉ birth of Xt. At yˢ season yᵉ Roman Ch yᵉ Greek Ch. yᵉ Eng Ch set apart 12 days
of holy time. There is something pleasing & becoming in giving some notice to yᵉ
occasion↓

Lines	*Page 37*
1	festival ⟨↑which is this day celebrated by Christian Chur↓⟩ welcome [addition and cancellation in pencil]
4	a ⟨personal⟩ Saviour
6	how ⟨far⟩ it
8–11	as ⟨the⟩ moments . . . force ⟨upon the⟩ in improving the arts, ⟨the laws⟩ the
12–13	↑whether by discovery of new region↓
21	& ⟨larger⟩ ↑more liberal↓

	Page 38
2–7	India. ↑{Insert A}↓ [On the preceding page, otherwise blank, a passage marked "A":] ↑{It . . . among ⟨nat⟩ tribes . . . law.↓
10–11	the ⟨Greek invasion⟩ ↑Macedonian invader↓ [emendation in pencil] . . . conque⟨sts.⟩rors.
12–13	opinion. ↑that these /evil/turbulent/ men were instruments of great benefit to the world.↓ [addition in pencil; variant in ink]
14	selfish ⟨men as Alexander & Caesar & Bonaparte⟩ [canceled in pencil and ink] ↑persons↓
17	Attila, they
23	¶ But ⟨obser⟩ we
25–26	↑not by them;↓ [in ink over pencil] . . . ↑great↓ fire of London ⟨↑AD 1666↓⟩ finally . . . city. ⟨It⟩ ↑The benefit↓
27–28	They ⟨sought⟩ [canceled in pencil and ink] were . . . insane↑,↓ [comma in pencil]

33–35   ¶ ↑We commemorate {this day} . . . race. ↑attended . . . mischief↓↓
             [last addition in ink over pencil; the pencil layer has "evil" for "mischief"]
35–38   empire ⟨these were the means by which benefit was bought to the
             human race⟩. [canceled in pencil and ink] But . . . is ⟨of⟩ an element
             of [end of line] ⟨of⟩ human
38–41   ↑not indirectly but directly↓ [in ink over pencil] the tamer of ↑savage↓
             . . . civilization↑;↓ . . . eye↑;↓ . . . order↑;↓ . . . heart↑,↓ [punctua-
             tion added in pencil]
44   of ⟨the⟩ spiritual

Page 39

1   spiritual↑.↓ [period in pencil]
5–6   A ⟨consummate⟩ child
9–10   not he said that . . . heaven.
12–16   ourselves. ¶ ⟨Now⟩ I wish to ⟨point⟩ ↑ask↓ [addition in pencil] your
             attention to ⟨two⟩ ↑some↓ circumstances of difference ⟨between⟩
             ↑which . . . interval↓ . . . by ⟨these⟩ ↑vulgar↓ . . . by ⟨Christ⟩
             ↑Jesus of Nazareth↓. ¶↑1.↓
17   their ⟨original⟩ design, & none of it ⟨designed⟩ ↑projected↓
20   direct ⟨intention⟩ ↑purpose↓
24   the ⟨go⟩ kingdom of heaven, is now, ⟨that⟩ as
26   ¶ ["2." is supplied to complement the "1." added by Emerson.]
             ↑Secondly;↓ ⟨That t⟩The good
29   end↑s↓
30   force of the his
33   that ⟨he contemplated a⟩ strife
37–38   ↑And . . . name↓

Page 40

1–2   ↑what was called↓ his c⟨hurch⟩ause. ↑It . . . cause.↓
16   truer ⟨copy⟩ likeness
18   ¶ ↑3.↓
19–21   ↑The . . . cause↓
22–23   it ⟨comes without observation.⟩ ↑is . . . ↑by↓ . . . ends.↓
25–26   swarming ⟨millions⟩ ↑nations↓ [addition in ink over pencil] . . .
             Christ, ⟨how do⟩ these numbers ⟨shrink⟩ ↑disappear↓.
28–35   who ⟨ha⟩ though . . . comfort ↑whom . . . good↓ [addition in
             pencil] . . . faithful ⟨persons of⟩ souls
40–42   ↑And . . . cause↓ ¶ ⟨These are the true apostles of religion these are
             they who mightily persuade us of the divinity of faith They are but a
             few but they hold the ark It is a mustard seed It is a little leaven in a great
             lump It is the overpowering persuasion of good actions of the gospel put
             in practice that enables it to keep its ground & gain ground ⟨in⟩ against
             all the skepticism and all the vice of society.⟩ ¶ It . . . the ⟨g⟩ word.

Page 41

1   Flesh, ⟨that reconciles men to God⟩ the
5   the ⟨spread⟩ ↑victories↓

10	to ⟨all men yᵉ gos⟩ every
11–14	↑be no . . . shall be↓ be no [in ink over the following in pencil:] The other movements on the world have spent yᵐselves these empires of Cyrus & Alexander & Caesar & Napoleon have
16	hatred. ⟨And⟩ But
36	good. ⟨All⟩Until

[Following the end of the sermon:] When we consider what his cause is, that it is the cause of moral truth we feel a confidence that nothing can shake that it must prevail. It will not come suddenly it will not come by observation [Luke 17:20], not by wars nor earthshakings nor by convulsions of society nor ⟨by⟩ to multitudes but to each mind alone in the improvement of its aims the conquest of its passions the purification of its thots its resemblance & so its union to God. ["It will . . . of its thots" in pencil]

Sermon CXXXIX

Manuscript: Six sheets folded to make four pages each; single leaves are inserted in the first two folios, and after the first, second, and third folios. Pages measure 25 x 20.2 cm. A quarter-sheet now taped to the verso of the last leaf was originally affixed to the recto of the same leaf with red sealing wax. The folios, single leaves, and quarter-sheet are sewn along the left margin with white thread. The fact that the stitching includes the removed quarter-sheet implies recent restoration.

[Above Bible text:] {Last night of the year 1831.

Lines	*Page 42*
Bible Text	⟨/Brethren/For/ if our heart⟨s⟩ condemn us↑,↓ ⟨not⟩God then ⟨we have confidence toward ⟨God;⟩⟨For⟩⟩ ↑is greater than our heart↓⟩ ⟨i⟩If our heart⟨s⟩ condemn us, God is greater than our heart⟨s⟩ & knoweth all things ↑x x x if our heart condemn us not then have we confidence toward God. I John. 3. 20, 21↓ [This complicated revision resulted from Emerson's having initially written the two verses, from memory, in reverse order; he tried to correct the error by revising I John 3:21 to produce the text of I John 3:20; canceling that effort, he crowded I John 3:21 between the text as he had written it and the first paragraph of the sermon. This revision casts important light on Emerson's method of composition: the fact that he does not make the memorial error of "hearts" for "heart" in the addition and the fact that the citation belongs to the added matter strongly imply that Emerson wrote the Bible text before he composed the sermon, that he relied on memory for the text, that he looked up the passage to confirm the wording, and that he made the correction before the first delivery.]
3	↑about to be↓ fulfilled; another season ⟨a⟩of
5–6	gloom. ⟨The air of /vast regions is loaded/populous countries is surcharged/ with pestilence. The⟩ The . . . ↑& the fear of change↓.
7–9	evil. ⟨The air of populous countries is surcharged with pestilence⟩ A frightful plague ↑baffling . . . science,↓ has ravaged Asia ⟨&⟩ Northern ↑& Central↓ Europe & now threatens ⟨England⟩ the South
10	¶ ↑In our own country↓ The

Page 43

2–5   {And . . . ↑few↓ . . . God}

6   this /mournful sunset/clouded evening/ [variant in pencil]

13–14   commemorate. [The following paragraph, in pencil, was added for
         the second delivery, January 3, 1836, in East Lexington:] ↑¶ Since we
         last assembled in this place another year has been completed. Another
         orbit of the planet we dwell upon has been fulfilled; another season of
         action ended; another portion of our decreasing life cut off. How
         various have been the effects of the departed year! How much
         admonition to man in its closing hours! Before it is yet wholly
         forgotten in yᵉ resistless pressure of new cares & daily vanities let me
         ask your attention to some reflections ⟨upon yᵉ⟩ that grow out of yᵉ
         hour↓ ¶ And

15–16   for ¶ ⟨2. What we have done with it⟩ ¶ 2. What

18   is ⟨Time⟩ a year? What is Time? ⟨It is only ⟨measured⟩ manifested
         by its use.⟩ Time,

19   What ⟨to us⟩ is

20   vices. ⟨The shoreless starless etern⟩ Time

21   ↑as yet↓ we ⟨softly⟩ slept

23   ↑before our birth↓,

27   ↑of 30 50 or 70 years↓.

28   is ⟨in⟩ what

29   its nature ↑of that mind↓. Time [emendation rejected as incomplete]

35–37   fuel time . . . growth time . . . ↑the play of↓ their bodily functions
         {time to man is the manner in which he answers the great end of his
         existence.} ¶ Time [The bracketed passage is revised below.]

39   the ⟨unfolding⟩ imitation

Page 44

4–5   love. ¶ ⟨2.⟩ Now

7   year ⟨wh⟩that

10   suppose ⟨there is⟩ ↑that↓

12   terms ⟨as plain &⟩ ↑far more↓

13   the ⟨c⟩ fact ↑to↓ [addition in pencil] . . . to ⟨press upon your⟩ ↑call
         your↓ [emendation in pencil]

14   Hour ⟨follows⟩ ↑steals↓

18–19   of ⟨so⟩ the . . . year. ⟨Meantime there is a fa⟩ ↑↑Ah, my brother,↓
         There . . . hour book.↓

22   secret ⟨but unerring sentence⟩ ↑verdict↓

23–25   ↑nothing but↓ . . . the ⟨present state⟩ ↑actual condition↓

25–26   see /the wond⟨rous⟩erful/what consummate/ [variant in pencil]

29   a ⟨nobler benevolence.⟩ ↑kinder heart.↓

30–31   ↑Do . . . him?↓

31   you ⟨governed⟩ ↑reined in↓

33–34   have ⟨placed⟩ ↑bettered↓ yourself in a ⟨much more desireable station
         & had wealth at command⟩ ↑worldly point of view↓

35   ↑increased↓

36   beings. {You [bracket in pencil]

40–42   Have you /spoken sharply to/reproached/ [variant in pencil] your /
         neighbor/brother/ [variant in pencil] & ⟨chuckled⟩ ↑↑laughed↓ in
         your sleeve↓ ⟨because you touched him⟩ ↑⟨bec⟩that your insult had
         galled him↓? you have ⟨made⟩ ↑soured↓ your own temper↑.↓ ⟨worse⟩.
         You ⟨are more⟩ ↑have let in↓ a devil ⟨than before⟩ ↑into your
         mind↓.

44–(45)1   a /better/more delicate/ [variant in pencil]

Page 45

3   a ⟨lying cheating drinking⟩ ↑false dishonest intemperate↓

4–5   is ⟨there.⟩ ↑not the less admirable.↓

8   is ⟨born⟩ ↑received↓;

10–14   but ⟨it⟩ whatever . . . you⟨r character.⟩. Every act↑ion↓ . . . ↑and of
         . . . the year↓ [addition in pencil] . . . are, ⟨added one stone to the
         pile⟩

14–15   ↑Nothing . . . himself.↓

16–18   brother, ⟨how you have spent⟩ ↑where is the record of↓ ⟨your⟩ ↑the↓
         . . . thoughts, ⟨the princip⟩ ↑your↓ habits, ⟨y⟩& your . . . distinct
         than ⟨this answer⟩ ↑its language↓ [last emendation in pencil]

19   ↑Hearken to the verdict.↓

21–22   things. ¶ ⟨There is the answer⟩ ¶ There

30   independant

33–35   be /used/valued/ . . . year ⟨I proceed to ask⟩ ↑let us proceed each to
         ask himself before God↓ 'how ⟨have you⟩ ↑he has↓

38   lie ⟨idle⟩ inactive.

39–(46)5   it. {You . . . dregs of ⟨poor performance by which we keep each
         other in countenance⟩ ↑custom↓ . . . mind⟨.⟩, ↑that star ↑that . . .
         it↓ that ⟨image⟩mirror . . . soul.↓ ¶ ⟨Time to you depends on what
         you can do with it not on what your brother or your friends have done
         or can do. Leave all & consult your own heart⟩ ¶ Especially ⟨take
         this view of⟩ ↑bend your thots upon↓ . . . views. ⟨Y⟩ As . . .
         deceived⟨.⟩ ↑as to your own merit.↓

Page 46

6   they, & ⟨y⟩ so

9–11   at ⟨the thought⟩ ↑it↓, . . . night↑—↓then

14–15   known. ¶ And for this reason ¶ And for this reason that if ⟨a man is
         accustomed⟩ death

18–20   drinks ⟨in dress & pride⟩ & . . . must ⟨be his ruin⟩ ↑appear . . .
         pleasures↓.

25   if ⟨you are accustomed⟩ your

33   time i.e. . . . proposed has

39   independant of death they

Page 47

3   us ⟨not⟩, God

5–6   done ⟨by us⟩ with . . . spending↑,↓ [emendations in pencil]

10–12   truth. ⟨Tomorrow is a new day. Tomorrow is⟩ ↑New days have
         come↓ a new year ↑opened↓. Neither time nor truth ⟨will⟩ stop when
         /this/the/ year ends. [emendations rejected as having been done for
         the second delivery]

15–17   made. ⟨If God shall spare us to another day⟩ ↑In this year↓ our
         [emendation rejected as having been made for the second delivery]
         . . . certain ⟨& momentous⟩ as

23–24   uncertainty ↑{↓in the verdict of God↑}↓ in the decision of the day of
         Judgment ↑or as to the↓. [additions in pencil, apparently to produce
         the reading as given]

25–28   {Doth . . . life.}

32–42   terms ⟨the⟩ ↑our↓ future fate. [In the lower right corner of the page is
         the following notation in pencil, apparently not part of the sermon:] "I
         had rather see yᵉ impressions of a godlike nature upon my own soul
         than have a vision from heaven, or an angel sent to tell me yᵗ my name
         was enrolled in yᵉ Book of Life." [On a quarter-sheet now taped to the
         last page of the MS but originally affixed with red sealing wax at this
         point (so as to cover the pencil inscription) is the following para-
         graph:] ↑/⟨le⟩Let us then/I exhort you then/ devote . . . characters,
         ⟨their love &⟩ what ⟨love⟩ is their love; ⟨what is their⟩ which . . .
         chastisments. ↑To . . . gloom↓ [addition in pencil] . . . strong then
         . . . heaven.↓ [On the verso of this quarter-sheet is a draft of the
         sermon's third paragraph (some text lost in the cutting of the right
         edge):] ["]Nothing is more precious than time, & no [thing?] less
         valued." St Bernard. ¶ Time the Teacher ¶ How many have seen their
         hop[es] shattered, their families ⟨wasted⟩ desolated, their strength
         wea[kened] their substance wasted the[ir] names dishonoured. How
         [many] have lost all that was dear & [unrecoverable word] seems a
         poor afterpiece. ¶ How many have lost groun[d in] the race of duty &
         usefulnes[s] [end of quarter-sheet verso] ¶ If

                              Page 48

4–7   in /solitude/yourself/, [variant in pencil] . . . irretrievabl⟨e⟩y
         ↑fixed↓, ["e" altered to "y" and "fixed" added in pencil] . . . further,
         ⟨&⟩before

9   Brethren, The

                          Sermon CXL

Manuscript: A single leaf followed by five sheets folded to make four pages each; pages
measure 25 x 20 cm. Though the single leaf has become separated, it once was sewn—
with the five stacked folios—along the left margin with white thread.

[Above Bible text:] Friendship. [in pencil]

Lines   *Page 49*
Bible Text   ⟨Let . . . I Cor. 10.24⟩
3   to ⟨a⟩ one

6–8   sanctioned th⟨is⟩ese . . . its ⟨relish⟩ capacity
12   noble. ⟨A⟩ The
18–22   us ⟨run instantly &⟩ take . . . us it . . . aid. ¶ ⟨But⟩ ↑As . . .
         strict↑er↓ society of ⟨Friendship⟩ ↑minds↓,↓

Page 50

15–16   knowledge, ↑for↓ love of virtue, ↑for love of pleasure,↓
17–18   evil. ⟨⟨They⟩ ↑Other men↓ are mirrors of ourselves. ⟨They are⟩ all
         our friends are living books in which we see the consequences of
         ⟨actions⟩ a great variety of actions exhibited. They are collectively a
         series of experiments by which every day the most important practical
         conclusions are taught us, & they confirm ⟨in⟩ by facts the ↑secret↓
         instructions of our minds. We learn ↑by↓ observing the bent & the
         effect of their various talents, what man can do. We see illustrated in
         their histories, the progress & end of every passion.⟩ ¶ These
19–21   little ⟨stricter⟩ narrower . . . of ⟨good⟩ ↑virtuous↓ friends; the benefi-
         [end of line]⟨cence of that provision that has made every one ac-
         quainted with some men who are possessed of some virtues in a high
         degree.
             ↑John Orpiment. Edward Ground.↓
             They form to a good man the /sweetness/ornament/solace/ of life
         Beautiful is the gift which the virtuous man confers upon the society
         in which he lives. He gives the warmth of life & reality to virtues
         which before were only commandments. He shows them in action,
         how possible & easy ⟨they⟩ ↑& graceful they↓ are, ⟨to be done⟩ &
         what honour they bring. ↑They confute every objection & parry
         every sneer at the romance of virtue↓ A good man is the liveliest
         revelation of God that can be. No description of God can ever be half
         so affecting as this clear image of him in a man.
             Every man can ⟨do⟩ practise some ↑one↓ virtue or disclose some
         peculiar talent ↑much↓ beyond ⟨the⟩ any other, & beyond the imita-
         tion of any other man. In witnessing that, we have been encouraged
         by seeing how far human nature has gone in one direction, & that
         success saves us from all foolish discouragements of the weakness of
         human nature on that side. And when in our tho'ts we put together
         the excellences of all the best persons we have an image that raises us
         above the attainments of any ⟨man⟩ mortal.⟩
             ⟨In the silence of night⟩ We
23   of ⟨temptation⟩ ↑discontent↓,
25   better ⟨th⟩ men
28–29   children. ↑the . . . temper.↓ ¶ ⟨A true friend is⟩ As
36   observes; "Though

Page 51

1–2   ↑whilst↓ . . . the ⟨theory⟩ image . . . friendship whilst ⟨it fills⟩ all
         ardent minds ⟨with great delight⟩ ↑have . . . it↓,
6   ↑in this world,↓
9   ↑alone↓

15   a ⟨barrier⟩ wall
16–20   feel. {And . . . there ⟨are still parts of our nature not⟩ is . . . other.} ¶
            ⟨Do⟩ ↑And hence,↓ ⟨we⟩We ⟨not⟩ see . . . day ⟨apparently⟩ intent
24   you⟨↑?↓ as⟩ ↑⟨as an⟩ ↑as the most↓ impressive & amazing ↑of↓
            fact↑s↓?↓
25–27   of ⟨their⟩ your . . . them? ¶ ⟨And⟩ ¶ Yes ⟨our common necessities⟩
            we
28–30   ↑And . . . unknown.↓ ¶ ⟨To every man he is a different person. ¶
            ⟨But⟩ Every man ⟨↑he meets↓⟩ according to his state of mind induces
            ⟨us to⟩ ↑the topics of the↓ convers⟨e⟩ation↑.↓ ⟨with him.⟩ And if a
            mind of higher order than yet he has found, should converse with him
            he would then deal with thoughts which have never yet parted from
            the silence of his own consciousness⟩ [After the cancellation, at the
            bottom of the page, is the following notation:] {The more friendship,
            the more egotism.} [end of page] ¶ For
31   ↑those↓
33–⟨52⟩3   ↑{↓You . . . limit.↑}↓ [brackets in pencil]
34–35   beyond ²{the state of your health} & ¹{the signs of the sky}.
37–38   sympathy / on / in regard to the same / ⟨religious⟩ literary

                              Page 52

1–3   are ⟨chosen⟩ ↑a↓ ⟨o⟩few . . . still ↑always I believe↓ with
7   ¶ ↑Thus . . . shared.↓
11–14   ↑& perish↓ unknown⟨,⟩; & ↑shall↓ . . . unsatisfied. No; ⟨⟨They⟩
            in a world where nothing was made in vain, they⟩ ↑{Insert X}↓ [On
            the facing page, otherwise blank, is a passage marked "X" written
            over a draft of the same in pencil:] ⟨↑↑It is a maxim of the wise so long
            confirmed that it has become a maxim of the ignorant that nothing
            was made in vain least of all that which is best & noblest in our
            nature. These unsatisfied desires↓⟩ {It is . . . nature.}↓ [end of Insert
            "X"] ↑These unsatisfied desires↓
15–16   {We . . . world.} This ⟨earnest⟩ ↑restless↓
23–24   continued / enjoyment / action / of them here↑,↓ [comma in pencil]
30–31   ↑And . . . end.↓
31–38   of / action / virtue / to be ⟨feeble⟩ ↑low↓ . . . to ⟨a⟩ vanity, . . .
            persist feel that you are / fighting / contending / . . . the ⟨society⟩
            ↑fellowship↓ . . . ↑all over the creation↓
42   not being independant of the body ⟨we cannot⟩ no

                              Page 53

2–4   are ⟨thus⟩ ↑for the time↓ . . . should ⟨f⟩ act . . . you ⟨cannot⟩ are
            . . . friend, persevere
6   not ⟨by⟩ neighborhood
8–12   ↑at↓ . . . faith; ⟨& tend⟩ unknown . . . roof. [Here follows a
            notation apparently inspired by the preceding paragraph and appar-
            ently written after the first delivery of the sermon:] ↑{Note. Society
            goes by affinity not by vicinage. Men mistake in compassing sea &
            land to get introduced into certain society. They are not in it, when

they are there. Leibnitz in his chamber at   sympathizes & associates
more truly with Newton commands his respect & love & stimulates
more of his actions than Sir John & Lady Jane in the parlor & within
sound of the voice of the sage.}

   ↑{"Let us but reflect how many men we have seen & known, &
acknowledge how little they have been to us, how little we to them—
& what must be our feelings? We meet the man of talent, without
conversing with him; the scholar, without learning from him; the
traveller, without seeking to gain information from him; the kind-[end
of line]hearted man, without making one effort to please him. And
alas this is not the case in transient intercourse alone. Thus it is that
societies & families treat their most valuable members,—towns, their
worthiest citizens—subjects, their best princes—nations, their most
excellent men." *Goethe*}↓↓ ¶ Once

14–24   ↑full of wisdom, & full of tenderness,↓ . . . mind⟨,⟩ can . . . soul?
[The remainder of the paragraph is an addition in ink over a draft of
the same in erased pencil:] ↑⟨⟨Our⟩ if it be true that our thots of God
are always more or less worthy as are our own characters is it not the
effect of our partial views & many offences that he has been clothed
by us with so much dread Has he not made these affections for the
contemplation & enjoyment of himself & when we become more
obedient shall we not perceive the meaning of the revelation that God
is love⟩If . . . characters⟨;⟩, is . . . Love"?↓

[The following notations appear after the end of the sermon:] Script. Prov. 27. Matt.
"receive as much again" &c. One Lord one faith God in all [to this point in pencil]

{The conversation between two men is necessarily limited to what is common ground
to both. A wise man meets an ignorant man, & this space is very narrow; he meets
another, & that space is much larger,—covers many more topics; he meets his friend, &
it is vastly enlarged, embracing all ⟨common⟩ ↑general↓ & all personal topics; but it
never, I believe covers the whole field of thought. There is always something unsaid that
is better than any thing that is said. There is always the ⟨certainty⟩ ↑sense↓ that the
communication is not perfect. 'One soul in two bodies,' as Aristotle defined friendship
[Quoted in Montaigne, "Of Friendship," *Essays* (London, 1693), 1:297]. And I suppose
there is always the certainty that if a greater & yet kindred mind should come, it would
quicken into expression tho'ts that now are recognized only.} 9 Jan.

{The communication never becomes one with the cogitation. "Counsel in yᵉ heart of
man is like deep water, but a man of understanding will draw it out⟨" Prov⟩ Most men
will proclaim ⟨his⟩ every one his own goodness but a faithful man who can find." Prov.
20; 5,6. [At the bottom of the page, the capital letter "R" is inscribed six times in pencil.]

Sermon CXLI

Manuscript (earlier version): Seven sheets folded to make four pages each, sewn along the
left margin with white thread. Pages measure 25 x 20.2 cm.

Lines   *Page 54*
7   the ⟨body.⟩ ↑flesh.↓
8–10   ↑And . . . self↓ This . . . religion ¶ ⟨I do not think⟩ ↑Few↓

14   of ⟨damned⟩ ↑accursed↓
21–24   religion↑.↓ ⟨that⟩ God ↑in his government↓ . . . us↑.↓ ⟨that⟩ our
                . . . us↑.↓, & ⟨that⟩ in . . . the ⟨universe⟩ ↑whole order of things↓
                we ⟨are as⟩ ↑act like↓ children who ↑think . . . or↓ shut their eyes↑.↓
                ⟨& think you cannot see them.⟩ We
26–⟨55⟩1   hurt ⟨ruin⟩ ↑or↓ . . . none ⟨in the universe⟩ ↑else↓ can harm us↑.↓
                ⟨⟨or⟩ but ourselves.⟩ ¶ Do thyself no harm. ⟨No one but yourself
                can harm you.⟩ No power ⟨↑can be↓⟩ in ⟨the universe⟩ ↑existence↓

Page 55

1–7   If ⟨instead of⟩ it . . . governs ⟨in⟩ the ⟨universe⟩ ↑world↓ . . . man.
                Do we . . . ↑in his own breast,↓
8–11   I ⟨make this incongruous⟩ put . . . enjoy ⟨f⟩ grace
17–19   & ↑He . . . for↓ . . . work⟨man⟩ to
20   ¶ ↑No; God . . . other↓ But ⟨the way by which mischief enters⟩ we
21   ↑much↓
23–27   itself—w⟨e⟩hen . . . myself, ↑⟨all good is vain⟩ all . . . vain,↓ . . .
                creation / what are they to me / the . . . Society /
28–29   ↑like . . . in↓ . . . a ⟨troubled⟩ ↑broken↓
33   ↑monarch of↓ Persia⟨n king⟩ was
35   sentence. ⟨The harm⟩ "Nothing
38–⟨56⟩3   ¶↑It . . . ye ⟨do⟩ ↑render↓ . . . apostles ¶ Who . . . good. ¶ That . . .
                reap.↓ [addition and emendation in pencil on an otherwise blank MS
                p. 11, opposite]

Page 56

6–8   it, ⟨that⟩ [end of line] that . . . that ⟨the least action h⟩ every . . . Day
                [end of MS p. 10; MS p. 12 blank except for the following notations:]
                ↑There is a sublime proverb of antiquity that the dice of God are
                always loaded. [Sophocles; see *JMN* 6:178 and 215; used in *Nature*
                (*CW* 1:25), "Compensation" (*CW* 2:60), and "Worship" (*W* 6:221)]
                     We reap our own fruit though
                     Love wins love, honesty confidence, veracity credit temperance
                health, & peevishness ill will curses rebound dishonesty produces
                distrust & yᵉ indignation↓ [all but the first sentence in pencil; end of
                MS p. 12] ¶ There
8–10   ↑The . . . effect.↓
12   surprise. ⟨But in this world⟩ [canceled in pencil] there
14–16   planted. ↑⟨T⟩As we . . . benefits ⟨but⟩ ⟨and⟩ ["and" canceled in
                pencil] all . . . do↓
20   independance
22   in ⟨some things⟩ ↑their success↓
30   ↑that↓
35–39   ↑¶ We . . . dart ⟨we⟩ that . . . wrongdoers.↓

Page 57

4–6   unexpected ⟨revolution⟩ ↑disturbance↓ . . . want of ⟨circumspection⟩
                prudence ⟨or foresight⟩. ↑He . . . but th⟨is⟩e observer . . . wasteful.↓

9   we ⟨expect⟩ conclude
13–14   misadventures ⟨ha⟩ befal
16   parents. ⟨Enter⟩ Risks
19   {We
22   frugality ⟨ar⟩is
25–26   ↑Because . . . mind.↓
34   action these
36   by ⟨fixing our attention upon⟩ ↑a steady confidence in↓

Page 58

7–8   it ²{shall seem to hiss you as you walk in the street ¹{ & shall ⟨really lower your reputation⟩ among ↑sensibly affect the impression you make upon↓ men.
10–11   temporary & ⟨only of contingent advantage⟩ ↑can . . . man↓ The sacrifice of principle is ⟨eternal⟩ ↑permanent↓
15–18   ↑¶ Therefore . . . the ⟨call⟩ warning . . . ⟨w⟩exhorting . . . how ⟨dearly⟩ ↑sorely↓ . . . gained.↓ [addition and emendations in pencil]
28   end. ⟨O⟩ ↑Look at the opening future &↓
33   our ⟨a⟩ pursuits,
41–43   ↑¶ Let . . . cannot ⟨stu⟩ possibly ⟨study too much⟩ meditate . . . ↑as if he ⟨mad⟩was making↓ . . . live↓ [addition and emendations in pencil]

Page 59

3   ↑and . . . them↓
5   of an future

Manuscript (later version): One sheet folded to make four pages, each measuring 24.7 x 20 cm, followed by: a single leaf (24.2 x 20 cm); a sheet folded to make four pages, each measuring 24.3 x 20 cm; two nested folios, the pages of which measure 24.3 x 20 cm and 24.7 x 20 cm; a single leaf measuring 24.3 x 20 cm (blank save for a single sentence in pencil on verso); two leaves measuring 24.2 x 20 cm, the second of which is blank; a folio, the pages of which measure 24.3 x 20 cm, with a blank leaf of the same dimensions inserted; three folios, the pages of which measure, respectively, 24.3 x 20 cm, 24.6 x 20 cm, and 24.3 x 20 cm; and a mutilated single leaf measuring 24.3 x 20 cm. Though the first folio has become detached, the entire gathering was sewn along the left margin with white thread. The second leaf of the first folio is torn across the middle.

141

Do thyself no harm. Acts 16, 28

It is a maxim which all the discoveries of science have uniformly confirmed—that every contrivance of nature has some good for its object. Benefit, the greatest benefit of the individual & of the whole is every where sought. The voice of religion is one with the voice of nature. It saith to every man Do thyself no harm. And I adopt these words in a more extensive sense than that conveyed in the passage of ⟨Scripture⟩ [canceled in pencil] sacred history from which they are taken because they conveniently express a general moral law which is taught throughout the Scriptures & which comprehends the whole of our duty.

Do thyself no harm. Few men consider how sacred a possession is locked up within the
narrow boundary of a human frame. Few men think how much is contained in the word
Thyself. Y[et it] [MS torn] is because of the all perceiving all embracing faculties of man
that the riches of nature are of any use. What would light be if there were no eye? What
would sweetness be if there were no taste? What would goodness be if there were no soul
to act? What would truth be if there were no mind to perceive. The world exists to us
only by our power of observation. It is the very wonder of our constitution this vast
comprehensiveness of the powers of thought. It does not take all men nor many men to
attain great felicity or to comprehend a great truth. One man & every man can. I am
capable of an infinite happiness. I am capable of an infinite misery. If it be rightly
considered then, in a man himself are contained Heaven, Hell, the knowledge of all truth
the possession of indefinite power, the relation to all things good & evil; & finally by
reason of the retribution↑s↓ which in the nature of things are affixed to every act a man is
in some sort the Providence to himself which dispenses the events of his l⟨ot⟩ife.

If self means all this↑,↓ [comma in pencil] it will be admitted we can hardly give too
much importance to the maxim Do thyself no harm. ↑Little as we are in the scale of
being we are all in all↓ [in pencil] For because thou art the universe to thyself if thou dost
⟨n⟩thyself no harm thou art safe; none else can harm thee.

⟨⟨For if⟩ ↑For, because thou art the universe to thyself if↓ thou dost thyself no harm
⟨all thou art the universe to thyself, &⟩ thou art safe; none else can harm thee—see next
page⟩ [in erased pencil on otherwise blank MS p. 5, a draft of text on MS p. 3 above]

1. Do thyself no harm & none else will or can. The apostle ↑Peter↓ [in ink over pencil
in the space left for it] asks with great truth Who is he that will harm you if ye be
followers of that which is good? ⟨No⟩ He might as well say Who *can*? No power in
existence can harm a virtuous mind. If it could be supposed that instead of the
benevolent power that governs in the world, we should be exposed to the tyranny of
supernatural agents. If it could be supposed, as the Hindoos suppose, that there are
malevolent deities and that ⟨he⟩ ↑such an one↓ should pursue with hatred an innocent
man. Is it not plain that so long as he kept his integrity so long as he was reconciled to
himself in the singleness of a clean conscience he would have a friend & refuge in his
own breast ⟨against⟩ from the most tremendous evils? that he would have a tranquillity
& a certain superiority in his single soul to all the ⟨Universe⟩ ↑powers↓ arrayed against
him. He might be crushed but still would be ⟨superior⟩ the better.

This is the very ⟨thot⟩ condition which under a false religion reason yet delighted to
contemplate. ↑A great man struggling with yᵉ storms of fate↓

⟨Seneca⟩

⟨Cato⟩

⟨Medea.⟩

⟨Some of the best poetry which has come down to us from the Romans is that in
which they describe ⟨Cato⟩ as taking part with the friends of liberty against Caesar
whilst the Gods took part with Caesar "The gods were on one side, ⟨Cato⟩ on the
other.⟨"⟩ was Cato."⟩

⟨{"Victrix causa diis placuit victaque Catoni"}⟩ [canceled in pencil; see *JMN* 6:79.]

When Caesar assailed & overturned the liberties of his country, Marcus Cato the most
virtuous of the Romans took part against him. Victory which in that age was esteemed
the decision of heaven declared itself for Caesar, so that the poet in reckoning the
strength of the parties, says "The gods were on one side, on the other was Cato."

Now who does not see that though the case supposed is an absurd one yet if it could be believed possible the real strength & superiority is forever on the side of the virtuous man though solitary unarmed & persecuted even by supernatural adversaries.

I put this impossible case ↑of a divine hostility to the good man↓ as the extreme one, & the more willingly because something like it has long been supposed in the popular theology that there are elect persons & reprobate persons who enjoy grace & suffer punishment ↑at the hands of God↓ without regard to merit.

I need not say yᵗ nothing can be more gross yⁿ such a low imagination of God. He cannot harm you because it is more alien to his nature to wrong you than i⟨s⟩t is to your own will. God is love. As far as science has explored as far as the heart has felt all the arrangements of the world are beneficent arrangements [&] [MS torn] the end everywhere sought is good.

⟨↑Has it occurred to each of us with the /clearness/force/ [variant uncertain and nearly illegible] that belongs to the thought that the compensations of the world are perfect; that no action not the least falls dead but every one is a seed & bears fruit after its kind, that what a man sows the same he always reaps↓⟩ [in erased pencil on otherwise blank MS p. 10]

This then is the first conclusion to be laid up in the mind that ⟨if⟩ there is an everlasting superiority in a virtuous mind to all outward evil; something unconquerable by any conceivable power. Do thyself no harm & none will harm you.

Secondly This leads at once to a↑nother↓ [addition in pencil] ⟨most⟩ ⟨momentous⟩ [second cancellation in pencil] consideration, I mean our own power to harm ourselves. ↑A man is his own worst enemy or best friend.↓ Though you are safe from others, you are in great danger from yourself; no man thinks in how great danger. And on ⟨this⟩ account ↑of the great law—↓which makes both our danger & safety—the ⟨great⟩ law which lies at the foundation of the moral universe, 'that all things are retributive.' This makes ⟨our actions⟩ every action of immense importance. ²{Take care how you act, for you⟨r⟩ are trifling with edge tools⟩ ↑can ruin yourself↓ ¹{Take care how you act, for you are every day dealing with you know not what ↑powers↓.} ↑{↓A [bracket added in pencil] man who acts without reflexion in yᵉ [end of MS p. 11] ⟨mighty circle of human affairs is a madman He is like one stricken blind & left to grope alone in the midst of the uproar & dangers of a crowded ⟨town⟩ ↑manufactory↓. He knows not where he walks, he knows not what he approaches. Here is fire ["Grammar" appears in light pencil above "Here is fire"] that will burn, gases that will ⟨explode⟩ ↑suffocate↓, water that will drown, ⟨wagons⟩ ↑wheels↓ that will crush him.↑}↓ [bracket added in pencil] ⟨⟨He that acts⟩ Every human agent is touching springs of unknown power that may bring down thunder upon him because all actions are retributive.↑}↓⟩ [bracket and cancellation in pencil] Whatever we do is ⟨attended⟩ ↑tracked↓ by inevitable consequences, & we are every moment providing future pleasure or pain. I find this lesson written over all nature. It is in the writings of the wise & the proverbs of the multitude. It is yᵉ observation of yᵉ East & West. On yᵉ tomb of Nushirvan, yᵉ ancient monarch of Persia, is written, "Thou shalt be paid exactly for what thou hast done, no more no less"⟩

⟨"All things," saith the son of Sirach, "are double one against another." What a man soweth he shall reap. 'Curses,' it is said, always recoil upon the head of him ⟨th⟩who utters them ↑The benevolent man really serves himself in serving others.↓ The thief steals from himself. The liar is never believed. And does not all the experience of this country repeat the ancient observation that when you ⟨fasten⟩ ↑put↓ a chain around the neck of a slave the other end fastens itself around your own.⟩

↑Inevitable consequences tread on yᵉ heels of every act↓ [in pencil]

⟨"All things," saith the son of Sirach, "are double one against the other" 'What a man soweth, he shall reap,' saith the apostle "The thief," says the proverb, "steals from himself." "Curses are like young chickens which always come home to roost."⟩

↑Has it ever occurred to each of us with the clearness which belongs to the thought that the compensations of the world are perfect; that no action—not the least—falls to the ground, but every one has its own consequence,—bears fruit after its kind. Natural Philosophers tell us that when a stone falls to the earth the earth also falls to the stone; that not an atom can be moved in any part of the globe without affecting the position also of every other ⟨part.⟩ ↑atom that if you move the air with your hand that movement propagates itself throughout the atmosphere.↓

Is it less true of actions? ⟨The least⟩Every action ⟨& the greatest are alike pursued by a proportionate⟩ ↑is tracked by inevitable↓ effect, ↑the least as well as the greatest↓ nothing is or can be done in vain. For every act reacts upon the doer. Is any man so thoughtless as to imagine that he can do a favor that shall not be repaid him? It is impossible. For in the very act of doing a kindness his heart is enlarged, he is better than he was. Does any man imagine he can withhold a favor ↑due from him↓ & not suffer the reproach of meanness? ⟨In the very act of⟩ It is impossible. In the very act of refusing, his heart is contracted, he is meaner than he was. ↑(A change has taken place in him which makes him the receiver of ↑a↓ blessing or of ↑a↓ curse)↓

I find this lesson written over all nature. It is in the writings of the wise, & the proverbs of the multitude. It is the observation of the East & West. On the tomb of Nushirvan the ancient monarch of Persia is written "Thou shalt be paid exactly for what thou hast done—no more—no less."

'All things,' saith the son of Sirach, 'are double one against another.' [Ecclesiasticus 42:24] What a man soweth he shall reap. Curses, it is said, always recoil upon the head of him who utters them. The benevolent man really serves himself in serving others. ↑A man is valued as he makes himself valuable↓ [in pencil] The thief steals from himself The liar is never believed And does not all the experience of this country repeat the ancient observation that when you put a chain around the neck of a slave the other end fastens itself around your own.↓ [With this paragraph, cf. "Compensation," CW 2:64.]

All actions are retributive. There is no such thing as good fortune nor bad fortune. We are are every day ⟨reaping the good or evil consequence⟩ ↑eating the sweet or bitter fruit↓ of our own doings. And every act of our will is entailing upon us distinct effects as sure as those that follow any material cause

This ↑as a↓ general truth is ↑partially↓ perceived by men. They believe when they reflect that the ↑events esteemed↓ most casual & contingent ⟨events⟩, clouds↑,↓ winds↑,↓ disease↑,↓ are bound in strict chains of cause & effect, ↑{↓agreeably to a sublime proverb of antiquity↑,↓ that "the dice of God are always loaded."↑}↓ [added punctuation and brackets in pencil] οι κυξοι Διος αει ευπιπτδοι [Emerson's note] The greater is our knowledge, with the more certainty do we predict events from seeing their causes, & if we were more wise, if we reached the science of angels↑,↓ [comma in pencil] we should see the certainty of more occurrences that now take us by surprize.

And in the eye of God every thing is seen to take place in order & by necessity.

⟨Men believe in the ⟨permanence⟩ uniformity of physical events. They believe that ⟨fire will always burn⟩ heat, & frost, water, salt, iron, air, electricity will never vary in their operation, but under yᵉ same circumstances produce ⟨yᵉ⟩ identical effects But they are slower to believe that the laws of moral nature are just as ⟨fixed⟩ immutable. Yet it is true. ↑There is no more confusion in the laws of morals than of vegetables↓ [in pencil on facing page] Each quality of the mind bears its own fruit (bears it always) & never bears any other. Temperance never produces the effect of intemperance Hatred never produces the effect of love Servility is never confounded in its consequence with independance any more than ⟨iron ↑wax↓ will⟩ wax will serve in the arts the office of iron ↑or oil exhibit in mixtures the properties of sugar.↓ Honour is different from dishonor in its beginning & middle & end. So love wins love; honesty, confidence; veracity credit; temperance, health; peevishness gets ill will; dishonesty, distrust & indignation; & curses are apt to rebound on yᵉ head of yᵉ imprecator.⟩

In their success men are generally very willing to see the strict connexion of cause & effect, to believe that what they reap is the genuine fruit of the seed they sowed. A man who has been industrious frugal & prudent enjoys his growing estate with keen satisfaction because he sees he is reaping his own fruit. He is very well pleased to say to his children or his friends that he has worked & ⟨watched⟩ ↑abstained↓ & studied & waited for this, & that the same force is in yᵉ same virtues for them. And none of us ever attained any great object of our ambition I suppose without being very willing to see & acknowledge our own fair share of merit in yᵉ same.

But yᵉ moment yᵗ instead of good we receive evil, we cease to see the effect of our own doings. We think then it is caused by others, we complain of being unfortunate We complain of our fellowmen who have wronged us or we speculate upon the inscrutable decrees of Providence that so chasten those whom God loveth. We will not see that we have opened our own breast to the dart that has hit us that we foresaw long ago the hour that has come upon us that we neglected the means of securing our good that we yielded to a temptation of which now we pay the penalty, and we ⟨curse⟩ ↑lament↓ [emendation in pencil] our ill-luck or we reproach our fellowmen. There is no luck good or bad & our fellowmen ⟨i⟩are not the wrongdoers.

Men do not discriminate. They expect from one virtue ↑in themselves↓ the reward of all ⟨in themselves⟩ ↑the virtues↓, and from one vice in another man, the ill consequence of all the vices. When a misfortune comes upon a man he ↑reckons up his virtues &↓ says, why should I suffer this? He does not consider that his faults draw blanks as well as his virtues draw prizes in ⟨⟨the great⟩ ↑w↓⟩ what he reckons th great lottery of Fate. ⟨The truth is,⟩ the misfortune that befalls a man which leads him to ⟨curse⟩ ↑blame↓ [emendation in ink over pencil] his hard fate or to accuse the prejudice or vices of all mankind, is generally the consequence of some subordinate part of his own character. Thus a man is industrious but he is rash & credulous, and whilst his industry tends steadily to enrich him his rashness & credulity tend ↑as surely↓ to put his property ⟨at⟩ in danger.

Or he has been very frugal & very prudent but he has been intemperate in his attention to his business & utterly negligent of his health His diseases then are as much his own work as his success in trade is his own.

Another man improves his mind & cultivates his benevolent affections & complains that the goods of the world are distributed in abundance to the unworthy the ignorant & the selfish. Why does he complain. He has sought good knowledge & good feelings & he has found them. Let the other man have also the wealth which he has exclusively sought. ↑If↓ You ⟨plant⟩ ↑sow↓ wheat you shall reap wheat but you must not expect melons. The proper fruit of virtue is not wealth but peace of mind, the love of God & of good men. The proper fruit of industry & frugality is not a strong constitution but a larger income.

⟨↑(I would go along with what has before been said to the same point) here it contradicts—↓⟩ [in erased pencil on otherwise blank MS p. 30]

⟨↑↑{↓Moreover [bracket in pencil] men are sensible that their own imprudence occasioned most of their ⟨mishaps.⟩ sufferings↓ The evils from which we suffer most frequently are avoidable evils. Your ship is lost, but you might have insured it. An inundation has ruined your farm; but you knew that a river was liable to floods & might have planted a more elevated soil. Your child causes you great vexation by his ill behaviour; but your indulgence made him headstrong. And so with many others. They might have been avoided.↑}↓⟩ [bracket in pencil]

Whilst thus we ought to feel that ⟨{we have forged & sharpened & aimed the weapon that has wounded us that}⟩ the evils we tax Providence with are our own making I am far from affirming that we could by any diligence or virtue escape all the evils that are so thick in the world. Although the consequences of all actions are fixed, yet every man is necessarily ignorant of many of those consequences for every one begins life in total ignorance Every day is however advancing the knowledge of man & so his dominion over nature raising him successively to the knowledge & so to the prevention of more & more evils. ↑And a deep conviction of this truth that we are the authors of our own happiness or misery will make us very careful what we do, will make us so vigilant that we shall ⟨detect the approaches of⟩ ↑shun giving occasion to↓ many evils↑.↓ ⟨in season to avoid them.⟩ Still some evils are not to be avoided↓

But it will be asked what difference does it make ⟨if⟩ whether we cause our own ⟨m⟩ evils, or they come to us by a fate, if we cause them through an *unavoidable* ignorance. The virtuous man is as much exposed to the pestilence the earthquake or the falling tower as the ⟨outlaw⟩ ↑thief or the adulterer↓. [emendation in ink over pencil] ⟨The⟩ Some evils are hereditary The virtuous man is the son of a sinful man & inherits the diseases of his parent. Risks must be incurred by good as well as bad men in the enterprizes of commerce. And death comes into the worthiest family by doors which no skill or diligence could keep shut & takes away the sweetness of life from the survivors. Why say then 'Do thyself no harm' if we are born to this ignorance which make harm inevitable.

I answer ⟨in the first place that a deep conviction of this fact that we are the authors of our own happiness or misery will make us very careful what we do; and, secondly;⟩ ↑⟨but⟩ admitting freely the fact that evils we could not avoid do ⟨follow our⟩ thwart the best laid plans & afflict the best men I am led to the third consideration ["3." inscribed in left margin, MS p. 33] that belongs to this subject; viz.↓ that there is a great difference never to be lost sight of between our circumstances & ourselves. And though it be impossible to preserve our *condition* in the world safe from many evils, it is possible to preserve our *souls* from any injury. ⟨So⟩ ↑Do *thyself* no harm, come what will to thy condition. So↓ vital ⟨& great⟩ [phrase circled in pencil, canceled in ink] is this distinction that it may be said that external evils are only apparent & not real. ↑⟨To⟩ harm ↑to↓ your fortunes is not harm to ⟨thyself⟩ ↑yourself↓↓ [last emendation in pencil] There is no real evil but that which touches the mind. The loss of property is to *fail* as a merchant but is not necessarily to fail as a man. The loss of friends is a severe privation but may /bring out new resources in the character./give you access to the sympathies of the invisible world./ [variant in pencil] The loss of health & the approach of death are necessary steps in Gods order to the glorification of the soul. Fear not that which kills the body & after that hath no more hurt that it can do

⟨The loss of character,⟩ ↑These are not absolute evils.↓ the loss of selfcommand, the loss of benevolent disposition, the loss of purity, the loss of simplicity, of speech & of action—↑the loss of honesty↓ these are real evils. These defile a man. And these are losses that can only befal us by our own consent.

Setting out then with the assured conviction that all actions are retributive, ⟨(believe that you alone can do yourself good or evil) and⟩ if you wish for the goods of this world secure them by prudence, & if you desire eternal riches secure them by virtue. So seek what you desire as to do your very self no harm.

Brethren this distinction ↑between our condition & our⟨selves⟩ ↑character↓↓ [addition in pencil] is one not of words but of things. And therefore a man cannot possibly make a greater mistake than to think he can gain any advantage by a vicious action. Never, never. The ⟨advantage the⟩ gain is apparent, is shortlived, is external;—the loss is real, the loss is lasting, and is a sacrifice of ↑the man↓ himself—it is actually a parting with a p⟨a⟩ort↑ion↓ of yourself. ⟨My friends if I could hope to⟩ ↑Happy above all others is that man who is able to↓ [emendation in pencil] bring home this simple truth which is in every bodys mouth to ⟨your⟩ ↑his own↓ [emendation in pencil] consciences, ⟨I⟩ this simple truth that a wrong action does ⟨you⟩ ↑him↓ [emendation in pencil] more harm than any misfortune, ⟨I should bless God that he had made me so useful.⟩ [cancellation in pencil] But though we have all our lifetime heard these words, yet so fatal is the blind which interest puts upon us that we cannot see the truth in our own case. My firm belief is, that a man who does a wrong action is like a man who deliberately should do an act that leads to utter insanity. It is to unclothe the soul of its understanding & affections yes of that by which it is a living soul. ⟨There⟩ ↑If ⟨the question could be put directly &⟩ the most unfortunate person of your acquaintance put before you I am persuaded there↓ is no money & no advantages in the world for which you would sell your powers of mind & receive in exchange ⟨the⟩ ↑this↓ narrow heart & feeble intellect↑.↓ ⟨of ⟨some⟩ ↑the most↓ unfortunate person of your acquaintance.⟩ And yet for a little ⟨money⟩ ↑gain↓ men are unconsciously ⟨doing⟩ ↑making↓ that very ⟨thing⟩ ↑exchange↓ whenever they take an unjust advantage. They are selling their benevolence their justice & their truth ↑and all wh. makes a ⟨ma⟩ soul beautiful & wise↓. ⟨They traffic for themselves⟩ ⟨ ↑It is not a traffic in flesh but in souls.↓ ⟩ [cancellation in pencil] Ah it is all hidden by years, the atrocity is not perceived because the change is not suddenly wrot; but what difference does it make in the real mischief or how is the calamity less? Here is one who began life an ardent ingenuous youth, with the light of heaven in his eye & its hope in his mind; tender hearted, scrupulously just, full of desires & designs of selfimprovement, & for the improvement of society. See him now with a seared conscience, accustomed to injustice,—his high intentions forgotten, sneering at plans of benevolence, & himself conniving at or cooperating in works of selfish oppression that once he would have denounced as abominable. Have the actions changed? Is evil become good, & good evil? Or is it that he has been perverted, depraved? Is it a soul that is lost.

Indeed indeed though this mistake is common & is called the way of the world, it is ⟨misery⟩ ↑the most pathetic misery↓ the ⟨most painful⟩ ↑worst↓ of all calamities. A man is tempted to take an unjust advantage of a poor man, & has gained a paltry sum by it,—hundreds or thousands if you will, but the largest sum so gained is paltry. Well he can ⟨enlarge⟩ enlarge his expenses, increase his business, & ⟨please himself with the thought that he is rich⟩ ↑the conveniences of living↓. But he has hardened his heart, he has bid farewell to the angels that were leading him onward; he has blinded his sense of right & wrong. He has said Honor depart. Depart from my face the clear & tranquil look with which I met my fellowmen, the unquestionable front of integrity. Depart from me forever the love & confidence of my associates, the affection of my dependents, the blessing of the poor ↑and above all the hope of growing wise & good.↓ ⟨For this consideration, for these dollars he has consented to be a mean narrowminded worthless person of low intentions & descending character. To be rich he has sold his hope as a man. And is not this a loss irreparable.⟩ [cancellation in pencil; all but last sentence canceled in ink also] Can any sorrow any misfortune compare with this sorrow & this misfortune.

Do thyself no harm then directly by seeking a selfish pleasure ↑at an expense of principle,↓ nor indirectly by injuring others. You can not be enriched by ill gotten gain but it mak⟨s⟩es you poorer. You cannot gain honor by any false pretension but are degraded. You cannot be refreshed by any intemperate morsel or draught but are chewing poison. If you injure others, it is to wound yourself through them. [end of page] ⟨desire eternal riches, secure them by virtue.⟩

↑Do thyself no harm for thou art immortal↓

⟨Do thyself no harm, then, for it follows from these laws of retribution that thou makest thyself; that what you do today ⟨is making⟩ ↑determines↓ what you shall be tomorrow. Who lays this to heart? Yet every one knows the effect of certain actions to end in fixed habits; the effect of certain postures to alter the form; the effect of the ⟨disposition⟩ temper in giving expression to the face, the effect of our peculiar ⟨bias⟩ tastes in determining the selection of our companions, of our books, of our calling, & our amusements, & lastly the effect of all these in determining what objects shall attract our attention in the general ⟨aspect⟩ ↑movement↓ of society. Does it not follow that wherever we go, we only converse with those objects which are like ourselves so that we do not so much see the general world which God made but only a world of our own eye. Every man has peculiar thoughts, peculiar dreams a peculiar set of friends & peculiar purposes. He is creating day by day a world for himself. Let him feel that he cannot possibly meditate too much the steps he is taking, the friends he is choosing the habits he is forming for it is as ⟨h⟩if he was making the world in which he shall live.

{Men act on a mistake & as if they came here to enjoy themselves whereas they came here to form themselves}⟩

⟨This last head seems to be rather a repetition of the Retribution consideration than a statement of the immeasureable weight added to the precept Do thyself no harm, by the fact of our immortality⟩ [In erased pencil, written over by the following paragraph:] Finally, brethren, these views acquire a great an immeasureable importance from the consideration of our immortal nature. ↑Do thyself no harm for thou art immortal.↓ Little evils become large, small errors become of enormous consequence, when they are regarded as continuing & propagating themselves as long as a rational mind can exist & act. Listen to your own heart & it shall tell you that there is something in you which need not fear the grave. ↑Then↓ Listen to your own experience & it will tell you that it is what you do today which determines what you shall be tomorrow, that wherever we go we converse with those objects only that are like ourselves, so that we do not so much see the general world that God made, as a particular world of our own eye. Every man has peculiar thoughts, peculiar dreams, a peculiar set of friends, & peculiar purposes. He is creating day by day a world for himself. When in the retirement of his thoughts he remembers that a human soul cannot perish he will feel that he cannot possibly meditate too heedfully the steps he is taking, the friends he is choosing, the habits he is forming; for it is as if he was making the world in which he shall live, & determining the good or evil of ages that open before ⟨you⟩ him. Therefore brethren I exhort you to listen heedfully to th⟨e⟩at voice of Gods benevolence which i⟨s⟩n every action of your life whispers to you Do thyself no harm.

Forego a temporary gratification, an animal delight an unjust gain that you may enjoy the deep reward of a peaceful conscience, of an ascending character of a joyful benevolence. ⟨God will never forget the least sacrifice that you make to duty⟩ Is there a single good action in all your life which you regret. There never was There never will be In human history there is not one ⟨God⟩ Be assured God will never forget the least sacrifice that you make to duty. By such actions & by such actions alone he makes men happy forevermore. [paragraph inscribed over a passage in erased pencil, extending over the entire page, of which only the words "esteemed" and "of the" have been recovered]

New Bedford 8 Dec. 1833.—35' [in pencil, followed by Emerson's pencil transcription of the last paragraph of the earlier text of Sermon CXLI, this version differing only in having "better" for the second "more" in the second sentence, "a future" for "an future" in the next-to-last sentence, and, in the last sentence, "wouldest" for "wouldst"]

Sermon CXLII

Manuscript: Five sheets folded to make four pages each; pages measure 24.2 x 20.1 cm; a single leaf (24.2 x 20 cm) is inserted into the last folio; folios stacked and sewn along the left margin with white thread.

Lines	*Page 60*
Bible Text	Matt. 28. 20 [in ink over pencil]
1	¶ ⟨It⟩ The
3–7	from ⟨fatal⟩ gross . . . shalt ⟨n⟩do . . . ↑ruling men↓
11–12	↑to him↓ . . . rays ⟨are coloured⟩ in
15	peculiar ⟨beauties or defects⟩ ↑qualities↓
17–23	↑¶ And . . . felt ⟨he⟩ ↑each↓ expressed as ⟨dis⟩ faithfully . . . people not . . . is yᵉ ⟨fault⟩ ↑defect↓ . . . it.↓ [paragraph and emendations in pencil]
24–25	these ⟨mat⟩ gross . . . views ⟨It is⟩ The
28–(61)3	Friend ⟨Let no one imagine that there can any⟩ ↑No↓ . . . arise↑s↓ . . . ↑as if . . . terrible↓ ⟨It is not only a change to ages; but it is just as much to individual minds; It is the good man to whom God shows himself good to the froward he shows himself froward.⟩ A

	Page 61
10–14	↑of different creeds↓ . . . ↑& every . . . him↓ [additions in pencil] ¶ ⟨We my friends ought to be thankful ⟨that⟩ ↑for↓⟩ ↑Such is the↓ this progressive character ⟨in our⟩ ↑of↓
17–19	God. ¶ ⟨But⟩ when . . . developed ⟨it is not by⟩ ↑the . . . by↓ authority ⟨that he must be guided⟩ but
22	the⟨ir⟩re
24–32	¶ ["1." supplied to complement Emerson's "2."] . . . the /absurd/ mistaken/ . . . regard ¶ If you ¶ If you would ⟨move a man⟩ awaken . . . and the most ⟨dreadful cons⟩ penalties . . . it. ⟨You are a W⟩ ↑How this man will hate you & execrate you! You are↓ . . . not ⟨love him⟩ ↑reverence his actions↓. ↑I . . . agreed↓ This . . . ↑of↓
34	↑in question↓.
37	by ⟨r⟩ painting

Page 62

4-11   ¶ Therefore . . . sin [The paragraph is in ink over the following in pencil:] Cease to require of us a different regard to him from y^t wh we shd. pay to ye same goodness & wisdom in every being. We do not know any other elements in rational nature y^n these two Let us love him as we wd love one who kept ye law & therefore gave it one who abased himself & so was exalted who was tempted as we are yet without sin ¶ ⟨We are supposing unnatural⟩ ↑Let . . . arbitrary↓ offices↑,↓ ⟨for him⟩; ↑but↓ that he ⟨does not merely⟩ ↑simply↓ benefit↑s↓ . . . others ⟨but⟩ ↑not↓

13-14   plan ⟨be⟩ & character become infinitely ⟨&⟩worthy

17-19   ↑2. Secondly; There is another ⟨sense⟩ & . . . understood.↓ [end of MS p. 11; MS p. 12 is blank, concluding the third folio. What follows on the fourth folio appears to have been written out of sequence, and early in the process of composition:] ¶ ⟨In the account given by Matthew of the parting discourse of our Saviour to his disciples before his ascension closes with these remarkable words Lo I am with you always even unto the end of the world. ¶ I conceive there are three senses in which Jesus may be conceived as present forever with his disciples in this world.⟩ ¶ ⟨1.⟩2 By

19   made ⟨th⟩ men

21   countrymen an obscure

25   details of the [end of page] his humble

28-29   ↑& ⟨it is⟩ ↑are↓ now moving west till ⟨it⟩ ↑they↓ meet⟨s⟩ his cradle in Bethlehem↓

30-31   But ⟨to leave⟩ ↑better than↓ . . . little, ⟨to⟩ think

32-35   prompt⟨s⟩ such . . . you," should

38   The⟨n⟩ memory

39-40   world. ¶ ⟨2⟩3. There

41-⟨63⟩1   religion. ↑not . . . truth.↓ ⟨T⟩He

Page 63

9-14   ↑Let . . . ears.↓ [in pencil] ¶ ⟨3⟩4. I do not know but ⟨to⟩by . . . these /⟨2⟩two/three/ . . . there is a third sense . . . disciples I

15   the ⟨thot⟩ duty

18-24   ↑But . . . imagine. ⟨{Our spirits lie in the spiritual world as our bodies in the natural}⟩ & perhaps . . . the ²porch & ¹entrance . . . of ⟨ou⟩ spiritual . . . them↓ [addition and emendations in pencil]

27-29   ↑our spirits lie in ye sp. world . . . all↓ [in pencil]

31-32   wrot ⟨an⟩ ↑ye same↓ ⟨effect⟩ ⟨up⟩ of [faulty emendation]

33   us to

33-34   ↑There . . . metaphor↓

35   ↑wh. is . . . heated lang↓

38-⟨64⟩6   that /we have/there is in ye human mind,/ . . . ↑entertained by some Xns↓ . . . & y^t ⟨ye good⟩ in . . . but ⟨we⟩ [canceled in pencil] the

Page 64

9-12   others ↑{↓& so ye Universe is one great family [The bracket, added in pencil, apparently indicates Emerson's intention to cancel the subse-

quent phrase, which is, in any event, repeated below.] ⟨yᵗ⟩ ⟨in God as
yᵉ waves are contained in yᵉ ocean⟩ [canceled in pencil] ↑&↓ [added
in pencil] If as I hold that ⟨noble⟩ principle of philosophy be ↑as↓
⟨true⟩ ↑sound↓ ["true" canceled and "sound" added in pencil] . . .
desireable is true ↑the moral . . . ↑included↓ . . . are cont. in yᵉ
ocean↓ [addition in pencil]

17   he ⟨m⟩ is not

Sermon CXLIII

Manuscript (earlier version): Four sheets folded to make four pages each; single leaves
are inserted in the first folio, between the first two folios (blank), in the second folio
(containing Insert "X"), between the second and third folios (containing Insert "A"), and
in the third folio (containing pencil inscriptions on the recto). All pages measure 24.2 x
20 cm. The gatherings are sewn along the left margin with white thread.

[The text of the earlier version follows:]

CXLIII.

Forgetting th⟨e⟩ose things ⟨that⟩ ↑which↓ are behind & reaching for⟨ward⟩th
↑un↓to those ↑things↓ wh. are before, I press toward the mark ⟨of⟩for yᵉ prize of yᵉ
high calling ⟨in Christ⟩ of God in Christ Jesus. Phil ⟨1⟩3. 13–14.

The Christian doctrine of the immortality of the soul gives the greatest importance to
all the events of this life as they in some degree affect the whole being of the soul.

Men in general are so entirely occupied with the particulars, as to give no attention to
the general course of their life. But though they ↑consider more the effect of single
actions &↓ [addition in ink over pencil; pencil layer has "regard" for "consider"] do not
⟨attend to it⟩ ↑take heed↓ that the course shall be serviceable on the whole, God does.
And if men would regard it, it would ⟨cheer⟩ ↑comfort↓ ⟨& ⟨console⟩ ↑instruct↓⟩
them to see that all this apparent disorder ↑of innumerable unconnected actions↓
[addition in ink over pencil] resolves itself into a great order ↑& is made by the Divine
Wisdom to produce the most beneficent results.↓

⟨When⟩ Look at the great throng the city presents ↑Consider the variety of callings &
pursuits↓ Here is one man ↑toiling↓ with a hod on his shoulder; and another with his
saw & tools; a third with his books; a fourth ⟨w⟩ driving bargains at the corners of the
streets; another ⟨is hasting to an⟩ ↑spreads his sail from the wharf toward yᵉ sea;
another, heals the sick; another draws a map; another is hasting to his↓ entertainment &
to dangerous pleasures; another is led to the jail between officers; another takes his seat
on a bench to judge him.

They do not perceive who make up this sad ⟨& merry⟩ ↑cheerful↓ [addition in ink
over pencil] scene that they ↑are↓ placed in these circumstances to learn the laws of the
universe, & that these various implements ⟨& outsides are only like⟩ ↑& callings
⟨shows⟩ serve the same use as↓ the ⟨boys⟩ ↑child's↓ [addition in ink over pencil] slate &
spelling book, wherewith he also learns his lesson, ⟨grumbling⟩ ↑murmuring all↓ the
while ↑at the necessity↓ & does not yet perceive that for his own good & not for
anothers it is taught him.

It ⟨is a matter⟩ well deserv⟨ing⟩es ⟨our⟩ attention how ⟨well suited⟩ ↑fit↓ are the various employments of men not only to occupy their attention & keep them from the misery of idleness but to engage ↑& invigorate↓ their faculties, to ⟨develop⟩ ↑form↓ the virtues, in short, to educate the man. It deserves attention how much every one is indebted to his ⟨profession.⟩ ↑↑calling↓ [cancellation and addition in ink over pencil] for his powers & for his enjoyments.↓ And it is curious to observe how complex is the action & reaction of a man upon his profession & his profession upon the man.

↑⟨There are two purposes answered by the general distribution of the work of society into various professions ⟨for⟩ and by each man's attention & ability being confined to some one ⟨i.e.⟩ his more efficient action is gained to the common good & secondly his own powers are revealed to him & gradually he is shown what his own peculiar talent is, which is every mans true ↑& eternal↓ calling from God his Maker.

It is to some remarks upon this last topic that I have to request your attention⟩ [passage in pencil, written over by the following in ink:] ⟨There are t⟩Two purposes ↑are↓ answered by the general distribution of the work of society into various professions and by each mans attention & ability being confined to some one; *first,* his more efficient action is gained to the common good; and, secondly; his own powers are revealed to him & gradually he is shown what his own peculiar talent is, which is every man's true & eternal calling from God his Maker.

It is to some remarks upon this last topic that I have to request your attention.↓

↑⟨Observing⟩ ↑On account of↓ the very remarkable effect which particular situations & duties have had on some men a great deal more power has been ascribed to thi⟨s⟩ngs ⟨cause⟩ ↑outward↓ than belongs to ⟨it⟩ ↑them↓.↓ We hear a great deal of the empire of circumstances o⟨f⟩ver the mind, but not enough of the empire of the mind over circumstances. ↑y^t ye mind is capable of exerting this power↓ [addition in pencil] ⟨But this is a doctrine of greatest importance & whilst we behold in /ye first/its passive submission/ [variant in pencil] ye benignity of God raising up the feeble race of man from barbarity to refinement↑,↓ ⟨in⟩ [emendation in pencil] the /second/action of ye will upon y^m/ [variant in pencil] is a truth of not ⟨less⟩ importance ⟨declaring⟩ ↑bespeaking↓ [emendation in pencil] the great gift of God in the endowment of the human race with Liberty.⟩

↑Both propositions contain truth, for the mind is capable of commanding & of being commanded by circumstances. In the fact that ⟨man is moulded⟩ the human character is much affected by the accidents of ⟨his⟩ country parentage & the like we trace the Divine Wisdom operating a progressive education of the race. At the same time it were treachery to our souls to overlook the other fact the power of man over his condition which bespeaks the great gift of God in the endowment of the human race with liberty.↓

Circumstances are of the greatest importance as instructors but they ⟨imply⟩ ↑suppose↓ a pupil. To say they make the man is to say the ⟨echo⟩ ↑air↓ makes the sound ⟨or the shadow is the cause of the substance.⟩ ↑which it only conveys↓ ↑or that it is the winds & not the pilot that brot the ship into harbour.↓

↑It is ⟨undeniably true⟩ ↑not to be denied↓ that all men are much influenced by the fortune of their birth & early associations & many men are passive↓ A man is born under the shadow of ancient institutions by the side of whose strength his own strength is insignificant. ⟨When he grows up⟩ Men are observed to be of their fathers' religion. Men frequently follow, especially in old countries, their fathers' profession. And so ⟨men say he⟩ ↑it is said man↓ is formed by these institutions ⟨But he is not. On the contrary observe⟩ ↑But observe on the other hand↓ how strong is the effect of individual character in each man to change the complexion of the same pursuits in his hands. In a degree he

⟨is⟩ always ↑is↓ affected by the nation, age, family, profession, friendships he falls upon; but he ⟨gives⟩ ↑exerts↓ influence as well as receives it. And that, in proportion to the strength of his character

↑I submit it to your thots whether there be not reason to think that↓ Every man is born with a peculiar character or ⟨with⟩ having a peculiar determination to some one pursuit or one sort of usefulness ⟨rather than another⟩. If he cultivate his powers & affections, this determination will presently appear. If he do not, he will yield to those ⟨chance ↑casual↓⟩ influences under which he first happens to fall; but as his character opens, there will be this ⟨a⟩ constant effort on the part of his mind to bend his circumstances to his character. Hence we continually see men ↑of strong character↓ changing the ⟨character⟩ ↑nature↓ of a profession in their hands. What different men have figured under the name of a *soldier,* from the bloody savage who was brother to the tiger & the wild boar, to the pious & gentle patriot who saved his country. How different has been the profession of the ⟨priesthood⟩ ↑ministers of religion↓ as it has fallen ⟨into⟩ ↑upon↓ different ⟨hands⟩ ↑men↓. One is a soldier, one a statesman, one an adviser of the kings conscience one a dispenser of ceremonies, one an almsgiver, one an ⟨alms⟩ beggar, one a petty tyrant, one a preacher, one a pastor

What entirely different professions are contained under the name of merchant ↑or lawyer↓ each individual pursuing those ↑parts↓ only or chiefly, for which his talents most qualify him ↑{Insert X} X {⟨In the world a⟩At present, society is served by a limited number of professions & each man according to his temper or the temper of his friends is thrown into one of these. But as society advances, no doubt, these pursuits will be infinite↑ly↓ [end of line] ly multiplied, & instead of a few professions, there will be almost as many callings as individuals. ↑Y

Y {This seems to be provided for in the infinite diversity of human taste & human character. ⟨o⟩One man loves agriculture, another commerce, another learning, another art; one would live on the mountains; another on the sea; one has skill in speech; another the brain in the hand; one loves the crowd; another to sit & study alone.↓ [Insert "X" continues.] Even now we occasionally see an individual forsake all the usual paths of life & show men a new one, better fitted than any other to his own powers}↓

And as any man discovers a taste of any new kind any new combination of powers he tends toward such places & duties as will give occasion for their exercise ⟨If a⟩ And this because ⟨no⟩ ↑great↓ powers ⟨like to⟩ ↑will not↓ sleep in a man's breast. Every thing was made for ⟨the greatest use & no man /will patiently submit to/⟨is content with⟩/ the ⟨silent⟩ the secret profession of ⟨/great/eminent/⟩ powers⟩ ↑use.↓ ⟨They will⟩ ↑Great powers↓ demand to be put in action the greater they are with the more urgency. [end of page] ⟨irresistible tone⟩ ↑urgency↓. ⟨So when⟩ Every man is uneasy until every power of his mind is in freedom & in action; ⟨there is therefore⟩ ↑& thence arises↓ a constant effort to take that attitude which will admit of this action

⟨{The practical consequence of this, is, that when a man's profession has been chosen for him against his ⟨will⟩ inclination, or when he has chosen it for himself before he was acquainted with the character of his own mind, if it admit of being bent to his character, it will be; if not, he will grow impatient of it & change it for one more suited to his genius}⟩ [canceled in pencil]

↑{Insert A} A {⟨Men have as yet learned so little to think & act for themselves⟩ ↑But men exercise their reflexion so little in this matter↓ that you see only rarely in society a man exactly suited to his profession. Often men seem entirely without suitableness to it, & ⟨the⟩ its duties are discharged ⟨lamely⟩ [canceled in pencil] without love & not only so but ⟨the⟩ men ↑in that condition↓ are but half ⟨men⟩ ↑themselves↓. [emendation in ink over pencil] powers unexerted slumber in them↑.↓ ⟨but o⟩On the other hand, we sometimes see ⟨a person⟩ ↑an individual↓ who seems to have fallen exactly into his right place. And what perfect satisfaction appears in his air & behaviour, how harmoniously all his powers are developed.} ↑and with what increased efficiency he works!↓↓

Let a man have that profession for which God formed him that he may be useful to mankind to the whole extent of his powers that he may ⟨delight⟩ find delight in the exercise of his powers, & do what he does with the full consent of his own mind

↑Every one knows well↓ What difference there is in the doing ⟨things⟩ ↑that we have↓ with all ones heart & the doing them against ones will If every man were engaged in those ↑innocent↓ things that he best loved, would not ⟨art &⟩ the wheels of society move with better speed & surer effect? Would not more be done & all be done better? And what an increase of happiness! for all labor would be pleasure.

These remarks are founded on the doctrine which I believe gains ⟨strength⟩ ↑faith↓ in every man's mind as he reflects, that every individual mind has its assigned province of action, a place which it was intended by God to fill, & ↑to↓ which always it is tending. It is that which the greatest cultivation of all his powers will enable him to do best. It is what that particular person was made to do. Every just act, every proper attention bestowed upon his mind makes this aim more distinct to hi⟨s⟩m↑.↓ ⟨mind⟩ It may be hidden from him for years. Unfavorable associations, ↑bad↓ advice, or his own perversity may fight against it But he will never be at ease, he will never act with efficiency, until he finds it. Whatever it be, it is his high calling. ⟨The delivery of the talent is the call.⟩ ↑This is his mark & prize This is permanent & infinite; all other callings are temporary are only means to bring out & present this distinctly before his eyes.↓ Many mistakes may be made in the search but every man who consults himself, the intimations of Divine Wisdom in his own mind, will constantly approach it. It is that state in which all the powers of the man are put in use and he who is steadfastly enlarging his views of what is true, & heroically doing what is right is ⟨irresistibly⟩ ↑fast↓ advancing toward this end.

↑In every good work trust thy own soul for yᵗ is yᵉ keepᵍ of yᵉ com [Ecclesiasticus 32:23]

Go forward & accept yᵉ gift of yr creation & resign yrself to his will by obeying yᵉ promptings of yr mind↓ [addition in pencil]

This end, this his high calling—let it be sacred in each man's mind. Let every mind rise to the perception that it was designed by the great Father of all for a peculiar good,—not to be benefitted only in common with nations, or with families, but as an individual. Be content then, humbly & wisely to converse with yourself; to learn what you can do, & what you cannot; to be deterred from attempting nothing ⟨in⟩ ↑out of↓ respect to the judgment of others, if it be not confirmed by your own judgment. Never take for granted a common opinion against the promptings of your heart, considering that another age will reverse all unfounded opinions & settle them anew. Nor ever consider that your ties in life, your obligations to your family, or ↑to↓ your benefactors, or ↑to↓ your creditors, or ↑to↓ your country ↑shut you out of your true field of action, by↓ forbid↑ding↓ you to correct the errors of choice of ⟨profession⟩ pursuit into which you have fallen. For you may constantly be tending towards this your use *through* all the common occupations & relations of life,—may constantly, by force of will, be bending them to that. The more distinctly we become acquainted with our powers & destiny, the more effectually do we exert ourselves to ⟨answer those ends⟩ give that direction to our common employments. The less do we serve our circumstances, & the more do they serve us.

⟨But consider further⟩ ↑Furthermore a pious mind will ⟨always b⟩feel assured↓ that God is always giving us freedom as fast as we are fit for it. He who has ⟨greatly⟩ adopted a ↑great↓ purpose ⟨which makes his life⟩ ↑with ardor↓ forsakes everything for it. ↑If his circumstances will admit of it he bends them to his purpose, if not he breaks them to it↓ It becomes to him father, mother, house & lands. The force of the feeling is his justification. He who does not feel his call with the same force remains where he is. ↑{Insert C} C {Or if there be any who feel a ↑painful↓ disproportion between their character & their condition & yet labor under a load of embarrassment to great to be removed, in the eternity of their nature & in the omnipotence of God is their hope. The circumstances change heaven & earth pass but the soul endures. There is no knot which death cannot untie and Jesus teaches us that death will bring a state of freedom↓ ⟨But⟩ death will presently come & will doubtless bring to all who ⟨are⟩ deserve it much more freedom than they now possess & will permit them to exert their virtues & talents with far more efficiency than they can at present.

Once more this the high calling of every soul is not in heaven, or over the sea, or existing in a heated imagination ⟨it⟩ or in a remote future, it may be served in this life as well as in the next it begins to be served whenever a man begins to act according to his conscience & he is leaving it whenever he violates his conscience. (It is your high calling *in Christ,* for the purpose of Christ was to redeem every soul from the bondage of sin to the glorious liberty of the sons of God that each might truly discern his own powers & duties.)

Finally; the high calling of every mind is full of infinite glory & joy & sweetness. Every man likes to do what he can do well. But this is to do what God made you to do best. It is no trifling no easy no short work. It is a work that demands severe exertion, your head & your heart, & it never will be done. But then it brings the strength it needs for it is embraced with the whole affection of the soul. It makes the day bright. It clothes the world with beauty & ⟨makes⟩ the face of God with smiles It is a path without an end, that beginning in the little pursuits of this world leads up to Gods right hand to pleasures forevermore.

Feb. 5. 1832. ↑plurima nix↓ [in pencil]
↑Federal St Feb. 12↓ [in pencil]

↑P. M.
{Callings of men in vulgar life useful to educe their powers & teach each man what is his 'high calling' or the use for which God made him. As a man discovers that let him sacredly follow it. It is different to every man. To one, poetry; to another, agriculture; to another, trade; to another, learning; to another, ethics; to another, the brain in the hand; to another, the state; to another, ⟨gr[?]⟩philosophy. Whatever it be, follow it. It is that state in which every power of a man is in full exercise & no power is demanded which he has not. ⟨According⟩ Every right exertion tends to show a man more distinctly what this is. According to the force of this call, i.e. according to yᵉ distinctness with which he sees his use, will be his efforts to bend his circumstances to it. If ⟨they won't⟩ ↑this profession cannot↓ be bent he will ⟨qui⟩ exchange ⟨them⟩ ↑it↓ for others more congenial to him. But the effect of the improvement of society & of individuals will be to multiply in↑de↓finitely the professions & instead of compelling each individual to bend himself to some unsuitable work to do that work he can. Blessed time & blessed men when each does that & only that for which he was made.↓

Manuscript (revised version): Five sheets folded to make four pages each; pages of the first three folios measure 24.2 x 20.1 cm, those of the last two folios measure 24.2 x 20.2 cm. Folios are stacked and cross-stitched along the spine with white thread; the first folio has become detached. A loose leaf measuring 23.8 x 20.3 cm is inserted into the first folio. On MS p. 1, the sermon number is written in lower case letters: "cxliii." The watermark "S & B / N H" appears on the last page.

Lines	Page 65
Bible Text	things ⟨th⟩which
6	↑of life↓
10	throng ⟨the city presents⟩ ↑in your streets↓. [emendation in pencil, apparently made for a delivery away from Boston]
13–15	↑another teaches the young↓ another . . . ↑another interprets the law↓ another [additions in pencil]
22–(66)16	good, ⟨& not⟩ [end of page] ↑& not . . . him.↓ [inscribed in pencil at the top of the inserted leaf; the sentence is also (and originally) completed at the top of MS p. 5: see below] ¶ ↑It is . . . our ⟨own⟩ mind↑s↓ [cancellation and addition in pencil] . . . this ⟨strange⟩ life↑,↓ [comma in pencil] . . . same. ⟨We shall⟩ ↑On . . . probably↓ . . . labor then . . . world.↓ [end of page] & not for another's, it is taught him. ¶ It well

	Page 66
22–25	¶ ↑Under this main design↓ Two ⟨main⟩ ↑particular↓ [addition and emendation in pencil] . . . one; ⟨1.⟩ first, . . . good; ⟨2.⟩ and,
27–36	is /to some remarks upon this last topic that I have to request your attention./to . . . now to ⟨invite⟩ ↑request↓ . . . behind to ⟨press forward⟩ reach . . . duties/ ¶ ⟨Observing⟩ On

	Page 67
26	bloody ⟨tyrant⟩ savage
34	↑most↓
40	inclination ⟨society would be no loser⟩, all

	Page 68
2	loves ⟨the⟩ a
7	in ⟨a⟩ ↑the↓ ⟨man's⟩human
11–12	action. ¶ ⟨Yet⟩Hitherto
21	↑there is↓
39	mind, will

	Page 69
1–5	↑It ought . . . duties & . . . them↓ [in pencil]
16	action⟨,⟩ by
25	ardor ⟨make⟩ postpones
37	possess⟨,—& will⟩↑.↓

Page 70

1–4   ↑Their . . . hearth.↓
5   mind⟨,⟩ is

[The following notation occurs, in pencil, after the end of the sermon:] This ought to be matter of serious reflexion to every man, to ascertain what is his true vocation. And for this end he ought to respect every doubt every misgiving every preference that touch his pursuits & not dismiss them till he has fully weighed & proved them.

No man ought to undertake any thing but that which God gives him
If it is true

Sermon CXLIV

Manuscript: Four sheets folded to make four pages each, stacked and inserted into a fifth folio whose pages are blank except for the third, which is the last inscribed page of the manuscript; folios stitched along the left margin with white thread. Pages of the outermost folio measure 24.8 x 20.3 cm; pages of the first inside folio measure 24.1 x 19.7 cm; pages of the remaining folios measure 24.8 x 20.4 cm. The watermark "J BUTLER" appears on the outermost folio. The manuscript is clearly a fair copy; since it was delivered fourteen times, the editors suppose it to be a relatively late version.

Lines   *Page 71*
1–2   said—the . . . doctrine is . . . ye perfect⟨"⟩ as

                                 Page 72
5–6   will ⟨have the⟩ speak
14–15   of ⟨h⟩His . . . serve ⟨h⟩Him

                                 Page 73
29   sense? ⟨i⟩Is

                                 Page 74
6–7   so ⟨gre⟩despotic
12   your ⟨labor⟩ work;
32   the ⟨operation⟩ occupation

                                 Page 75
2   clothed ⟨in⟩with

                                 Page 76
3   with ⟨an eye⟩ a . . . drag ⟨y⟩every
28   of ⟨r⟩Reason. . . . would ⟨make⟩ ↑renew↓

Sermon CXLV

Manuscript: Six sheets folded to make four pages each; sewn along the left margin with white thread. Pages measure 24.3 x 20.1 cm.

Lines   *Page 77*
4–5   ↑300 years . . . that land.↓

7	Harvey↑: now known to all↓
15	in ⟨virtue⟩ ↑morals↓.
17–18	↑some↓ . . . entirely ⟨obsolete⟩ without . . . nations. ⟨One⟩ ↑A single↓ savage↑, or two or three↓
24	the ⟨whole⟩ ↑great↓ [emendation in ink over pencil] body of the people ⟨among us⟩ have ↑risen to↓ [cancellation and addition in pencil]
27	multitude. ⟨Every⟩ All

Page 78

5	that ⟨o⟩by
7–9	↑Hence ⟨comes⟩ ↑arises↓ . . . ↑& this . . . urge.↓↓ ["& this . . . urge." in pencil] ¶ ⟨I wish to speak of the sacred duty of judging for ourselves what is right.⟩ [canceled in pencil] Is
11–12	yet /one can hardly speak with confidence/it . . . admitted/ [variant in pencil] but . . . not⟨,⟩ to
18–19	some ⟨remarks upon⟩ reason↑s↓ . . . right, & ⟨the advantage⟨s⟩ & duty⟩ ↑some remarks upon the↓
22	which ⟨h⟩ find
25	therefore, ⟨it⟩ ↑there↓ must be ↑some↓ good ↑in it.↓
28–29	recommend ⟨it.⟩ ↑it, . . . fault.↓
31–32	have ⟨been in habits⟩ allowed
35–39	on ⟨m⟩ society . . . heroes. ¶ ⟨"not all that heralds rake from coffined clay, / Nor florid prose, nor honied lies in rhyme / Can ⟨san⟩ blazon evil deeds, or consecrate a crime."⟩ ¶ ⟨In the next place⟩ ↑But it is said ⟨is⟩Have we . . . say the↓ Scripture is ⟨not of itself⟩ a . . . conduct ⟨for the plain reason that it needs the⟩ ↑we . . . aid of↓ human ⟨reason⟩ ↑spirit↓
40–⟨79⟩3	read ⟨it⟩. This . . . have ⟨spoken⟩ alluded . . . men. ¶ ⟨3. Thirdly. ⟨Consider the origin⟩ What is ⟨the origin of⟩ the soul? It is our nearest means of knowing the will of God. It is the voice of God which the soul utters. Any other instruction must be indirect second hand traditional this is our access to the Father himself the Source of all wisdom. For what is the origin of the soul? In the obscure generation of man we trace no origin to the soul It is no child of the father or of the mother The parents are as utterly ignorant as the bird of the formation of her egg⟩ ¶ There

Page 79

8–18	interpreter ↑{Insert X} X {Why . . . the ⟨Scriptures⟩ ↑human race↓ . . . ↑that has no record↓ . . . creation ⟨ce⟩ thought . . . ↑however great is↓ th⟨e⟩at being ⟨that⟩ ↑who↓ . . . ↑He↓ . . . a ⟨sp⟩ ray . . . light}↓ ¶ ⟨And it is the duty & the advantage of using this gift, which all of you will bear me witness is very little used, that I wish to urge upon you.⟩ [canceled in pencil and ink] ¶ Settle . . . that ↑it↓ . . . to it, ⟨a⟩so . . . examination; ⟨that it is to discriminate between⟩ [canceled in pencil and ink] ↑⟨all ⟨it must dispose all its tho'ts in one of two classes either⟩that it must dispose all its thots in one of two

classes, either↓ ["all . . . classes either" in pencil, overwritten by "that
. . . classes, either" in ink] . . . consideration, ⟨&⟩ ↑or↓

20–24   business; ⟨the⟩ your . . . day ⟨under⟩ before

37   ↑or inscrutable mysteries↓

40   long ⟨sla⟩ Slavery

42   mankind ⟨[indeterminate canceled word: either "will" or "with"]⟩ &

44   diminished; ↑only recently↓

44–(80)1   recently ⟨has Prison discipline been introduced⟩ ↑that decency . . .
Prisons.↓ ⟨Only⟩ ↑It is but↓

Page 80

3–4   schools; & ⟨impr⟩ Bankrupt . . . Insane⟨,⟩↑.↓ these

10   and ⟨every one may see⟩ is ⟨deceived by⟩ abused by ⟨a thousand⟩
↑great↓

13   to ⟨orders of nobility⟩ the

15–16   ↑instead . . . trust↓.

17   Already ⟨this⟩ the

19–20   truth who have [end of page] who find out the secrets of ⟨nature⟩ the
elements; the ⟨men of science⟩ ↑untiring inquirers↓ [emendation in
pencil] . . . of ⟨numbers⟩ ↑matter↓,

26–27   knowledge ⟨the teachers of truth shall be more honoured ↑by us,↓ [in
ink over "by us" in pencil] than the officers of the state.⟩ ↑shall . . .
obtain more.↓ [cancellation and addition in pencil]

29   more ⟨discret⟩ reason

30   to ⟨add to their wealth⟩ ↑make . . . fortune↓

31   otherwise; ⟨but⟩ for,

33–(81)1   pleasures, ⟨&⟩ ↑when↓ . . . men ⟨studiously⟩ ↑strictly↓ limit their
⟨years of toil⟩ ↑exertion↓

Page 81

4   open [end of page] new

6   mankind; ⟨nor accept it settled forever⟩ ↑& do not begin ⟨by taking
it for granted⟩ ↑by . . . settled↓↓

8   the ⟨common⟩ ↑vulgar↓

9–10   ↑borrow . . . they↓

20   half ⟨or⟩ so

24   health ⟨a firm religious belief,⟩ the power

27–29   the ⟨possession⟩ power of acquiring truth. ⟨In another age⟩ ↑It . . .
that↓ Men . . . ↑wisdom↓ they have. ⟨I dare affirm⟩ ↑It is supposed↓

31–35   age, ⟨the knowledge men⟩ what . . . ignorance. ¶ ⟨Finally⟩ ↑In
short,↓ . . . the⟨y⟩ eye

42–(82)2   Yet ⟨men never remember it⟩ in many cases ↑very worthy↓ men
⟨continually⟩ act . . . opinion Every . . . injustice? But

Page 82

4–6   defrauded; ⟨to wit,⟩ Defrauding ↑is worse↓, & Malice, & Slan-
der↑.↓ ⟨are worse.⟩ We . . . which ⟨command⟩ ↑enjoin↓

13   ↑too↓

26–27 man ⟨himself⟩ who . . . in ⟨all⟩ his ↑farthest↓ ["all" canceled and
 "farthest" added in pencil]
33 will⟨l⟩ make

Sermon CXLVI

Manuscript: A single leaf measuring 24.2 x 20.1 cm, followed by five sheets folded to
make four pages each (the pages of the first two folios measure 24.3 x 20 cm; pages of the
last three folios measure 24.3 x 20.2 cm); followed by two leaves, the second of which is
blank, each measuring 24.3 x 20 cm; a leaf (containing Insert "A" and other material)
measuring 24.3 x 20 cm is inserted into the third folio. Folios are stacked and sewn along
the left margin with white thread.

[Below Bible text:] ↑Rom. 8.26↓ [in pencil]

Lines	*Page 83*

3–4 of ⟨human life⟩ ↑Providence↓ . . . of ⟨philosophy⟩ ↑reflexion↓
 [emendation in pencil] . . . object ⟨the deliverance of the human soul
 from its enemies & a gradual communication of the power to stand
 alone⟩ ↑to assist ⟨the hu⟩man ⟨soul⟩ in . . . cultivation↓.
5 more ⟨wonderful⟩ ↑admirable↓
6–10 a ⟨wonderful⟩ providence . . . him; ⟨calls out⟩ ↑awakens↓ . . . quits
 the⟨m⟩se for . . . better ⟨apparatus⟩ ↑series↓
10–12 This ⟨genius⟩ ↑guardian↓ . . . operating ⟨to perfect⟩ more . . . man
 & ⟨fit him for freedom⟩ ↑enable . . . alone↓.
14 ↑¶ Let . . . discipline↓
16–18 ↑Tis . . . softness [conjectural "nor" obscured by the stitching of the
 MS] impenetrable to his plough↓
19–20 ↑All . . . otherwise↓
21–24 breathe ⟨What⟩ ↑Another observation↓ . . . singular ⟨is that b⟩ The
 air . . . one, & & one
25–26 ↑by experimenters↓ . . . support ⟨breathing⟩ ↑respiration↓

Page 84

2–5 discovered ⟨but taken from the tops of mountains or the bottom of
 mines this uniform proportion is always kept which is best suited to
 the health of man. Every step that science makes brings to light some
 new instance as conspicuous & beautiful of ⟨b⟩ wise contrivance.⟩
 [canceled in pencil] ¶ In . . . admirably ⟨⟨suited⟩ are indispensable⟩
 ↑adjusted↓ to the ⟨development⟩ ↑unfolding↓
7–14 profession ⟨learning⟩ becoming . . . truth. ⟨He is⟩ ↑& thereby↓
 [emendation in pencil] . . . power that is greater freedom. ↑But . . . It
 ⟨puts⟩ holds . . . vice.↓ ¶ ⟨2. The second aid which⟩ ↑⟨2⟩3. But . . .
 nature↓ is afforded ⟨man⟩ ↑to each individual↓ i⟨s⟩n the aid which
 /{the moral sentiments of mankind furnish ⟨in aid⟩ ↑to↓ the ⟨of⟩
 formation of his principles}/Society furnishes to yᵉ moral senti-
 ments/
16 And /it/this/ might do ⟨to say so⟩ if

18–21   nation ⟨sanctions⟩ ↑commends↓ . . . murder↑.↓ ⟨& all sorts of abominations⟩ ¶ Even in the best ⟨ages⟩ days . . . pure ⟨but as to frown down⟩ but

22   ↑virtuous↓

22–23   It i⟨t⟩s altogether ↑too fluctuating↓ unworthy

24   be the ⟨sentiments⟩ reason

25–32   us. ¶ ⟨But ↑although it will not do to make so uncertain a judgment yᵉ rule↓ of how great advantage is it to men that whilst ⟨this is⟩ ↑the individ. reason↓ yet feeble & speaks with a stifled voice, the ⟨virtue⟩ first steps of virtue are upheld by a dependance on the moral sentiments of our fellow men⟨.⟩, ↑which tho' in one place they may allow ⟨one⟩ ↑particular↓ vice↑s↓ are always just in the majority of cases.↓⟩ ¶ ↑{Insert X} X {But . . . in ⟨one⟩ ↑every↓ [emendation in pencil] . . . vices, ⟨yet they are⟩ in . . . yet /of/ none can be blind to/ [variant in pencil] how great advantage is it to . . . dependance . . . community.}↓

34   conform him self, willing⟨ly⟩ or unwilling, to the ⟨rules⟩ good

35–(85)3   must ⟨not cheat⟩ be . . . kindness. ⟨In these⟩ ↑A free↓ Indulgence . . . itself. ¶ ⟨In⟩ ↑By↓

Page 85

6–10   injured ⟨if it was supposed⟩ ↑at the intimation↓ . . . from ⟨taking unjust advantages of⟩ ⟨their⟩ ↑assaulting or defrauding↓ . . . gratifying ⟨their⟩ ↑any criminal↓ passion⟨s⟩ out . . . law. ⟨If⟩ [end of line] ↑And ⟨for⟩ a . . . society ⟨this is true as to capital offences⟩ ↑do . . . statute↓.↓ [end of line] ↑If↓ . . . rare. ↑among them.↓

10–13   the ⟨judgments⟩ restraints of public opinion ↑which makes the law.↓ ⟨This is an arm of might⟩ ¶ The . . . in ⟨aid of our own⟩ ↑assisting the↓

16   hard⟨y⟩ly . . . to ⟨go⟩ ↑fly↓

17–18   have ⟨been⟩ advanced . . . fixed ⟨original⟩ principles . . . practi⟨c⟩se

23   all ⟨stand⟩ are

24–25   them ⟨alone⟩ in . . . presently ⟨w⟩seen

26–27   safeguard ⟨am⟩ in . . . to ⟨a⟩ thousand↑s↓

31–37   be ⟨far⟩ ↑one of↓ [emendation in pencil] . . . aid which . . . virtue ¶ ↑↑Insert A A↓ [addition in pencil] {He is ↑yet↓ far from ⟨truth &⟩ ↑the kingdom↓ heaven ↑who . . . society,↓ . . . live ⟨as⟩ with that decency ⟨& p⟩ ↑&↓ . . . requires⟨.⟩ ↑to be as bad as he dares.↓ . . . example↑,↓ . . . take ⟨a secondary⟩ the . . . principle.}↓

Page 86

3–6   feet. ¶ ⟨Jesus came to deliver men from the bondage of death unto life, & to sanctify a peculiar people [Cf. Hebrews 2:15 and Titus 2:14.] ¶ self cultivation ¶ ⟨M⟩ Wonderful adaptation of the world to man in all parts of his organization ¶ 1 Of the material world to the formation of his body; its elements to his food; its air to his respiration; ⟨its⟩ & the cultivation of the earth & the pursuit of his accommodation upon it, to the development of all his powers ↑child⟨is⟩ at his toys, is learning nat. phil.↓ ¶ 2. Of the moral sentiments of men to ↑aid↓ the formation of his principles to keep him safe whilst they are forming. ¶ 3. Of ⟨the⟩ External Religion, of a regard to what God shall give or do⟩ ¶ ⟨The universal⟩ Does . . . & the ⟨common d⟩ vulgar

18–20   this ⟨strong⟩ unwillingness ↑to . . . society↓ which ⟨exists⟩ is . . . men ⟨to outrage the feelings of society⟩ exists [The cancellation and addition of this phrase is in fact a relocation indicated by a caret.]

22   in ⟨the⟩ perfect

24–25   with /that more elevated ⟨class of men⟩ [canceled in pencil] who/ those who have reached ground & / [variant in pencil] . . . are /a very important aid/not without use/.

29–30   independant . . . ↑unspeakable↓

32–35   it." ¶ ⟨3.⟩ ↑4.↓ . . . religion↑.↓ ⟨such⟩ By . . . as ⟨a being far removed from us clothed in outward majesty &⟩ external

38   external ⟨punishment⟩ infliction

40   threats. ⟨And⟩ Men

Page 87

1–2   the ⟨clouds⟩ storm his manifestation, ⟨nor⟩ ↑They . . . in↓

5   ↑religious↓

7   they ⟨det⟩ hinder

8   supply ⟨food⟩ occupation

13–15   reward. ⟨It is a most⟩ ↑We . . . the↓ . . . that ⟨worships⟩ ↑kneels to↓ a supposed deity ⟨in the heavens⟩ ↑⟨amon⟩above the stars↓ . . . ↑Him . . . universe;↓

17   a ⟨truly⟩ [canceled in pencil] spiritual

21–24   another ⟨but⟩ & feel . . . present, {that . . . him} that

30   soul ⟨he⟩ external

38–39   ↑from religion of Moses to r. of Xt; from letter of yᵉ gospel to yᵉ spirit↓,

40–(88)1 soul su⟨perior⟩fficient to . . . richly ⟨accomplished it⟩ ↑endowed it↓.

Page 88

1   ↑capable↓

3–5   & ⟨ad⟩ use . . . itself ⟨And⟩ In

8–11   ¶ ↑Judge . . . these ⟨aids⟩ ↑means↓ . . . you↓ [addition in pencil]

13   ¶ 1 ⟨W⟩ Virtuous

14–16   feels ⟨it⟩ ↑virtuous conduct in itself↑ to be of immense importance— ⟨virtuous conduct in itself⟩ as [The cancellation and addition is in fact a relocation of the phrase indicated by a caret.] . . . principle. ⟨What⟩ Let

23–24   salvation↑.↓ ⟨with fear & trembling⟩ ¶ Let

26–27   from ⟨meaner⟩ ↑lower↓ motives to ⟨worthier⟩ ↑more excellent↓;

[The following notations occur upside down relative to the sermon text on the last inscribed page of the manuscript:] Others contend yᵗ Jesus ascended into heaven in visible pomp

1. Altho' we shd concede yᵗ Luke was yᵉ only witness of yˢ fact it is not proved yᵗ faith shd. not be given to yˢ testim. Which of yᵉ classic authors was present at all yᵉ events related in his book. All historical faith falls to yᵉ ground if you only believe yᵉ ocular witness. But yˢ fact is attested by Pet, Paul, John in Rev, & author of Heb.

2 Nature of death lies in separation of spirit from body. If it is true

Sermon CXLVII

Manuscript: Six sheets folded to make four pages each; pages measure 24.3 x 20.2 cm. The folios are stacked and sewn along the left margin with white thread.

Lines	Page 89
Bible Text	this giving [comma supplied from the King James version] . . . 1 Peter 1; 5,6,7.
2–3	them, ⟨by which⟩ to
6	↑to right action↓ [in ink over pencil]
8	dogma⟨s⟩ of [canceled in pencil]
9–10	if ⟨a⟩ humble ⟨origin⟩ circumstances . . . with ⟨humble⟩ contracted
13–15	is, ↑The disciples . . . men. So far from its being a narrow↓ [in ink over the following in pencil:] And surely it is not not a new thing in the world that poverty & truth shd. dwell together or that exalted virtue shd. be found ⟨under⟩ in humblest walks of life So far from narrow
18–19	↑the↓ human ⟨nature⟩ ↑soul↓ [first addition and cancellation in pencil; "soul" added in ink over pencil] . . . divine & ⟨nearest in interest⟩ ↑most beloved↓ . . . works ⟨to⟩ ↑by↓
20–(90)1	any / view / theory / of / man / life / . . . to ⟨the whole⟩ every

	Page 90
5	↑speaks . . . sect↓ [in pencil]
6	peasants war?
9–11	↑Not . . . oil ⟨pomp⟩ ↑friends↓ . . . charity.↓
12–17	Christianity. ⟨It appeals to nothing in us⟩ ↑that . . . anything↓ . . . feelings ⟨to the angels in us to the rudiments & seeds of the divine nature. ⟨Let us attend further to the Apostolic advice.⟩⟩ ↑This . . . man, ⟨as sublime & infinite as that in⟩ ¶ Let . . . a ⟨more⟩ further . . . advice.↓
19	↑quite↓
20–22	↑They . . . eye.↓
24	will ⟨be rendered⟩ ↑appear↓ more just ⟨in our version⟩ by
26–27	*this giving* [It is unclear whether Emerson understood the phrase as he wrote it (without the comma, here as in the opening sermon text) or as he read it in the Bible (with the comma, as here emended); given Emerson's laxness in punctuation, it is quite possible that he was conscious of the authorized reading and paused after "this" in the delivery.] . . . *strength.* ("And with this very view, employing your utmost earnestness" Wakefield.) ⟨that is⟩ to

30   that ⟨it⟩ this
33   Christ" Acts 24.24
36   which ⟨there is⟩ not
38   epistles↑?↓ . . . thee⟨?⟩."

Page 91

2   ↑it↓
3   a ⟨good⟩ virtuous
8   ↑depraved↓
12–13   this ⟨is entirely in⟩ ↑exclusively↓ regard↑s↓ ⟨to⟩ the
15   a ⟨good faith in the truth⟩ ↑cheerful . . . by Xt↓ [emendation in
            pencil]
19–20   word ⟨rendered⟩ ↑here translated↓ virtue ⟨in the original requires
            the limitation⟩ ↑though . . . yet↓ . . . languages ⟨is⟩ expresses . . .
            fortitude⟨. The⟩ or
21   And ⟨it⟩ in
24–27   And ⟨with⟩ ↑to↓ *fortitude, knowledge.* Faith & Fortitude & ⟨Knowl-
            edge⟩. Faith . . . good. ⟨In a⟩ These virtues themselves ⟨can have no
            great extent⟩ of . . . force ⟨until⟩ except
27–28   knowledge, ⟨read⟩ ↑understand↓
29   ↑& welcome↓
34–37   these ⟨wonderful⟩ powers of your ⟨own⟩ mind ↑of . . . observe↓ . . .
            perfectly ⟨to⟩ ↑with↓ . . . you ⟨rejoice in⟩ ↑understand↓ . . . &
            ⟨understand⟩ ↑sympathize with↓ all they feel? ⟨↑They all beseech
            you ⟨to⟩ Add to your faith knowledge.↓⟩ What
41–42   state. ↑⟨Who⟩ Does . . . less make⟨s⟩ the best ⟨friend ruler⟩ ↑son↓
            . . . friend?↓

Page 92

2–5   is ⟨finding out⟩ ↑laying open↓ . . . exact ⟨co⟩ deductions
8   by ⟨cultivation⟩ ↑use↓, & ⟨languish⟩ ↑perish↓ by ⟨neglect⟩ ↑disuse↓;
9   judgment, yᵗ
12   treasures. ⟨Fear & scorn⟩ this [rejected as incomplete emendation]
19   to ⟨gain⟩ add
22–23   nature the . . . so ⟨full⟩ disgusting
24–28   is ⟨almost offensive⟩ ↑not permitted↓ . . . to /censure/condemn/ it.
            And yet ⟨it⟩ standing . . . vice, & ⟨it⟩ the
30–40   temperate. ⟨A⟩ In . . . appetites. ↑But to leave so large a considera-
            tion rather fit for the moral philosopher than the preacher↓ [addition
            rejected as incomplete; the next paragraph shows that Emerson
            reconsidered the decision to leave the subject] ¶ To . . . temperance.
            ↑↑{↓Suffer [bracket in pencil] . . . to ⟨c⟩so . . . society ⟨are⟩in . . .
            the ⟨good⟩ ↑faithful↓ . . . ↑of accomplishing . . . good.↓ . . . so-
            cieties ⟨ag⟩ to . . . can be↓
42   have ⟨been⟩ guided

Page 93

1–2   ↑God . . . scare↓
3–4   you↑r excess↓ for gout & /rheumatism/atrophy/

5-8   ↑How . . . when↓ The . . . which the swine did eat. ↑which the swine
           did eat.↓ It . . . which ⟨lives with⟩ ↑faithfully follows↓ . . . a
           ⟨walking sermon⟩ ↑perpetual lesson↓
9   ↑is↓
17-19   speak ⟨to the young⟩ in . . . hastily ⟨n⟩enumerate
23-26   a ⟨h⟩ close . . . ↑always↓ . . . ↑of men, ↑by . . . nature↓↓ ["by . . .
           nature" in pencil] . . . devils ⟨out⟩ of
35   the ⟨many⟩ whole

Page 94

1   among m the
3-4   not like your words to be . . . ↑to be intelligible↓
6   the ⟨mob⟩ ↑multitude↓
7   be ⟨beautiful⟩ a . . . but ⟨your⟩ a
8   the ⟨decoration⟩ kingly
14-17   heart it . . . it ⟨is⟩ ↑comes to be↓ . . . it ⟨has⟩ ↑gains↓ over the body;
           ↑/It is/When you are temperate you are/↓ always ↑conscious yᵗ it is↓
           . . . God. & ⟨{preparing the mind for the exercise of holiest}⟩ ↑you
           are prepared for↓ contemplati⟨ons⟩ng
21-22   or ⟨are⟩ you . . . ↑they are↓ wearied ⟨out⟩ ↑down↓
26   ↑Add . . . patience↓
34   of ⟨friends⟩ our
35   *with ⟨love of Christians⟩ brotherly*
36-37   the ⟨p⟩ benevolence . . . mankind. ↑& further yᵉ brute creation.↓
           [addition in ink over pencil]

Page 95

1   God ⟨brotherly⟩ &
4-5   any /comparison of manuscripts/examination of yᵉ orig tongue/
           [variant in pencil] . . . soberness & ⟨ag⟩ uttered
8-11   most ⟨important⟩ material, . . . them. ⟨And it would be well if⟩ ↑I
           exhort you↓ every day we would /repeat/read/ them /meditatively/
           seriously this night/ in our chambers, ↑& repeat them every day↓
           [two variants and final addition in pencil; emendation rejected on the
           ground of sense] until

Sermon CXLVIII

Manuscript: Six sheets folded to make four pages each; single leaves occur before the
first folio, within the second folio (containing Insert "A" on the verso), within the third
folio (blank), and between the third and fourth folios (blank). Pages of the first three
folios measure 24.3 x 20.2 cm.; all other pages measure 24.3 x 20 cm. The gathering is
sewn along the left margin with white thread.

[Above Bible text:] SUNDAY SCHOOLS

Deut 6. 6,7 ⟨↑speaking of yᵐ when thou sittest in thine house & when thou walkest by yᵉ
way & when thou liest down & when thou risest up↓⟩ [added in pencil; canceled by

being erased and overwritten by the following revised opening, added for the second or
third delivery and therefore excluded from the clear text:] ↑I was happy to learn on the
last Sabbath that renewed efforts are now being made in this church to revive the Sunday
School for the religious education of children. I comply gladly with the suggestion made
by some of its friends that it might not be unprofitable to solicit the attention of the
congregation to the important objects of this institution.↓

Lines	Page 96
1–7	{It . . . & ⟨t⟩so . . . Society.} ↑I believe↓ No [addition rejected as probably related to the omission of the previous sentence in the second or third delivery] . . . the ⟨growth⟩ ↑prosperity↓ [emendation in pencil] of th⟨is⟩e [emendation in pencil and ink] ↑general↓ [in pencil] ⟨institution⟩ ↑undertaking↓ ↑of . . . branch↓ ["of . . . branch" in pencil] . . . importance↑,↓ [comma in pencil] . . . influence ⟨among⟩ ↑in↓
8	pleasure ⟨the⟩ ↑an↓ [emendation rejected as late]
10	attention / successively to some/ to a brief review/ [variant in pencil]
12	is ⟨for⟩ an
13	is ⟨much.⟩ ↑not without importance↓ [emendation in pencil]
15–16	manufactures, ⟨war, peace,⟩—all are addressed to the⟨⟨i⟩m⟩se classes
19	this ⟨knowledge⟩ ↑belief↓.
21	abstain⟨.⟩ ↑& so . . . temperate.↓
24–26	a ⟨general⟩ moral . . . young↑. It . . . age↓ [addition in pencil]

	Page 97
3	¶ Out [first part of paragraph written between the lines of an earlier pencil notation:] People dont believe enough in yᵉ power of education Remember yᵉ Spartans Pestalozzi lived for them
4–8	↑with↓ . . . ↑light of↓ true divinity that / moved/ won/ . . . ↑shining↓ in the↑ir↓
10–15	↑earthly↓ [in pencil] . . . dew." ¶ ⟨But I must leave these reflexions to say that always it must be pleasing in the eye of God & man to see the strength of this influence directed to yᵉ period of life & in yᵗ way yᵗ leads to yᵉ most hope for yᵉ human society⟩ ↑We . . . more ⟨i⟩emphasis . . . soon.↓ [addition in pencil]
17	↑or an immoral↓
18	enough↑,↓ is↑,↓ [commas in pencil]
25	the ⟨mo⟩ excellent
32	with ⟨{approbation &}⟩ hope [brackets in pencil]

	Page 98
2–3	pleasure ⟨to ⟨see⟩⟩ ["see" canceled separately in pencil] ↑⟨beloved⟩the deliverance of↓ [ink over pencil] . . . blessed ⟨saved from offence {and angels rescued.}⟩ [brackets in pencil] ↑out . . . world.↓ [last addition in ink over "that must needs be in yᵉ world" in pencil] ¶ ↑And . . . it.↓ [addition in pencil]
10–12	is ⟨usual⟩ I believe the . . . to ⟨be on⟩ ↑give↓
16	indispensable ⟨for⟩ ↑to↓ [emendation in pencil]

22   ¶ ↑And this /is important/is seen/ [variant in pencil] in another view↓
24–25   girl ⟨is⟩ ↑shows↓ . . . which ⟨it presents⟩ ↑the same child exhibits↓
25–30   ↑who . . . children &↓ who ⟨sees⟩ ↑goes a stranger into↓ /a/a
            large/ [variant in pencil] school ⟨of children⟩, [canceled in pencil] is
            . . . of ⟨the⟩ idle, . . . teacher; ⟨& he is afflicted by the thought⟩ ↑He
            . . . conclusion↓ . . . ↑prematurely↓
32   wholly /vanish/effaced/
32–33   ↑It . . . Conquer↓
34–41   each ⟨child⟩ ↑individual↓ [emendation in pencil] . . . application. ¶
            ⟨Any one may notice this in yᵉ /plays/common language/ [variant in
            pencil] of children yᵗ confidence ↑each child feels↓ yᵗ he who knows
            yᵐ best will like yᵐ best ⟨ie to say if⟩ as much as to say if ⟨he were
            stripped to the⟩ ↑this↓ [emendation in pencil] heart ↑were laid open↓
            [addition in pencil] there wd. be found a fountain of tenderness &
            goodness ⟨there⟩.⟩ ["there" canceled in pencil; paragraph written in
            ink over the notation "Dick you know me" in pencil] ¶ ↑{Insert A} A
            {The . . . says Give it me send it me, for ["Give . . . for" circled in
            pencil, apparently to cancel] *you know me* ↑wh. is no obscure↓
            [addition in pencil] . . . ↑& truth.↓↓ ["& truth." in pencil]

                                        Page 99
1   character, ↑this↓
7–10   pupil. ¶ ↑{Insert B} B {On . . . the ⟨degree of advantage wh.⟩
            ↑efficacy of↓ [emendation in pencil] a Sunday School ⟨can afford⟩
            [canceled in pencil] ⟨wh⟩ a fact ["a fact" circled in pencil, apparently
            to cancel] which . . . pupils.↓
12–14   admit of↑.↓ ⟨thus⟩ ↑↑Thus↓ he becomes yᵉ discoverer ⟨of great
            merit⟩ & encourager, of . . . its teaching↓ . . . itself↑,↓ [comma
            added in pencil] &
21–24   ↑In . . . uni⟨versal⟩form . . . discipline↓ [in pencil] ↑A . . . place.↓
            ⟨And⟩ [canceled in pencil] certainly ⟨to⟩by . . . or ⟨without⟩
            ↑until↓ . . . teaching, ⟨punishment⟩ ↑a coercive system↓ [emenda-
            tion in ink over pencil]
26   teaching, ⟨Henry Pestalozzi⟩ &
30   ↑of the power↓
34–35   laughed out ⟨of him⟩ ↑or . . . him↓
38   ↑at Stantz↓
39   ↑vicious↓
42–(100)6   convincing ⟨Pestalozzi⟩ ↑him↓ . . . offence." ⟨"if necessity had not
            forced him out of his o⟨wn⟩ld ways he shd. hardly have come to that
            childlike state of mind in which it was possible for him freely &
            willingly to follow yᵉ path of nature.⟩ [canceled in pencil; see Biber,
            Henry Pestalozzi, 33–34; end of page] ¶ ↑Delightful account↓ [in
            pencil] ¶ "At

                                        Page 100
8   existence.⟨"⟩ To
17   on ⟨yᵐ⟩ theirs

21–25	ceased↑;↓ . . . children↑,↓ . . . kind↑,↓ . . . domestic↑,↓ were thus converted↑,↓ in a short time↑,↓ . . . circle↑,↓ in wh↑ich↓ [all additions in pencil] . . . exist." ¶ ⟨"He taught we are told⟩ He
28–30	yᵉ ⟨hear⟩ mind . . . ↑on . . . teacher↓
32–34	¶ ↑It . . . remarks↓ [in pencil]
37–40	in yᵉ love of k. & . . . acquiring they . . . were / {daily} / perpetually / [the Biber text has "perpetually" at this point]

Page 101

1	principle↑,↓ ⟨& the⟩ must [emendation in pencil]
5	occupation ⟨before so little⟩ ↑oftener↓
6–8	But ⟨this is eminently⟩ ↑that . . . peculiar↓ applicabl⟨e⟩ility ↑of . . . teaching↓ to the *Sunday School*. There ↑are no punishments;↓
13–14	welfare. ¶ ⟨Too much can hardly be expected from this institution, if it were made to yield all it can. It is a direct personal relation established between you & your little friends whereby you ⟨b⟩ are constituted their counsellor & friend⟩ ¶ 4. I ⟨need not⟩ ↑mt.↓
17–19	↑But this need har⟨l⟩dly be . . . effects; for↓ It . . . direction. ⟨What⟩ Too
22–27	whole ⟨/youthful/infant/⟩ population ↑of children↓ . . . duties; ↑{The . . . reformed.↓ what . . . of ⟨pure⟩ ↑well informed↓
31	that ⟨make⟩ now
33	of ⟨vir⟩ knowledge
36–(102)5	instruction ⟨gi⟩ brings . . . imparted ⟨{I wish only to call your attention, all you who have time & attention to bestow, to the rich reward which you shall deserve & obtain.}⟩ No⟨t⟩r . . . but ↑but I wd. call ⟨your⟩ ↑the↓ [emendation in pencil] . . . charity↓ . . . ↑which . . . obtain↓ namely . . . the ⟨holy⟩ day ↑of rest↓

Page 102

7–8	has ²{the consciousness of the approbation of God}, ¹{the consciousness of having . . . country} &
13–15	We ⟨ask your⟩ ↑ask parents . . . ask the↓ interest ↑of all↓ & we ask ⟨your⟩ ↑the↓ assistance ⟨in⟩ of . . . & the ⟨disposition to give it⟩ ↑will,↓ [last emendation in pencil]
15–16	institution ⟨a⟩ in
20–22	his ⟨assistance⟩ ↑help↓ [emendation in pencil] . . . ↑if . . . so↓ [addition in pencil]

Sermon CXLIX

Manuscript: Five sheets folded to make four pages each; pages measure 24.3 x 20.2 cm. Two leaves of the same dimensions are included in the sewing between the first and second and the fourth and fifth folios. A leaf measuring 24.7 x 19.5 cm, once attached with red sealing wax to the first page of the fourth folio, has become detached. The folios are stacked and sewn with white thread along the left margin.

Lines	*Page 103*
2–5	that ⟨our⟩ we . . . virtues. ⟨We must begin somewhere.⟩ [canceled in

pencil and ink] ⟨You⟩ ↑We↓ must ⟨show⟩ ↑know↓ the exact ⟨nature⟩
↑amount↓ of ⟨your⟩ ↑the↓ demand upon our ⟨hands⟩ way

5–6   ↑We . . . begin.↓ [added in ink over the following in pencil:] We must
know that it is practicable & we must know where to begin

7–15   ourselves ⟨or enjoining the law of duty upon others⟩ to ⟨fix direct⟩
concentrate ⟨the⟩ ↑our↓ endeavours on one point↑, & . . . observation.↓ [addition in ink over pencil] ⟨Let not⟩ ↑It . . . that↓ the mind
be ↑not↓ . . . in ⟨mind⟩ ↑view↓ . . . ↑leave it↓ . . . the ⟨store⟩
↑counting house↓,

21   ↑only↓

21–23   the ⟨glory⟩ ↑divine mark↓ . . . universal ⟨applicability⟩ ↑fitness↓
. . . minds. ⟨And unt⟩ And . . . spiritual ⟨knowledge⟩ ↑growth↓.
[last emendation in ink over pencil]

24–(104)1   ↑We . . . poor what . . . mean ⟨if⟩ than . . . attain↓ [addition in
pencil]

Page 104

1–3   Eyes." ↑the . . . disagreeable↓ [addition in pencil]

4   the ⟨fact⟩ truth

5   see, ⟨↑each↓⟩ a ↑one a↓

8   life. ⟨In a good life there wd. be no dull days⟩ "Good

12–22   good ⟨of peace of mind,⟩ ↑on its pillars↓ . . . justice, ⟨↑of content-
ment↓⟩—the . . . on ⟨any⟩ ↑the↓ . . . sky. ¶ ⟨And⟩ ↑My friends,↓
[addition in ink over pencil] . . . new ⟨commercial⟩ ↑project or
business↓ [emendation in pencil] . . . sweeter, ⟨to⟩ more . . . holy. ¶
⟨Let me⟩ ↑And . . . day; to↓

26–35   heaven⟨.⟩: ↑to excite, . . . man [in ink over the following in pencil:]
⟨to excite if it were possible in every one of us attention to himself to
arouse in each, to the youngest⟩ [The ink inscription continues, with
verses canceled in pencil:]

        ⟨"Who, not content that former worth stand fast,
        Looks forward persevering to the last,
        From well to better, daily self surpast."⟩

    ↑who . . . better↓↓ ["who . . . better" added in pencil]

    ↑And the first of these virtues for whose cultivation every condition
affords room is self-command.↓ [in ink over the following in pencil:]
⟨And the first of these virtues ↑for↓ whose cultivation every condition
affords room⟩ [The ink inscription continues:]

    1. ["1." rejected because Emerson supplies no "2."] ⟨Temperance.⟩
Self Command ⟨especially⟩ in that . . . animal ⟨appetites⟩ ↑nature↓
. . . food⟨.⟩; & chastity. ¶ ⟨Early⟩ Philosophers

Page 105

4–7   ↑enemies, the↓ ⟨e⟩passions↑,↓ have ⟨shut his ear to⟩ hidden his favor
from us. ¶ ↑↑Why need I praise Temperance?↓ ¶ All the animal
gratifications it is the part of Self Command to restrain. And they are
all connected—all beneficent whilst under the law of the mind, all
debasing when they attain mastery. The God of Nature has sur-

rounded us with warnings against license which every one in the privacy of his own meditation will do well to heed. In general I will only make one remark upon all, that ancient observation has shown a mysterious yet habitual connexion between sensuality & all that is most hideous in human nature. It has been noticed that there is in history a close connexion between sensuality & cruelty, which though not always distinctly traceable in individuals, is yet very easily seen in large masses of men, & which, by an unknown process hidden in the depths of our nature, makes devils of malice out of men who have gratified their pleasant tastes.↓ [These two paragraphs, drawn from Sermon CXLVII (see p. 93) are rejected as a late addition.] ¶ Why . . . Temperance ⟨(of which I had recent occasion to speak somewhat in detail.)⟩ And [cancellation rejected as a late emendation]

8	↑true↓
14	him ⟨let him⟩ ⟨master⟩ ↑conquer↓
15–17	ounces, ⟨eleven⟩ ↑twelve↓ or ⟨twelve⟩ ↑fourteen↓ . . . purpose. ⟨To Tempe⟩ Its
20–23	person. ⟨It⟩ The . . . ↑one in↓ the ↑weariest day &↓ [last addition in ink over pencil] . . . tho'ts. ↑⟨&⟩ of . . . injured.↓ [addition in ink over "of . . . injured" in pencil]
24	↑comes . . . life↓ all men
29	↑one↓
34	us. ⟨The only⟩ Now
36–37	↑This . . . therein.↓

Page 106

3	adviser, ⟨instead of⟩ ↑& changing his opinions↓
9	↑with↓
11	neighbor's ⟨coat & hat⟩ ↑garments↓ [emendation in pencil]
13	↑a final↓ deliverance from th⟨is⟩ese
15–17	duties ⟨to⟩ command his tongue, ⟨to⟩ eat ↑a↓ lighter meal⟨s⟩, ⟨to⟩ rise earlier, ⟨to⟩ work harder, ⟨to⟩ do . . . strictly ⟨to⟩ adhere
19	his ⟨coat & hat⟩ ↑garments↓ [emendation in pencil]
21	every ⟨expression⟩ ↑feature↓
23	things↑—↓in [addition in pencil]
25	lot↑,↓ [comma in pencil] convinced that ↑our↓
27–29	↑Know thyself.↓ Let ⟨every one⟩ ↑each↓ [both additions in ink over pencil] . . . duty↑,↓ [comma in pencil]
31	being. /He is/Do you not see that while you sit alone to find what is your duty you have/That humble soul is/ attaining [variants in pencil]

Page 107

1	↑whether . . . labor,↓ [in pencil]
6	↑&↓
17	independance
21–22	days. ↑when ⟨men thot⟩ public opinion allowed it to use the ax & the fagot.↓

23	times ⟨when men tho't it right⟩. Every
25–26	↑malevolence . . . deportment↓
28	the⟨ir⟩ convenience
29–30	grey ⟨in⟩ at the fire side ↑in . . . virtues↓
33	↑of distress↓
34	th⟨e⟩ at necessity
40	known. ⟨See whether in your⟩ "If

Page 108

5	dependance
12–14	↑And . . . fail ⟨to add to the amount of human happiness⟩ to create . . . to ⟨call out charity⟩ reprove . . . happiness.↓ [addition and emendations in pencil]
27	admit⟨s⟩ equally
31	visionary. ⟨Surely⟩ I . . . nor ⟨un⟩ love
35	↑No . . . existent.↓
36–(109)1	the ⟨Principle⟩ ↑good God↓ [emendation in pencil] . . . it ⟨glows⟩ ↑warms↓ . . . of ⟨obeying⟩ submitting

Page 109

1	that ⟨reference⟩ acknowledgment
5	privelege . . . not ↑⟨slowly⟩ reluctantly↓ [ink over pencil]
11–18	independant . . . condition. ↑B [on the previous page, a passage marked "B":] {I need . . . in ⟨y⟩ the . . . endeavor.}↓ [end of Insert "B"] ↑To . . . day↓ [addition in ink over the following in pencil:] ⟨To practise these virtues wd be to meditate all the day on the law of the Lord⟩
20	ourselves; ⟨occasions⟩ ↑objects↓

Sermon CL

Manuscript: Five sheets folded to make four pages each; single leaves follow the first and second folios. The gathering is stacked and sewn along the left margin with white thread. Pages measure 24.3 x 20.2 cm.

[Above Bible text:] FAST DAY

Lines	*Page 110*
Bible Text	Is ⟨this the⟩ ↑it such a↓
2	the ⟨anniversary⟩ religious
5	↑the↓
5–11	a ⟨highly becoming accommodation of the apostolic institutions to these last days as a carrying on of the sacred history as a ⟨blessing⟩ consecration of our privileges by a devout retrospection as ⟨a⟩ ↑another↓ verse of the penitential psalm of centuries making music in the ear of God⟩ and as a↑n↓ ⟨historical⟩ invaluable . . . degenerate ⟨de⟩ posterity . . . disuse↑; as a . . . priveleges . . . piety.↓

12–22	that ⟨the ver actual state of the Fast Day among us,⟩ the actual state of the public feeling with regard to ⟨it⟩ ↑the Fast Day;↓ the . . . ↑in this instance↓ . . . inconsistency ⟨of⟩ ↑between↓ . . . ↑by multitudes↓ . . . that ⟨the institution should⟩ an . . . that ⟨it S a⟩ Sabbath . . . remembrances. ¶ ⟨The⟩ However ↑time . . . settle↓ these questions↑,↓ ⟨may be settled,⟩ that . . . ↑matter↓, is, ⟨{that these are all forms & it is really of very little consequence how they are settled provided it never be lost sight of that like all other good forms they suppose a substance} although these are forms⟩ ↑that . . . mere forms.↓
24	And ⟨it is of extreme importan &⟩ though
26–(111)5	For, ⟨if⟩ rightly . . . but ⟨have their roots in the nature of man. [illegible word]⟩ ↑↑are as old as the world &↓ [addition in pencil] are . . . man.↓ ¶ ↑"Men . . . actions"↓ [end of page] ¶ ↑And I ⟨desire⟩ ↑propose↓ [emendation in pencil] . . . obligation↓ [end of page; added paragraphs in pencil]

Page 111

6	found ⟨in⟩ to
10	essence? ⟨It⟩ ↑The . . . depend,↓
13	lead ⟨men⟩ ↑the soul↓
16	↑privation &↓ [ink over pencil]
17–24	ostentatious↑,↓ . . . vices↑,↓ . . . men↑,↓ [commas added in ink over pencil] the Nazarite ↑among the ancient Jews↓, the [end of page] ↑of the later↓ . . . Spartan, ⟨the Christian monk⟩ the . . . ↑from the naked sage in ⟨the⟩ [canceled in pencil] ancient India⟨n desart⟩ [canceled in pencil] down . . . Latrappe↓ . . . its ⟨capability of pouring contempt⟩ ↑power . . . serenity.↓
26	↑in hunger & penance↓ . . . ↑India↓ ["India" in ink over pencil]
28	the ⟨wild animal⟩ ↑gnawing fox↓

Page 112

1–2	from ⟨meat⟩ animal . . . pulse ⟨on⟩ grew
4	↑guilty of↓
9	thinks ⟨His will⟩ ↑agreable to Him↓ can acheive
16–18	↑clad↓ . . . upon ⟨heroic⟩ ↑the↓ . . . have ⟨starved themselves⟩ ↑been . . . rack↓ . . . knowledge & ⟨enjoy⟩ the
19–20	victories ⟨in a bad cause⟩ ↑of savage fanaticism↓ . . . in ⟨a good⟩ working
30–32	independance . . . luxury⟨.⟩ ↑worth . . . sacrifices.↓ ↑How . . . want said Socrates.↓

Page 113

1	than ⟨{the {vanity of such an ornament or the pride of independance.}⟩ ↑a vain pride.↓
2–5	↑the time it saves↓ ²{the increase . . . benevolence, ¹{the mastery . . . propensities} & . . . us ⟨these⟩ this [brackets and numerals in pencil]
6	¶ 2. (Humiliation.) The

8   cry ⟨Unc⟩ like
12–13   dependant . . . nature. ⟨W⟩ Self
15   that ⟨the wisest⟩ he
18   their ⟨view⟩ insight
21   require ⟨the⟩ ↑acts & words of↓
22   very ⟨cant⟩ ↑byword↓
26   true ⟨act⟩ ↑office↓ . . . . a ⟨watchful⟩ jealousy of its↑elf↓ ⟨own⟩ a
29–30   a ⟨perpetual⟩ ↑permanent↓ principle. [end of MS p. 14; p. 15 is
                blank; at the bottom of p. 16, written upside down relative to the rest
                of the text:] ⟨cxlix⟩ ↑cl↓ [end of MS p. 16] ¶ 3. Prayer.
31   ↑& worse than↓

Page 114

2–6   or ⟨(at home)⟩ their bedside; ↑These . . . prayer. And if↓ if these ⟨do
                not⟩ are only strings of words; ⟨↑These are only the vehicles↓⟩ if . . .
                wasted ⟨blasphemous⟩ ↑hypocritical↓ breath; ↑These are not
                prayers↓ . . . come /continually/familiarly/ into the soul ↑flow . . .
                will↓
9–10   prayers ⟨are granted.⟩ ↑God is every day granting ↑to the righteous
                man & to the sinner↓, . . . mind.↓
11   the ⟨true⟩ ↑effectual↓
16–22   ↑An . . . to the ⟨whole⟩ ↑our↓ . . . mankind.↓ ¶ ⟨And⟩ And . . . a
                ⟨perpetual⟩ ↑lasting↓ . . . thought. ¶ ⟨And thus,⟩ ↑On . . . obliga-
                tion.↓
23   temperance↑;↓ {& self command} We
25–26   ↑in↓ what manner the ⟨F⟩Annual
30   *social & ⟨public⟩ ↑political↓*
34–35   the ⟨colossal⟩ vice ↑when . . . length↓ which they ⟨entertain⟩
                tolerate . . . miniature; as ⟨men⟩ the
40–41   ↑a great duty↓ in old kingdoms ⟨a great duty⟩ where

Page 115

2–4   weak; ↑if . . . manners;↓ [addition in ink over pencil; the pencil layer
                lacks the phrase "in high places"] . . . approve ⟨the⟩ ↑such↓ . . . . as
                ⟨much⟩ ↑truly↓ . . . our ↑tongues ⟨advised⟩ ↑gave↓ the counsel,↓
                hands
7–8   public ⟨purity⟩ honesty, . . . religion, ⟨it is⟩ ↑they are↓ . . . act
                ⟨&⟩thereupon
17   whom ⟨a⟩ one
20   offer ⟨the⟩ just

Sermon CLI

Manuscript: Five sheets folded to make four pages each; single leaves follow the second,
third, and fourth folios, while a single leaf is inserted into the fourth folio. Pages measure
24.3 x 20.2 cm. The fascicle is sewn along the left margin with white thread.

Lines   *Page 116*
3–4   observances. ↑to . . . access.↓ [addition in pencil]

6   rose ⟨no pain without it⟩ ↑no↓ ⟨poison without its antidote⟩ no evil [second cancellation in pencil]

10   much ⟨reduced⟩ ↑contracted↓ by ⟨long⟩ ↑chronic↓

Page 117

1–23   hath ⟨set the world in man's heart⟩ made . . . heart. ¶ ⟨In⟩ ↑It is most true in↓ [in ink over "It is ⟨true⟩ most true" in pencil] . . . ↑& virtue.↓ [ink over "& virtue" in pencil] ¶ ⟨⟨There is within our reach a world of pleasure & advantage of which we have yet made very little use.⟩ Do not look so far as to overlook the mark. ⟨It would be of great use to us if we wd accustom ourselves to reflect upon the right use of the senses; upon the extent of their powers, & the five worlds to which they are inlets.⟩⟩ ¶ ↑I . . . remarks↑, 1.↓ . . . sorrow.↓ ¶ ↑1. First; . . . organs.↓

10–11   ↑the↓ dependance . . . ↑nook of↓

13–15   firmament↑,↓ ⟨mine, & so of⟩ ↑and↓ all it enlightens⟨;⟩ ↑in some sort, mine;↓ . . . & ⟨religion⟩ ↑piety↓ [addition in ink over pencil] . . . ↑the↓ touch, & ↑the↓ smell↑,↓ [comma in ink over pencil]

19   enjoy. ⟨Also b⟩Brethren, if ↑it were possible↓

26–29   desart. ↑{Insert X} X {Why . . . untiring ⟨ingenuity⟩ industry . . . servant.}↓

30   who ⟨they say⟩ was

33   ↑at length↓

35   more ⟨piety⟩ true

39–(118)1 power." (Galen apud Abernathy p.) ¶ ⟨↑I need not point at what wonders this little instrument has executed under the genius of painters sculptors engravers architects but wd rather point to its daily cunning, its untiring industry.↓⟩ [added and canceled in pencil] ¶ So

Page 118

2   & ⟨no⟩ ↑of none↓ more familiar↑ly↓ ⟨proof of it can be quoted⟩ ↑spoken↓ than of ⟨the value they put upon the eye who are losing it⟩ ↑the eye↓.

7   ↑ascertained . . . spots↓.

8–16   death↑.↓ ⟨& all the intelligent men in Europe felt it as a public calamity.⟩ ↑{Insert A} A {He . . . ↑for me↓ is shrunk ⟨for me⟩ into . . . it⟨"⟩ So . . . calamity}↓

17–20   priveleged, . . . come." ¶ ⟨"Alas!" he himself says, "I am become totally & irreparably blind so that this heaven this earth this universe which with wonderful observations I had enlarged a hundred & thousand times beyond yᵉ belief of bygone ages henceforward ⟨is⟩ for me is shrunk into yᵉ narrow space which I myself fill in it.⟨"⟩ ⟨So it pleases God, it shall therefore please me also."⟩ ¶ ⟨He had ⟨declared⟩ boasted yᵗ he never wd cease using yᵉ senses God had given him in declaring yᵉ glory of his works.⟩⟩ ¶ ⟨So it was with⟩ ↑The same calamity befel↓

25   virtue; and that [end of page] and that by

29–30   really /valuable/useful/ . . . ↑by every man↓

30   was ⟨the⟩ ↑said in↓
33   with ⟨as an idle spectator of others⟩ ↑⟨unimproved⟩ seeing . . .
            live.↓ . . . virtue, ⟨either⟩ but

Page 119

3   explore ⟨its⟩ ↑a nation's↓
5–11   if ⟨this⟩ ↑it↓ . . . by ⟨travel⟩ ↑going abroad↓. For ⟨the young ar⟩ you
            very often may he⟨re⟩ar people . . . like, ⟨Us⟩ & . . . & ⟨ha⟩enjoyed
            great trusts. ↑True Wisdom says to you↓ [in ink over "True Wisdom
            teaches" in pencil] Use
16–20   ↑stay↓ . . . much /fact/instructive experience/, . . . ↑not . . . vir-
            tue.↓
23   by /travelling/being much abroad/ . . . nature,↑—↓as
31–(120)1   in ⟨a glas⟩ water, . . . man.' ¶ ⟨⟨Instead⟩ Not however to⟩ ↑I would
            not↓ . . . true., (for I know we need the help of others to know
            ourselves,) ↑{Insert B} B {Far . . . one from [end of line] from the . . .
            more ⟨various⟩ than he has used.}↓ [in ink over erased pencil; the
            pencil layer has "opportunities" for "advantages" in the second
            sentence and "the cultivating" for "cultivating" in the third, where,
            also, "multiplying" is lacking and "various" is uncanceled] I will ask
            ⟨if it were not wis⟩ any

Page 120

5–7   with ⟨20⟩twenty . . . nature ⟨in extenso⟩ as
11–12   a ⟨p⟩ grown
13–15   ↑To↓ Almost . . . family ⟨is brot into⟩ ↑have come↓ . . . feasting,
            ⟨ma⟩ funerals,
20–21   ↑'no duty . . . broke',↓ than when ⟨duties are left & callings broken⟩
            ↑you make it a distin⟨g⟩ct object↓
23   their ⟨glad⟩ ↑cheerful↓
25   ↑Because . . . heart.↓
39   & ⟨now⟩ chiefly

Page 121

2   ↑wherever . . . principle↓
4   because ⟨w⟩ our
10–11   incessant ⟨impulse⟩ prompting . . . nature ⟨all⟩ of
17   of ⟨our⟩ God

Sermon CLII

Manuscript: Four sheets folded to make four pages each; the pages of the first folio
measure 24.3 x 20.1 cm, those of the second and fourth 24.3 x 20.2 cm, and those of the
third 24.1 x 19.8 cm. A leaf measuring 24.3 x 19.9 cm follows the first folio. Two leaves
follow the second folio; a leaf is inserted into the third folio; and a leaf follows the third
folio (each of these four leaves measures 24.3 x 20.2 cm). Folios are sewn along the left
margin with white thread. The sermon is numbered "152" at the top of MS p. 1.

Lines	Page 123
3	¶ 1. All [Emerson switches to roman numerals for subsequent headings.]
8–9	forgotten. ¶ ⟨{"Thou mad'st all nature beauty to his eye / And music to his ear."}⟩ ¶ He
17	↑have↓ use↑d↓
24	pe⟨pet⟩rpetuated . . . which ⟨brought to a minute examination⟩ but
31–32	intention ¶ ⟨P⟩ ↑To this point I quote with pleasure the remarks of Paley↓ [in ink over "To this point I quote" in pencil] "The
34	prospect /on/upon/

	Page 124
8	That ⟨little⟩ ↑small↓
10–13	many ⟨geometers⟩ ↑architects↓ to form [end of line] of it, . . . employed. ⟨But leaving other points of interest I speak of on⟩ ↑And . . . attention↓ the . . . ↑is constructed↓
16–19	naturalist ⟨↑(↓suspecting yᵗ yˢᵉ angles mt be chosen to spare wax,↑)↓⟩ [parentheses in ink over pencil] proposed . . . cell ⟨of this description⟩ ↑with . . . strength↓ . . . possible ⟨matter⟩ ↑wax↓ [last emendation in ink over pencil]
34–37	invariable ⟨mixture of the⟩ composition of the ⟨el⟩atmosphere . . . ↑in the case of water↓ to the general law by which ⟨liquids⟩ bodies

	Page 125
6–7	ends." [traces of an erased pencil draft of this paragraph (beneath the ink version) reveal no variation; end of page] ¶ ⟨Well then⟩ when . . . progress⟨,⟩ ↑of *man*↓
9–19	talents ↑the ⟨combination⟩ ↑unconscious cooperation↓ . . . speech & ⟨good⟩ ↑brave↓ . . . known↓ And when . . . ↑after↓ becom⟨es⟩-ing ⟨conscious⟩ ↑aware↓ . . . come↑s↓ . . . attraction ⟨seems to⟩ reign↑s↓ . . . power, ⟨I am⟩ ↑it is↓ . . . exists ⟨to which I can trust,⟩ in
23–24	order. ¶ ⟨And I learn⟩ The
29–32	in ⟨h⟩Him . . . whole, ⟨from⟩ the . . . secure. ⟨Shall I doubt the preservation of my life who see this annual resurrection of nature from the dust who see the south wind blow & green herbage run over the regions of winter.⟩ ¶ It . . . these ⟨spe⟩ observations . . . off they
35	the ⟨care⟩ thot

	Page 126
2–3	nature. ¶ ⟨He spoke wisely who on being asked if he did not fear to die? replied, 'No I see no reason for dying.'⟩ ¶ II In
8	herbage runs over [This seems to be a copying error: note that the word is "run" in the corresponding canceled passage.]
24–34	grave.' [end of page] ¶ ⟨Connexion with spiritual life⟩ ¶ ↑⟨[Inde-cipherable capital letter]⟩ {Why [The canceled letter suggests that Emerson intended the paragraph as an insert, then decided that he was satisfied with its position as written.] . . . actions, built . . .

temperance, ⟨of diligence⟩ of . . . more?⟩↓ [end of page] ¶ ⟨This is
life within life⟩ [end of page] ¶ Shall

36   in ⟨h⟩Him

37   dead, his

40–(127)1   life. ¶ ⟨⟨[indecipherable number or letter]⟩ 2.⟩ ↑III.↓ All

                              Page 127

2   ↑possessing↓ [in ink over pencil]

3   nature ⟨obeying⟩ ↑having↓ laws wholly /new/its own/ [emendation
                  and variant in ink over pencil]

5   which ⟨he cannot for⟩ material nature ↑never commands.↓ [cancella-
                  tion and addition in ink over pencil]

6   allegory ⟨of⟩ ↑by . . . in↓ [addition in ink over "by which his mind is
                  instructed" in pencil]

10   emphasis; ⟨that then⟩ ↑as if↓

12   that ⟨his life is renewed⟩ ↑he is born again↓

16–18   nature [end of line] it . . . nothing ⟨that⟩ ↑so↓

26–27   worth. ⟨This then is the highest sense in which ⟨the soul⟩ ↑man↓
                  lives unto God Thus heaven lives unto him, ↑and all its host of holy
                  beings,↓ & thus every soul ↑& all its orders of holy beings↓ [addition
                  in pencil] lives unto him in proportion to the progress it hath made.⟩
                  ¶ No . . . God ⟨in this highest sense⟩ when . . . ↑habitual↓

29–30   is ⟨character wisdom⟩ to . . . animal ⟨propensities⟩ ↑indulgence↓;

32–33   ↑lives unto him↓

37   ↑in its virtue↓

[Following the end of the sermon is a passage written for the fifth delivery, July 10, 1836,
at Concord. It refers to the death, the previous day, of Hersey Bradford Goodwin, junior
pastor to Ezra Ripley:] My friends, I have asked your attention to this sentiment now
because although the language & precepts of Jesus have an everlasting pertinence to
human nature, yet this seemed to address itself to the present hour & to its heavy tidings.
⟨Y⟩our pastor & friend shall never more return to our solemn assembly. Here he shall
break no more to us the bread of life. His pleasant voice we shall no more hear. Now
when the increasing experience & acquaintance with you for several years had fitted him
to give & you to receive the benefits of his office, he is hurried out of your sight in the
bloom of manly beauty, in the innocency of his life, in the preparation & first fruits of
his strength.—↑I leave to others the sad satisfaction of drawing his character & praising
his virtues↓

   The voice of this event is, "Unto God he yet lives." Let not the ⟨curtain⟩ horizon of
this world fall like a curtain over our prospect. ⟨Let us f⟩Follow him with the eyes of
hope & faith & love whither he is gone nor let the bell that tolls for a friend knock on our
hearts like a knell but like ⟨a kind⟩ a kindly solemn admonition from the other world
whither we too are bound. Let us see him safe, and alive, & born again to a better life,
& to vast attai↑n↓ments in the eternal power of God So shall our souls even now thro'
the abundance of spiritual life transcend the limits & the sorrows of [end of line] of time,
&, by living unto God, live with all the children of God.

Sermon CLIII

Manuscript: Four sheets folded to make four pages each; pages measure 24.3 x 20.2 cm. A leaf of the same size follows the first folio; the second folio contains a nested folio (the pages of which measure 24 x 19.6 cm) fastened by a pin to the left margin, as well as a loose leaf of the same size (these are MS pp. 9–14 and contain added material); a leaf measuring 24.3 x 20.2 cm follows the second folio; a leaf of the same measurements follows the third folio (bearing the watermark "S & B / N H"). The folios are sewn along the left margin with white thread.

[Below the Bible text Emerson inscribed a second text for a later delivery:] The mercy of the Lord is from everlasting to everlasting upon them that fear him, ↑xxxx↓ to such as keep his covenant & to those who remember his commandments to do them Ps. 103, 17–18

Lines	Page 129
Bible Text	them ⟨who⟩that . . . Lord ⟨God⟩ of
1–6	¶ ⟨The⟩ ↑A↓ sentiment . . . soul. ⟨that his strength is sufficient for our weakness.⟩ that . . . ↑ac↓counted ⟨as nothing⟩ ↑vile↓ in comparison. ↑This . . . Psalms.↓
7–8	↑that noble strain of↓ /Habakkuk ⟨in the prophecy⟩/⟨the⟩ prophecy/ ↑which . . . age.↓
11–12	↑This . . . Jesus.↓
14	¶ If ⟨this be true⟩ the . . . ↑shall be↓
15–17	true ⟨the cares of every day are commonly sweetened⟩ the . . . provided ⟨that⟩ ↑in↓ . . . day ⟨in⟩ among industrious persons ⟨shall⟩ a . . . insensible ⟨of⟩ ↑to↓
19–21	We ⟨would feel a more real & deep-seated⟩ ↑demand a better↓ . . . last, ⟨or whether it may⟩ be ⟨dissipated like the morning⟩ cloud
22	our ⟨understandings.⟩ reason.
23–(130)1	it ⟨more worthy of⟩ ↑fit that↓ rational beings ⟨to⟩ ↑should↓ . . . is ⟨ne⟩also

	Page 130
2–5	of ⟨your⟩ ↑the↓ . . . not ⟨win your ↑hearts↓ attention the furnishing you with all amusements⟩ ↑carry with it ⟨the⟩ peace . . . no, nor↓ . . . gratify ¶ ⟨God draws the curtain of darkness around you every night & is continually sending us into solitude⟩ ¶ There
9–12	sees ⟨that⟩ distinctly . . . happy ⟨and he will not be able⟩ ↑he sees it with pain,—& ⟨happy⟩blessed . . . able↓ . . . ↑of conscience↓ [last addition in pencil]
12–15	↑It makes itself heard, ⟨that voice of conviction⟩ ↑in every worthy soul↓ above . . . curtain⟨s⟩ of darkness over ⟨you⟩ ↑us↓ . . . solitude.↓
16–18	all, ⟨there are⟩ ↑& which . . . bitter↓ . . . from ⟨severe trials of their fortitude.⟩ ↑misfortunes . . . to ⟨the⟩ ↑severe↓ trial.↓
19	away. ⟨Dear friends are taken away by death.⟩ Unforeseen
21	who ⟨take away their⟩ ↑hinder them from↓

21–23   livelihood; ⟨They lose⟩ their health ↑is wasted;↓ . . . the ⟨life of our⟩ ↑altered character of their↓ friends has ceased to ⟨become⟩ ↑make their life↓

25–27   ¶ These ⟨pressing wants⟩ ↑infirmities↓ . . . ↑& crosses of our condition↓ . . . religion. ↑{A} A ⟨This is the claim of religion that it is a consolation a medicine the oil of joy the anchor of hope⟩It . . . hope.↓ [ink over pencil]

28   the ⟨truth⟩ ↑import↓

30–31   satisfies ⟨blesses⟩ [canceled in pencil and ink] those . . . ↑& by means of↓ [addition in pencil]

37–42   who ⟨by circumstances⟩ far . . . their s⟨u⟩ituation . . . dependant . . . own ⟨cannot awaken⟩ ↑are yet excluded from↓ . . . ↑& unhappy↓ . . . years; ⟨and the friendless; & the mourner; & the poor⟩ I

Page 131

3   sad ⟨events⟩ ↑conditions↓

5–11   Th⟨e⟩at circumstance ↑in their case↓ which [end of MS p. 8; the inscription continues on MS p. 15 (cognate with p. 8), following the inserted folio and single leaf:] ⟨most forcibly awakens your pity, is that they ⟨appear⟩ are ↑often↓ unconscious that there are pleasures accessible to them that will set them far above pity. Yes, here is the consolation which religion addresses to the unhappy. ↑Fear God↓ Set yourself with diligence to keep your Father's law. Be a ministering angel to the wants of others. Withdraw your eye from too close a criticism on your own *lot* compared with others & fix it upon your *duties*.⟩ [The canceled passage is rewritten at the top of MS p. 9, at the beginning of an added passage occupying MS pp. 9–14:] ↑most . . . above pity.↓ ¶ ⟨It is the most pathetic part of the real tragedies which we see taking place around us in life that the sufferers do not help themselves as they might.⟩ They . . . overlooked. ¶ ⟨Let us compare the different resources ↑⟨of yᵉ hum. understanding & yᵉ religious heart⟩of the mere understanding & of the religious heart↓ [ink over pencil] Religion says to them all one thing In your character find consolation. Fear God & keep his commandments.⟩ See

13–16   that /calamity/mortification/ . . . certain ⟨possessions⟩ ↑accomplishments↓

18–19   ↑But . . . returns.↓

20   for ⟨what is denied⟩ ↑the . . . taken↓

23–38   great; ⟨the⟩ He makes . . . attention ↑but h⟨e⟩is ↑pale cheek↓ . . . youth.↓ ["of youth" written around canceled "The" which appears to be an earlier false start of a paragraph] ¶ ⟨Less innocently the childless or bereaved parent contrasts his solitude with the gratified affections of others. The impoverished with the successful; the sick ⟨with the sound;⟩ ↑grows paler at the approach of robust & glowing youth↓⟩ the rejected with the accepted candidate⟩ [incomplete cancellation] ¶ But more ⟨unfortunate⟩ ↑an object of pity↓ . . . men & wo⟨men who ⟨are eaten up by a vulgar⟩ ↑have unhappily placed their↓ ambition for⟩↑men, whose eye is ever upon ⟨rank in life⟩ ↑place in society,↓ who . . . upon↓ . . . world, ⟨for⟩ ↑upon↓ connexions, high society ⟨faultless dress⟩ unexceptionable ⟨dress &⟩ appearance, ⟨& to wh⟩ ↑&↓ influence⟨, & to whom wealth has been denied.⟩↑.↓ They ⟨occupy⟩ compare . . . issue. ⟨Before those whom they reckon of better condition they lead a life of ⟨constant⟩ ↑studied↓ deference, & take their revenge in envy & slander in other company⟩ ↑Especially . . . them ⟨the⟩ ↑sentiments↓ most impertinent ⟨& deplorably ignorant sentiments expressed⟩ ↑& betraying miserable ignorance↓ as if the ⟨sufferer⟩ individual . . . by.↓

39   Religion ⟨says⟩ utters . . . word. ⟨In your chara⟩ You

Page 132

7–8   opening ⟨of your eye to⟩ ↑acquaintance with↓ new worth ⟨to⟩ ↑with↓ virtue ⟨to⟩ ↑with↓ usefulness, ⟨shall⟩ you

14   your⟨'s⟩ nor any man's ↑opinion,↓ but drawn from ⟨a reverent regard to⟩ the

20–27   persons ⟨who⟩ ↑who . . . by↓ spend↑ing↓ . . . of a↑n insect or a↓ plant. ⟨↑How much more↓⟩ Shall . . . nature; ⟨& shall we not honour him who occupies himself⟩ ↑how . . . is ⟨his⟩the . . . but↓ . . . be⟨.⟩, ↑in . . . design.↓

39   rich that soul ⟨in man or woman⟩ I

Page 133

6–9   poor ¶ ↑⟨In a⟩A cheerful . . . attainment↓

10   this /duty/rule/ . . . often ⟨kept⟩ fulfilled

12–13   persisting & ⟨great⟩ extreme

14   is ⟨best⟩ the

16–28   out ⟨r⟩concerning . . . spirit; ↑Insert B B {Or . . . dissipation ⟨are⟩ become . . . Virtue} ↑These . . . purpose↓↓ & . . . world. ⟨↑{Insert B}↓⟩ But . . . ↑ere long↓ . . . peace; ⟨but⟩ ↑that↓ God striketh ⟨thro⟩ ↑down↓ the proud; and ↑we learn↓ [added in pencil] . . . ↑our↓ first tho'ts. ↑{↓"First . . . coincide."↑}↓ [brackets in pencil]

29–30   condition↑?↓ ⟨or suffer under grievous affliction? Make an experiment of⟩ ↑Try↓ this ⟨great⟩ remedy ⟨in⟩of

34–35   {He . . . wound}

Page 134

5–6   to ⟨God. I call it personal relation for want of a better term.⟩ ↑its Maker.↓

8–9   ↑But . . . him.↓ ⟨But⟩ we

10–11   God. ⟨And⟩ By . . . consent ↑to↓

12–14   virtue ⟨is the only ⟨preparation⟩ ↑discipline↓⟩ ↑alone can introduce us↓ . . . a ⟨common⟩ principle

22–27   object ⟨of amazement⟩ ↑which . . . faculties↓. ⟨The⟩ Look . . . him [end of page] ¶ ↑when . . . Eye↓ [addition in pencil; end of page]

28   to ⟨act⟩ make

35–40   ↑lead to the↓ a discovery . . . ↑with↓ more ↑favor↓

Page 135

1   by ⟨a reference to⟩ this

[Following the end of the sermon is this passage in pencil:] The Lord is a sun & shield the Lord will give grace & glory No good thing will he withhold from them that walk uprightly. O Lord of hosts blessed is yᵉ man yᵗ trusteth in thee

Sermon CLIV

Manuscript: A leaf followed by four sheets folded to make four pages each; single leaves follow the first and second folios. Pages measure 24.3 x 20.2 cm. The fascicle is sewn along the left margin with white thread.

Lines	*Page 136*
Bible Text	⟨Much⟩ ↑Great↓
3–4	a ⟨comm⟩ law which is /true/sacred/ [variant in pencil]
6	↑This . . . duty↓ [in pencil]
8	howe⟨r⟩ver
9	man ⟨in his right⟩ ↑of sane↓

Page 137

2   ↑found pleasure in↓ whisper⟨ed⟩ing to himself ⟨alone with delight⟩ that . . . ↑or lewd,↓

3   owed ⟨allegiance⟩ ↑obedience↓

4   when /it/this law/

9–10   ¶ ↑1 And . . . soul↓

12   man. [The following passage was probably added for a late delivery:] ↑See how the weeks fly by us. See how fast we lose ⟨our⟩ old faces & meet new ones, how [end of line] how fast the town changes & its fashions pass away↓ Not

17   often ⟨change⟩ ↑alter↓

18–19   should ⟨often wonder⟩ ↑soon . . . opinions↓

22–23   to /{withdraw ourselves from action}/give . . . life/ & meditate upon the ⟨strange⟩ ↑shifting↓

35–43   for ⟨an⟩ ↑another man's↓ . . . strange do⟨ctrine⟩gma ↑⟨whether⟩ ↑that↓ the souls of infants are unregenerate ⟨whether⟩ ↑that↓ Faith comes by Justification or Justification by Faith some arbitrary particular assertion↓ . . . Christ; ⟨which⟩ ↑& they . . . dispute & the↓ doctrine is wholly . . . generation⟨;⟩. ⟨b⟩But . . . doctrine ⟨they⟩ ↑the disputants↓

Page 138

1   run ⟨through⟩ ↑under↓

3–4   ↑though they should discussed . . . angels↓.

6   the ⟨fathers of⟩ doctors of ⟨Nice or Dort⟩ ↑Westminster or Rome↓

8   true ⟨seat⟩ ↑centre↓

11   princ↑i↓ple of ↑equi↓poise

12–15   ↑the↓ . . . life ⟨have⟩ have wounded. ⟨There are many tra⟩ If . . . those we⟨e⟩ meet

16	the ⟨bright⟩ ↑fair↓ hopes of parents /cut down/destroyed/
17-23	young ⟨men⟩ ↑persons↓ . . . changed ⟨we shd find⟩ the flush of youth /turned pale/is gone/, the joyfulness of its ⟨manners⟩ ↑behaviour↓ exchanged for the ⟨cautious mechanical⟩ ↑negligent↓ [emendation in pencil] manners of ⟨laborious & unpleasing⟩ ↑hard↓ life ⟨We sh⟩ limited . . . conversation [end of page] ⟨We shd find⟩ ↑There is↓ . . . beauty ⟨↑now↓⟩ ↑is↓ [emendation rejected for sense] changed & ⟨cold⟩ ↑reserved↓, . . . hopeful, ⟨condemned⟩ ↑much altered↓ [emendation in pencil] . . . misfortunes ⟨thwarted⟩ ↑afflicted by unkindness↓
25-29	friend, ⟨lonely⟩ toiling alone ↑L {L There . . . ↑dependant↓ . . . unhappiness.}↓ [The insert is very possibly, though not certainly, a late addition.]
31-(139)3	frame↑, a . . . end?↓ [addition in ink over an unpunctuated version of the same in pencil; end of MS p. 10] ¶ ↑not . . . themselves.↓ [This added paragraph occupies MS p. 8, the verso of the leaf following the first folio; MS p. 7, the recto of the leaf, contains the last paragraph before heading "2" on MS p. 9. Since this added paragraph could not reasonably have concluded the discussion under heading "1," the editors incline to the belief that Emerson wished to add to the inscription on MS p. 10, and found MS p. 8 the nearest blank page; still, the placement of the text is conjectural.]
34-39	that ⟨are⟩ ↑are↓ saved: . . . are remov⟨ed⟩↑ed↓ . . . from ⟨th⟩ ⟨sad⟩ ↑fatal↓ . . . contrition, do not ⟨mourn⟩ ↑mourn↓ . . . angels ⟨but mourn for yourselves⟩ ↑But . . . mourn↓
39-(139)1	these. ↑X X {There . . . those wh⟨ich⟩om . . . dishonored.↓

Page 139

2	of ⟨life⟩ middle
4	disasters the
8	casts ⟨off⟩ the
13	that ⟨savors⟩ ↑⟨sweetens⟩ flavors↓
16	↑amidst . . . works↓ have a ⟨light⟩ serenity
21	↑again to him.↓. ⟨It s⟩ & makes
25-26	the /talents/faculties/ [variant in pencil]
29-31	is ⟨also the⟩ ↑also . . . in a↓ path ⟨of⟩ ↑that↓ ever widen⟨ing⟩s & never end⟨ing⟩s↑.↓ ⟨improvement.⟩ It
32	with ⟨those⟩ his
35	Far ⟨from it⟩ ↑otherwise↓.
36	because h⟨e⟩is ↑acts↓
39-(140)4	a ⟨wret⟩ poor patriot who is ⟨not⟩ a ⟨good⟩ ↑negligent↓ . . . poor. ⟨↑Can he love↓⟩ ↑{for when . . . there?}↓

Page 140

5	↑among our↓
6	dependance upon you ⟨is the⟩ does
8	his ⟨household⟩ ↑family↓
12	with ⟨it⟩ the

14–15   The ⟨pains⟩ difficulties of virtue disappear. ⟨The husbandman⟩
          ↑He↓ that ⟨went⟩ ↑goeth↓ forth ⟨to sow⟩ & weep⟨ing⟩eth bearing
          precious seed ↑shall doubtless↓ ⟨shall ⟨return with joy in harvest⟩⟩
          ↑come again with rejoicing↓

16   no ⟨joy⟩ ↑pleasure↓

20–21   ↑for↓ . . . & ⟨resume his evil⟩ come

24–25   of ⟨happiness of⟩ heaven

27   of ⟨David⟩ ↑Solomon↓ 'The

30–31   law. ¶ ↑To conclude with ⟨two⟩three reflexions. ¶ 1↓ Does [addition re-
          jected as having been written for the second delivery, January 5, 1834]

33–35   world ⟨convince⟩ speak . . . truth ⟨& yᵉ character of Deity⟩ ↑that
          . . . him↓.

38–(141)1 believe,—↑tho↓ . . . nature? ¶ ↑2.↓ [addition rejected as belonging to
          the second delivery] And . . . obeyed ⟨by us⟩?

Page 141

8–10   it. ¶ [The following passage was added for the second delivery, on the
          evening of January 5, 1834, at the Friend Street Chapel:] ↑3. But
          thirdly my friends is it not a joyful fact. Are you not glad it is so?
          ⟨When your minister asked me to come ⟨down⟩ & speak a word to
          you this evening, I considered whether I had anything to say;⟩ and it
          seemed to me that there was nothing more fit on ⟨the first Sunday of
          the New Year,⟩ ↑amid the grievous commercial embarrassments by
          which our community has been so much distressed↓ than to come &
          congratulate you upon this ⟨blessed⟩ ↑enduring↓ inheritance to which
          you & I & all men are born, this life of our life, & soul of our soul,
          which never was born, & never grows old, which proceeding eter-
          nally from God in heaven, is his witness in each of our minds that he is
          there present. It has lost none of its freshness for you & me. Here at
          this moment this quiet prompter is peacefully but distinctly uttering
          his assent to every truth his approbation of every right purpose, his
          instruction for the present hour. It offers to lead us to wisdom &
          virtue in this year to ⟨bless⟩ make the year happy with more than
          prosperity, & to make it new in a more glorious sense than because it
          is just begun; to make ⟨it⟩ ↑time↓ new by bringing us to perceive that
          the whole creation is new every moment by the constant providence
          & interposition of God; & we are new ⟨re⟩creatures every moment
          ⟨by⟩ ↑through↓ a larger acknowledgment of his presence & a living
          communion with him. ¶ ↑Know the relief the refreshment of this thot
          ¶ to come out from the distracting cares of the week, the trials of a
          season of unprecedented anxiety & disappointment in our commer-
          cial community makes us glad↓↓ [last two paragraphs in pencil] ¶ My
          . . . uncertainty ⟨in the course of all⟩ ↑is in every↓ . . . enterprize
          ⟨Much⟩ Over

11–15   But ⟨this⟩ one . . . ↑that . . . to ⟨do⟩ ↑discharge↓ those ⟨things⟩ ↑ob-
          ligations↓ . . . us.↓. ["discharge" and "obligations" in pencil and ink]
          These things let us ⟨cultivate⟩ perform . . . be ⟨today⟩ ↑at the time↓,

17–18   forward. ↑in our everlasting progress.↓

Sermon CLV

Manuscript: Four sheets folded to make four pages each; pages measure 24.3 x 20.2 cm. Two leaves are inserted into the first folio; the first of these measures 24 x 19.3 cm and is not included in the sewing. (Internal evidence conclusively shows that the leaf is misplaced; the question Emerson refers to on the recto of this leaf as "asked just now" occurs on the recto of the first leaf of the second folio. The editors conjecture that it was intended to introduce the discussion under heading "3" and therefore suppose that it was originally laid in immediately before the third folio, where that discussion begins.) A leaf (containing Insert "A") follows the first folio; two single leaves follow the second folio; a leaf measuring 23.9 x 19.9 cm follows the third folio; all other leaves measure 24.3 x 20.2 cm. The folios are sewn along the left margin with white thread. Below the Bible text on MS p. 1 is a large "S" in pencil.

Lines	Page 142
3	the ⟨pulpit & the press⟩ ↑teachers of the gospel↓
5–6	& ⟨b⟩ethical books . . . of ⟨blame⟩ ↑↑pity or↓ execration ⟨or pity⟩↓.
6–7	And ⟨to⟩ ↑even at↓ this day a ⟨large⟩ great . . . speak ⟨well⟩ ↑kindly↓
11–12	↑as God made it,↓ & because I ⟨am⟩ repent
13	highly ⟨of⟩ concerning
14	despises. ⟨I cannot think he has I ever communed with himself.⟩ I
15–18	which ⟨is⟩ every mans own self⟨.⟩ is; . . . good—its . . . such / partial/false/ & /self contradictory/impertinent/ ⟨terms⟩ sentiments
19	language ⟨use⟩ ↑employ↓
23	ignorant ⟨of himself⟩ of

	Page 143
1	what ⟨wd.⟩ shall
3–6	[The following emendations are rejected as probably belonging to a late delivery:] to ⟨present⟩ ↑speak of↓ the ⟨dignity of⟩ ↑place↓ [emendation in ink over pencil] the human soul ↑holds↓ [addition in pencil] among the works of God, under ↑a↓ three↑fold↓ view⟨s⟩ which . . . mind. ¶ ↑1. And, in the first place, that which awakens my admiration in the view of man, is, the ⟨↑{↓unimaginable↑}↓⟩ [brackets in pencil] extent of human consciousness. ⟨I wish to suggest⟩ Let us fix our attention on the really unlimited comprehensiveness of the soul of man.↓ [end of MS p. 6] ↑The unimaginable extent of human consciousness.↓ [This notation seems to be the source and occasion of the revised introduction to the first discussion, as inscribed on MS p. 6.] ¶ ⟨1.⟩ To
6–7	more ⟨you⟩ ↑he↓ think↑s↓, . . . soon ⟨you are⟩ ↑he is↓
10–11	contemplation. ↑⟨Is not t⟩That . . . mind⟨?⟩.↓
11–15	the ⟨meaning⟩ ↑measure↓ of self ↑the . . . thoughts↓? ⟨What is it that is involved⟩ ↑Add . . . is↓ . . . consciousness? Let . . . yourself? Is
16	↑&↓ all that you ⟨believe⟩ ↑imagine↓?

17   it ⟨rolled⟩ ↑existed & grew↓
18   eternity, ⟨unobserved⟩ ↑unknown↓.
18–19   another, but
23–31   you↑r conscious self↓ . . . ↑the society of the living↓ . . . action⟨,⟩ to
              . . . child; ↑A A {The . . . idea of ⟨God of⟩ one . . . work.↓ [In ink
              over the following in pencil:] The single fact that the mind is capable
              of forming & cannot help forming a knowledge of God, feeling that it
              does not exist by itself but was made by another & made ⟨to do his
              will⟩ to love the wisest & best of all beings the Creator of this glorious
              nature the Supreme Good, God, ⟨should⟩ seems to ennoble the
              whole work. [end of pencil inscription] and
32–35   consciousness ⟨is⟩ enlarg⟨ing⟩es ⟨& including more worlds in its
              deep abyss⟩ ↑& embraces . . . nature↓ [addition in ink over "facts
              more truth" in pencil] . . . horizon. ⟨⟨We are⟩I am fearfully &
              wonderfully made ⟨thus comprizing all being in ours.⟩ ↑& that my
              soul knoweth right well↓⟩ ¶ This . . . God↑.↓ ⟨&⟩ ↑And↓
37–38   ↑Say . . . well.↓

                            Page 144
10–11   ↑& more common↓ [ink over pencil] . . . nature↑,↓ [comma in
              pencil] . . . be ⟨⟨thus⟩ [canceled in pencil and ink] contemned⟩
              ↑slightly ⟨accounted⟩ esteemed↓.
12–13   he ⟨is⟩ accounts . . . creatures—⟨He is⟩ God
15   & ⟨finish⟩ ↑termination↓ of the ↑visible↓
16   each ⟨to⟩from
23   the ⟨tulip⟩ ↑lily↓
25   speak) ⟨lavished⟩ ↑displayed↓ . . . decoration ⟨& the painting⟩ of
26   ↑& bats,↓
32   ¶ Thus . . . manner. [written above and below a pencil inscription:
              "We give ↑their↓ name to"]
35   ↑the dog↓
37–(145)5   life ¶ ⟨And as man has been made⟩ ↑Judge how↓ capable ⟨of⟩ ↑man
              is of↓ mastering all this ⟨rich⟩ knowledge, of ⟨gov⟩ commanding
              nature ⟨by⟩ ↑thro'↓ observing its laws ⟨so⟩ ↑by seeing what↓ he hath
              ↑already↓ done ⟨it⟩. Men go t⟨oo⟩o & fro ⟨& knowledge is
              increased.⟩ ↑& knowledge . . . man.↓ ↑And . . . gives.↓ [last addi-
              tion in ink over pencil] the

                            Page 145
8   unnoticed, ⟨the⟩ ⟨nor ↑the↓ reptile in its hiding place⟩ nor
19–26   to ⟨humble⟩ ↑shame↓ . . . merits. ¶ [The following passage, the
              conclusion of an earlier draft of the sermon (possibly, though not
              definitely, earlier than the first delivery form), occurs upside down at
              the bottom of the page:] ⟨yet apprehended to that which is in store for
              he who said what shall a man give in exchange for his soul came into
              the earth to bring immortality to light. ¶ May 13, 1832 [end of page;
              the editors conjecture that the loose leaf (verso blank) now inserted
              in the first folio originally occupied a position here, before the third

folio (see the manuscript note, above):] ↑{I . . . accursed? whether
. . . himself.}↓

27–29   reason ⟨why I venerate the⟩ ↑which . . . the↓ nature . . . individuals,
I see ⟨under the vices of⟩ ↑running through↓ . . . ↑under the vices↓

Page 146

6–9   To ⟨discuss them always is like those trades⟩ ↑be . . . frame↓ . . .
body. ¶ ⟨But p⟩Present . . . ↑a measure affecting↓

17–19   him. ↑& it . . . soul.↓

20–21   personal; ↑would . . . place.↓ those

28   man. ⟨This is at once the inmost⟩ Thus

33–36   ↑in Alpine peaks↓ . . . ↑at . . . mines↓, . . . nature.) [end of page]
⟨freedom⟩ ⟨great noise⟩ [end of page] ¶ It

38–40   much ⟨attention⟩ ↑study↓ . . . be ⟨given⟩ bestowed . . . be ⟨allowed⟩
suffered

Page 147

1–2   produce. ⟨It⟩ ↑The survey of ⟨our⟩ what we have received↓ [emenda-
tions in pencil]

3   ↑my friend↓

13–14   life it . . . ↑tends . . . difficult↓ [addition in pencil] separates

18–27   thoughts it . . . inhabitant. ⟨What would it profit a man though he
should gain the whole world & lose his own soul? But a⟩Above
[cancellation in pencil and ink] all ↑remember that↓ . . . day. ⟨Who
can sin when he realizes the faith of immortality. Give not that which
is holy unto dogs. Cast not the pearl of great price before swinish
passions. [cf. Matthew 7:6] But study to show thyself approved before
God [II Timothy 2:15] in the assured conviction that thou shalt never
die.⟩ ↑Is . . . these ⟨body⟩ members ↑Is it wise then as ⟨we⟩ ↑we↓
[emendation in pencil] . . . ↑we possessed↓ . . . What will it profit a
man &c↓↓ ["Is it wise . . . &" in pencil and ink; text supplied from
Mark 8:36–37] ¶ May 13, 1832 [Although Emerson placed the dateline
immediately after the canceled passage and wrote the added passage
around it, the fact does not assist in determining the date or dates of
the various inscriptions: the addition may have been made before the
first delivery, or, on the hypothesis that the dateline merely repeats the
date of first delivery as given in an earlier version (e.g., the canceled
conclusion on MS p. 18), the entire conclusion, as we have it, may
represent a late revision.]

Sermon CLVI

Manuscript: Four sheets folded to make four pages each; pages of the first three folios
measure 24.3 x 20.1 cm, those of the fourth folio 23.8 x 20.3 cm. A leaf measuring 24.3 x
20.1 cm (with the watermark "S & B / N H") follows the first folio; a leaf of the same
measurements is inserted into the second folio; a blank leaf measuring 24.3 x 20.3 cm
follows the second folio; a leaf measuring 24.3 x 20.1 cm is inserted into the third folio; a
leaf measuring 24.3 x 20.4 cm follows the third folio. The folios are sewn along the left
margin with white thread.

Lines   Page 148
Bible Text   ⟨Where envying is, there is confusion & every evil work. James 3. 16⟩
              ↑Charity envieth not 1 Cor. 13. 4↓
1–3   ¶ ⟨Jesus & his apostles⟩ ⟨↑The Scriptures↑⟩ ⟨↑St Paul↓⟩ ["St Paul"
              added in ink over "St Paul &" in pencil] ↑Charity . . . general↓
5–13   condemnation. ¶ ²{⟨⟨↑Still↓⟩ This circumstance would not com-
              mand⟩ ↑But it is not that it is set down in the Bible↓ our attention any
              more than the ↑tithe or↓ . . . ↑still↓ . . . vitals} [faulty emendation;
              the editors have been compelled to interpolate the words "that it
              commands" to restore the sense] ¶ ¹{⟨And⟩ yet ⟨an evil affection
              awakens so little attention that⟩ it . . . vice.} ¶ ⟨And i⟩In . . . of
              ⟨coveting the⟩ covetousness—wishing ⟨to⟩ ↑we could↓ . . . in ⟨imag-
              ination⟩ ↑thought↓—
14–17   consequent ⟨security⟩ sureness . . . ↑with . . . folly.↓
22–23   of ⟨our⟩ ↑an↓ . . . if ⟨h⟩envy
27–(149)4   unhappy ⟨jealousy⟩ ↑principle↓. ⟨I see⟩ ↑Who . . . pain↓ . . . who
              ⟨w⟩have . . . the ⟨well⟩ happily

                                    Page 149
5   this ⟨devil's work⟩ ↑bad affection↓ [emendation in ink over pencil]
7–10   society ⟨the⟩ it . . . him, he . . . that ⟨corporation⟩ ⟨company⟩ law,
              /⟨or that school⟩/or that college/↑, or that corporation.↓
14–18   manufacturers) [end of page; the following uncompleted paragraph is
              rejected:] ¶ There exists in every country a party hostile to the
              standing institutions who stand ready to abase whatever is exalted, to
              [end of page] ¶ At . . . ↑the kingdom of↓ [over "yᵉ kingd" in pencil]
              France propose ↑under . . . philanthropy↓ . . . machinery ⟨o⟩ used
              . . . property ⟨of the rich⟩ ↑from the hands ⟨of them who⟩ ↑that↓
              hold it↓ & distribute it anew ⟨on their own principles⟩ according
20   ↑It . . . land.↓
27–35   moon. ↑And the amount↓ ¶ ⟨⟨In short it is almost a settled principle
              that we do not love any body or any thing that is better than we &
              ours.⟩ And so all the happiness of the world is my sorrow & but for
              fear but for decency I should ⟨utter⟩ ↑show↓ my hatred to every
              person that wore better clothes ↑possessed more friends↓ lived in a
              better house or had more wisdom & power than I have⟩ ¶ ⟨To this
              ⟨evil principle⟩ seed of wo Jesus came to teach benevolence. He said
              not only thou shalt not commit adultery but thou shall not lust after
              licentious pleasure, thou shalt not *hate* thy ⟨neig⟩ enemy love him
              serve him⟩ ¶ ↑And the amount of it is ⟨what⟩ that . . . not. ↑Insert A
              A ↑{They . . . it.↓ . . . themselves. ⟨They would all have some people
              under them; why not then have some people above them."⟩↓ [end of
              Insert "A"] . . . ↑like the Athenian↓ . . . Just.↓

                                    Page 150
1–6   ¶ ↑This . . . that ⟨which pr⟩ whose fruit↑, St James saith,↓ . . . kill.↓
8   other. ⟨But this principle⟩ ↑In . . . envy↓

11–16	which ²nature or ¹art had . . . of ²nature & ¹art. In that ⟨unhappy⟩ ↑disastrous↓ . . . principle ⟨prevailed the reign of terror⟩ ↑usurped the sceptre of power↓ . . . ↑ferocious↓ [in pencil] . . . ↑& confiscated their estates;↓
20	it ⟨is⟩ rules. ⟨It ⟨would⟩ goes to make all merit dangerous to the wearer.⟩ It
21–22	would ⟨raze⟩ ↑demolish all↓ the ⟨ornaments of⟩ architecture ↑& besmear all elegance↓ it
24–29	beasts. ¶ ⟨With regard to t⟩ This feeling of malevolence ⟨not⟩ in great avowed extravagant ⟨measure for that⟩ ↑indulgence↓ is very rare ↑or the world would be uninhabitable↓; but ⟨to⟩ the least degrees of ⟨such as⟩ ↑it,↓ . . . ↑are common. Upon the whole subject↓
30–34	That /it/this feeling/ ⟨argues⟩ is . . . itself ¶ ⟨That⟩ It . . . used" it
36–(151)3	himself ↑a a ⟨t⟩ There . . . portion↓ . . . forever 'In

Page 151

4	from others [written around the stray phrase "⟨The possessions⟩"]
8	the ⟨dispositions you⟩ temper
12	¶ 2. ⟨It is not⟩ The
15	God↑,↓ ⟨It shuts you out⟩ ⟨forbids you to⟩ ↑makes you incapable of↓ receiv⟨e⟩ing
17–21	↑How . . . heart↓
25–27	itself⟨,⟩. ⟨i⟩It would love nothing. ⟨Like Napoleon i⟩It . . . ↑that incarnation . . . of↓ . . . every ⟨thing⟩ object
28–29	would ⟨write great ⟨N.⟩ N⟩ ↑read . . . top↓ . . . ↑but the syllables of its own ⟨wretched⟩ [canceled in pencil] name↓. ⟨O my friends it is a sad uncomfortable inmate⟩ And
31–32	inmate. ¶ ⟨The angel trumpets that announced the Messiah proclaimed Peace on earth & goodwill to men. [Luke 2:14] Compare the two principles Christianity taught the divine secret of converting all the happiness I witness into my happiness, of enjoying the genius virtue beauty riches health favor triumph of my fellows as so much kindness done to me so much pain spared to me so much occasion on my part of gratitude to God.⟩ ¶ But
36–37	happiness ⟨I⟩ ↑we↓ witness into ⟨my⟩ ↑our↓ happiness↑.↓ ⟨of⟩ ↑It teaches me to↓ enjoy⟨in⟩ the
40–(152)10	¶ ↑I exhort you therefore↓ Cultivate ⟨I beseech you⟩, my . . . from ⟨me⟩us . . . in him. [paragraph written over the following in pencil:] ⟨Can any p⟩ Could any possession any talent bestow upon a good man half the pleasure he derives from rejoicing with all those who rejoice. Let us be content that other people have virtues & blessings. Let us delight in them. Far be it from us to cast censure or doubt upon the deserts of others A man without virtue ⟨s⟩is ever ready to suspect the purity of others but he who is conscious of his own worth believes & reveres the worth of other men

[Following the end of the sermon is an earlier draft of the concluding paragraph:]
⟨Cultivate I beseech you this generous ⟨happiness⟩ ↑goodwill↓ It is of inestimable

importance ⟨to you &⟩ to your happiness & to your usefulness. ⟨Just in proportion to a man's own powers of thought & action is ⟨his⟩ the generosity of his delight in other men's.

A man who has done noble things himself knows he loses nothing by praising his friend: but⟩ ["Just . . . but" canceled in pencil] it is the life of an angel ↑the course of that man↓ [addition in pencil] which ↑whilst it↓ never forgives any sin to itself, apologizes for every offence of another, casts a glance of pleasure at all innocent enjoyments & of unmixed delight at all mens gratifications ⟨&⟩ ↑& even out of the midst of its own defeats↓ offers ⟨an⟩up ardent thanksgiving for other mens joy ⟨as for his own.⟩. Truly he that loveth is born of God & dwelleth in God & God in him.⟩

{The gospel knoweth our welfare better than we know it ourselves. ⟨⟨The⟩ It was an admirable maxim of ancient wisdom⟩ Men think at least they may lawfully indulge malevolent feelings toward the worthless & wicked those that have injured us. It was an admirable maxim of ancient wisdom which said "Would you be revenged on your enemy Live as you ought & you have done it to purpose." [see *JMN* 4:20] Yet Christianity goes one step higher in enjoining love to him   if he hunger feed him; if he thirst, give him drink. [Romans 12:20] "Only Charity admitteth of no excess."} [Francis Bacon; see *JMN* 6:181]

Sermon CLVII

Manuscript: When Emerson delivered Sermon CLVII for the second time—at Waltham, November 30, 1834, on the occasion of the eclipse—he replaced the first six manuscript pages with a newly written eight-page introduction; in the course of this substitution one leaf (the last two pages of the superseded original inscription) was torn out and lost. The lost text was apparently closely related to a journal entry of May 26, 1832 (*JMN* 4:25–26), which Emerson used again in 1834 to make the transition from the new introduction to the old body of the sermon. The lost material and the related revisions make it impossible to offer a coherent text of the first-delivery form; the editors have therefore elected to present the text in second-delivery form, with the new introduction. The textual notes below give as much evidence as exists about the first-delivery form.

The manuscript consists of five sheets folded to make four pages each; pages of the first folio measure 24.3 x 20.3 cm, those of the other four folios 24.3 x 20.1 cm. The first leaf of the second folio has been torn out (leaving evidence of inscription on the recto and verso of the stub), and inserted in its place is a leaf measuring 24.3 x 20.1 cm. A leaf measuring 24.3 x 20.1 cm follows the second folio, and leaves measuring 25 x 20 cm are laid in after the fourth and within the fifth folio. The gathering (exclusive of the two loose leaves and the new introduction) is sewn along the left margin with white thread.

The substitute introduction prepared for the second delivery consists of two sheets folded to make four pages each, which are not sewn; pages of the first folio measure 25 x 20 cm, those of the second measure 24 x 19.7 cm. The text of the original introduction follows:

clvii

Astronomy. [in ink over "Influence of Astronomy on Theology" in pencil]

God that made the world & all things therein seeing that he is Lord of heaven & earth dwelleth not in temples made with hands; neither is worshipped with mens hands as though he needed any thing, seeing he giveth to all life & breath & all things; ⟨{& hath made of one blood all nations of men to dwell on all the face of the earth & hath determined the times before appointed, & the bounds of their habitation; that they mt. seek the Lord if haply they mt. feel after him & find him; though he be not far from every one of us.—}⟩ [brackets in ink over pencil; cancellation in ink] Forasmuch, then, as we are the offspring of God we ought not to think yᵗ yᵉ Godhead is like to gold or silver or stone graven by art & man's device And yᵉ times of this ignorance God overlooked but now commandeth all men every where to repent Because he hath appointed a day in which he will judge yᵉ world in righteousness by that man whom he hath ordained, whereof he hath given assurance unto all men in that he hath raised him from yᵉ dead Acts 17. 24—&c

⟨I quote all these memorable words of St Paul ⟨to show that⟩ because they may serve as one out of many passages to show that the Scriptures claim to come from the same ⟨b⟩Being that made the heavens & the earth; that the God of nature, & the God of the bible are affirmed to be the same, that the ⟨Divine P⟩ Father of Jesus Christ is the Divine Providence in whose wisdom & love all beings are embosomed.

↑The lesson which the heavenly bodies teach the human mind is not learned by some men because they are never out of sight↓ [added in pencil]

Since this is so,—↑since↓ the records of the divine ⟨dispensations⟩ dealings ↑with men↓ claim no other origin than the author of nature, we may expect that they are to be read by the light of nature; that ⟨the progress of⟩ ↑more↓ knowledge of his works, will enable us⟩ [end of page] better to ⟨interpret⟩ ↑understand↓ his word; and that religion will become purer & truer by the ⟨triumphs o⟩ progress of science

This consideration ought to secure our interest in the book of nature. ⟨We ought to⟩ ↑The lover of truth will↓ look at all the facts which every year science is bringing to light with ⟨eager⟩ curiosity as the commentary & exposition, say rather, the ⟨continuation⟩ ↑sequel↓ of the revelation which our Creator is giving us of himself.

With this view I am led to offer you some reflexions ⟨upon⟩ that are suggested by the present state of the science of astronomy, ↑some thoughts↓ upon the influence which the wonderful discoveries men have made ⟨in⟩ of the extent & plan of the universe have had upon religious opinion. [end of MS p. 3; MS p. 4 is blank; the next leaf (MS pp. 5–6) has been torn out leaving the following traces of inscription:] [two lines of text] / of / It / to a / ra / [approximately seven lines of text] / & / you c / But D / yo / if / th [end of MS p. 5] n / ts / som / [three or four lines] / ⟨only⟩ / fac / te / [five or six lines] / ned [end of MS p. 6]

[Although the Bible text does not appear in the MS of the revised introduction, Emerson alludes in the fourth paragraph to "the passage which I have read from the New Testament"; the editors believe this could refer only to the passage given at the beginning of the first-delivery version (see above).]

Lines	Page 153
1–⟨155⟩33	[The substitute introduction is headed: "Preached on the day of Solar Eclipse at Waltham Nov 30 1834"] ¶ ↑↑{↓The [bracket in pencil] remarkable . . . of the science↓

3–(154)4   fact. {⟨But⟩ Nature [cancellation in pencil; rejected as a late emenda-
tion] . . . men↑.↓ ⟨And⟩ though)} ⟨w⟩We [period, cancellation,
second bracket, and capitalization of "we" in pencil. Emerson's pencil
emendations are evidently done for the third delivery, to remove the
immediate reference to the eclipse; the editors therefore reject the
several pencil emendations from the clear text.] . . . light though
["though" circled in pencil] . . . air. This we forget ↑in . . . light↓,
. . . his ⟨bright limb⟩ southern

Page 154

7–8   they ⟨foresaw⟩ ↑anticipated↓ the fatal consequence ⟨⟨o⟩if⟩ ↑should↓
that shadow ⟨should⟩ continue to ⟨hide⟩ ↑cover↓ his ⟨beams⟩ ↑face↓.

8–10   throughout animal . . . ↑of our globe↓ . . . still ⟨& die⟩ ↑enough↓ &
the ⟨earth⟩ shad⟨ow⟩e

12   are ⟨never⟩ likely never quite to ⟨lose their knowledge of⟩ ↑forget↓
[emendation in pencil] ⟨our indebtedness⟩ how

14–16   ¶ ↑{↓This . . . predicted↑}↓ ⟨It reminds us⟩ [brackets and cancellation in pencil; emendations rejected] impressively . . . human ⟨mind⟩
↑intellect↓.

16–17   the ⟨m⟩ littleness

25–26   only the [end of page] the knowledge . . . ↑of brute matter↓

29   made ⟨many⟩ the

35–38   that /make/associate/ astronomy . . . religion. ⟨Religion⟩ ↑It . . .
sentiment Religion↓ . . . paths & ⟨it looks like⟩ ↑the . . . as↓ a
⟨degree⟩ ↑sort↓

Page 155

2–4   God. ¶ ⟨For Religion is the knowledge of man's position & duties as
they flow from the superhuman & we feel at once that all the Universe
is on the same side with us of *that* line making one creature⟩ ¶ Then
. . . all /{opinion especially these}/our/ [brackets and variant in
pencil; emendation rejected] speculations

7–8   them ⟨↑to leave untold the attributes & influences of our Sun.↓⟩
↑Nothing else in nature has the grandeur & influence upon the mind↓

11–13   ↑Syrian↓ . . . before⟨.⟩ ⟨T⟩the human race was. We are ⟨but⟩ new

14–16   with ⟨unquestionable signs⟩ ↑wrinkles↓ of immense age, but ⟨the
human race⟩ ↑its inhabitant↓ . . . eternity ↑long . . . now↓

17   hence ⟨most⟩ ↑it↓ naturally ⟨it⟩ happened

18–21   they ⟨readily⟩ were . . . & ⟨how⟩ let . . . th⟨is⟩e opinion . . . moral
⟨&⟩influence upon the ⟨⟨life⟩lives⟩ ↑lives↓

33–39   science ¶ ⟨In the next place, it cannot be too much considered how
much the progress of this science⟩ ↑But a↑n↓ ⟨far more⟩ important
. . . astronomy↓ has ↑been to↓ correct⟨ed⟩ & exalt⟨ed⟩ our views of
God, & humble⟨d⟩ our view of ourselves. ⟨It is known to all to
whom I speak that⟩ ¶ ⟨It was an old sarcasm upon⟩ ¶ ↑In all ancient
spec↓ [in pencil] ↑In all ancient speculation↓ Men . . . must ⟨be like
him in⟩ ↑resemble human↓ nature. ⟨Astrono⟩ Even . . . ↑infant↓
. . . idolatry ⟨gave⟩ ↑imputed to↓

40–43   th⟨i⟩es↑e↓ . . . worlds ⟨to which we belong⟩ that . . . must ⟨be⟩
          have

Page 156

1–4   the ↑human↓ blood . . . the ⟨muscles raise the limbs⟩ ↑strength . . .
          ground↓ . . . Jupiter. ¶ ⟨To e⟩Each ⟨then⟩ of . . . ↑therefore↓ . . .
          must ⟨belong a race of inhabit⟩ be

9   has ⟨ordained⟩ ↑assigned↓

14–15   place ⟨it⟩ ↑the science of astronomy↓ . . . ↑the doctrines of↓ [addi-
          tion in ink over "yᵉ doctrines" in pencil]

19   illuminate ⟨t⟩ &

20–23   ↑the time of↓ Galileo & Newton ⟨since⟩ it . . . ball ⟨f⟩on . . . that
          ⟨it⟩ it . . . which ⟨it⟩ ↑were↓ . . . them; ↑And not only ⟨s⟩the earth↓

27   ↑of the stars↓

27–28   ↑They . . . shop.↓

33–(157)2 round. ¶ ⟨We⟩ ↑When . . . we↓ . . . in ⟨an obscure⟩ a . . . &
          ⟨altogether⟩ ↑quite↓ . . . the ⟨br⟩ millions . . . revealed↑.↓ ⟨to us.⟩
          It was the ⟨inevitable⟩ effect of this ⟨enlargement to make as great a⟩
          ↑⟨of our⟩ ↑⟨correction &⟩ new↓ knowledge↓↑, to make an equal↓
          [This unusually complex revision requires an explanation: Emerson
          first inserted "of our knowledge" after "enlargement," then canceled
          "enlargement of our" and inserted in its place "correction & new,"
          then canceled "correction &," and finally added the comma after
          "knowledge" and the phrase "to make an equal" having canceled the
          phrase "to make as great a".] . . . science. ⟨The earth seemed no⟩
          ↑for . . . any↓ longer↑, as↓

Page 157

7   redemption ⟨↑as it↓ occupied⟩ as

9–10   ↑'The . . . vengeance'↓

13–14   the ⟨th⟩ ↑theological↓

15–16   popular [end of page] ↑doctrine.↓ Newton

21–26   ↑so revolted them↓ the . . . than /↑{↓God↑}↓/ an intelligent Cause/.
          [brackets and variant in pencil; apparently this emendation was per-
          formed when the following incomplete and evidently abandoned para-
          graph was inscribed, also in pencil; presumably neither the emen-
          dation nor the addition formed part of the sermon as delivered and
          they are therefore rejected from the clear text] ¶↑⟨And I cannot but
          esteem it an inevitable⟩ When the student of Nature quitting the
          simplicity & perfectness of natural laws came into the churches &
          colleges to learn the character of God they there⟨f⟩ found such gross
          & unworthy views of him as not agreed but contrasted with their
          own conclusions respecting the cause of Nature, & as with one voice
          they rejected these creeds. Others finding no congenial faith, rejected
          all, rejected the hope & consolation of man, and in yᵉ face of yᵗ
          divine↓ ¶ In . . . to ⟨command the view⟩ send

31–37   wonderful ⟨mass of evidence to⟩ pro⟨ve⟩ofs ↑of↓ . . . systems, ⟨&⟩
          reaching . . . cannot ⟨co⟩ weigh . . . ever increasing surprise and
          delight. ⟨T⟩One . . . ↑fatal↓

37–(*158*)9   A ⟨second inquirer⟩ ↑more searching observer↓ . . . ↑when,↓ after
⟨in⟩ a . . . equilibrium↑.↓ ⟨and i⟩It . . . ↑an error . . . other↓ . . . is
⟨no loose pin no lawless particle⟩ no . . . God. ¶ ⟨And⟩ ↑Cheered by
these results↓ . . . planet ⟨rolls on⟩ ↑gravitates to↓ . . . ↑each . . .
orbit↓ [in ink over pencil] as ⟨s⟨af⟩urely⟩ ↑surely↓ [cancellation and
addition in pencil] . . . from ⟨the hive⟩ ↑its dark cell↓

Page 158

11   invisible ⟨hand⟩ guide
14–28   ↑thus↓ . . . have /↑{↓added . . . God.↑}↓/reconciled the greatness of
nature to the greatness of the mind/ [brackets and variant in pencil; rejected as a probable late emendation] ⟨Indeed it is an awful an adorable
Being but as merciful as affectionate in his care as he is surpassing in
wisdom.⟩ ↑Once . . . Wisdom↓ [end of page] ¶ L ¶ ⟨I proceed to say
that as this enlargement to our religious views this correction of error &
this more generous consideration of God's government comes to our
minds inevitably by the progress of this science so it cannot be doubted
that it was designed. ↑The times of that ignorance God overlooked↓
Though slow yet it was the sure result of the divine faculties with which
he endowed his children. ↑⟨G⟩He opened the heavens to ⟨man⟩them
to reform ⟨his⟩their religion & to educate the mind↓ God meant to enlarge their views of him. God never meant to shut up & chill & be-
numb his children with error & fear. He meant they should know &
love him & he rewards every exertion of their faculties by more just
knowledge of Himself.⟩ ¶ ⟨↑B {If we could carry the N.T. to the
inhabitant's of other worlds, we might ⟨have⟩ ↑need↓ to leave Jewish
Xy & Roman Xy, Paul & Apollos & Cephas & Luther & Socinus, but
the moral law, justice & mercy would be at home in every climate &
world where life is.}↓⟩ [end of page] ↑L ¶ I proceed . . . Himself↓
24   thereby ⟨s⟩teach
27–28   a ⟨juster⟩ higher . . . by ⟨a⟩more
32   are. ⟨It⟩ On
34–35   neither ⟨bond no⟩ Jew nor Greek. ↑Here . . . blood↓
38–(*159*)5   We ⟨feel⟩ ↑are assured↓ . . . regions, in . . . God ↑Insert B B {that
. . . Luther, & Socinus but yᵉ moral law justice & mercy wd. be . . .
is.↓ [end of Insert "B"; the editors take the canceled version of the
insert (see above) as authority to supply the comma after "law," but
decline to interpret "justice & mercy" as either an appositive or as
elements in a list] that ↑we can go↓ nowhere ↑but↓ ⟨will⟩ wisdom
↑will not↓ [faulty emendation] be ⟨less⟩ valuable [end of page] ⟨nor⟩
↑and↓ justice ⟨less⟩ venerable ⟨nor⟩ ↑&↓ humility ⟨less⟩ ↑&↓
[faulty emendation] suitable ⟨⟨nor⟩ ↑&↓ truth ⟨less⟩ sacred⟩ ⟨nor⟩
↑&↓ diligence ⟨less⟩ useful ⟨nor⟩ ↑&↓ ⟨charity divine.⟩ ↑& truth,
sacred, & charity divine.↓

Page 159

11–13   ourselves; ⟨that the only⟩ that . . . the ⟨princ⟩ standard . . . judged.
¶ [The following paragraph is inscribed in ink on both sides of a leaf

loosely laid in at this point; it is rejected from the clear text as a probable late addition.] ↑The greatest enlargement that our views of the solar system or of the Creation can attain can never throw the least shade upon the truths upon moral truth upon the truths which it was the office of Jesus to unfold. *Can never* throw a shade upon them! Not only so but they lose all brightness & greatness themselves by the comparison. There is a time when in the human mind busied before in objects of matter the voice is heard ⟨in the so⟩ Hunger & thirst after righteousness [Matthew 5:6] That ⟨ho⟩ word⟨s⟩ is like another morn risen on midnoon. [Milton, *Paradise Lost*, V, 310-11] It is a new heaven & a new earth. [Revelation 21:1] The outward Creation great as it was pales away & is dull & dim. We feel that millions of suns & systems, new & deeper reaches into the infinite void help us not. they are mere additions of number & magnitude which let them ⟨go⟩ reach as far as they will, have no life & can never touch the human heart. We then feel that there is no grandeur like moral grandeur. Before one act of courage of love of self-devotion all height & distance are ineffectual & the stars withdraw their shining. [Joel 2:10, 3:15] This only is real absolute independent of all circumstance & all change↓

14	our faith ⟨to⟩ the
18	¶ ↑The . . . hands↓
20–21	the↑m↓ ⟨scripture which came by human hands⟩ Let . . . from th⟨em⟩is ↑source↓
26	God↑.↓ ⟨by⟩ the

Sermon CLVIII

Manuscript: A leaf followed by five sheets folded to make four pages each; single leaves are inserted into the fourth and fifth folios and single leaves follow the fourth and fifth folios; pages measure 25 x 20.2 cm; sewn along the left margin with white thread. The third folio is not included in the sewing.

Lines	*Page 160*
Bible Text	⟨Of old hast thou laid the foundation of the earth & the heavens are the work of thy hands They shall perish but thou ⟨remainest⟩ shall endure yea all of them shall wax old as doth a garment; as a vesture thou shall [half a line of space] but thou art the same & thy years shall have no end Ps 102, 25.6⟩
	fathers ⟨s⟩hath . . . you & . . . ↑to me↓ . . . Exod 3. 14
5	faculties⟨,⟩ are
8–9	repose ¶ ⟨It is the ready steadfast c⟩ ¶ Man
11	he ⟨s⟩ could

	Page 161
6	And i⟨n⟩t is
13	Paul. As

20–25   away ¶ ⟨But this is error.⟩ Men ⟨do⟩ make . . . religion they . . .
         they ⟨do⟩ see . . . them they . . . life. ¶ ⟨I⟩ We

31–32   ↑traces of↓

33–36   ↑That . . . proceeds↓ ¶ ⟨This is taught by reason & by Scripture⟩
         What

37   ↑hostile↓

Page 162

1–3   origin to . . . life ⟨back⟩ & . . . who ["who" is emphasized by being
         traced over several times] is that whence, to . . . God: to worship it:
         &

11   & [how] [MS torn] much in ↑our↓

13   just [con]ception [MS torn]

20   But [he] had [MS torn]

21   seen [by] the eye [MS torn]

24   fagots the . . . incorrup[ti]ble [MS torn]

28   bundles A No the

29   ↑Divine↓

30–31   God &c [Emerson normally uses "&c" to stand for the remainder of
         a passage from scripture, and while he may here have had Exodus 3:6
         in mind, it is not clear how he would have finished this sentence, or
         indeed whether he would have quoted from the Bible.] ¶ ⟨And ⟨so⟩
         surely reason ⟨&⟩ [canceled in pencil] ⟨religion⟩ ⟨↑scripture↓⟩
         [canceled in pencil] teach⟩ ↑⟨1. Our reason⟩1 My reason & experi-
         ence teach↓ /me/us this/ [rejected variant in pencil] to [Emerson
         wrote, in pencil, "1. Our reason & experience teach" then wrote over
         the first words in ink: "1 My reason"; the capital letter looks much
         more like a "B" though a badly formed "M" is possible and makes
         better sense. The number "1." is rejected because Emerson canceled
         the "2." at page 164, line 4.]

37–38   us. ¶ ⟨The more improvement⟩ As

Page 163

4   ¶ /And/And . . . you/ have [variant in pencil]

6–7   before. ⟨Now that⟩ ↑And when↓ [emendation in pencil] the cloud of
         yesterday ["of yesterday" circled in pencil, apparently to indicate that
         the omission of the phrase is part of the variant that follows] /has
         broke/shall break/ [variant in pencil] . . . cheerful ⟨radiance⟩
         ↑beam↓ . . . he ⟨went up⟩ rose

13   when ⟨the waters⟩ God ⟨said⟩ ↑saw↓

14–15   ¶ ↑Is . . . obstruction↓ On the contrary ↑God . . . eternity↓

19   the ⟨generous⟩ social

23–27   ↑Why . . . strong.↓ ¶ ⟨Well⟩ ↑What hinders↓ then will [Emerson
         neglected to cancel "will"] ↑that↓ you ⟨not⟩ ↑should↓ . . . in ⟨your⟩
         behalf ⟨as⟩ of

28–30   outstre⟨c⟩tched . . . ↑when . . . it↓

31–32   ↑There . . . renewed↓

36–(164)4   ↑And . . . is. [in ink over the same in pencil] {Thoughts . . . new.↓ ¶
⟨And so every moment demands a new religion What is religion? I
understand it to be ⟨the acknowledgment⟩ the ⟨cordial⟩ acknowledgment ↑in the heart↓ that all our being is derived from God & so is
to be ⟨held⟩ used according to his laws. The amount of good which
every being possesses is the measure of his debt to God. For the soul
perceives God to be the source of all being & whatever is, is from him.
I↑n yᵉ next place↓⟩ [addition in pencil] ¶ ↑⟨2.⟩ [canceled in pencil] As
. . . continually↓

Page 164

5   ↑to our reason↓ [in pencil] . . . never ceasing
8   a ↑per↓pe⟨r⟩tual
15–16   therefore ⟨the whole amount of our⟩ whatever faculties ⟨I have⟩
↑each has↓, [emendation in pencil] . . . to /me/him/ [variant in
pencil]
21–25   laws. ¶ ⟨Therefore⟩ For . . . persuasion ⟨to⟩with
32   ↑& a former age↓. [in pencil]
33   Providence↑;↓ [semicolon in pencil]
36   directly↑,↓ . . . ↑to offer its homage↓ [additions in pencil]
37–38   the ⟨peculiar⟩ liveliest . . . nature. ⟨We⟩The . . . the ⟨s⟩concealed
41   The ⟨idea of⟩ supposition

Page 165

2   beautiful. ⟨The acquisition of virtues is to us the dri⟩ ↑Moral . . .
old↓
13–15   all the [sentence not completed, though there was space on the page
for several more lines; end of page] ¶ ↑The Scriptures teach it↓ [in ink
over "The SS teach it" in pencil] ¶ This ↑is↓
20–21   the ⟨instr⟩ Teacher . . . wisdom ⟨of God⟩ &

[Following the end of the sermon is a notation in pencil:] And no where more plainly
than in the remarkable passage in yᵉ text

Sermon CLIX

Manuscript: Five sheets folded to make four pages each; the pages of the first three folios
measure 24.3 x 20.2 cm; those of the fourth and fifth measure 25 x 20.2 cm; a leaf
measuring 25 x 20.2 cm is inserted into the fourth folio; sewn along the left margin with
white thread.

Lines   *Page 166*
1   question ⟨of⟩ ↑put by↓
4–6   answer. ¶ ⟨↑Though we cannot↓⟩ ↑Infinite . . . is. ⟨But we⟩Man
. . . seeks.↓
7   ↑large↓
10–11   which ⟨was hidden from⟩ ↑began to be shown to↓ the first man ⟨&⟩
in
13–14   more ⟨largely⟩ ↑liberally↓

16–17	achievements. ²{This is the cause that never goes backward.} ¹{This is the treasure that never is diminished.} Battles
20–21	forevermore ¶ ⟨It is now a wide⟩ ¶ ⟨This⟩ ↑Truth↓ is what is ↑already↓
22	well as ⟨↑a↓⟩ ↑the↓
26–(167)1	there ⟨was⟩ ↑were↓ some ⟨one⟩ to serve as ⟨a⟩ connecting link↑s↓ ⟨a⟩ keeper↑s↓ & transmitter↑s↓

Page 167

3	¶ Every ⟨single⟩ mans life ⟨leads to results that⟩ ↑tends to↓
7–9	much ⟨advanced⟩ ↑manifested↓ by ↑the ruin of↓ . . . it. ¶ ⟨Truth What is often meant by⟩ ↑One . . . word↓
11	But ⟨forget not that that⟩ this
12–13	This ⟨that I speak of⟩ is ↑only↓ . . . world↑.↓, ⟨taken together⟩— but th⟨at⟩e other
19–21	duration. It ¶ This . . . knowledge ⟨the pursuit of⟩ which leads ever inward ⟨to⟩ from
23	¶ 2. The ["2." is rejected because Emerson supplies no "1."] . . . ↑this↓ connexion↑,↓ ⟨with this⟩ is,
25–27	¶ ↑Truth is . . . is⟨,⟩ to . . . by it↓
30–31	him ⟨are⟩ ↑in a romance↓ never ⟨were⟩ ↑happened↓ . . . in ⟨the⟩ ↑a↓ romance⟨s,⟩ or
34	↑so↓
35–36	the ⟨pages⟩ ↑fiction↓ where it is ⟨done⟩ ¶ If this order were ⟨not⟩ contradicted
39	that ⟨for⟩ which
42–(168)4	it? ¶ ⟨Truth is agreeable to the nature of man⟩ ↑⟨Indeed⟩ ↑Truth is ↑so↓ . . . that↓ . . . him.↓

Page 168

6	they ⟨love⟩ ↑approve↓.—
8	unsound? ⟨Someth⟩ A
14	fears. The [end of page] The reason
16	desireable.
19	↑↑the↓ True & ↑the↓ best . . . thing↓
21–22	desireable . . . be ⟨de⟩conceived . . . urgently de⟨si⟩manded
25–26	policy. ⟨Why do we say so.⟩ ↑What do we mean?↓
27	& ⟨among⟩ ↑for↓
30	affirms ⟨that fact as a⟩ ↑the↓
31	¶ ↑In short↓ We
35–37	the ⟨tru⟩ declaration . . . truth. ¶ ⟨Consider⟩ It
40–(169)7	is ⟨most⟩ ↑especially↓ . . . receive. ⟨¶ Now brethren consider I pray you that⟩ The . . . ↑and an . . . follow.↓ ↑And . . . Paul. ↑Good . . . it↓ . . . truth.↓ ¶ ⟨Now⟩For, . . . you ⟨that⟩ what . . . improving ⟨conclusions⟩ ↑reasonings↓ . . . character. ↑that . . . knowledge.↓

Page 169

9–11	led ⟨year by year⟩ ↑gradually↓ to irresistible conclusions↑—to . . . see.↓

12	such /midges/atoms/ ⟨as⟩ we
20–21	that ⟨was⟩ ever ⟨raised⟩ gave . . . may ⟨have⟩ borrow . . . but ⟨to⟩ stop it we cannot here
23	overthrow ⟨do⟩ have
25	think ⟨of⟩ the doctrines they reverence ⟨as⟩ ↑to be↓
33–34	nature. ¶ ⟨Consider o⟩Once more, ⟨brethren, that⟩ the appointed way ⟨& the only way⟩ in
39	see, ⟨is⟩ ↑gives↓ always the ⟨path⟩ ↑title↓

Page 170

2	that ⟨our⟩ ↑the↓
6–7	↑It . . . examination↓
17	in ⟨that clear declaration⟩ ↑the discoveries↓
20–26	↑becoming↓ spirit ⟨of truth⟩, to . . . God. ⟨Let us serve the truth⟩ Believing . . . truth, ⟨but⟩ ↑we↓ . . . apprehen⟨e⟩ded . . . but th⟨e⟩is . . . behind, I & reaching

Sermon CLX

Manuscript: Five sheets folded to make four pages each; a leaf follows the second folio; two leaves follow the third folio; and a leaf follows the fifth folio. Pages of the second folio and the leaf that follows it measure 24.3 x 20.2 cm; all others measure 25 x 20.2 cm. A strip measuring approximately 4.5 x 19.8 cm (containing Insert "B") was once attached with red sealing wax to the lower right corner of the last page of the fourth folio. The gathering is sewn along the left margin with white thread.

Lines	*Page 171*
5	¶ ↑{↓My [bracket in pencil] . . . occasion of ⟨our⟩ meeting ⟨after⟩ ↑you↓
7	↑recent↓
13–16	with ↑the↓ . . . God."↑}↓ [bracket in pencil] ⟨↑How often does the thot occur that God is unknown in the world, that He is forgot by whom are all things. Men do not even desire this species of knowledge.↓⟩ ¶ ⟨My friends I invite your thoughtful attention to this subject. I wish we might arouse one another to ⟨som fron something like⟩ the attention which is due to it. I wish we might awake each other from the ⟨sleep⟩ ↑indifference↓ in which we all indulge to what is truly great & good, ⟨that we might open our faculties to the knowledg⟩ whilst we count all other knowledge good we might count this the supreme good; perceive this to be the grandest thought in the universe of thought that in this knowledge many men who think themselves most wise are profoundly ignorant indeed, that the highest knowledge men have on this subject must be profound ignorance, to perceive that so far from being a dull dead speculative thought it is quick with life & giveth life—that it is the education of man that the knowledge of God is commensurate with the knowledge of yourself ⟨that the increase of it is the increase of power to your hands & of peace in your bosom,⟩ that it comes not by sleepy contemplations but by righteous & energetic actions⟩ ¶ Does

Page 172

2–3   dull. ¶ ⟨But my friends that which I stand here to urge is the infinite blessing of an increasing knowledge of God.⟩ ↑But↓ What

6   of ⟨men⟩ states, if we see ↑not↓ & ask not⟨hing⟩ why

8–9   men—⟨if⟩ to . . . spring ⟨by⟩ which

10   & ⟨control⟩ persuade

13–14   conversing ⟨with⟩ by . . . unreal ⟨mockery⟩ &

17–19   works. ⟨It should be⟩ ↑But↓ . . . moment⟨,⟩ to . . . ↑to every one↓ . . . ↑it shd. be↓ . . . God—⟨to come⟩ to

22   ¶ And ⟨↑{↓this ↑{↓is ↑{↓possible as well as right.↑}↓⟩ This has God↑}↓ provided [brackets in pencil; cancellation in pencil and ink]

23–25   is ⟨as⟩precisely . . . devils. ⟨All over the world such as the ⟨man is such ⟨will h⟩ are his descriptions of God,⟩ ↑civilization, such is the religion.↓⟩ ⟨tell me what is his worship & you tell me what is the worshipper.⟩ ↑Describe . . . ↑he worships,↓ . . . ↑to you↓ the man.↓

26–28   is ⟨a very plain⟩ ↑therefore an important↓ truth, ⟨to him who ponders it⟩ that every ⟨adv⟩ step . . . the ⟨more true⟩ better

29   more ⟨clearly⟩ ↑plainly↓ appear by considering ⟨attentively⟩ ⟨↑as I propose to do↓⟩ the

31–32   consider ⟨in succession the more striking⟩ ↑⟨the successive⟩ the successive↓ . . . ascertained ⟨T⟩that

34–35   but ⟨it is⟩ there

37–40   as ⟨exist in ⟨India⟩ Indostan⟩ those . . . Ganges. ¶ ⟨Let me proceed to enumerate the successive ⟨stages⟩ ↑steps by↓ which men ascend to a better knowledge of God.⟩ ↑With . . . God.↓

Page 173

1–2   important ⟨step⟩ ↑moment↓ . . . look ⟨at⟩ ↑in↓

3–4   Omnipresent. ⟨↑but in their own heart & soul↓⟩ ↑He is ⟨the principle⟩ the Soul ⟨that which is⟩ within all nature↓

5–15   any ⟨vehicle⟩ finite . . . image. ↑{Insert A} A {What . . . men ⟨come up⟩ ↑gathered↓ . . . effect!}↓ ⟨But⟩ I . . . idolat⟨e⟩ry & ⟨the grossest⟩ ignorance . . . the ⟨pra⟩ form

20   to the ⟨memory⟩ ↑remembrance↓

23   slaughtered ⟨at once⟩ before

30–38   ↑Yet . . . all ⟨great⟩ ↑high↓ . . . only ⟨be⟩ exist . . . to ⟨this⟩ ↑a↓ heavenly worship, ⟨from⟩ to the ⟨costly⟩ giving . . . economy.↓ [These added sentences appear to be crowded in a space left for them in the middle of the paragraph.] And the ⟨perception⟩ ↑conviction↓ that God is not ⟨thus⟩ to be ⟨pleased⟩ ↑propitiated . . . altar,↓ . . . ↑first↓ . . . oblations' ⟨indicates⟩ ↑shows the dawning of↓ . . . humanity↑.↓ ⟨dawning⟩ ¶ 3.

Page 174

2–5   the ⟨cholera⟩ ↑mechanism of the heavens↓ or the ⟨Famine⟩ ↑heaving Sea↓; . . . good ⟨in the making⟩ ↑unfinished↓;

7–8   the ⟨wrath⟩ spite

10   be ⟨beheld⟩ ↑looked upon↓. They⟨↑}↓⟩ try [bracket in pencil]

12–13   ↑Still . . . judgments.↓

15–17   seen, ²{that our misfortunes are our best friends}; ¹{that out of all
           evil issues good;} & . . . Want, ⟨Adversity⟩ Difficulty,

22   danger It [It is unclear whether the sentence ending "danger" is a
           rhetorical question or an exclamation; the editors have supplied a
           period, not wishing to interpret arbitrarily.]

35–41   fraudulent. ⟨Certainly, my friends, this is not an error confined to
           savages or to Jews or to Catholics. Beware if it have not infected our
           minds. Do⟩ [Emerson had space on the page to complete this sentence
           if he had wished; it appears to have been abandoned, then canceled,
           without loss of text. End of MS page 16; page 17 is blank; page 18 has
           only some hymn notations in pencil (here omitted); the text resumes
           on MS p. 19.] ¶ But . . . breathe & ⟨&⟩act . . . ↑perhaps↓

Page 175

1–4   felt, ⟨it⟩ that soul ⟨will arrive at⟩ ↑is on its way to↓ all good. ¶ And
           ⟨surely it must be plain⟩ ↑it cannot be doubted↓ . . . ↑upon earth↓.

8–12   us. ⟨that God dwells in the human soul.⟩ It . . . our ⟨attention⟩
           [canceled in pencil and ink] search . . . from ⟨things outward⟩
           ↑without↓ . . . the ⟨fullest⟩ ↑brightest↓ . . . depths of [end of line] of
           our

13   to ⟨fathom⟩ understand . . . I ⟨will not endeavour⟩ ↑know not how↓

19–20   never ⟨abases⟩ hurts, . . . nature, ⟨without us⟩ &

25   duty ⟨to power⟩ &

28   can ⟨make⟩ ↑domesticate↓

31–(176)4 yet ⟨if it be carefully considered⟩ ↑who . . . felt↓ its truth↑?↓
           ⟨appears. It will be felt⟩ ↑Every man knows↓ . . . very ⟨far⟩ distinct
           from selfishness. ⟨It will be felt⟩ ↑Every man knows↓ . . . voice↑.↓
           [period in pencil] ⟨It will be felt⟩ ↑Every man knows↓ . . . a ⟨serene⟩
           praise . . . the ⟨trumpet⟩ ↑eloquence↓ . . . cold. ⟨It is felt in the
           bosom of every man, such is the majesty that reigns there, that no
           man was ever benefitted by a⟩ ↑{Insert B} [On a slip of paper at one
           time attached to MS p. 22, containing a passage marked "B":] {Every
           . . . universe, ⟨but⟩ and . . . at ⟨odds⟩ discord with himself. He
           ⟨knows⟩ ↑believes↓ . . . bad↓ [a line from "of present" to the end of
           the insert; end of Insert "B"] ⟨bad action⟩, [faulty cancellation in
           pencil] & . . . ever ⟨really a sufferer from⟩ ↑harmed by↓

Page 176

11–12   ↑He . . . Spirit.↓ [in ink over pencil; "Eternal" is capitalized in the
           pencil version]

14   incapab⟨a⟩le

26–27   man. ↑in . . . this?↓ Is it not to ⟨divest⟩ ↑redeem↓ him ⟨of⟩ ↑from↓

29   his ⟨ey⟩ roving

32   could ⟨come up to the fact⟩ increase

35–(177)7 stars. [The following addition, in pencil, is rejected as a probable late
           emendation:] ↑Let us not undervalue the very lowest aid: let us not
           ⟨un⟩ neglect ⟨the⟩ any custom, any form, in which sincere hearts

have found aid & expression to their thots: but let us use all ⟨aids⟩ ↑forms↓ as aids as instruments to a closer converse with God in his chosen temple the Heart↓ ¶ ⟨My . . . God.⟩ [The cancellation of the final paragraph (which terminates with the date "Sept. 2. 1832") is rejected as a probable late emendation.]

37   nearer / access / approach / [variant in pencil]
39   which ⟨h⟩ we

Page 177

1–5   person.') ⟨Let us⟩ ↑I beseech you↓ then ⟨to⟩ ⟨↑that we may↓ make ⟨so much⟩ ↑that↓ effort of mind as to bring it home to our own thoughts, that the glory of our nature⟩ ↑Let us then lay . . . have↓ is ⟨in⟩ this ⟨alliance⟩ privilege . . . God; ↑Let us ⟨[unrecovered letter]⟩ reflect↓ . . . he ⟨becomes⟩ makes . . . us; ⟨&⟩ that . . . the ⟨slightest⟩ ↑faintest↓ . . . shall ⟨rise⟩ expel every ⟨hostile⟩ advers⟨e⟩ary . . . unfold ⟨an⟩ new

[Following the end of the sermon is a substitute conclusion:] ¶ ↑My friends the world runs after an external religion an external God but let all whose affections & understandings are so far cultivated open their hearts to the unspeakable gift of an inward revelation of the Divinity. Every man that has been born has been born with this priv⟨e⟩ilege of access to the Eternal. The reason why so few men have found the Father is that so few men watch their own minds. But if a man will reve⟨n⟩rently watch his own thoughts he will find that a verdict which is indeed divine is there rendered upon every act, & that God is inviting him to renounce a wretched dependance upon human censure & human praise, by writing his own sentence there in letters of light. This is the gospel of glad tidings which Jesus Christ brot to men It is glad tidings of great joy to him who hath ears to hear.↓ [Cf. Luke 2:10; Matthew 11:15, Mark 4:9, Luke 8:8]

Sermon CLXI

Manuscript (earlier version): Three sheets folded to make four pages each; folio pages measuring, respectively, 25 x 20.2 cm, 24.3 x 20.2 cm, and 24.3 x 20.1 cm. The first folio is followed by two leaves each measuring 24.3 x 20.2 cm; the second folio is followed by a leaf also 24.3 x 20.2 cm; the third folio is followed by two leaves (measuring, respectively, 25 x 20.2 cm and 24.3 x 20.2 cm). The entire gathering is sewn along the left margin with white thread.

[The text of the earlier version follows:]

clxi.
O. S.

In the sweat of thy face shall thou eat bread, ⟨all the days of thy life⟩ till thou return unto the ground. Genesis 3, 19.

Never surely was any prophecy more strictly fulfilled than this ancient word. We all smart under the operation of the curse. If there is good in it we are slow to own it.

'Poverty' saith an old observation, 'is a good which all hate.' We loudly complain of the hard necessity which drives us all, as with the cart whip, to our labor. A little respite, we cry, a time to take breath. What is life for, if it is all to be spent in ⟨work⟩ ↑toil↓? but our complaints are not heard, or are not regarded. The stern law still is enforced, & the earth is incessantly shaken with the din of human industry.

We see ⟨its⟩ the fulfilment ↑of the divine sentence↓ with our eyes. We fulfil it with our own hands. See this army of strong men which pours out of the doors of all these streets as the sun rises. Hear the incessant noise of their thousand trades all day long. Go into the stores & see the unwearied pen of the clerk, the anxious brow of the merchant & the diligent feet that run to & fro on his errands all day.

↑On every estate↓ In every office, in every shop, in every manufactory, ⟨in every bank⟩ ↑in every ship↓, there is still the same ⟨toil⟩ ↑labor↓ under new forms, the toiling of the brains & the sweat of the face. Or go ⟨into the house⟩ ↑under the domestic roof↓ & see the cares of every family, the endless duties of the laboring woman, of the mother, the wife, & the ⟨daughter⟩ ↑maiden↓ Leave the town & ⟨go⟩ ↑walk↓ into the fields, you have exchanged the machinery but the farmer works as hard as the mechanic; or cross the seas or travel to the northern pole or ⟨to⟩ go southward to the line, and wherever the human race hold any possessions enjoy any comforts, the same painful means are everywhere the price of bread.

My friends, this universal law does not prevail without being a universal benefit. And it will help to reconcile us to our own part in it,—⟨it⟩ & will ⟨at least⟩ make the hum of labor sound more cheerfully in our ears, if we accustom ourselves to review the specific benefits that arise to man out of it. Moreover ⟨there is always a handful of men released by circumstances⟩ ↑the circumstances of some men release them if only their nature would also release them↓ from this necessity; and the temptation is continually coming to every man to forego some of the good he might obtain for the sake of being ⟨released⟩ ↑set free↓ from this continual labor. This temptation is full of danger. There is no end to the perils of idleness. It is the mother of all mischief.

I invite you then to consider some of the ⟨more⟩ general advantages which flow to the human race out of this law of our constitution. And this subject I shall consider in four points. Labor makes man 1. healthful & powerful; 2. safe; 3. useful; 4. happy.

1. The first advantage of this law of our nature is that it confers upon us health & strength. The ⟨ruddy⟩ red cheek & the ⟨cunning⟩ ↑nimble↓ hand belong to the laborer not to the sluggard ⟨It is the plain intent of every⟩ ↑Man is by nature a Workman as much as a fish is a swimmer or a bird ⟨a flyer⟩ designed for flight↓ It is written all over this wonderful frame ⟨of ours⟩, it is writ on every limb & artery & nerve, *This is for use*. There is not a sense nor an organ nor a drop of blood in the whole anatomy that hath not its prescribed office. ↑It is true of the voluntary & of the involuntary functions↓ The heart beats at the centre, day & night, year after year, & never stops till the soul is called from the flesh. The lungs heave as long. ⟨We are fearfully & wonderfully made [Psalms 139:14] &⟩ disease begins the moment one ⟨pa⟩ member fails to perform its function. So is it with all the voluntary actions of the frame. The still hand becomes ⟨p⟩ numb. The life of every sense & limb depends on its use. And the finer powers that seem to mediate betwixt the body & the soul, health & cheerfulness exist only in the active frame. ↑As the health so also do the powers ⟨of the⟩ grow by use.↓ 'A full grown man,' says the political economist, 'is an accumulated capital.' The habit of years has qualified him to produce effects ⟨every day⟩ that are more wonderful every day & that would seem (if the intermediate steps were not seen, & only the first & last works compared)

quite miraculous. He that does nothing is poorer than he that has nothing. ↑What ⟨a miracle⟩ power has its use given to↓ Galileos eye↑; or to↓ Galens hand↑?↓ [sentence marked off by heavy vertical ink lines in either margin] ↑What wonderful skill does the dullest eye acquire in measuring distances by a glance that by a little shade of grey or green discerns this to be water & that to be stone at the distance of miles! What cunning doth not the hand ↑of the sculptor the engraver the painter↓ acquire by long use It has no more muscles than the hand of a boy, no more flexibility. ⟨Yet the sculptor the engraver the painter ⟨the⟩ as well as ↑in↓ the mechanic arts—what divine power has not labor given⟩ ↑⟨Let⟩ ↑Has not↓ the observation of every one of you ⟨answer whether⟩ confirmed the experience of the world that Labor gives health & /wonderful/new/ [variant in pencil] powers /to the frame/every day/ [variant in pencil] Not ⟨the⟩ less ⟨wonderful⟩ but much more amazing is the skill acquired by practi⟨s⟩ce in all mental labor.↓↓

2 Industry is safe. The safety of him who is engaged in lawful labor is so conspicuous when contrasted with the dangers of the idle that it seems well bought at any price. Working in your own calling is like dwelling in a sanctuary which no enemies dare approach. ↑Walls of stone or an army of guards are a less sure defence from danger than is the discharge of our duties.↓ It is a preventive to all dangers It elevates you above danger. Would you be revenged of your enemy ⟨live as you ought⟩ ↑work in your calling↓ & you are nobly avenged. But the danger of idle hands is so great that the proverbs of all nations abound with warnings against it.

The fact is, leisure, absolute leisure, doing nothing would not be dangerous but deadly. For the life of all our powers is their action. ⟨There is only this difference in the effect of leisure upon different persons that there are some persons in the world who can employ themselves without affairs in books & in contemplation & some who cannot. Some of the most industrious persons that ever lived ↑& some of the most useful too↓ have been almost incapable of any manual labor or any management of affairs.⟩ ↑{Insert A} A {Leisure, in the sense of doing nothing, belongs to no human being. There are many persons in every community who ⟨w⟩are called men of leisure, because they never work with their hands. Some of the most diligent workmen that ever lived & the most productive workmen too have been of this description ⟨Certainly⟩ there is a great difference ↑between the sorts of activity↓ [addition in ink over "between" in pencil] among men↑,↓ [comma in pencil] for to /stop the bodily activity/bind the hands/ of some men would be to condemn them to idleness whilst another class of men habitually employ themselves without affairs in books or in ⟨contemplation⟩ ↑study↓. [emendation in pencil] ↑but↓ God demands of every man constant action ⟨No man⟩ The call of ⟨duty⟩ ↑nature↓ upon the rich & the poor upon the scholar or the mechanic is incessant. But there needs a necessity a little ⟨sterner⟩ ↑harsher↓ than the mere call ⟨of duty⟩ to lead us into our own good↓ [end of Insert "A"] ↑It is true↓ [in ink over pencil] There have been some ⟨too⟩ [cancel in ink over pencil] who needed no other taskmaster to set them their stint of labor than their own insatiable curiosity in seeking after scientific or religious truth. But these instances are rare. Most men, men of study as well as of business need some other regulator than their own humour. They need the compulsion of a stated work to guard them from themselves—from this besetting temptation besetting all men to relax effort, & fold the hands. Moreover most men need not only the discipline of method & required amount of labor but need also a due proportion of active duty, of conversation & dealing with their fellowmen, ↑a mixture↓ of privations & pains & obstacles to keep the moral system in tone & invigorate the understanding. ↑"If thou dost not want labour for *food* thou mayest for *physick*," said William Penn And all wise men have prescribed ⟨it⟩ to themselves the mixture of contemplation with active business of some sort.↓

⟨But to most⟩ ↑A few↓ [emendation in ink over pencil] men of study ↑may task themselves but↓ [in pencil and ink] & to all other men of active employments it needs very little observation of what takes place around us, to see how much danger would follow the removal of the common necessity

For repose, so sweet to labor, is very quickly irksome, and the faculties must be employed in good or evil. It is not a choice between inaction & work, but between doing good or doing harm. By our nature, work we must. ⟨We cannot be still.⟩ We are miserable without excitement The head will be busy & the body ⟨must be moved⟩ ↑in motion↓ & if you do not provide them with honest employment they will carve out mischief for themselves. Something must excite us & if you will not furnish the brain with innocent ⟨thots⟩ ↑⟨materials⟩ subjects↓, it will be a shop of mischievous purposes, of unfriendly thoughts, of foul imaginations. There is no virtue can be preserved in sloth. The idle man—you know him in the street by his roving eye, by his discontented malevolent expression. He meddles with his neighbors affairs to their hurt

But benevolence is just as naturally generated in the breast of the industrious man. He comes ⟨out of⟩ ↑from↓ his desk or work-room & looks ↑abroad↓ with senses & soul ready to draw keen enjoyment from every object He hath the innocence of childhood. There is refreshment to him in the face of the sky & the countenance of man. They remind him of the thousand thousand cheerful works that have proceeded around him whilst he has been engrossed ⟨in⟩ ↑with↓ his own. He has not been soured or belittled by the gossip of the bar-room. He is spotless from the crimes into which the idlers have been drawn He has not wrought himself into a fever in the little politics of the ward. He has not ⟨made himself obnoxious to⟩ bound himself by rash promises to rash men to ↑any↓ criminal engagements; he has not made himself obnoxious to men; he has not made himself ↑an object of↓ the grief of angels, & the disapprobation of God. [end of MS p. 13]

↑Idle men no leisure

Busy men

The recreations of busy men shame the idle↓ [end of MS p. 14]

3. It makes men useful. It not only makes men innocent it makes them useful. It makes them useful 1 to others & then to themselves & out of this self-good accrues again a larger benefit to the world. It is a ⟨small thing⟩ good thing amid the ⟨distracting⟩ manifold temptations of the world to do no harm; but it is a far better to do it great service. And who is it, I pray you, who have done all the good that is or has been on earth. It is ⟨poor men⟩ the poor. Poor men & poor women laboring for their bread with wits sharpened by their wants pinched by cold driven by hunger straitened by debt striving to make their wants fewer and their labors more lucrative, these have been the benefactors of the world. It is these stern necessities ⟨of ours⟩ that we are ashamed of & which we mourn, that ⟨are the active⟩ have invented all the arts, & multiplied the comforts & finished the great improvements of social life. Every thing that is great & good cost labor, & watching, & contention & sacrifice.

And every individual in the whole ↑working↓ community however his hands have been employed who has done his duty feels the lively satisfaction of having contributed his part to the prosperity of the state

In the next place, he has been useful to himself. By the providence of God it is ordered that no man should faithfully use his talent without receiving personal benefit there-from. His power is increased; his acquaintance with himself is increased; his knowledge of human nature & human duty is increased. The great truths of religion are opened to him who works in his own vocation as in a book. One does not need to study many volumes nor to run over many lands nor to be acquainted with hundreds of men & variety of manners

There is a religion of Common Sense that lies in the mind of simple men who have had no other instruction than their bible & their daily observation in a very confined business which is amply sufficient for the guidance of the man in all common questions of duty. For God has provided that the Conscience, the domestic god, the eye of the soul, should grow up in man in every condition & therefore has prepared the experience by which it is to be formed to grow like grass in every place. ↑Every one has his own way of getting it.↓ [in ink over "To every one are his own means" in pencil] Books supply it to ⟨one man⟩ ↑the scholar↓ [addition in ink over pencil] courts supply it to / another man / the statesman /, ↑the ways of↓ children to ⟨another⟩ ↑the schoolmaster course of yᵉ season & growing corn to the farmer↓ and the petty details of the smallest employment in which any one is habitually engaged, speak a moral language to every man, ⟨are very significant⟩ ↑↑&↓ ⟨&⟩are preachers↓ to him of his duties.

↑That is to say↓ As every man has in his own personal experience very striking illustrations of the ⟨gospel⟩ ↑moral↓ maxims ⟨so⟩ that Honesty is the best policy that ↑the↓ lazy take the most pains, Time is money or the like—↑examples↓ that more convince him than any other proofs, so every man has in his own handiwork familiar & pointed illustrations of all religious truth ⟨Every⟩ And this because moral truth is the soul of the ⟨whole⟩ universe & is expressed as much by every minute change as by great ones.

E Thus in England formerly every trade was a mystery & ⟨was⟩ ↑its details were↓ spiritually improved into symbols & mementos of all doctrines & all duties ↑wh. ↑were↓ printed in prose or rhyme & sold at village fairs in stitched sheets↓ and as it has been said "every craftsman had as it were two versions of his bible, one in yᵉ common language of the country, another in yᵉ acts objects & products of his own particular craft."

But every one to whom I speak, if he has ever reflected upon the objects↑,↓ ⟨of⟩ whatever they be⟨,⟩ which daily occupy his attention will have observed in them this peculiar property of conveying a moral & religious instruction that only wants an attentive eye & ear to make it effectual on his heart & life.

4. And, in the fourth place, Labor makes men *happy*. For this divine instruction which it conveys is the ⟨best⟩ highest kind of happiness. In the way to which I have alluded, the industrious man gathers a daily wisdom, a conviction of the eternal value & beauty of veracity, of diligence, of kindness, of perseverance, & of faith, even out of the ⟨homely & narrow⟩ ↑trivial↓ details of a very narrow employment. He is made acquainted with himself He learns what he can do; how his powers compare with other men's; what sweetness leisure has for him, & how soon it becomes wearisome & what sweetness there is in labor. This solid wisdom is an enlargement of his mind & is so much preparation for enterprize, for higher duties, more comprehensive undertakings; it is so much food for meditation & ⟨convers⟩ discourse. And so he is daily made more fit to serve effectually his family, his neighbors, his town his country & to contribute his quota of service to the improvement of the human race. And this consciousness will give the most sensible satisfaction to every good mind.

Moreover these are steps in a path which has no end. Fitness to live is fitness to die. He who is making himself more useful to his fellowmen is becoming a better servant of God. True preparation for this world is a preparation for all the worlds in the government of God.

Mere labor to be sure will not suffice to make us wise & good, & ⟨so⟩ ↑therefore↓ happy. Labor is the safe & appointed place of man, but he must labor with a pious mind, with a conviction that the blessing is from ⟨a⟩ the Lord. ↑A wi Let a man distinguish his usefulness from the usefulness of a windmill or a waterwheel. Let his be voluntary.↓ Then his increasing wisdom will dictate such changes in his ⟨pursuit &⟩ employment of his time as will ⟨cont⟩ enable him to act with greater effect & will most powerfully exercise his abilities, so that we shall continually approach that state in which we do what we are most fit to do & what we love best & so the bitterness of the curse will pass away, & the sentence upon man, 'In the sweat of thy face shalt thou eat bread' will be seen & felt to be a blessing.

Therefore, brethren, seeing that the constitution of this world is fitted to make all our work benefit the workman, to make us more strong more safe useful & happy for all our labor, let us be diligent in our business; let us comply with Gods law; let us not be weary in well doing. ⟨a⟩ Above all, let us by our faithful & thankful disposition, call down on our labor the divine blessing. Then go forth in your duties how high, how humble soever,—to your store, to your work-yard, to your office, to your study, to your household,—& every where feel that you are by these present temporary works ⟨f⟩ training up yourself for higher duties, for a heavenly society, for endless usefulness.

September 2,
1832

Manuscript (later version): Six sheets folded to make four pages each; folio pages measure 24 x 19.8 cm; sewn along the left margin with white thread.

Lines	Page 178
2–3	The /good/ alleviation/ [variant in pencil] . . . own. ⟨Poverty saith⟩ It
5	say↑,↓ [comma in pencil]
7	regarded the
14–(179)1	every ⟨estate⟩ ↑⟨farm⟩ wharf↓ in . . . ship↑,↓ . . . forms↑,↓ [commas in pencil]

	Page 179
6	seas ⟨or⟩ travel [canceled in pencil]
9	¶ ↑In . . . life↓ [in pencil]
11–12	to /consider/ observe narrowly/ [variant in pencil] . . . it ↑nay whether it be not altogether an advantage↓. [addition in ink over "nay whether it be not all advantage" in pencil]
13–14	of ⟨such⟩ meditation⟨s⟩ ↑upon the laws of ⟨of⟩ our condition↓ is to ⟨make the⟩ reconcile . . . doom↑,↓ [comma in pencil]
19–20	task. ⟨But a ⟨just⟩ ⟨thorough⟩ ↑better↓ understanding of the ⟨effect⟩ influence which this law ⟨produce⟩ exerts upon our worldly condition ⟨would lead us perhaps⟩ ↑is always modifying, & may come at last↓ to reverse our opinions & practices.⟩ ¶ ↑But . . . it↓

25–26   him↑,↓ [comma in pencil] . . . sword the ⟨spade⟩ ↑plough↓ . . . map
         ⟨or⟩ the . . . implement ⟨If he does nothing⟩ ⟨It is not necessary that
         he should even use⟩ [last cancellation in pencil] ↑He . . . using↓ [in
         pencil]

30   is ⟨What or⟩ [canceled in pencil] How . . . live ⟨were⟩ ↑it needed↓

32–37   of th⟨is⟩e . . . ↑in important respects↓ [addition in pencil] ¶ ⟨1. In
         the first place I observe that⟩ ↑1. Labor . . . faculties.↓ ⟨i⟩It . . . laws
         ↑is↓ . . . penalties. ⟨The health of the body & the mind can only by
         labor be gained & secured.⟩ Man

40   secured. ⟨It begins⟩ ↑This instruction is given↓

41   frame ⟨of ours⟩it is . . . nerve *This*

                         Page 180

8–9   ↑Inaction . . . death↓

14   only ⟨the⟩his

15–16   its ⟨inimitable⟩ ↑/exquisite/miraculous/↓ [cancellation and variants
         in pencil] . . . as ↑watchmakers hand or the surgeons↓ the

19   power ⟨acquired⟩ which

23–24   source.—⟨To omit entirely⟩ ↑To consider↓ at present the ⟨point⟩
         ↑subject↓ of intellectual labor ↑would . . . far↓ [all emendations in
         pencil]

25   it ⟨a conspicuous⟩ ↑an all important↓ [emendation in pencil]

28–29   ↑Tho this . . . a↑n↓ ⟨hard⟩ interpreter . . . attention↓ [in pencil]

34–35   ↑you are rising . . . time↓

39   the ⟨experience⟩ ↑opinions↓ [emendation in pencil]

                         Page 181

1–2   ↑↑(↓It . . . devil.↑)↓↓ [parentheses in pencil]

11   man you

21   spotless from [end of page] from the

22–23   poli⟨cs⟩tics of the /ward/parish/.

23   promises ⟨to⟩ ↑with↓

27   ↑at↓

28   hindrance, ⟨t⟩an

32   duties↑, to . . . lofty & exertion↓ [addition in pencil]

33–34   ↑The . . . character↓ [in pencil]

36   And ⟨we find that⟩ ↑thus↓ [emendation in pencil]

38–40   ↑our↓ . . . than ⟨safe⟩ ↑innocent↓ . . . makes ⟨⟨them⟩ ↑men↓⟩men
         . . . accrues ⟨a larger⟩ again

                         Page 182

1   is ⟨a⟩ far

15–16   ↑It is . . . lived.↓

19   ¶ Again ⟨it⟩ industrious

20   than ⟨idle men⟩ that

22   off ⟨more⟩ better fruits from their ⟨le⟩recreation than the ⟨best⟩
         most

25–26	always ⟨holds⟩ ↑sets↓ before his eyes↑—↓to . . . usefulness↑—↓to [all emendations in pencil]
31	speak ⟨a⟩ever
33	genius ⟨information⟩ knowledge culture? ⟨To do n⟩ To

Page 183

1	rewards ⟨his⟩ fidelity
3	↑who↓
18–22	¶ ↑Need . . . by ⟨const⟩ faithful . . . from ⟨absorbing⟩ griefs ↑that threatened to overwhelm us↓ . . . remarked The . . . heal.↓ [paragraph and emendations in pencil]
26–28	↑As . . . truths↓ ¶ ⟨But⟩ ↑Yet, . . . lackest.↓ it
31	him /work/produce good/ in [variant in pencil; rejected]
35–38	If ⟨the laborer⟩ ↑man↓ [emendation in pencil] . . . reflexion, ⟨let him⟩ ↑if he will↓ . . . unhappy; ⟨let him⟩ ↑if he will↓ . . . employment; ⟨let him⟩ ↑if he will↓

Page 184

4–8	¶ ↑The . . . blessed.↓

Sermon CLXII

Manuscripts: Sermon CLXII, the so-called "Lord's Supper" sermon, is represented by two separate and complete holograph manuscripts, designated A and B by the Houghton Library staff. Manuscript A, which serves here as copy-text, was the one Emerson read from on September 9, 1832, the occasion of its only delivery. Manuscript B, lacking hymn citations, is a revised fair copy, most probably prepared soon after the event to be circulated among friends. This was the copy given by Emerson to Cyrus Bartol in August, 1857 (see *L* 5:81–82); Bartol's daughter returned it to Edith Emerson Forbes in April, 1920, and in April, 1933, it was conveyed to Harvard. Manuscript B was also the source of the sermon's first publication, in Octavius Brooks Frothingham, *Transcendentalism in New England* (New York, 1876), 363–80. (It seems clear that this printing was approved by Emerson: see *JMN* 16:478 and *The Letters of Ellen Tucker Emerson*, ed. Edith E. W. Gregg [Kent, Ohio, 1982], 2:193.) Frothingham's text was in turn adopted for the posthumous Riverside edition of Emerson's *Miscellanies* (1884). The Riverside text, which introduces a number of typographical errors, was reprinted in all later collected editions. The sermon as Emerson delivered it to his congregation is here published for the first time. Two late nineteenth-century manuscript copies also exist, but lack authority: Houghton Manuscript C, in an unidentified nineteenth-century hand, is simply a copy of Manuscript B. A hand-written copy of Manuscript A, prepared in 1883 by Mary Sherwood Brown, is contained in volume 61 of the Second Church Records, deposited at the Massachusetts Historical Society. The full text of Manuscript B is given following the notes to the text from Manuscript A.

Manuscript A: Eight sheets folded to make four pages each; pages measure 24.3 x 20.2 cm. Leaves of the same dimensions occur after the first folio, within and after the third folio, after the fourth folio, within and (containing Insert "A" on recto) after the seventh folio. All are sewn along the left margin with white thread, though the final leaf and folio have become detached. The editors speculate that the leaf following the first folio is in fact the remnant of a previous first folio, the first leaf of which was canceled and discarded prior to the sermon's delivery; the canceled portions of the text on the remaining leaf were rewritten on the substitute first folio.

Lines	*Page 185*
Bible Text	joy ⟨of⟩ ↑in↓
5–8	whether ⟨it⟩ mixed . . . be ⟨poured out⟩ ↑served↓ . . . broken, ⟨it⟩ ↑the questions↓ has been . . . church, ⟨the question to who[m] [MS torn] it⟩ ↑who↓ . . . be ⟨kept⟩ ↑prepared↓
8–9	Church ⟨since the 9th Century the bread only is given to the laity & ⟩ once . . . ↑& then forbidden↓ to partake. ⟨but⟩ since
14–15	the ⟨occasion of the Reformation⟩ ↑main controversy between Ch. of England & Ch. of Rome↓.
16–(*186*)1	↑In↓ The . . . maintained that that it . . . ↑not a sacrifice but↓

Page 186

3–15	¶ ↑If . . . . ¶ ⟨It⟩ And . . . . ¶ I allude . . . ↑so far . . . agreed,↓ . . . particular. ¶ ⟨My Christian friends, I have⟩ ↑Having↓ recently / paid/made/ [variant rejected] . . . subject, ⟨& been⟩ ↑I was↓ led to ⟨embrace⟩ the ⟨opinion⟩ ↑conclusion↓ . . . opinions↓ [end of MS p. 3; MS p. 4 blank] ¶ ⟨It is now ⟨a little⟩ near ⟨4⟩200 years since the Society of the Quakers denied its authority altogether & gave good reasons for ⟨its⟩ ↑their↓ disuse of it. ¶ I mention these facts to show that there has always been the widest room for difference of opinion upon this particular & that it is not as some have imagined an unheard of question. ¶ It is my opinion that Jesus did not intend ⟨that the observance⟩ to establish an institution for perpetual observance when he ate the Passover with his disciples. It is also my opinion that it is not expedient to celebrate it as we do. I shall endeavour to state distinctly my reasons for these two opinions.⟩ ¶ An
21–22	(14.22) ¶ ⟨In⟩ St Luke . . . words. 'This
26–29	facts. ⟨Here are⟩ Two . . . occasion. ⟨⟨& John certainly a most attentive listener.⟩⟩ Neither . . . to ⟨establish an ordinance⟩ ↑set . . . permanent↓.
31	omitted ⟨this⟩ such
32–(*187*)1	¶ ↑Neither . . . of↓ St Mark ⟨also who was not present⟩ who . . . facts↑.↓ ⟨omits this material one of Do this in remembrance.⟩ It

Page 187

2	↑that we know↓ for ⟨doubting⟩ ↑rejecting↓
3–11	I ⟨on⟩ have only ⟨considered⟩ ↑brought↓ ["brought" written over an unrecovered word which has been finger-wiped] . . . a ⟨great pe⟩ ↑solemn↓ . . . all ⟨men⟩ mankind, . . . manner ↑in . . . slight↓ that the ⟨words⟩ intention of ⟨perpetuity⟩ ↑remembering it↓ sh⟨d.⟩ould . . . two ⟨out of⟩ ↑among the↓ . . . happened! ¶ ⟨But what did⟩ ↑Still . . . that↓ this expression ⟨which⟩ ↑This do &c↓ had . . . present ⟨ *This do in remembrance of me,* ⟩ ↑What did it↓

12	expression. ⟨He⟩ ↑Jesus↓
14	wishes ⟨his d⟩ the
21–25	see ⟨meaning⟩ ↑natural feeling↓ . . . friends; ⟨but I cannot bring myself to believe that he looked beyond⟩ I . . . ↑& meant↓
31–32	↑wd. easily . . . impression↓
33	It ⟨will be⟩ ↑is then↓
39	after ⟨the same⟩ ↑a prescribed↓

Page 188

1	earth.' ⟨H⟩ and . . . table. ⟨Then⟩ It
17	calls ⟨himself b⟩ the
23–26	not ⟨understand⟩ ↑comprehend↓ . . . ↑actually↓ eaten ⟨with our teeth⟩ ↑that . . . commandment↓ he
28–32	life." ¶ ⟨Whilst⟩ ¶ Whilst . . . others ⟨which⟩ particularly . . . ↑at least↓
33	they ⟨shou⟩ ought

Page 189

1–2	↑forever↓, . . . compare ⟨it⟩ with
5–6	↑If . . . authority.↓ [in pencil]
7	Sand⟨i⟩emanians. It has been ↑very properly↓
8–10	↑1.↓ ⟨b⟩Because it was ↑a↓ . . . ↑2.↓ because . . . & ⟨they⟩ ↑all↓ understand⟨i⟩ that humility is the ⟨main⟩ thing ⟨taught⟩ ↑signified↓.
11	& ⟨the⟩ ↑its↓ bread & wine were ⟨also⟩ typical & ⟨the love⟩ do
13–14	¶ These ⟨are the⟩ views ⟨which the examination⟩ of . . . Supper ⟨suggests to me that⟩ ↑lead me to esteem↓ it ⟨was⟩ an
16–19	however {from . . . Corinthians} that . . . bread as ⟨a symbol⟩ & drank wine as symbols. ¶ I cannot ¶ I look upon this ⟨f circumstance⟩ ↑fact↓
22–24	event↑ful↓ ⟨which⟩ ↑evening↓ . . . them they, . . . ↑furthermore↓ . . . done ⟨by⟩ with peculiar propriety by ⟨his⟩ them,
32	nothing ⟨more⟩ to
34	was ⟨perfectly but⟩ ↑but↓
39–40	persons ⟨the most⟩ conclusive . . . institution. ⟨It does, & chiefly because of the expression he uses *I have received of the Lord*.⟩ ↑I . . . stands.↓

Page 190

1–5	seems. ⟨{That passage, the ⟨1⟩eleventh . . . decency ⟨as wel n⟩ not . . . supper.}⟩ [cancellation rejected as having most likely been done in the course of the revision that resulted in Manuscript B, where in fact a different sentence is substituted]
6–7	↑{in y^t Chapter}↓ . . . to ⟨correct⟩ ↑censure↓
8	nowadays ⟨to⟩ as
9–11	To ⟨show them⟩ ↑make↓ . . . which ↑this↓
16	that ⟨was⟩ ↑might be↓
17–18	↑So . . . possess.↓

21–22   the ⟨S⟩second . . . ↑he tells them↓
26   that ⟨the⟩ ↑this↓
30   single ⟨error⟩ expectation
33–(191)5   rite⟨.⟩ when once established. ⟨↑It was to be left to↓ Time
             ⟨however⟩ the great instructor gradually opened the eyes of the
             disciples to the meaning of their masters words. Time modified their
             ↑too↓ literal interpretation of his words. Time which enlarged their
             numbers taught them the impracticability of a community of goods.
             Time pacified & ⟨he⟩ ended one after another the fierce disputes
             about meats offered to idols about circumcision & uncircumcision
             about gifts of tongues & the deportment of women & antichrist
             Time which has overtaken the gnostic & the ⟨bishop⟩ early contro-
             versies wh the question of the intent of this rite the white robe the
             consecrated pall the extreme unction has yet ⟨yet⟩ preserved to us the
             use of this rite which seems to have no better foundation than those
             frivolous disputes.⟩ ¶ We . . . perpetual. ¶ 2. It . . . Evangelists. ¶
             ⟨Time has ⟨cont⟩ which has destroyed so many trifles that seemed
             huge matters once, has magnified also what then seemed small. Time
             has every day unfolded more & more the sublime spiritual sense of
             the gospel of Christ. The words the dogmas of apostles & bishops &
             sects are dropped one after another but the eternal truths come out
             like stars & take their place forever in the firmament. This process
             will go on.⟩ ¶ ⟨I have . . . that ⟨much⟩ many . . . men ⟨very slowly
             perceived the design of his gospel⟩ ↑more . . . virtue↓, . . . coun-
             tries.⟩ [paragraph canceled lightly in pencil; cancellation rejected as
             probably having been done in the course of the revision that produced
             Manuscript B, where it appears revised and repositioned] ¶ Admit-
             ting . . . perpetuity ⟨I do not⟩ that . . . ↑for us↓.

Page 191

6   ↑We . . . things.↓
11–12   ages? ¶ ⟨I come⟩ But
13   accepted ⟨in⟩ ↑under↓
19   in ⟨its⟩ administering
20–21   language ⟨us⟩ you
37   offices of [end of page] of Christ

Page 192

10   this that ⟨that⟩ the
13–14   I ⟨can not help feeling⟩ ↑apprehend↓
15–16   actions. ⟨We⟩ ↑Most men↓ . . . to ⟨many of us⟩ ↑some persons↓
18–20   ↑It . . . be ⟨perfectly in harmony with⟩ ↑animated by↓ our feelings;
             that ⟨we⟩ our . . . operative↓
21   this ⟨objection entitled⟩ ↑difficulty↓
23   ordinance. ⟨That represents⟩ ↑It is↓ my own ⟨case.⟩ ↑objection.↓
26   contemplated ⟨its becoming⟩ ↑to make↓ permanent—this mode of
             commemoration ⟨so agre⟩ every
29–31   {For . . . thought} ↑For↓

35   to ⟨good⟩ works . . . awaken ↑a↓
40–(193)2   but ⟨it⟩ an . . . it which ⟨is at war with the free spirit of divine
                      truth.⟩ ↑which never . . . any ⟨ordinance.⟩ ↑form.↓ M.F the k. of G.
                      is not &c↓ ↑{Insert X} X {Forms . . . end}↓ [last two brackets in
                      pencil and ink]

Page 193

3–11   principles. ⟨It is not at Mount Gerizim nor yet at Jerusalem he said
                      where men should worship the Father God is a spirit & must be
                      worshipped in spirit & truth. [John 4:24] The kingdom of God is
                      within you [Luke 17:21] the kingdom of God is not meat or drink but
                      righteousness & peace & joy of the holy Ghost.⟩ ↑If↓ . . . own
                      ⟨evidence⟩ reason, . . . not ⟨to us⟩ its . . . themselves that . . . itself.
                      ⟨It is no⟩ ↑I am not engaged to Xy by↓ decent forms it is no saving
14–26   life, ⟨its suitableness to my soul,⟩ the . . . onward. ⟨This was a
                      revolution in the world.⟩ ⟨It is not in this religion to exalt any form as
                      a form into a duty whether in itself suitable or not.⟩ [last cancellation
                      in pencil] ¶ ↑{Insert A} A ↑{↓Freedom . . . Christianity ⟨Its institu-
                      tions⟩ It . . . us.↑}↓↓ [the words "Insert A" and "A" in ink over
                      pencil; second set of brackets in pencil] ¶ The ¶ ⟨Therefore This is
                      strongly felt by me.⟩ ↑And . . . others↓ I have labored ⟨because⟩ to
                      . . . ↑though↓ I have ⟨shown the caus⟩ gone . . . Paul⟨.⟩, ⟨But s⟩ ↑I
                      feel that↓ . . . it ⟨i⟩In . . . ↑or those of Luke or John↓
26   ↑seem to↓
28–31   which ⟨we bless the name of Jesus & thank God for his gift ⟨is⟩
                      ↑was↓ ⟨that⟩ ⟨he⟩to redeem⟨ed⟩ us from⟩ ↑Jesus . . . from↓ . . . &
                      ⟨taught⟩ ↑teach↓ . . . soul. ⟨To him all forms are indifferent.⟩ ↑The
                      . . . full idols & ordinances↓
35–40   were ⟨frivolous⟩ ↑shadows↓, . . . to ⟨your feelings⟩ ↑their under-
                      standings↓ or not. ¶ ⟨Until⟩ Is . . . to ⟨hold back the⟩ turn back the
                      hand⟨s⟩ on
41   that ⟨righ⟩ not

Page 194

4–5   ¶ There ⟨are⟩ remain . . . state ⟨I will only name one⟩ ↑There is one
                      on wh. I had intended to say a few words↓ the
9–11   ↑& yᵉ claim of authority↓ . . . ordinance, ⟨& the claim of authority⟩
                      & . . . purpose m⟨t⟩ight
16–18   say that ⟨I⟩ the . . . is ⟨simply⟩ ↑shortly↓ . . . desire, ⟨the only
                      principle on which⟩ ↑in↓ . . . minister ⟨should be held that he⟩ ↑to↓
                      do nothing which ⟨he⟩ ↑I↓ cannot do with ⟨his⟩ ↑my↓ whole heart.
                      ⟨But that is the whole matter.⟩ ↑⟨Having⟩ Having . . . all.↓
24–25   is ⟨esteemed⟩ an
27   has ⟨many⟩ some
29   its ⟨demands may well⟩ ↑claims↓ oppress↑es↓

Manuscript B: This MS is the fair copy presented in 1857 to the Rev. C. A. Bartol. It is
bound in marbled boards with leather spine, and with marbled end papers. The sermon
consists of thirty pages measuring 25 x approximately 19.8 cm.

The first page of the sermon is preceded by a leaf inscribed on the recto: "Given by R. W. Emerson / To C. A. Bartol / R. W. Emerson's Sermon on the Communion Service. / in his handwriting" [first two lines in Bartol's hand; last two lines in an unknown hand in pencil]. The last sermon page is followed by two blank leaves.

The kingdom of God is not meat and drink; but righteousness and peace and joy in the holy Ghost. Romans 14; 17.

In the history of the Church no subject has been more fruitful of controversy than the Lord's Supper. There never has been any unanimity in the understa[nd]ing [inscription runs off the edge of the page] of its nature, nor any uniformity in the mode of celebrating it. Without considering the frivolous questions which have been hotly debated as to the posture in which men should partake of it, or whether mixed or unmixed wine should be served, whether leavened or unleavened bread should be broken, the questions have been settled differently in every church, who should be admitted to the feast, & how often it should be prepare[d.] [inscription runs off the edge of the page] In the Catholic Church ⟨if⟩ infants were at one time permitted & then forbidden to partake; and since the ninth century, the laity receive the bread only, the cup being reserved to the priesthood. So as to the time of the solemnity. In the fourth Lateran Council, it was decreed that every believer should communicate at least once in a year at Easter. Afterwards it was determined that ⟨it should⟩ this sacrament should be received three times in the year, at Easter, Whitsuntide, & Christmas. But more important controversies have arisen respecting ⟨the⟩its nature↑.↓ ⟨of this rite.⟩ The famous question of the Real Presence was the main controversy between the Church of England & the Church of Rome. The doctrine of the Consubstantiation taught by Luther, was denied by Calvin. In the Church of England, Archbishops Laud & Wake maintained that the elements were an Eucharist or sacrifice of thanksgiving to God; Cudworth & Warburton, that this was not a sacrifice, but a sacrificial feast; and Bishop Hoadly, that it was neither a sacrifice, nor a feast after sacrifice, but a simple commemoration. And finally, it is now near two hundred ⟨s⟩ years since the Society of Quakers denied the authority of the rite altogether, & gave good reasons for disusing it.

I allude to these facts only to show that so far from the Supper being a tradition in which men are fully agreed, there has always been the widest room for difference of opinion upon this particular.

Having recently given particular attention to this subject, I was led to the conclusion that Jesus did not intend to establish an institution for perpetual observance when he ate the passover with his disciples; and, further, to the opinion, that it is not expedient ⟨for⟩ to celebrate it as we do. I shall now endeavour to state distinctly my reasons for these two opinions.

I. The authority of the rite.

An account of the last Supper of Christ with his disciples is given by the four evangelists Matthew, Mark, Luke & John.

In St Matthew's Gospel {Matt. xxvi. 26–30} [Emerson's footnote] are recorded the words of Jesus in giving bread and wine on that occasion to his disciples, but no expression occurs intimating that this feast was hereafter to be commemorated.

In St Mark {Mark xiv. 22} [Emerson's footnote] the same words are recorded, and still with no intimation that the occasion was to be remembered.

St Luke {Luke xxii 15} [Emerson's footnote] after relating the breaking of the bread, has these words 'This do in remembrance of me.'

In St John, although other occurrences of the same evening are related, this whole transaction is passed over without notice.

Now observe the facts. Two of the evangelists, namely, Matthew & John, were of the twelve disciples & were present on that occasion. Neither of them drops the slightest intimation of any intention on the part of Jesus to set up anything permanent. John, especially, the beloved disciple, who has recorded with minuteness the conversation & the transactions of that memorable evening has quite omitted such a notice. Neither does it appear to have come to the knowledge of Mark who though not an eyewitness relates the other facts. This material fact that the occasion was to be remembered, is found in Luke alone who was not present. There is no reason, however, that we know, for rejecting the account of Luke. I doubt not, the expression was used by Jesus. I shall presently consider its meaning. I have only brought these accounts together, that you may judge whether it is likely that a solemn institution, to be continued to the end of time by all mankind, as they should come, nation after nation, within the influence of the Christian religion, would have been established in this slight manner, ↑—↓in a manner so slight, that the intention of commemorating it, should not appear, from their narrative, to have caught the ear or dwelt in the mind of the only two among the twelve who wrote down what happened.

Still we must suppose that the expression, *This do in remembrance of me*, had come to the ear of Luke, from some disciple who was present. What did it really signify? It is a prophetic & an affectionate expression. Jesus is a Jew sitting with his countrymen, celebrating their national feast. He thinks of his own impending death, & wishes the minds of his disciples to be prepared for it. 'When hereafter,' he says to them, you shall keep the passover, it will have an altered aspect ⟨to⟩in your eyes. It is now a historical covenant of God with the Jewish nation. Hereafter, it will remind you of a new covenant sealed with my blood. In years to come, as long as your people shall come up to Jerusalem to keep this feast, the connexion which has subsisted between us, will give a new meaning in your eyes, to the national festival, as the anniversary of my death.'—I see natural feeling & beauty in the use of such language from Jesus, a friend to his friends; I can readily imagine that he was willing & desirous, when his disciples met, his memory should hallow their intercourse, but I cannot bring myself to believe that in the use of such an expression he looked beyond the living generation, beyond the abolition of the festival he was celebrating, & the scattering of the nation, & meant to impose a memorial feast upon the whole world.

↑{↓Without presuming to fix precisely the purpose in the mind of Jesus, you will see that many opinions may be entertained of his intention, all consistent with the opinion that he did not design ⟨the⟩ a perpetual ordinance. He may have foreseen that his disciples would meet to remember him, & that with good effect. It may have crossed his mind that this would be easily continued a hundred or a thousand years, as men more easily transmit a form than a virtue, & yet have been altogether out of his purpose to fasten it upon men in all times & all countries.↑}↓ [brackets in pencil]

But though the words, *Do this in remembrance of me*, do not occur in Matthew Mark or John, and though it should be granted us that, taken alone, they do not necessarily import so much as is usually thought yet many persons are apt to imagine that the very striking & formal manner in which this eating & drinking is described, indicates a striking & formal purpose to found a festival. And I admit that this impression might probably be left upon the mind of one who read only the passages under consideration in the New Testament. But this impression is removed by reading any narrative of the mode in which the ancient or the modern Jews have kept the passover. It is then perceived that the leading circumstances in the gospels, are only a faithful account of that ceremony. Jesus did not celebrate the passover, & afterwards the supper, but the Supper *was* the passover. He did with his disciples exactly what every master of a family in Jerusalem was doing at the same hour with his household. It appears that the Jews ate the lamb & the unleavened bread, & drank wine after a prescribed manner. It was the custom for the master of the feast to break the bread & to bless it, using this formula, which the Talmudists have preserved to us, "Blessed be thou, o Lord, our God, the king of the world, who hast produced this food from the earth,—" & to give it to every one at the table. It was the custom for ⟨for⟩ [canceled in pencil and ink] the master of the f⟨east⟩amily to take the cup which contained the wine, & to bless it, saying, "Blessed be thou, o Lord, who givest us the fruit of the vine,"—and then to give the cup to all. Among the modern Jews who in their dispersion retain the passover, a hymn is ↑also↓ sung after this ceremony, specifying the twelve great works done by God for the deliverance of their fathers out of Egypt.

But still it may be asked, why did Jesus use expressions so extraordinary & emphatic as these, "This is my body which is broken for you Take; Eat. This is my blood which is shed for you. Drink it."—I reply, they are not extraordinary expressions from him. They were familiar in his mouth. He always taught by parables & symbols. It was the national way of teaching & was largely used by him. Remember the readiness which he always showed to spiritualize every occurrence. He stooped & wrote on the sand. He admonished his disciples respecting the leaven of the Pharisees. He instructed the woman of Samaria respecting living water. He permitted himself to be anointed, declaring that it was for his interment. He washed the feet of his disciples. These are admitted to be symbolical actions & expressions. Here, in like manner, he calls the bread his body & bids the disciples eat. He had used the same expression repeatedly before. The reason why St John does not repeat ⟨the⟩ [canceled in pencil and ink] his words on this occasion seems to be that he had reported a similar discourse of Jesus to the people of Capernaum more at length already. {John vi, 27 & seq.} [Emerson's footnote] He there tells the Jews—"Except ye eat the flesh of the Son of Man & drink his blood, ye have no life in you." And when the Jews on that occasion complained that they did not comprehend what he meant, he added for their better understanding, & as if for our understanding, that we might not think that his body was to be actually eaten, that he only meant, *we should live by his commandment*. He closed his discourse with these explanatory expressions. "The flesh profiteth nothing;—the *words* that I speak to you, they are spirit, & they are life."

Whilst I am upon this topic, I cannot help remarking that it is not a little singular that we should have preserved this rite & insisted upon perpetuating one symbolical act of Christ whilst we have totally neglected all others, particularly one other which had at least an equal claim to our observance. Jesus washed the feet of his disciples & told them, that 'as he had washed their feet, they ought to wash one anothers feet,⟨'⟩ for he had given them an example, that they should do as he had done to them.' I ask any person who believes the Supper to have been designed by Jesus to be commemorated forever, to go & read the account of it in the other gospels, & then compare with it the account of this transaction in St John, & tell me if this be not much more explicitly authorized than the supper. It only differs in this, that we have found the Supper used in

New England, & the washing of the feet, not. But if we had found it an established rite in our churches; on grounds of mere authority, it would have been impossible to have argued against it. That rite is used by ⟨by⟩the Church of Rome, & by the Sandemanians. It has been very properly dropped by other Christians. Why? For two reasons; 1; because it was a local custom, & unsuitable in western countries; & 2; because it was typical, & all understand that humility is the thing signified. But the passover was local too, & does not concern us; and its bread & wine were typical, & do not help us to understand the redemption which they signified.

These views of the original account of the Lord's Supper lead me to esteem it an occasion full of solemn & prophetic interest, but never intended by Jesus to be the foundation of a perpetual institution.

It appears however in Christian history that the disciples had very early taken advantage of these impressive words of Christ to hold religious meetings where they broke bread & drank wine as symbols.

I look upon this fact as very natural in the circumstances of the Church. The disciples lived together; they threw all their property into a common stock; they were bound together by the memory of Christ & nothing could be more natural than that this eventful evening should be affectionately remembered by them, that they, Jews like Jesus, should adopt his expression↑s↓ & his type↑s↓, &, furthermore, that what was done with peculiar propriety by them his personal friends,—with less propriety should come to be extended to their companions also. In this way, religious feasts grew up among the early Christians. They were readily adopted by the Jewish converts who were familiar with religious feasts, & also by the Pagan converts whose idolatrous worship had been made up of sacred festivals, & who very readily abused these to gross riot, as appears from the censures of St Paul. Many persons consider this fact the observance of such a memorial feast by the early disciples, decisive of the question whether it ought to be observed by us. For my part, I see nothing to wonder at, in its originating with them; all that is surprizing, is that it should exist among us. ⟨It had great propriety⟩ ↑There was↓ good reason ⟨that⟩ for his personal friends to remember their friend & repeat his words. It was only too probable that among the half converted Pagans & Jews, any rite any form would find favour, whilst yet unable to comprehend the spiritual character of Christianity.

The circumstance, however, that St Paul adopts these views, has seemed to many persons conclusive in favour of the institution. I am of opinion that it is wholly upon the epistle to the Corinthians, & not upon the gospels that the ordinance stands. ↑Upon this matter of St Pauls view of the Supper, a few important considerations must be stated.↓

The end which he has in view in the eleventh chapter of the first Epistle, is, not to enjoin upon his friends to observe the Supper, but to censure their abuse of it. We quote the passage nowadays as if it enjoined attendance upon the Supper, but he wrote it merely to chide them for drunkenness. To make their enormity plainer he goes back to the origin of this religious feast to show what ⟨that⟩ ↑sort of↓ feast ↑that↓ was, out of which this riot of theirs came, & so relates the transactions of the last Supper. '*I have received of the Lord,*' he says, '*that which I delivered to you.*' By this expression, it is often thought that a miraculous communication is implied, but certainly without good reason, if it is remembered that St Paul was living in the lifetime of all the apostles who could give him an account of the transaction, and it is contrary to all reason & to all experience, to suppose that God should work a miracle to convey information that could so easily be got by natural means. So that the import of the expression ↑is,↓ that he had received the story of eyewitnesses such as we also possess.

But there is a material circumstance which diminishes our confidence in the correctness of the apostle's view; and that is, the observation that his mind had not escaped the prevalent error of the primitive church, the belief, namely, that the second coming of Christ would shortly occur, until which time, he tells them, this feast was to be kept. Elsewhere he tells them, that, at that time the world would be burnt up with fire, & a new government established, in which the Saints would sit on thrones; so slow were the disciples, during the life, & after the ascension of Christ, to receive the idea which we receive, that his second coming was a spiritual kingdom,—the dominion of his religion in the hearts of men, to be extended gradually over the whole world.

In this manner, I think we may see clearly enough how this ancient ordinance got its footing among the early Christians, & this single expectation of a speedy reappearance of a temporal Messiah, which kept its influence even over so spiritual a man as St Paul, would naturally tend to preserve the use of the rite when once established.

We arrive then at this conclusion, *first*, That it does not appear from a careful examination of the account of the Last Supper in the Evangelists, that it was designed by Jesus to be perpetual; *secondly*; that it does not appear that the opinion of St Paul, all things considered, ought to alter our opinion derived from the evangelists.

One general remark before quitting this branch of the subject. We ought to be ⟨careful⟩cautious in taking even the best ascertained opinions & practices of the primitive church, for our own. If it could be satisfactorily shown that they esteemed it authorized & to be transmitted forever, that does not settle the question for us. We know how inveterately they were attached to their Jewish prejudices & how often ↑even↓ the influence of Christ failed to enlarge their views. On every other subject succeeding times have learned to form a judgment more in accordance with the spirit of Christianity than was the practice of the early ages.

But it is said, Admit that the rite was not designed to be perpetual. What harm doth it? Here it stands, generally accepted, under some form, by the Christian world, the undoubted occasion of much good; is it not better it should remain?

II. This is the question of Expediency.

I proceed to state a few objections that in my judgment lie against its use in its present form.

1. If the view which I have taken of the history of the institution be correct, then the claim of authority should be dropped in administering it. You say, every time you celebrate the rite, that Jesus enjoined it, & the whole language you use, conveys that impression⟨,⟩. ⟨b⟩But if you read the New Testament as I do, you do not believe he did.

2. It has seemed to me that the use of this ordinance tends to produce confusion in our views of the relation of the soul to God. It is the old objection to the doctrine of the Trinity, that the true worship was transferred from God to Christ, or that such confusion was introduced into the soul, that an undivided worship was given nowhere. Is not that the effect of the Lord's Supper? I appeal now to the convictions of communicants, & ask such persons whether they have not been occasionally conscious of a painful confusion of thought between the worship due to God, & the commemoration due to Christ. For, the service does not stand upon the basis of a voluntary act, but is imposed by authority. It is an expression of gratitude to Christ, enjoined by Christ. There is an endeavour to keep Jesus in mind, whilst yet the prayers are addressed to God. I fear it is the effect of this ordinance to clothe Jesus ⟨↑in↓⟩ with an authority which he never claimed, & which distracts the mind of the worshipper. I know our opinions differ much respecting the nature & offices of Christ, & the degree of veneration ↑to↓ which ⟨is due to him⟩ he

is entitled. I am so much a Unitarian as this, that I believe the human mind cannot admit but one God, and that every effort to pay religious homage to more than one being, goes to take away all right ideas. I appeal, brethren, to your individual experience. In the moment when you make the least petition to God, though it be but a silent wish that he may approve you, or add one moment to your life,—do you not, in the very act, necessarily exclude all other beings from your thought? In that act, the soul stands alone with God, & Jesus is no more present to the mind, than your brother or your child.

But is not Jesus called in Scripture the Mediator? He is the Mediator in that only sense in which possibly any being can mediate between God and man, that is, an Instructer of man. He teaches us how to become like God. And a true disciple of Jesus will receive the light he gives most thankfully, but the thanks he offers, & which an exalted being will accept, are not *compliments*,—commemorations,—but the use of that instruction.

3. Passing other objections, I come to this, that the *use of the elements* however suitable to the people & the modes of thought in the East, where it originated, is foreign & unsuited to affect us. Whatever long usage & strong association may have done in some individuals to deaden this repulsion, I apprehend that their use is rather tolerated than loved by any of us. We are not accustomed to express our thoughts or emotions by symbolical actions. Most men find the bread and wine no aid to devotion, & to some, it is a painful impediment. To eat bread, is one thing; to love the precepts of Christ & resolve to obey them is quite another.

The statement of this objection leads me to say that I think this difficulty wherever it is felt, to be entitled to the greatest weight. It is alone a sufficient objection to the ordinance. It is my own objection. This mode of commemorating Christ is not suitable to me. That is reason enough why I should abandon it. If I believed that it was enjoined by Jesus on his disciples, & that he even contemplated ⟨the⟩ making permanent this mode of commemoration—every way agreeable to an Eastern mind, and yet, on trial, it was disagreeable to my own feelings, I should not adopt it. I should choose other ways which, as more effectual upon me, he would approve more. For I choose that my remembrances of him should be pleasing, affecting, religious. I will love him as a glorified friend, after the free way of friendship, and not pay him a stiff sign of respect, as men do to those whom they fear. A passage read from his discourses, a moving provocation to works like his, any act or meeting which tends to awaken a pure thought, a glow of love, an original design of virtue, I call a worthy, a true commemoration.

4. Fourthly, The importance ascribed to this particular ordinance is not consistent with the spirit of Christianity. The general object & effect of this ordinance is unexceptionable. It has been & is, I doubt not, the occasion of indefinite good; but an importance is given by Christians to it, which never can belong to any form.

My friends, the Apostle well assures us that "the kingdom of God is not meat or drink; but righteousness, and joy, & peace in the holy Ghost." I am not so foolish as to declaim against forms. Forms are as essential as bodies; but to ⟨adhere to one form⟩ exalt *particular* forms, to adhere to one form, a moment after it is outgrown, is ⟨not more⟩ unreasonable, ⟨than⟩ ↑and↓ it is alien to the spirit of Christ. If I understand the distinction of Christianity, the reason why it is to be preferred over all other systems, & is divine, is this, that it is a moral system; that it presents men with truths which are their own reason, & enjoins practices that are their own justification; that if miracles may be said to have been its evidence to the first Christians, they are not its evidence to us, but the doctrines themselves; that every practice is Christian which praises itself, and every practice unchristian which condemns itself. I am not engaged to Christianity by decent forms, or saving ordinances, it is not usage, it is not what I do not understand, that binds me to it—let these be the sandy foundation of falsehoods What I ⟨love⟩ revere & obey in it, is, its reality its boundless charity, its deep interior life, the rest it gives to my mind, the echo it returns to my thoughts, the perfect accord it makes with my reason through all its representation of God & his Providence; and the persuasion & courage that come out thence to lead me upward & onward. Freedom is the essence of this faith. It has for its object simply to make men good & wise. Its institutions, then, should be as flexible as the wants of men. That form out of which the life & suitableness have departed, should be as worthless in its eyes, as the dead leaves that are falling around us.

And, therefore, although, for the satisfaction of others, I have laboured to show by the history, that this rite was not intended to be perpetual; although I have gone back to weigh the expressions of Paul, I feel that here is the true point of view. In the midst of considerations as to what Paul thought, & why he so thought, I cannot help feeling that it is time misspent to argue to or from ⟨the⟩his convictions, or those of Luke or John, respecting any form. I seem to lose the substance in seeking the shadow. That ↑for↓ which Paul lived & died so gloriously; that for which Jesus gave himself to be crucified; the end that animated the thousand martyrs & heroes who have followed his steps, was to redeem us from a formal religion and teach us to seek our wellbeing in the reformation of the soul. The whole world was full of idols & ordinances. The Jewish was a religion of forms. The Pagan was a religion of forms; it was all body,—it had no life;—and the Almighty God was pleased to qualify & send forth a man to teach men that they must serve him with the heart; that, only that life was religious which was thoroughly good; that, sacrifice was smoke, & forms were shadows; and this man lived & died true to this purpose, & now, with his blessed words & life before us, Christians must contend that it is a matter of vital importance—really a duty—to commemorate him by a certain form, whether that form be agreeable to their understandings or not.

Is not this to make vain the gift of God? Is not this to turn back the hand on the dial? Is not this to make men—to make ourselves forget that not forms but duties, not names but righteousness & love, are enjoined, and that in the eye of God there is no other measure of the value of any one form than the measure of its use.

There remain some practical objections to the ordinance into which I shall not now enter. There is one on which I had intended to say a few words—I mean the unfavorable relation in which it places that numerous class of persons who abstain from it merely from disinclination to the rite.

Influenced by these considerations, I have proposed to the brethren of the church, to drop the use of the elements & the claim of authority in the administration of this ordinance, & have suggested a mode in which a meeting for the same purpose might be held free of objection.

My brethren have considered my views with patience & candor, and have recommended unanimously an adherence to the present form. I have therefore been compelled to consider whether it becomes me to administer it. I am clearly of opinion that I ought not. This discourse has already been so far extended, that I can only say that the reason of my determination is shortly this—It is my desire in the office of a Christian minister, to do nothing which I cannot do with my whole heart. Having said this, I have said all. I have no hostility to this institution. I am only stating my want of sympathy with it. Neither should I ever have obtruded this opinion upon other people, had I not been called by my office to administer it. That is the end of my opposition, that I am not interested in it. I am content that it stand to the end of the world, if it please⟨s⟩ men & please heaven, & I shall rejoice in all the good it produces.

As it is the prevailing opinion & feeling in our religious community that it is an indispensable part of the pastoral office to administer this ordinance, I am about to resign into your hands that office which you have confided to me. It has many duties for which I am feebly qualified. It has some which it will always be my delight to discharge, according to my ability, wherever I exist. And whilst the recollection of its claims oppresses me with a sense of my unworthiness, I am consoled by the hope that no time & no change can deprive me of the satisfaction of pursuing & exercising its highest functions.

September 9, 1832.

Sermon CLXIII

Manuscript: Four sheets folded to make four pages each; single leaves have been inserted in each folio; a leaf measuring 24.3 x 19.8 cm is attached with red sealing wax to the lower right corner of the last page of the first folio. All other pages measure 24.3 x 20.2 cm. All except the tipped-in leaf are sewn along the left margin with tan thread.

[Below the Bible text:] {Palimpsest [In several previous instances, Emerson marked the original manuscript "Princeps Edit." and the corresponding revised version "Palimpsest"; no "Princeps Edit." for Sermon CLXIII appears to have survived.]

Lines	*Page 195*
1–2	it ⟨operates⟩ produces gloomy impressions ⟨²Truth is cheerful.⟩ ⟨¹⟩Wisdom is goodnatured. ↑Truth is cheerful↓
4–5	↑Nothing . . . divinities↓ ⟨With t⟩The
6–9	↑It . . . mind↓ The
10	Still ⟨a barbarous⟩ ↑that favored↓
14	Father. and
17	↑if the . . . mind↓ [ink over pencil; the pencil layer has "brot" for "bro't" and "us" for "the mind"]

	Page 196
2–3	↑at least not uniformly nor usually↓ as the ⟨Cheerer⟩ Comforter,
4–6	than ⟨a dispenser of love.⟩ ↑an . . . heart.↓ How ↑strictly associated↓ has it been ⟨kept for funerals &⟩ ↑with sickness &↓ death, death
6–11	It ⟨is al⟩ holds . . . world. ¶ ⟨I conceive this to be wrong very wrong.⟩ ↑Is . . . views of ⟨Xty⟩ Christianity?↓
12	↑often↓ [in pencil]
13–18	↑teacher of↓ living↑.↓ ⟨philosopher.⟩ He . . . present⟨.⟩, ↑& death . . . view.↓ ⟨It is a departure from his spirit & is unnatural & pernicious.⟩ ↑{Insert B.} B {To . . . pernicious.↓ The faults of ⟨ministers⟩ ↑religion & religious men↓ [last emendation in ink over pencil]
19–(197)2	the ⟨joy⟩ overflowing . . . felicity ⟨& he that thinks so⟩ must . . . loves. ¶ ⟨It is the common language of religious persons to say, ⟨r⟩Remember thou must die. Lead a good life because your future well being depends on it. In the pursuits of life never forget they must shortly terminate. I do not like this language. I say What have I to do

with death? Think on living.⟩ ¶ ↑⟨I think it⟩ ↑Here↓ [cancellation
and addition in pencil] . . . relief↓

26–27   ↑satisfactory↓ feeling ⟨of⟩ nor ⟨contemplate⟩ obtain ⟨any⟩ ↑such a↓
             . . . it ⟨that can⟩ ↑as to↓

28–29   ↑And . . . desire.↓

31   indifferenc⟨y.⟩e [emendation in pencil and ink] ↑to it.↓

31–33   1 that ⟨we are not to think of⟩ ↑our business is not↓ dying but ⟨of⟩
             living 2. ⟨t⟩That . . . ↑with↓draw

39   which ⟨I ca⟩ my thoughts can rest. ⟨God has⟩ ↑I will dismiss it
             forever. God has↓

Page 197

1   moment ⟨I⟩ recall ⟨my⟩ thought [cancellations rejected as an
             incomplete revision]

4–5   ↑What . . . death?↓

5–8   of ⟨your⟩ my . . . the /loathsome/unpleasing/ [variant in pencil]
             . . . it. ⟨But present me⟩ What

10–11   ↑then↓ . . . & ⟨teaches⟩ feels ⟨its⟩ a lofty

12   last ⟨pangs⟩ moments

14–18   ¶ ↑The . . . in ⟨dying but in li⟩ getting . . . fit ⟨to be⟩ for any
             world.↓ ¶ ⟨With this sentiment I do not approve the common
             language⟩ ↑Good men say↓

18   wha⟨ll⟩t

19   world. ⟨Whatever you may think there is nothing about them in the
             New Testament And death is mere darkness.⟩ It

25–26   its ⟨future⟩ being ↑best for the future↓ . . . is ⟨happ⟩ best

28   man ⟨& no⟩ ⟨n⟩has

29–36   end? ↑{Insert A} A {Certainly . . . ↑the mode↓ [in pencil] . . . a
             ²speaking ¹reasoning . . . reason ⟨for⟩ at . . . men↓

Page 198

1   aspirations⟨.⟩ ↑for . . . inaccessible.↓

3   that ⟨he has in send⟩ ↑in↓ appointing ⟨the⟩ ↑our↓

7–10   fitness ⟨is⟩ for . . . is ⟨a⟨n⟩⟩ ↑a↓ . . . their ⟨⟨use⟩ power & use and
             so it⟩ ↑use,↓

11   duty ⟨to count any⟩ because

13–14   ↑It . . . earth.↓ [in ink over pencil; pencil layer lacks commas]

16–21   ↑so often↓ . . . concerning ⟨their friends⟩ ↑the departed↓. ↑A . . .
             preparation.↓ ⟨They⟩ ↑We↓ . . . satisfaction ⟨relat⟩ intimating
             the↑ir↓ willingness ⟨of the departed⟩ to . . . act. ¶ ⟨⟨They⟩ But⟩
             The

22   ↑in my judgment↓

27–28   ↑without it, would be↓ . . . continual ⟨contemplation⟩ ↑prayer.↓
             [emendation in ink over pencil]

33–34   mode . . . appearance. [in ink over pencil; pencil layer lacks punctua-
             tion]

36–37   so.' ¶ ⟨Men have not⟩ But

40–41   at ⟨a fairy tale⟩ ↑some . . . good↓

44   day ⟨Has yet your soul come out into mature & free action or does it lie a poor slave to the senses & to custom. ¶ Consider what it is to be a man.⟩ These

Page 199

2–11   imagined. ⟨It is a secret to you & to the Universe who⟨s⟩ you are & what is your destiny & only your action can publish it⟩ They . . . hell. ↑{Insert X} X {What . . . heaven↑?↓ [question mark in ink over pencil] ⟨I⟩ any thing by *description*⟨,⟩? any . . . the N. T⟨.⟩? If . . . knowledge of some ⟨decided improvement⟩ ↑reformation . . . politics,↓ [addition in ink over pencil; pencil layer lacks commas] . . . society,—⟨that is,⟩ ↑you have then acquired↓ . . . souls.}↓

15–16   say & ⟨how you act that it is⟩ ↑do↓—in homely duties, ⟨unmentioned ways⟩ ↑trivial particulars↓.

21   a ⟨praised⟩ ↑graceful↓

25   with ⟨change⟩ ↑decay↓.

27   ↑in the Christian ethics↓

29   philanthropy, ⟨⟨is⟩ conveys to the soul that has acquired it no image & no fear of death⟩ ↑is . . . mortality↓.

32–33   ↑Do . . . Father,↓ . . . pure; be ⟨kind⟩ meek; Live well. ⟨Live singly⟩ ↑Sin . . . life.↓ [addition in ink over pencil; pencil layer lacks punctuation]

35   this ⟨is⟩falls . . . taken, ⟨that he⟩ that

39   us ⟨feel⟩ that [cancellation rejected as an incomplete emendation]

Page 200

2–5   ↑Let not us ⟨who⟩ believe . . . body let . . . Soul}↓ We are to ⟨act⟩ ↑act↓,

7   But ⟨life⟩ the

10–11   only ⟨a clean conscience⟩ ↑the . . . intentions↓,

20   be ⟨deranged⟩ ↑impaired↓.

26   so ⟨good⟩ ↑precious↓

27   ↑in↓

29–30   never ⟨die.⟩ ↑perish.↓

Sermon CLXIV

Manuscript (earlier version): Seven sheets folded to make four pages each. The first folio is preceded by a leaf (containing sermon outline on verso). The lower right corner of the first page of the third folio has been torn out with no apparent loss of text. The third folio contains a leaf with pencil inscription on recto and verso. A leaf follows the fourth folio. Folio pages and leaves measure 24.3 x 20.1 cm. The folios are sewn along the left margin with white thread.

[The text of the earlier version follows:]

clxiv.
The Genuine Man.

Some men doubt if they have a right to follow [end of MS p. 1; "The . . . follow" in pencil]

All partial excellences have been shown
To us remains the work of forming *entire Men*
The man less considered than the circumstances
Importance of the distinction to us.
    Marks of the genuine man
    1. He believes in himself
    2. He speaks the truth
    3 He thinks the truth
    4 He acts the truth
    Grandeur of this character & its identity with religious life

    Stand therefore having your loins girt about with truth   Ephes. 6. 14
    ↑The New Man which after God is created in righteousness & true holiness↓ [addition in pencil; Ephesians 4:24]

    ↑We hear the opinion often expressed that ⟨great⟩ ⟨↑men are in a state of mind↓⟩ this is an age of great improvement↓ [addition in pencil] It is thought that juster views of human nature are gaining ground than have yet prevailed Men are beginning to see with more distinctness what they ought to be, that is, what true greatness is. What was called ⟨true⟩ greatness, they have discovered to be an imposture. We stand on tiptoe looking for a brighter age whose signs & forerunners have already appeared. ↑If it be so let us rejoice. Certainly the times past have failed & the welfare of men still is only hoped for↓ [addition in pencil]
    It seems to be left to us to commence the best of ⟨works⟩ all works. ⟨Already some⟩ ⟨n⟩Nations ↑long before us↓ have made desolating wars & gained bloody victories. Others have invented useful & elegant arts. Others have reared grand temples & beautiful palaces Others have bred great kings—terrible to their enemies & to their subjects; have produced ingenious artists inspired poets, eloquent orators, wise judges, brave soldiers, rich ↑me⟨n,⟩rchants,↓ benevolent ↑⟨men⟩ benefactors,↓ learned ⟨men⟩ ↑scholars↓. Let them all have their due praise To us has been committed by Providence the higher & holier work of forming *men*, ⟨free⟩ true & entire men.
    ⟨The world has always waited for such ⟨creations⟩ ↑children↓ but has waited hitherto in vain.⟩ A finished man—Who has seen↑?↓ ⟨such a ⟨being⟩ ↑creation↓?⟩ ["being" canceled in pencil; "creation" added in pencil; the entire phrase canceled in ink] Men are everywhere, on the land & sea, in mountains & mines; cities & fields swarm with them They are reckoned by thousands & myriads & millions. Yet where to find one who is that which he should be that which his Maker designed. There is a plan ⟨with⟩in us, we have not seen executed out of us.
    Survey the whole circle of your acquaintance of your neighborhood of your town & if you can fix upon one complete man, a man independent of his circumstances ⟨who a man⟩ ↑a mind which↓ fills & satisfies your idea of the perfection of human nature—one whom you venerate *as a man*; ⟨& not because he belongs to a particular family or occupies an office or possesses a large estate but⟩ whose value to your eye ⟨arises⟩ ↑⟨results⟩ consists↓ entirely ⟨from⟩ ↑in↓ the richness of his own nature, ↑in↓ the ability & dispositions you suppose him to possess, & not because he belongs to a particular

family, or ⟨occupies⟩ ↑fills↓ ⟨an⟩ ↑a certain↓ [last emendation in pencil] office or possesses a large estate, or is preceded by a great reputation.

There is nothing for the most part less considered than the essential man. The circumstances are much more attended to.

⟨In common language we say the rich & the great⟩ ↑Ordinarily↓ When we speak of great men we mean great circumstances. ⟨↑In that view of greatness↓⟩ The man is the least part of himself. We hear the wheels of his carriage. We see the company that walk with him. We read his name often in the newspapers—but *him* ↑the soul of him↓ the praised, the blamed, the enriched, & accompanied, we know not. ↑What manner & quality & colour of character he has by which he is that particular person & no other. Silsbee Tazewell Grundy Barbour—they are mere names—present no specific idea.↓ You sit in the same room with him & yet *himself* you see not. ⟨Every body is sensible of the absolute ignorance in which we ⟨stand of the real character⟩ of ↑There are↓ persons who seem ↑live in the statehouse↓ to move in procession & whose names are always ⟨before the public.⟩ ↑in the newspaper & yet of whose real character we are in total ignorance↓⟩ [last sentence emended and canceled in pencil; entire paragraph also struck through with light diagonal line in pencil, though apparently the intention was not to cancel it, as the paragraph appears in the revised version]

↑All are sensible that↓ The eminence which men are acquiring in society every day is of an extremely artificial character & can be gotten & given to almost any man The error lies in supposing we know those people best whose names or faces we see most. ↑frequently.↓

But not only ⟨a little⟩ ↑an inferior↓ man is thus ⟨frequently⟩ often magnified ⟨into a great man⟩ but ⟨in⟩ men of real ability owe to this ⟨trumpeting⟩ ↑noise & pomp↓ the largest part of their eclat. ↑It aids & doubles their greatness.↓ Whichever way the great man turns, whatever he saith or doth ↑he is never considered on his naked merits↓ his fame wins for him, argues for him, commands for him. Who can resist this influence & feel that the reason of Caesar is really no more weighty than ⟨the reason of his servant⟩ ↑our own↓.

We meet a prosperous person The imagination is first excited & the judgment a little shaken by the renown of his name Then he is announced by all sort of cheerful & respectful attentions. Then every word comes loaded with the weight of his professional character. Then there still is another fence of fine plausible manners, & ⟨melodious⟩ ↑polished↓ speech, & the men are very few who have the firmness of nerve to go behind all these inclosures, & with an undazzled eye penetrate unto & measure & weigh the man himself; & the men are fewer still who can bear the scrutiny. Behind all this splendid barricade of circumstances is often found a poor shrunken distorted almost imperceptible object who when exposed is found helpless & unhappy.

Is it not true in your experience brethren that ↑thus↓ the man is the least part of himself. Arts & professions, wealth & office, manners & religion are screens which conceal lameness & imperfection of character. ↑The eye is so entertained with the out parade that↓ Rarely does any body concern himself with the state of the real person that moves under all ⟨this parade⟩. The whole world goes after externals & ⟨man man⟩ ↑the soul↓ [emendation in pencil] Gods image & likeness [Genesis 1:26] is overlooked. Is it not true that men do not think highly, reverently of their own nature? ⟨In the insane world i⟩It is counted a small thing to injure the truth or to sacrifice a scruple of conscience to the opinion & practice of all society or to the obvious need of getting a decent livelihood. Yet it is to sacrifice the substance for the shadow it is to sacrifice themselves for pottage. [The two preceding sentences are struck through with two diagonal lines in pencil; with the second, cf. Genesis 25:34] ⟨Does it⟩ ↑To some persons it may↓ sound strange that we say People do not think enough of themselves. Does ↑not↓ the Apostle Paul, ↑they↓ say, ↑teach↓ that a man ought not to think highly of himself Do⟨es all the world⟩ ↑we not↓ [emendation in ink over pencil] say of a ⟨coxcomb⟩ ↑trifler↓ [addition in pencil] that he thinks too much of himself. Let us draw the distinction between a right & a wrong estimate of ones self

   There are two ways of speaking of self; one, when we speak of ²{the whole self that which comprehends a mans whole being, ⟨all he is,⟩} & the other when we speak of ¹{his low & partial self as when he is said to be selfish.}

   ⟨I speak now⟩ of that self of which Jesus said What can a man give in exchange for his soul, [Matthew 16:26; Mark 8:37] & in that sense, when you say of a man that he thinks too much of himself I say, ⟨that⟩ ↑no, the fault is that↓ he does not think of himself at all. He has not got so far as to know himself. He thinks of his ⟨coat⟩ dress, he thinks of his money, he thinks of his comely person, & pleasant voice, he thinks of the pretty things he has got to say & do,—but the eternal reason which shines within him, the immortal life that dwells at the bottom of his heart ↑he↓ knows not. he is not great enough—not good enough—not ⟨brave⟩ ↑man↓ [emendation in pencil] enough to go in & converse with that celestial scene. Very likely he is so utterly unacquainted with himself,—has lived so on the outside of his world, that he does not yet believe in its existence. ⟨Long & weary road that lies before him! Painful perhaps frightful convulsions that he must suffer before the twilight of that inner day can dawn upon his understanding!⟩

   It seems to me brethren as if we wanted nothing so much as a habit of ↑steadily↓ fixing the eye upon this higher self, the habit of ⟨sep⟩ distinguishing between our circumstances & ourselves the practice of rigorous scrutiny into our own daily life to learn how much there is of our own action & how much is not genuine but imitated or mercenary the advantage of arriving at a precise notion of a genuine man such as all good & great persons have aimed to be,—such as Jesus designed to be & to make many become, such, in short, as in the language of the Scriptures is ↑the New Man,↓ created after God in righteousness & true holiness. [end of MS p. 12; text of MS pp. 13–14 is entirely in pencil:]

   ↑And this is my object in the present discourse to draw the picture of the Genuine Man—

   {I think *very* few such have ever lived}

   But it is essential that he shd. believe in himself because that is the object in view to ⟨act on⟩ raise up a great counterbalance to the engrossing ⟨uses⟩ of riches of popularity of the love of life in the man & make him feel that all these ought to be his servants & not ⟨his⟩ masters that He is as great nay much greater than any of these: to make him feel that ⟨he may becom⟩ whereas the consequence of most men now depends on their wealth or their popularity; he is capable of being & ought to become ⟨su⟩ a man so rich & so commanding by the simple force of his character that wealth or poverty wd. be an unnoticed accident that his ↑solitary↓ opinion & his support to any cause whatever would be like the acclamation of ⟨a nation⟩ the world in its behalf

   This as we shall see is the secret of all true greatness the development of the inward nature the raising it to its true place to absolute sovereignty ⟨preferring⟩ ↑hearkening↓ this voice which to most men sounds so faint & insignificant above the thunder of the laws & the customs of mankind. And it is founded & can only be founded in religion. It can only prefer this self because it esteems it to speak the voice of God.

   This example of public life is only a glaring instance of the manner in which we are dazzled by circumstances but you & I ⟨ar⟩ in the most private condition are quite as apt to make the same mistake. A failure in trade is ⟨th⟩ called *ruin* tho' it may only call out the faculties & resources of his character The death of a parent or ⟨frie⟩ relative on whom a family depends is esteemed an irreparable loss How many ⟨fe⟩ women are brot up in the belief that a↑n↓ ⟨c⟩advantageous connexion in life is essential to their respectability & comfort & grow up in ignorance of their own resources.↓ [end of MS p. 14; end of pencil inscription]

Let me have your attention then ↑{↓& not that only but your critical judgment if I speak to any young person engaged in the formation of his character let him compare my account with his own experience↑}↓ [brackets in pencil] in ⟨marking⟩ ↑⟨pointing out⟩ dwelling↓ ["pointing out" canceled and "dwelling" added in pencil] the conspicuous marks of the genuine man.

It is the essence of truth of character that a man should follow his own thought; that he should not be accustomed to adopt his motives or modes of action from any other but should follow the leading of his own mind like a little child.

Vulgar people act from a great variety of motives ↑sometimes from principle↓ sometimes from prejudice sometimes from the expectations other people have of them sometimes from ⟨interest⟩ ↑mean calculation↓ sometimes from superstition. The genuine man is always consistent for he has but one leader. He acts always in character because he acts always *from* his character. He is accustomed to pay implicit respect to the dictates of his own reason & to obey them without asking why. He therefore speaks what he thinks. He acts his thought. He acts simply & up to the highest motives he knows of.

The excellence of this character ⟨is only to be appreciated⟩ ↑will appear↓ by comparing it with the way of the world. In all our intercourse with men we are obliged to make much allowance for what is said out of complaisance & what is said from self-interest. ⟨It is thought to be a proof of wisdom & knowledge of the world⟩ ↑What is meant by "k. of yᵉ world" is it not↓ [emendation in pencil] to be suspicious—not to confide too much in kind words or first impressions

And sad it is to see how much dissimulation exists There are some people who never appear to speak from their thought—very well behaved people too to whom it never seems to have occurred that they ought to act themselves. They are always plotting. They always have one meaning on their lips & another in their heart; ↑often↓ not so much from a design to deceive, as to make themselves agreeable to their company. ↑(↓It is being agreeable at an immense expense. It cannot deceive any one many times & it cuts up all confidence at the root & undoes the complaisant person↑)↓ [parentheses in pencil]

I have seen a person who really never heard with the ear his real intents. He never put off the mask ⟨but⟩ ↑& while every one wondered why one should take so much unnecessary pains he↓ was content to carry that cartload of dishonesty from morning t⟨o⟩ill night winter & summer for forty years & more. ↑Some people who live only for appearance Apicius sold his house but kept the balcony to see & be seen↓ [addition in pencil; see *JMN* 5:52 and 6:170; used in "The Present Age," *EL* 2:163]

From such painful folly it is refreshing to come into the pure air & free sunshine of the genuine man. All this imposture seems to him needless & irksome This duplicity shows that there is no sufficient power of reason within the mind that practises it to counterbalance the temptation of acting from external motives. ↑The person is conscious that his intentions are mean & need concealment.↓ But where the mind has no low ends, & is satisfied of the ⟨fitness⟩ rectitude of its purpose, it assumes no veil—it needs none—but goes ⟨directly⟩ to its object openly, & by the shortest way. He is transparent. His intention shines through all his words & deeds. It was nobly said by ⟨Drusus⟩ ↑an old Roman↓ when the masons offered for a hundred crowns to build him a house such that nobody in ⟨Rome⟩ ↑the city↓ could look into it: "I will give you twice so much money", he said, "if you will build me a house so that all Rome can see every part of it." It was well said by George Fox the Quaker, "That which I am in words—I am the same in life." It was to the same purpose that an eminent religious teacher of the last generation, Emanuel Swedenborg, said of his writings, that, "they would be found another self."

But to come a little closer to this matter to show more particularly how the genuine man speaks & acts, & what is meant by his following implicitly the leading of his own mind. It was happily said of a great man, "that he was content to stand by, & let reason argue for him." [see *JMN* 4:38, 44, and 212; and *Sermons* 2:69] That is precisely the impression ⟨conveyed⟩ left on your mind whenever you talk with a truth speaker, that it is not he who speaks, so much as reason that speaks through him You are not dealing with a mere man but with something higher & better than any man—with the voice of Reason common to him & ⟨to⟩ you & all men. It is as if you conversed with Truth & Justice

This man has the generosity of spirit to give himself up to the guidance of God ↑& lean upon the laws of nature↓ [ink over pencil; pencil layer has "the Creation" for "nature"] & ↑he parts with his individuality leaves all tho't of private stake personal feeling↓ in compensation he has in some sort the strength of the whole, as each limb of the ⟨body⟩ ↑human system↓ is able to draw to its aid the whole ⟨force⟩ weight of the body His heart beats pulse for pulse with the heart of the Universe.

⟨So much for *speech*; not less remarkable is the *action* of the genuine man.⟩ [canceled in pencil]

↑↑To some this may seem a vague expression There is this supreme ⟨reason⟩ Universal reason in your mind which is not yours or mine or any mans but is the Spirit of God in us all. The more it is trusted, the more it shows itself trustworthy↓ [paragraph in pencil]

By the genuine man I understand something more than a man who speaks the literal truth. There are I hope many men who aim to do this, & this though a commendable is not the highest virtue, but the genuine man speaks in the spirit of truth. He is one who recognizes his right to examine for himself every opinion every practice that is received in society & who accepts or rejects it for himself He is one who though calm & cheerful is in earnest & nothing can make a man calm & cheerful but the belief that he is advancing toward his true ends. Being thus in earnest & examining all things he does what he does & speaks whatever he says with all his heart & soul, & so the effect upon the hearer is that you have his whole being a warrant for every word.↓

He is distinguished by the heartiness with which he gives himself to the affairs that engage his attention, ⟨follow the⟩ following the advice of the Apostle—himself a high example of this sincerity—"Whatsoever ye do, do it *heartily*, as unto the Lord, & not as unto men." And this appears first in the choice of his pursuit.

It is plain to all observers that some men have been formed for public life for the management of general affairs of a robust fabric of soul that needs the rough discipline of ⟨co⟩ hot contention, of ⟨great⟩ ↑deep↓ stakes, of great antagonists, & a vast theatre Others as manifestly are born to benefit men by the advancement of science↑,↓ [comma in pencil] by

Others ⟨promote⟩ ↑embrace↓ [emendation in ink over pencil] the mechanick arts &

find no pleasure like that of exercising their own ingenuity to valuable ends Others delight in the bustle of commerce Others have quieter yet scarcely less effectual means of serving their fellow men in gentle offices of compassion or instruction. But to each is his own mode & the genuine man finds his way to that for which he is fitted. Therein he delights & moves with freedom & joy. You shall see others & this is the great fault of ⟨many⟩ men that they ⟨do not give themselves to their work they only half act they⟩ in all public business—they do not give themselves to the affairs they undertake↑,↓ [comma in pencil] they only half act—they speak much, & do much, & yet do not embark themselves fairly & frankly, for better for worse, in the cause but are ever looking around to see what chance there is for their particular advantage. ⟨Not so the ge⟩ ↑It is only the *means* to him of a private end↓ And you never get a perfect confidence in them Not so the genuine man He fairly espouses his cause. He grows in its success he faints in its failure It is his own cause & his life is in it. All men understand this difference at a glance & feel who does his work /professionally/as a task/ [variant in pencil] & who does it with the heart.

I am led in connexion with these views of genuineness of character to remark upon the stability that belongs to it. "Be ye steadfast immoveable—" says Paul, an injunction that cannot be complied with, except by him who possesses truth of character.

By listening to this inward Voice, by following this invisible Leader, it is in the power of a man to cast off from himself the responsibility of his words & actions & to make God responsible for him. It is beautiful, it is venerable to see the majesty which belongs to the man who leans directly upon a principle. He has a confidence ⟨not to be moved⟩ that it cannot fail him. ↑It is affirmed to him as by oath of God. The conviction that possesses him is equal to the pledge As God liveth it shall be so.↓ Whilst he rests upon it, he has nothing to do with consequences; he is above them. he has nothing to do with the effect of his example; he is following Gods finger & cannot go astray. ↑God will take care of the issues.↓ He may walk in the frailty of the flesh with the firm step of an archangel.

{Whilst I follow my conscience I know I shall never be ashamed. When I have followed it, I know my conduct is capable of explanation, tho' I have wholly forgotten the circumstances. {Webster & Hayne—Adams & Stephenson} [see *JMN* 3:184] Integrity defies the sun to find a flaw in its texture. Scipio burned his African accounts

Finally in answer to any (if such there be) who shall say, 'this quality is good, but is there not something better?' I would add one remark, that ⟨a⟩ the conviction must be produced in our minds ⟨of the⟩ that *this truth of character is identical with a religious life*; that they are one & the same thing; that this voice of your own mind is the voice of God; that the reason why you are bound to reverence it, is because it is the direct revelation of your Makers Will not written in books many ages since nor attested by distant miracles but in the flesh & blood in the faculties & emotions of your constitution. ↑that Jesus Christ came into the world for this express purpose to teach men to prefer the soul to the body.↓ ↑For who is this invisible Guide & Light this Reason↓ [last addition in pencil]

Until this conviction is wrought & acted on a man can never be ↑said to have↓ fairly set out on his journey of improvement, for, this alone can teach him how to blend his religion with his daily labor, so that every act shall be done with the full consent of his head & his heart, ⟨instead of⟩ ↑& he shall not↓ regard⟨ing⟩ his business as so much interruption or so much injury to his religious life, & leav⟨ing⟩e his faith at home, when he goes to his store.

↑The sabbath was made for man not man for the sabbath, & Religion⟨s⟩ is made for man's benefit not for Gods.↓ [addition in pencil]

And yet who knows not that crowds of men are acting on that error, that their religious character is something separate from their daily actions—quite external—like a dress ↑to wear↓ or a chamber ↑to lodge in↓, & that ⟨mer⟩ ⟨commerce⟩ ↑trade↓ is to get them money, & prayers & sermons are to get them virtue, but either would be hurt by being joined with the other.

If instead of this, he worked with love in his favourite calling; if he saw in every days labor, that he was thereby growing more skilful & more wise; that he was cooperating with God in his own education so that every dollar he earned was a medal of so much real power, the fruit & the means of so much real goodness; if neither his work [end of line] ⟨nor⟩ing h⟨is⟩ours nor his rest were lost time, but all was helping him onward, would not his heart sing for joy—Would not the day be brighter & even the night light about him Would not ↑company be more pleasant & even↓ solitude be sociable ⟨& company pleasant to him & all⟩ ↑&↓ his life ↑reveal↓ a new heaven & a new earth to his purer eyes?

⟨Would⟩ ↑Were↓ it not ⟨be⟩ an unspeakable blessing to the world the appearance of such men in its affairs, who should show us how much radiance may belong to mere character, who should show us that honour may dwell in a small tenement as well as in a state house, & that there is no place that will not shine under the light of virtues.

We do not know how rich we are. [line drawn across the page]

What is the practical end of the views we have taken? This, & this only,—Be genuine.—Be girt with truth. ⟨Be⟩ Aim in all things at all times to be that with⟨out⟩↑in↓ which you ⟨are⟩ ↑would appear↓ with⟨in⟩out. Commune with your own heart that you may learn what it means to be true to yourself ↑& follow steadily↓. God would have you introduce another standard of success than that which prevails in the world. When you go home at night, and cast your thoughts on your condition, fix them upon your character: instead of asking whether this day has made you richer, or better known, or what compliments have you received,—you shall ask⟨—⟩am I more just—am I more useful—more patient—more wise what have I learned—what new truth has been disclosed to me?

Then you will have an interest in yourselves. You will be watching the wonderful opening & growth of a human character, the birth & growth of an angel that has been born, but never will die—who was designed by his maker to be a growing benefit to the world, & to find his own happiness in forever enlarging the knowledge, multiplying the powers, & exalting the pleasures of others.

21 October, 1832.

⟨⟨Now I am afraid that the⟩ I said just now that to us was committed the formation of men. That cannot however be done by many To himself to himself it is committed & if he fails to form it the conspiring world cannot do it for him. When once we assume that charge ↑the cultiv. of our own nature,↓ all men can help us; but none, if we are wanting to ourselves; so true is that melancholy aphorism of the Swiss philosopher, that, If a man will not help himself, there is no one in the wide world who is either able or willing to help him. [i.e., Pestalozzi: see *JMN* 4:19–20] It is essential to a man's genuineness of character that he should feel that he has a right to be original, to follow the dictates of his own judgment. ↑People say, It will do for men of original mind, &c. You are an original mind or if not were made for one↓ That he has a ⟨r⟩higher right to speak his own thought & to act it, than any king or any public can give him by dignities or by admiration That he derives his right from the Creator of the world who made him a new being, with some thoughts that never were in any other being with a plan & determination of character peculiar & novel in the universe. But you are a stranger to that originality & strength for you never give it play. You depart from your own convictions & copy other people & say what they say—& so you have not found out what you are—& others do the same & ⟨s⟩hence it happens that all society presents the same tame ⟨ & timid mediocrity⟩ & uninteresting mediocrity ⟨instead⟩ whatever is striking & singular being scowled upon lest it should offend & ground down to one ⟨dull⟩ ↑uniform↓ face.⟩

The genuine man never fears to avow his opinion.

[The following is in erased pencil:] Danger that such as Carlisle shd forsake the Cause that the flood of degeneracy bad example shd sweep him down by reason of his ceasing to look inward & be true to himself—Easy to accept pensions & grow fat & rank w [several illegible words] to stand alone & without sympathy fear of [illegible word] cowering [illegible words] Bonapartes & his respectable [several illegible lines; cf. *JMN* 4:52–53]

Manuscript (later version): Six sheets folded to make four pages each. The first three folios measure 24 x 19.4 cm, and the last three 25.1 x 20.1 cm. A leaf measuring 24 x 19.7 cm is inserted in the second folio. That folio is followed by a leaf measuring 24.3 x 19.4 cm and another leaf which once belonged to a folio, the first page having been torn away, leaving fragments of letters, and now measuring 24 x 19.4 cm. The third folio contains a leaf (23.8 x 20.1 cm) with an erased pencil inscription (MS p. 18); it is followed by a leaf (24 x 19.6 cm) with erased pencil at top verso, and a leaf measuring 24 x 19.4 cm. The first two folios (and leaf within the second folio) are stitched in one place with double black thread. The rest of the components are fastened by a straight pin. There are several illegible passages in erased pencil—presumably drafts for the ink inscription, though not enough has been recovered to be certain.

Lines	Page 201
Bible Text	mind &—put
4	greatness↑,↓ [comma in pencil]
7	Character↑,↓ then↑,↓ indeed↑, it↓ is left to us↑,↓ [additions in pencil]
13–14	↑due↓ . . . work ["us . . . work" circled in pencil]
18	his ⟨m⟩Maker

	Page 202
8–9	us. ⟨Some men whose names are as familiar to us as our own⟩ ↑⟨Especially is this true of men in public life.⟩ A . . . life↓
10	himself. ⟨There are⟩ We
15	in ⟨almost⟩ ↑nearly↓
24–25	own? ¶ ⟨You meet a prosperous person⟩ Consider

	Page 203
4–21	substance. ⟨⟨↑{Insert X}↓⟩ [added in pencil and erased] Fix your eye steadily upon this distinction, & see if we are not habitually forming

our views of what is worth pursuing, according to the commonly
received notions, & forgetting that the formation of our character is
our main concern.⟩ [canceled in pencil and ink] ¶ ⟨It seems to me↑,↓
brethren↑,↓ [commas in pencil] as if we wanted nothing so much as
the habit of distinguishing betwixt our circumstances & ourselves,
the habit of rigorous scrutiny into our own daily life to learn how
much there is of our own action & how much is not genuine but
imitated & mercenary; the advantage of arriving at a precise notion
of a genuine⟩ ¶ ↑In . . . genuine↓ [ink over erased pencil draft of the
same] man such ⟨Jesus designed to be & to make many become⟩ as
all good & great persons have aimed to be; such as Jesus /designed to
be/⟨was⟩/, [variant in erased pencil] &

24–26   ↑to this topic,↓ [addition in ink over erased pencil] . . . ↑compare &↓
28   himself. ⟨People⟩ In
30   strange↑,↓ [comma in pencil]
32–37   ↑selfish or a↓ . . . himself. ⟨Let us draw a distinction between a right
         & a wrong estimate of oneself.⟩ There . . . partial ⟨passions⟩ ↑self↓,
         . . . ↑of the prodigal son↓ "And when he ⟨returned⟩ ↑came↓ to
         himself,—"; and,
40–41   & ⟨pleasant voice⟩ ↑graceful manners↓ . . . he ⟨has⟩ is

Page 204

4   ↑yet↓
9–12   perfection. ⟨It is necessary that he should feel⟩ ↑Far from being
         daunted↓ when he comes ⟨↑⟨↓every day↑⟩↓⟩ [parentheses and can-
         cellation in pencil] in contact with ⟨great advantages⟩ [canceled in
         pencil and ink] ↑⟨the exhibition of⟩ the . . . feel↓ [addition in ink
         over erased pencil] . . . great,↑—↓nay,↑—↓much [dashes in pencil]
13–16   that, w⟨e⟩hereas . . . & ↑so↓ . . . that, ↑his↓ . . . be ⟨an unnoticed
         accident⟩ ↑of trifling importance↓,— [last emendation in pencil]
18   highly↑—↓since [dash in pencil]
38–41   it. ¶ ⟨2. It follows from this self-regard that the genuine man is a lover
         & servant of truth. And this in every sense. He speaks the truth & he
         seeks the truth & he acts the truth.⟩ [canceled in pencil and ink] ¶ ⟨2.
         And [illegible word] truth of the genuine man that⟩ [erased pencil] ¶
         ↑2. This . . . truth.↓ [A largely unrecovered erased pencil draft of this
         paragraph occurs on the same page.]

Page 205

2   complaisance↑,↓ [comma in pencil]
3   ↑Indeed↓ What . . . world↑?↓" [additions in pencil]
6–7   thought very . . . too↑,↓ [comma in pencil] . . . occurred ⟨that they
         ought to act themselves⟩ that
11–14   company. ⟨I have seen a⟩ ↑There are↓ person↑s↓ . . . hear⟨d⟩ with
         the ear ⟨his⟩their real intents. ⟨He⟩They . . . wonder⟨ed⟩s why . . .
         pains ⟨he was⟩ ↑they are↓ . . . night↑,↓ [all emendations in pencil]
23–25   Roman↑,↓ [comma in pencil] when ⟨the⟩ ↑some↓ [emendation in ink
         over pencil] . . . money↑,↓ he replied↑,↓ if [commas in pencil]

31–32   this ↑a higher . . . this,↓ [addition in ink over pencil]

33–37   motives ⟨of⟩ or . . . from ⟨oth⟩ any other↑,↓ [comma in pencil] . . .
         child. ¶ ⟨Vulgar people⟩ ↑Most men↓ [emendation in pencil] . . .
         them↑,↓ [comma in pencil]

38   consistent↑,↓ [comma in pencil]

Page 206

1   in ⟨C⟩character↑,↓ [comma in pencil]

2–3   implicit ⟨deference⟩ respect . . . reason. ⟨↑{↓& to obey them with-
         out asking why↑}↓⟩ ↑As↓ [brackets and "As" in pencil] He . . .
         thinks. He acts his

4–6   with. ¶ ⟨↑{↓But to come a little closer to this matter to show more
         particularly with what sort of truth the genuine man speaks & acts,
         & what is meant by his following implicitly the leading of his own
         mind. It was happily said of a great man, "that he was content to stand
         by, & let reason argue for him." That is precisely the impression left
         on your mind whenever you talk with a truth speaker, that it is not he
         who speaks so much as reason that speaks thro' him. You are not
         dealing with a mere man but with something higher & better than
         any man,—with the voice of reason common to him & you & all
         men. It is as if you conversed with Truth & Justice.↑}↓⟩ [brackets and
         cancellation in pencil] ¶ ↑And . . . action;↓ [An erased pencil draft of
         this sentence occurs two pages later.] ¶ ↑3. I . . . that↓ His [addition in
         ink over erased pencil]

15–16   even with ⟨the⟩ [canceled in pencil and ink] abuses↑,↓ but must
         conform↑,↓ ⟨& swallow some camels⟩ ↑& take . . . it↓. [last
         emendation in pencil]

17   correct ⟨these⟩ abuses↑,↓ [cancellation in pencil; comma in ink over
         pencil] & . . . life↑,↓

22   conforming him [end of page] ⟨& moves therein⟩ himself to ⟨its
         blind usages⟩ ↑corrupt modes↓,

24   his ⟨h↑e↓ar⟩ heart.

25–26   love. ⟨↑{↓He carries the same power into every cause he approves.
         You shall see others,—& this is the great fault of men in all public
         business—that they do not give themselves to the affairs they under-
         take; they only half act; they speak much, they do many things, & yet
         do not embark themselves fairly & frankly, for better for worse, in
         the cause, but are ever looking round to see what chance there is for
         their own particular advantage It is only the *means* to them of their
         private ends. And you never get a ⟨con⟩ perfect confidence in them.
         Not so the genuine man. He fairly espouses his cause. He grows in its
         success; he faints in its failure. It is his own Cause, & his life is in
         it. All men understand this difference at a glance, & feel who does
         his work ⟨professionally⟩ ↑perfunctorily↓, & who does it with the
         heart.↑}↓⟩ [brackets and cancellation in pencil] ¶ ⟨There is a main
         consideration belonging to this subject on which I find I have not yet
         touched. It is this. You must work after your own fashion & not after
         that of any body else. You must be virtuous & wise in your own way

as much as you must speak in your own tone & not mimic other
people [one or two illegible words] not [two or three illegible words]
nor use strong expressions in favor of popular virtues & [two or three
illegible words] as Temperance [illegible word] then do not affect [il-
legible word] There is something that does seem to you good & wise
Praise that Commend that Forward that by all the means in your
power & not the less because you find your self in the minority no nor
even if you should find yourself alone.⟩ [This paragraph, in erased
pencil, occupies MS p. 18.] ¶ It

33   are↑,↓ ⟨several⟩ perhaps,

Page 207

1   something—be⟨a⟩ assured,
4–6   character, the . . . himself,—a fit object for his ⟨exertions,⟩ ↑advo-
                      cacy,↓ bestows
20   desireable
40–(208)2   ↑Jesus did . . . in us↓ [in pencil]

Page 208

9–11   worked ⟨with love⟩ in . . . ↑in the . . . *love*↓— [cancellation and
                      addition in pencil]
29–33   birth & ⟨growth⟩ breeding . . . exal⟨l⟩ting

[Following the end of the sermon, upside down in pencil:]
C. C. Emerson
  17 Court St.

Sermon CLXV

Manuscript: Seven sheets folded to make four pages each. The first folio, the pages of
which measure 25 x 20.3 cm, is followed by a leaf measuring 24.6 x 20.2 cm; pages of the
second and third folios measure 24.6 x 20.2 cm; the third folio is followed by leaves
measuring, respectively, 22.8 x 18.5 cm and 24.7 x 20.1 cm. Pages of the last four folios
measure 25 x 20.3 cm. The folios are sewn along the left margin with white thread. The
sermon is numbered "165" on MS p. 1. An additional leaf, measuring 24.8 x 20.2 cm and
currently filed with Sermon CLXVI, manifestly belongs to this sermon and seems to fit
between MS pp. 6 and 7 (i.e., a second single leaf following the first folio).

[Above the Bible text:] ↑{A Discourse preached at the Second Church in Boston Oct 27.
1833.—↓ [in pencil]

Lines   *Page 209*
1   ¶ ⟨↑{↓One . . . pertinency.↑}↓⟩ [The first four paragraphs were
                      bracketed and canceled in pencil for deliveries after the first. The
                      cancellation is rejected, as is the paragraph, also in pencil, that was
                      substituted for them:] ↑I wish to invite your attention to ⟨so⟩ a con-
                      sideration of the prospects of society in reference to religious instruc-
                      tion; of that change which [written over erased "to the subject of
                      that"] seems to be taking place under our eyes in the opinions of men

on religious questions; of that Teaching which all men are waiting for
& of that Teacher who has been predicted & hath not yet come.↓

4   world⟨,⟩ God

Page 210

17   is ⟨the end of⟩ the

18   earth. ⟨He that has no ambition to be taught.⟩ It

21   lesson, ⟨that fruit⟩ is the ⟨cause⟩ reason

30   hope ⟨and this⟩ ↑or↓ raise⟨s⟩ man

32–33 you /believe/discern/ [variant in pencil] ⟨that⟩ that . . . within
    ⟨influences⟩ reach

37–38 preparation [end of MS p. 6; the editors conjecture that a leaf now
    filed with Sermon CLXVI, containing one canceled and one uncan-
    celed paragraph (verso blank), originally followed at this point:] ¶
    ⟨He looked upon a Teacher as the highest want of the soul as the
    greatest gift of God. He looked upon a Teacher in the light in which
    all wise & good men have regarded that gift He had a clear &
    steadfast conviction of the existence of an inner world compared with
    which the outer was chips & husks & ashes.⟩ ¶ I

Page 211

1–7   the ⟨rem⟩ memorable . . . text. [T]hey [MS torn] . . . Teacher ⟨as⟩in
    . . . that ⟨gift as the highest want of the soul⟩ ↑good,↓ . . . soul. [end
    of inscribed leaf; text resumes on MS p. 7:] ¶ ⟨The language of Jesus
    Christ himself is sufficiently remarkable⟩ He assured . . . ↑now;↓
    . . . he ⟨was gone⟩ ↑had departed↓

11–16 this? ⟨What but this amiable & holy prophet⟩ He . . . to ⟨their
    heathenish mind⟨s⟩,⟩ ↑the Jewish mind,↓ . . . dawn. ¶ ⟨Th⟩Here
    are promises ⟨here⟩ whose . . . unfolded. ⟨1.⟩ That

20–21 the ⟨lies⟩ ↑falsehoods↓

21–28 moment ⟨& the wise man is richer by his losses & better by his sins.
    That every moment⟩ from . . . Father ⟨sends⟩ accumulates . . .
    race⟨;⟩ from . . . countless ⟨events⟩ ↑occurrences↓ the ⟨accumulat-
    ing⟩ ↑growing↓ . . . stars ⟨darted⟩ ↑which beam↓

29   but ⟨h⟩He

30–31 ↑He is never silent.↓

31   by ⟨some one of them⟩ ↑him↓.

32–34 of ⟨events⟩ society, . . . ↑with it↓ this beneficent ⟨fruit in its issue⟩
    ↑effect↓

37   ↑cheerful↓

39–41 ↑continually being↓ revealed. ⟨↑Not only the piety of humble pas-
    tors↓⟩ The ↑rival↓ . . . ↑the pious . . . labored↓

Page 212

3–5   race. ¶ ⟨It is of this class of truths—that which is called moral truth to
    which I would confine myself. It is ⟨this whic⟩ the capacity for this
    that makes man a religious being Herein lies all the depth & majesty

of his nature. ⟨He⟩ ↑Jesus↓ promised his disciples a larger measure of ⟨knowledge⟩ truth than yet had been imparted to them No promise has been more punctually fulfilled. The high value set by him upon this instruction, & the promise of fuller intelligence which he makes them, will aid us in forming just views of the present & of the future ¶ ↑I speak of course of that which is called Moral Truth—of that ↑high↓ [addition in pencil] class of facts to which these promises relate. ↑recognized in every breast.↓ The name "Duty" the word "I ought" suppose it. It ↑is↓ his capacity for this that makes man a religious being. All the grand sentiments that ever were addressed to him would be ridiculous, if this part of his constitution were wanting. In the value that is set upon this nature consists the welfare & hope of society. In the cultivation of this nature, & not in ships or cities, consists the prosperity & progress of nations. The high value which Jesus sets upon this nature in the expressions that have been quoted, the solemnity with which he promises the means of its nourishment may guide us into some just views of the past the present & the future state of the world in this respect.↓⟩ [last paragraph canceled in pencil and ink] ¶ 1. ⟨Jesus promised his disciples a larger measure ⟨↑of this truth.↓⟩ of truth than yet had been imparted ↑to↓ them No promise has been more punctually fulfilled. The first effect of it (& this also seems to have been within the foresight of that Teacher) has been to adjust our views of his gospel.⟩ [cancellation in pencil and ink] ↑Let . . . regarded.↓ [in ink over erased pencil]

9   ↑not↓ being ⟨less⟩ [canceled in pencil and ink] adored. He has had↑, . . . know,↓

16   world ⟨waxes⟩ ↑grows↓

20–23   showing ⟨that⟩ ↑a↓ . . . all ⟨thinkers that come after⟩ ↑the lovers . . . truth↓.

24–28   whether ⟨this⟩ ↑it↓ . . . whether ⟨this⟩ it . . . the ⟨ages that preceded⟩ age

29   ↑particular↓

34   ↑notwithstanding this occasional character↓

37–40   ¶ But ⟨this⟩ in . . . great ⟨& glorious⟩ affirmation . . . opens ⟨the way⟩ ↑an entrance↓

42–(213)21 the ⟨reality & eternity⟩ existence of the ⟨invisible & eternal⟩ ↑spiritual↓ world. ⟨But it is not the only nor the last affirmation. There shall be a thousand more. Very inconsistent would it be with a soul so possessed with this love of the real & the unseen as Christ's, to set bounds to the discoveries of that illimitable ocean. None knew better than he that every soul occupies a new position & that if the stars cannot be counted nor the sea sands numbered⟩ [end of MS p. 14; MS pp. 15–16 are an added leaf. Upside down at the bottom of p. 15 is the canceled sentence "I believe that every thing technical, sectarian, parabolical will come to an end".] ¶ ↑⟨It is the most emphatic affirmation of the existence of the spiritual world a recognition of that unexhausted inexhaustible mine of thought which raises the soul of man into a new & endless career⟩ [canceled in pencil and ink] And . . . scholars.↓ ¶ ⟨2. In the second place⟩ Christ

Page 213

1–4	moral⟨s⟩ ↑nature↓ [emendation in pencil] . . . saw, ⟨& said⟩ & proved . . . he ⟨⟨had knowledge of⟩ saw⟩ ↑saw↓ . . . of ⟨the⟩ external
5–6	↑And . . . Jesus.↓ [in ink over erased pencil; only the conclusion of the pencil draft is legible: "of Jesus ⟨in the⟩ as an history of the past."]
7–8	↑What . . . growth.↓ . . . truth ⟨is⟩ ↑was↓
9	of ⟨moral⟩ spiritual
11–12	the ⟨unseen &⟩ real . . . discoveries ⟨of⟩ ↑in↓ that illimitable ⟨ocean⟩ ↑region↓.
16	truth ⟨I⟩have
22	the ⟨c⟩future
25	than ⟨the⟩ ↑this↓
26	tardy ⟨operations⟩ expansion of the ↑worldly↓
27	scholar. ⟨What else⟩ ↑This, . . . intimated↓
28–31	↑what is called↓ . . . is⟨;⟩, they . . . perverse ⟨stiffnecked⟩ [canceled in pencil and ink] generation

Page 214

1–6	seed↑—↓it . . . leaven,↑—↓it . . . pearl↑—↓but . . . it↑,↓ [additions in pencil] . . . from ⟨assembly to assembly⟩ ↑house to house,↓ . . . with ⟨sublime⟩ sympathy . . . preparing ⟨minds⟩ ↑hearts↓ . . . ↑lofty &↓
8–13	the ⟨larger applications⟩ ↑enlargement↓ . . . ↑in its effects↓. In the place ↑of the . . . antiquity↓ [addition in ink over erased pencil] . . . few ⟨Phenicians⟩ ↑Corinthians,↓ . . . ↑of the Mediterran[ean]↓ [inscription runs off the page] for piracy & ⟨war⟩ conquest, . . . the ⟨world⟩ ↑globe↓ . . . pacific & ⟨legal⟩ ↑equitable↓
17	the ⟨D⟩diffusion
23–24	'it ⟨was⟩is . . . men. ↑(↓A [addition in pencil]
32–34	fruitfulness↑,↓ . . . represent.↑)↓ [additions in pencil]
35	¶ III.
41	from ⟨that⟩ what

Page 215

1	teach↑i↓ng
10–12	head &↑,↓ . . . theology↑,↓ . . . Christ↑,↓ again↑,↓ . . . all↑,↓ [commas in pencil]
14	*my* relation . . . *my* relation [underscoring added in pencil]
25	him⟨self,⟩, that

Page 216

12	faith↑,↓ . . . me↑,↓ [commas in pencil]
13	I am the Father. [Emerson misquotes John 14:11.]
15–16	¶ {I . . . farther ⟨influence⟩ ↑opening↓ . . . mind↑,↓ [emendation and comma in pencil]

23   to ⟨foretell⟩ ↑portray↓
27–28   ↑especially . . . source.↓.

                                        Page 217
10–12   ¶ {It . . . the ⟨assurance⟩ ↑belief↓ . . . future, & ⟨perceives⟩ ↑is
                            conscious↓
17–29   within.} ¶ ⟨↑{↓May . . . him.↑}↓⟩ [second pair of brackets and
                            cancellation in pencil; rejected as a late emendation]

[Following the end of the sermon is a substitute conclusion, dated March 15, 1834, the
day before the second delivery:] ¶ Be assured, brethren, that a disposition to use the light
we have, to serve God according to our best knowledge, is the certain way of acquiring
new truth. *If ye will do the will of my Father, ye shall know of the doctrines.* [John 7:17]
This spirit is the spirit of Truth This is he that when he comes, shall guide you into all
truth. For he shall not speak of man,—of anything finite or mortal. He shall speak of
that which is within & above man,—that which he heareth from God, the source of
truth. And whatsoever he heareth from God, that shall he speak And he shall show you
things to come.

                                   Sermon CLXVI
Manuscript: The manuscript is incomplete, consisting of one sheet folded to make four
pages, each measuring 25.1 x 20 cm. The folio has what appear to be pinholes from prior
sewing. An additional loose sheet currently filed with the manuscript actually belongs to
Sermon CLXV (see above). The sermon is numbered "166" on MS p. 1.

Lines   *Page 218*
Bible Text   ↑⟨As⟩ ↑As in water↓ face answereth to face, ⟨in [illegible word] so
                            doth the⟩so . . . Prov. 27. 19↓ [in pencil]
5–6   the ⟨c⟩troop
9–11   Divine ⟨Disposer⟩, [canceled in pencil] & . . . circle. ↑A↓ [in pencil]
                            ¶ ⟨↑{↓So universal are these laws that the world has hardly heard of a
                            man or a woman ⟨that⟩ ↑who↓ was absolutely alone.↑}↓⟩ [brackets
                            in pencil; cancellation in pencil and ink] ¶ ⟨It is a striking feature of
                            our condition that amidst all this provision for the dependence of men
                            each man is by his consciousness separated wholly from all other men
                            & so separated as to be ⟨absolutely⟩ alone with God⟨.⟩↑; that in the
                            most intimate society we are solitary. There is an apparent conflict
                            between our social & our solitary duties which ⟨is⟩a just understand-
                            ing of them will remove. And the study of these relations has the high-
                            est interest to reflecting persons as it throws light upon the inmost
                            mechanism of our being↓ ¶ I wish to invite your attention to ⟨a⟩
                            conside↑r↓ [end of line] ⟨ration of man in his two relations the
                            solitary & the social⟩ ↑⟨the true⟩ what are the offices which we
                            perform to each other the lowest & the highest uses↓ ⟨of the uses⟩
                            which man subserves to man, of the ⟨mutual⟩ ↑reciprocal↓ influence
                            of society & solitude⟩ ¶ Thus every man ↑even↓
14   feel ⟨the⟩a deep⟨est⟩ interest

15–17	bread. ⟨he could not support⟩ their aversion. ↑would make him unhappy.↓ ¶ But ⟨a reflecting man⟩ ↑he↓ . . . certain ⟨in his constitution⟩, that,
20–21	↑from . . . men↓ . . . interior ⟨s⟩Self,
22–24	↑Mixed . . . contact↓ [in ink over "as we . . . contact" in pencil] Conversing . . . conspiring ↑with↓, . . . an /↑inaccessible↓ island ↑floating↓/incommunicable privacy/ [additions and variant in pencil]

Page 219

1	twofold ⟨property—a duplicity⟩ ↑nature↓
2–7	duties⟨, a practical question of great importance⟩ which . . . ↑to settle,↓ . . . society. ⟨This is no speculative question no question for colleges but one for the bosom thought of every person to whom I speak.⟩ ¶ Our . . . man ⟨as his mind is expanded to meet them⟩ to . . . of /↑{↓every↑}↓/different/ [brackets and variant in pencil] condition, character, ↑early↓ [in pencil]
11	acquaintance. ⟨None but⟩ ↑The . . . himself↓ has observed that
15	¶ On [The paragraph is written over an erased pencil passage, from which the following phrases have been recovered: "arrangements is good . . . minutest particular. And the ⟨good⟩ ↑pious↓ man will perceive & partake of the . . . these are good . . . the sensual & selfish . . . covet & enjoy . . . & unthankful . . . cultivate the society of their fellow men with . . . single . . . advantage".]
16–17	contemplation? ⟨All⟩ Nothing is ⟨so⟩ [cancellation in pencil, rejected for sense] manifest
18–19	Nay ⟨to accomplish great benevolent ends by⟩ ↑by↓ [cancellation in pencil and ink; addition in pencil] . . . ↑some↓
21	yet ⟨born⟩ ↑awakened↓

Sermon CLXVIII

Manuscript: Six sheets folded to make four pages each; pages of the first four folios measure 24.8 x 20.2 cm; those of the last two folios measure 24.1 x 19.7 cm. Two single leaves occur after the fourth folio, one after the fifth folio, and two within the sixth folio; each single leaf measures 24 x 19.7 cm. The sermon is numbered "168" in green pencil. The folios are sewn along the left margin with black and brown thread.

[Above the Bible text:] ↑Sermon after the death of George Sampson↓ [in pencil]

Lines	*Page 221*
Bible Text	unto ⟨a⟩ m⟨a⟩en
3–4	flesh, ⟨they⟩we only know that ⟨↑t↓he⟩ ↑⟨departed⟩our brother↓
6–7	↑although . . . trusted,↓
10–11	withdrawn. ¶ ⟨Yet I think that⟩ whilst ↑however↓ . . . griefs ⟨↑{↓the danger is rather that we should esteem it too little than too much because↑}↓⟩ ↑yet↓ [brackets in pencil; "yet" in ink over pencil]
14	which ⟨is to come⟩ ↑shall be↓, [emendation in ink over pencil]
16	give ⟨a sanction⟩ ↑leave↓

Page 222

24–25	I ↑{↓after . . . him↑}↓ to [brackets in pencil]
29–30	character! ⟨What⟩ How . . . virtues. There
36	↑there↓
39	in ⟨private⟩ ↑this↓ famil⟨ies⟩y

Page 223

5	of ⟨his⟩ ↑Mr Sampson's↓
7–9	↑I . . . them,↓ [ink over pencil] . . . of ⟨them⟩ ↑the features of his soul↓ [addition in ink over erased pencil] . . . me↑, in . . . observer.↓ [addition in ink over erased pencil; the legible portion of the pencil layer reads: "⟨⟨belonged to them⟩ presented yᵐselves to the observer⟩"]
19–20	respects. ⟨{Insert X}⟩ ¶ He
26	de⟨s⟩ception.
33–34	far ⟨superior⟩ ↑remote↓ . . . remark ⟨to⟩from

Page 224

5–6	best ⟨minds which ⟨prompts⟩ ↑makes↓ them ⟨to⟩ contemn the⟩ ↑minds . . . the↓ [addition in ink over illegible erased pencil]
11	see↑i↓ng . . . tenderness ⟨of⟩in
18	dignity ⟨to⟩upon
23	morning ⟨has⟩which
25	¶ Aware [This paragraph is written over the following erased pencil draft:] Aware of of these infinite relations ⟨t⟩he conformed his life to them. He had no surface action. [several illegible words] act of the whole man. He had no courtesy that did not spring [illegible word] love no firmness that was not sense of duty no modesty that was not humility no cheerfulness but it was trust no attention to your words but it was love of truth Thus was he all principle
27	court⟨i⟩esy
33	should ⟨be⟩ cultivate
36–37	information, ⟨& with⟩ & . . . any ⟨one who had⟩ ↑who↓
40	because ⟨his⟩ they

Page 225

3–8	he ⟨was too⟩ would . . . opposition↑; & therefore . . . world.↓ [addition in ink over erased pencil; pencil layer has "an opinion" for "any sentiment"] ¶ He ⟨had a strong⟩ was . . . of ⟨a⟩ remaining
12	↑to↓
15–16	to ⟨exaggerate the value of the⟩ ↑overestimate the↓ opinions & ⟨of⟩ the
20–21	contemplation ↑&↓ ⟨&⟩for . . . not ⟨⟨a clergyman⟩ ↑an author,↓ nor⟩ a
24–26	↑so↓ . . . him ⟨a⟩ ↑some↓ . . . in ⟨it⟩the
28	his ²appearance or ¹manners
29	↑He . . . singularity.↓
31	& ⟨entered with warmth into⟩ ↑& . . . upon↓

33   listened ⟨care⟩ ↑heed-↓[end of line] fully to ↑men of↓
35–36   on ⟨&⟩ ↑↑to the last,↓ . . . one↓
39–40   he ⟨served⟩ ↑shared↓ . . . but ⟨a⟩ ↑the support of his↓

Page 226

2   ↑Boston Port Society↓
6   to ⟨whatever was good & wise⟩ ↑every judicious movement↓
10   ↑a↓ virtuous
12   work ⟨⟨{if it should please God⟩ for long & happy years—} as
15–16   the ⟨courage⟩ ↑confidence↓ . . . ↑in . . . minded↓
18–30   the ⟨vigor of his youth⟩ ↑midst of society↓? ¶ ⟨How shall I speak of
          him as a friend,—since the truest statement of his generous carriage
          would sound like exaggeration to strangers, & they who have enjoyed
          his confidence do not need to be reminded of his ↑true &↓ noble
          heart. ↑All of us who knew him are the debtors of his love.↓ His
          ⟨passion for a friend⟩ ⟨↑idea of friendship↓⟩ ↑idea of friendship↓ is a
          ⟨trait in⟩ ↑part of↓ his character ↑It haunted him like a passion↓ He
          has carried it with him all unsatisfied into that spiritual world whither
          he is gone. His whole life might be called a search after a friend.
          There was no sacrifice he would not count it a joy to make for the sake
          of those he loved. I may say his friendship was a species of religion, for
          he was accustomed to say that the habit of recalling the image of a
          reverenced friend was a powerful restraint upon any unworthy
          purpose.⟩ ¶ ↑How . . . purpose.↓

Page 227

1–4   year ↑X X {He . . . frame ↑He . . . Father}↓↓ [The two "X"s, the
          brackets, and the last sentence are in pencil.]
9   he ⟨would⟩ ↑could not↓
14–17   charity. ⟨And the words "praise & glory" he thot contributed little to
          the life of a prayer.⟩ At . . . teaching↑, . . . him↓ [addition in ink over
          erased pencil]
19   presented ⟨to those⟩ the
23   made ⟨a⟩the
23–27   we ⟨scarcely⟩hardly ["scarcely" lightly struck through in pencil, then
          overwritten "hardly" in ink] ⟨↑hardly knew how to↓⟩ [addition in
          pencil; erased] separated him from ⟨them⟩ ↑his deeds↓, . . . us. ⟨Yet
          was h⟨e⟩is a life from which preachers might well quote both single
          virtues & general habits to illustrate many a ⟨virt⟩ text, & he alone
          of all the hearers should ⟨perhaps⟩ be unconscious that his own
          portrait was drawn.⟩ [sentence canceled in pencil and ink] ¶ Of . . .
          mind, ⟨it would⟩ ↑of . . . would↓ scarcely occur to ⟨his friends⟩
          ↑any observer↓
33   ↑He . . . virtues.↓ [ink over erased pencil]
39   ↑He . . . ↑the↓ . . . adored↓ [in pencil]

Page 228

4   his ⟨short⟩ virtues,

Sermon CLXIX

Manuscripts: Two manuscripts survive, a heavily revised earlier version, the source of the first three deliveries, and a later version, source of the final five deliveries. The date of the revision can be confidently assigned to the period of February and March 1835. In an undated letter to Lydia Jackson, Emerson wrote: "Lidian what have you done with my Plymouth sermon. [Emerson had delivered the sermon at Plymouth as a Wednesday lecture, January 21, 1835.] I forgot twice to take it away. All that is important is to keep it out of sight. If you have left it at P. do not let it be lent again & if you have it in Boston seal it up for me. I have a copy of it that I shall presently finish & bring it to more connected & luminous conclusions, I hope, than when at P." (*L* 1:440). This letter, which is misdated by Rusk as "March *c.* 4, 1835," conveyed Carlyle's first letter to Emerson, to be lent to Mrs. Bliss. Since Mrs. Bliss had Carlyle's letter on February 24 (see *L* 1:439), Emerson's could have been written no later than February 23, a date consistent with other events he alludes to. Thus, the revised version of the sermon would have been first preached at Waltham on March 29, 1835.

Manuscript (earlier version): Seven sheets folded to make four pages each; the first folio is preceded by a leaf (the lower right-hand third of which is torn away) containing, in pencil, sermon number, hymn numbers, and a verse. Pages of the first folio measure 24.8 x 20.2 cm, those of the other six folios 24 x 19.6 cm (except for the fifth folio, which measures 24 x 19.8 cm). The fifth folio contains a leaf which also measures 24 x 19.8 cm; a leaf measuring 24 x 19.6 cm follows the last folio. The folios are sewn along the left margin with black thread.

[The text of the earlier version follows:]

169

I am fearfully & wonderfully made. ↑marvellous are thy works;↓ and that my soul knoweth right well. Ps. 139. 14

Every body knows that he is wonderfully made. And yet it ⟨has⟩ ↑will↓ occur⟨red to me⟩ [emendation and cancellation in ink over pencil] sometimes ⟨that it ↑is↓⟩ [addition in pencil] ↑to a thoughtful mind as↓ [addition in ink over "to a thoughtful mind" in pencil] strange, ↑that↓ people ⟨are not oftener overcome with⟩ ↑do not continually break out into expressions of↓ astonishment at themselves. When an Asiatic prince came to Paris & was asked what ⟨he saw⟩ ↑seemed to him↓ most surprizing ↑in that capital↓ he replied "to find himself there." With better reason a man might say that ⟨he⟩to himself ↑his own↓ existe⟨d⟩nce in the world was more ⟨marvellous⟩ ↑amazing↓ than any other fact. I believe ⟨almost no⟩ ↑few↓ person↑s↓ ⟨does⟩ perceive the exceeding ⟨strangeness⟩ ↑marvel↓ of their own constitution, & yet it is more wondrous than any fiction that was ever conceived "Truth is strange—stranger than fiction."

The proposition that 'we are wonderfully made,' is applied by people generally to the external constitution of men & admitted without debate and without afterthought. And ⟨surely⟩ ↑undoubtedly↓ our ⟨external⟩ ↑physical↓ constitution is ingenious enough to justify the expression

The fine contrivance ⟨that appears⟩ in every part of our frame, the perfect fitting of ⟨part to p⟩ the members, & the admirable working of the whole machine transcend all praise: Then, the ⟨g⟩fitness of man to the earth; & his peaceful dwelling among the cattle, the birds, & the fish, turning the Earth into his garden & pleasure ground, the ⟨change⟩ ↑round↓ of the seasons, ⟨the remote⟩ ↑and the universal↓ order↑,↓ ⟨of the planets,⟩ is all set down in the books. The external fitness is wonderful indeed;—but I doubt if to those who saw this only, it would have ever occurred ↑(↓in the first instance↑)↓ [parentheses in pencil] to remark upon the marvel. It has been said with some ingenuity of conjecture that 'without ⟨s⟩ the phenomenon of sleep, we should be atheists;' because, if we had no experience of the interruption of the activity of the Will "⟨it⟩ ↑we↓ could never be bro't to a sense & acknowledgment of its dependence on the Divine Will." {N.J.M. Nov 1832 With more assurance it may be said of the things apprehended by the senses, that they are so nicely grooved into one another that ⟨one⟩ the sight of one suggests the next preceding & this the next before, that the understanding ↑would↓ runs forever in the round of second causes, ⟨so that we see men go through life & die at 70 years & die without surprize⟩ ↑but that the Reason sometimes grows impatient of the narrow circlet, & demands tidings of the First Cause.↓ Were there not graver considerations to be remembered, there is something almost comic in seeing such a creature as is a man growing up with perfect senses & faculties & going in & out for 70 years amid the shows of nature & of humanity, making up his mouth every day ⟨⟨at some⟩ into⟩ ↑to express↓ all degrees of surprize at every impertinent trifle, & never suspecting all the time that it is even /singular/remarkable/ [variant in pencil] he should exist.

But ↑superficial views will not always satisfy us↓ it will not always suffice us to ask why this bone is thus terminated & be answered that it may fit that socket or why is this animal thus configured & be answered that the residence & the food of the animal requires such frame but the question ⟨arises⟩ ↑starts up↓ and almost with terror within us, why the animal ⟨exist⟩ or any animal exists? to what farther end its being has regard beyond this nice tissue of neighboring ⟨considerations⟩ ↑facts?↓ why organization, why order exist? Nay why this interrogator exists, & what he is? Indeed if you will steadily contemplate the ⟨mere⟩ ↑bare↓ fact of your existence as a man, it is one of such bewildering astonishment that it seems ⟨more rational⟩ ↑it were the part of reason↓ to spend one's lifetime in a trance of wonder↑; altogether more rational to lift ones hands in blank amazement↓ than ⟨th⟩ to assume the least shadow of ⟨pride or⟩ dogmatism⟨.⟩ or pride.

I say these things because I think ⟨a man has not yet ar⟩ that man's mind has not yet arrived at a just perception of his own position & duties in the Creation who is not yet alive to the ⟨astonishment⟩ miracle that surrounds him "Let others wrangle," said ↑the pious↓ Augustin, "I will wonder." It is related of the wisest man in the ancient world the Athenian Socrates that on one occasion he stopped short in his walk & stood stock still in a fast contemplation from sunset to sunrise in a rapture of amazement.

⟨A⟩ ↑But we may be conscious of the mystery without always saying so. Certainly; & a↓ man might be well forgiven his omission to express his admiration of that which *is*, if his employments ↑indicated any sense of his powers & relations

But see the oddity of his demeanor. This little creature set down he knows not how amid all the sublimities of the moving Universe ⟨gifted⟩ sharpsighted enough to find out the movement not only of the sphere he inhabits but of all the spheres in the depths around him, and not only so, but ⟨(more powerful still)⟩ capable by the subtle powers of intellect & affection of acting upon remote men as upon himself: Yes, & from his little hour extending the arms of his influence through thousands of years, & to millions of millions of rational men: Nay, by means of Virtue of entering instantly upon a life that seems to make the whole grandeur of the Creation pale & ⟨shadowy⟩ ↑visionary↓—Yet this little creature quite unmindful of these vast prerogatives struts about with immense activity to ⟨get⟩ ↑procure↓ various meats to eat, & stuffs to wear, and ⟨chiefly⟩ ↑most of all↓ salutations & marks of respect from his fellows. He seems to think it quite natural he should be here, & things should be as they are,—so natural, as not ↑to↓ deserve a second thought: And the moment he has got a neat house ⟨on⟩ to sit down & to eat & to sleep in, he is so possessed with a sense of his importance, that he not only thinks he deserves much more attention than if he knew the whole order of the creation, but he expect⟨ed⟩s confidently great deference from his fellow men.

⟨ It is related of the wisest man of the ancient world the Athenian Socrates that on one occasion he stopped short in his walk and in a steadfast contemplation he stood stockstill from sunset to sunrise in ⟨c⟩a ⟨ravishment⟩ ↑rapture↓ of amazement.⟩

We go so gravely about our ordinary trifl⟨es⟩ing employments that we are apt to lose the sense of the absurdity of much that we do. We allow by our acquiescence a man that has more houses & ships & farms than his neighbors, to assume consequence in his manners on that ground. Although we know very well, when we ⟨think⟩ ponder the matter, that if instead of a few ↑thousand↓ acres of land, or a a ⟨few⟩ ↑score of↓ ships or houses, he owned the entire property of the civilized world, he would be as much in the dark, as mortal, & as ⟨self-⟩↑in↓sufficient ↑to himself↓ as he is now. He could not then solve ⟨by⟩ ↑not so much as↓ one word ↑of↓ the vast mystery that envelopes us; he would not have a particle more of real power ↑In the great All↓ he would be the very insect he is now.

Yet the extent & consistency of the world's farce keeps each particular puppet in countenance, and we go on in the universal hunt for station & ⟨extent of⟩ ⟨real estate⟩ ↑land↓ & horses ⟨& coaches⟩ & ships & stocks & attentions & compliments, hiding the inanity of the ↑whole↓ thing in the ⟨confusion⟩ ↑multitude↓ of the particulars. Is it not as if one should have a nest of a hundred boxes & nothing in the last box?

And ↑hence the wise laughter of↓ the ancient philosopher Democritus ⟨affected to laugh at⟩ ↑who made ⟨j⟩a jest of↓ all human society & pursuits. No wise man he said could keep his countenance in view of such utter folly.

⟨↑{↓There is much that is ludicrous in the solemnity with which we labor year after year until we fall sick & die in the work of taking a little from that heap & adding it to this other which we are pleased to call *mine*. We have no leisure to laugh we are so intent upon the work. We keep each other in countenance and as all are agreed to consider it in the ludicrous language of the world 'the main chance,' the nonsense of the whole thing is carefully kept out of sight↑}↓⟩ [brackets in pencil; cancellation in pencil and ink]

But why call it ludicrous? is it not necessary that we ⟨get⟩ ↑acquire↓ property?— Assuredly it is. Let us carefully distinguish ↑between wisdom & folly.↓. We are of an animal constitution & have animal wants, which must be supplied & indispensably ⟨require⟩ ↑demand↓ continual exertion. This whole ⟨fab⟩ matter of Commerce,—a net woven round every man—grows out of it & it needs & it is good that every man should do his part & one ↑sow the field & one weave the cloth, & one draw the contracts & one↓ plough the sea & one build the ship one throw the harpoon ⟨& one weave the cloth & one sow the field & one draw the contracts⟩ Theres much that is wonderful but nothing that is ludicrous in this simply considered

The ludicrous part of it is in the acting as if it were the ultimate end; just that for which we lived; & the entire oversight of the end for which this is only means. ⟨And then the purseproud man he is the chief actor in the farce⟩ ↑The proud man, the sensualist, the denier of divine power, the avaricious, the selfish↓ By such earthworms the wonder of our being is not perceived. they are merely ⟨upper⟩ ↑the highest class of↓ animals, and like ants & horses & elephants, they do not perceive any thing extraordinary in their life.

⟨But⟩ ↑And what remedy? What can save us from this capital error, or repair it? The exercise of↓ Reason, the act of reflexion redeems a man at once out of this brutishness. the man ⟨that⟩ ↑who↓ reflects *is* a man, & not an animal. I take it to be a⟨n⟩ ↑main↓ [cancellation in pencil; addition in ink over pencil] object of that education which this world administers to each soul↑,↓ [comma in pencil] to touch the springs of wonder in us, & ⟨awaken us⟩ make us ⟨wide awake⟩ ↑alive↓ to the marvel of our condition. ↑That done all is done.↓ Before, he was so wrongheaded, so at discord with things around him, that he ⟨did not p⟩ was ⟨lud⟩ ridiculous: now, he is at one with all He accepts his lot: he perceives the great astonishment. He adores. Awaked to truth & virtue ⟨But not only⟩ he perceives ⟨how⟩ ↑the↓ wonder⟨fully he is made⟩ ↑he did not perceive before↓: ↑Moreover↓ the chief wonders of the human condition begin with the act of reason.

Let me ⟨enumerate⟩ ↑for more accurate consideration separate↓ a few of the particulars that ⟨most⟩ amaze the contemplative ⟨man⟩ spirit.

1. See how ⟨magically⟩ ↑cunningly↓ constructed are all things in such a manner as to make each being the centre⟨.⟩ ↑of the Creation.↓ ⟨Ea⟩ You seem to be the a point or focus upon which all objects, all ages ⟨all⟩ concentrate their influence Nothing past but affects *you*. Nothing remote but through some means reaches *you*. Every superficial grain of sand ⟨in this most wonderful creation⟩ may be considered as the ⟨centre⟩ ↑fixed point↓ round which all things revolve↑,↓ [comma in pencil] so intimately is it allied to all, & so truly do all turn as if for it alone. This is true in the lowest natures, to the least leaf or moss. ↑Who has ever selected one individual from the annual reproduction of nature without profounder astonishment.↓ ⟨Behold⟩ ⟨⟨See the little⟩ ↑Look at that summer↓⟩ ↑Who has not seen the summer↓ blackberry lifting his polished surface a few inches from the ground⟨.⟩? How did that little chemist extract from ⟨that⟩ ↑the↓ sand bank the spices & sweetness it has concocted in its cells? By ⟨no⟩any cheap or ⟨petty⟩ ↑accidental↓ means↑? Not so;↓ but the whole creation has been at the cost of its ⟨formation⟩ ↑↑birth &↓ [addition in pencil] nurture↓ ⟨The sun⟩ ↑A globe of fire↓ near a hundred millions of miles distant in the great space has been ⟨shining upon it⟩ ↑flooding it with light & heat↓ as if he shone for no other. It is six or seven months of that ↑t↓he ↑sun↓ has made the tour of the heavens ↑every day↓ over this ⟨little⟩ ↑tiny↓ sprout before it could bear its fruit. The sea has evaporated its countless tuns of water into the atmosphere that the rain of heaven might wet the roots of this little vine The elastic air exhaled from all ↑live↓ creatures & all minerals ⟨ & all⟩ yielded this small pensioner the gaseous aliment it required: the earth by the ↑attraction of its↓ mass ⟨of⟩ determined its form & size; & when we consider how the earths attraction is fixed at ⟨its amount⟩ this moment ⟨by the⟩ in equilibrium by the ⟨thousand c⟩ innumerable attractions, on every side, of ⟨remote⟩ ↑distant↓ bodies,↑—↓we shall see that the berry's form & history is determined by causes & agents the most prodigious & remote.

What then shall we say of the manner in which ⟨a⟩one man is made the centre round which all things ⟨revolve⟩ ↑roll↓ & upon which all things scatter ⟨in⟩gifts. ⟨Morning & evening summer & winter have⟩ ↑Let us take one from the crowd not one of the sons of prosperity but a poor solitary virtuous man ↑the humblest↓ who is capable of reflection↓ He stands on the top of the world: he is the centre of the horizon. Morn↑ing↓ & even↑ing↓ lavish their sweetness & their solemnity upon his senses; summer &

winter bring to ⟨you⟩ ↑him↓ the instruction of their harvests & their storms. All that he
sees & hears, gives him a lesson. Do not the ages that are past record their experience for
his ⟨behoof⟩ ↑tuition↓ & millions of millions of rational spirits epitomize their fate for
his behoof. ⟨Am I⟩ ↑Is he↓ not continually moved to joy or grief by things said a
thousand years ago? ⟨I⟩ ↑He↓ understand↑s↓ them ⟨my⟩ ↑His↓ soul embraces the act or
the sentiment as if it were done or said for ⟨me⟩ ↑him↓ only. Is not ⟨my⟩ ↑this↓ condition
different for every one of the men that has acted upon the world. See how much ⟨Jesus
Christ⟩ ↑Luther see how much Columbus↓ has affected ⟨my⟩ ↑this↓ condition. ⟨Colum-
bus⟩ and all the inventors of arts. Do they not give ⟨me⟩ ↑him↓ the unshared total
benefit of their wisdom? Does not Socrates & Solomon & Bacon & Shakspear counsel
him alone. Does not Jesus live for him only? Does not God exist for him only? & Right,
& Wrong, & Wisdom & Folly? the whole of Pleasure; & of Pain and all the Heaven of
thought Are they not all poured into his bosom as if the world had no other child?

    And this perfect world exists thus entire to every man, to the poorest ⟨laborer ↑dig↓ in
the ditch⟩ drover in the mountains, the poorest laborer in his ditch. Quite independent
of his work, are his wonderful endowments. There is enough ⟨in⟩ ↑in↓ him, (grant him
capable of thought & virtue) to puzzle and outwit all our philosophy The history of one
man, inasmuch as it is searching & profound, is as valuable as the history of a nation.
Thoroughly acquaint me with the heart of one living man—though the humblest—& what
can Italy or England teach me more, with all their wars & all their laws? Sharpen the
insight of these obtuse perceptions of /mine/ours/ & show /me/us/ [variants in ink over
pencil] the motives, the fancy, the affection, the distorting & colouring lenses ⟨this⟩that
pauper makes use of & the redeeming power that still sets him right after countless errors
& that promises him a kingdom of heaven whilst he shuffles about in his ⟨barn⟩ ↑field↓,
and ⟨I⟩ ↑we↓ shall be able to do without Tacitus ↑Hume↓ [in pencil] & Clarendon.

    2. Thus, in the first place, is ⟨an intelligent being like⟩ man ⟨n⟩placed in the focus, at
the heart of the world. But that is only half of his power. That is merely to receive
influence. ↑He receives only to impart↓ [addition in pencil] He ⟨has more to do⟩ ↑is
appointed to action↓ [emendation in pencil] He is an active being & is not designed to be
an idle eye before which Nature passes in panorama but is by his action enabled to learn
the irresistible properties of moral nature perceived only by the mind as laws difficult to
be grasped or defined yet everywhere working out their inevitable results to the last jot
& tittle in human affairs whereupon if a man fall it will grind him to powder. There is
nothing in material nature, certainly nothing in fiction so splendid & perfect as the law
of Compensations,—the law according to which not an act is done by any moral being
but draws after it its inevitable fruit which no chance & no art can elude.

[The following passage, down to and including the quotation from St. Bernard, is in
erased pencil:] ⟨the irresistible properties of moral nature perceived only by the mind as
laws difficult to be grasped or defined yet every where working out their inevitable
results to the last jot & tittle in human affairs. whereupon if a man fall it will grind him
to powder. There is nothing in material nature certainly nothing in fiction so splendid &
perfect as the law of compensations the law according to which not an act is done by any
moral being but draws after it its inevitable fruit wh. ⟨without any possibility⟩ no
chance and no art can elude

    "Nothing can work me mischief except myself the harm which I sustain I carry about
with me, & am never a real sufferer ⟨except⟩ ↑but↓ by my own fault
                              St Bernard⟩

⟨2. Thus in the first place ⟨the whole⟩ he is the focus of all. But that is merely to ⟨see⟩ ↑receive influence↓. He has more to do he is an active being & is ⟨to learn bu⟩ not to be an idle eye before which Nature passes in panorama but ⟨an active⟩ by his action enabled to learn the ⟨amazing properties of moral nature, for example⟩ [canceled in pencil and ink] the law of Compensations.⟩ He is to learn that the Creation is so magically woven that nothing can do him any ⟨harm⟩ ↑mischief↓ but himself; that an invisible ⟨immortal⟩ [canceled in pencil] fence surrounds his whole being, which forever defends him from all ⟨harm⟩harm ⟨↑mischief↓⟩ he wills to resist; that the whole Creation cannot bend him whilst he stands upright; but on the other hand ²{that every act of his, is↑,↓ ⟨ins⟩ not hereafter, but instantaneously judged & rewarded;} ¹{that the lightning loiters by the speed of Retribution} that every generous effort impulse of his is to its full amount compensated by the instant enlargement ennobling of his soul; ⟨every⟩ that his patience disarms calamity; his love brightens the sun; his purity destroys temptation; ↑Whilst falsehood is a foolish suicide & is never believed; selfishness separates itself from ⟨m⟩the happy human family idleness whips itself with discontent; malice multiplies foes.↓ [addition in pencil] ⟨s⟩So that ever it seems, as some have maintained, that he is solicited by good & by evil spirits & that he gives himself up to them whose bidding he does and they labor continually to make him more entirely their own, & induce ⟨to⟩him to confirm his last action by repetition & by fresh energy of the same kind.

⟨Now is it not much, is it ↑not↓ the greatest kindness to ⟨open the mind of⟩ make the revelation of these laws to the ignorant mind⟩ ↑To open to ourselves, to open to others these laws—is it not worth living for↓ to make the slavish soul acquainted with the mighty secrets of its own power, that by self renouncement a kingdom of heaven of which indeed he had no conception begins at once in his heart;—by the high act of yielding his will, a total sacrifice,—that little individual heart becomes dilated as with the presence & inhabitation of the Spirit of God

⟨2⟩3 Shall I ⟨say⟩ ↑select↓ ["Shall . . . ↑select↓" circled in pencil] a third trait of our human condition so wonderful which only begins with reflexion is that it turns all our Evil to good. Thus the moment Reason assumes its empire over a man, he finds that he has nothing low & injurious in him but it is, under this dominion, the root of power & beauty; ⟨his lusts, [illegible word];⟩ ⟨his⟩ that which was debasing him, will now prove the very sinew of his character; his petulance, is the love of order; ⟨h⟩ out of his natural necessities grew this complex structure of civilization

Nay what he blushes for, & reckons his weakness, because it is different from other men whom he admires,—the odds are, it is what he should throw himself on his knees & thank God for, as his crowning gift. For there is somewhat peculiar in every man, which, is, on that account, apt to be neglected, but which must be let grow, & suffered to give direction to the other faculties, if he would attain his acme & be dear & honorable to his brethren.

↑He finds that whatever disadvantages he has labored under; whatever uncommon exertions he has been called to make; whatever poverty; what sickness; what unpopularity; what mistake; yes even what deep sin he has been given up to commit; when once ⟨his soul⟩ is awaked to truth & Virtue, ⟨to⟩ ↑touched with↓ the veneration of the Almighty Father & stung with the insatiable desire of making every day his soul more perfect—then all these the /darkest/worst/ calamities the sorest sorrows are changed are glorified he owns his deep debt to them & see with {even /exstatic admiration/rapture/} the omnipresent energy of the God who transforms all things into the divine↓ [paragraph in pencil]

And what is this Admiration? What is it but a perception of his true position in the Universe & his consequent obligations This is the whole moral & end of such views as I present. I desire a man to consider ⟨well⟩ ↑faithfully↓ in solitude & silence the unknown Nature within him, that he may not sink ⟨beneath⟩ ↑into↓ [emendation in pencil] his own contempt, & be a spectacle of folly to the Universe. ↑X X {I would have him open his eyes to true wonder that he may never more be agitated by trifles. I would have him convinced that by the act of his own Will alone can that which is most worth his study be disclosed to him.}↓ I would have him open his eyes to see that the unreflecting laborer is a brute; that the reflecting laborer only is a man. Let him consider that all riches though convenient to the senses cannot profit *him*↑self↓, but that a true thought a worthy deed puts him at once into harmony with the real & eternal. Let him consider that if he loves respect, he must seek it in what really belongs to a Man & not in any thing accidental such as fortune or appearance.

Instead of making it his pride to be announced as a person of consideration in the state or in his profession or in the fashionable world or as a rich or a travelled or a powerful man let him delight rather to make himself known in all companies by his action & by his discourse as one who has attained unto selfcommand; one who has thought in earnest upon the questions of human duty; one who carries with hi⟨m⟩s ↑presence↓ [writeover and addition in ink over pencil] the terrors & the beauty of justice; and who, even in the moment when ⟨you⟩ ↑his friends↓ ignorantly ⟨bl⟩censure him, is privy to the virtuous action he has performed, & those he has in hand. {It is a ⟨law⟩ maxim of state that that an ambassador carries his country with him, so that he & they who belong to him, are not amenable to the laws of the country where they reside, but to their own. ⟨t⟩The good man always carries his country with him. The miracle which his soul contemplates is so much more to him than all outward objects & events that wherever God is there is he at home.}

What is in ⟨a⟩this admiration? Is it not the fountain of religion in his ⟨heart⟩ ↑soul↓. What is it but an acknowledgment of the incomprehensible? not a sight only but a love & adoration of the Wisdom & Love which breathes through the Creation into ⟨his⟩the heart. What ⟨but⟩ does the world inspire but a lofty Faith that all will be, that all is well, that the Father who thus vouchsafes to reveal himself in all that ↑is↓ great & all that is lovely, will not forsake the child whom every hour & every event & Memory & Hope educate. What does it intimate but presages of an in⟨t⟩finite & a perfect life? What but an assured Trust through all evil & danger & Death.

⟨↑Why should we fear Disease let it come in what unwonted forms it will⟨,⟩? when the soul has once awakened to duty & love no change that merely touches the body can affect its everlasting ⟨be⟩peace. It is defended & ⟨blessed by⟩ ↑embosomed in↓ the love of God.↓⟩ [paragraph added and canceled in pencil]

↑Brethren I aim in ⟨these thots⟩ ↑presenting these truths↓ to awaken the /divine/ devout/ spirit in ⟨man⟩ ↑us↓ not to specify single duties. If a man will admit these thots, will listen to the ⟨call⟩ ↑pleadings of God thro the voice↓ of Nature ↑&↓ the wonders of human life, ⟨↑to the↓⟩ he will then be not less but more disposed to a faithful performance of his specific duties. He will feel that though all else is visionary & may come to nothing the love of God remains forever the attributes of the human soul ↑remain forever,↓ that Duty which is Gods law is never one moment relaxed & only in a sacred obedience to it ⟨e⟩in every moment in every alternative do we bring ourselves into unity & accord with good spirits & with God our Father↓ [paragraph added in pencil]

Manuscript (later version): Eight sheets folded to make four pages each; pages of the first six folios measure 24.8 x 20.1 cm, those of the last two folios 24.8 x 20 cm. The pages of the last folio are blank. The folios are sewn along the left margin with white thread; also secured just below the middle of the back margin with black thread.

[Below the Bible text:] S [in pencil]

Lines	*Page 229*
1	¶ ⟨Every body knows that he is wonderfully made. And yet it will occur sometimes to a thoughtful mind as strange that people do not continually break out into expressions of astonishment at themselves.⟩ When
3	that to himself,
4	the ⟨exceeding⟩ marvel
6–7	fiction." ¶ ⟨The proposition that 'we are wonderfully made,' is applied by people generally to the external constitution of men & admitted without debate, & without afterthought. And undoubtedly our physical constitution is ingenious enough to warrant the remark.⟩ ¶ The
12	wonderful, ⟨indeed⟩;—but

	Page 230
7	of ⟨wonder⟩ surprize
12–22	why is this animal is thus . . . or any any animal . . . is? ¶ ⟨Indeed, if you will steadily contemplate⟩ the bare . . . man ⟨it⟩ is . . . pride. ¶ ⟨I say these things because I think that man's mind has not yet arrived at a just perception of his own position & duties in the creation, who is not yet alive to the miracle that surrounds him.⟩ "Let
28	powers & ⟨dut⟩ relations.
31–36	movement ⟨not only⟩ of . . . inhabits, ⟨but⟩ ↑&↓ of ⟨all⟩ the . . . by ⟨the subtle powers of⟩ intellect . . . himself: Yes, & ⟨his⟩from . . . that ⟨seems to⟩ makes

	Page 231
9	of the ⟨civilized⟩ world,
11	solve not so much
13	the ⟨very⟩ insect
21	such ⟨utter⟩ folly.
22–25	property?—⟨Assuredly it is. Let us carefully distinguish between wisdom & folly We are of an animal constitution &⟩ ↑Yes. We↓ . . . supplied, ⟨& indispensably demand continual exertion. This whole matter of⟩ Commerce— . . . of ⟨it,⟩ ↑them↓ ⟨and it needs, & it is good, that⟩ every . . . part, ⟨and⟩ one
28	were ⟨the ultimate end;⟩ just
31	perceived⟨,⟩: they
36–38	reflects, is . . . ↑The ox . . . consider↓ [in pencil]

	Page 232
4	man ⟨becomes⟩ perceives

21	if ⟨he⟩ ↑it↓
23	water ⟨into the atmosphere⟩ that
38–39	past, ⟨record⟩ ↑report↓ . . . rational ⟨men⟩spirits

Page 233

1	different ⟨from every⟩ for
2	↑Newton, Grotius, Jefferson Franklin↓
5–6	alone? ⟨Does not⟩ Jesus live↑s as↓ for him only? ⟨Does not⟩ God exist↑s↓ for him only? and Right & Wrong, & Wisdom & Folly? the
8–9	child? ¶ ⟨And this⟩ ↑The↓ perfect world exists ⟨thus entire⟩ to
10–11	his ⟨wonderful⟩ endowments.
12–20	philosophy. ↑{↓The . . . Sharpen ⟨the insight of⟩ these . . . Clarendon.↑}↓ [brackets in pencil]
21	¶ 2. Thus ⟨in the first place⟩ is ↑each↓ man placed ⟨as in the focus—as⟩ at
22	is ⟨merely⟩ to
22–26	He is ⟨an active being &⟩ is not . . . in ⟨panorama⟩ ↑review↓, [addition and last cancellation in pencil] . . . results ⟨to the last jot & tittle⟩ in
29–30	which ⟨not⟩ an act ⟨is⟩ done . . . being ⟨but⟩ draws after it its ⟨e⟩inevitable
31–(234)4	only ⟨acti⟩ by . . . action. ⟨He is to learn that⟩ the Creation . . . himself; ⟨that⟩ an . . . his ⟨whole⟩ being, which ⟨forever⟩ defends . . . resist; ⟨that⟩ the . . . hand, ⟨that⟩ every act of his, is⟨, not hereafter but⟩ instantaneously judged & rewarded: ⟨that⟩ the . . . retribution; ⟨that⟩ every . . . is, ⟨to its full amount,⟩ compensated . . . soul; ⟨that⟩ his . . . suicide & ⟨is never⟩ ↑destroys↓ belie⟨ved⟩f;

Page 234

6–7	seems ⟨(as some have maintained)⟩ that . . . spirits & ⟨that⟩ he . . . labor ⟨to make unceasingly⟩ to
11–14	with the ⟨mighty⟩ secret . . . which ⟨indeed⟩ he . . . will⟨, a total sacrifice,⟩ that
21–22	the ⟨very⟩ sinews . . . order [end of line] out
23	↑trait↓
40	obligations. ⟨t⟩This

Page 235

18	action he he has
20–21	Wisdom & ⟨l⟩Love
22	all ⟨is⟩will be,

Sermon CLXX

Manuscript: Nine sheets folded to make four pages each; pages measure 20.1 x 12.5 cm. The seventh folio is followed by two leaves measuring, respectively, 20 x 12.4 cm and 20.1 x 12.5 cm. The folios are sewn along the left margin with black thread.

Lines   *Page 236*

3   ↑one↓

6   good ⟨a⟩definition

8–10   ↑You . . . congra↑tu↓lation↓ . . . of ⟨s⟩ divine

14–16   which ⟨whe⟩ make . . . how⟨ever⟩ different soever may be our
             ⟨ordinary⟩ employments

18–20   those ⟨thoughts &⟩ subjects . . . ↑subjects↓

25–27   Faith ⟨the⟩ when . . . one thing & feel [Emerson failed to complete
             the sentence, leaving off in the middle of the last line on MS p. 3.] ¶ I
             choose

                                   Page 237

6–7   certain & ⟨imminent⟩ ↑terrific↓

9–10   ↑to↓ other men ⟨wait⟩ the ↑heat & cold are tempered by their↓
             gradual changes ⟨of the heat & cold⟩ of

12   the W. Indies

14   planet ↑t↓he ⟨is still⟩ ↑sea↓ shut↑s him↓ up

19–21   work. ↑upon . . . reef↓

22   become ⟨w⟩acquainted

27   life that

29   that ⟨in⟩ when

31   him; But

34–40   all Set . . . above &c ¶ And . . . satisfaction ↑for . . . life.↓ ¶ ⟨An
             affection set on things above is

                 1. an obligation to duty
                 2. a source of contentment
                 3. a ground of union with men
                 4. an immortal good.⟩ ¶ Set

                                   Page 238

12–14   says K. of God is within you ¶ 1 A religious [The numeral "1" seems to
             relate to Emerson's original (and rejected) positioning of his outline
             of topics, and is therefore rejected.]

18   hatred. [following this paragraph is a line across the page]

19   ↑the same as if it sd.↓

24–33   thou? ¶ ⟨Set your affections on things within⟩ [at the bottom of the
             page, set off by a long curved line] ¶ I . . . truths ⟨contained in this
             implied in th⟩ that . . . Apostle ¶ 1. . . . good ¶ The service [omitted
             Roman numeral supplied] . . . mind. w ¶ Here

35   practicable ⟨in⟩ to

38–(239)3   housekeeper & ⟨s⟩ prate . . . of ⟨philanthropy⟩ generosity . . .
             heathen & ⟨save⟩ the reform

                                   Page 239

7–8   ↑Whatsoever . . . Duty.↓ [written over "Its"—a false start of the next
             paragraph]

11–13   end, ⟨is⟩—the end for which ⟨religion⟩ ↑the affection on t. a.↓ was
             . . . removing ⟨the⟩ stumbling . . . helps ⟨A⟩Forevermore

16–21   feel ⟨a⟩the . . . rain. ⟨if his⟩ Well . . . the ⟨sea⟩ ↑waters↓ . . .
         immortal ↑trace↓ . . . them ¶ ⟨The Port Society, good men & God are
         the sailor's friends. But no society can help him much; only himself.⟩
         Man

24   he ⟨feels ⟨if⟩⟩ ↑laments that↓ he has been defeated ⟨it is no great
         matter [end of line] it is no great matter if⟩ the

26   orators ⟨philosophers⟩ great

30–34   Yet ⟨I do not think⟩ whilst . . . ↑overboard↓

35   ↑cold &↓

                              Page 240

2   much ⟨of⟩?

5   shrink ⟨would they open their hearts to the remembrance of God
         who is looking at them all the while⟩ to

8   me⟨e⟩re

14–15   man. ¶ ⟨A true affection⟩ Yes

22–23   toil not &c ¶ Now [It seems probable, though not certain, that
         Emerson would have finished the quotation from the better-known
         version in Matthew ("neither do they spin") rather than from Luke
         ("they spin not").]

27–29   down ⟨though in a bar⟩ though . . . never ⟨one⟩for ⟨m⟩one

31   men though

34   ↑Anger Slander↓

35   ↑& so . . . together↓

36   you ⟨s⟩would ⟨be⟩ have

39–(241)1 alone [end of line] they . . . appearance. [end of page] ⟨different thing
         is done from what we think to do & perhaps they play the most
         important part who seem to do the least. In those calm moments
         when the sky of the soul is no longer overcast, when the clouds
         separate, & God shines in, & trifles disappear we have a vision of his
         sufficiency & of our own insignificance & of the truth that entire
         trust & gratitude is our fittest thought. Then enters the great God
         into the heart of mortal man. Then first is he united to the human
         race⟩ ¶ The

                              Page 241

2–11   to ⟨wor⟩plant . . . ships & ⟨so is hi⟩ many . . . race this . . . him he
         cares not for ⟨him⟩them . . . him he . . . interest also he

13–15   comfort he ⟨j⟩grudges . . . him he is ⟨calculating on⟩ ↑awaiting↓
         . . . ↑else↓ . . . H⟨im⟩e then

20   ¶ ↑Is it not true↓ The moment God enters /the/my/ soul

22   sun ⟨shine⟩ warms

28–30   it is for [end of page; remainder of passage supplied from Psalms
         133:1] ¶ ↑In saying yᵗ ground of union↓ My [Emerson must surely, for
         clarity, have interpolated some phrase into this abbreviated notation;
         "the religious sentiment" is selected from the outline of topics.] . . .
         pray—⟨whilst you⟩ your

32	out ⟨to⟩from
34–35	honor ⟨him⟩the heavens bows to

Page 242

2	I ⟨beseech⟩ entreat
5–6	I say An . . . mind ⟨is in itself⟩ declares
11	life they
17	us ⟨much as the court or common where we played ball or drove hoop do now.⟩ But
22–23	part. ↑{The . . . ever↓
25–26	heaven. ¶ ⟨As you make progress in Virtue you will not think how much you have done, ⟨o⟩ no indeed but how little the best man says Be merciful to me a sinner [Luke 18:13] He ⟨does not think on what he has done who⟩ ↑All that he↓ has done ⟨much⟩ does not ↑lead him to↓ think on what he has done but prepares him to think justly of himself & resolutely of his duties It is a very bad sign to hear a man speak much of what he has done.⟩ ¶ And
29	obscurest ⟨st⟩place
39	short if . . . has ⟨enter⟩ passed

Sermon CLXXI

Manuscript: Six sheets folded to make four pages each; pages measure 24.9 x 20.2 cm. The gathering is sewn along the left margin with white thread.

Lines	Page 244
12–13	↑it is . . . but↓ . . . ↑them↓
15	persons ⟨no more grateful images than sickness or⟩ ↑as disagreeable as↓ a jail. It ⟨is⟩ ↑needs↓
17–19	↑the delivery . . . call &↓ . . . minds.—For ⟨it is as obviously communicated⟩ ↑it . . . opened↓ . . . private ⟨good⟩ behoof, ⟨f⟩but

	Page 245
8–10	for ⟨regulating⟩ preserving . . . is ⟨more⟩ ↑as much↓ . . . office, ⟨than⟩ ↑as↓
12–13	better ⟨have⟩ ↑eat↓ . . . than ⟨that⟩ ↑suffer↓ the soul ⟨should⟩ ↑to↓
15	wise ⟨& good⟩ man,
18	rendered ⟨us⟩ by
22–32	offices of ⟨priests⟩ the . . . God, ⟨made up⟩ ↑composed↓ . . . Teacher; ⟨in short⟩ of . . . of ⟨God⟩ ↑truth↓ . . . man. ⟨Even more touching because they come more within the reach of our affections⟩ These

	Page 246
3	ask ⟨them⟩ whether . . . charming ⟨to offer⟩ than the ⟨company⟩ sweet
9	of ⟨no particular⟩ ↑different↓

11–15   ↑They characterise the world X X {I speak . . . of in⟨sight⟩ward
         light ↑whose . . . study↓↓ [last addition in pencil] . . . ↑We . . .
         fortune↓
19–20   com↑i↓ng . . . gone that
24–27   the ⟨cle⟩ priesthood . . . clergy. ⟨But⟩ ↑But . . . wants↓ the . . .
         when ⟨the bulk of⟩ the
31–35   ↑↑Then . . . said↓ "Once" ⟨said an ancient church⟩ "once . . . golden
         priests, ⟨but⟩ now . . . wooden priests."↓
37–40   people. ⟨It is obvious to all men how great a revolution⟩ has ⟨been
         going on in the character of the clergy & their relation to the laity
         during the last century in Europe & in America⟩ ↑According . . .
         centuries The . . . adulterated with↓ ⟨T⟩the

                              Page 247
2   always ⟨b⟩ inclines
4   broke ⟨up⟩ ↑in pieces↓
12–15   ↑the blood . . . skirts↓ . . . ↑spiritual↓ captain. ↑Men . . . race↓
17–20   of men. Men . . . inquire ⟨for⟩ each . . . the ⟨universe⟩ joy
25   now ⟨offers⟩ solicits
27   drops ⟨entirely⟩ all
28   him ⟨a⟩ ↑/any/the least/↓ [cancellation and variants in pencil]
30   men [end of line] as
32   parts. ⟨The⟩ It
37   upon ⟨untruth⟩ a false
40   to the office⟨r⟩ &

                              Page 248
2–4   thought & ⟨of⟩ the . . . imparts ¶ ⟨Now t⟩The
4   as ⟨certain⟩ sure
5   ounce, ⟨of⟩let it be high, or
18   principles ⟨of⟩ in
23   to ⟨humble⟩ ↑subdue↓
25–28   find ⟨in⟩ that . . . than all [end of page] all tongues
31–33   but ⟨noble⟩ invigorating . . . what⟨e⟩soever . . . valuable. ⟨It opens
         the door to unlimited improvement for⟩ ↑If . . . respect↓

                              Page 249
3   circumstances ⟨which⟩ into
4   ↑as . . . it,↓
10   ↑that he assumed it↓
11   of ⟨worldly⟩ wealth
23   friendly /man/spirit/
28   the ⟨manliness &⟩ independence
32–34   scholar & ⟨preserved amidst his⟩ used the ⟨op⟩leisure . . . ↑best↓
         popular ⟨literature⟨s⟩⟩ ↑books↓

                              Page 250
4–5   ↑heightened his interest in ⟨his⟩the . . . time↓
9   patience, of ⟨compassion,⟩ kindness,

10	the ⟨dignity⟩ power
13	be ⟨the⟩ restraints
14	all ⟨who⟩ on
20	us ⟨&⟩ as
21–22	church if ⟨we⟩ our . . . when ⟨an⟩ old

Occasional Discourses and Sermon Fragments

[Sermon Fragment]

Manuscript: Two loose leaves followed by a sheet folded to make four pages; pages measure 24.6 x 20.1 cm. Emerson numbered pages 2 through 8 in the upper right (recto) or upper left (verso) corners, the only sermon manuscript thus paginated. It lacks a sermon number and listing of hymns, while the Bible text lacks the usual citation. The MS bears no evidence of having been stitched, and appears not to have been delivered. The manuscript is incomplete, breaking off in the middle of a sentence at the very end of MS p. 8 (in a passage duplicated in the following "Draft Sermon"). The "Draft Sermon" and the "Sermon Fragment" are evidently of much earlier composition than either of the two sermons (LVI and CXXXIII) that Emerson preached on II Corinthians 4:3.

Lines	*Page 253*
Bible Text	[Citation supplied]
6	elements ⟨before⟩ to
8	to ⟨the⟩ all
11–18	lowest↑, namely in barbarous ⟨society⟩ ↑nations↓.↓ The daily toil of [end of page] of the . . . & /maintain/keep/ a ↑good↓ . . . ↑the surrender . . . govern^t,↓ . . . ↑done with a view↓ . . . of the ⟨original⟩ ↑gradual↓ formation of th⟨is⟩at
21–22	this is is a . . . to ⟨tho⟩ civilized men seems ↑almost↓ worthless. And the ⟨enh⟩ great⟨er⟩ &

	Page 254
4	our ⟨certaint⟩ convictions
7–16	& li⟨f⟩ves of a hosts of good men . . . prosper. ²{But in . . . great sacrifices,} and ¹{we shall . . . & toil.} ¶ The . . . rests ⟨its⟩the
18–23	us ⟨in⟩ ↑with↓ . . . procured ⟨by⟩ but
30	perished ⟨here⟩ among
38	forfeiture ⟨a⟩of

	Page 255
18–22	his ⟨s⟩Son . . . iniquity ⟨in⟩ ↑that may deface↓
26	these ⟨perverse⟩ traditionary
32	↑the mass of society↓

[Draft Sermon on the Evidences of Christianity]

Manuscript: A single leaf followed by three leaves pasted together along the left margin, followed by a folio with a leaf pasted along the margin of the last page, followed by a folio with a leaf pasted along the margin of the first page; pages measure 24.6 x 20.1 cm.

At the top of MS p. 1 is the following inscription in the hand of James Elliot Cabot: "This paper was found among Mr Emerson's Sermons. I do not know upon what occasion it was read. Perhaps the Thursday Lecture?" In fact, it appears to be an early sermon, very probably a revision of the "Sermon Fragment" above, never delivered. Emerson has rearranged sections of the sermon by placing letters "A" through "L" at the beginnings of paragraphs. The original sequence of inscription is as follows:

A. "The freedom . . ." (page 256, line 1)
B. "But in the Providence . . ." (page 256, line 21)
C. "It is with reason . . ." (page 256, line 28)
J. "The authority . . ." (page 259, line 31)
K. "The objections . . ." (three paragraphs, the last canceled; page 259, line 42)
G. "There are also . . ." (two paragraphs; page 258, line 31)
H. "Such was the doctrine . . ." (two paragraphs; page 259, line 13)
I. "But we cannot attempt . . ." (page 259, line 27)
L. "It is a defensible . . ." (page 261, line 9)
D. "And what are the pretensions . . ." (two paragraphs; page 256, line 32)
E. "There is an objection . . ." (page 257, line 29)
F. "We think the objection . . ." (two paragraphs; page 258, line 1)

Lines	Page 256
19–20	path ⟨on⟩in . . . ↑solemnly↓
24–26	felt ⟨how burdensome⟩ with . . . be⟨e⟩tween
33	votaries ⟨the⟩ all

	Page 257
3	each pre⟨f⟩ser⟨r⟩ved
9	nature of the ↑other↓
13–15	of ⟨lo⟩God . . . perfect, ⟨but⟩it . . . man it
25	faith ⟨Th⟩both
32–34	denied the . . . eccles. hist. that . . . doctrines wh. J. C. came
35–36	↑a revolut. in mens ms. took place↓
41–42	such contrad. ⟨rea⟩ lights?

	Page 258
1	of ⟨C⟩Xns on
4	that fut. happ. & mis. depended
10–12	superstit. mind . . . of the[ir] Teacher [portion of word obscured by glue; the inscription may actually be "the"]
12–14	habit of hum. mind . . . the nat. of association with a contin[ual] effort [ending of word obscured by glue]
20–21	the corrup. of . . . the circum. that
25–26	minds contin. operates . . . this div. revelation.
28–29	false opin. of men like ↑casting off↓ . . . hum prej.
31	¶ ↑There . . . in evid.↓
33	↑been↓
41	beget ⟨obedience⟩ conviction

	Page 259
9	the ⟨condition⟩ existence
11	↑the uses of affliction↓

17	empire, the Rom Emp was
25	an evid. of . . . the ⟨c⟩bloody
28–29	only ⟨e⟩testimony . . . internal evid. is
34	↑reason &↓
35	downfal

Page 260

1	historical ⟨d⟩speculators
5	↑men or↓

Page 261

2	↑great↓
8	eternal. ¶ ⟨The remarks wh. naturally suggest themselves to me at this time, & which it is proposed to arrange are brief notices of this internal evidence drawn from the wants it was proposed to supply & the manner in which it has supplied them.⟩ [end of section labeled "K"]
12	transmit. ↑it;↓ It
13	"J. C. died
15	to hum. belief a practical ⟨belief⟩ religion

"Right Hand of Fellowship"

Manuscript: Three sheets folded to make four pages each; three folios nested and sewn through the center fold with light brown thread; pages measure 24.9 x 20.1 cm.

Right Hand of Fellowship.
at the ordination of Revd H. B Goodwin;
Concord, 1830.

Right Hand of Fellowship—
At Mr Goodwins ordination at Concord

The ancient custom of offering a new pastor the expression of the sympathy of the churches is no unsuitable rite ↑in the ceremonies of Ordination↓ & hath ⟨its⟩ ↑a deep↓ foundation in reason. There is no sympathy so strong as that between ↑the↓ good ⟨men⟩, & no feeling which Christianity ↑has↓ do⟨th⟩ne ⟨so⟩ m⟨uch⟩ore to ⟨create.⟩ foster.

Whilst men are in the darkness wh vice produces, each individual is a sect by himself, each is a self-seeker, with his hands against every man, & every man's hands against him. Each ↑forgetful of all other rights & feelings↓ is straining every nerve to build up his own sordid advantage, yea ⟨building it if it so happen out of the materials⟩ tearing down his neighbours happiness, if need be, to build up his own. ⟨Ea⟩ His eye is blind his ear is deaf to the great ⟨law⟩ ↑harmonies↓ by which God has yoked social & selfish good ⟨Just⟩of his children. Just in proportion as men grow ↑wiser &↓ better their efforts converge to a point. For as *truth is one*, ⟨they⟩ ↑in seeking it, they↓ all aim to conform their actions to one standard. When intelligent men talk together it is remarkable ⟨how many p⟩ ↑how↓ much they think alike, how many positions are taken for granted, that are disputed inch by inch in the conversation of ignorant persons. The more intelligent men are, the more is this unanimity,—as is attested by the ⟨vulgar⟩ ↑common↓ wonder when two ⟨decidedly great⟩ ↑minds of unquest sup.↓ minds ⟨differ⟩ ↑come to opp. con.↓. [emendations in this sentence in pencil] As it is with the mind so it is with the heart. As ⟨both⟩ ↑two↓ minds agreeing with truth do mutually agree, so if their affections are right with God, they are square with each other.

Christianity claims to teach the perfection of human nature & eminently therefore does it teach the unity of the Spirit. It is not only in its peculiar injunctions but by all its operation—⟨it is⟩ [canceled in pencil] a law of love. It does by its revelation of God & the true purpose & true action of life—⟨accomplish its end of⟩ ↑operate↓ binding up of ⟨soldering⟩ together & not ↑to↓ distinguishing & sep⟨e⟩arating. It proclaimed peace, ⟨& wd. sheath the sword of selfish passion⟩ [canceled in pencil] But it speaks first to its own disciples. Be of one mind Else with what countenance shd the church say to the world ↑of men,↓ Love one another.

And thousands & thousands of hearts have heard the commandment & anon with joy received it. All men on who⟨m⟩se souls the light of Gods revelation shineth ↑under whatever apparent differences↓ [in pencil] are of one mind, work together, whether consciously or not for ⟨on⟨ce⟩e⟩ one & the same good. Faces that never beheld each other are lighted by it with the same expression. Hands that were never clasped toil unceasingly at the same work. This it is which makes the omnipotence of truth in the keeping of feeble men—this fellowship in all its servants ⟨Though each gives but a mite it is all thrown in the same heap.⟩ [canceled in pencil] Gods truth! it is that electric spark which flies instantaneously thro countless hands that make the chain, & not like ↑each form of↓ [in pencil] error depending ↑for its repute↓ [in pencil] on the powers of here & there a solitary mind ↑that espouses it↓ [in pencil] combines hosts for its support ↑& makes them cooperate↓ across mountains & oceans yea & ages of time.

This is what was meant in that beautiful sentiment of the ancient Stoics, that God ha⟨s⟩d so intimately linked all wise men to each other that if one should only lift his finger in Rome all the rest were benefitted by it tho' in Egypt, or Asia. This that one body in Christ of which all men are ↑the↓ members.

↑Sir↓ It is this sentiment, which is recognized in the ancient & simple rite of the churches. God has bound heart to heart by invisible & ⟨indissoluble connexions.⟩ ↑eternal bands,↓ by oneness of nature, of duty, & of hope. To us, is one Lord, one faith, one baptism. And in acknowledgment of these divine connexions, existing between us, *the Christian Churches, whose organ I am, do offer you, my brother, this right hand of their fellowship.* They greet you by me, to the exalted relations on which now you are entering; they give you a solemn welcome to great duties, to honourable sacrifices↑,↓ [in pencil] to ⟨endless⟩ ↑unremitting↓ studies↑,↓ [in pencil] & to the eternal hope of all souls. They exhort you to all pious resolutions; and they pledge to you by this sign their sympathy, their aid, & their intercession. They say to you that so long as in purity of heart you do the work ⟨of God⟩ ↑to which you are set↓ in this vineyard of ⟨his⟩ ↑the Lord↓, you are not alone, but you shall be secure of the love & the furtherance of all righteous men In every hour of perplexity or suffering they shall ↑encourage &↓ aid ↑& bless↓ you by desire, & by word, & by action. ↑And when the day of success comes to you & you see around you in this garden of the Lord the fruit of yʳ virtues & the light of yʳ example & the truth you teach shine forth together—in that day a kindred joy shall touch our hearts We shall be glad ⟨for⟩ ↑with↓ you & give thanks with you & hope for you↓

Sir it is with sincere pleasure that I speak for the Churches on this occasion & on this spot hallowed to all by so many patriotic & to me by so many affectionate recollections. I feel a peculiar right to welcome you hither to the home & the ⟨church⟩ ↑temple↓ of my fathers. I believe the church, whose pastor you are, will forgive me the allusion, if I express the ↑extreme↓ interest ↑which↓ every man feels in the scene of the trials & labours of his ancestors. F⟨our⟩ive out of seven of your predecessors ⟨have been my relations⟩ ↑are my↓ kindred. They are in the dust who bind my attachment to this place—but not all. I cannot help congratulating you that one survives, to be your friend & counsellor as he has ⟨mine⟩ been mine. I heartily rejoice to see their labours ↑& a portion of his↓ resting on one who comes with such ability & as I trust with such devout feeling to the work. Suffer me then, as for them, to offer you my hand, ⟨& to⟩ ↑and↓ receive with it↑, my brother↓ [adddition in pencil] my best wishes & prayers for your success in your great undertaking, & for your everlasting welfare.

[Preliminary Notes for Sermon LXXXIV]

Manuscript: One sheet folded to make four pages; pages measure 25 x 20.2 cm.

Lines	Page 265
6	that ⟨a n⟩ an
17–18	his ⟨observations⟩ ↑speculations↓
22	what [t]hey [MS torn]
24	none t⟨o⟩hat

	Page 266
2	intends ⟨means⟩ by
4	by ⟨k⟩his
7	↑of tho't↓
10	↑human↓
15–16	sideways ⟨P⟩How
29	of ⟨the⟩ facts.

"Address at the Dedication of Second Church Vestry Feb. 28, 1831."

Manuscript: Five sheets folded to make four pages each; pages measure 25 x 20.1 cm. The lower right-hand corner of the last folio leaf is torn away without loss of text. Sewn along the left margin with white thread.

[The title is underlined in the MS.]

Lines	Page 267
1	companions sake,
6–10	shall ⟨stand⟩ ↑endure↓; . . . earth ⟨from⟩ ↑on↓
13–18	then ⟨proposed⟩ ↑on . . . voted↓ . . . ↑for this purpose,↓ [in ink over pencil] & ⟨after⟩ ↑it . . . after↓ [emendation in ink over pencil] . . . Vestry, ⟨to⟩ ↑the . . . would↓ [emendation in ink over pencil]
19	this ⟨la⟩ offer
23–26	will ⟨yet⟩ continue . . . purpose↑,↓ in a ⟨clear⟩ ↑full↓ [comma and emendation in pencil] . . . be ⟨cheerfully⟩ given [cancellation in pencil; "given . . . inconvenience." in ink over pencil, save that the comma is in ink only]
27–28	those ⟨simple⟩ epochs

Page 268

3	night↑?↓ [addition in ink over pencil]
3–4	the ⟨kindred⟩ former . . . Vestry↑?↓ [addition in ink over pencil]
5–13	order↑—↓not [addition in pencil] ⟨to⟩ ↑a↓ concert ↑of↓ . . . political ⟨partisans⟩ ↑agents↓ . . . party; ⟨it⟩not a meeting to arrange ⟨a company for⟩ [canceled in pencil and ink] speculations in trade: ↑tis↓ . . . hospital↑;↓ No↑;↓ [added punctuation in pencil] . . . came, ⟨&⟩and . . . it ⟨& to ask what he really means we should think & do⟩ &
21	God↑,↓ at least *in words*↑,↓ [commas in pencil; underscoring in pencil and ink]
24	in ⟨the⟩ every just ⟨thot⟩ conception
27	his ⟨country⟩ ↑city↓ [emendation in ink over pencil]
32–35	eye—in [end of line] ↑in↓closed . . . mind, ⟨not to be demolished by mortal⟩ which . . . ↑the *goods* of↓

Page 269

3	a ⟨man⟩ creature
6–7	we ⟨are⟩ have, . . . we ⟨dedicate⟩ have
8	us, ⟨W⟩for
12–13	explanation ⟨of the sense⟩ of . . . its ⟨i⟩text
13	to ⟨conduct the⟩ aid
14	↑I know↓ This
18–21	↑we hold↓ . . . into ⟨or imposing⟩ any compact of opinion ⟨upon⟩ ↑with↓ his brethren ↑or . . . them↓.
30	assembl⟨y⟩↑ing↓,
32–33	↑form↓ correct ⟨our⟩ opinions . . . to ⟨right⟩ ↑correct↓
34	↑be↓ arm↑ed↓ ⟨our⟩ with
36–(270)2	gives ⟨superiority⟩ authority . . . & acrimony [these two words circled in pencil]

Page 270

7–9	three ⟨purposes⟩ things, . . . duty ⟨for⟩ which
10	↑with the↓
22	afraid ⟨when⟩ of
23	↑I see in God↓
29	this ⟨room⟩ hall.
30–31	sensualist, ⟨There was⟩ ↑he saw↓ no beauty in the flowers, ⟨to h⟩
35	men ⟨to whom⟩ ↑in whose eyes↓ [emendation in ink over pencil]

Page 271

3–5	world. ⟨The house of⟩ I . . . places. ⟨The⟩A . . . ↑in my eyes↓ than ⟨the splendour⟩ ↑many conveniences↓
8	Athens ⟨& of France⟩ they
10–11	↑In . . . seen↓
13	& ⟨the⟩ plants their law, & ⟨the⟩ stones
15	of ⟨r⟩Revelation,
19	from ⟨us be a single⟩ this

Second Discourse on the Death of George Sampson

Lines	Page 275
37	Yes, [The editors have conjecturally emended the copy-text, which has "Yet,".]

[Thanksgiving Sermon: Fragment]

Manuscript: One sheet folded to make four pages; folio pages measure 24.6 x 20.1 cm. The single list of hymns on MS p. 1 is headed "N.Y.C."

Lines	Page 281
5	business, ⟨to suspend the routine of common duties⟩ &
6–9	the ⟨pleasant⟩ duty [canceled in pencil] . . . to ⟨cease from magnifying⟩ ↑cover up↓ . . . ↑count our pleasures,↓ . . . sympathize (⟨if⟩ I

Lines	Page 282
3–4	of ⟨consanguinity⟩ ↑kindred↓ . . . brightened, & ⟨the strength of the whole⟩ new
7–8	the ⟨family⟩ ↑domestic↓ . . . recollection of ↑all↓
10	all pervading
14	by th⟨e⟩is /light of this day/ anniversary/ [emendation and variant in pencil]
16	house of ⟨prayer⟩ God.
16–17	the ⟨f⟩Father
29	herbs & ⟨balsams &⟩ drugs

[Thanksgiving Sermon: Introduction]

Manuscript: A single leaf measuring 25.2 x 20.5 cm.

Lines	Page 283
3	feelings. ⟨It is⟩ The
8	enumeration of of Gods
12	order a [end of page] some of
13	social ⟨fellowship⟩ ↑joy↓

[Sermon Fragment]

Manuscript: A single leaf measuring 24.9 x 20.2 cm.

Lines	Page 284
1	any on[e] sect [MS torn]
4	↑punctual↓

Appendix B

The following variants appear in Butts's broadside printing:

[Title] Rev. Mr Emerson's Letter to the Second Church and Society.

["Letter." at the head of the second leaf recto of the pamphlet is omitted as redundant on a broadside printed on recto only.]

Line   *Page 305*
3   cannot
20   above all if
28   if, in this manner,

CUMULATIVE INDEX TO VOLUMES 1-4

A

Abernethy, John: *Physiological Lectures,* 4:124n6; quoted, 4:117
Abraham, 2:219n4, 264; 3:175, 218; 4:60, 161, 162, 163
Abstinence, 2:154
Achan, 2:164n2
Actions, 2:19, 20, 120, 128, 153, 186, 189, 217-18, 220-21, 230, 241, 245, 247, 251-54; 4:205-7; motives for, 3:265-69. *See also* Principles
Adam, 1:193, 299; 2:76; 4:157, 161, 163, 178, 207, 246
Addison, Joseph, 3:246
Admiration, 4:28-29, 234
Aesop, 4:24n5
Affection, 2:193; and reason, 2:49; for Christ, 2:118-19, 120
Affections, 1:220-23, 244, 272-77, 288-89; 2:20, 21, 23, 76, 98-99, 110, 166-70, 187, 193, 200, 203, 215, 235, 247; development of, 2:157; in children, 2:173
Africa, 3:48; 4:27
Afterlife, 1:61, 69, 72, 99, 117-18, 126, 132, 138-39, 140, 268-71, 285-87, 309-11; 2:19, 176-80, 181, 183, 188; 3:14-15, 21, 27-28, 33-34, 74, 98, 102-4, 149, 192-94, 195-96, 214, 217-20. *See also* Heaven; Immortality
Aeschylus, 3:235n4
Agesilaus, 1:201
Ahlstrom, Sydney, 1:30
Aiken, John, 4:104n2
Alcibiades, 1:143; 4:230n5
Alcott, Amos Bronson, 4:221n, 226n11
Alden, Timothy, 1:103
Alexander the Great, 3:60; 4:37
Alfred, 2:29
Algiers, 3:43, 48
Ambition, 1:66-67, 76, 160; 2:39, 41, 44, 127, 198
America, 4:211, 259; God's feeling for, 2:212; duties of, 2:213-15; and religious liberty, 2:215; as Zion, 2:215
American Indian. *See* Native Americans
American Revolution, leaders of, 2:213
American Sunday School Union, 2:95n7; 4:80n4

American Temperance Society, 4:80n4
American Unitarian Association, 1:5, 12; 4:292. *See also* Unitarianism
Amherst (Massachusetts), 4:42n2
Amsdorff, Nicholas von, 2:48
Ananias, 3:125
Anniversary Sermon, Second Church, Boston (LXIX), 2:156-61
Antinomianism, 1:25; 2:148
Antipater, 3:230; 4:97
Antonines, 4:174
Apollos, 4:159
Aquinas, St. Thomas, 1:282n6
Arabian proverb, 4:238
Archimedes, 4:155
Arethusa, 2:79n3
Arianism, 2:187-88
Aristides, 1:282; 4:149, 222
Aristocracy, 3:43
Aristotle, 1:84n17, 276n3; 4:125n7; quoted, 1:85; 4:51
Arius, 2:187n3
Asia, 3:57, 68; 4:27, 42, 62, 155, 259, 263
Assyria, 4:38
Astronomy, 2:29, 140; 4:153-59
Atheism, 1:105, 204, 205; 2:63, 87, 90; 3:129-30, 178. *See also* Skepticism
Atlantic Ocean, 4:240
Atonement, 2:187; 4:215
Attila, 3:250; 4:38
Augusta (Georgia), 4:289
Augustine, Archbishop of Canterbury, 3:238
Augustine, Saint, 1:143n7, 153; 3:89; quoted, 4:230
"Aurem Pythagoreum Carmen," 1:163n3
Authority, 4:60-62
Avarice, 2:37, 44, 145, 198; as perversion of duty, 2:39

B

Baal, 2:138; 3:252
Bacchus, 2:145
Bacon, Sir Francis, 3:66, 123, 142; 4:233; *The Advancement of Learning,* 1:84n16, 163n3, 276-77n3, 280n2; 3:263; quoted, 4:133; "Apophthegms New and Old," 3:172n5, quoted, 3:60; "Colors of Good

and Evil," 1:163n3; De Augmentis Scientiarum, 3:225n8; "Of Death," quoted, 3:30; "Of Fortune," quoted, 3:171; "Of Friendship," quoted, 2:67; "Of Great Place," quoted, 1:58; "Of Love," 4:119n13; "Of Marriage and Single Life," quoted, 1:64; Novum Organum, quoted, 3:149; "Of Simulation and Dissimulation," 3:261n2

Bailey, Samuel: Essays on the Formation and Publication of Opinions, quoted, 4:57, 107-8

Baltic, 4:241

Bancroft, George, 3:55n9

Bank of the United States, 4:217n23

Bankruptcy laws, 4:80

Baptism, 1:238; 2:148

Baptists, 3:129

Barbauld, Anna Letitia, 3:231, 246; 4:104n2

Barbauld, Rochemont, 3:231n7

Bardesanes: Dialogue of Destiny, 3:38n18

Barish, Evelyn, 1:9

Barrett, Samuel, 1:21

Bartol, Cyrus A., 4:185

Bay Psalm Book, 3:246n3

Beauty, 1:298-99; and spiritual nature of man, 2:146

Beecher, Lyman, 1:5; "The Faith Once Delivered to the Saints," 1:5

Belief, 3:255

Belknap, Jeremy, 3:244n, 246, 248

Bell, Andrew, 3:231

Beneficence, 2:133-34, 153, 197, 201, 207-8, 223

Benevolence, 2:31, 34, 116, 133-36, 150, 168, 169, 183, 184, 187, 193, 196, 209, 210, 249, 259, 266; 4:82, 107

Benevolent Fraternity of Christian Churches for the Support of the Ministry at Large, 4:278

Benhadad, 1:176

Bernard of Clairvaux, 1:105; quoted, 4:55

Bessus of Poeonia, 1:194

Bethlehem, 4:39, 62

Bethune, John E. D.: Lives of Eminent Persons, quoted, 4:118nn8-9

Bias, King of Priene, 4:162, 268

Biber, Edward, 3:222n4, 229n2, 230n4; quoted, 4:97, 99-101

Bible: Emerson's views of, 1:30-31, 150; 2:19, 187-88, 201; 3:17, 92, 185-86, 225, 246, 257; 4:159, 207, 242

Bible societies, 4:214

Black Hawk War, 3:141; 4:115n11

Bliss, Daniel, 4:264n8

Body, versus spirit, 2:144-50

Bonaparte, Napoleon, 1:227; 2:39, 267; 3:250; 4:30, 151

Book of Common Prayer, 2:24

Books, 3:184-88, 197, 227, 229

Boston, 3:46-47; 4:42n2

Boston Female Asylum, 3:226n

Boston Port Society, 4:226

Boston Prison Discipline Society, 2:68n3; 4:80n4

Boswell, James, 1:282n5; 4:149n4

Brahma, 2:138

Brown, Thomas, 1:59n9

Browne, Sir Thomas, 1:84n17; 2:30n1; Hydrotaphia, 3:69n; Pseudodoxia Epidemica, 4:111n3; Religio Medici, quoted, 4:34

Bryant, William Cullen, 1:94n1

Buckingham. See Villiers, George

Buckminster, Joseph Stevens, 1:4, 8

Buell, Lawrence, 1:22

Bulkeley, Edward, 4:264n8

Bulkeley, Peter, 4:264n8

Bunyan, John, 1:169; 4:245n6

Burke, Edmund, 1:281n3; 2:168; 4:180n3; quoted, 1:88, 164; 2:120, 243

Butler, Joseph, 1:24, 283n9; 3:222n2; quoted, 2:151, 363

Byron, Admiral John, 2:93, 222

Byron, George Gordon, Lord, 2:169n12; Childe Harold's Pilgrimage, 4:227n13; Don Juan, quoted, 4:104, 229

C

Cabot, James Elliot, 1:16

Cadmus, 1:286

Caecus, Appius Claudius, 1:156

Caesar, 1:218, 227; 2:267; 4:38

Caiaphas, 2:120

Cain, 1:82

Callings. See Vocations

Calumny, 1:185-90, 295; 2:155, 164

Calvin, John, 1:105, 153; 2:19, 20; 3:26, 99; 4:185

Calvinism, 1:3-5, 24, 26, 154; 2:19, 186, 189, 248; 3:127, 246; 4:55n1, 198; Channing on, 1:6

Cameron, Kenneth W., 1:151n4; 2:216, 235n5, 238n1; 4:178n, 241n12, 244n, 249n14, 267n2, 272n

Cape Verde islands, 4:292

Capernaum, 4:188

Capital punishment, 4:79

Cappe, Catherine, 4:80n4

Carlyle, Thomas, 3:220n15; translation of Novalis in "Characteristics," quoted, 4:86, 225; "Signs of the Times," quoted, 4:163; translation of Goethe's Wilhelm Meister's Apprenticeship, quoted, 4:196n5, 197n6

Castelli, Benedetto, quoted, 4:118

Castlereagh, Robert Stewart, 2:128n8

Catholic Church, 1:149-50, 152; 2:248; 3:35, 37, 63, 127, 165, 188; 4:185, 189

Cato, 2:32; 4:222
Cephas. *See* Peter
Change, 1:93–97; 296–300; fear of,
2:127–28; moral world immune from,
1:97–99, 261–62; human nature immune
from, 1:169, 172. *See also* Time
Channing, William Ellery, 1:4, 6–9, 19, 21,
24; 2:186, 213*n1*, 243*n2*, 247*n2*, 263;
tutors Emerson, 1:8–9; "The Demands
of the Age on the Minister," 1:19; "Evidences of Christianity," 1:9; *Evidences of
Revealed Religion*, 1:9; "Unitarian Christianity," 1:4, 5
Character, 2:216; 3:94, 103, 109–10, 131,
149, 188, 212, 226, 233, 262–64; improvement of, 2:119, 125, 128, 153, 165, 227;
4:25–26, 39, 247–49; standard of, 2:266;
unity of, 3:264, 265. *See also* Genuine
Man; Sampson, George Adams
Charity, 1:160, 180, 301–6; 2:90–91, 116,
178, 183, 196–200, 206, 209–11, 222, 239;
3:86–87, 89, 156, 196, 226, 229; 4:94,
148–52, 225–26, 278–79
Charlemagne, 4:38
Charles I, King of England, 3:139
Charles X, King of France, 4:149*n3*
Chemistry, 4:83–84
Cherokees, 3:47
Chesterfield, Lord. *See* Stanhope, Philip
Dormer
Children, conscience of, 2:173; education
of, 2:28–29, 172–74; 4:96–102; virtues of,
2:171–75
Chilo (Chilon), quoted, 2:41
China, 4:237
Christian Examiner, 3:244*n*
Christianity, 2:122, 192, 206, 209, 223,
238, 244, 254, 256; 3:99; 4:162, 172,
268; divisions within, 2:19–20, 186–91;
and Jewish Law, 2:56, 58; and paganism, 2:57, 58, 119; teachings of, 2:82,
90, 263; 4:151, 195; excellence of, 2:111,
123; coincident with morals, 2:152–53;
3:64–67, 118, 180, 251; and social code,
2:196; influence of, 3:63–64, 66, 184;
truth of, 3:186–87; 4:40–41, 170, 212,
262–64; early history of, 3:238–39, 240;
4:246–47; progress of, 3:239–40; 4:40–
41; consists in keeping the commandments, 3:249–53; perversions of the truth
of, 4:39–40; sects of, 4:159; evidences
of, 4:253–61
Christian life, 3:152–57; defined, 1:175–
76
Christmas sermon: XIII, 1:141–48; LX,
2:108–11; CXXXVIII, 4:37–41
Church, as temple of God, 2:252
Church of England, 4:185
Cicero, 3:165*n10*, 221*n1*; 4:122*n1*, 162*n6*

Circumcision, 3:251
Civil unrest, 4:42
Civilization, 2:25, 234; 4:254; good of,
2:93–94
Clarendon, Edward Hyde, first Earl of,
4:233
Clarke, James Freeman, 1:16, 17
Clarkson, Thomas: *A Portraiture of
Quakerism*, 4:185*n*, 185–89*nn1–18*
Clay, Henry, 4:110*n*
Clement, Saint, 3:186
Cleobulus, quoted, 2:41
Cole, Phyllis, 1:3
Coleridge, Samuel Taylor, 1:27, 30, 285*n1*;
3:33*n5*; *Aids to Reflection*, 2:126*n3*,
228*n3*; 3:217*nn7–8*; *Biographia Literaria*,
quoted, 2:95; *The Friend*, 2:183*n5*, 349,
360; 3:224*n6*, quoted, 3:83, 85*n2*; 4:68*n2*,
125*n7*; *The Statesman's Manual*, 3:190*n3*,
quoted, 3:139
Collins, Anthony, 4:32
Columbus, Christopher, 2:27, 109, 233*n2*;
4:233, 266
Commandments, 2:55, 124, 159, 164, 165,
169, 171, 180, 201, 203, 204–5, 221, 241,
254, 262, 266; obedience to, 2:40, 47,
249; 3:249–53; 4:132–33; practice of,
2:120, 123. *See also* Law
Compensation, 1:78–84, 130; 4:233, 254; as
innate retribution, 4:55–59
Confession, 3:128
Confucius, 4:146
Conger, George Perrigo, 1:276*n3*
Conscience, 1:62, 72, 116–17, 159, 175, 177,
180, 191–96, 289, 292; 2:21, 80, 193, 195,
204, 208, 222, 224, 225, 228, 253, 254;
3:64, 77, 205, 234, 257, 268; 4:52, 69–70,
79, 141, 183, 238; as proof of God's
existence, 1:191, 195–96; 4:175; versus
action, 2:45; in children, 2:173
Consolation. *See* Religion
Constitution: of the United States, 3:142,
213; 4:254; of France, 3:213
Consubstantiation, 4:185
Contentment. *See* Tranquility
Conversation, 3:260–62, 263
Cook, Captain James, 2:93
Copernican System, 2:238; 4:157
Corinth, 3:186
Cornelius, 3:251
Cousin, Victor, 3:222*n3*; 4:216*n17*
Covetousness, 3:85
Cowper, William, 3:246
Cromwell, Oliver, 1:227
Crucifixion, 2:106
Cudworth, Ralph, 4:186
Custom, 3:99, 242, 260; defined, 3:239
Cyprian, Saint, 1:118*n10*
Cyrus, 4:38

D

Dante Alighieri, 1:134*n1*

David, 1:114, 136, 275; 2:152; 3:76, 130, 143, 150, 212, 246, 260; 4:23, 49, 138, 143, 161, 195, 242

Davis, Merrell R., 1:27

Davy, Sir Humphry, 4:84*n3*

Death, 1:307–11; 2:30, 35, 112, 128, 129, 177, 179, 190, 193, 210, 240, 241; 3:27, 39, 105, 169; 4:23, 126, 138–39, 203, 217, 221–28; fear of, 2:182–85; 3:29–34, 68–73, 84, 103–5, 205, 214, 215–16, 219; 4:49; preparation for, 2:24, 181, 185; second, 2:135; joy of, 3:117. *See also* Immortality

De Britaine, William, 1:187*n4*, 376; 4:238*n2*

Deception, 2:216–17

Declaration of Independence, 2:215*n3*

Delphi, 4:106*n12*

Demetrius of Phaleria, 1:186–87

Democritus, 4:231

Derby, Elizabeth, 3:232

Dewey, Orville, 4:250*n15*

De Scudery, Georges, quoted, 1:87

Diffusion of Useful Knowledge, associations for, 4:214

Diligence, 1:209–10; 2:178, 187; 4:90

Disease, 4:42, 81, 200

D'Israeli, Isaac, 1:188*n5*

Doddridge, Philip, 1:98*n10*; 3:246

Dominic, Saint, 1:105

Domitian, 4:174

Dorr, Elizabeth, 3:232

Dort (Holland), 1:170

Double consciousness, 4:215

Doubt, 2:239; 3:258. *See also* Skepticism

Dryden, John, 1:129*n4*; "On the Death of a Very Young Gentleman," quoted, 4:97

Dueling, 3:37–38, 242

Duty, 1:252–53; 2:26, 30–32, 34–35, 39, 41–42, 45, 47, 55, 91, 134, 150, 152, 153, 156, 158–60, 167, 183, 188, 196, 199, 204, 206, 209, 224, 228, 231, 233–34, 239, 242, 245, 246, 247, 250, 263, 266; 3:34, 49, 55, 64, 65, 76, 84–91, 94, 96, 98, 105, 112, 123, 129, 140, 148, 151, 153–54, 164–65, 175, 180, 200, 203, 208, 218–19, 226, 236, 237, 239, 253, 264, 267; 4:47, 127, 132, 136–41, 199, 238–39

E

Earth, 4:229, 232–33

Easter, 4:185

Echo, 2:79*n3*

Eclipse, solar, 4:153–59

Economy, political, 2:126*n5*, 133; 4:225; law of, 2:78, 142

Eden, 4:151, 163, 207

Edgeworth, Maria, 3:231

Edgeworth, Richard Lovell, 3:231*n7*

Education, 2:188; 3:226–32; 4:254; of the Will, 3:224; defined, 3:227; Massachusetts State Board of, 4:80*n4*. *See also* Religious education

Edwards, Jonathan, 1:25

Egypt, 4:161, 188, 263

Election, doctrine of, 1:152, 275

Eliot, Samuel A., 4:278*n18*

Elizabeth I, Queen of England, 3:139

Eloquence: defined, 3:262

Elstowe, Friar, 1:252*n3*

Emerson, Charles Chauncy, 1:3, 11; 4:144*n7*, 291

Emerson, Edward Bliss, 1:11

Emerson, Ellen Tucker, 1:10, 12–14, 16, 382; 3:101*n*

Emerson, Lidian. *See* Jackson, Lydia

Emerson, Mary Moody, 1:3, 8, 88*n14*, 110*n5*, 117*n8*, 123*n5*, 294*n7*; 2:20*n5*, 24*n17*, 332, 334; 3:116*n7*, 147*n6*; 4:171*n1*

Emerson, Phebe Bliss, 4:264*n8*

Emerson, Ralph Waldo: resignation from Second Church, 1:2–3, 17–18; pietism of, 1:7–8; keeps school, 1:8, 9; licensed to preach, 1:10; health of, 1:10, 12–13, 17; as supply preacher, 1:10–11; preaching style of, 1:11–12, 16; becomes pastor of Second Church, 1:13–14, 232–33*n4*; relations with Ware, 1:14–15; ministerial duties, 1:15–16; theology of, 1:23–28; and supernaturalism, 1:28–30, 31; first anniversary as pastor of Second Church, 2:156

—Works: "Address on Education," 4:101*n16*; "Ben Jonson, Herrick, Herbert, Wotton," 2:398; 4:104*n3*; Blotting Book Psi, 2:150*n22*; "Chaucer," 3:114*n3*; "Circles," 1:27; 3:139*n6*; "Compensation," 1:78*n*, 79*nn3–5*; 164*n4*; 2:198*n4*, 248*n5*; 4:55*nn4–5*; "Country Life," 4:116*n4*; "Demonology," 4:215*n14*; Divinity School Address, 1:2, 19, 20, 23, 28; 2:149*n18*; 4:57*n13*, 159*n12*, 160*n*; "Doctrine of Hands," 2:126*n5*; "Education," 4:101*n16*; "English Literature: Introductory," 4:144*n8*; *English Traits*, 1:84*n17*, 264*n5*; 3:149*n12*, 261*n3*; "Ethical Writers," 2:90*n2*, 103*n1*; 3:88*n10*; 4:216*n18*; "Ethics," 1:63*n1*, 78*n1*, 163*n3*, 164*n4*, 294*n5*; 2:198*n4*, 220*n5*, 248*n5*, 253*n7*, 398; 3:153*n3*; 4:55*n4*, 57*n13*, 244*n1*; "Experience," 4:193*n22*, 233*n9*; "Fate," 3:41*n5*, 57*n*; "Friendship," 4:51*n8*; "General Views," 1:283*n9*; 2:151*n1*; 3:222*n2*; "Genius," 2:398; "George Fox," 1:247*n4*; 2:235*n8*; "The Heart," 4:133*n9*; "Historic Notes of Life and Letters in New England," 1:110*n5*; 2:186; "Immortality," 1:283*n9*; 2:151*n1*; 3:222*n2*; 4:197*n*; "The

Individual," 1:110*n5;* "Introductory" (Human Culture series), 2:105*n4;* 3:193*n11;* "John Milton," 4:215*n14;* "Literature," 2:398; "Literature" (first lecture), 4:182*n12;* "Lord Bacon," 4:215*n14;* "Manners," 1:264*n11;* "Martin Luther," 2:48*n2;* 4:110–11*n1;* "Mary Moody Emerson," 1:294*n7;* "Milton," 4:215*n14;* "Modern Aspects of Letters," 4:163*n9,* 182*n12;* "The Naturalist," 4:158*n8;* "Natural Religion," 4:174*n7; Nature,* 1:20, 23, 28, 283*n9;* 2:146*n7,* 151*n1,* 201*n,* 206*n,* 235*n5;* 3:37*n15,* 166*n12,* 222*n2,* 242*n9;* 4:144*n8,* 193*n22,* 239*n6;* "Old Age," 2:103*n2;* "Pan," 3:55*n9;* "Plutarch," 2:90*n2;* 3:88*n10;* 4:216*n18;* "The Poet," 1:23; 2:398; 4:242*n14;* "Politics," 1:164*n4,* 247*n4;* 2:162*n1;* "The Preacher," 4:246*n9;* "The Protest," 3:236*n10;* 4:151*n11;* "Prudence," 4:108*n17,* 116*n4;* "Quotation and Originality," 3:114*n3;* "Reforms," 2:42*n4;* "The Relation of Man to the Globe," 2:140*n3;* 4:84*n3;* "Religion," 1:112*n12;* 2:218*n2;* 3:66*n2,* 230*n5;* 4:248*n13; Representative Men,* 1:61*n16;* "The School," 3:55*n9;* "Self-Reliance," 2:398; 3:236*n10;* 4:34*n9,* 151*n11;* "Shakspear" (second lecture), 1:193*n5;* "Society," 1:85*n2;* 2:186*n,* 195*n3;* 4:86*n6;* "The Sovereignty of Ethics," 4:233*n12;* "Spiritual Laws," 1:112*n12,* 294*n5;* 2:218*n2;* 3:153*n3,* 230*n5,* 264*n8;* 4:182*n12,* 244*n1,* 248*n12;* "The Superlative," 2:155*n8;* "Swedenborg," 1:280*n2;* "Trades and Professions," 4:182*n12;* "The Transcendentalist," 2:186*n;* 4:215*n14;* "The Uses of Natural History," 2:140*n3,* 195*n3;* 4:104*n2,* 118*n9,* 124*n6,* 133*n13,* 197*n7;* "Water," 4:24*n4;* "The Young American," 2:38*n7*

Emerson, William (grandfather), 4:264*n8*

Emerson, William (father), 1:8; 3:244*n;* 4:84*n3*

Emerson, William (brother), 1:2, 11, 13; 4:250*n15,* 285

England, 3:85, 139, 238–39; 4:27, 42*nn1–2,* 233, 241. *See also* Great Britain

Envy, 2:198; 3:195, 225; 4:148–52

Epicharmus, 1:80*n7*

Epicurus, 1:63–64, 115, 289*n8;* 4:112, 119*n13*

Erasmus, Desiderius, 1:153; 3:26

Erie Canal, 2:114*n7*

Essenes, 4:111*n2*

Europe, 3:47, 63, 68, 139, 152; 4:27, 30, 42, 62, 77, 209*n,* 211, 259

Eusebius, 3:38*n18*

Evangelical Missionary Society, 1:304, 305; 2:211

Evangelical Treasury, 1:301; 2:206, 210, 211; 3:87*n4;* 4:289, 292

Everett, Edward, 4:261*n9*

Evil, 2:29, 119, 147, 164, 182–83, 187, 193, 199, 200, 203, 204, 209, 210, 217, 218, 239, 241, 245, 253, 264; 3:57–58, 65, 103, 130, 154, 170, 210, 212–13, 230; 4:116, 234; as "merely privative," 4:57*n13,* 174

Example: force of, 1:69, 70–76, 123–24, 171; source of, 2:144; as motive for action, 3:265–69

F

Faith, 2:20, 23, 61, 92, 176, 182, 184, 185, 187, 223, 224, 225, 227, 238, 240, 243, 254; 3:94, 97–100, 108, 118, 129, 186, 190–91, 214, 249, 254–55; and works, 2:46–50; 3:95, 100, 155; 4:35, 90–91; justification by, 3:127; 4:137; defined, 3:191

Fame, 2:123

Fast Day sermon: XVII, 1:167–72; LXX, 2:162–65; CXIII, 3:138–44; CL, 4:110–15

Fasting, 4:111–13

Fate, 3:120; 4:174

Fear, 2:130, 187, 190, 191, 203; 3:51 56, 114, 136, 209, 219. *See also* Death, fear of

Federal Street Church, 4:291

Felix, 2:219; 4:90

Fénelon, Francois de Salignac de La Mothe-, 1:105, 282; 2:20, 210, 229, 264, 400; 3:26, 88, 187; 4:63*n8,* 146

Fichte, Johann Gottlieb, 3:209*n5*

Flattery, 2:155

Fletcher, Andrew, 4:31

Follen, Charles, 4:285

Fontenelle, Bernard le Bovier de, 2:28*n5;* 4:156*n;* quoted 2:195

Forbearance, 3:241–42

Forgiveness, 1:256–59; 3:176

Fortitude, 1:210; 4:91

Foscolo, Ugo, 1:134*n1*

Fourth of July sermon: XLII, 1:312–16; LXXX, 2:212–15

Fox, George, 2:235*n8;* 4:205

France, 3:48; 4:27, 42*n1,* 157, 271; unrest in, 4:149. *See also* French Revolution

Franklin, Benjamin, 1:282; 2:266; 4:43*n4,* 233

Frederic of Prussia, 2:26

Freedom, 2:245, 247; 3:205–9, 216. *See also* Independence

Free will, 2:34, 52, 71–75, 79, 84–85, 120, 178, 261; 3:175. *See also* Liberty

French Revolution, 3:48, 165; 4:150, 211

Friendship, 2:118, 120, 123; 3:77, 226, 262; 4:49–53

Frothingham, N. L., 1:233*n4*

Frothingham, O. B., 1:17; 4:278n18
Fuller, Margaret, 1:16; 4:122n, 171n
Fuller, Thomas: *Gnomologia,* 3:59n3;
    4:116n3, 118n7, 122n1, 139n6
Furies, 4:174
Future, 2:125–26, 204

G

Galen, 4:117
Galileo, 4:118, 156
Gannett, Ezra Stiles, 1:10, 11, 12, 19, 233n4
Gannett, William C., 4:278n18
Garrison, William Lloyd, 4:115n11
Geneva, 4:138
Genius, 2:146–47
Gentleness, 1:260–65
Genuine Man, 4:201–8, 224n5
Geology, 2:140; 3:68
Gerando, Marie Joseph de: *Histoire Com-
    paree des Systemes de Philosophie,*
    3:190n3
German scholars, 4:259–60
Germany, 4:27
Ghosts, 1:267–68
Gibbon, Edward, 4:234n14
Gilbert, Sir Humphrey, 1:252n3
Gilead, 2:240
"Gloria Patri," 4:87n8
God: present in the soul, 1:26–28; 2:21, 24,
    197; 3:111, 125, 175; 4:121, 174–77, 208,
    215, 216, 234, 238, 240, 242; ideas of,
    1:108–11, 130, 143–47, 152, 197, 203–7,
    222–23, 255–56; 2:22, 61–65, 138–40,
    238–39, 241, 242, 243, 256–58, 261;
    4:60–61, 86–88, 268–71; and Nature,
    2:21; benevolence of, 2:22; 3:147–48,
    170; 4:106, 108–9, 116–21, 210; object
    of human concern, 2:138–43, 222, 224,
    237–41; 3:49–50, 116–17, 191–92, 203–4;
    Xenophon's proof of, 2:141; moral char-
    acter of, 2:257–58; 3:81, 129, 177–78;
    4:137; omnipresence of, 3:42–43, 77, 98,
    121, 258; 4:27, 47, 173; replaces self,
    3:44; object of love, 3:51–52, 105, 127,
    130, 135, 137, 180; 4:104, 195, 217; fear
    of, 3:52, 143, 182, 253; 4:60–62; as Par-
    ent, 3:64, 75, 87–88, 90, 104, 107–8;
    4:143, 154, 159, 162, 165, 174–76, 195,
    211, 216, 227, 234, 282; proportions the
    burden to our strength, 3:75–78, 214;
    perfectly wise and good, 3:102, 114, 124,
    178; is infinite, 3:116; 4:94; as Creator,
    3:121, 155, 159, 253; 4:43, 92, 112, 134,
    142–44, 151, 154–59, 162, 174, 178–84,
    201, 204, 207, 215, 219, 248, 281; source
    of truth, 3:122; 4:166–70; trust in, 3:145–
    50, 235; 4:207, 237; unity of, 3:221;
    4:160; is love, 3:243; 4:270; as Reality,
    4:31; likeness to, 4:62, 192; living to,

4:122–28, 135, 152; sufficiency of, 4:129–
    35; omnipotence of, 4:139, 224; eternity
    of, 4:160–65; knowledge of, 4:171–77;
    false views of, 4:172, 174. *See also*
    Spirit, Holy
Godliness, 1:219–24; 4:94
Goethe, Johann Wolfgang von: on St. Philip
    Neri, 2:385–86; *Wilhelm Meister's Ap-
    prenticeship,* quoted, 4:196
Golden Rule, 2:136, 209; 3:84, 240, 242;
    4:49. *See also* Luke 6:31 in the Index of
    Biblical References
Goldsmith, Oliver: "The Deserted Village,"
    quoted, 3:136; "Retaliation: A Poem,"
    quoted, 2:189
Goodwin, Hersey Bradford, 4:122n,
    244–50, 262–64, 290
Government, 2:162–65; 4:114–15
Grace, 2:201, 223; 3:127
Gratitude, 1:135, 138, 151, 294, 313; 2:187;
    4:23–24
Gray, Thomas: "Ode on the Pleasure Aris-
    ing from Vicissitude," 3:46
Great Awakening, 1:3. *See also* Second
    Great Awakening
Great Britain, 3:85. *See also* England
Greece, 4:37, 38
Greeks, 4:174, 245
Greenwood, Francis William Pitt, 1:23;
    3:244n, 248; 4:291–92, 304n
Grief, 4:221
Grotius, Hugo, 4:233
Guilt, 2:125, 187, 258; 3:221
Gymnosophists, 4:111

H

Habit, 1:273; 2:28, 76–81, 85, 98, 100, 107,
    160, 166, 168, 203, 233, 239, 243; 4:75,
    114; evil, 2:120, 190, 262
Hakluyt, Richard, 1:252n3
Haman, 2:261n14
Hancock Sunday School, 2:95, 211; 4:96
Happiness, 1:64–69, 134–35, 138, 154, 280,
    286–90; 2:86, 101, 155, 218, 259–62; of
    New England, 1:168, 283
Hare, Augustus and Julius: *Guesses at
    Truth,* 4:133n10; quoted, 4:29
Harrington, James, 2:166n3
Harvey, William, 4:77
Hastings, James, 2:188n3
Hazlitt, William, 2:235n7
Heaven, 1:287–90; 2:99–101, 180, 184, 193,
    225, 235, 259, 261; 3:24–25, 27–28, 78,
    105, 135, 192–94, 260; 4:54, 133, 143, 199,
    238, 255; defined, 2:99; 3:249. *See also*
    Afterlife; Immortality
Hedge, Frederic Henry, 1:11; 4:286n2, 289
Hell, 1:286; 2:184; 3:192–94; 4:54
Heraclitus, 3:190n3

Herbert, George: "The Elixir," quoted, 3:236; "Sinne," quoted, 2:126
Heroes, interest in, 2:225
Herrick, Robert: "The Rose," 4:116n3
Herschel (planet). *See* Uranus
Herschel, Sir William, 4:155–56n3
Hezekiah, 3:46; 4:282
Higher Criticism, 1:29
Hinduism, 3:64
Hoadly, Benjamin, 4:186
Hobart, Nathaniel: "Life of Swedenborg," 4:205n9
Hobbes, Thomas, 2:30n1; *Behemoth,* quoted, 3:163
Holbrook, Josiah, 2:95n7
Holiness: defined, 3:262
Holland, 4:237
Holmes, Oliver Wendell, 1:9
Holy Ghost, body as temple of, 2:252–55; 4:175
Home, 4:208; pleasures and blessings of, 4:25, 118
Homer, 3:116; *Iliad,* 1:135
Honesty, 2:178, 183
Honor, 4:31–33
Hopkins, John, 3:246n3
Hopkins, Samuel, 1:26; 2:33; 4:127n15
Horace, quoted, 2:258
Howard Benevolent Society, 1:291; 3:84n
Howard, John, 1:227, 282; 4:63
Howe, Daniel Walker, 1:7, 18
Howe, Samuel Gridley, 4:80n4
Humboldt, Baron Alexander von, 2:93
Hume, David, 1:24, 64n2; 2:50; 4:105n6
Humiliation, 4:110, 113
Humility, 1:160, 161–66, 210; 2:90–91, 99, 222–26
Hutcheson, Francis, 1:17; *An Inquiry Into the Original of Our Ideas of Duty and Virtue,* 2:197n2; 3:43n10
Hutchison, William, 1:17
Hymns, 3:245–48; 4:291–92
Hypocrisy, 2:148, 220, 223

I

Idumea, 4:90
Ignatius, of Antioch, 3:110
Ignorance, 1:128, 130, 283
Imagination, 3:255
Imitation, dangers of, 2:73, 264–67
Immortality, 2:19, 23, 74, 88, 90, 145, 147, 176, 178, 193, 255, 263; 3:24, 31–33, 77, 152, 154, 218, 247, 258; 4:46, 65, 120, 134, 195–200, 242, 259, 265. *See also* Afterlife; Heaven
Improvement, 2:25, 28, 38, 40, 228, 230, 232–34, 246, 249. *See also* Man, improvement of
Independence, 1:293, 312–16; 2:127–29, 190, 224; 4:105; and imitation, 2:73

India, 4:38, 42n2, 111
Indians. *See* Native Americans
Individuality, 2:264
Industry, 2:222
Inspiration, 3:119, 121, 123, 129
Intemperance, 2:145
Irish laborers, 4:241
Irving, Washington, 2:233n2; 4:265n, 266n2
Isaac, 3:218; 4:162
Isaiah, 3:140
Ishmael, 1:190
Italy, 4:27, 233

J

Jackson, Andrew, 4:110n, 217n23
Jackson, Lydia (Lidian Jackson Emerson), 1:260n
Jacob, 3:218; 4:162
Jagannath, 1:151n4, 312
James, 1:185, 212; 2:48, 70, 245; 3:82, 109, 215, 221, 223, 233; 4:129, 150
James II, King of England, 3:139
Japan, 4:146
Jealousy, 2:190
Jefferson, Thomas, 2:162n1, 212n, 215nn3–4; 4:233
Jeremiah, 3:140, 142
Jerusalem, 4:158, 187
Jesus Christ, 1:29–30, 86–92, 142–48, 153, 162, 173, 251, 253, 262, 275, 278, 279, 311, 315–16; 2:23, 28, 57–58, 108–11, 141, 169, 185, 222, 247, 253, 255; 3:23, 27, 33–36, 40, 42, 43, 47, 51, 63–67, 70, 71, 72, 73, 76, 78, 79, 82, 84, 88, 94, 99, 101, 102, 103, 104, 108, 114, 120–21, 122, 123, 127, 130, 131, 135, 137, 140, 143, 148, 150, 151–52, 155, 156, 159, 164, 172, 184, 188, 191, 203, 204, 205, 209, 218, 219, 225, 228, 236, 240, 247, 249–50, 252, 263, 264; 4:32, 36, 37, 39, 46, 49, 79, 91, 97–98, 106, 109, 122–23, 126, 129, 134–35, 142, 145, 154, 158, 161, 176–77, 211, 227, 233, 245; and Sermon on the Mount, 2:97; 3:250, 255; example of, 2:109, 217; 4:203, 207–8; his love to mankind, 2:118–23, 217; 3:179–83; teachings of, 2:122, 129, 136, 157, 171–75, 192–95, 204, 217, 257, 262; 4:150, 163–65, 196, 199, 238, 240, 248, 269; authority of, 2:192–95, 247; 3:180–81, 250; salvation through, 2:201; 4:55–56, 83, 150, 257; proper regard to, 4:61–64, 212–13; misconceptions of, 4:103, 222; as moral guide, 4:159, 170, 192–94. *See also* Language; Lord's Supper
Jewish culture, 4:161, 173, 187–93, 195, 210–11, 245
John, 1:315; 2:253; 3:24, 28, 56, 120, 179, 195, 213, 252; 4:49, 129, 134, 186, 193

Johnson, Samuel, 1:282; 3:113n1; quoted, 4:149; *The Adventurer,* quoted, 4:112n6; *The Idler,* quoted, 4:105, 112n6; *Life of Dryden,* 1:129n4; *Diary,* 1:208n; *The Rambler,* 1:63n1, 227n4; 2:263n; quoted, 2:102-3, 316, 354; 4:116
John the Baptist, 3:127, 249
Jonathan, 4:49
Jonson, Ben, 2:66n1
Joseph, 3:138
Jove, 2:138. *See also* Jupiter
Judas, 2:106
Judea, 4:161
Judgment, 3:36-39, 137, 215, 251, 258; 4:54
Jupiter (god), 2:219; 3:252. *See also* Jove
Jupiter (planet), 4:118, 155-56
Justice, 2:125, 222
Justin Martyr, 3:186-87
Juvenal, quoted, 1:63

K

Kalinevitch, Karen, 4:267n2
Keith, Sir William, 3:54
Kempis, Thomas à, 1:282; 3:187-88; 4:270
Kent, William, 1:12
King, Gedney, 4:285, 292, 293, 294
Kingdom of God (of heaven), 3:23, 24, 27, 28, 99, 154, 167, 194, 210; 4:121n16; defined, 3:249
Knowledge, 1:278-84, 287-88, 290; 2:22, 26, 126-29, 132, 177, 179, 194, 207, 222, 227, 228, 231-36, 237, 242; 3:223, 242; 4:77, 91-92, 144-45, 210, 265-66; and improvement, 2:228-30; essential to freedom, 3:205-6. *See also* Wisdom; God, knowledge of
Knox, John, 1:105
Knox, Vicesimus, 1:209n2; 2:42n4; 4:178n1, 180n4, 181n6, 182n12, 248n13
Koran, 1:293; 3:118

L

Labor, 4:178-84
Lacedaemonians. *See* Spartans
Laertius, Diogenes, *Lives of Eminent Philosophers,* 2:42n4; 4:112n6
Lafayette, Marquis de, 2:68n3; 3:213
Lagrange, Count Joseph Louis, 4:158
Lancaster, Joseph, 3:231
Landor, Walter Savage, *Imaginary Conversations,* 4:202n2
Language: theological, 4:142, 198-99; of Jesus, 4:145, 176, 187-88, 212-14, 216. *See also* Speech
Laplace, Pierre Simon Marquis de, 4:158n8
Last Judgment, 2:30n2
Lateran Council, fourth, 4:185
Lathrop, John, 1:14

Laud, Archbishop William, 4:185
Law, and mercy, Christian, 2:121-22, 193, 206, 210; of nature, 2:139, 141, 142; perfection of, 2:148 2:152; civil, 2:163; Jewish, 2:192; of love, 2:196; "Law of the Lord," 2:127, 134, 187, 248, 254; 3:126-31, 177-78, 221-22, 258
Lazarus, 2:74; 3:197
Learning. *See* Truth
Leighton, Robert, 3:88-89; 4:230n4; quoted, 3:89
Leonidas, 2:32; 3:66
Lessing, Gotthold Ephraim, 3:13
Liberty, 3:205, 258; 4:27. *See also* Free will; Independence
Likeness, 3:190, 204
Locke, John, 1:105
Lodestone, 2:20
London, great fire of, 4:38
Lord's Prayer, 2:244; 3:175-76
Lord's Supper, 1:17, 238-39, 247-48; 2:56-60, 148, 242, 262; 3:181; 4:171n1, 185-94, 227n12, 292-94
Lothrop, J. K., 4:285
Louis Philippe, 4:42n1, 149n3
Love, 1:109-12, 274-76; 2:23, 41, 122, 123, 136, 187, 190, 191, 196, 200, 201, 203, 209, 210, 211, 231, 241, 243, 247, 248, 258, 260; 3:51-56, 87, 99-100, 130-31, 197, 219, 225, 229, 231, 240-43, 247; 4:29-30, 46, 99, 127, 133, 227, 238; to God, 4:28, 33-34, 53
Loyalty, 4:30
Luke, 1:89; 4:186-87, 193
Lunatic Asylum, State, at Worcester, 4:80n4
Lust, 2:145; 4:242
Luther, Martin, 1:105n7, 261, 262, 282; 2:29, 48; 3:26, 72; 4:159, 185, 233; quoted, 4:110-11
Lyceum, 2:95
Lying, 3:59
Lynn (Massachusetts), 4:42n3
Lyons (France), 4:149n3

M

Mackenzie, Sir Alexander, 2:93
Mackintosh, Sir James, 3:239nn1-2; *A General View of the Progress of Ethical Philosophy,* quoted, 4:31n5
Mackintosh, Peter, 4:291, 294, 295
Mahomet, 3:14, 64
Mammon, 3:227
Man: character of, 1:114-19; 3:155, 160-61; defined, 1:115, 134, 200-201, 229, 276-77; perfection of, 2:38, 49; improvement of, 2:51-55, 58-60, 61-63, 66, 76, 119-20, 141, 175, 183, 223; 4:103-9, 204; moral nature of, 2:56, 144-50, 198, 208; 3:64-66, 81, 151, 163, 224; 4:142-47,

166-70; standard idea of, 2:69; spiritual nature of, 3:23, 32, 148, 258; averse to God, 3:61; naturally Christian, 3:65; as child of God, 3:87-88, 89, 116, 186, 208-9; has nothing of his own, 3:113, 202-3; as sensualist, 3:189-90; made for God's love, 3:52; and wonder of Creation, 4:229-35

Manicheanism, 3:57

Mann, Horace, 4:80n4

Marivaux, Pierre Carlet de Chamblain de, 1:288n5

Mark, 4:186

Marriage, 1:238

Martha, 2:25, 28

Martineau, Harriet, 1:16

Marvell, Andrew, 1:270n6; "Bermudas," 1:212n6

Mary, 2:28, 74

Material world, 1:93-97, 244-49, 276. See also Nature

Materialists, 2:30

Mather, Cotton, 1:1, 243n10; 4:269n7

Mather, Increase, 1:1, 243n10

Matthew, 4:186

McGiffert, Arthur Cushman, Jr.: Young Emerson Speaks, 1:2, 33; 3:2435n1

Meditation, 2:120

Mediterranean, 4:214

Melanchthon, Philip, 1:105

Mercury (planet), 4:155

Mercy, 2:19, 152, 169, 208, 211, 258, 262

Methodists, 3:127, 129, 257

Mexico, 3:49

Millennialism, 1:21-22

Millennium, 1:112

Milman, Henry Hart, 1:132n14

Milner, Joseph and Isaac: The History of the Church of Christ, 4:110-11n1

Milton, John, 2:229, 264; 4:118; Areopagitica, 4:265; quoted, 2:86; 4:78; "Comus," quoted, 4:93; "Il Penseroso," quoted, 1:244; "Of Reformation in England," quoted, 2:91; Paradise Lost, 4:245n5; quoted, 1:58, 108, 109, 157, 187, 212; 2:157; 3:74, 219; Paradise Regained, 4:113n9; Sonnet XIX, quoted, 2:250; "To Mr. Cyriack Skinner upon His Blindness," quoted, 2:157

Mind, 1:70, 226, 227, 235, 258, 276, 278-84; 2:145, 146, 147; 4:24, 31, 167; and perception of God, 2:19, 20, 64; 4:45-46; versus matter, 2:30; changes in, 2:103; power of, 2:149

Minister, as preacher, 1:233-37; as preacher and pastor, 2:156; 4:227, 244-50; duties of, 1:15-16, 233-43; 2:156-61, 196; 4:194, 293-96; relation to congregation, 2:156; 4:247

Miracles, 2:360; 3:13, 79-83, 121-22, 185; 4:24, 190

Miriam, 3:246

Moderation, 2:125, 244

Modesty, 2:125, 135, 266

Montaigne, Michel Eyquem de, 1:80n7, 284; "Against Idleness," quoted, 60; "Apology for Raimond de Sebonde," 1:232n3; quoted, 1:115; "Of Conscience," quoted, 1:194; "Of Cruelty," 4:112-13n7; "Of Custom," quoted, 1:293; "Defence of Seneca and Plutarch," 4:111-12n3; "Of Democritus and Heraclitus," 4:231n6; "Of the Education of Children," quoted, 3:114; "Of Experience," 4:112-13n7; "Of Friendship," quoted, 4:50, 51n6; "Of Pedantry," quoted, 4:97; "Of Solitude," quoted, 1:270, 284; "Upon Some Verses of Virgil," quoted, 1:187; "Of Vanity," 4:63n11, 241n12, 263n4

Montesquieu, Charles de Secondat, Baron de La Brède et de: The Persian Letters, quoted, 4:50n4, 218n1

Moore, George, quoted, 2:216n; 4:178n

Moral design, 2:142. See also Providence, design of

Moral excellence, 2:27, 41, 109, 263

Moral law, 2:44, 78-79, 86, 193; 3:152

Moral sense, 1:7, 24-28, 116-17, 288; 2:204; 4:77-82, 85

Moral slavery, 2:201

Moral truth, 2:194; 4:158, 163, 165

Moral world, 1:97-99, 244-49, 276; 2:202, 208; 4:144

Mordecai, 2:261; 3:106

Mortalist heresy, 2:30n11; 3:33n5

Moses, 2:141, 264; 3:36, 158, 179, 191, 223n5, 236; 4:60, 139, 146, 161, 195, 269; Mosaic law, 4:110

Mott, Wesley T., 1:29; 4:121n16

Mount Gerizim, 4:158

Mount of Olives, 3:137; 4:39

Mount Sinai, 3:158, 164, 179, 251

Mount Sion, 4:61

Murder, 2:145

Music, 3:244

Muzzy, Artemas B., 4:291

N

Naaman, 1:176-78

Napoleon. See Bonaparte, Napoleon

Native Americans, 2:95; 3:54; 4:115, 162, 254, 268. See also Black Hawk War; Cherokees; Seminoles

Natural religion. See Religion, natural

Nature, 2:139, 202, 208; 3:66, 71, 81, 130, 149, 155; 4:153, 253; laws of, 2:21; as mirror of the soul, 2:146, 219, 248. See also Material world; Man, and wonder of Creation

Nazirites, 4:111
Neri, St. Philip, 2:385–86
Nero, 1:231; 4:174
Neuhof (Switzerland), 4:97
Newell, William, 4:291
New England, 4:25, 110, 189, 281–82
New Jerusalem, Church of. *See* Swedenborgianism
Newton, Sir Isaac, 1:105, 310; 2:28, 29, 229, 233, 266; 3:61, 66, 72, 110, 123; 4:29, 156, 157, 225, 233, 266; quoted, 2:151
New York City, Second Unitarian Church of, 4:250
Niles, Hezekiah, 2:106n6
Noah, 3:158; 4:60
Norton, Andrews, 1:4, 25, 29, 30; 4:290
Novalis, quoted, 4:86, 225
Numa. *See* Pompilius Numa
Nushirvan, 4:55

O
Octavian, 1:143n8
Ordinance of Nullification (South Carolina), 4:115n11
Original sin, 1:152. *See also* Sin
Overton, Richard, 2:30n1
Ovid, 2:79; 4:202n2, 216n17
Owen, John, 3:222n3

P
Packer, Barbara, 1:29
Paganism, 2:57, 58, 119, 139; 4:193, 195
Pain, 3:106–7, 149, 258
Paley, William, 3:26; *Moral and Political Philosophy,* quoted, 4:74–75, 123–24; *Natural Theology,* 2:238n1; quoted 2:71
Paris, 4:229
Parkman, Francis, 1:233n4
Parnassus, 2:126n3
Pascal, Blaise: *Pensées,* quoted, 2:167–68
Passover, 4:187–92
Past, 2:201–2, 204
Patience, 3:94
Patriotism, 2:165, 213–15
Paul, 1:74, 110–11, 122, 143, 159, 209, 224, 225, 227, 229, 231–32, 247, 253, 267; 2:22, 39, 57, 90, 107, 119, 157, 170, 180, 192, 219, 229, 247, 252; 3:34, 72, 82, 88, 93, 99, 110, 121–22, 123, 125, 149, 169, 186, 189, 195, 210, 212, 213, 219, 251; 4:32, 35, 62, 82, 129, 148, 159, 161, 169, 170, 171, 189–91, 193, 203, 238
Paulinus, Bishop of Nola, 1:183–84
Pausanias, 1:226n2
Peabody, Elizabeth Palmer, 4:221n
Peace of mind, 3:134–37
Peace societies, 4:214
Penitence, 1:167–68; 2:187; 3:140

Penn, William, 1:282; 3:54; quoted, 4:179
Pennsylvania, 3:54
Pentecost, 3:122; 4:217n24
Perfection, 2:22, 106, 111, 129, 132, 145, 147, 148, 151, 168, 170, 188, 197, 217, 227, 230, 243, 249, 263, 265; 3:217, 225, 253, 263. *See also* Man, improvement of
Periander, quoted, 2:41
Perkins Institute for the Blind, 4:80n4
Perseverance, 2:102–7
Persia, 4:38
Persius, 1:270n5
Peru, 4:237
Pestalozzi, Johann Heinrich, 3:222, 229, 230, 231; 4:97, 99–101
Peter, 1:179, 261; 2:170n14; 3:88, 93, 110, 124, 195, 251; 4:89, 90, 91, 93, 129, 159
Pharaoh, 4:269
Pharisees, 3:121, 250; 4:188
Philo Judaeus, 1:276n3
Phocion, 3:172
Piety, 4:94; at home, 1:120–26
Pilate, Pontius, 1:88, 90–91; 4:166
Pilgrims, 4:269n7
Pindar: *Olympian Odes,* quoted, 4:24
Pisistratus, 1:286
Pittacus, quoted, 2:41
Plato, 1:61, 143, 187, 226n2; 2:229; 4:125n7; *Phaedo,* 4:113n9; "Symposium," 4:230n5
Plautus: *Bacchides,* quoted, 4:227
Plutarch, 1:282; 2:50; 3:172n5; "How a Man May Be Sensible of His Progress in Virtue," quoted, 2:43; "Life of Agesilaus," quoted, 1:201; "Life of Alexander," 4:37n2, 111n2; "Life of Aristides," 4:149n5; "Life of Demetrius," 4:112–13n7; "Life of Gaius Marius," quoted, 1:105; "Life of Lycurgus," 4:111n3; "Life of Pericles," 4:132; "Life of Pompey," 4:216n19; "Life of Pyrrhus," quoted, 3:49; "Life of Themistocles," quoted, 3:241; *Morals,* 4:37n2; quoted, 1:246, 4:205n8
Plymouth Rock, 1:141
Poetry, 3:244
Poland, 4:42n1
Politicians, 2:164
Politics, 2:94; 3:115–16, 141, 198; 4:114–15, 225
Polo, Marco, 1:212n6
Polytheism, 2:139
Pompilius Numa, 2:29
Pope, Alexander, 1:135n5; "Elegy to the Memory of an Unfortunate Lady," quoted, 2:113; "Epistle to Dr. Arbuthnot," quoted, 1:198; *Essay on Man,* 3:61n8; quoted, 1:153; "The Universal Prayer," quoted, 4:156
Portugal, 3:49
Potter, William J., 1:17

Poverty, 4:182
Power, 3:114-16, 121, 122, 124-25, 141, 196, 197-99, 206; defined, 3:262
Prayer, 1:55-62, 233; 2:22, 28, 61-62, 120, 126, 148-50, 159, 170, 185, 187, 190, 217; 3:61, 77, 92, 95, 100, 128, 176; 4:110, 113-14; efficacy of, 2:23, 245; natural, 2:139; duty of, 2:242-45; object of, 2:242-45
Preaching. See Minister, as preacher
Preparation, 2:90, 127, 147, 178, 179, 190, 202
Press, 2:163-64
Pride, 1:162-66; 2:135, 136, 183, 198, 222, 225; 3:85, 112-17, 137, 201, 207
Priestley, Joseph, 1:215; 2:28
Primary School Committee, 4:225
Principles, 2:26, 128, 130, 209, 246, 247, 251-55, 263; as separate from actions, 1:179-84, 294; 2:46; 4:58
Prison reform, 4:80, 214
Prodigal Son, 4:93, 145, 203
Professions. See Vocations
Prophecy, 3:122-23
Property, 3:113, 135, 141, 183, 211, 213, 242. See also Wealth
Providence, 2:22, 23, 34, 43, 75, 83, 85, 96, 114, 149, 159, 162, 168, 177, 178, 184, 187, 200, 201-2, 205, 207, 211, 215, 230, 233, 244, 252, 258, 260, 261; 3:45-46, 58-59, 75-77, 80, 96, 102, 108, 155, 158, 187-88, 197, 215, 230, 262, 267; 4:27, 56-57, 60, 72, 75, 83, 122, 125, 134, 139, 154, 157, 164, 184, 195, 197, 199, 201, 211, 213, 226, 227, 242, 246, 253-56, 259; doctrine of, 2:139, 142; design of, 2:141-42; 4:200; favors the good, 3:210-14
Prudence, 3:212
Psalmody, 3:245-48
Ptolemy, 4:155
Puritans, 1:141, 169, 261; 2:215; 3:138-40, 141; 4:259
Putnam, George, 4:291
Pyrrhonism, 1:27
Pythagoreans, 4:111, 112

Q
Quakers, 2:235n8; 3:127, 242; 4:185n, 186, 215n15

R
Rabirius, 1:306n8; 2:380
Raikes, Robert, 4:80n4
Railroad, 3:49
Rancé, Abbot Armand de, 4:111n2
Ray, John: A Compleat Collection of English Proverbs, 4:139n6
Reason, 2:98, 126, 129, 145, 166, 192, 206,

235, 265; in struggle with vice, 2:44-45, 49; and affection, 2:49; and idea of God, 2:49, 138, 142; 4:175; purposes of, 2:203; 4:231-34; and senses, 2:238; and virtue, 2:224; and faith, 3:18-19, 163, 165; 4:175; 4:73-74
Réaumur, René Antoine Ferchault de, 4:124
Reckoning of moral accounts, importance of at year's end, 2:112-17
Reed, Sampson, 2:238n1; 4:223n4, 224n6; quoted, 2:235; 4:229
Reformation, 2:48; 3:37, 258; 4:101, 247, 259
Regeneration, 2:46; 3:69, 71, 73, 92, 127
Reid, Thomas, 1:7
Religion, 2:22, 24, 119, 122, 125, 138, 145, 151, 152, 157, 160, 183, 199, 237, 246, 260, 263, 267; 4:284; natural, 1:224; 2:20, 138-39, 196; practical, 2:20, 88; 4:154; purposes of, 2:52-55, 88-90, 238; defined, 2:54, 61; 3:44, 249, 254-59; 4:236-43; and views of God, 2:62-63, 237-41; teachings of, 2:82; and equality of men, 2:240; and prayer, 2:242; offers consolation, 3:13-17, 69-73, 101-5, 107-11, 143, 170-73, 213-14; 4:131, 134, 139; "experimental," 3:94; received individually, 3:201-2; and society, 4:209-17. See also Christianity
Religious education, 3:162-63
Religious opinion: progress of, 1:107, 149-54, 179; 3:128
Repentence, 2:169
Reputation, 2:220
Responsibility, 2:83; opposed to selfishness, 2:132-37; 4:73
Resurrection, 2:106, 183; 3:103; 4:23-24, 126. See also Mortalist heresy
Retribution. See Compensation
Revelation, 2:22, 23, 24, 109, 115, 121, 122, 141, 142, 149, 176, 182, 188, 203, 204, 206, 231, 246, 261; 3:13, 18, 19-20, 82, 118, 121, 159, 177; 4:246, 259, 269
Revivals, 3:127-29
Righteousness, 1:214-18
Right Hand of Fellowship, 4:262-64
Ripley, Rev. Ezra, 1:10, 233n4; 4:122n, 244n, 249n14, 264n8, 291
Ripley, Rev. Samuel, 1:10, 232-33n4
Robbins, Chandler, 1:1, 15; 4:217n24
Robertson, William, 1:282
Robinson, Rev. John, 4:269n7
Roman Empire, 4:62, 259
Romans, 4:174, 245
Rome, 4:138, 146, 205, 263
Romulus, 2:29n6
Rose, Anne C., 4:278n18
Rousseau, Jean Jacques, 3:229n2, 231n7
Russia, 4:42n1

S

Saadi: *The Gulistan,* 3:25*n7*

Sabbath, 1:100–106, 204; 2:38, 40, 160, 254, 262; 3:158–68; 4:110

Sacrifice, of self to God, 2:246–50

Sadducees, 4:123

Saint-Evremond, Charles de Marguetel de Saint-Denis, quoted, 4:29–30

St. Petersburg, 4:237

Sallust, quoted, 1:155

Salvation, 2:201–5, 209, 230, 255, 267; 3:127, 129, 205, 209, 228, 233, 249; importance of Faith and Works to, 2:46, 48; and obedience to moral law, 2:47; defined, 2:201; 3:253

Samaria, 4:90, 188

Samaritans, 3:186; 4:260

Sampson, George Adams, 4:51*n7*, 199*n8*, 207*n11*, 221–28, 272–80, 285*n1*, 290–94

Sampson, Hillman B., 4:226*n11*

Samson, 1:262

Samuel, 3:180

Sanctification, 3:119, 121, 219

Sandemanians, 4:189

Saturn (planet), 4:118, 155

Saul, 3:239

Saurin, Jacques, 1:110*n5*; quoted, 4:157

Science, 1:129, 297–98; 2:29, 93–94, 139–40, 207, 230, 236, 251; 3:206, 221–22; 4:79, 124–25, 145, 265–66. *See also* Astronomy; Chemistry; Geology

Scotland, 3:85; 4:42*n2*

Scott, Sir Walter: *The Heart of Midlothian,* quoted, 4:108

Scougal, Henry, 1:28, 282; 2:239*n2*; 3:89, 187; 4:242*n16*

Seamen's Bethel, Boston, 4:236

Seamen's societies, 4:214

Second Church, Boston, 1:1, 8, 13–14; 2:56; 4:209, 213*n8*, 217*n24*; repairs to, 4:171; vestry of, 4:267–71, 291–92; records of, 4:285–303; letter from Emerson to, 4:304–6;

Second Coming, 4:190

Second Great Awakening, 1:18

Sects, 2:19–20, 186–91, 253; 3:55–56, 95, 126–27, 129, 249, 254

Segur, Philip de: *History of the Expedition to Russia, Undertaken by the Emperor Napoleon,* quoted, 4:30

Self, 2:132–34; 3:43, 95; 4:54–59, 143, 145, 203–4, 218

Self-command, 1:210–12, 290, 295; 2:42–45, 82, 100, 107, 154, 190, 225; defined, 2:43; 4:104–5, 127

Self-denial, 2:129–30, 204; 3:156–57, 229

Self-examination, 3:132–33, 143

Self-improvement, 4:71–76

Self-indulgence, 2:129; 4:52

Self-interest, 2:163, 209

Selfishness, 2:27, 29, 133–37, 150, 154, 164, 167, 168, 169, 193, 196, 198, 199, 200, 262; 4:151, 234

Self-knowledge, 1:226–27; 2:267; 4:147. *See also* Wisdom

Self-love, 2:132, 134, 136, 251; 3:85–87, 90, 127, 129, 139, 180, 207, 264. *See also* Selfishness

Self-reliance, 2:157, 263–67; 3:201–4; 4:218

Seminoles, 4:115*n11*

Seneca, Lucius Annaeus, 2:50; 4:119*n13; De Beneficiis,* 1:306; 2:380; "De Providentia," 3:88*n10,* quoted 2:20; 4:216; *Epistulae Morales,* 3:190*n4;* quoted, 1:366; "On the Renown Which My Writings Will Bring You," 2:115*n22*

Senses, 4:117–18, 173

Sermon on the Mount, 2:97–101; 4:150*n9,* 159. *See also* Matthew 5–7 in the Index of Biblical References

Seven Sages, 2:42*n4;* quoted, 2:41–42

Sewel, William: *The History of the . . . Quakers,* 4:205*n9*

Sexes, distinction between, 2:147

Shaftesbury, Anthony Ashley Cooper, Third Earl of, 3:130

Shakespeare, William, 3:213*n5,* 215*n4;* 4:29, 233; *Antony and Cleopatra,* quoted, 1:193; *As You Like It,* quoted, 4:118; *Hamlet,* 2:147*n10;* 4:181*n7;* quoted, 1:308–9; 3:267; *I Henry VI,* 1:99*n13; Henry VIII,* quoted, 1:68; *Macbeth,* quoted, 1:306; *Othello,* quoted, 1:125; *The Tempest,* quoted, 1:125; 2:105

Sibley, J. L., 4:289

Sickness. *See* Disease

Sidney, Sir Philip, 3:66; 4:32

Sidon, 4:90

Silas, 2:22; 3:149; 4:35

Sin, 1:118–19, 154, 167, 169, 171, 195, 248, 275, 312; 2:23, 126, 129–30, 134, 136, 142, 144, 145, 148, 153, 154, 187, 190, 191, 193, 195, 201, 203, 204, 224, 225, 226, 241, 253, 254, 255, 257, 258, 261; 3:34, 41, 42, 52–56, 57, 61–62, 65, 67, 73, 78, 90, 95, 98, 124, 126, 130, 136, 140, 143, 153, 155, 176, 182, 202, 205, 208, 225, 239, 255; 4:48; forgiveness of, 1:255–59, 292; defined, 3:264; of sensuality and cruelty, 4:93. *See also* Original sin

Skepticism, 1:206, 255; 2:44, 87, 90, 110, 124–25, 176, 193. *See also* Atheism

Skill, defined, 3:262

Slavery, 3:38, 43, 47, 59, 205, 206; 4:79, 115, 214, 241

Smith, Adam, 2:69*n4;* quoted, 1:61, 79, 192

Smith, Walter B., 2:114n7
Society, 2:23, 142, 196, 217, 218, 232, 246; 3:260; advantages of, 2:25, 83-84; 4:26-27, 84-86; evils of, 2:25-26; and individual, 2:82-86; 4:33-34, 209-17, 218-19
Socinus, 4:159
Socrates, 1:192, 227, 310; 2:29, 39, 141, 229, 264; 3:213; 4:146, 230, 233; quoted, 4:112, 113n9, 174
Sodom, 1:188
Solitude, advantages of, 2:25, 77, 84-86, 121; 4:244
Solomon, 1:114, 128, 157, 212, 250, 253, 264, 309; 2:42, 166, 167, 169, 222, 267; 3:149, 215; 4:116-17, 120, 140, 150, 233
Solon, quoted, 2:41; 4:216
Sophocles, 3:235n4
Soul, 2:20, 27, 28, 39, 106, 117, 194, 197, 218, 219, 228, 229, 239, 245, 247, 248, 254, 258; 3:69-70, 90, 98, 102-3, 108, 110, 193, 213, 218-19, 227-28, 236, 258; related to God, 2:20-23, 89, 199, 236; death of, 2:30n1; education of, 2:88-91; 4:83-88, 142-47, 265-66; as colony of Heaven, 2:99; infinite strength of, 3:77-78; 4:46
Spain, 3:49; 4:27, 237
Sparta, 3:227, 230
Spartans, 4:97, 105, 111
Speech, 2:66-70; 3:263-64; 4:204-7; and knowledge, 2:68-70. See also Language
Spence, Joseph, 2:128n9, 151n2, 210n10
Spirit, 2:252-53; attributes of, 2:145-49; Holy, 3:119-25, 128; versus body, 2:144-50
Spiritual discernment, 3:189-94
Spiritual influence: reciprocal nature of, 3:174-78, 236-37
Stabler, Edward, 2:149n18
Staël, Madame de, 1:112n12; Germany, 3:13n1, 229n2; quoted, 2:195; 3:230; 4:98n7, 265
Stanhope, Philip Dormer, Lord Chesterfield, quoted, 2:155
Stantz, 4:99-100
Steele, Anne, 3:246
Sterne, Laurence: A Sentimental Journey, 376n2
Sternhold, Thomas, 3:246n3
Stephen, Saint, 3:110
Stewart, Dugald, 1:7; 2:260n13; 4:75n6; quoted, 4:133
Stoddard, Solomon, 2:59n8
Stoics, 1:275; 2:29; 3:20-21, 88; 4:111, 245
Stow, John, 1:252n3
Stylites, Saint Simeon, 4:112
Suetonius, 1:143n8
Suffering, 1:68-69, 94, 133-34, 246, 250; 2:202

Suicide, 2:128; 3:106, 193
Sunday school, 3:168; 4:80, 96-102, 212, 214, 275
Sunday School Society, 4:226
Swedenborg, Emanuel: The Apocalypse Revealed, 3:264n8; quoted, 4:205
Swedenborgianism, 3:127, 257, 268; 4:241n12. See also Reed, Sampson
Swift, Jonathan, quoted, 2:128; 3:193
Switzerland, 4:42n1, 97
Sympathy, 2:101, 235, 261; with Christ, 2:120

T
Tacitus, 1:231; 4:233
Talent, 3:196, 199, 263
Talmud, 4:187
Tamur, destroyed by Vishnu, 2:32
Taylor, Edward Thompson, 4:236n
Taylor, Jeremy, 1:118n10, 208n, 282; 2:20; 3:106; quoted, 1:87
Teacher, God's gift of, 4:210-13, 215, 245, 257-58
Tell, William, 4:29
Temperance, 1:181, 209, 291, 295; 2:31, 154, 178, 193, 222; 3:38, 95, 130, 207, 211, 225, 233, 251; 4:92-94, 105, 112, 206, 242; as reform movement, 4:79, 80, 214
Temptation, 3:57-62, 78, 81, 103, 109, 183, 190, 214, 228-29, 233-37, 253, 260
Tertullian: Apologeticus, 3:99n6
Thanksgiving Day sermon: XII, 1:133-40; LVII, 2:92-96; XCVII, 3:45-50; CXXXVI, 4:23-27; fragment, 4:281-82; introduction, 4:283
Themistocles, 3:241
Theological School at Cambridge, 4:290
Thought, 2:126-27; freedom of, 3:21-22
Tiberius, 3:261
Time, 1:155-60, 226; 3:219; 4:43-48, 73, 76, 164, 170, 199, 242; change wrought by, 1:93-96, 182-83
Timothy, 2:219
Tischer, John Frederick William, 1:262n4
Toplady, Augustus Montague, 4:160n1
Tranquility, 4:106, 207, 239-40
Transcendentalism, 1:16, 17, 22, 25, 29, 31-32
Transfiguration, 2:243n5
Transubstantiation, 2:57
Trappist monks, 4:111
Travel, 4:118-19, 254
Trinitarianism, 2:186-91; 3:120, 247
Trinity, 2:187; 4:191
Tripoli, 3:43
Truth, 1:180, 197-202, 206, 281; 2:26, 109, 123, 127, 141, 147, 155, 179, 190, 193-95, 202, 216, 217, 221, 224, 225, 230, 234-

36, 238, 243, 247, 248, 252, 253, 254, 265, 267; 3:13, 21, 23, 37, 67, 72, 114, 118, 126–27, 128, 173, 201–2, 205–6, 225, 249, 253, 255, 260–64; 4:130, 166–70; scientific, 2:251; and falsehood, 3:18, 130, 228; love of, 3:26–27, 32, 118, 129; 4:204; search for, 3:184–88, 201; unity of, 3:221–23; in conversation, 3:260–62

Tucker, Abraham, 1:294*n5*; 3:153*n3*; 4:244*n1*

Tuckerman, Joseph, 4:278*n18*

Turkey, 4:237

Turner, Nat, 4:42*n1*

Tyre, 4:90

U

Union, 4:115

Unitarianism, 1:3; doctrines of, 1:4–7; and art, 1:22–23; critics of, 2:19 4:269. *See also* American Unitarian Association; Channing, William Ellery

Unitarian-Trinitarian conflict, 2:186–91

Unitarians, 2:187*n3*, 189

Upham, Charles W., 1:233*n4*

Uranus, 4:155–56

Usefulness, 3:219, 228, 233, 250

Ussher, James, 4:163*n12*

V

Vanini, Lucilio, 3:222

Vanity, 2:138, 155

Venus, 2:145

Vergil, 1:143

Vespasian, 1:159–60

Vice, 2:19, 22, 26, 106, 120, 135, 137, 138, 145, 152, 164, 165, 183, 193, 200, 202, 217, 219, 224, 225, 229, 248, 254; 3:142, 152, 153, 170, 191, 195, 221, 224–25, 232; 4:133, 256; is slavery, 3:207–8, 233–34; among pagans, 3:238

Villiers, George, Duke of Buckingham, 1:264*n11*; 4:32

Virgin, Holy, 2:138

Virtue, 2:21, 22, 23, 24, 29, 31–34, 37, 40, 41, 49–50, 54, 89, 91, 106–7, 109, 111, 120–24, 125–28, 130, 132–34, 136–37, 143, 146–48, 151, 153–54, 178, 179, 183, 185, 187, 189–91, 192, 193, 194, 196–97, 199, 202, 206, 209, 217–21, 222–26, 227–31, 232, 239, 240, 244, 248, 254, 261, 265; 3:28, 58, 66, 93, 108–10, 137, 153, 175, 177–78, 181, 190, 195, 203, 221, 232; 4:133, 230, 256; advantages of, 2:31; defined, 2:41, 136; 3:25, 151, 222, 233–34, 236, 258, 268; and free will, 2:72–75; and government, 2:164–65; and good-heartedness, 2:166–70; among pagans, 3:19–20; preferable to success, 3:172–73; unity of,

3:223–25; 4:89–95, 240–41; in action, 4:44

Vishnu, destroys Tamur, 2:32

Vocations, 4:65–70, 178–84, 208, 223, 225–28, 231, 236–37, 239, 242, 244–50, 265, 273–79

Voltaire, 2:50

W

Waddington, George: *A History of the Church,* quoted, 3:186–87

Wake, Archbishop William, 4:185

Wakefield, Gilbert: *A Translation of the New Testament,* quoted, 4:90*n3*, 121*n16*

Walker, Rev. James, 4:288

Wallace, Sir William, 4:29

Waller, Edmund: "Of the Last Verses in the Book," quoted, 1:268

War, 3:37–38, 59

Warburton, William, 4:186

Ward, Robert Plummer: *Tremaine,* quoted, 2:151; 3:222

Ware, Rev. Henry, Jr., 1:1, 4, 8, 11, 13–15, 16, 24, 242*n8*, 304; 2:114; 3:68*n*; 4:213*n8*, 285, 288, 289; "The Doctrine of Probation," 1:6; "The Faith Once Delivered to the Saints," 1:5–6; *The Formation of the Christian Character,* 1:7

Washington, D.C., Unitarian Church in, 4:289

Washington, George, 1:227, 282; 2:215*n4*, 266; 3:66, 72, 205; 4:29, 63, 222

Waterford (Maine), 4:171*n1*

Watts, Isaac, 3:246; "An Hymn for the Lord's Day Evening," quoted, 2:36

Wayland, Francis, 4:80*n4*

Wealth, 2:127–29, 134, 229; 3:86, 110, 113, 135, 195, 196–97, 213, 216; pursuit of, 1:77–84, 214–16; 2:123; 4:80–81

Webster, Daniel, 2:95*n7*

Wesley, John, 1:282; 3:99

West Indies, 3:152; 4:237

Westminster, 4:138

White, Henry Kirke, 1:109*n3*

White Mountains, 4:171*n1*, 185*n*

Wilberforce, William, 1:103

Will, 2:102, 104, 105, 106, 126; 4:229. *See also* Free will

Winslow, Edward, *Hypocrisie Unmasked,* 4:269*n7*

Wisdom, 1:128–32, 157–58, 278; 2:28, 110, 125, 127, 210, 217, 218, 232, 234–35, 242, 243, 252, 258; 3:114, 119–20, 122–24, 228; 4:219, 226; defined, 3:262. *See also* Knowledge; Self-knowledge

Women, 3:227

"Wood 'n' Ware Debate," 2:186*n*

Woods, Leonard, 2:186*n*

Worcester, Samuel, 2:186*n*

Wordsworth, William: quoted, 3:148; *The Excursion,* quoted, 1:102; 3:71, 104, 177, 208; 4:32, 123; "Lines Composed a Few Miles above Tintern Abbey," 4:226n10; "Peter Bell, A Tale," quoted, 4:270; *Poems Dedicated to National Independence and Liberty,* quoted, 4:31

Work. *See* Labor; Vocations

Works, 2:165, 188, 197; 3:95, 97, 155–56, 250; and Faith, 2:46–50; defined, 2:47. *See also* Actions

Worldliness, 2:87–88, 91

Worship, 3:97–98, 166–68, 202, 245; 4:34

X
Xenophon, 2:141; 4:105n6

Y
Young, Charles L., 1:80n7
Young, Edward: *Night Thoughts,* quoted, 8, 54, 84, 181, 225; 3:107, 137, 192; 4:125n8, 157n7, 216n20

Z
Zoroastrianism, 3:57n

Index of Biblical References in Volumes 1–4

Genesis
1:2, **1**:234
1:3, **2**:258; **3**:40
1:11, **2**:207
1:11-12, **2**:265
1:20, **2**:207
1:24, **2**:207
1:26, **1**:97; **2**:56, 113, 120, 208, 218, 252,
  256; **3**:54, 204; **4**:134, 143, 411
1:26-27, **1**:277, 302; **4**:241
1:27, **1**:146; **4**:43
1:31, **2**:92; **4**:163, 281
2:2, **4**:281
2:7, **1**:97; **2**:208; **4**:36, 163
2:18, **2**:84; **4**:283
3:3-10, **1**:257
3:8, **1**:193
3:19, **1**:101; **2**:115, 144; **3**:159; **4**:149, 151,
  166, 178, 388
4:7, **2**:59
4:15, **1**:82
6:3, **2**:80
7:4, **3**:158
8:22, **1**:298
16:12, **1**:190; **4**:262
18:25, **3**:148
18:32, **1**:188
25:29-34, **3**:199
25:34, **4**:412
35:39, **2**:160
49:24, **2**:246

Exodus
3:6, **4**:162
3:13-14, **4**:160
3:14, **4**:269
4:16, **3**:115
7, **2**:164
10:21, **3**:153
12:8, **2**:156
15:8, **2**:257
16:22-30, **3**:158
19:5, **2**:168
20:1-17, **2**:124; **3**:164, 191, 252
20:3, **3**:179, 182
20:4, **4**:173
20:5, **1**:106
20:8, **3**:158

20:9-10, **3**:166
20:13, **2**:124
20:15, **3**:183
20:16, **3**:130
20:19, **3**:179
22:21, **3**:138
23:9, **3**:138
23:22, **2**:168
25:8, **4**:195
29:45-46, **4**:195
34:7, **1**:106
34:35, **4**:139

Leviticus
13:45, **4**:113
19:2, **3**:88
19:18, **1**:259; **4**:133

Numbers
9:11, **2**:156
35:34, **4**:195

Deuteronomy
5:7-21, **2**:124
5:17, **2**:124
6:6-7, **4**:96
11:29, **4**:158
14:2, **2**:165
26:5, **3**:138
28:23, **2**:258
28:37, **2**:114
30:11-14, **4**:136, 1141
30:14, **3**:42
32:47, **2**:237
33:25, **3**:74
34:1, **1**:104

Joshua
9:23-27, **2**:229
24:15, **1**:97; **2**:201; **4**:28

Judges
5:20, **1**:270
14:5-6, **1**:262

I Samuel
3:9, **3**:180
5, **2**:48

10:11, 3:239

II Samuel
22:10, 2:256
22:11, 2:208

I Kings
17:4-6, 2:142

II Kings
1:10, 1:57
4, 1:134
5:1-14, 1:176
20:12-17, 3:46; 4:282

I Chronicles
16:29, 1:106; 3:182
28:2, 2:256
28:9, 1:98

II Chronicles
20:20, 1:93

Esther
5:13, 2:261; 3:106

Job
1:21, 1:116; 2:51; 3:29, 214
1:22, 3:41, 102
3:1-3, 1:132
3:14, 1:74
4:8, 4:72
5:7, 1:134; 3:14, 106
14:1, 1:267
23:8-9, 2:242
28:28, 1:131
29:13, 2:209
31:40, 2:248
32:8, 2:144
36:4, 1:57
38:7, 4:122, 154
38:11, 1:61; 2:105
42:5, 2:21, 180

Psalms
2:4, 2:256
2:11, 2:190
8:2, 4:97
8:4, 4:134
8:6, 4:144
11:4, 2:257
12:1, 2:114; 3:138
13:43, 2:215
14:1, 2:63
14:3, 2:152; 3:93
16:10, 4:126
18:10, 2:208
18:26, 2:136
19:7, 3:126

19:8, 2:30
22:6, 3:226
23:4, 1:98, 240, 307; 4:195
24:3-5, 2:46
24:4, 4:270
25:14, 3:136, 182
29:2, 1:106; 3:182
30:5, 1:69
32:9, 4:74
33:6, 3:120
34:8, 3:149
34:12-14, 4:133
34:22, 3:145
36:9, 4:128
37:3, 2:256; 3:150
37:7, 3:150
37:25, 3:76
39:13, 1:68
41:4, 1:256
42:5, 2:157; 3:143; 4:121
42:11, 2:157; 4:121
43:5, 2:157; 4:121
44:1, 2:212
46:2, 1:98
47:7, 3:244
49:7, 2:72; 3:72
50:7, 4:161
51:6, 3:260
53:3, 2:152; 3:93
55:14, 1:71; 2:160
68:6, 4:25, 283
73:26, 1:240
74:16-17, 1:296
77:9, 4:163
78:25, 2:147
84:11, 4:121
84:11-12, 4:129
85:10, 3:119
86:17, 4:195
90:5-6, 1:299
90:10, 2:259; 4:75
90:12, 1:155
91:6, 4:200
92:1, 1:133
94:9, 1:109
94:11, 3:22
95, 3:247
95:4-5, 2:256
98:8, 2:146
99:5, 2:256
100:3, 4:23, 164
101, 3:247
102:25-27, 4:381
103:2, 2:92
103:16, 4:276
103:17-18, 4:365
104:8, 2:208
104:33, 4:23
106:1-2, 4:23

107:21, 3:43, 45
107:43, 4:281, 307
112:7, 1:96
116:11, 3:93, 260
119:97, 4:103
119:100, 4:138
119:105, 4:86
119:165, 4:136
121:1, 3:150
126:5, 3:144
126:6, 4:140
133:1, 4:241
136:5, 3:120
139:6, 2:24
139:14, 4:143, 229, 389, 428
144:15, 2:162
146:2, 4:23
147:20, 1:136

Proverbs
1:26-27, 4:195
2:3-4, 4:92
3:6, 2:24
3:13, 1:127
3:15, 4:272
3:17, 1:127
4:6-7, 1:128
4:7, 1:284
4:18, 2:55
4:23, 2:166, 167
6:11, 3:119
6:16-17, 1:166
6:23, 4:140
8:3, 2:257
8:27-30, 3:120
9:1-5, 2:257
9:10, 3:114
10:2, 4:81
10:7, 2:111; 3:139; 4:250
10:9, 2:216
11:2, 2:222
13:12, 2:139
13:14, 4:128
13:24, 1:134
14:10, 2:142; 3:182
14:14, 2:267; 3:201
14:27, 4:128
14:30, 4:150
15:1, 1:264
16:18-19, 2:222
16:32, 1:212; 2:41
19:2, 1:391
19:8, 2:232
19:16, 4:136
20:56, 4:326
22:17-21, 3:184
22:29, 4:119, 180, 184, 225
23:7, 2:248; 3:191
23:23, 4:92

23:31, 1:58
27:19, 2:219; 4:119, 218, 247
28:26, 3:149
31:28, 1:76, 124

Ecclesiastes
1:14, 1:115, 250
2:2, 2:169
2:14, 3:215
3:1-8, 4:120
3:4, 1:135
3:11, 1:371
3:11-12, 4:116
3:15, 3:132
3:21, 3:119
5:8, 3:150
7:2, 1:85; 3:140
8:12, 3:215
9:2, 3:215
9:4, 3:138
9:5-6, 1:309
9:7, 3:215
9:10, 1:250; 2:107
9:11, 3:145
11:1, 1:60-61, 304; 3:266
11:3, 1:118
11:9, 3:215
11:40, 2:28
12:7, 4:166
12:13, 2:41; 3:251; 4:131
12:19, 3:264

Isaiah
1:3, 4:231
1:13, 4:173
2:22, 4:36
3:15, 1:60; 2:37
5:7, 4:263
5:12, 1:60
7:14, 2:24
9:6, 1:139
9:6-7, 4:37
10:13, 2:255
10:14, 2:261
11:9, 1:76
13:22, 3:140
21:6-12, 4:245
21:11-12, 4:224
24:7, 3:140
28:10, 13, 4:279
29:13, 2:257
30:18, 3:175
40:3, 1:110-11
40:10, 1:69; 4:105
40:12, 1:109, 205
49:13, 4:195
49:15, 1:138
50:10, 3:106
51:3, 4:195

51:12, 4:195
52:7, 4:244
52:8, 4:245
53:2, 3:131, 182
53:3, 1:68, 88; 2:23, 110, 195, 240; 3:172;
    4:239
54:8, 2:256, 262
55:8, 2:317
55:12, 2:146, 257
57:19-21, 3:132
58:4, 1:171
58:5, 1:171; 4:110
58:8, 4:269
58:13, 1:106
59:14, 3:141, 145
60:11, 2:36
61:3, 4:130
62:11, 1:69
64:4, 1:132
64:6, 3:127
65:17, 3:73
66:1, 3:147
66:22, 3:73
66:24, 1:195; 2:19

Jeremiah
2:13, 3:15; 4:131
2:34, 4:247
5:17, 3:140
6:4, 3:142
6:16, 4:131
8:22, 1:119; 2:240
9:23-24, 3:112
13:23, 2:76
17:7, 3:149
18:8, 2:256
33:22, 4:213

Ezekiel
12:19, 2:116
18:20, 4:45
37:1-14, 3:256

Daniel
3, 1:134
3:19-21, 1:315
3:24-25, 1:75
12:4, 2:74; 4:145

Hosea
8:7, 4:107
10:8, 1:193

Joel
1:14, 1:167
2:10, 4:381
2:31, 1:60
3:15, 4:381

Amos
8:9, 3:140

Jonah
1:3-4, 1:208
3:9, 2:256

Micah
6:7, 1:177
6:8, 2:159, 169; 3:124; 4:165

Nahum
1:3, 2:256

Habakkuk
2:2, 2:38; 3:177
2:14, 1:76
3:17-18, 1:139; 4:129
3:18, 1:240

Zechariah
4:10, 3:138

Malachi
4:1, 3:38

Ecclesiasticus
32:23, 2:400; 4:341
42:24, 1:78; 2:198, 248; 4:331

Wisdom of Solomon
4:8, 1:157; 3:71
4:8-9, 4:221

Matthew
1:23, 2:24, 240; 4:121, 175, 195
2:4-12, 1:134
3:2, 1:167; 3:249
3:3, 1:110-11
4:4, 3:165
4:10, 3:179
4:11, 4:129
4:16, 4:41
4:17, 1:167; 2:169
5-7, 2:97-101; 4:159
5:1-11, 3:34
5:3, 2:99, 180; 3:27, 70, 100, 180
5:3-4, 3:171
5:3-6, 2:255
5:3-8, 3:181
5:3-10, 4:35
5:4, 4:195
5:5-9, 1:174
5:6, 4:127, 381
5:7, 1:161; 2:199, 211; 3:123, 174, 218
5:8, 2:30, 61, 65, 99, 180, 222; 3:22, 100,
    180; 4:36, 176
5:9, 2:144
5:11-12, 3:171

5:12, 1:148, 187, 224
5:13, 3:93
5:14, 2:53, 97, 165; 3:218
5:18, 4:63, 69, 76, 136
5:21-22, 3:252, 255; 4:150
5:27-28, 3:252, 255; 4:150
5:28, 3:195
5:29-30, 4:277
5:39, 2:90
5:39-40, 3:241
5:43, 4:133
5:43-44, 3:238
5:43-46, 3:38
5:44, 2:199; 3:180
5:45, 1:303; 2:110, 182; 3:45; 4:308
5:46, 2:53
5:48, 1:283, 291; 2:90; 3:88, 225; 4:71
6:2, 1:262; 2:97, 154; 3:108
6:3, 1:247
6:4, 1:98
6:5, 3:202
6:6, 1:98, 145; 2:82, 84; 3:34, 202; 4:78
6:8, 3:111
6:9, 3:27, 108
6:9-10, 2:62
6:9-15, 3:176
6:10, 2:244; 3:40
6:12, 1:255
6:13, 3:62; 4:83, 88
6:17, 3:140
6:18, 1:98
6:19, 2:97
6:20, 2:98
6:20-21, 1:97
6:21, 2:97
6:22, 3:23
6:24, 3:227
6:26, 2:97
6:28, 2:97, 265; 4:106, 240
6:28-30, 3:38
6:30, 1:300
6:33, 3:78
7:1-2, 2:199
7:2, 4:56
7:5, 3:65
7:6, 3:182, 4:373
7:7, 3:123, 136, 174; 4:175
7:7-8, 2:149, 245; 3:175
7:12, 2:41, 209; 3:56; 4:49, 62
7:13, 1:81; 3:60
7:13-14, 4:105
7:14, 1:73; 3:133
7:16, 2:46, 48, 97; 3:250
7:16-20, 1:55; 3:43
7:17, 3:266
7:20, 2:216, 255
7:21, 2:49; 3:100, 250; 4:199
7:23, 3:174; 4:279
7:26, 2:50

7:28, 2:357
7:29, 2:192; 3:123; 4:208
8:5-10, 3:20
8:20, 1:88; 2:110
8:27, 1:298
9:13, 2:59
9:28-35, 4:91
9:36, 1:242
10:7, 4:39
10:14, 1:169
10:18-19, 3:123
10:22, 1:68; 3:235
10:28, 1:293
10:29, 4:123
10:29-30, 1:260
10:30, 3:111
10:32, 1:92
10:34, 3:16
10:34-35, 4:39
10:35, 4:45
10:35-37, 4:69
10:42, 1:83, 306; 2:152, 199; 3:232
11:5, 2:211
11:15, 4:388
11:28, 2:36, 262; 3:15
11:29, 1:166; 2:222; 4:131
11:30, 1:173
12:12, 3:168
12:25, 4:55
12:25-26, 3:23
12:31-32, 3:120
12:33, 2:251
12:36, 3:22
12:37, 1:190
12:43-45, 3:235
12:50, 3:47
13:12, 2:234; 3:60, 72
13:15, 3:24
13:17, 1:148
13:18-23, 3:21
13:24-30, 2:34
13:31, 4:41, 214
13:37-43, 2:34
13:46, 2:152; 4:214
13:57, 4:222
14:16-17, 3:120
15:11-20, 2:166
15:14, 3:153
15:18, 20, 4:57
16:6-12, 4:188
16:18, 1:261; 3:55
16:19, 3:177
16:24, 2:129; 3:180
16:26, 2:263, 267; 4:277, 412
17:2, 2:243
17:5, 4:241
17:20, 1:390; 3:122; 4:41, 214
18:3, 2:171, 173
18:6, 3:232

18:7, 4:98
18:8, 3:39; 4:270
18:10, 2:171
18:21–22, 3:34
18:22, 2:107
19:17, 2:74; 3:164, 181, 249
19:19, 1:112, 259; 2:259; 4:133
19:21, 1:302; 2:90, 239
19:23, 3:195
19:26, 2:126
19:27, 4:169
19:28, 3:195
20:27, 3:56
21:16, 4:97
21:42, 3:100
21:44, 2:148; 4:61, 169, 233
22:21, 1:218
22:30, 2:147
22:31–32, 3:33
22:37, 1:154; 2:34; 4:193
22:37–39, 2:29, 190, 254
22:39, 4:133
23:5, 4:148
23:12, 2:222
23:23, 1:167
23:25, 3:229
24:13, 1:231
24:35, 2:111; 4:69, 76
24:51, 4:280
25, 1:106
25:1–13, 3:98
25:14–30, 2:54, 73; 3:162; 4:250
25:21, 1:76, 124; 2:260; 4:47
25:21–23, 4:183
25:23, 2:151, 155; 4:47
25:25, 2:19
25:31–46, 4:64
25:32–33, 3:193
25:40, 1:121
25:41, 3:39; 4:47
26:18, 2:57
26:26, 4:186
26:26–28, 4:188
26:39, 3:214
26:40, 1:142, 154, 176
26:41, 1:210; 2:44; 3:98
26:42, 3:180, 191
26:53, 3:108
26:56, 1:88
27:6–8, 1:86
27:24, 1:88
27:25, 1:88
27:38, 2:240
27:39–40, 1:90
27:51, 1:90
27:62–65, 1:91
28:2–4, 1:91
28:6, 4:23
28:20, 1:91; 2:240; 3:103; 4:60

Mark
1:13, 4:129
1:22, 3:123; 4:208
2:16, 3:268
2:17, 2:59
2:27, 1:100; 3:158
3:24–25, 4:55
3:35, 4:199
4:9, 4:388
4:22, 2:220
4:25, 2:234
4:26–29, 2:113
4:31, 4:41, 214
4:39, 1:89
4:41, 1:298
5:42, 4:232
6:4, 4:222
6:11, 1:169
6:34, 1:242
7:15, 20, 23, 4:57
7:25–30, 3:20
8:15–21, 4:188
8:18, 2:189
8:34, 2:129, 326
8:36, 4:277; 4:373
8:36–37, 3:236, 412
8:37, 4:142
9:7, 4:241
9:41, 1:83, 306
9:43, 4:277
9:44, 1:195
9:47, 4:277
9:48, 1:195
9:50, 3:93
10:14, 2:171, 174
10:15, 1:166
10:16, 2:171
10:17–18, 2:110
10:21, 1:302; 2:90, 239; 4:183
10:27, 2:126
10:28, 4:169
10:29–30, 4:34, 69
10:44, 3:197
11:23, 3:122
11:24, 1:380
12:10, 3:100
12:17, 1:218; 3:23
12:25, 2:147
12:26–27, 3:33
12:30, 1:121, 154; 2:34, 148; 3:15
12:30–31, 2:29, 190, 254; 3:22, 70
12:30–33, 4:193
12:31, 2:159; 4:133
12:33, 4:133
12:34, 4:85, 103
12:42, 2:152
12:42–44, 1:302; 2:33
13:12, 4:45
13:13, 1:231

13:31, 2:111; 4:63, 69, 76
13:33, 3:98
14:8, 4:188
14:22, 4:186
14:22–24, 4:188
14:37, 1:154
14:38, 2:44; 3:57, 98
14:50, 1:88
15:30–32, 1:90
15:38, 1:90
16:1, 4:188
16:6, 4:23
16:19, 1:91

Luke
1:30, 3:51
1:79, 4:41
2:7, 2:240
2:10, 1:148; 2:110; 4:41, 388
2:11, 1:141
2:13–14, 1:144
2:14, 1:142, 148; 2:196; 3:67; 4:375
2:29, 1:213; 2:181
2:49, 3:153
2:52, 4:39
3:4, 3:127
4:24, 4:222
5:11, 4:169
5:32, 2:59
6:25, 2:19
6:27–28, 2:111, 199
6:29, 2:90
6:31, 2:41, 132, 137, 209; 4:49, 62
6:35, 2:199
6:36, 3:33, 88
6:37–38, 2:248; 4:56
6:39, 3:153
6:42, 3:65
6:46, 1:111
6:48, 3:94
7:11–15, 1:134
7:50, 4:90
8:1, 3:24
8:8, 4:388
8:18, 2:234
8:25, 1:298
9:5, 1:169
9:23, 3:151
9:25, 4:277
9:35, 4:241
9:54, 1:57
9:54–56, 2:59
9:55, 2:229; 3:236
9:58, 1:88
9:60, 3:15
9:62, 3:100
10:20, 4:39
10:24, 1:148
10:27, 2:29, 34, 148, 190, 204; 3:22, 33,

44, 51, 66, 201, 218, 240, 241; 4:133,
193
10:30–37, 2:33
10:33–34, 1:147
10:34, 4:260
10:41–42, 2:25
10:42, 2:41, 178; 3:249
11:2, 2:244; 3:27
11:4, 3:62; 4:83, 88
11:9, 3:136, 174; 4:175
11:9–10, 2:149, 245
11:10, 3:175
11:17, 4:55
11:24–26, 3:235
11:34, 3:23
12:1, 4:188
12:2, 1:201
12:6–7, 1:260; 2:138
12:7, 3:111
12:8, 1:91
12:11–12, 3:123
12:27, 2:254, 265; 4:106, 240
12:28, 1:300
12:33, 1:283, 302, 306; 2:380
12:33–34, 1:97
12:46, 4:280
12:48, 2:149; 4:73
12:57, 4:77
13:4, 4:57
13:7, 3:155; 4:182
13:19, 4:41, 214
13:27, 3:174; 4:279
14:26, 3:15
14:27, 3:137
14:34, 3:93
15:7, 1:151; 4:140
15:10, 1:151
15:16, 4:93
15:17, 4:145, 203
16:13, 3:227
16:17, 4:69, 76
16:19–31, 2:133; 3:197
16:31, 2:179; 3:42, 191
17:6, 4:41, 214
17:10, 2:199
17:20, 1:151
17:20–21, 4:275
17:21, 1:206, 287; 2:24, 99; 3:194, 214;
4:121, 175, 215, 238, 399
17:24, 2:83
18:1, 2:242
18:9–14, 3:250
18:13, 4:439
18:14, 2:34
18:17, 1:166; 2:171
18:22, 1:302; 2:90–91, 239; 4:183
18:42, 4:90
19:40, 4:271
20:18, 2:148; 4:61, 169, 233

20:25, 1:218
20:34, 3:29
20:35, 2:147
20:36, 2:14
20:37-38, 3:33
20:38, 4:122, 135
21:2, 2:152
21:2-4, 1:302; 2:33
21:33, 2:111; 4:63, 69, 76
22:17-19, 2:53
22:19, 2:56; 3:181; 4:186
22:19-20, 4:188
22:42, 2:23; 3:38, 40, 137, 250
22:53, 3:23
23:4, 2:357
23:30, 1:193
23:34, 1:90, 262; 3:44; 4:173
23:45, 1:90
24:6, 4:23
24:15-16, 1:70
24:32, 3:131
24:37, 3:119
24:45, 4:35

John
1:1, 3:114, 120; 4:242
1:3, 2:21; 3:121
1:4, 4:242
1:8, 3:127
1:9, 3:37, 152; 4:140
1:10, 2:256; 3:69, 172
1:14, 2:109; 4:41
1:18, 3:42, 52
1:29, 1:262
1:42, 4:159
1:50, 4:214
2:3-9, 1:238
3:2, 3:79; 4:245
3:3, 4:127, 165
3:5-8, 3:69
3:6, 2:148; 3:23
3:7, 4:127, 165
3:11, 4:246
3:19, 2:113
3:36, 4:195
4:7-15, 4:188
4:10-14, 3:23; 4:165
4:14, 2:74, 262
4:24, 3:119; 4:399
4:42, 3:186
4:44, 4:222
5:24, 2:147; 3:69; 4:127
5:26, 3:69
5:30, 3:95
5:35, 4:139
5:44, 3:95
5:45, 3:36
6:12, 2:113
6:27, 3:57; 4:402

6:35, 3:23, 250; 4:245
6:48, 4:245
6:53, 4:188
6:54-55, 4:165
6:63, 3:70; 4:188
7:16-17, 1:153
7:17, 3:42; 4:176, 424
7:24, 4:240
7:34, 1:240
7:38, 3:250
7:46, 3:264
8:6-8, 4:188
8:7, 2:261
8:11, 3:73
8:12, 2:167, 239; 3:36
8:23, 4:273
8:31-36, 1:315
8:32, 2:221; 3:22, 184, 206; 4:82
8:36, 3:22
8:44-47, 3:22
8:45, 4:213
8:51, 1:311
10, 1:242
10:30, 3:180
11:25, 2:57, 74; 3:36; 4:199
11:25-26, 1:311
11:26, 4:199
11:33, 2:58
11:33-44, 2:184
11:35, 2:169
11:52, 2:144
13-17, 4:186
13:5, 4:188
13:8, 4:280
13:14-15, 4:188
14:2, 3:28, 103
14:6, 2:170; 3:250; 4:63, 258
14:6-14, 3:263
14:10, 1:145; 2:253
14:10-11, 4:216
14:10-13, 4:143
14:12, 4:214
14:15, 2:204; 3:204
14:16, 4:195, 213
14:16-21, 4:211
14:17, 4:175, 195, 211
14:21, 3:174
14:23, 2:253
14:26, 4:195
14:27, 3:16
14:28, 4:216
15:5-6, 2:64
15:10, 1:273; 2:65, 122; 3:179, 204
15:14, 2:118
15:15, 2:118, 119
15:19, 4:273, 274
15:26, 4:195, 211
16:7, 4:195, 213
16:12-13, 3:23

16:13, 4:175, 209
16:16, 1:240
17:1-5, 2:57
17:1-26, 3:250
17:3, 2:187; 4:165
17:4, 1:89
17:5, 4:242
17:11-16, 4:274
17:14, 4:273, 274
17:16, 4:273
17:21, 2:195
17:21-22, 2:255
17:21-23, 1:275; 2:90
18:36, 3:24
18:38, 4:166
19:30, 1:90
19:34, 2:120
20:21, 2:110
20:25, 3:129
21:18, 1:95

Acts
1:19, 1:86
2:1-4, 3:122
2:3, 2:49
2:20, 1:60
3:19, 3:33, 218; 4:246
5:1-11, 3:125
5:29, 2:86
5:41, 3:149
7:57, 2:111
7:59, 3:119
8:23, 3:205
9:6, 4:238, 259
9:10, 4:238, 259
9:15, 3:181
9:18, 2:132
10:14, 3:20
10:34, 3:125, 203; 4:57, 162
10:34-35, 1:179; 3:20, 251
10:42, 4:64
13:4-12, 1:166
14:12, 2:219
14:17, 4:166
15:36-41, 3:22
16:25, 2:22; 3:149; 4:35
16:28, 4:54, 328
16:30, 2:187
16:31, 3:15
17:19, 1:110-11
17:24-25, 29-31, 4:153, 376-77
17:28, 1:96, 145, 207; 2:19; 4:173
17:31, 1:148; 3:36; 4:64
18:24-19:1, 4:159
20:35, 2:135; 4:214
24:16, 1:75
24:24, 4:90
24:26, 2:219
28:1-6, 2:219

Romans
1:14-25, 2:110
1:16, 1:231
1:20, 1:203
2:4, 2:80
2:5-9, 1:117
2:7, 1:139; 2:247
2:9, 3:258
2:11, 3:125, 203
2:14, 1:230; 4:74, 83, 184
2:14-15, 1:191
2:15, 1:217
2:29, 3:252; 4:87, 150
5:3, 3:210
6:5, 2:128
6:11, 4:279
6:23, 2:241; 3:205
7:6, 4:269
7:23, 2:44
8:1, 3:15, 28
8:4, 3:28
8:5-11, 3:27
8:9, 3:99, 204; 4:195, 272
8:9-10, 3:218
8:9-11, 4:175
8:10, 3:36
8:14, 1:179
8:16, 1:380; 2:144, 239; 3:88, 186
8:17, 2:122
8:18, 3:124
8:19, 1:143
8:21, 1:143; 3:205
8:26, 4:347
8:27, 1:98
8:28, 2:143; 3:149, 210
8:31, 3:210
9:26, 2:144
10:8-10, 4:238
10:10, 3:22
12:1, 2:246
12:2, 2:124, 128, 250; 3:33; 4:273
12:3, 4:203
12:5, 4:263
12:15, 4:152
12:19, 2:70
12:20, 4:376
13:7, 1:218
13:9, 2:124; 4:133
13:10, 1:224; 4:133
13:11, 2:75
13:12, 2:112; 4:48
13:34, 2:124
14:4, 1:186
14:5, 2:138; 3:265
14:7, 2:170
14:8, 3:33, 90
14:10, 3:35; 4:275
14:12, 2:71, 72, 254; 3:22
14:17, 3:16, 25, 99; 4:185, 400

14:22, 3:94, 97
15:13, 3:13, 16

I Corinthians
1:10, 4:263
1:21, 2:157
1:23, 1:85, 173
1:24, 3:36, 204; 4:165
1:26–27, 3:52
1:26–31, 3:116
1:27, 1:87
2:9, 1:95, 132; 4:161–62, 268
2:9–10, 1:118
2:10, 2:337; 3:128
2:11, 3:119
2:14, 2:180; 3:27, 131, 170, 189
3:6–8, 3:21
3:7, 2:158
3:13, 3:38
3:16, 2:144, 145, 148, 252; 3:88, 90; 4:175, 195
3:21, 1:225; 2:149
3:21–22, 1:225
4:3, 3:169
4:7, 1:182; 3:89, 111
4:12, 1:267
5:6, 4:41, 214
5:6–7, 3:164
6:2, 2:25
6:7, 4:82
6:9–10, 3:27
6:19, 4:175
6:19–20, 2:251, 255
7:19, 3:251
7:31, 2:24
8:5, 1:161
8:28, 2:176
9:18, 3:123
9:26, 3:213
10:1–31, 4:189
10:4, 2:253
10:12, 2:51, 54
10:24, 2:196; 3:253; 4:49
10:31, 2:244
11:20–34, 4:189
11:23, 4:190
11:23–26, 3:181
11:29, 2:57
12:4–11, 3:122
12:12–14, 4:263
12:26, 2:118
12:27, 2:302
12:28, 3:122
13:1, 2:72; 4:138
13:3, 1:110; 2:199
13:4, 4:148
13:4–5, 1:160
13:8, 1:132
13:12, 2:176, 185, 235; 3:124, 194, 214

14:32, 3:123
15:19, 1:266; 2:62
15:22, 3:36; 4:126, 161
15:26, 2:181
15:28, 1:183; 3:130
15:31, 3:69
15:41, 2:235
15:51–52, 3:15
15:53, 3:28
15:55, 3:105
15:56–57, 1:408

II Corinthians
1:3–7, 4:195
2:9, 3:103
2:16, 3:230
3:6, 2:188; 3:35; 4:26, 87, 150, 269
3:14–16, 4:167
3:16, 3:41
3:17, 1:312
3:18, 2:243–44
4:3, 3:254; 4:253
4:3–4, 2:87
4:4, 3:19
4:5, 1:238
4:6, 3:63; 4:47
4:7, 3:101, 214; 4:142
4:9, 2:190
4:16, 3:16, 190; 4:147
4:18, 1:131, 244; 2:51; 4:260
5:1, 3:101; 4:104, 270
5:10, 3:35; 4:275
5:17, 1:68
5:23, 1:242
6:1, 2:90, 156
6:2, 1:290; 2:201, 203; 3:62, 220
6:8, 1:83, 196
7:4, 3:149
7:6, 4:195
9:7, 2:371
9:8, 4:116
11:23–33, 3:210
12:10, 3:169
13:1, 3:98
13:8, 4:166

Galatians
2:7–8, 2:110
2:9, 4:262
2:20, 3:36
3:24, 3:36
3:26, 2:144
3:28, 4:158
4:4, 2:108
4:8–10, 2:138
4:19, 3:36; 4:274
5:1, 1:315; 2:190
5:9, 3:164; 4:41, 214
5:13, 2:134

5:14, 4:133
5:16, 3:15, 218
5:24, 4:273
6:2, 1:124
6:4, 2:405
6:4-5, 2:186
6:5, 2:82
6:7, 1:77, 236; 2:232; 3:178; 4:56, 72
6:9, 2:102, 104, 106; 3:235; 4:184
6:10, 2:198; 3:195
6:14, 2:119

Ephesians
1:17, 3:119
2:1, 2:64
2:5, 2:64
3:14-19, 3:99
3:17, 4:278
3:21, 3:124
4:5, 4:263
4:6, 4:159
4:13, 4:274
4:14, 1:200
4:20, 3:36
4:22-24, 2:247
4:23-24, 4:201
4:24, 4:410
5:14, 3:36
5:15, 2:51
5:15-16, 4:109
5:16, 3:33, 218; 4:76
6:6, 4:193
6:8, 1:159; 3:178
6:13, 3:169
6:14, 1:197; 4:208, 410

Philippians
1:21, 3:33, 36, 204
1:27, 4:263
2:12, 4:88
2:13, 3:88, 205
2:22, 4:263
3:7-8, 2:119
3:13, 1:153; 2:51
3:13-14, 1:67; 4:65, 170, 338
3:14, 2:249
3:20, 1:285
4:7, 3:137; 4:267
4:8, 1:141; 3:34, 218
4:11, 1:63; 3:90
4:13, 2:107; 3:78

Colossians
1:9-10, 4:171
1:12, 2:245; 4:115
1:23, 4:41
2:2, 2:84
2:5, 4:63
2:13, 2:64

2:19, 2:84
3:2, 1:224; 4:236
3:3, 3:182
3:4, 1:148; 3:36, 204
3:11, 4:158
3:17, 2:244
3:23, 3:92; 4:206
4:5, 4:76
4:11, 2:90

I Thessalonians
5:17, 1:55; 2:244
5:21, 2:158

II Thessalonians
3:13, 4:184

I Timothy
1:19, 4:259
2:5, 4:192
2:7, 4:245
4:8, 1:294; 2:165; 3:210, 220
4:12, 1:70
5:4, 1:120, 154
5:25, 1:81
6:7, 2:179; 3:216
6:17, 4:117

II Timothy
1:1, 4:245
1:7, 3:22, 119
1:10, 3:218
1:14, 4:175, 195
2:15, 4:373
3:15, 1:131, 229; 3:194
3:17, 2:24
4:2, 2:158
4:8, 1:90

Titus
1:15, 2:129
2:12, 1:208, 214, 219, 272
2:13-14, 4:83
2:14, 2:165; 4:101, 348
3:2, 1:185

Hebrews
1:3, 4:36, 177
1:14, 2:209; 3:119
2:6, 4:134
2:10, 3:213; 4:172
2:14-15, 3:29
2:15, 4:348
3:12, 2:37, 168
4:1, 2:180
4:3-11, 2:241
4:15, 1:86; 4:62
6:1, 4:71
6:12, 4:280

6:17, 4:280
6:18-19, 2:36
6:19, 1:247; 2:35; 3:182; 4:87, 130
8:6, 4:192
9:11, 4:270
9:15, 4:192
11:1, 1:147
11:6, 1:207; 3:94; 4:140
11:9, 4:280
11:13, 4:51
11:16, 1:290; 2:165
11:38, 1:76
12:1, 1:73, 200, 247
12:2, 1:69; 4:274
12:6, 1:134; 4:56
12:14, 1:83; 3:251
12:18-22, 4:61
12:22, 2:126
12:23, 1:56, 60, 76, 126, 200, 247; 3:109;
    4:280
12:24, 4:192
12:28, 1:149
13:2, 4:271
13:8, 1:262; 3:216; 4:274
13:16, 2:206
13:20, 4:126

James
1:12, 3:109, 233
1:13, 2:258; 3:60
1:17, 3:118, 178
1:22, 4:40
1:27, 1:110, 147, 253; 2:254; 4:223
2:8, 4:133
2:10, 1:73; 2:223; 3:221
2:17-18, 3:155
2:19, 4:248
2:23, 2:219
3:2, 1:212; 2:66, 70
3:5, 1:74
3:16, 4:150, 374
3:8, 1:185
3:17, 1:260; 3:61
4:4, 4:273
4:6, 4:270
4:7, 3:60, 123
4:8, 3:123, 174, 190
4:14, 2:61, 112; 3:215
5:12, 2:172
5:15-16, 2:245
5:16, 4:113

I Peter
1:16, 4:270
1:23, 4:127
2:9, 1:148
2:11, 3:33
2:21, 1:91
2:23, 1:190, 262

3:10-11, 4:133
3:13, 4:56
3:15, 3:154
3:22, 4:70
4:7, 2:170; 3:98
4:8, 1:301
4:10, 1:82
5:1, 3:124, 237
5:5, 4:270

II Peter
1:4, 2:144; 3:88, 124; 4:87, 89
1:5, 1:278; 2:227, 231
1:5-7, 4:89
1:8, 2:231
1:10, 1:154
1:19, 4:39
3:8, 2:117; 3:77, 216; 4:115, 316
3:13, 1:240; 3:73

I John
1:5, 2:22
2:16, 4:260
3:14, 2:147; 3:69
3:17, 2:199
3:18-23, 3:56
3:20-21, 4:42, 320
3:23, 3:33; 4:263
4:4-7, 3:56
4:7, 4:152, 263, 270
4:8, 1:143; 2:41; 3:56, 243; 4:53, 55, 195,
    270
4:11, 2:123
4:12, 2:253
4:12-13, 4:152
4:16, 1:143; 4:53, 55, 195
4:18, 1:110; 2:122, 190; 3:51, 219
5:2, 2:144
5:3, 3:252
5:5, 3:20
5:14, 3:150

Jude
1:9, 1:262
1:14, 1:140

Revelation
1:17-18, 3:168
1:18, 3:177
2:7, 1:258, 289
2:10, 2:111
4, 3:24
4:8, 1:145
4:9, 2:202
6:12, 1:60
9:12, 3:35
10:6, 3:34, 219
14:7, 4:154
14:11, 1:291

14:13, 3:232
21:1, 1:138; 3:73; 4:208, 381
21:4-5, 2:202
21:6, 4:128, 133
21:8, 2:135
21:23, 2:231
21:25, 2:36

22:1, 4:133
22:2, 1:86; 3:181; 4:37
22:5, 4:88
22:11, 1:218; 3:60
22:12, 1:69
22:15, 3:22
22:17, 4:133